The Z Shell Manual

Version 5.7.1
Updated February 3, 2019

Original documentation by Paul Falstad

This is a texinfo version of the documentation for the Z Shell, originally by Paul Falstad.

Permission is granted to make and distribute verbatim copies of this manual provided the copyright notice and this permission notice are preserved on all copies.

Permission is granted to copy and distribute modified versions of this manual under the conditions for verbatim copying, provided also that the entire resulting derived work is distributed under the terms of a permission notice identical to this one.

Permission is granted to copy and distribute translations of this manual into another language, under the above conditions for modified versions.

Table of Contents

1 The Z Shell Manual

This document has been produced from the texinfo file `zsh.texi`, included in the `Doc` sub-directory of the Zsh distribution.

1.1 Producing documentation from zsh.texi

The texinfo source may be converted into several formats:

The Info manual

> The Info format allows searching for topics, commands, functions, etc. from the many Indices. The command '`makeinfo zsh.texi`' is used to produce the Info documentation.

The printed manual

> The command '`texi2dvi zsh.texi`' will output `zsh.dvi` which can then be processed with *dvips* and optionally *gs* (Ghostscript) to produce a nicely formatted printed manual.

The HTML manual

> An HTML version of this manual is available at the Zsh web site via:
>
> `http://zsh.sourceforge.net/Doc/`.
>
> (The HTML version is produced with *texi2html*, which may be obtained from `http://www.nongnu.org/texi2html/`. The command is '`texi2html --output . --ifinfo --split=chapter --node-files zsh.texi`'. If necessary, upgrade to version 1.78 of texi2html.)

For those who do not have the necessary tools to process texinfo, precompiled documentation (PostScript, dvi, PDF, info and HTML formats) is available from the zsh archive site or its mirrors, in the file `zsh-doc.tar.gz`. (See Section 2.2 [Availability], page 2, for a list of sites.)

2 Introduction

Zsh is a UNIX command interpreter (shell) usable as an interactive login shell and as a shell script command processor. Of the standard shells, zsh most closely resembles *ksh* but includes many enhancements. It does not provide compatibility with POSIX or other shells in its default operating mode: see the section Section 4.2 [Compatibility], page 7.

Zsh has command line editing, builtin spelling correction, programmable command completion, shell functions (with autoloading), a history mechanism, and a host of other features.

2.1 Author

Zsh was originally written by Paul Falstad `<pf@zsh.org>`. Zsh is now maintained by the members of the zsh-workers mailing list `<zsh-workers@zsh.org>`. The development is currently coordinated by Peter Stephenson `<pws@zsh.org>`. The coordinator can be contacted at `<coordinator@zsh.org>`, but matters relating to the code should generally go to the mailing list.

2.2 Availability

Zsh is available from the following HTTP and anonymous FTP site.

```
ftp://ftp.zsh.org/pub/
https://www.zsh.org/pub/ )
```

The up-to-date source code is available via Git from Sourceforge. See `https://sourceforge.net/projects/zsh/` for details. A summary of instructions for the archive can be found at `http://zsh.sourceforge.net/`.

2.3 Mailing Lists

Zsh has 3 mailing lists:

`<zsh-announce@zsh.org>`
> Announcements about releases, major changes in the shell and the monthly posting of the Zsh FAQ. (moderated)

`<zsh-users@zsh.org>`
> User discussions.

`<zsh-workers@zsh.org>`
> Hacking, development, bug reports and patches.

To subscribe or unsubscribe, send mail to the associated administrative address for the mailing list.

```
<zsh-announce-subscribe@zsh.org>
<zsh-users-subscribe@zsh.org>
<zsh-workers-subscribe@zsh.org>
```

```
<zsh-announce-unsubscribe@zsh.org>
<zsh-users-unsubscribe@zsh.org>
<zsh-workers-unsubscribe@zsh.org>
```

YOU ONLY NEED TO JOIN ONE OF THE MAILING LISTS AS THEY ARE NESTED. All submissions to *zsh-announce* are automatically forwarded to *zsh-users*. All submissions to *zsh-users* are automatically forwarded to *zsh-workers*.

If you have problems subscribing/unsubscribing to any of the mailing lists, send mail to `<listmaster@zsh.org>`. The mailing lists are maintained by Karsten Thygesen `<karthy@kom.auc.dk>`.

The mailing lists are archived; the archives can be accessed via the administrative addresses listed above. There is also a hypertext archive, maintained by Geoff Wing `<gcw@zsh.org>`, available at `https://www.zsh.org/mla/`.

2.4 The Zsh FAQ

Zsh has a list of Frequently Asked Questions (FAQ), maintained by Peter Stephenson `<pws@zsh.org>`. It is regularly posted to the newsgroup *comp.unix.shell* and the *zsh-announce* mailing list. The latest version can be found at any of the Zsh FTP sites, or at `http://www.zsh.org/FAQ/`. The contact address for FAQ-related matters is `<faqmaster@zsh.org>`.

2.5 The Zsh Web Page

Zsh has a web page which is located at `https://www.zsh.org/`. This is maintained by Karsten Thygesen `<karthy@zsh.org>`, of SunSITE Denmark. The contact address for web-related matters is `<webmaster@zsh.org>`.

2.6 The Zsh Userguide

A userguide is currently in preparation. It is intended to complement the manual, with explanations and hints on issues where the manual can be cabbalistic, hierographic, or downright mystifying (for example, the word 'hierographic' does not exist). It can be viewed in its current state at `http://zsh.sourceforge.net/Guide/`. At the time of writing, chapters dealing with startup files and their contents and the new completion system were essentially complete.

2.7 See Also

man page sh(1), man page csh(1), man page tcsh(1), man page rc(1), man page bash(1), man page ksh(1)

IEEE Standard for information Technology - Portable Operating System Interface (POSIX) - Part 2: Shell and Utilities, IEEE Inc, 1993, ISBN 1-55937-255-9.

3 Roadmap

The Zsh Manual, like the shell itself, is large and often complicated. This section of the manual provides some pointers to areas of the shell that are likely to be of particular interest to new users, and indicates where in the rest of the manual the documentation is to be found.

3.1 When the shell starts

When it starts, the shell reads commands from various files. These can be created or edited to customize the shell. See Chapter 5 [Files], page 8.

If no personal initialization files exist for the current user, a function is run to help you change some of the most common settings. It won't appear if your administrator has disabled the **zsh/newuser** module. The function is designed to be self-explanatory. You can run it by hand with '`autoload -Uz zsh-newuser-install; zsh-newuser-install -f`'. See also Section 26.11 [User Configuration Functions], page 489.

3.2 Interactive Use

Interaction with the shell uses the builtin Zsh Line Editor, ZLE. This is described in detail in Chapter 18 [Zsh Line Editor], page 183.

The first decision a user must make is whether to use the Emacs or Vi editing mode as the keys for editing are substantially different. Emacs editing mode is probably more natural for beginners and can be selected explicitly with the command `bindkey -e`.

A history mechanism for retrieving previously typed lines (most simply with the Up or Down arrow keys) is available; note that, unlike other shells, zsh will not save these lines when the shell exits unless you set appropriate variables, and the number of history lines retained by default is quite small (30 lines). See the description of the shell variables (referred to in the documentation as parameters) `HISTFILE`, `HISTSIZE` and `SAVEHIST` in Section 15.6 [Parameters Used By The Shell], page 99. Note that it's currently only possible to read and write files saving history when the shell is interactive, i.e. it does not work from scripts.

The shell now supports the UTF-8 character set (and also others if supported by the operating system). This is (mostly) handled transparently by the shell, but the degree of support in terminal emulators is variable. There is some discussion of this in the shell FAQ, `http://www.zsh.org/FAQ/`. Note in particular that for combining characters to be handled the option `COMBINING_CHARS` needs to be set. Because the shell is now more sensitive to the definition of the character set, note that if you are upgrading from an older version of the shell you should ensure that the appropriate variable, either `LANG` (to affect all aspects of the shell's operation) or `LC_CTYPE` (to affect only the handling of character sets) is set to an appropriate value. This is true even if you are using a single-byte character set including extensions of ASCII such as `ISO-8859-1` or `ISO-8859-15`. See the description of `LC_CTYPE` in Chapter 15 [Parameters], page 85.

3.2.1 Completion

Completion is a feature present in many shells. It allows the user to type only a part (usually the prefix) of a word and have the shell fill in the rest. The completion system in zsh is programmable. For example, the shell can be set to complete email addresses in arguments to the mail command from your `~/.abook/addressbook`; usernames, hostnames, and even remote paths in arguments to scp, and so on. Anything that can be written in or glued together with zsh can be the source of what the line editor offers as possible completions.

Zsh has two completion systems, an old, so called `compctl` completion (named after the builtin command that serves as its complete and only user interface), and a new one, referred to as `compsys`, organized as library of builtin and user-defined functions. The two systems differ in their interface for specifying the completion behavior. The new system is more customizable and is supplied with completions for many commonly used commands; it is therefore to be preferred.

The completion system must be enabled explicitly when the shell starts. For more information see Chapter 20 [Completion System], page 242.

3.2.2 Extending the line editor

Apart from completion, the line editor is highly extensible by means of shell functions. Some useful functions are provided with the shell; they provide facilities such as:

`insert-composed-char`
> composing characters not found on the keyboard

`match-words-by-style`
> configuring what the line editor considers a word when moving or deleting by word

`history-beginning-search-backward-end`, etc.
> alternative ways of searching the shell history

`replace-string`, `replace-pattern`
> functions for replacing strings or patterns globally in the command line

`edit-command-line`
> edit the command line with an external editor.

See Section 26.7 [ZLE Functions], page 455, for descriptions of these.

3.3 Options

The shell has a large number of options for changing its behaviour. These cover all aspects of the shell; browsing the full documentation is the only good way to become acquainted with the many possibilities. See Chapter 16 [Options], page 110.

3.4 Pattern Matching

The shell has a rich set of patterns which are available for file matching (described in the documentation as 'filename generation' and also known for historical reasons as 'globbing') and for use when programming. These are described in Section 14.8 [Filename Generation], page 72.

Of particular interest are the following patterns that are not commonly supported by other systems of pattern matching:

`**`   for matching over multiple directories

`|`   for matching either of two alternatives

`~`, `^`   the ability to exclude patterns from matching when the **EXTENDED_GLOB** option is set

`(...)`   glob qualifiers, included in parentheses at the end of the pattern, which select files by type (such as directories) or attribute (such as size).

3.5 General Comments on Syntax

Although the syntax of zsh is in ways similar to the Korn shell, and therefore more remotely to the original UNIX shell, the Bourne shell, its default behaviour does not entirely correspond to those shells. General shell syntax is introduced in Chapter 6 [Shell Grammar], page 10.

One commonly encountered difference is that variables substituted onto the command line are not split into words. See the description of the shell option **SH_WORD_SPLIT** in Section 14.3 [Parameter Expansion], page 52. In zsh, you can either explicitly request the splitting (e.g. `${=foo}`) or use an array when you want a variable to expand to more than one word. See Section 15.2 [Array Parameters], page 86.

3.6 Programming

The most convenient way of adding enhancements to the shell is typically by writing a shell function and arranging for it to be autoloaded. Functions are described in Chapter 9 [Functions], page 24. Users changing from the C shell and its relatives should notice that aliases are less used in zsh as they don't perform argument substitution, only simple text replacement.

A few general functions, other than those for the line editor described above, are provided with the shell and are described in Chapter 26 [User Contributions], page 423. Features include:

promptinit

> a prompt theme system for changing prompts easily, see Section 26.6 [Prompt Themes], page 453,

zsh-mime-setup

> a MIME-handling system which dispatches commands according to the suffix of a file as done by graphical file managers

zcalc   a calculator

zargs   a version of `xargs` that makes the `find` command redundant

zmv   a command for renaming files by means of shell patterns.

4 Invocation

4.1 Invocation

The following flags are interpreted by the shell when invoked to determine where the shell will read commands from:

-c

> Take the first argument as a command to execute, rather than reading commands from a script or standard input. If any further arguments are given, the first one is assigned to $0, rather than being used as a positional parameter.

-i

> Force shell to be interactive. It is still possible to specify a script to execute.

-s

> Force shell to read commands from the standard input. If the -s flag is not present and an argument is given, the first argument is taken to be the pathname of a script to execute.

If there are any remaining arguments after option processing, and neither of the options -c or -s was supplied, the first argument is taken as the file name of a script containing shell commands to be executed. If the option PATH_SCRIPT is set, and the file name does not contain a directory path (i.e. there is no '/' in the name), first the current directory and then the command path given by the variable PATH are searched for the script. If the option is not set or the file name contains a '/' it is used directly.

After the first one or two arguments have been appropriated as described above, the remaining arguments are assigned to the positional parameters.

For further options, which are common to invocation and the set builtin, see Chapter 16 [Options], page 110.

The long option '--emulate' followed (in a separate word) by an emulation mode may be passed to the shell. The emulation modes are those described for the emulate builtin, see

Chapter 17 [Shell Builtin Commands], page 139. The '--emulate' option must precede any other options (which might otherwise be overridden), but following options are honoured, so may be used to modify the requested emulation mode. Note that certain extra steps are taken to ensure a smooth emulation when this option is used compared with the emulate command within the shell: for example, variables that conflict with POSIX usage such as path are not defined within the shell.

Options may be specified by name using the -o option. -o acts like a single-letter option, but takes a following string as the option name. For example,

```
zsh -x -o shwordsplit scr
```

runs the script scr, setting the XTRACE option by the corresponding letter '-x' and the SH_WORD_SPLIT option by name. Options may be turned *off* by name by using +o instead of -o. -o can be stacked up with preceding single-letter options, so for example '-xo shwordsplit' or '-xoshwordsplit' is equivalent to '-x -o shwordsplit'.

Options may also be specified by name in GNU long option style, '--*option-name*'. When this is done, '-' characters in the option name are permitted: they are translated into '_', and thus ignored. So, for example, 'zsh --sh-word-split' invokes zsh with the SH_WORD_SPLIT option turned on. Like other option syntaxes, options can be turned off by replacing the initial '-' with a '+'; thus '+-sh-word-split' is equivalent to '--no-sh-word-split'. Unlike other option syntaxes, GNU-style long options cannot be stacked with any other options, so for example '-x-shwordsplit' is an error, rather than being treated like '-x --shwordsplit'.

The special GNU-style option '--version' is handled; it sends to standard output the shell's version information, then exits successfully. '--help' is also handled; it sends to standard output a list of options that can be used when invoking the shell, then exits successfully.

Option processing may be finished, allowing following arguments that start with '-' or '+' to be treated as normal arguments, in two ways. Firstly, a lone '-' (or '+') as an argument by itself ends option processing. Secondly, a special option '--' (or '+-'), which may be specified on its own (which is the standard POSIX usage) or may be stacked with preceding options (so '-x-' is equivalent to '-x --'). Options are not permitted to be stacked after '--' (so '-x-f' is an error), but note the GNU-style option form discussed above, where '--shwordsplit' is permitted and does not end option processing.

Except when the *sh/ksh* emulation single-letter options are in effect, the option '-b' (or '+b') ends option processing. '-b' is like '--', except that further single-letter options can be stacked after the '-b' and will take effect as normal.

4.2 Compatibility

Zsh tries to emulate *sh* or *ksh* when it is invoked as sh or ksh respectively; more precisely, it looks at the first letter of the name by which it was invoked, excluding any initial 'r' (assumed to stand for 'restricted'), and if that is 'b', 's' or 'k' it will emulate *sh* or *ksh*. Furthermore, if invoked as su (which happens on certain systems when the shell is executed by the su command), the shell will try to find an alternative name from the SHELL environment variable and perform emulation based on that.

In *sh* and *ksh* compatibility modes the following parameters are not special and not initialized by the shell: ARGC, argv, cdpath, fignore, fpath, HISTCHARS, mailpath, MANPATH, manpath, path, prompt, PROMPT, PROMPT2, PROMPT3, PROMPT4, psvar, status, watch.

The usual zsh startup/shutdown scripts are not executed. Login shells source `/etc/profile` followed by `$HOME/.profile`. If the ENV environment variable is set on invocation, `$ENV` is sourced after the profile scripts. The value of ENV is subjected to parameter expansion, command substitution, and arithmetic expansion before being interpreted as a pathname. Note that the `PRIVILEGED` option also affects the execution of startup files.

The following options are set if the shell is invoked as **sh** or **ksh**: NO_BAD_PATTERN, NO_BANG_HIST, NO_BG_NICE, NO_EQUALS, NO_FUNCTION_ARGZERO, GLOB_SUBST, NO_GLOBAL_EXPORT, NO_HUP, INTERACTIVE_COMMENTS, KSH_ARRAYS, NO_MULTIOS, NO_NOMATCH, NO_NOTIFY, POSIX_BUILTINS, NO_PROMPT_PERCENT, RM_STAR_SILENT, SH_FILE_EXPANSION, SH_GLOB, SH_OPTION_LETTERS, SH_WORD_SPLIT. Additionally the BSD_ECHO and IGNORE_BRACES options are set if zsh is invoked as **sh**. Also, the KSH_OPTION_PRINT, LOCAL_OPTIONS, PROMPT_BANG, PROMPT_SUBST and SINGLE_LINE_ZLE options are set if zsh is invoked as **ksh**.

4.3 Restricted Shell

When the basename of the command used to invoke zsh starts with the letter 'r' or the '-r' command line option is supplied at invocation, the shell becomes restricted. Emulation mode is determined after stripping the letter 'r' from the invocation name. The following are disabled in restricted mode:

- changing directories with the **cd** builtin
- changing or unsetting the EGID, EUID, GID, HISTFILE, HISTSIZE, IFS, LD_AOUT_LIBRARY_PATH, LD_AOUT_PRELOAD, LD_LIBRARY_PATH, LD_PRELOAD, MODULE_PATH, module_path, PATH, path, SHELL, UID and USERNAME parameters
- specifying command names containing /
- specifying command pathnames using **hash**
- redirecting output to files
- using the **exec** builtin command to replace the shell with another command
- using `jobs -Z` to overwrite the shell process' argument and environment space
- using the ARGV0 parameter to override `argv[0]` for external commands
- turning off restricted mode with `set +r` or `unsetopt RESTRICTED`

These restrictions are enforced after processing the startup files. The startup files should set up PATH to point to a directory of commands which can be safely invoked in the restricted environment. They may also add further restrictions by disabling selected builtins.

Restricted mode can also be activated any time by setting the RESTRICTED option. This immediately enables all the restrictions described above even if the shell still has not processed all startup files.

5 Files

5.1 Startup/Shutdown Files

Commands are first read from **/etc/zshenv**; this cannot be overridden. Subsequent behaviour is modified by the RCS and GLOBAL_RCS options; the former affects all startup files, while the second only affects global startup files (those shown here with an path starting with a **/**). If one of the options is unset at any point, any subsequent startup file(s) of the corresponding type will not be read. It is also possible for a file in $ZDOTDIR to re-enable GLOBAL_RCS. Both RCS and GLOBAL_RCS are set by default.

Commands are then read from $ZDOTDIR/**.zshenv**. If the shell is a login shell, commands are read from **/etc/zprofile** and then $ZDOTDIR/**.zprofile**. Then, if the shell is interactive, commands are read from **/etc/zshrc** and then $ZDOTDIR/**.zshrc**. Finally, if the shell is a login shell, **/etc/zlogin** and $ZDOTDIR/**.zlogin** are read.

When a login shell exits, the files $ZDOTDIR/**.zlogout** and then **/etc/zlogout** are read. This happens with either an explicit exit via the **exit** or **logout** commands, or an implicit exit by reading end-of-file from the terminal. However, if the shell terminates due to **exec**'ing another process, the logout files are not read. These are also affected by the RCS and GLOBAL_RCS options. Note also that the RCS option affects the saving of history files, i.e. if RCS is unset when the shell exits, no history file will be saved.

If ZDOTDIR is unset, HOME is used instead. Files listed above as being in **/etc** may be in another directory, depending on the installation.

As **/etc/zshenv** is run for all instances of zsh, it is important that it be kept as small as possible. In particular, it is a good idea to put code that does not need to be run for every single shell behind a test of the form 'if [[-o rcs]]; then ...' so that it will not be executed when zsh is invoked with the '-f' option.

5.2 Files

```
$ZDOTDIR/.zshenv
$ZDOTDIR/.zprofile
$ZDOTDIR/.zshrc
$ZDOTDIR/.zlogin
$ZDOTDIR/.zlogout
${TMPPREFIX}* (default is /tmp/zsh*)
/etc/zshenv
/etc/zprofile
/etc/zshrc
/etc/zlogin
/etc/zlogout (installation-specific - /etc is the default)
```

Any of these files may be pre-compiled with the **zcompile** builtin command (Chapter 17 [Shell Builtin Commands], page 139). If a compiled file exists (named for the original file plus the **.zwc** extension) and it is newer than the original file, the compiled file will be used instead.

6 Shell Grammar

6.1 Simple Commands & Pipelines

A *simple command* is a sequence of optional parameter assignments followed by blank-separated words, with optional redirections interspersed. For a description of assignment, see the beginning of Chapter 15 [Parameters], page 85.

The first word is the command to be executed, and the remaining words, if any, are arguments to the command. If a command name is given, the parameter assignments modify the environment of the command when it is executed. The value of a simple command is its exit status, or 128 plus the signal number if terminated by a signal. For example,

```
echo foo
```

is a simple command with arguments.

A *pipeline* is either a simple command, or a sequence of two or more simple commands where each command is separated from the next by '|' or '|&'. Where commands are separated by '|', the standard output of the first command is connected to the standard input of the next. '|&' is shorthand for '2>&1 |', which connects both the standard output and the standard error of the command to the standard input of the next. The value of a pipeline is the value of the last command, unless the pipeline is preceded by '!' in which case the value is the logical inverse of the value of the last command. For example,

```
echo foo | sed 's/foo/bar/'
```

is a pipeline, where the output ('foo' plus a newline) of the first command will be passed to the input of the second.

If a pipeline is preceded by 'coproc', it is executed as a coprocess; a two-way pipe is established between it and the parent shell. The shell can read from or write to the coprocess by means of the '>&p' and '<&p' redirection operators or with 'print -p' and 'read -p'. A pipeline cannot be preceded by both 'coproc' and '!'. If job control is active, the coprocess can be treated in other than input and output as an ordinary background job.

A *sublist* is either a single pipeline, or a sequence of two or more pipelines separated by '&&' or '||'. If two pipelines are separated by '&&', the second pipeline is executed only if the first succeeds (returns a zero status). If two pipelines are separated by '||', the second is executed only if the first fails (returns a nonzero status). Both operators have equal precedence and are left associative. The value of the sublist is the value of the last pipeline executed. For example,

```
dmesg | grep panic && print yes
```

is a sublist consisting of two pipelines, the second just a simple command which will be executed if and only if the **grep** command returns a zero status. If it does not, the value of the sublist is that return status, else it is the status returned by the **print** (almost certainly zero).

A *list* is a sequence of zero or more sublists, in which each sublist is terminated by ';', '&', '&|', '&!', or a newline. This terminator may optionally be omitted from the last sublist in the list when the list appears as a complex command inside '(...)' or '{...}'. When a sublist is terminated by ';' or newline, the shell waits for it to finish before executing the next sublist. If a sublist is terminated by a '&', '&|', or '&!', the shell executes the last pipeline in it in the background, and does not wait for it to finish (note the difference from other shells which execute the whole sublist in the background). A backgrounded pipeline returns a status of zero.

More generally, a list can be seen as a set of any shell commands whatsoever, including the complex commands below; this is implied wherever the word 'list' appears in later descriptions. For example, the commands in a shell function form a special sort of list.

6.2 Precommand Modifiers

A simple command may be preceded by a *precommand modifier*, which will alter how the command is interpreted. These modifiers are shell builtin commands with the exception of `nocorrect` which is a reserved word.

-            The command is executed with a '-' prepended to its `argv[0]` string.

`builtin`   The command word is taken to be the name of a builtin command, rather than a shell function or external command.

`command [ -pvV ]`
    The command word is taken to be the name of an external command, rather than a shell function or builtin. If the `POSIX_BUILTINS` option is set, builtins will also be executed but certain special properties of them are suppressed. The `-p` flag causes a default path to be searched instead of that in `$path`. With the `-v` flag, `command` is similar to `whence` and with `-V`, it is equivalent to `whence -v`.

`exec [ -cl ] [ -a argv0 ]`
    The following command together with any arguments is run in place of the current process, rather than as a sub-process. The shell does not fork and is replaced. The shell does not invoke `TRAPEXIT`, nor does it source `zlogout` files. The options are provided for compatibility with other shells.

    The `-c` option clears the environment.

    The `-l` option is equivalent to the `-` precommand modifier, to treat the replacement command as a login shell; the command is executed with a `-` prepended to its `argv[0]` string. This flag has no effect if used together with the `-a` option.

    The `-a` option is used to specify explicitly the `argv[0]` string (the name of the command as seen by the process itself) to be used by the replacement command and is directly equivalent to setting a value for the `ARGV0` environment variable.

`nocorrect`
    Spelling correction is not done on any of the words. This must appear before any other precommand modifier, as it is interpreted immediately, before any parsing is done. It has no effect in non-interactive shells.

`noglob`   Filename generation (globbing) is not performed on any of the words.

6.3 Complex Commands

A *complex command* in zsh is one of the following:

if *list* then *list* [elif *list* then *list*] ... [else *list*] fi

>   The if *list* is executed, and if it returns a zero exit status, the then *list* is executed. Otherwise, the elif *list* is executed and if its status is zero, the then *list* is executed. If each elif *list* returns nonzero status, the else *list* is executed.

for *name* ... [in *word* ...] *term* do *list* done

>   Expand the list of *word*s, and set the parameter *name* to each of them in turn, executing *list* each time. If the 'in *word*' is omitted, use the positional parameters instead of the *word*s.

>   The *term* consists of one or more newline or ; which terminate the *word*s, and are optional when the 'in *word*' is omitted.

>   More than one parameter *name* can appear before the list of *word*s. If N names are given, then on each execution of the loop the next N *word*s are assigned to the corresponding parameters. If there are more *name*s than remaining *word*s, the remaining parameters are each set to the empty string. Execution of the loop ends when there is no remaining *word* to assign to the first *name*. It is only possible for in to appear as the first *name* in the list, else it will be treated as marking the end of the list.

for (([*expr1*] ; [*expr2*] ; [*expr3*])) do *list* done

>   The arithmetic expression *expr1* is evaluated first (see Chapter 11 [Arithmetic Evaluation], page 31). The arithmetic expression *expr2* is repeatedly evaluated until it evaluates to zero and when non-zero, *list* is executed and the arithmetic expression *expr3* evaluated. If any expression is omitted, then it behaves as if it evaluated to 1.

while *list* do *list* done

>   Execute the do *list* as long as the while *list* returns a zero exit status.

until *list* do *list* done

>   Execute the do *list* as long as until *list* returns a nonzero exit status.

repeat *word* do *list* done

>   *word* is expanded and treated as an arithmetic expression, which must evaluate to a number *n*. *list* is then executed *n* times.

>   The repeat syntax is disabled by default when the shell starts in a mode emulating another shell. It can be enabled with the command 'enable -r repeat'

case *word* in [[(] *pattern* [| *pattern*] ...) *list* (;; | ;& | ;|)] ... esac

>   Execute the *list* associated with the first *pattern* that matches *word*, if any. The form of the patterns is the same as that used for filename generation. See Section 14.8 [Filename Generation], page 72.

>   Note further that, unless the SH_GLOB option is set, the whole pattern with alternatives is treated by the shell as equivalent to a group of patterns within parentheses, although white space may appear about the parentheses and the vertical bar and will be stripped from the pattern at those points. White space may appear elsewhere in the pattern; this is not stripped. If the SH_GLOB option

is set, so that an opening parenthesis can be unambiguously treated as part of the case syntax, the expression is parsed into separate words and these are treated as strict alternatives (as in other shells).

If the *list* that is executed is terminated with `;&` rather than `;;`, the following list is also executed. The rule for the terminator of the following list `;;`, `;&` or `;|` is applied unless the **esac** is reached.

If the *list* that is executed is terminated with `;|` the shell continues to scan the *patterns* looking for the next match, executing the corresponding *list*, and applying the rule for the corresponding terminator `;;`, `;&` or `;|`. Note that *word* is not re-expanded; all applicable *patterns* are tested with the same *word*.

select *name* [**in** *word ... term*] **do** *list* **done**

where *term* is one or more newline or `;` to terminate the *words*. Print the set of *words*, each preceded by a number. If the **in** *word* is omitted, use the positional parameters. The `PROMPT3` prompt is printed and a line is read from the line editor if the shell is interactive and that is active, or else standard input. If this line consists of the number of one of the listed *words*, then the parameter *name* is set to the *word* corresponding to this number. If this line is empty, the selection list is printed again. Otherwise, the value of the parameter *name* is set to null. The contents of the line read from standard input is saved in the parameter `REPLY`. *list* is executed for each selection until a break or end-of-file is encountered.

(*list*)   Execute *list* in a subshell. Traps set by the **trap** builtin are reset to their default values while executing *list*.

{ *list* }   Execute *list*.

{ *try-list* } **always** { *always-list* }

First execute *try-list*. Regardless of errors, or **break**, **continue**, or **return** commands encountered within *try-list*, execute *always-list*. Execution then continues from the result of the execution of *try-list*; in other words, any error, or **break**, **continue**, or **return** command is treated in the normal way, as if *always-list* were not present. The two chunks of code are referred to as the 'try block' and the 'always block'.

Optional newlines or semicolons may appear after the **always**; note, however, that they may *not* appear between the preceding closing brace and the **always**.

An 'error' in this context is a condition such as a syntax error which causes the shell to abort execution of the current function, script, or list. Syntax errors encountered while the shell is parsing the code do not cause the *always-list* to be executed. For example, an erroneously constructed **if** block in **try-list** would cause the shell to abort during parsing, so that **always-list** would not be executed, while an erroneous substitution such as `${*foo*}` would cause a run-time error, after which **always-list** would be executed.

An error condition can be tested and reset with the special integer variable `TRY_BLOCK_ERROR`. Outside an **always-list** the value is irrelevant, but it is initialised to -1. Inside **always-list**, the value is 1 if an error occurred in the **try-list**, else 0. If `TRY_BLOCK_ERROR` is set to 0 during the **always-list**, the error condition caused by the `try-list` is reset, and shell execution continues normally after the end of `always-list`. Altering the value during the `try-list` is not useful (unless this forms part of an enclosing `always` block).

Regardless of `TRY_BLOCK_ERROR`, after the end of `always-list` the normal shell status `$?` is the value returned from `try-list`. This will be non-zero if there was an error, even if `TRY_BLOCK_ERROR` was set to zero.

The following executes the given code, ignoring any errors it causes. This is an alternative to the usual convention of protecting code by executing it in a subshell.

```
{
    # code which may cause an error
} always {
    # This code is executed regardless of the error.
    (( TRY_BLOCK_ERROR = 0 ))
}
# The error condition has been reset.
```

An `exit` command (or a `return` command executed at the outermost function level of a script) encountered in `try-list` does *not* cause the execution of *always-list*. Instead, the shell exits immediately after any `EXIT` trap has been executed.

`function` *word* ... [()] [*term*] { *list* }
word ... () [*term*] { *list* }
word ... () [*term*] *command*

where *term* is one or more newline or ;. Define a function which is referenced by any one of *word*. Normally, only one *word* is provided; multiple *words* are usually only useful for setting traps. The body of the function is the *list* between the { and }. See Chapter 9 [Functions], page 24.

If the option `SH_GLOB` is set for compatibility with other shells, then whitespace may appear between the left and right parentheses when there is a single *word*; otherwise, the parentheses will be treated as forming a globbing pattern in that case.

In any of the forms above, a redirection may appear outside the function body, for example

```
func() { ... } 2>&1
```

The redirection is stored with the function and applied whenever the function is executed. Any variables in the redirection are expanded at the point the function is executed, but outside the function scope.

`time` [*pipeline*]

The *pipeline* is executed, and timing statistics are reported on the standard error in the form specified by the `TIMEFMT` parameter. If *pipeline* is omitted, print statistics about the shell process and its children.

`[[` *exp* `]]`   Evaluates the conditional expression *exp* and return a zero exit status if it is true. See Chapter 12 [Conditional Expressions], page 36, for a description of *exp*.

6.4 Alternate Forms For Complex Commands

Many of zsh's complex commands have alternate forms. These are non-standard and are likely not to be obvious even to seasoned shell programmers; they should not be used anywhere that portability of shell code is a concern.

The short versions below only work if *sublist* is of the form '{ *list* }' or if the SHORT_LOOPS option is set. For the if, while and until commands, in both these cases the test part of the loop must also be suitably delimited, such as by '[[...]]' or '((...))', else the end of the test will not be recognized. For the for, repeat, case and select commands no such special form for the arguments is necessary, but the other condition (the special form of *sublist* or use of the SHORT_LOOPS option) still applies.

if *list* { *list* } [elif *list* { *list* }] ... [else { *list* }]

> An alternate form of if. The rules mean that

>
> ```
>     if [[ -o ignorebraces ]] {
>       print yes
>     }
> ```
>
> works, but
>
> ```
>     if true {  # Does not work!
>       print yes
>     }
> ```
>
> does *not*, since the test is not suitably delimited.

if *list* *sublist*

> A short form of the alternate if. The same limitations on the form of *list* apply as for the previous form.

for *name* ... (*word* ...) *sublist*

> A short form of for.

for *name* ... [in *word* ...] *term* *sublist*

> where *term* is at least one newline or ;. Another short form of for.

for (([*expr1*] ; [*expr2*] ; [*expr3*])) *sublist*

> A short form of the arithmetic for command.

foreach *name* ... (*word* ...) *list* end

> Another form of for.

while *list* { *list* }

> An alternative form of while. Note the limitations on the form of *list* mentioned above.

until *list* { *list* }

> An alternative form of until. Note the limitations on the form of *list* mentioned above.

repeat *word* *sublist*

> This is a short form of repeat.

case *word* { [[(] *pattern* [| *pattern*] ...) *list* (;;|;&|;|)] ... }

> An alternative form of case.

select *name* [in *word ... term*] *sublist*
> where *term* is at least one newline or ;. A short form of select.

function *word ...* [()] [*term*] *sublist*
> This is a short form of function.

6.5 Reserved Words

The following words are recognized as reserved words when used as the first word of a command unless quoted or disabled using disable -r:

do done esac then elif else fi for case if while function repeat time until select coproc nocorrect foreach end ! [[{ } declare export float integer local readonly typeset

Additionally, '}' is recognized in any position if neither the IGNORE_BRACES option nor the IGNORE_CLOSE_BRACES option is set.

6.6 Errors

Certain errors are treated as fatal by the shell: in an interactive shell, they cause control to return to the command line, and in a non-interactive shell they cause the shell to be aborted. In older versions of zsh, a non-interactive shell running a script would not abort completely, but would resume execution at the next command to be read from the script, skipping the remainder of any functions or shell constructs such as loops or conditions; this somewhat illogical behaviour can be recovered by setting the option CONTINUE_ON_ERROR.

Fatal errors found in non-interactive shells include:

- Failure to parse shell options passed when invoking the shell
- Failure to change options with the set builtin
- Parse errors of all sorts, including failures to parse mathematical expressions
- Failures to set or modify variable behaviour with typeset, local, declare, export, integer, float
- Execution of incorrectly positioned loop control structures (continue, break)
- Attempts to use regular expression with no regular expression module available
- Disallowed operations when the RESTRICTED options is set
- Failure to create a pipe needed for a pipeline
- Failure to create a multio
- Failure to autoload a module needed for a declared shell feature
- Errors creating command or process substitutions
- Syntax errors in glob qualifiers
- File generation errors where not caught by the option BAD_PATTERN
- All bad patterns used for matching within case statements
- File generation failures where not caused by NO_MATCH or similar options
- All file generation errors where the pattern was used to create a multio
- Memory errors where detected by the shell
- Invalid subscripts to shell variables

- Attempts to assign read-only variables
- Logical errors with variables such as assignment to the wrong type
- Use of invalid variable names
- Errors in variable substitution syntax
- Failure to convert characters in `$'...'` expressions

If the `POSIX_BUILTINS` option is set, more errors associated with shell builtin commands are treated as fatal, as specified by the POSIX standard.

6.7 Comments

In non-interactive shells, or in interactive shells with the `INTERACTIVE_COMMENTS` option set, a word beginning with the third character of the `histchars` parameter ('#' by default) causes that word and all the following characters up to a newline to be ignored.

6.8 Aliasing

Every eligible *word* in the shell input is checked to see if there is an alias defined for it. If so, it is replaced by the text of the alias if it is in command position (if it could be the first word of a simple command), or if the alias is global. If the replacement text ends with a space, the next word in the shell input is always eligible for purposes of alias expansion. An alias is defined using the `alias` builtin; global aliases may be defined using the `-g` option to that builtin.

A *word* is defined as:

- Any plain string or glob pattern
- Any quoted string, using any quoting method (note that the quotes must be part of the alias definition for this to be eligible)
- Any parameter reference or command substitution
- Any series of the foregoing, concatenated without whitespace or other tokens between them
- Any reserved word (`case`, `do`, `else`, etc.)
- With global aliasing, any command separator, any redirection operator, and '(' or ')' when not part of a glob pattern

Alias expansion is done on the shell input before any other expansion except history expansion. Therefore, if an alias is defined for the word `foo`, alias expansion may be avoided by quoting part of the word, e.g. `\foo`. Any form of quoting works, although there is nothing to prevent an alias being defined for the quoted form such as `\foo` as well.

When `POSIX_ALIASES` is set, only plain unquoted strings are eligible for aliasing. The `alias` builtin does not reject ineligible aliases, but they are not expanded.

For use with completion, which would remove an initial backslash followed by a character that isn't special, it may be more convenient to quote the word by starting with a single quote, i.e. `'foo`; completion will automatically add the trailing single quote.

6.8.1 Alias difficulties

Although aliases can be used in ways that bend normal shell syntax, not every string of non-white-space characters can be used as an alias.

Any set of characters not listed as a word above is not a word, hence no attempt is made to expand it as an alias, no matter how it is defined (i.e. via the builtin or the special parameter `aliases` described in Section 22.20 [The zsh/parameter Module], page 354). However, as noted in the case of `POSIX_ALIASES` above, the shell does not attempt to deduce whether the string corresponds to a word at the time the alias is created.

For example, an expression containing an = at the start of a command line is an assignment and cannot be expanded as an alias; a lone = is not an assignment but can only be set as an alias using the parameter, as otherwise the = is taken part of the syntax of the builtin command.

It is not presently possible to alias the '((' token that introduces arithmetic expressions, because until a full statement has been parsed, it cannot be distinguished from two consecutive '(' tokens introducing nested subshells. Also, if a separator such as && is aliased, \&& turns into the two tokens \& and &, each of which may have been aliased separately. Similarly for \<<, \>|, etc.

There is a commonly encountered problem with aliases illustrated by the following code:

```
alias echobar='echo bar'; echobar
```

This prints a message that the command `echobar` could not be found. This happens because aliases are expanded when the code is read in; the entire line is read in one go, so that when `echobar` is executed it is too late to expand the newly defined alias. This is often a problem in shell scripts, functions, and code executed with 'source' or '.'. Consequently, use of functions rather than aliases is recommended in non-interactive code.

Note also the unhelpful interaction of aliases and function definitions:

```
alias func='noglob func'
func() {
    echo Do something with $*
}
```

Because aliases are expanded in function definitions, this causes the following command to be executed:

```
noglob func() {
    echo Do something with $*
}
```

which defines `noglob` as well as `func` as functions with the body given. To avoid this, either quote the name `func` or use the alternative function definition form 'function func'. Ensuring the alias is defined after the function works but is problematic if the code fragment might be re-executed.

6.9 Quoting

A character may be *quoted* (that is, made to stand for itself) by preceding it with a '\'. '\' followed by a newline is ignored.

A string enclosed between '$'' and ''' is processed the same way as the string arguments of the `print` builtin, and the resulting string is considered to be entirely quoted. A literal ''' character can be included in the string by using the '\'' escape.

All characters enclosed between a pair of single quotes ('') that is not preceded by a '$' are quoted. A single quote cannot appear within single quotes unless the option `RC_QUOTES` is set, in which case a pair of single quotes are turned into a single quote. For example,

> `print ''''`

outputs nothing apart from a newline if `RC_QUOTES` is not set, but one single quote if it is set.

Inside double quotes (`""`), parameter and command substitution occur, and '\' quotes the characters '\', ''', '"', '$', and the first character of `$histchars` (default '!').

7 Redirection

If a command is followed by & and job control is not active, then the default standard input for the command is the empty file `/dev/null`. Otherwise, the environment for the execution of a command contains the file descriptors of the invoking shell as modified by input/output specifications.

The following may appear anywhere in a simple command or may precede or follow a complex command. Expansion occurs before *word* or *digit* is used except as noted below. If the result of substitution on *word* produces more than one filename, redirection occurs for each separate filename in turn.

< *word*   Open file *word* for reading as standard input. It is an error to open a file in this fashion if it does not exist.

<> *word*   Open file *word* for reading and writing as standard input. If the file does not exist then it is created.

> *word*   Open file *word* for writing as standard output. If the file does not exist then it is created. If the file exists, and the CLOBBER option is unset, this causes an error; otherwise, it is truncated to zero length.

>| *word*
>! *word*   Same as >, except that the file is truncated to zero length if it exists, even if CLOBBER is unset.

>> *word*   Open file *word* for writing in append mode as standard output. If the file does not exist, and the CLOBBER option is unset, this causes an error; otherwise, the file is created.

>>| *word*
>>! *word* Same as >>, except that the file is created if it does not exist, even if CLOBBER is unset.

<<[-] *word*

        The shell input is read up to a line that is the same as *word*, or to an end-of-file. No parameter expansion, command substitution or filename generation is performed on *word*. The resulting document, called a *here-document*, becomes the standard input.

If any character of *word* is quoted with single or double quotes or a '\', no interpretation is placed upon the characters of the document. Otherwise, parameter and command substitution occurs, '\' followed by a newline is removed, and '\' must be used to quote the characters '\', '$', ' ' ' and the first character of *word*.

Note that *word* itself does not undergo shell expansion. Backquotes in *word* do not have their usual effect; instead they behave similarly to double quotes, except that the backquotes themselves are passed through unchanged. (This information is given for completeness and it is not recommended that backquotes be used.) Quotes in the form $'...' have their standard effect of expanding backslashed references to special characters.

If <<- is used, then all leading tabs are stripped from *word* and from the document.

<<< *word*   Perform shell expansion on *word* and pass the result to standard input. This is known as a *here-string*. Compare the use of *word* in here-documents above, where *word* does not undergo shell expansion.

<& *number*
>& *number*

    The standard input/output is duplicated from file descriptor *number* (see man page dup2(2)).

<& -
>& -   Close the standard input/output.

<& p
>& p   The input/output from/to the coprocess is moved to the standard input/output.

>& *word*
&> *word*   (Except where '>& *word*' matches one of the above syntaxes; '&>' can always be used to avoid this ambiguity.) Redirects both standard output and standard error (file descriptor 2) in the manner of '> *word*'. Note that this does *not* have the same effect as '> *word* 2>&1' in the presence of multios (see the section below).

>&| *word*
>&! *word*
&>| *word*
&>! *word*   Redirects both standard output and standard error (file descriptor 2) in the manner of '>| *word*'.

>>& *word*
&>> *word*   Redirects both standard output and standard error (file descriptor 2) in the manner of '>> *word*'.

>>&| *word*
>>&! *word*
&>>| *word*
&>>! *word*   Redirects both standard output and standard error (file descriptor 2) in the manner of '>>| *word*'.

If one of the above is preceded by a digit, then the file descriptor referred to is that specified by the digit instead of the default 0 or 1. The order in which redirections are specified is significant. The shell evaluates each redirection in terms of the (*file descriptor*, *file*) association at the time of evaluation. For example:

> ... 1>*fname* 2>&1

first associates file descriptor 1 with file *fname*. It then associates file descriptor 2 with the file associated with file descriptor 1 (that is, *fname*). If the order of redirections were reversed, file descriptor 2 would be associated with the terminal (assuming file descriptor 1 had been) and then file descriptor 1 would be associated with file *fname*.

The '|&' command separator described in Section 6.1 [Simple Commands & Pipelines], page 10, is a shorthand for '2>&1 |'.

The various forms of process substitution, '<(*list*)', and '=(*list*)' for input and '>(*list*)' for output, are often used together with redirection. For example, if *word* in an output redirection is of the form '>(*list*)' then the output is piped to the command represented by *list*. See Section 14.2 [Process Substitution], page 50.

7.1 Opening file descriptors using parameters

When the shell is parsing arguments to a command, and the shell option `IGNORE_BRACES` is not set, a different form of redirection is allowed: instead of a digit before the operator there is a valid shell identifier enclosed in braces. The shell will open a new file descriptor that is guaranteed to be at least 10 and set the parameter named by the identifier to the file descriptor opened. No whitespace is allowed between the closing brace and the redirection character. For example:

> ... {myfd}>&1

This opens a new file descriptor that is a duplicate of file descriptor 1 and sets the parameter `myfd` to the number of the file descriptor, which will be at least 10. The new file descriptor can be written to using the syntax >&$myfd.

The syntax {*varid*}>&-, for example {myfd}>&-, may be used to close a file descriptor opened in this fashion. Note that the parameter given by *varid* must previously be set to a file descriptor in this case.

It is an error to open or close a file descriptor in this fashion when the parameter is readonly. However, it is not an error to read or write a file descriptor using <&$*param* or >&$*param* if *param* is readonly.

If the option `CLOBBER` is unset, it is an error to open a file descriptor using a parameter that is already set to an open file descriptor previously allocated by this mechanism. Unsetting the parameter before using it for allocating a file descriptor avoids the error.

Note that this mechanism merely allocates or closes a file descriptor; it does not perform any redirections from or to it. It is usually convenient to allocate a file descriptor prior to use as an argument to **exec**. The syntax does not in any case work when used around complex commands such as parenthesised subshells or loops, where the opening brace is interpreted as part of a command list to be executed in the current shell.

The following shows a typical sequence of allocation, use, and closing of a file descriptor:

```
integer myfd
exec {myfd}>~/logs/mylogfile.txt
print This is a log message. >&$myfd
exec {myfd}>&-
```

Note that the expansion of the variable in the expression `>&$myfd` occurs at the point the redirection is opened. This is after the expansion of command arguments and after any redirections to the left on the command line have been processed.

7.2 Multios

If the user tries to open a file descriptor for writing more than once, the shell opens the file descriptor as a pipe to a process that copies its input to all the specified outputs, similar to *tee*, provided the `MULTIOS` option is set, as it is by default. Thus:

```
date >foo >bar
```

writes the date to two files, named 'foo' and 'bar'. Note that a pipe is an implicit redirection; thus

```
date >foo | cat
```

writes the date to the file 'foo', and also pipes it to cat.

Note that the shell opens all the files to be used in the multio process immediately, not at the point they are about to be written.

Note also that redirections are always expanded in order. This happens regardless of the setting of the `MULTIOS` option, but with the option in effect there are additional consequences. For example, the meaning of the expression `>&1` will change after a previous redirection:

```
date >&1 >output
```

In the case above, the `>&1` refers to the standard output at the start of the line; the result is similar to the **tee** command. However, consider:

```
date >output >&1
```

As redirections are evaluated in order, when the `>&1` is encountered the standard output is set to the file **output** and another copy of the output is therefore sent to that file. This is unlikely to be what is intended.

If the `MULTIOS` option is set, the word after a redirection operator is also subjected to filename generation (globbing). Thus

```
: > *
```

will truncate all files in the current directory, assuming there's at least one. (Without the `MULTIOS` option, it would create an empty file called '*'.) Similarly, you can do

```
echo exit 0 >> *.sh
```

If the user tries to open a file descriptor for reading more than once, the shell opens the file descriptor as a pipe to a process that copies all the specified inputs to its output in the order specified, provided the `MULTIOS` option is set. It should be noted that each file is opened immediately, not at the point where it is about to be read: this behaviour differs from **cat**, so if strictly standard behaviour is needed, **cat** should be used instead.

Thus

```
sort <foo <fubar
```

or even

```
sort <f{oo,ubar}
```

is equivalent to 'cat foo fubar | sort'.

Expansion of the redirection argument occurs at the point the redirection is opened, at the point described above for the expansion of the variable in >&$myfd.

Note that a pipe is an implicit redirection; thus

```
cat bar | sort <foo
```

is equivalent to 'cat bar foo | sort' (note the order of the inputs).

If the MULTIOS option is *unset*, each redirection replaces the previous redirection for that file descriptor. However, all files redirected to are actually opened, so

```
echo Hello > bar > baz
```

when MULTIOS is unset will truncate 'bar', and write 'Hello' into 'baz'.

There is a problem when an output multio is attached to an external program. A simple example shows this:

```
cat file >file1 >file2
cat file1 file2
```

Here, it is possible that the second 'cat' will not display the full contents of file1 and file2 (i.e. the original contents of file repeated twice).

The reason for this is that the multios are spawned after the cat process is forked from the parent shell, so the parent shell does not wait for the multios to finish writing data. This means the command as shown can exit before file1 and file2 are completely written. As a workaround, it is possible to run the cat process as part of a job in the current shell:

```
{ cat file } >file >file2
```

Here, the {...} job will pause to wait for both files to be written.

7.3 Redirections with no command

When a simple command consists of one or more redirection operators and zero or more parameter assignments, but no command name, zsh can behave in several ways.

If the parameter NULLCMD is not set or the option CSH_NULLCMD is set, an error is caused. This is the *csh* behavior and CSH_NULLCMD is set by default when emulating *csh*.

If the option SH_NULLCMD is set, the builtin ':' is inserted as a command with the given redirections. This is the default when emulating *sh* or *ksh*.

Otherwise, if the parameter NULLCMD is set, its value will be used as a command with the given redirections. If both NULLCMD and READNULLCMD are set, then the value of the latter will be used instead of that of the former when the redirection is an input. The default for NULLCMD is 'cat' and for READNULLCMD is 'more'. Thus

```
< file
```

shows the contents of file on standard output, with paging if that is a terminal. NULLCMD and READNULLCMD may refer to shell functions.

8 Command Execution

If a command name contains no slashes, the shell attempts to locate it. If there exists a shell function by that name, the function is invoked as described in Chapter 9 [Functions], page 24. If there exists a shell builtin by that name, the builtin is invoked.

Otherwise, the shell searches each element of `$path` for a directory containing an executable file by that name. If the search is unsuccessful, the shell prints an error message and returns a nonzero exit status.

If execution fails because the file is not in executable format, and the file is not a directory, it is assumed to be a shell script. `/bin/sh` is spawned to execute it. If the program is a file beginning with '`#!`', the remainder of the first line specifies an interpreter for the program. The shell will execute the specified interpreter on operating systems that do not handle this executable format in the kernel.

If no external command is found but a function `command_not_found_handler` exists the shell executes this function with all command line arguments. The return status of the function becomes the status of the command. If the function wishes to mimic the behaviour of the shell when the command is not found, it should print the message '`command not found:` cmd' to standard error and return status 127. Note that the handler is executed in a subshell forked to execute an external command, hence changes to directories, shell parameters, etc. have no effect on the main shell.

9 Functions

Shell functions are defined with the `function` reserved word or the special syntax '*funcname* ()'. Shell functions are read in and stored internally. Alias names are resolved when the function is read. Functions are executed like commands with the arguments passed as positional parameters. (See Chapter 8 [Command Execution], page 24.)

Functions execute in the same process as the caller and share all files and present working directory with the caller. A trap on `EXIT` set inside a function is executed after the function completes in the environment of the caller.

The `return` builtin is used to return from function calls.

Function identifiers can be listed with the `functions` builtin. Functions can be undefined with the `unfunction` builtin.

9.1 Autoloading Functions

A function can be marked as *undefined* using the `autoload` builtin (or '`functions -u`' or '`typeset -fu`'). Such a function has no body. When the function is first executed, the shell searches for its definition using the elements of the `fpath` variable. Thus to define functions for autoloading, a typical sequence is:

```
fpath=(~/myfuncs $fpath)
autoload myfunc1 myfunc2 ...
```

The usual alias expansion during reading will be suppressed if the `autoload` builtin or its equivalent is given the option `-U`. This is recommended for the use of functions supplied with the zsh distribution. Note that for functions precompiled with the **zcompile** builtin command the flag **-U** must be provided when the **.zwc** file is created, as the corresponding information is compiled into the latter.

For each *element* in **fpath**, the shell looks for three possible files, the newest of which is used to load the definition for the function:

element.**zwc**

> A file created with the **zcompile** builtin command, which is expected to contain the definitions for all functions in the directory named *element*. The file is treated in the same manner as a directory containing files for functions and is searched for the definition of the function. If the definition is not found, the search for a definition proceeds with the other two possibilities described below.
>
> If *element* already includes a **.zwc** extension (i.e. the extension was explicitly given by the user), *element* is searched for the definition of the function without comparing its age to that of other files; in fact, there does not need to be any directory named *element* without the suffix. Thus including an element such as '**/usr/local/funcs.zwc**' in **fpath** will speed up the search for functions, with the disadvantage that functions included must be explicitly recompiled by hand before the shell notices any changes.

element/*function*.**zwc**

> A file created with **zcompile**, which is expected to contain the definition for *function*. It may include other function definitions as well, but those are neither loaded nor executed; a file found in this way is searched *only* for the definition of *function*.

element/*function*

> A file of zsh command text, taken to be the definition for *function*.

In summary, the order of searching is, first, in the *parents of* directories in **fpath** for the newer of either a compiled directory or a directory in **fpath**; second, if more than one of these contains a definition for the function that is sought, the leftmost in the **fpath** is chosen; and third, within a directory, the newer of either a compiled function or an ordinary function definition is used.

If the **KSH_AUTOLOAD** option is set, or the file contains only a simple definition of the function, the file's contents will be executed. This will normally define the function in question, but may also perform initialization, which is executed in the context of the function execution, and may therefore define local parameters. It is an error if the function is not defined by loading the file.

Otherwise, the function body (with no surrounding '*funcname*() {...}') is taken to be the complete contents of the file. This form allows the file to be used directly as an executable shell script. If processing of the file results in the function being re-defined, the function itself is not re-executed. To force the shell to perform initialization and then call the function defined, the file should contain initialization code (which will be executed then discarded) in addition to a complete function definition (which will be retained for subsequent calls to the function), and a call to the shell function, including any arguments, at the end.

For example, suppose the autoload file **func** contains

```
func() { print This is func; }
```

```
   print func is initialized
```

then 'func; func' with `KSH_AUTOLOAD` set will produce both messages on the first call, but only the message 'This is func' on the second and subsequent calls. Without `KSH_AUTOLOAD` set, it will produce the initialization message on the first call, and the other message on the second and subsequent calls.

It is also possible to create a function that is not marked as autoloaded, but which loads its own definition by searching `fpath`, by using 'autoload -X' within a shell function. For example, the following are equivalent:

```
myfunc() {
  autoload -X
}
myfunc args...
```

and

```
unfunction myfunc    # if myfunc was defined
autoload myfunc
myfunc args...
```

In fact, the `functions` command outputs 'builtin autoload -X' as the body of an autoloaded function. This is done so that

```
eval "$(functions)"
```

produces a reasonable result. A true autoloaded function can be identified by the presence of the comment '# undefined' in the body, because all comments are discarded from defined functions.

To load the definition of an autoloaded function `myfunc` without executing `myfunc`, use:

```
autoload +X myfunc
```

9.2 Anonymous Functions

If no name is given for a function, it is 'anonymous' and is handled specially. Either form of function definition may be used: a '()' with no preceding name, or a 'function' with an immediately following open brace. The function is executed immediately at the point of definition and is not stored for future use. The function name is set to '(anon)'.

Arguments to the function may be specified as words following the closing brace defining the function, hence if there are none no arguments (other than $0) are set. This is a difference from the way other functions are parsed: normal function definitions may be followed by certain keywords such as 'else' or 'fi', which will be treated as arguments to anonymous functions, so that a newline or semicolon is needed to force keyword interpretation.

Note also that the argument list of any enclosing script or function is hidden (as would be the case for any other function called at this point).

Redirections may be applied to the anonymous function in the same manner as to a current-shell structure enclosed in braces. The main use of anonymous functions is to provide a scope for local variables. This is particularly convenient in start-up files as these do not provide their own local variable scope.

For example,

```
variable=outside
function {
  local variable=inside
  print "I am $variable with arguments $*"
} this and that
print "I am $variable"
```

outputs the following:

```
I am inside with arguments this and that
I am outside
```

Note that function definitions with arguments that expand to nothing, for example 'name=; function $name { ... }', are not treated as anonymous functions. Instead, they are treated as normal function definitions where the definition is silently discarded.

9.3 Special Functions

Certain functions, if defined, have special meaning to the shell.

9.3.1 Hook Functions

For the functions below, it is possible to define an array that has the same name as the function with '_functions' appended. Any element in such an array is taken as the name of a function to execute; it is executed in the same context and with the same arguments as the basic function. For example, if $chpwd_functions is an array containing the values 'mychpwd', 'chpwd_save_dirstack', then the shell attempts to execute the functions 'chpwd', 'mychpwd' and 'chpwd_save_dirstack', in that order. Any function that does not exist is silently ignored. A function found by this mechanism is referred to elsewhere as a 'hook function'. An error in any function causes subsequent functions not to be run. Note further that an error in a **precmd** hook causes an immediately following **periodic** function not to run (though it may run at the next opportunity).

chpwd   Executed whenever the current working directory is changed.

periodic   If the parameter PERIOD is set, this function is executed every $PERIOD seconds, just before a prompt. Note that if multiple functions are defined using the array periodic_functions only one period is applied to the complete set of functions, and the scheduled time is not reset if the list of functions is altered. Hence the set of functions is always called together.

precmd   Executed before each prompt. Note that precommand functions are not re-executed simply because the command line is redrawn, as happens, for example, when a notification about an exiting job is displayed.

preexec   Executed just after a command has been read and is about to be executed. If the history mechanism is active (regardless of whether the line was discarded from the history buffer), the string that the user typed is passed as the first argument, otherwise it is an empty string. The actual command that will be executed (including expanded aliases) is passed in two different forms: the second argument is a single-line, size-limited version of the command (with things like function bodies elided); the third argument contains the full text that is being executed.

zshaddhistory

Executed when a history line has been read interactively, but before it is executed. The sole argument is the complete history line (so that any terminating newline will still be present).

If any of the hook functions returns status 1 (or any non-zero value other than 2, though this is not guaranteed for future versions of the shell) the history line will not be saved, although it lingers in the history until the next line is executed, allowing you to reuse or edit it immediately.

If any of the hook functions returns status 2 the history line will be saved on the internal history list, but not written to the history file. In case of a conflict, the first non-zero status value is taken.

A hook function may call 'fc -p ...' to switch the history context so that the history is saved in a different file from the that in the global HISTFILE parameter. This is handled specially: the history context is automatically restored after the processing of the history line is finished.

The following example function works with one of the options INC_APPEND_HISTORY or SHARE_HISTORY set, in order that the line is written out immediately after the history entry is added. It first adds the history line to the normal history with the newline stripped, which is usually the correct behaviour. Then it switches the history context so that the line will be written to a history file in the current directory.

```
zshaddhistory() {
  print -sr -- ${1%%$'\n'}
  fc -p .zsh_local_history
}
```

zshexit Executed at the point where the main shell is about to exit normally. This is not called by exiting subshells, nor when the **exec** precommand modifier is used before an external command. Also, unlike **TRAPEXIT**, it is not called when functions exit.

9.3.2 Trap Functions

The functions below are treated specially but do not have corresponding hook arrays.

TRAP*NAL* If defined and non-null, this function will be executed whenever the shell catches a signal **SIG***NAL*, where *NAL* is a signal name as specified for the **kill** builtin. The signal number will be passed as the first parameter to the function.

If a function of this form is defined and null, the shell and processes spawned by it will ignore **SIG***NAL*.

The return status from the function is handled specially. If it is zero, the signal is assumed to have been handled, and execution continues normally. Otherwise, the shell will behave as interrupted except that the return status of the trap is retained.

Programs terminated by uncaught signals typically return the status 128 plus the signal number. Hence the following causes the handler for `SIGINT` to print a message, then mimic the usual effect of the signal.

```
TRAPINT() {
  print "Caught SIGINT, aborting."
  return $(( 128 + $1 ))
}
```

The functions `TRAPZERR`, `TRAPDEBUG` and `TRAPEXIT` are never executed inside other traps.

`TRAPDEBUG`

> If the option `DEBUG_BEFORE_CMD` is set (as it is by default), executed before each command; otherwise executed after each command. See the description of the `trap` builtin in Chapter 17 [Shell Builtin Commands], page 139, for details of additional features provided in debug traps.

`TRAPEXIT` Executed when the shell exits, or when the current function exits if defined inside a function. The value of `$?` at the start of execution is the exit status of the shell or the return status of the function exiting.

`TRAPZERR` Executed whenever a command has a non-zero exit status. However, the function is not executed if the command occurred in a sublist followed by '`&&`' or '`||`'; only the final command in a sublist of this type causes the trap to be executed. The function `TRAPERR` acts the same as `TRAPZERR` on systems where there is no `SIGERR` (this is the usual case).

The functions beginning 'TRAP' may alternatively be defined with the `trap` builtin: this may be preferable for some uses. Setting a trap with one form removes any trap of the other form for the same signal; removing a trap in either form removes all traps for the same signal. The forms

```
TRAPNAL() {
 # code
}
```

('function traps') and

```
trap '
 # code
' NAL
```

('list traps') are equivalent in most ways, the exceptions being the following:

- Function traps have all the properties of normal functions, appearing in the list of functions and being called with their own function context rather than the context where the trap was triggered.

- The return status from function traps is special, whereas a return from a list trap causes the surrounding context to return with the given status.

- Function traps are not reset within subshells, in accordance with zsh behaviour; list traps are reset, in accordance with POSIX behaviour.

10 Jobs & Signals

10.1 Jobs

If the MONITOR option is set, an interactive shell associates a *job* with each pipeline. It keeps a table of current jobs, printed by the **jobs** command, and assigns them small integer numbers. When a job is started asynchronously with '&', the shell prints a line to standard error which looks like:

```
[1] 1234
```

indicating that the job which was started asynchronously was job number 1 and had one (top-level) process, whose process ID was 1234.

If a job is started with '&|' or '&!', then that job is immediately disowned. After startup, it does not have a place in the job table, and is not subject to the job control features described here.

If you are running a job and wish to do something else you may hit the key ^Z (control-Z) which sends a TSTP signal to the current job: this key may be redefined by the **susp** option of the external **stty** command. The shell will then normally indicate that the job has been 'suspended', and print another prompt. You can then manipulate the state of this job, putting it in the background with the **bg** command, or run some other commands and then eventually bring the job back into the foreground with the foreground command **fg**. A ^Z takes effect immediately and is like an interrupt in that pending output and unread input are discarded when it is typed.

A job being run in the background will suspend if it tries to read from the terminal.

Note that if the job running in the foreground is a shell function, then suspending it will have the effect of causing the shell to fork. This is necessary to separate the function's state from that of the parent shell performing the job control, so that the latter can return to the command line prompt. As a result, even if **fg** is used to continue the job the function will no longer be part of the parent shell, and any variables set by the function will not be visible in the parent shell. Thus the behaviour is different from the case where the function was never suspended. Zsh is different from many other shells in this regard.

One additional side effect is that use of **disown** with a job created by suspending shell code in this fashion is delayed: the job can only be disowned once any process started from the parent shell has terminated. At that point, the disowned job disappears silently from the job list.

The same behaviour is found when the shell is executing code as the right hand side of a pipeline or any complex shell construct such as **if**, **for**, etc., in order that the entire block of code can be managed as a single job. Background jobs are normally allowed to produce output, but this can be disabled by giving the command 'stty tostop'. If you set this tty option, then background jobs will suspend when they try to produce output like they do when they try to read input.

When a command is suspended and continued later with the **fg** or **wait** builtins, zsh restores tty modes that were in effect when it was suspended. This (intentionally) does not apply if the command is continued via 'kill -CONT', nor when it is continued with **bg**.

There are several ways to refer to jobs in the shell. A job can be referred to by the process ID of any process of the job or by one of the following:

%*number*   The job with the given number.

%*string*   The last job whose command line begins with *string*.

%?*string*   The last job whose command line contains *string*.

%%   Current job.

%+   Equivalent to '%%'.

%–   Previous job.

The shell learns immediately whenever a process changes state. It normally informs you whenever a job becomes blocked so that no further progress is possible. If the NOTIFY option is not set, it waits until just before it prints a prompt before it informs you. All such notifications are sent directly to the terminal, not to the standard output or standard error.

When the monitor mode is on, each background job that completes triggers any trap set for CHLD.

When you try to leave the shell while jobs are running or suspended, you will be warned that 'You have suspended (running) jobs'. You may use the **jobs** command to see what they are. If you do this or immediately try to exit again, the shell will not warn you a second time; the suspended jobs will be terminated, and the running jobs will be sent a SIGHUP signal, if the HUP option is set.

To avoid having the shell terminate the running jobs, either use the *nohup* command (see man page nohup(1)) or the **disown** builtin.

10.2 Signals

The INT and QUIT signals for an invoked command are ignored if the command is followed by '&' and the MONITOR option is not active. The shell itself always ignores the QUIT signal. Otherwise, signals have the values inherited by the shell from its parent (but see the TRAP*NAL* special functions in Chapter 9 [Functions], page 24).

Certain jobs are run asynchronously by the shell other than those explicitly put into the background; even in cases where the shell would usually wait for such jobs, an explicit **exit** command or exit due to the option ERR_EXIT will cause the shell to exit without waiting. Examples of such asynchronous jobs are process substitution, see Section 14.2 [Process Substitution], page 50, and the handler processes for multios, see the section Multios in Chapter 7 [Redirection], page 19.

11 Arithmetic Evaluation

The shell can perform integer and floating point arithmetic, either using the builtin **let**, or via a substitution of the form $((...)). For integers, the shell is usually compiled to use 8-byte precision where this is available, otherwise precision is 4 bytes. This can be tested, for example, by giving the command '**print - $((12345678901))**'; if the number appears unchanged, the precision is at least 8 bytes. Floating point arithmetic always uses the 'double' type with whatever corresponding precision is provided by the compiler and the library.

The `let` builtin command takes arithmetic expressions as arguments; each is evaluated separately. Since many of the arithmetic operators, as well as spaces, require quoting, an alternative form is provided: for any command which begins with a '`((`', all the characters until a matching '`))`' are treated as a quoted expression and arithmetic expansion performed as for an argument of `let`. More precisely, '`((...))`' is equivalent to '`let "..."`'. The return status is 0 if the arithmetic value of the expression is non-zero, 1 if it is zero, and 2 if an error occurred.

For example, the following statement

```
(( val = 2 + 1 ))
```

is equivalent to

```
let "val = 2 + 1"
```

both assigning the value 3 to the shell variable `val` and returning a zero status.

Integers can be in bases other than 10. A leading '`0x`' or '`0X`' denotes hexadecimal and a leading '`0b`' or '`0B`' binary. Integers may also be of the form '*base*#*n*', where *base* is a decimal number between two and thirty-six representing the arithmetic base and *n* is a number in that base (for example, '`16#ff`' is 255 in hexadecimal). The *base*# may also be omitted, in which case base 10 is used. For backwards compatibility the form '[*base*]*n*' is also accepted.

An integer expression or a base given in the form '*base*#*n*' may contain underscores ('`_`') after the leading digit for visual guidance; these are ignored in computation. Examples are `1_000_000` or `0xffff_ffff` which are equivalent to `1000000` and `0xffffffff` respectively.

It is also possible to specify a base to be used for output in the form '[#*base*]', for example '[#16]'. This is used when outputting arithmetical substitutions or when assigning to scalar parameters, but an explicitly defined integer or floating point parameter will not be affected. If an integer variable is implicitly defined by an arithmetic expression, any base specified in this way will be set as the variable's output arithmetic base as if the option '`-i` *base*' to the `typeset` builtin had been used. The expression has no precedence and if it occurs more than once in a mathematical expression, the last encountered is used. For clarity it is recommended that it appear at the beginning of an expression. As an example:

```
typeset -i 16 y
print $(( [#8] x = 32, y = 32 ))
print $x $y
```

outputs first '8#40', the rightmost value in the given output base, and then '8#40 16#20', because `y` has been explicitly declared to have output base 16, while `x` (assuming it does not already exist) is implicitly typed by the arithmetic evaluation, where it acquires the output base 8.

The *base* may be replaced or followed by an underscore, which may itself be followed by a positive integer (if it is missing the value 3 is used). This indicates that underscores should be inserted into the output string, grouping the number for visual clarity. The following integer specifies the number of digits to group together. For example:

```
setopt cbases
print $(( [#16_4] 65536 ** 2 ))
```

outputs '0x1_0000_0000'.

The feature can be used with floating point numbers, in which case the base must be omitted; grouping is away from the decimal point. For example,

```
zmodload zsh/mathfunc
print $(( [#_] sqrt(1e7) ))
```

outputs '3_162.277_660_168_379_5' (the number of decimal places shown may vary).

If the `C_BASES` option is set, hexadecimal numbers are output in the standard C format, for example '0xFF' instead of the usual '16#FF'. If the option `OCTAL_ZEROES` is also set (it is not by default), octal numbers will be treated similarly and hence appear as '077' instead of '8#77'. This option has no effect on the output of bases other than hexadecimal and octal, and these formats are always understood on input.

When an output base is specified using the '[#base]' syntax, an appropriate base prefix will be output if necessary, so that the value output is valid syntax for input. If the `#` is doubled, for example '[##16]', then no base prefix is output.

Floating point constants are recognized by the presence of a decimal point or an exponent. The decimal point may be the first character of the constant, but the exponent character `e` or `E` may not, as it will be taken for a parameter name. All numeric parts (before and after the decimal point and in the exponent) may contain underscores after the leading digit for visual guidance; these are ignored in computation.

An arithmetic expression uses nearly the same syntax and associativity of expressions as in C.

In the native mode of operation, the following operators are supported (listed in decreasing order of precedence):

`+ - ! ~ ++ --`
    unary plus/minus, logical NOT, complement, {pre,post}{in,de}crement

`<< >>`   bitwise shift left, right

`&`   bitwise AND

`^`   bitwise XOR

`|`   bitwise OR

`**`   exponentiation

`* / %`   multiplication, division, modulus (remainder)

`+ -`   addition, subtraction

`< > <= >=`
    comparison

`== !=`   equality and inequality

`&&`   logical AND

`|| ^^`   logical OR, XOR

`? :`   ternary operator

`= += -= *= /= %= &= ^= |= <<= >>= &&= ||= ^^= **=`
    assignment

,   comma operator

The operators '&&', '||', '&&=', and '||=' are short-circuiting, and only one of the latter two expressions in a ternary operator is evaluated. Note the precedence of the bitwise AND, OR, and XOR operators.

With the option `C_PRECEDENCES` the precedences (but no other properties) of the operators are altered to be the same as those in most other languages that support the relevant operators:

```
+ - ! ~ ++ --
```
          unary plus/minus, logical NOT, complement, {pre,post}{in,de}crement

`**`   exponentiation

`* / %`   multiplication, division, modulus (remainder)

`+ -`   addition, subtraction

`<< >>`   bitwise shift left, right

```
< > <= >=
```
          comparison

`== !=`   equality and inequality

`&`   bitwise AND

`^`   bitwise XOR

`|`   bitwise OR

`&&`   logical AND

`^^`   logical XOR

`||`   logical OR

`? :`   ternary operator

```
= += -= *= /= %= &= ^= |= <<= >>= &&= ||= ^^= **=
```
          assignment

,   comma operator

Note the precedence of exponentiation in both cases is below that of unary operators, hence '-3**2' evaluates as '9', not '-9'. Use parentheses where necessary: '-(3**2)'. This is for compatibility with other shells.

Mathematical functions can be called with the syntax 'func(args)', where the function decides if the *args* is used as a string or a comma-separated list of arithmetic expressions. The shell currently defines no mathematical functions by default, but the module `zsh/mathfunc` may be loaded with the `zmodload` builtin to provide standard floating point mathematical functions.

An expression of the form '##x' where *x* is any character sequence such as 'a', '^A', or '\M-\C-x' gives the value of this character and an expression of the form '#*name*' gives the value of the first character of the contents of the parameter *name*. Character values are according to the character set used in the current locale; for multibyte character handling the option MULTIBYTE must be set. Note that this form is different from '$#*name*', a standard parameter substitution which gives the length of the parameter *name*. '#\' is accepted instead of '##', but its use is deprecated.

Named parameters and subscripted arrays can be referenced by name within an arithmetic expression without using the parameter expansion syntax. For example,

```
((val2 = val1 * 2))
```

assigns twice the value of $val1 to the parameter named val2.

An internal integer representation of a named parameter can be specified with the **integer** builtin. Arithmetic evaluation is performed on the value of each assignment to a named parameter declared integer in this manner. Assigning a floating point number to an integer results in rounding towards zero.

Likewise, floating point numbers can be declared with the **float** builtin; there are two types, differing only in their output format, as described for the **typeset** builtin. The output format can be bypassed by using arithmetic substitution instead of the parameter substitution, i.e. '${*float*}' uses the defined format, but '$((*float*))' uses a generic floating point format.

Promotion of integer to floating point values is performed where necessary. In addition, if any operator which requires an integer ('&', '|', '^', '<<', '>>' and their equivalents with assignment) is given a floating point argument, it will be silently rounded towards zero except for '~' which rounds down.

Users should beware that, in common with many other programming languages but not software designed for calculation, the evaluation of an expression in zsh is taken a term at a time and promotion of integers to floating point does not occur in terms only containing integers. A typical result of this is that a division such as **6/8** is truncated, in this being rounded towards 0. The **FORCE_FLOAT** shell option can be used in scripts or functions where floating point evaluation is required throughout.

Scalar variables can hold integer or floating point values at different times; there is no memory of the numeric type in this case.

If a variable is first assigned in a numeric context without previously being declared, it will be implicitly typed as **integer** or **float** and retain that type either until the type is explicitly changed or until the end of the scope. This can have unforeseen consequences. For example, in the loop

```
for (( f = 0; f < 1; f += 0.1 )); do
# use $f
done
```

if **f** has not already been declared, the first assignment will cause it to be created as an integer, and consequently the operation 'f += 0.1' will always cause the result to be truncated to zero, so that the loop will fail. A simple fix would be to turn the initialization into 'f = 0.0'. It is therefore best to declare numeric variables with explicit types.

12 Conditional Expressions

A *conditional expression* is used with the `[[` compound command to test attributes of files and to compare strings. Each expression can be constructed from one or more of the following unary or binary expressions:

-a *file*   true if *file* exists.

-b *file*   true if *file* exists and is a block special file.

-c *file*   true if *file* exists and is a character special file.

-d *file*   true if *file* exists and is a directory.

-e *file*   true if *file* exists.

-f *file*   true if *file* exists and is a regular file.

-g *file*   true if *file* exists and has its setgid bit set.

-h *file*   true if *file* exists and is a symbolic link.

-k *file*   true if *file* exists and has its sticky bit set.

-n *string*   true if length of *string* is non-zero.

-o *option*   true if option named *option* is on. *option* may be a single character, in which case it is a single letter option name. (See Section 16.1 [Specifying Options], page 110.)

When no option named *option* exists, and the `POSIX_BUILTINS` option hasn't been set, return 3 with a warning. If that option is set, return 1 with no warning.

-p *file*   true if *file* exists and is a FIFO special file (named pipe).

-r *file*   true if *file* exists and is readable by current process.

-s *file*   true if *file* exists and has size greater than zero.

-t *fd*   true if file descriptor number *fd* is open and associated with a terminal device. (note: *fd* is not optional)

-u *file*   true if *file* exists and has its setuid bit set.

-v *varname*
               true if shell variable *varname* is set.

-w *file*   true if *file* exists and is writable by current process.

-x *file*   true if *file* exists and is executable by current process. If *file* exists and is a directory, then the current process has permission to search in the directory.

-z *string*   true if length of *string* is zero.

-L *file*   true if *file* exists and is a symbolic link.

-O *file*   true if *file* exists and is owned by the effective user ID of this process.

-G *file*   true if *file* exists and its group matches the effective group ID of this process.

-S *file* true if *file* exists and is a socket.

-N *file* true if *file* exists and its access time is not newer than its modification time.

file1 -nt *file2*
> true if *file1* exists and is newer than *file2*.

file1 -ot *file2*
> true if *file1* exists and is older than *file2*.

file1 -ef *file2*
> true if *file1* and *file2* exist and refer to the same file.

string = *pattern*
string == *pattern*
> true if *string* matches *pattern*. The two forms are exactly equivalent. The '=' form is the traditional shell syntax (and hence the only one generally used with the **test** and [builtins); the '==' form provides compatibility with other sorts of computer language.

string != *pattern*
> true if *string* does not match *pattern*.

string =~ *regexp*
> true if *string* matches the regular expression *regexp*. If the option RE_MATCH_PCRE is set *regexp* is tested as a PCRE regular expression using the **zsh/pcre** module, else it is tested as a POSIX extended regular expression using the **zsh/regex** module. Upon successful match, some variables will be updated; no variables are changed if the matching fails.
>
> If the option BASH_REMATCH is not set the scalar parameter MATCH is set to the substring that matched the pattern and the integer parameters MBEGIN and MEND to the index of the start and end, respectively, of the match in *string*, such that if *string* is contained in variable **var** the expression '${var[$MBEGIN,$MEND]}' is identical to '$MATCH'. The setting of the option KSH_ARRAYS is respected. Likewise, the array **match** is set to the substrings that matched parenthesised subexpressions and the arrays **mbegin** and **mend** to the indices of the start and end positions, respectively, of the substrings within *string*. The arrays are not set if there were no parenthesised subexpresssions. For example, if the string 'a short string' is matched against the regular expression 's(...)t', then (assuming the option KSH_ARRAYS is not set) MATCH, MBEGIN and MEND are 'short', 3 and 7, respectively, while **match**, **mbegin** and **mend** are single entry arrays containing the strings 'hor', '4' and '6', respectively.
>
> If the option BASH_REMATCH is set the array BASH_REMATCH is set to the substring that matched the pattern followed by the substrings that matched parenthesised subexpressions within the pattern.

string1 < *string2*
> true if *string1* comes before *string2* based on ASCII value of their characters.

string1 > *string2*
> true if *string1* comes after *string2* based on ASCII value of their characters.

exp1 -eq *exp2*

> true if *exp1* is numerically equal to *exp2*. Note that for purely numeric comparisons use of the ((...)) builtin described in Chapter 11 [Arithmetic Evaluation], page 31, is more convenient than conditional expressions.

exp1 -ne *exp2*

> true if *exp1* is numerically not equal to *exp2*.

exp1 -lt *exp2*

> true if *exp1* is numerically less than *exp2*.

exp1 -gt *exp2*

> true if *exp1* is numerically greater than *exp2*.

exp1 -le *exp2*

> true if *exp1* is numerically less than or equal to *exp2*.

exp1 -ge *exp2*

> true if *exp1* is numerically greater than or equal to *exp2*.

(*exp*)   true if *exp* is true.

! *exp*   true if *exp* is false.

exp1 && *exp2*

> true if *exp1* and *exp2* are both true.

exp1 || *exp2*

> true if either *exp1* or *exp2* is true.

For compatibility, if there is a single argument that is not syntactically significant, typically a variable, the condition is treated as a test for whether the expression expands as a string of non-zero length. In other words, [[$var]] is the same as [[-n $var]]. It is recommended that the second, explicit, form be used where possible.

Normal shell expansion is performed on the *file*, *string* and *pattern* arguments, but the result of each expansion is constrained to be a single word, similar to the effect of double quotes.

Filename generation is not performed on any form of argument to conditions. However, it can be forced in any case where normal shell expansion is valid and when the option EXTENDED_GLOB is in effect by using an explicit glob qualifier of the form (#q) at the end of the string. A normal glob qualifier expression may appear between the 'q' and the closing parenthesis; if none appears the expression has no effect beyond causing filename generation. The results of filename generation are joined together to form a single word, as with the results of other forms of expansion.

This special use of filename generation is only available with the [[syntax. If the condition occurs within the [or test builtin commands then globbing occurs instead as part of normal command line expansion before the condition is evaluated. In this case it may generate multiple words which are likely to confuse the syntax of the test command.

For example,

```
[[ -n file*(#qN) ]]
```

produces status zero if and only if there is at least one file in the current directory beginning with the string 'file'. The globbing qualifier N ensures that the expression is empty if there is no matching file.

Pattern metacharacters are active for the *pattern* arguments; the patterns are the same as those used for filename generation, see Section 14.8 [Filename Generation], page 72, but there is no special behaviour of '/' nor initial dots, and no glob qualifiers are allowed.

In each of the above expressions, if *file* is of the form '/dev/fd/*n*', where *n* is an integer, then the test applied to the open file whose descriptor number is *n*, even if the underlying system does not support the /dev/fd directory.

In the forms which do numeric comparison, the expressions *exp* undergo arithmetic expansion as if they were enclosed in $((...)).

For example, the following:

```
[[ ( -f foo || -f bar ) && $report = y* ]] && print File exists.
```

tests if either file foo or file bar exists, and if so, if the value of the parameter report begins with 'y'; if the complete condition is true, the message 'File exists.' is printed.

13 Prompt Expansion

13.1 Expansion of Prompt Sequences

Prompt sequences undergo a special form of expansion. This type of expansion is also available using the -P option to the print builtin.

If the PROMPT_SUBST option is set, the prompt string is first subjected to *parameter expansion*, *command substitution* and *arithmetic expansion*. See Chapter 14 [Expansion], page 45.

Certain escape sequences may be recognised in the prompt string.

If the PROMPT_BANG option is set, a '!' in the prompt is replaced by the current history event number. A literal '!' may then be represented as '!!'.

If the PROMPT_PERCENT option is set, certain escape sequences that start with '%' are expanded. Many escapes are followed by a single character, although some of these take an optional integer argument that should appear between the '%' and the next character of the sequence. More complicated escape sequences are available to provide conditional expansion.

13.2 Simple Prompt Escapes

13.2.1 Special characters

%%   A '%'.

%)   A ')'.

13.2.2 Login information

%l
The line (tty) the user is logged in on, without '/dev/' prefix. If the name starts with '/dev/tty', that prefix is stripped.

%M
The full machine hostname.

%m
The hostname up to the first '.'. An integer may follow the '%' to specify how many components of the hostname are desired. With a negative integer, trailing components of the hostname are shown.

%n
$USERNAME.

%y
The line (tty) the user is logged in on, without '/dev/' prefix. This does not treat '/dev/tty' names specially.

13.2.3 Shell state

%#
A '#' if the shell is running with privileges, a '%' if not. Equivalent to '%(!.#.%%)'. The definition of 'privileged', for these purposes, is that either the effective user ID is zero, or, if POSIX.1e capabilities are supported, that at least one capability is raised in either the Effective or Inheritable capability vectors.

%?
The return status of the last command executed just before the prompt.

%_
The status of the parser, i.e. the shell constructs (like 'if' and 'for') that have been started on the command line. If given an integer number that many strings will be printed; zero or negative or no integer means print as many as there are. This is most useful in prompts PS2 for continuation lines and PS4 for debugging with the XTRACE option; in the latter case it will also work non-interactively.

%^
The status of the parser in reverse. This is the same as '%_' other than the order of strings. It is often used in RPS2.

%d
%/
Current working directory. If an integer follows the '%', it specifies a number of trailing components of the current working directory to show; zero means the whole path. A negative integer specifies leading components, i.e. %-1d specifies the first component.

%~
As %d and %/, but if the current working directory starts with $HOME, that part is replaced by a '~'. Furthermore, if it has a named directory as its prefix, that part is replaced by a '~' followed by the name of the directory, but only if the result is shorter than the full path; Section 14.7 [Filename Expansion], page 69.

%e
Evaluation depth of the current sourced file, shell function, or eval. This is incremented or decremented every time the value of %N is set or reverted to a previous value, respectively. This is most useful for debugging as part of $PS4.

%h
%!
Current history event number.

%i
The line number currently being executed in the script, sourced file, or shell function given by %N. This is most useful for debugging as part of $PS4.

%I   The line number currently being executed in the file %x. This is similar to %i, but the line number is always a line number in the file where the code was defined, even if the code is a shell function.

%j   The number of jobs.

%L   The current value of $SHLVL.

%N   The name of the script, sourced file, or shell function that zsh is currently executing, whichever was started most recently. If there is none, this is equivalent to the parameter $0. An integer may follow the '%' to specify a number of trailing path components to show; zero means the full path. A negative integer specifies leading components.

%x   The name of the file containing the source code currently being executed. This behaves as %N except that function and eval command names are not shown, instead the file where they were defined.

%c
%.
%C   Trailing component of the current working directory. An integer may follow the '%' to get more than one component. Unless '%C' is used, tilde contraction is performed first. These are deprecated as %c and %C are equivalent to %1~ and %1/, respectively, while explicit positive integers have the same effect as for the latter two sequences.

13.2.4 Date and time

%D   The date in *yy-mm-dd* format.

%T   Current time of day, in 24-hour format.

%t
%@   Current time of day, in 12-hour, am/pm format.

%*   Current time of day in 24-hour format, with seconds.

%w   The date in *day-dd* format.

%W   The date in *mm/dd/yy* format.

%D{*string*}

     string is formatted using the **strftime** function. See man page strftime(3) for more details. Various zsh extensions provide numbers with no leading zero or space if the number is a single digit:

     %f   a day of the month

     %K   the hour of the day on the 24-hour clock

     %L   the hour of the day on the 12-hour clock

     In addition, if the system supports the POSIX **gettimeofday** system call, %. provides decimal fractions of a second since the epoch with leading zeroes. By default three decimal places are provided, but a number of digits up to 9 may be given following the %; hence %6. outputs microseconds, and %9. outputs nanoseconds. (The latter requires a nanosecond-precision `clock_gettime`; systems lacking this will return a value multiplied by the appropriate power of 10.) A typical example of this is the format '`%D{%H:%M:%S.%.}`'.

The GNU extension `%N` is handled as a synonym for `%9.`.

Additionally, the GNU extension that a '–' between the `%` and the format character causes a leading zero or space to be stripped is handled directly by the shell for the format characters d, f, H, k, l, m, M, S and y; any other format characters are provided to the system's strftime(3) with any leading '–' present, so the handling is system dependent. Further GNU (or other) extensions are also passed to strftime(3) and may work if the system supports them.

13.2.5 Visual effects

%B (%b)   Start (stop) boldface mode.

%E   Clear to end of line.

%U (%u)   Start (stop) underline mode.

%S (%s)   Start (stop) standout mode.

%F (%f)   Start (stop) using a different foreground colour, if supported by the terminal. The colour may be specified two ways: either as a numeric argument, as normal, or by a sequence in braces following the %F, for example %F{red}. In the latter case the values allowed are as described for the `fg zle_highlight` attribute; Section 18.7 [Character Highlighting], page 221. This means that numeric colours are allowed in the second format also.

%K (%k)   Start (stop) using a different bacKground colour. The syntax is identical to that for %F and %f.

%{...%}   Include a string as a literal escape sequence. The string within the braces should not change the cursor position. Brace pairs can nest.

A positive numeric argument between the % and the { is treated as described for %G below.

%G   Within a %{...%} sequence, include a 'glitch': that is, assume that a single character width will be output. This is useful when outputting characters that otherwise cannot be correctly handled by the shell, such as the alternate character set on some terminals. The characters in question can be included within a %{...%} sequence together with the appropriate number of %G sequences to indicate the correct width. An integer between the '%' and 'G' indicates a character width other than one. Hence %{seq%2G%} outputs seq and assumes it takes up the width of two standard characters.

Multiple uses of %G accumulate in the obvious fashion; the position of the %G is unimportant. Negative integers are not handled.

Note that when prompt truncation is in use it is advisable to divide up output into single characters within each %{...%} group so that the correct truncation point can be found.

13.3 Conditional Substrings in Prompts

%v   The value of the first element of the **psvar** array parameter. Following the '%' with an integer gives that element of the array. Negative integers count from the end of the array.

%(*x.true-text.false-text*)

Specifies a ternary expression. The character following the *x* is arbitrary; the same character is used to separate the text for the 'true' result from that for the 'false' result. This separator may not appear in the *true-text*, except as part of a %-escape sequence. A ')' may appear in the *false-text* as '%)'. *true-text* and *false-text* may both contain arbitrarily-nested escape sequences, including further ternary expressions.

The left parenthesis may be preceded or followed by a positive integer n, which defaults to zero. A negative integer will be multiplied by -1, except as noted below for '**l**'. The test character x may be any of the following:

!	True if the shell is running with privileges.
#	True if the effective uid of the current process is n.
?	True if the exit status of the last command was n.
_	True if at least n shell constructs were started.
C	
/	True if the current absolute path has at least n elements relative to the root directory, hence / is counted as 0 elements.
c	
.	
~	True if the current path, with prefix replacement, has at least n elements relative to the root directory, hence / is counted as 0 elements.
D	True if the month is equal to n (January $= 0$).
d	True if the day of the month is equal to n.
e	True if the evaluation depth is at least n.
g	True if the effective gid of the current process is n.
j	True if the number of jobs is at least n.
L	True if the **SHLVL** parameter is at least n.
l	True if at least n characters have already been printed on the current line. When n is negative, true if at least **abs**(n) characters remain before the opposite margin (thus the left margin for **RPROMPT**).
S	True if the **SECONDS** parameter is at least n.
T	True if the time in hours is equal to n.
t	True if the time in minutes is equal to n.

v   True if the array `psvar` has at least n elements.

V   True if element n of the array `psvar` is set and non-empty.

w   True if the day of the week is equal to n (Sunday = 0).

%<*string*<
%>*string*>
%[*xstring*]

Specifies truncation behaviour for the remainder of the prompt string. The third, deprecated, form is equivalent to '%*xstring*x', i.e. x may be '<' or '>'. The *string* will be displayed in place of the truncated portion of any string; note this does not undergo prompt expansion.

The numeric argument, which in the third form may appear immediately after the '[', specifies the maximum permitted length of the various strings that can be displayed in the prompt. In the first two forms, this numeric argument may be negative, in which case the truncation length is determined by subtracting the absolute value of the numeric argument from the number of character positions remaining on the current prompt line. If this results in a zero or negative length, a length of 1 is used. In other words, a negative argument arranges that after truncation at least n characters remain before the right margin (left margin for `RPROMPT`).

The forms with '<' truncate at the left of the string, and the forms with '>' truncate at the right of the string. For example, if the current directory is '/home/pike', the prompt '%8<..<%/' will expand to '..e/pike'. In this string, the terminating character ('<', '>' or ']'), or in fact any character, may be quoted by a preceding '\'; note when using `print -P`, however, that this must be doubled as the string is also subject to standard `print` processing, in addition to any backslashes removed by a double quoted string: the worst case is therefore '`print -P "%<\\\\<<..."`'.

If the *string* is longer than the specified truncation length, it will appear in full, completely replacing the truncated string.

The part of the prompt string to be truncated runs to the end of the string, or to the end of the next enclosing group of the '%(' construct, or to the next truncation encountered at the same grouping level (i.e. truncations inside a '%(' are separate), which ever comes first. In particular, a truncation with argument zero (e.g., '%<<') marks the end of the range of the string to be truncated while turning off truncation from there on. For example, the prompt '%10<...<%~%<<%# ' will print a truncated representation of the current directory, followed by a '%' or '#', followed by a space. Without the '%<<', those two characters would be included in the string to be truncated. Note that '%-0<<' is not equivalent to '%<<' but specifies that the prompt is truncated at the right margin.

Truncation applies only within each individual line of the prompt, as delimited by embedded newlines (if any). If the total length of any line of the prompt after truncation is greater than the terminal width, or if the part to be truncated contains embedded newlines, truncation behavior is undefined and may change in a future version of the shell. Use '%-n(1.*true-text*.*false-text*)' to remove parts of the prompt when the available space is less than *n*.

14 Expansion

The following types of expansions are performed in the indicated order in five steps:

History Expansion
> This is performed only in interactive shells.

Alias Expansion
> Aliases are expanded immediately before the command line is parsed as explained in Section 6.8 [Aliasing], page 17.

Process Substitution
Parameter Expansion
Command Substitution
Arithmetic Expansion
Brace Expansion
> These five are performed in left-to-right fashion. On each argument, any of the five steps that are needed are performed one after the other. Hence, for example, all the parts of parameter expansion are completed before command substitution is started. After these expansions, all unquoted occurrences of the characters '\','' and '"' are removed.

Filename Expansion
> If the `SH_FILE_EXPANSION` option is set, the order of expansion is modified for compatibility with *sh* and *ksh*. In that case *filename expansion* is performed immediately after *alias expansion*, preceding the set of five expansions mentioned above.

Filename Generation
> This expansion, commonly referred to as *globbing*, is always done last.

The following sections explain the types of expansion in detail.

14.1 History Expansion

History expansion allows you to use words from previous command lines in the command line you are typing. This simplifies spelling corrections and the repetition of complicated commands or arguments.

Immediately before execution, each command is saved in the history list, the size of which is controlled by the `HISTSIZE` parameter. The one most recent command is always retained in any case. Each saved command in the history list is called a history *event* and is assigned a number, beginning with 1 (one) when the shell starts up. The history number that you may see in your prompt (see Chapter 13 [Prompt Expansion], page 39) is the number that is to be assigned to the *next* command.

14.1.1 Overview

A history expansion begins with the first character of the `histchars` parameter, which is '!' by default, and may occur anywhere on the command line, including inside double quotes (but not inside single quotes '...' or C-style quotes $'...' nor when escaped with a backslash).

The first character is followed by an optional event designator (Section 14.1.2 [Event Designators], page 46) and then an optional word designator (Section 14.1.3 [Word Designators], page 47); if neither of these designators is present, no history expansion occurs.

Input lines containing history expansions are echoed after being expanded, but before any other expansions take place and before the command is executed. It is this expanded form that is recorded as the history event for later references.

History expansions do not nest.

By default, a history reference with no event designator refers to the same event as any preceding history reference on that command line; if it is the only history reference in a command, it refers to the previous command. However, if the option `CSH_JUNKIE_HISTORY` is set, then every history reference with no event specification *always* refers to the previous command.

For example, '!' is the event designator for the previous command, so '!!:1' always refers to the first word of the previous command, and '!!$' always refers to the last word of the previous command. With `CSH_JUNKIE_HISTORY` set, then '!:1' and '!$' function in the same manner as '!!:1' and '!!$', respectively. Conversely, if `CSH_JUNKIE_HISTORY` is unset, then '!:1' and '!$' refer to the first and last words, respectively, of the same event referenced by the nearest other history reference preceding them on the current command line, or to the previous command if there is no preceding reference.

The character sequence '^*foo*^*bar*' (where '^' is actually the second character of the `histchars` parameter) repeats the last command, replacing the string *foo* with *bar*. More precisely, the sequence '^*foo*^*bar*^' is synonymous with '!!:s^*foo*^*bar*^', hence other modifiers (see Section 14.1.4 [Modifiers], page 47) may follow the final '^'. In particular, '^*foo*^*bar*^:G' performs a global substitution.

If the shell encounters the character sequence '!"' in the input, the history mechanism is temporarily disabled until the current list (see Chapter 6 [Shell Grammar], page 10) is fully parsed. The '!"' is removed from the input, and any subsequent '!' characters have no special significance.

A less convenient but more comprehensible form of command history support is provided by the `fc` builtin.

14.1.2 Event Designators

An event designator is a reference to a command-line entry in the history list. In the list below, remember that the initial '!' in each item may be changed to another character by setting the `histchars` parameter.

!   Start a history expansion, except when followed by a blank, newline, '=' or '('. If followed immediately by a word designator (Section 14.1.3 [Word Designators], page 47), this forms a history reference with no event designator (Section 14.1.1 [Overview], page 46).

!!	Refer to the previous command. By itself, this expansion repeats the previous command.
!*n*	Refer to command-line *n*.
!-*n*	Refer to the current command-line minus *n*.
!*str*	Refer to the most recent command starting with *str*.
!?*str*[?]	Refer to the most recent command containing *str*. The trailing '?' is necessary if this reference is to be followed by a modifier or followed by any text that is not to be considered part of *str*.
!#	Refer to the current command line typed in so far. The line is treated as if it were complete up to and including the word before the one with the '!#' reference.
!{...}	Insulate a history reference from adjacent characters (if necessary).

14.1.3 Word Designators

A word designator indicates which word or words of a given command line are to be included in a history reference. A ':' usually separates the event specification from the word designator. It may be omitted only if the word designator begins with a '^', '$', '*', '-' or '%'. Word designators include:

0	The first input word (command).
n	The *n*th argument.
^	The first argument. That is, 1.
$	The last argument.
%	The word matched by (the most recent) ?*str* search.
x-*y*	A range of words; *x* defaults to 0.
*	All the arguments, or a null value if there are none.
*x****	Abbreviates '*x*-$'.
x-	Like '*x****' but omitting word $.

Note that a '%' word designator works only when used in one of '!%', '!:%' or '!?*str*?:%', and only when used after a !? expansion (possibly in an earlier command). Anything else results in an error, although the error may not be the most obvious one.

14.1.4 Modifiers

After the optional word designator, you can add a sequence of one or more of the following modifiers, each preceded by a ':'. These modifiers also work on the result of *filename generation* and *parameter expansion*, except where noted.

a	Turn a file name into an absolute path: prepends the current directory, if necessary; remove '.' path segments; and remove '..' path segments and the segments that immediately precede them.

This transformation is agnostic about what is in the filesystem, i.e. is on the logical, not the physical directory. It takes place in the same manner as when changing directories when neither of the options CHASE_DOTS or CHASE_LINKS is set. For example, '/before/here/../after' is always transformed to '/before/after', regardless of whether '/before/here' exists or what kind of object (dir, file, symlink, etc.) it is.

A   Turn a file name into an absolute path as the 'a' modifier does, and *then* pass the result through the realpath(3) library function to resolve symbolic links.

Note: on systems that do not have a realpath(3) library function, symbolic links are not resolved, so on those systems 'a' and 'A' are equivalent.

Note: foo:A and realpath(foo) are different on some inputs. For realpath(foo) semantics, see the 'P' modifier.

c   Resolve a command name into an absolute path by searching the command path given by the PATH variable. This does not work for commands containing directory parts. Note also that this does not usually work as a glob qualifier unless a file of the same name is found in the current directory.

e   Remove all but the part of the filename extension following the '.'; see the definition of the filename extension in the description of the r modifier below. Note that according to that definition the result will be empty if the string ends with a '.'.

h   Remove a trailing pathname component, leaving the head. This works like 'dirname'.

l   Convert the words to all lowercase.

p   Print the new command but do not execute it. Only works with history expansion.

P   Turn a file name into an absolute path, like realpath(3). The resulting path will be absolute, have neither '.' nor '..' components, and refer to the same directory entry as the input filename.

Unlike realpath(3), non-existent trailing components are permitted and preserved.

q   Quote the substituted words, escaping further substitutions. Works with history expansion and parameter expansion, though for parameters it is only useful if the resulting text is to be re-evaluated such as by eval.

Q   Remove one level of quotes from the substituted words.

r   Remove a filename extension leaving the root name. Strings with no filename extension are not altered. A filename extension is a '.' followed by any number of characters (including zero) that are neither '.' nor '/' and that continue to the end of the string. For example, the extension of 'foo.orig.c' is '.c', and 'dir.c/foo' has no extension.

s/l/r[/]   Substitute *r* for *l* as described below. The substitution is done only for the first string that matches *l*. For arrays and for filename generation, this applies to each word of the expanded text. See below for further notes on substitutions.

The forms 'gs/*l*/*r*' and 's/*l*/*r*/:G' perform global substitution, i.e. substitute every occurrence of *r* for *l*. Note that the g or :G must appear in exactly the position shown.

See further notes on this form of substitution below.

    &   Repeat the previous s substitution. Like s, may be preceded immediately by a g. In parameter expansion the & must appear inside braces, and in filename generation it must be quoted with a backslash.

    t   Remove all leading pathname components, leaving the tail. This works like 'basename'.

    u   Convert the words to all uppercase.

    x   Like q, but break into words at whitespace. Does not work with parameter expansion.

The s/*l*/*r*/ substitution works as follows. By default the left-hand side of substitutions are not patterns, but character strings. Any character can be used as the delimiter in place of '/'. A backslash quotes the delimiter character. The character '&', in the right-hand-side *r*, is replaced by the text from the left-hand-side *l*. The '&' can be quoted with a backslash. A null *l* uses the previous string either from the previous *l* or from the contextual scan string *s* from '!?*s*'. You can omit the rightmost delimiter if a newline immediately follows *r*; the rightmost '?' in a context scan can similarly be omitted. Note the same record of the last *l* and *r* is maintained across all forms of expansion.

Note that if a '&' is used within glob qualifiers an extra backslash is needed as a & is a special character in this case.

Also note that the order of expansions affects the interpretation of *l* and *r*. When used in a history expansion, which occurs before any other expansions, *l* and *r* are treated as literal strings (except as explained for HIST_SUBST_PATTERN below). When used in parameter expansion, the replacement of *r* into the parameter's value is done first, and then any additional process, parameter, command, arithmetic, or brace references are applied, which may evaluate those substitutions and expansions more than once if *l* appears more than once in the starting value. When used in a glob qualifier, any substitutions or expansions are performed once at the time the qualifier is parsed, even before the ':s' expression itself is divided into *l* and *r* sides.

If the option HIST_SUBST_PATTERN is set, *l* is treated as a pattern of the usual form described in Section 14.8 [Filename Generation], page 72. This can be used in all the places where modifiers are available; note, however, that in globbing qualifiers parameter substitution has already taken place, so parameters in the replacement string should be quoted to ensure they are replaced at the correct time. Note also that complicated patterns used in globbing qualifiers may need the extended glob qualifier notation (#q:s/.../.../) in order for the shell to recognize the expression as a glob qualifier. Further, note that bad patterns in the substitution are not subject to the NO_BAD_PATTERN option so will cause an error.

When HIST_SUBST_PATTERN is set, *l* may start with a # to indicate that the pattern must match at the start of the string to be substituted, and a % may appear at the start or after an # to indicate that the pattern must match at the end of the string to be substituted. The % or # may be quoted with two backslashes.

For example, the following piece of filename generation code with the `EXTENDED_GLOB` option:

```
print *.c(#q:s/#%(#b)s(*).c/'S${match[1]}.C'/)
```

takes the expansion of `*.c` and applies the glob qualifiers in the `(#q...)` expression, which consists of a substitution modifier anchored to the start and end of each word (`#%`). This turns on backreferences (`(#b)`), so that the parenthesised subexpression is available in the replacement string as `${match[1]}`. The replacement string is quoted so that the parameter is not substituted before the start of filename generation.

The following `f`, `F`, `w` and `W` modifiers work only with parameter expansion and filename generation. They are listed here to provide a single point of reference for all modifiers.

`f`   Repeats the immediately (without a colon) following modifier until the resulting word doesn't change any more.

`F:`*expr*`:`   Like `f`, but repeats only *n* times if the expression *expr* evaluates to *n*. Any character can be used instead of the ':'; if '(', '[', or '{' is used as the opening delimiter, the closing delimiter should be ')', ']', or '}', respectively.

`w`   Makes the immediately following modifier work on each word in the string.

`W:`*sep*`:`   Like `w` but words are considered to be the parts of the string that are separated by *sep*. Any character can be used instead of the ':'; opening parentheses are handled specially, see above.

14.2 Process Substitution

Each part of a command argument that takes the form '`<(`*list*`)`', '`>(`*list*`)`' or '`=(`*list*`)`' is subject to process substitution. The expression may be preceded or followed by other strings except that, to prevent clashes with commonly occurring strings and patterns, the last form must occur at the start of a command argument, and the forms are only expanded when first parsing command or assignment arguments. Process substitutions may be used following redirection operators; in this case, the substitution must appear with no trailing string.

Note that '`<<(`*list*`)`' is not a special syntax; it is equivalent to '`< <(`*list*`)`', redirecting standard input from the result of process substitution. Hence all the following documentation applies. The second form (with the space) is recommended for clarity.

In the case of the `<` or `>` forms, the shell runs the commands in *list* as a subprocess of the job executing the shell command line. If the system supports the `/dev/fd` mechanism, the command argument is the name of the device file corresponding to a file descriptor; otherwise, if the system supports named pipes (FIFOs), the command argument will be a named pipe. If the form with `>` is selected then writing on this special file will provide input for *list*. If `<` is used, then the file passed as an argument will be connected to the output of the *list* process. For example,

```
paste <(cut -f1 file1) <(cut -f3 file2) |
tee >(process1) >(process2) >/dev/null
```

cuts fields 1 and 3 from the files *file1* and *file2* respectively, pastes the results together, and sends it to the processes *process1* and *process2*.

If `=(...)` is used instead of `<(...)`, then the file passed as an argument will be the name of a temporary file containing the output of the *list* process. This may be used instead of the `<` form for a program that expects to lseek (see man page lseek(2)) on the input file.

There is an optimisation for substitutions of the form `=(<<<`*arg*`)`, where *arg* is a single-word argument to the here-string redirection `<<<`. This form produces a file name containing the value of *arg* after any substitutions have been performed. This is handled entirely within the current shell. This is effectively the reverse of the special form `$(<`*arg*`)` which treats *arg* as a file name and replaces it with the file's contents.

The `=` form is useful as both the `/dev/fd` and the named pipe implementation of `<(...)` have drawbacks. In the former case, some programmes may automatically close the file descriptor in question before examining the file on the command line, particularly if this is necessary for security reasons such as when the programme is running setuid. In the second case, if the programme does not actually open the file, the subshell attempting to read from or write to the pipe will (in a typical implementation, different operating systems may have different behaviour) block for ever and have to be killed explicitly. In both cases, the shell actually supplies the information using a pipe, so that programmes that expect to lseek (see man page lseek(2)) on the file will not work.

Also note that the previous example can be more compactly and efficiently written (provided the `MULTIOS` option is set) as:

```
paste <(cut -f1 file1) <(cut -f3 file2) > >(process1) > >(process2)
```

The shell uses pipes instead of FIFOs to implement the latter two process substitutions in the above example.

There is an additional problem with `>(`*process*`)`; when this is attached to an external command, the parent shell does not wait for *process* to finish and hence an immediately following command cannot rely on the results being complete. The problem and solution are the same as described in the section *MULTIOS* in Chapter 7 [Redirection], page 19. Hence in a simplified version of the example above:

```
paste <(cut -f1 file1) <(cut -f3 file2) > >(process)
```

(note that no `MULTIOS` are involved), *process* will be run asynchronously as far as the parent shell is concerned. The workaround is:

```
{ paste <(cut -f1 file1) <(cut -f3 file2) } > >(process)
```

The extra processes here are spawned from the parent shell which will wait for their completion.

Another problem arises any time a job with a substitution that requires a temporary file is disowned by the shell, including the case where '`&!`' or '`&|`' appears at the end of a command containing a substitution. In that case the temporary file will not be cleaned up as the shell no longer has any memory of the job. A workaround is to use a subshell, for example,

```
(mycmd =(myoutput)) &!
```

as the forked subshell will wait for the command to finish then remove the temporary file.

A general workaround to ensure a process substitution endures for an appropriate length of time is to pass it as a parameter to an anonymous shell function (a piece of shell code that is run immediately with function scope). For example, this code:

```
() {
```

```
    print File $1:
    cat $1
} =(print This be the verse)
```

outputs something resembling the following

```
    File /tmp/zsh6nUOkS:
    This be the verse
```

The temporary file created by the process substitution will be deleted when the function exits.

14.3 Parameter Expansion

The character '$' is used to introduce parameter expansions. See Chapter 15 [Parameters], page 85, for a description of parameters, including arrays, associative arrays, and subscript notation to access individual array elements.

Note in particular the fact that words of unquoted parameters are not automatically split on whitespace unless the option SH_WORD_SPLIT is set; see references to this option below for more details. This is an important difference from other shells.

In the expansions discussed below that require a pattern, the form of the pattern is the same as that used for filename generation; see Section 14.8 [Filename Generation], page 72. Note that these patterns, along with the replacement text of any substitutions, are themselves subject to parameter expansion, command substitution, and arithmetic expansion. In addition to the following operations, the colon modifiers described in Section 14.1.4 [Modifiers], page 47, in Section 14.1 [History Expansion], page 45, can be applied: for example, ${i:s/foo/bar/} performs string substitution on the expansion of parameter $i.

In the following descriptions, 'word' refers to a single word substituted on the command line, not necessarily a space delimited word. With default options, after the assignments:

```
    array=("first word" "second word")
    scalar="only word"
```

then $array substitutes two words, 'first word' and 'second word', and $scalar substitutes a single word 'only word'. This may be modified by explicit or implicit word-splitting, however. The full rules are complicated and are noted at the end.

${*name*}   The value, if any, of the parameter *name* is substituted. The braces are required if the expansion is to be followed by a letter, digit, or underscore that is not to be interpreted as part of *name*. In addition, more complicated forms of substitution usually require the braces to be present; exceptions, which only apply if the option KSH_ARRAYS is not set, are a single subscript or any colon modifiers appearing after the name, or any of the characters '^', '=', '~', '#' or '+' appearing before the name, all of which work with or without braces.

If *name* is an array parameter, and the KSH_ARRAYS option is not set, then the value of each element of *name* is substituted, one element per word. Otherwise, the expansion results in one word only; with KSH_ARRAYS, this is the first element of an array. No field splitting is done on the result unless the SH_WORD_SPLIT option is set. See also the flags = and s:*string*:.

${+*name*} If *name* is the name of a set parameter '1' is substituted, otherwise '0' is substituted.

${*name*-*word*}
${*name*:-*word*}

> If *name* is set, or in the second form is non-null, then substitute its value; otherwise substitute *word*. In the second form *name* may be omitted, in which case *word* is always substituted.

${*name*+*word*}
${*name*:+*word*}

> If *name* is set, or in the second form is non-null, then substitute *word*; otherwise substitute nothing.

${*name*=*word*}
${*name*:=*word*}
${*name*::=*word*}

> In the first form, if *name* is unset then set it to *word*; in the second form, if *name* is unset or null then set it to *word*; and in the third form, unconditionally set *name* to *word*. In all forms, the value of the parameter is then substituted.

${*name*?*word*}
${*name*:?*word*}

> In the first form, if *name* is set, or in the second form if *name* is both set and non-null, then substitute its value; otherwise, print *word* and exit from the shell. Interactive shells instead return to the prompt. If *word* is omitted, then a standard message is printed.

In any of the above expressions that test a variable and substitute an alternate *word*, note that you can use standard shell quoting in the *word* value to selectively override the splitting done by the SH_WORD_SPLIT option and the = flag, but not splitting by the s:*string*: flag.

In the following expressions, when *name* is an array and the substitution is not quoted, or if the '(@)' flag or the *name*[@] syntax is used, matching and replacement is performed on each array element separately.

${*name*#*pattern*}
${*name*##*pattern*}

> If the *pattern* matches the beginning of the value of *name*, then substitute the value of *name* with the matched portion deleted; otherwise, just substitute the value of *name*. In the first form, the smallest matching pattern is preferred; in the second form, the largest matching pattern is preferred.

${*name*%*pattern*}
${*name*%%*pattern*}

> If the *pattern* matches the end of the value of *name*, then substitute the value of *name* with the matched portion deleted; otherwise, just substitute the value of *name*. In the first form, the smallest matching pattern is preferred; in the second form, the largest matching pattern is preferred.

${*name*:#*pattern*}

> If the *pattern* matches the value of *name*, then substitute the empty string; otherwise, just substitute the value of *name*. If *name* is an array the matching array elements are removed (use the '(M)' flag to remove the non-matched elements).

${*name*: | *arrayname*}

> If *arrayname* is the name (N.B., not contents) of an array variable, then any elements contained in *arrayname* are removed from the substitution of *name*. If the substitution is scalar, either because *name* is a scalar variable or the expression is quoted, the elements of *arrayname* are instead tested against the entire expression.

${*name*:**arrayname*}

> Similar to the preceding substitution, but in the opposite sense, so that entries present in both the original substitution and as elements of *arrayname* are retained and others removed.

${*name*:^*arrayname*}

${*name*:^^*arrayname*}

> Zips two arrays, such that the output array is twice as long as the shortest (longest for ':^^') of **name** and **arrayname**, with the elements alternatingly being picked from them. For ':^', if one of the input arrays is longer, the output will stop when the end of the shorter array is reached. Thus,
>
> ```
> a=(1 2 3 4); b=(a b); print ${a:^b}
> ```
>
> will output '1 a 2 b'. For ':^^', then the input is repeated until all of the longer array has been used up and the above will output '1 a 2 b 3 a 4 b'.
>
> Either or both inputs may be a scalar, they will be treated as an array of length 1 with the scalar as the only element. If either array is empty, the other array is output with no extra elements inserted.
>
> Currently the following code will output 'a b' and '1' as two separate elements, which can be unexpected. The second print provides a workaround which should continue to work if this is changed.
>
> ```
> a=(a b); b=(1 2); print -l "${a:^b}"; print -l "${${a:^b}}"
> ```

${*name*: *offset*}

${*name*: *offset*: *length*}

> This syntax gives effects similar to parameter subscripting in the form $*name*[*start*,*end*], but is compatible with other shells; note that both *offset* and *length* are interpreted differently from the components of a subscript.
>
> If *offset* is non-negative, then if the variable *name* is a scalar substitute the contents starting *offset* characters from the first character of the string, and if *name* is an array substitute elements starting *offset* elements from the first element. If *length* is given, substitute that many characters or elements, otherwise the entire rest of the scalar or array.
>
> A positive *offset* is always treated as the offset of a character or element in *name* from the first character or element of the array (this is different from native zsh subscript notation). Hence 0 refers to the first character or element regardless of the setting of the option KSH_ARRAYS.
>
> A negative offset counts backwards from the end of the scalar or array, so that -1 corresponds to the last character or element, and so on.
>
> When positive, *length* counts from the *offset* position toward the end of the scalar or array. When negative, *length* counts back from the end. If this

results in a position smaller than *offset*, a diagnostic is printed and nothing is substituted.

The option `MULTIBYTE` is obeyed, i.e. the offset and length count multibyte characters where appropriate.

offset and *length* undergo the same set of shell substitutions as for scalar assignment; in addition, they are then subject to arithmetic evaluation. Hence, for example

```
print ${foo:3}
print ${foo: 1 + 2}
print ${foo:$(( 1 + 2))}
print ${foo:$(echo 1 + 2)}
```

all have the same effect, extracting the string starting at the fourth character of `$foo` if the substitution would otherwise return a scalar, or the array starting at the fourth element if `$foo` would return an array. Note that with the option `KSH_ARRAYS` `$foo` always returns a scalar (regardless of the use of the offset syntax) and a form such as `${foo[*]:3}` is required to extract elements of an array named `foo`.

If *offset* is negative, the - may not appear immediately after the : as this indicates the `${name:-word}` form of substitution. Instead, a space may be inserted before the -. Furthermore, neither *offset* nor *length* may begin with an alphabetic character or & as these are used to indicate history-style modifiers. To substitute a value from a variable, the recommended approach is to precede it with a `$` as this signifies the intention (parameter substitution can easily be rendered unreadable); however, as arithmetic substitution is performed, the expression `${var: offs}` does work, retrieving the offset from `$offs`.

For further compatibility with other shells there is a special case for array offset 0. This usually accesses the first element of the array. However, if the substitution refers to the positional parameter array, e.g. `$@` or `$*`, then offset 0 instead refers to `$0`, offset 1 refers to `$1`, and so on. In other words, the positional parameter array is effectively extended by prepending `$0`. Hence `${*:0:1}` substitutes `$0` and `${*:1:1}` substitutes `$1`.

`${name/pattern/repl}`
`${name//pattern/repl}`
`${name:/pattern/repl}`

Replace the longest possible match of *pattern* in the expansion of parameter *name* by string *repl*. The first form replaces just the first occurrence, the second form all occurrences, and the third form replaces only if *pattern* matches the entire string. Both *pattern* and *repl* are subject to double-quoted substitution, so that expressions like `${name/$opat/$npat}` will work, but obey the usual rule that pattern characters in `$opat` are not treated specially unless either the option `GLOB_SUBST` is set, or `$opat` is instead substituted as `${~opat}`.

The *pattern* may begin with a '#', in which case the *pattern* must match at the start of the string, or '%', in which case it must match at the end of the string, or '#%' in which case the *pattern* must match the entire string. The *repl* may be an empty string, in which case the final '/' may also be omitted. To quote the final '/' in other cases it should be preceded by a single backslash; this is not necessary if the '/' occurs inside a substituted parameter. Note also that the '#', '%' and '#%' are not active if they occur inside a substituted parameter, even at the start.

If, after quoting rules apply, ${*name*} expands to an array, the replacements act on each element individually. Note also the effect of the I and S parameter expansion flags below; however, the flags M, R, B, E and N are not useful.

For example,

```
foo="twinkle twinkle little star" sub="t*e" rep="spy"
print ${foo//${~sub}/$rep}
print ${(S)foo//${~sub}/$rep}
```

Here, the '~' ensures that the text of $sub is treated as a pattern rather than a plain string. In the first case, the longest match for t*e is substituted and the result is 'spy star', while in the second case, the shortest matches are taken and the result is 'spy spy lispy star'.

${#*spec*} If *spec* is one of the above substitutions, substitute the length in characters of the result instead of the result itself. If *spec* is an array expression, substitute the number of elements of the result. This has the side-effect that joining is skipped even in quoted forms, which may affect other sub-expressions in *spec*. Note that '~', '=', and '~', below, must appear to the left of '#' when these forms are combined.

If the option POSIX_IDENTIFIERS is not set, and *spec* is a simple name, then the braces are optional; this is true even for special parameters so e.g. $#- and $#* take the length of the string $- and the array $* respectively. If POSIX_IDENTIFIERS is set, then braces are required for the # to be treated in this fashion.

${^*spec*} Turn on the RC_EXPAND_PARAM option for the evaluation of *spec*; if the '^' is doubled, turn it off. When this option is set, array expansions of the form *foo*${*xx*}*bar*, where the parameter *xx* is set to (*a b c*), are substituted with '*fooabar foobbar foocbar*' instead of the default '*fooa b cbar*'. Note that an empty array will therefore cause all arguments to be removed.

Internally, each such expansion is converted into the equivalent list for brace expansion. E.g., ${^var} becomes {$var[1],$var[2],...}, and is processed as described in Section 14.6 [Brace Expansion], page 68, below: note, however, the expansion happens immediately, with any explicit brace expansion happening later. If word splitting is also in effect the $var[*N*] may themselves be split into different list elements.

${=*spec*} Perform word splitting using the rules for SH_WORD_SPLIT during the evaluation of *spec*, but regardless of whether the parameter appears in double quotes; if the '=' is doubled, turn it off. This forces parameter expansions to be split into separate words before substitution, using IFS as a delimiter. This is done by default in most other shells.

Note that splitting is applied to *word* in the assignment forms of *spec* *before* the assignment to *name* is performed. This affects the result of array assignments with the A flag.

${~*spec*}   Turn on the GLOB_SUBST option for the evaluation of *spec*; if the '~' is doubled, turn it off. When this option is set, the string resulting from the expansion will be interpreted as a pattern anywhere that is possible, such as in filename expansion and filename generation and pattern-matching contexts like the right hand side of the '=' and '!=' operators in conditions.

In nested substitutions, note that the effect of the ~ applies to the result of the current level of substitution. A surrounding pattern operation on the result may cancel it. Hence, for example, if the parameter foo is set to *, ${~foo//*/*.c} is substituted by the pattern *.c, which may be expanded by filename generation, but ${${~foo}//*/*.c} substitutes to the string *.c, which will not be further expanded.

If a ${...} type parameter expression or a $(...) type command substitution is used in place of *name* above, it is expanded first and the result is used as if it were the value of *name*. Thus it is possible to perform nested operations: ${${foo#head}%tail} substitutes the value of $foo with both 'head' and 'tail' deleted. The form with $(...) is often useful in combination with the flags described next; see the examples below. Each *name* or nested ${...} in a parameter expansion may also be followed by a subscript expression as described in Section 15.2 [Array Parameters], page 86.

Note that double quotes may appear around nested expressions, in which case only the part inside is treated as quoted; for example, ${(f)"$(foo)"} quotes the result of $(foo), but the flag '(f)' (see below) is applied using the rules for unquoted expansions. Note further that quotes are themselves nested in this context; for example, in "${(@f)"$(foo)"}", there are two sets of quotes, one surrounding the whole expression, the other (redundant) surrounding the $(foo) as before.

14.3.1 Parameter Expansion Flags

If the opening brace is directly followed by an opening parenthesis, the string up to the matching closing parenthesis will be taken as a list of flags. In cases where repeating a flag is meaningful, the repetitions need not be consecutive; for example, '(q%q%q)' means the same thing as the more readable '(%%qqq)'. The following flags are supported:

\#   Evaluate the resulting words as numeric expressions and output the characters corresponding to the resulting integer. Note that this form is entirely distinct from use of the # without parentheses.

If the MULTIBYTE option is set and the number is greater than 127 (i.e. not an ASCII character) it is treated as a Unicode character.

%   Expand all % escapes in the resulting words in the same way as in prompts (see Chapter 13 [Prompt Expansion], page 39). If this flag is given twice, full prompt expansion is done on the resulting words, depending on the setting of the PROMPT_PERCENT, PROMPT_SUBST and PROMPT_BANG options.

@   In double quotes, array elements are put into separate words. E.g., '"${(@)foo}"' is equivalent to '"${foo[@]}"' and '"${(@)foo[1,2]}"' is the same as '"$foo[1]" "$foo[2]"'. This is distinct from *field splitting* by the f, s or z flags, which still applies within each array element.

A   Convert the substitution into an array expression, even if it otherwise would be scalar. This has lower precedence than subscripting, so one level of nested expansion is required in order that subscripts apply to array elements. Thus `${${(A)name}[1]}` yields the full value of *name* when *name* is scalar.

This assigns an array parameter with '`${...=...}`', '`${...:=...}`' or '`${...::=...}`'. If this flag is repeated (as in '`AA`'), assigns an associative array parameter. Assignment is made before sorting or padding; if field splitting is active, the *word* part is split before assignment. The *name* part may be a subscripted range for ordinary arrays; when assigning an associative array, the *word* part *must* be converted to an array, for example by using '`${(AA)=name=...}`' to activate field splitting.

Surrounding context such as additional nesting or use of the value in a scalar assignment may cause the array to be joined back into a single string again.

a   Sort in array index order; when combined with '`O`' sort in reverse array index order. Note that '`a`' is therefore equivalent to the default but '`Oa`' is useful for obtaining an array's elements in reverse order.

b   Quote with backslashes only characters that are special to pattern matching. This is useful when the contents of the variable are to be tested using `GLOB_SUBST`, including the `${~...}` switch.

Quoting using one of the **q** family of flags does not work for this purpose since quotes are not stripped from non-pattern characters by `GLOB_SUBST`. In other words,

```
pattern=${(q)str}
[[ $str = ${~pattern} ]]
```

works if `$str` is '`a*b`' but not if it is '`a b`', whereas

```
pattern=${(b)str}
[[ $str = ${~pattern} ]]
```

is always true for any possible value of `$str`.

c   With `${#name}`, count the total number of characters in an array, as if the elements were concatenated with spaces between them. This is not a true join of the array, so other expressions used with this flag may have an effect on the elements of the array before it is counted.

C   Capitalize the resulting words. 'Words' in this case refers to sequences of alphanumeric characters separated by non-alphanumerics, *not* to words that result from field splitting.

D   Assume the string or array elements contain directories and attempt to substitute the leading part of these by names. The remainder of the path (the whole of it if the leading part was not substituted) is then quoted so that the whole string can be used as a shell argument. This is the reverse of '`~`' substitution: see Section 14.7 [Filename Expansion], page 69.

e   Perform single word shell expansions, namely *parameter expansion*, *command substitution* and *arithmetic expansion*, on the result. Such expansions can be nested but too deep recursion may have unpredictable effects.

f   Split the result of the expansion at newlines. This is a shorthand for 'ps:\n:'.

F   Join the words of arrays together using newline as a separator. This is a shorthand for 'pj:\n:'.

g:*opts*: Process escape sequences like the echo builtin when no options are given (g::).
         With the o option, octal escapes don't take a leading zero. With the c option, sequences like '^X' are also processed. With the e option, processes '\M-t' and similar sequences like the print builtin. With both of the o and e options, behaves like the print builtin except that in none of these modes is '\c' interpreted.

i   Sort case-insensitively. May be combined with 'n' or 'O'.

k   If *name* refers to an associative array, substitute the *keys* (element names) rather than the values of the elements. Used with subscripts (including ordinary arrays), force indices or keys to be substituted even if the subscript form refers to values. However, this flag may not be combined with subscript ranges. With the KSH_ARRAYS option a subscript '[*]' or '[@]' is needed to operate on the whole array, as usual.

L   Convert all letters in the result to lower case.

n   Sort decimal integers numerically; if the first differing characters of two test strings are not digits, sorting is lexical. Integers with more initial zeroes are sorted before those with fewer or none. Hence the array 'foo1 foo02 foo2 foo3 foo20 foo23' is sorted into the order shown. May be combined with 'i' or 'O'.

o   Sort the resulting words in ascending order; if this appears on its own the sorting is lexical and case-sensitive (unless the locale renders it case-insensitive). Sorting in ascending order is the default for other forms of sorting, so this is ignored if combined with 'a', 'i' or 'n'.

O   Sort the resulting words in descending order; 'O' without 'a', 'i' or 'n' sorts in reverse lexical order. May be combined with 'a', 'i' or 'n' to reverse the order of sorting.

P   This forces the value of the parameter *name* to be interpreted as a further parameter name, whose value will be used where appropriate. Note that flags set with one of the typeset family of commands (in particular case transformations) are not applied to the value of *name* used in this fashion.

         If used with a nested parameter or command substitution, the result of that will be taken as a parameter name in the same way. For example, if you have 'foo=bar' and 'bar=baz', the strings ${(P)foo}, ${(P)${foo}}, and ${(P)$(echo bar)} will be expanded to 'baz'.

         Likewise, if the reference is itself nested, the expression with the flag is treated as if it were directly replaced by the parameter name. It is an error if this nested substitution produces an array with more than one word. For example, if 'name=assoc' where the parameter assoc is an associative array, then '${${(P)name}[elt]}' refers to the element of the associative subscripted 'elt'.

q   Quote characters that are special to the shell in the resulting words with backslashes; unprintable or invalid characters are quoted using the $'\NNN' form, with separate quotes for each octet.

    If this flag is given twice, the resulting words are quoted in single quotes and if it is given three times, the words are quoted in double quotes; in these forms no special handling of unprintable or invalid characters is attempted. If the flag is given four times, the words are quoted in single quotes preceded by a $. Note that in all three of these forms quoting is done unconditionally, even if this does not change the way the resulting string would be interpreted by the shell.

    If a q- is given (only a single q may appear), a minimal form of single quoting is used that only quotes the string if needed to protect special characters. Typically this form gives the most readable output.

    If a q+ is given, an extended form of minmal quoting is used that causes unprintable characters to be rendered using $'...'. This quoting is similar to that used by the output of values by the **typeset** family of commands.

Q   Remove one level of quotes from the resulting words.

t   Use a string describing the type of the parameter where the value of the parameter would usually appear. This string consists of keywords separated by hyphens ('-'). The first keyword in the string describes the main type, it can be one of 'scalar', 'array', 'integer', 'float' or 'association'. The other keywords describe the type in more detail:

   local   for local parameters

   left   for left justified parameters

   right_blanks
      for right justified parameters with leading blanks

   right_zeros
      for right justified parameters with leading zeros

   lower   for parameters whose value is converted to all lower case when it is expanded

   upper   for parameters whose value is converted to all upper case when it is expanded

   readonly for readonly parameters

   tag   for tagged parameters

   export   for exported parameters

   unique   for arrays which keep only the first occurrence of duplicated values

   hide   for parameters with the 'hide' flag

   hideval   for parameters with the 'hideval' flag

   special   for special parameters defined by the shell

u   Expand only the first occurrence of each unique word.

U   Convert all letters in the result to upper case.

v   Used with **k**, substitute (as two consecutive words) both the key and the value of each associative array element. Used with subscripts, force values to be substituted even if the subscript form refers to indices or keys.

V   Make any special characters in the resulting words visible.

w   With ${#*name*}, count words in arrays or strings; the **s** flag may be used to set a word delimiter.

W   Similar to **w** with the difference that empty words between repeated delimiters are also counted.

X   With this flag, parsing errors occurring with the **Q**, **e** and **#** flags or the pattern matching forms such as '${*name*#*pattern*}' are reported. Without the flag, errors are silently ignored.

z   Split the result of the expansion into words using shell parsing to find the words, i.e. taking into account any quoting in the value. Comments are not treated specially but as ordinary strings, similar to interactive shells with the **INTERACTIVE_COMMENTS** option unset (however, see the **Z** flag below for related options)

               Note that this is done very late, even later than the '(**s**)' flag. So to access single words in the result use nested expansions as in '${${(z)foo}[2]}'. Likewise, to remove the quotes in the resulting words use '${(Q)${(z)foo}}'.

0   Split the result of the expansion on null bytes. This is a shorthand for 'ps:\0:'.

The following flags (except **p**) are followed by one or more arguments as shown. Any character, or the matching pairs '(...)', '{...}', '[...]', or '<...>', may be used in place of a colon as delimiters, but note that when a flag takes more than one argument, a matched pair of delimiters must surround each argument.

p   Recognize the same escape sequences as the **print** builtin in string arguments to any of the flags described below that follow this argument.

               Alternatively, with this option string arguments may be in the form $*var* in which case the value of the variable is substituted. Note this form is strict; the string argument does not undergo general parameter expansion.

               For example,

```
sep=:
val=a:b:c
print ${(ps.$sep.)val}
```

               splits the variable on a :.

~   Strings inserted into the expansion by any of the flags below are to be treated as patterns. This applies to the string arguments of flags that follow ~ within the same set of parentheses. Compare with ~ outside parentheses, which forces the entire substituted string to be treated as a pattern. Hence, for example,

```
[[ "?" = ${(~j.|.)array} ]]
```

treats '|' as a pattern and succeeds if and only if **$array** contains the string '?' as an element. The ~ may be repeated to toggle the behaviour; its effect only lasts to the end of the parenthesised group.

j:*string*:   Join the words of arrays together using *string* as a separator. Note that this occurs before field splitting by the **s:***string***:** flag or the **SH_WORD_SPLIT** option.

l:*expr*::*string1*::*string2*:

Pad the resulting words on the left. Each word will be truncated if required and placed in a field *expr* characters wide.

The arguments :*string1*: and :*string2*: are optional; neither, the first, or both may be given. Note that the same pairs of delimiters must be used for each of the three arguments. The space to the left will be filled with *string1* (concatenated as often as needed) or spaces if *string1* is not given. If both *string1* and *string2* are given, *string2* is inserted once directly to the left of each word, truncated if necessary, before *string1* is used to produce any remaining padding.

If either of *string1* or *string2* is present but empty, i.e. there are two delimiters together at that point, the first character of **$IFS** is used instead.

If the **MULTIBYTE** option is in effect, the flag **m** may also be given, in which case widths will be used for the calculation of padding; otherwise individual multibyte characters are treated as occupying one unit of width.

If the **MULTIBYTE** option is not in effect, each byte in the string is treated as occupying one unit of width.

Control characters are always assumed to be one unit wide; this allows the mechanism to be used for generating repetitions of control characters.

m   Only useful together with one of the flags **l** or **r** or with the **#** length operator when the **MULTIBYTE** option is in effect. Use the character width reported by the system in calculating how much of the string it occupies or the overall length of the string. Most printable characters have a width of one unit, however certain Asian character sets and certain special effects use wider characters; combining characters have zero width. Non-printable characters are arbitrarily counted as zero width; how they would actually be displayed will vary.

If the **m** is repeated, the character either counts zero (if it has zero width), else one. For printable character strings this has the effect of counting the number of glyphs (visibly separate characters), except for the case where combining characters themselves have non-zero width (true in certain alphabets).

r:*expr*::*string1*::*string2*:

As **l**, but pad the words on the right and insert *string2* immediately to the right of the string to be padded.

Left and right padding may be used together. In this case the strategy is to apply left padding to the first half width of each of the resulting words, and right padding to the second half. If the string to be padded has odd width the extra padding is applied on the left.

s:*string*:   Force field splitting at the separator *string*. Note that a *string* of two or more characters means that all of them must match in sequence; this differs from the treatment of two or more characters in the IFS parameter. See also the = flag and the SH_WORD_SPLIT option. An empty string may also be given in which case every character will be a separate element.

For historical reasons, the usual behaviour that empty array elements are retained inside double quotes is disabled for arrays generated by splitting; hence the following:

```
line="one::three"
print -l "${(s.:.)line}"
```

produces two lines of output for one and three and elides the empty field. To override this behaviour, supply the '(@)' flag as well, i.e. "${(@s.:.)line}".

Z:*opts*: As z but takes a combination of option letters between a following pair of delimiter characters. With no options the effect is identical to z. (Z+c+) causes comments to be parsed as a string and retained; any field in the resulting array beginning with an unquoted comment character is a comment. (Z+C+) causes comments to be parsed and removed. The rule for comments is standard: anything between a word starting with the third character of $HISTCHARS, default #, up to the next newline is a comment. (Z+n+) causes unquoted newlines to be treated as ordinary whitespace, else they are treated as if they are shell code delimiters and converted to semicolons. Options are combined within the same set of delimiters, e.g. (Z+Cn+).

:*flags*: The underscore () flag is reserved for future use. As of this revision of zsh, there are no valid *flags*; anything following an underscore, other than an empty pair of delimiters, is treated as an error, and the flag itself has no effect.

The following flags are meaningful with the ${...#...} or ${...%...} forms. The S and I flags may also be used with the ${.../...} forms.

S Search substrings as well as beginnings or ends; with # start from the beginning and with % start from the end of the string. With substitution via ${.../...} or ${...//...}, specifies non-greedy matching, i.e. that the shortest instead of the longest match should be replaced.

I:*expr*: Search the *expr*th match (where *expr* evaluates to a number). This only applies when searching for substrings, either with the S flag, or with ${.../...} (only the *expr*th match is substituted) or ${...//...} (all matches from the *expr*th on are substituted). The default is to take the first match.

The *expr*th match is counted such that there is either one or zero matches from each starting position in the string, although for global substitution matches overlapping previous replacements are ignored. With the ${...%...} and ${...%%...} forms, the starting position for the match moves backwards from the end as the index increases, while with the other forms it moves forward from the start.

Hence with the string

```
which switch is the right switch for Ipswich?
```

substitutions of the form ${(SI:*N*:)string#w*ch} as *N* increases from 1 will match and remove 'which', 'witch', 'witch' and 'wich'; the form using '##'

will match and remove 'which switch is the right switch for Ipswich',
'witch is the right switch for Ipswich', 'witch for Ipswich' and
'wich'. The form using '%' will remove the same matches as for '#', but in
reverse order, and the form using '%%' will remove the same matches as for '##'
in reverse order.

B Include the index of the beginning of the match in the result.

E Include the index one character past the end of the match in the result (note
this is inconsistent with other uses of parameter index).

M Include the matched portion in the result.

N Include the length of the match in the result.

R Include the unmatched portion in the result (the *Rest*).

14.3.2 Rules

Here is a summary of the rules for substitution; this assumes that braces are present around
the substitution, i.e. `${...}`. Some particular examples are given below. Note that the Zsh
Development Group accepts *no responsibility* for any brain damage which may occur during
the reading of the following rules.

1. *Nested substitution*

   If multiple nested `${...}` forms are present, substitution is performed from the
   inside outwards. At each level, the substitution takes account of whether the
   current value is a scalar or an array, whether the whole substitution is in double
   quotes, and what flags are supplied to the current level of substitution, just as
   if the nested substitution were the outermost. The flags are not propagated
   up to enclosing substitutions; the nested substitution will return either a scalar
   or an array as determined by the flags, possibly adjusted for quoting. All the
   following steps take place where applicable at all levels of substitution.

   Note that, unless the '(P)' flag is present, the flags and any subscripts apply
   directly to the value of the nested substitution; for example, the expansion
   `${${foo}}` behaves exactly the same as `${foo}`. When the '(P)' flag is present
   in a nested substitution, the other substitution rules are applied to the value
   before it is interpreted as a name, so `${${(P)foo}}` may differ from `${(P)foo}`.

   At each nested level of substitution, the substituted words undergo all forms
   of single-word substitution (i.e. not filename generation), including command
   substitution, arithmetic expansion and filename expansion (i.e. leading ~ and
   =). Thus, for example, `${${:-=cat}:h}` expands to the directory where the `cat`
   program resides. (Explanation: the internal substitution has no parameter but
   a default value =cat, which is expanded by filename expansion to a full path;
   the outer substitution then applies the modifier `:h` and takes the directory part
   of the path.)

2. *Internal parameter flags*

   Any parameter flags set by one of the **typeset** family of commands, in particular
   the -L, -R, -Z, -u and -l options for padding and capitalization, are applied
   directly to the parameter value. Note these flags are options to the command,

e.g. '`typeset -Z`'; they are not the same as the flags used within parameter substitutions.

At the outermost level of substitution, the '`(P)`' flag (rule **4.**) ignores these transformations and uses the unmodified value of the parameter as the name to be replaced. This is usually the desired behavior because padding may make the value syntactically illegal as a parameter name, but if capitalization changes are desired, use the `${${(P)foo}}` form (rule **25.**).

3. *Parameter subscripting*

If the value is a raw parameter reference with a subscript, such as `${var[3]}`, the effect of subscripting is applied directly to the parameter. Subscripts are evaluated left to right; subsequent subscripts apply to the scalar or array value yielded by the previous subscript. Thus if `var` is an array, `${var[1][2]}` is the second character of the first word, but `${var[2,4][2]}` is the entire third word (the second word of the range of words two through four of the original array). Any number of subscripts may appear. Flags such as '`(k)`' and '`(v)`' which alter the result of subscripting are applied.

4. *Parameter name replacement*

At the outermost level of nesting only, the '`(P)`' flag is applied. This treats the value so far as a parameter name (which may include a subscript expression) and replaces that with the corresponding value. This replacement occurs later if the '`(P)`' flag appears in a nested substitution.

If the value so far names a parameter that has internal flags (rule **2.**), those internal flags are applied to the new value after replacement.

5. *Double-quoted joining*

If the value after this process is an array, and the substitution appears in double quotes, and neither an '`(@)`' flag nor a '`#`' length operator is present at the current level, then words of the value are joined with the first character of the parameter `$IFS`, by default a space, between each word (single word arrays are not modified). If the '`(j)`' flag is present, that is used for joining instead of `$IFS`.

6. *Nested subscripting*

Any remaining subscripts (i.e. of a nested substitution) are evaluated at this point, based on whether the value is an array or a scalar. As with **3.**, multiple subscripts can appear. Note that `${foo[2,4][2]}` is thus equivalent to `${${foo[2,4]}[2]}` and also to `"${${(@)foo[2,4]}[2]}"` (the nested substitution returns an array in both cases), but not to `"${${foo[2,4]}[2]}"` (the nested substitution returns a scalar because of the quotes).

7. *Modifiers*

Any modifiers, as specified by a trailing '`#`', '`%`', '`/`' (possibly doubled) or by a set of modifiers of the form '`:...`' (see Section 14.1.4 [Modifiers], page 47, in Section 14.1 [History Expansion], page 45), are applied to the words of the value at this level.

8. *Character evaluation*

Any '`(#)`' flag is applied, evaluating the result so far numerically as a character.

9. *Length* Any initial '#' modifier, i.e. in the form ${#*var*}, is used to evaluate the length of the expression so far.

10. *Forced joining*

    If the '(j)' flag is present, or no '(j)' flag is present but the string is to be split as given by rule 11., and joining did not take place at rule 5., any words in the value are joined together using the given string or the first character of $IFS if none. Note that the '(F)' flag implicitly supplies a string for joining in this manner.

11. *Simple word splitting*

    If one of the '(s)' or '(f)' flags are present, or the '=' specifier was present (e.g. ${=*var*}), the word is split on occurrences of the specified string, or (for = with neither of the two flags present) any of the characters in $IFS.

    If no '(s)', '(f)' or '=' was given, but the word is not quoted and the option SH_WORD_SPLIT is set, the word is split on occurrences of any of the characters in $IFS. Note this step, too, takes place at all levels of a nested substitution.

12. *Case modification*

    Any case modification from one of the flags '(L)', '(U)' or '(C)' is applied.

13. *Escape sequence replacement*

    First any replacements from the '(g)' flag are performed, then any prompt-style formatting from the '(%)' family of flags is applied.

14. *Quote application*

    Any quoting or unquoting using '(q)' and '(Q)' and related flags is applied.

15. *Directory naming*

    Any directory name substitution using '(D)' flag is applied.

16. *Visibility enhancement*

    Any modifications to make characters visible using the '(V)' flag are applied.

17. *Lexical word splitting*

    If the '(z)' flag or one of the forms of the '(Z)' flag is present, the word is split as if it were a shell command line, so that quotation marks and other metacharacters are used to decide what constitutes a word. Note this form of splitting is entirely distinct from that described by rule 11.: it does not use $IFS, and does not cause forced joining.

18. *Uniqueness*

    If the result is an array and the '(u)' flag was present, duplicate elements are removed from the array.

19. *Ordering*

    If the result is still an array and one of the '(o)' or '(O)' flags was present, the array is reordered.

20. RC_EXPAND_PARAM

    At this point the decision is made whether any resulting array elements are to be combined element by element with surrounding text, as given by either the RC_EXPAND_PARAM option or the '^' flag.

21. *Re-evaluation*

Any '(e)' flag is applied to the value, forcing it to be re-examined for new parameter substitutions, but also for command and arithmetic substitutions.

22. *Padding*

Any padding of the value by the '(l. *fill.*)' or '(r. *fill.*)' flags is applied.

23. *Semantic joining*

In contexts where expansion semantics requires a single word to result, all words are rejoined with the first character of IFS between. So in '${(P)${(f)lines}}' the value of ${lines} is split at newlines, but then must be joined again before the '(P)' flag can be applied.

If a single word is not required, this rule is skipped.

24. *Empty argument removal*

If the substitution does not appear in double quotes, any resulting zero-length argument, whether from a scalar or an element of an array, is elided from the list of arguments inserted into the command line.

Strictly speaking, the removal happens later as the same happens with other forms of substitution; the point to note here is simply that it occurs after any of the above parameter operations.

25. *Nested parameter name replacement*

If the '(P)' flag is present and rule 4. has not applied, the value so far is treated as a parameter name (which may include a subscript expression) and replaced with the corresponding value, with internal flags (rule 2.) applied to the new value.

14.3.3 Examples

The flag f is useful to split a double-quoted substitution line by line. For example, ${(f)"$(<*file*)"} substitutes the contents of *file* divided so that each line is an element of the resulting array. Compare this with the effect of $(<*file*) alone, which divides the file up by words, or the same inside double quotes, which makes the entire content of the file a single string.

The following illustrates the rules for nested parameter expansions. Suppose that $foo contains the array (bar baz):

"${(@)${foo}[1]}"

This produces the result b. First, the inner substitution "${foo}", which has no array (@) flag, produces a single word result "bar baz". The outer substitution "${(@)...[1]}" detects that this is a scalar, so that (despite the '(@)' flag) the subscript picks the first character.

"${$(@)foo}[1]}"

This produces the result 'bar'. In this case, the inner substitution "${(@)foo}" produces the array '(bar baz)'. The outer substitution "${...[1]}" detects that this is an array and picks the first word. This is similar to the simple case "${foo[1]}".

As an example of the rules for word splitting and joining, suppose `$foo` contains the array '`(ax1 bx1)`'. Then

`${(s/x/)foo}`

> produces the words 'a', '1 b' and '1'.

`${(j/x/s/x/)foo}`

> produces 'a', '1', 'b' and '1'.

`${(s/x/)foo%%1*}`

> produces 'a' and ' b' (note the extra space). As substitution occurs before either joining or splitting, the operation first generates the modified array (ax bx), which is joined to give "ax bx", and then split to give 'a', ' b' and ''. The final empty string will then be elided, as it is not in double quotes.

14.4 Command Substitution

A command enclosed in parentheses preceded by a dollar sign, like '`$(...)`', or quoted with grave accents, like '``...``', is replaced with its standard output, with any trailing newlines deleted. If the substitution is not enclosed in double quotes, the output is broken into words using the `IFS` parameter.

The substitution '`$(cat foo)`' may be replaced by the faster '`$(<foo)`'. In this case *foo* undergoes single word shell expansions (*parameter expansion, command substitution* and *arithmetic expansion*), but not filename generation.

If the option `GLOB_SUBST` is set, the result of any unquoted command substitution, including the special form just mentioned, is eligible for filename generation.

14.5 Arithmetic Expansion

A string of the form '`$[exp]`' or '`$((exp))`' is substituted with the value of the arithmetic expression *exp*. *exp* is subjected to *parameter expansion, command substitution* and *arithmetic expansion* before it is evaluated. See Chapter 11 [Arithmetic Evaluation], page 31.

14.6 Brace Expansion

A string of the form '*foo*{*xx,yy,zz*}*bar*' is expanded to the individual words '*fooxxbar*', '*fooyybar*' and '*foozzbar*'. Left-to-right order is preserved. This construct may be nested. Commas may be quoted in order to include them literally in a word.

An expression of the form '{*n1..n2*}', where *n1* and *n2* are integers, is expanded to every number between *n1* and *n2* inclusive. If either number begins with a zero, all the resulting numbers will be padded with leading zeroes to that minimum width, but for negative numbers the - character is also included in the width. If the numbers are in decreasing order the resulting sequence will also be in decreasing order.

An expression of the form '{*n1..n2..n3*}', where *n1*, *n2*, and *n3* are integers, is expanded as above, but only every *n3*th number starting from *n1* is output. If *n3* is negative the numbers are output in reverse order, this is slightly different from simply swapping *n1* and *n2* in the case that the step *n3* doesn't evenly divide the range. Zero padding can be specified in any of the three numbers, specifying it in the third can be useful to pad for example '{-99..100..01}' which is not possible to specify by putting a 0 on either of the first two numbers (i.e. pad to two characters).

An expression of the form '{c1..c2}', where c1 and c2 are single characters (which may be multibyte characters), is expanded to every character in the range from c1 to c2 in whatever character sequence is used internally. For characters with code points below 128 this is US ASCII (this is the only case most users will need). If any intervening character is not printable, appropriate quotation is used to render it printable. If the character sequence is reversed, the output is in reverse order, e.g. '{d..a}' is substituted as 'd c b a'.

If a brace expression matches none of the above forms, it is left unchanged, unless the option BRACE_CCL (an abbreviation for 'brace character class') is set. In that case, it is expanded to a list of the individual characters between the braces sorted into the order of the characters in the ASCII character set (multibyte characters are not currently handled). The syntax is similar to a [...] expression in filename generation: '-' is treated specially to denote a range of characters, but '^' or '!' as the first character is treated normally. For example, '{abcdef0-9}' expands to 16 words 0 1 2 3 4 5 6 7 8 9 a b c d e f.

Note that brace expansion is not part of filename generation (globbing); an expression such as */{foo,bar} is split into two separate words */foo and */bar before filename generation takes place. In particular, note that this is liable to produce a 'no match' error if *either* of the two expressions does not match; this is to be contrasted with */(foo|bar), which is treated as a single pattern but otherwise has similar effects.

To combine brace expansion with array expansion, see the ${^spec} form described in Section 14.3 [Parameter Expansion], page 52, above.

14.7 Filename Expansion

Each word is checked to see if it begins with an unquoted '~'. If it does, then the word up to a '/', or the end of the word if there is no '/', is checked to see if it can be substituted in one of the ways described here. If so, then the '~' and the checked portion are replaced with the appropriate substitute value.

A '~' by itself is replaced by the value of $HOME. A '~' followed by a '+' or a '-' is replaced by current or previous working directory, respectively.

A '~' followed by a number is replaced by the directory at that position in the directory stack. '~0' is equivalent to '~+', and '~1' is the top of the stack. '~+' followed by a number is replaced by the directory at that position in the directory stack. '~+0' is equivalent to '~+', and '~+1' is the top of the stack. '~-' followed by a number is replaced by the directory that many positions from the bottom of the stack. '~-0' is the bottom of the stack. The PUSHD_MINUS option exchanges the effects of '~+' and '~-' where they are followed by a number.

14.7.1 Dynamic named directories

If the function zsh_directory_name exists, or the shell variable zsh_directory_name_functions exists and contains an array of function names, then the functions are used to implement dynamic directory naming. The functions are tried in order until one returns status zero, so it is important that functions test whether they can handle the case in question and return an appropriate status.

A '~' followed by a string *namstr* in unquoted square brackets is treated specially as a dynamic directory name. Note that the first unquoted closing square bracket always terminates *namstr*. The shell function is passed two arguments: the string **n** (for name) and *namstr*. It should either set the array **reply** to a single element which is the directory corresponding to the name and return status zero (executing an assignment as the last statement is usually sufficient), or it should return status non-zero. In the former case the element of reply is used as the directory; in the latter case the substitution is deemed to have failed. If all functions fail and the option NOMATCH is set, an error results.

The functions defined as above are also used to see if a directory can be turned into a name, for example when printing the directory stack or when expanding %~ in prompts. In this case each function is passed two arguments: the string **d** (for directory) and the candidate for dynamic naming. The function should either return non-zero status, if the directory cannot be named by the function, or it should set the array reply to consist of two elements: the first is the dynamic name for the directory (as would appear within '~[...]'), and the second is the prefix length of the directory to be replaced. For example, if the trial directory is **/home/myname/src/zsh** and the dynamic name for **/home/myname/src** (which has 16 characters) is **s**, then the function sets

```
reply=(s 16)
```

The directory name so returned is compared with possible static names for parts of the directory path, as described below; it is used if the prefix length matched (16 in the example) is longer than that matched by any static name.

It is not a requirement that a function implements both **n** and **d** calls; for example, it might be appropriate for certain dynamic forms of expansion not to be contracted to names. In that case any call with the first argument **d** should cause a non-zero status to be returned.

The completion system calls 'zsh_directory_name c' followed by equivalent calls to elements of the array zsh_directory_name_functions, if it exists, in order to complete dynamic names for directories. The code for this should be as for any other completion function as described in Chapter 20 [Completion System], page 242.

As a working example, here is a function that expands any dynamic names beginning with the string p: to directories below **/home/pws/perforce**. In this simple case a static name for the directory would be just as effective.

```
zsh_directory_name() {
  emulate -L zsh
  setopt extendedglob
  local -a match mbegin mend
  if [[ $1 = d ]]; then
    # turn the directory into a name
    if [[ $2 = (#b)(/home/pws/perforce/)([^/]##)* ]]; then
      typeset -ga reply
      reply=(p:$match[2] $(( ${#match[1]} + ${#match[2]} )) )
    else
      return 1
    fi
  elif [[ $1 = n ]]; then
    # turn the name into a directory
```

```
        [[ $2 != (#b)p:(?*) ]] && return 1
        typeset -ga reply
        reply=(/home/pws/perforce/$$match[1])
    elif [[ $1 = c ]]; then
      # complete names
      local expl
      local -a dirs
      dirs=(/home/pws/perforce/*(/:t))
      dirs=(p:${^dirs})
      _wanted dynamic-dirs expl 'dynamic directory' compadd -S\] -a dirs
      return
    else
      return 1
    fi
    return 0
}
```

14.7.2 Static named directories

A '~' followed by anything not already covered consisting of any number of alphanumeric characters or underscore ('_'), hyphen ('-'), or dot ('.') is looked up as a named directory, and replaced by the value of that named directory if found. Named directories are typically home directories for users on the system. They may also be defined if the text after the '~' is the name of a string shell parameter whose value begins with a '/'. Note that trailing slashes will be removed from the path to the directory (though the original parameter is not modified).

It is also possible to define directory names using the -d option to the **hash** builtin.

When the shell prints a path (e.g. when expanding %~ in prompts or when printing the directory stack), the path is checked to see if it has a named directory as its prefix. If so, then the prefix portion is replaced with a '~' followed by the name of the directory. The shorter of the two ways of referring to the directory is used, i.e. either the directory name or the full path; the name is used if they are the same length. The parameters $PWD and $OLDPWD are never abbreviated in this fashion.

14.7.3 '=' expansion

If a word begins with an unquoted '=' and the **EQUALS** option is set, the remainder of the word is taken as the name of a command. If a command exists by that name, the word is replaced by the full pathname of the command.

14.7.4 Notes

Filename expansion is performed on the right hand side of a parameter assignment, including those appearing after commands of the **typeset** family. In this case, the right hand side will be treated as a colon-separated list in the manner of the **PATH** parameter, so that a '~' or an '=' following a ':' is eligible for expansion. All such behaviour can be disabled by quoting the '~', the '=', or the whole expression (but not simply the colon); the **EQUALS** option is also respected.

If the option `MAGIC_EQUAL_SUBST` is set, any unquoted shell argument in the form '*identifier=expression*' becomes eligible for file expansion as described in the previous paragraph. Quoting the first '=' also inhibits this.

14.8 Filename Generation

If a word contains an unquoted instance of one of the characters '*', '(', '|', '<', '[', or '?', it is regarded as a pattern for filename generation, unless the `GLOB` option is unset. If the `EXTENDED_GLOB` option is set, the '^' and '#' characters also denote a pattern; otherwise they are not treated specially by the shell.

The word is replaced with a list of sorted filenames that match the pattern. If no matching pattern is found, the shell gives an error message, unless the `NULL_GLOB` option is set, in which case the word is deleted; or unless the `NOMATCH` option is unset, in which case the word is left unchanged.

In filename generation, the character '/' must be matched explicitly; also, a '.' must be matched explicitly at the beginning of a pattern or after a '/', unless the `GLOB_DOTS` option is set. No filename generation pattern matches the files '.' or '..'. In other instances of pattern matching, the '/' and '.' are not treated specially.

14.8.1 Glob Operators

*   Matches any string, including the null string.

?   Matches any character.

[...]   Matches any of the enclosed characters. Ranges of characters can be specified by separating two characters by a '-'. A '-' or ']' may be matched by including it as the first character in the list. There are also several named classes of characters, in the form '[:*name*:]' with the following meanings. The first set use the macros provided by the operating system to test for the given character combinations, including any modifications due to local language settings, see man page ctype(3):

  [:alnum:]
          The character is alphanumeric

  [:alpha:]
          The character is alphabetic

  [:ascii:]
          The character is 7-bit, i.e. is a single-byte character without the top bit set.

  [:blank:]
          The character is a blank character

  [:cntrl:]
          The character is a control character

  [:digit:]
          The character is a decimal digit

[:graph:]
>
> The character is a printable character other than whitespace

[:lower:]
>
> The character is a lowercase letter

[:print:]
>
> The character is printable

[:punct:]
>
> The character is printable but neither alphanumeric nor whitespace

[:space:]
>
> The character is whitespace

[:upper:]
>
> The character is an uppercase letter

[:xdigit:]
>
> The character is a hexadecimal digit

Another set of named classes is handled internally by the shell and is not sensitive to the locale:

[:IDENT:]
>
> The character is allowed to form part of a shell identifier, such as a parameter name

[:IFS:] The character is used as an input field separator, i.e. is contained in the **IFS** parameter

[:IFSSPACE:]
>
> The character is an IFS white space character; see the documentation for **IFS** in Section 15.6 [Parameters Used By The Shell], page 99.

[:INCOMPLETE:]
>
> Matches a byte that starts an incomplete multibyte character. Note that there may be a sequence of more than one bytes that taken together form the prefix of a multibyte character. To test for a potentially incomplete byte sequence, use the pattern '[[:INCOMPLETE:]]*'. This will never match a sequence starting with a valid multibyte character.

[:INVALID:]
>
> Matches a byte that does not start a valid multibyte character. Note this may be a continuation byte of an incomplete multibyte character as any part of a multibyte string consisting of invalid and incomplete multibyte characters is treated as single bytes.

[:WORD:] The character is treated as part of a word; this test is sensitive to the value of the **WORDCHARS** parameter

Note that the square brackets are additional to those enclosing the whole set of characters, so to test for a single alphanumeric character you need

'[[:alnum:]]'. Named character sets can be used alongside other types, e.g. '[[:alpha:]0-9]'.

[^...]

[!...]   Like [...], except that it matches any character which is not in the given set.

<[x]-[y]>   Matches any number in the range x to y, inclusive. Either of the numbers may be omitted to make the range open-ended; hence '<->' matches any number. To match individual digits, the [...] form is more efficient.

Be careful when using other wildcards adjacent to patterns of this form; for example, <0-9>* will actually match any number whatsoever at the start of the string, since the '<0-9>' will match the first digit, and the '*' will match any others. This is a trap for the unwary, but is in fact an inevitable consequence of the rule that the longest possible match always succeeds. Expressions such as '<0-9>[^[:digit:]]*' can be used instead.

(...)   Matches the enclosed pattern. This is used for grouping. If the KSH_GLOB option is set, then a '@', '*', '+', '?' or '!' immediately preceding the '(' is treated specially, as detailed below. The option SH_GLOB prevents bare parentheses from being used in this way, though the KSH_GLOB option is still available.

Note that grouping cannot extend over multiple directories: it is an error to have a '/' within a group (this only applies for patterns used in filename generation). There is one exception: a group of the form (*pat*/)# appearing as a complete path segment can match a sequence of directories. For example, foo/(a*/)#bar matches foo/bar, foo/any/bar, foo/any/anyother/bar, and so on.

x|y   Matches either x or y. This operator has lower precedence than any other. The '|' character must be within parentheses, to avoid interpretation as a pipeline. The alternatives are tried in order from left to right.

^x   (Requires EXTENDED_GLOB to be set.) Matches anything except the pattern x. This has a higher precedence than '/', so '^foo/bar' will search directories in '.' except './foo' for a file named 'bar'.

x~y   (Requires EXTENDED_GLOB to be set.) Match anything that matches the pattern x but does not match y. This has lower precedence than any operator except '|', so '*/*~foo/bar' will search for all files in all directories in '.' and then exclude 'foo/bar' if there was such a match. Multiple patterns can be excluded by 'foo~bar~baz'. In the exclusion pattern (y), '/' and '.' are not treated specially the way they usually are in globbing.

x#   (Requires EXTENDED_GLOB to be set.) Matches zero or more occurrences of the pattern x. This operator has high precedence; '12#' is equivalent to '1(2#)', rather than '(12)#'. It is an error for an unquoted '#' to follow something which cannot be repeated; this includes an empty string, a pattern already followed by '##', or parentheses when part of a KSH_GLOB pattern (for example, '!(*foo*)#' is invalid and must be replaced by '*(!(*foo*))').

x##   (Requires EXTENDED_GLOB to be set.) Matches one or more occurrences of the pattern x. This operator has high precedence; '12##' is equivalent to '1(2##)', rather than '(12)##'. No more than two active '#' characters may appear together. (Note the potential clash with glob qualifiers in the form '1(2##)' which should therefore be avoided.)

14.8.2 ksh-like Glob Operators

If the KSH_GLOB option is set, the effects of parentheses can be modified by a preceding '@', '*', '+', '?' or '!'. This character need not be unquoted to have special effects, but the '(' must be.

@(...)   Match the pattern in the parentheses. (Like '(...)'.)

*(...)   Match any number of occurrences. (Like '(...)#', except that recursive directory searching is not supported.)

+(...)   Match at least one occurrence. (Like '(...)##', except that recursive directory searching is not supported.)

?(...)   Match zero or one occurrence. (Like '(|...)'.)

!(...)   Match anything but the expression in parentheses. (Like '(^(...))'.)

14.8.3 Precedence

The precedence of the operators given above is (highest) '^', '/', '~', '|' (lowest); the remaining operators are simply treated from left to right as part of a string, with '#' and '##' applying to the shortest possible preceding unit (i.e. a character, '?', '[...]', '<...>', or a parenthesised expression). As mentioned above, a '/' used as a directory separator may not appear inside parentheses, while a '|' must do so; in patterns used in other contexts than filename generation (for example, in **case** statements and tests within '[[...]]'), a '/' is not special; and '/' is also not special after a '~' appearing outside parentheses in a filename pattern.

14.8.4 Globbing Flags

There are various flags which affect any text to their right up to the end of the enclosing group or to the end of the pattern; they require the EXTENDED_GLOB option. All take the form (#X) where X may have one of the following forms:

i   Case insensitive: upper or lower case characters in the pattern match upper or lower case characters.

l   Lower case characters in the pattern match upper or lower case characters; upper case characters in the pattern still only match upper case characters.

I   Case sensitive: locally negates the effect of i or l from that point on.

b   Activate backreferences for parenthesised groups in the pattern; this does not work in filename generation. When a pattern with a set of active parentheses is matched, the strings matched by the groups are stored in the array $match, the indices of the beginning of the matched parentheses in the array $mbegin, and the indices of the end in the array $mend, with the first element of each array corresponding to the first parenthesised group, and so on. These arrays are not otherwise special to the shell. The indices use the same convention as does parameter substitution, so that elements of $mend and $mbegin may be used in subscripts; the `KSH_ARRAYS` option is respected. Sets of globbing flags are not considered parenthesised groups; only the first nine active parentheses can be referenced.

For example,

```
foo="a string with a message"
if [[ $foo = (a|an)' '(#b)(*)' '* ]]; then
  print ${foo[$mbegin[1],$mend[1]]}
fi
```

prints '`string with a`'. Note that the first parenthesis is before the (`#b`) and does not create a backreference.

Backreferences work with all forms of pattern matching other than filename generation, but note that when performing matches on an entire array, such as ${*array#pattern*}, or a global substitution, such as ${*param//pat/repl*}, only the data for the last match remains available. In the case of global replacements this may still be useful. See the example for the `m` flag below.

The numbering of backreferences strictly follows the order of the opening parentheses from left to right in the pattern string, although sets of parentheses may be nested. There are special rules for parentheses followed by '#' or '##'. Only the last match of the parenthesis is remembered: for example, in '`[[ abab = (#b)([ab])# ]]`', only the final '`b`' is stored in `match[1]`. Thus extra parentheses may be necessary to match the complete segment: for example, use '`X((ab|cd)#)Y`' to match a whole string of either '`ab`' or '`cd`' between '`X`' and '`Y`', using the value of `$match[1]` rather than `$match[2]`.

If the match fails none of the parameters is altered, so in some cases it may be necessary to initialise them beforehand. If some of the backreferences fail to match — which happens if they are in an alternate branch which fails to match, or if they are followed by `#` and matched zero times — then the matched string is set to the empty string, and the start and end indices are set to -1.

Pattern matching with backreferences is slightly slower than without.

B   Deactivate backreferences, negating the effect of the `b` flag from that point on.

cN,M The flag (`#c`N,M) can be used anywhere that the `#` or `##` operators can be used except in the expressions '`(*/)#`' and '`(*/)##`' in filename generation, where '`/`' has special meaning; it cannot be combined with other globbing flags and a bad pattern error occurs if it is misplaced. It is equivalent to the form {N,M} in regular expressions. The previous character or group is required to match between N and M times, inclusive. The form (`#c`N) requires exactly N matches; (`#c,`M) is equivalent to specifying N as 0; (`#c`N,) specifies that there is no maximum limit on the number of matches.

m   Set references to the match data for the entire string matched; this is similar to backreferencing and does not work in filename generation. The flag must be in effect at the end of the pattern, i.e. not local to a group. The parameters `$MATCH`, `$MBEGIN` and `$MEND` will be set to the string matched and to the indices of the beginning and end of the string, respectively. This is most useful in parameter substitutions, as otherwise the string matched is obvious.

For example,

```
arr=(veldt jynx grimps waqf zho buck)
print ${arr//(#m)[aeiou]/${(U)MATCH}}
```

forces all the matches (i.e. all vowels) into uppercase, printing 'vEldt jynx grImps wAqf zhO bUck'.

Unlike backreferences, there is no speed penalty for using match references, other than the extra substitutions required for the replacement strings in cases such as the example shown.

M   Deactivate the m flag, hence no references to match data will be created.

a*num*   Approximate matching: *num* errors are allowed in the string matched by the pattern. The rules for this are described in the next subsection.

s, e   Unlike the other flags, these have only a local effect, and each must appear on its own: '(#s)' and '(#e)' are the only valid forms. The '(#s)' flag succeeds only at the start of the test string, and the '(#e)' flag succeeds only at the end of the test string; they correspond to '^' and '$' in standard regular expressions. They are useful for matching path segments in patterns other than those in filename generation (where path segments are in any case treated separately). For example, '*((#s)|/)test((#e)|/)*' matches a path segment 'test' in any of the following strings: test, test/at/start, at/end/test, in/test/middle.

Another use is in parameter substitution; for example '${array/(#s)A*Z(#e)}' will remove only elements of an array which match the complete pattern 'A*Z'. There are other ways of performing many operations of this type, however the combination of the substitution operations '/' and '//' with the '(#s)' and '(#e)' flags provides a single simple and memorable method.

Note that assertions of the form '(^(#s))' also work, i.e. match anywhere except at the start of the string, although this actually means 'anything except a zero-length portion at the start of the string'; you need to use '(""~(#s))' to match a zero-length portion of the string not at the start.

q   A 'q' and everything up to the closing parenthesis of the globbing flags are ignored by the pattern matching code. This is intended to support the use of glob qualifiers, see below. The result is that the pattern '(#b)(*).c(#q.)' can be used both for globbing and for matching against a string. In the former case, the '(#q.)' will be treated as a glob qualifier and the '(#b)' will not be useful, while in the latter case the '(#b)' is useful for backreferences and the '(#q.)' will be ignored. Note that colon modifiers in the glob qualifiers are also not applied in ordinary pattern matching.

u   Respect the current locale in determining the presence of multibyte characters in a pattern, provided the shell was compiled with MULTIBYTE_SUPPORT. This overrides the MULTIBYTE option; the default behaviour is taken from the option. Compare U. (Mnemonic: typically multibyte characters are from Unicode in the UTF-8 encoding, although any extension of ASCII supported by the system library may be used.)

U   All characters are considered to be a single byte long. The opposite of u. This overrides the MULTIBYTE option.

For example, the test string `fooxx` can be matched by the pattern `(#i)FOOXX`, but not by `(#l)FOOXX`, `(#i)FOO(#I)XX` or `((#i)FOOX)X`. The string `(#ia2)readme` specifies case-insensitive matching of `readme` with up to two errors.

When using the ksh syntax for grouping both `KSH_GLOB` and `EXTENDED_GLOB` must be set and the left parenthesis should be preceded by `@`. Note also that the flags do not affect letters inside `[...]` groups, in other words `(#i)[a-z]` still matches only lowercase letters. Finally, note that when examining whole paths case-insensitively every directory must be searched for all files which match, so that a pattern of the form `(#i)/foo/bar/...` is potentially slow.

14.8.5 Approximate Matching

When matching approximately, the shell keeps a count of the errors found, which cannot exceed the number specified in the `(#anum)` flags. Four types of error are recognised:

1.   Different characters, as in `fooxbar` and `fooybar`.

2.   Transposition of characters, as in `banana` and `abnana`.

3.   A character missing in the target string, as with the pattern `road` and target string `rod`.

4.   An extra character appearing in the target string, as with `stove` and `strove`.

Thus, the pattern `(#a3)abcd` matches `dcba`, with the errors occurring by using the first rule twice and the second once, grouping the string as `[d][cb][a]` and `[a][bc][d]`.

Non-literal parts of the pattern must match exactly, including characters in character ranges: hence `(#a1)???` matches strings of length four, by applying rule 4 to an empty part of the pattern, but not strings of length two, since all the ? must match. Other characters which must match exactly are initial dots in filenames (unless the `GLOB_DOTS` option is set), and all slashes in filenames, so that `a/bc` is two errors from `ab/c` (the slash cannot be transposed with another character). Similarly, errors are counted separately for non-contiguous strings in the pattern, so that `(ab|cd)ef` is two errors from `aebf`.

When using exclusion via the ~ operator, approximate matching is treated entirely separately for the excluded part and must be activated separately. Thus, `(#a1)README~READ_ME` matches `READ.ME` but not `READ_ME`, as the trailing `READ_ME` is matched without approximation. However, `(#a1)README~(#a1)READ_ME` does not match any pattern of the form `READ?ME` as all such forms are now excluded.

Apart from exclusions, there is only one overall error count; however, the maximum errors allowed may be altered locally, and this can be delimited by grouping. For example, `(#a1)cat((#a0)dog)fox` allows one error in total, which may not occur in the `dog` section, and the pattern `(#a1)cat(#a0)dog(#a1)fox` is equivalent. Note that the point at which an error is first found is the crucial one for establishing whether to use approximation; for example, `(#a1)abc(#a0)xyz` will not match `abcdxyz`, because the error occurs at the 'x', where approximation is turned off.

Entire path segments may be matched approximately, so that '`(#a1)/foo/d/is/available/at/the/bar`' allows one error in any path segment. This is much less efficient than without the `(#a1)`, however, since every directory in the path must be scanned for a possible approximate match. It is best to place the `(#a1)` after any path segments which are known to be correct.

14.8.6 Recursive Globbing

A pathname component of the form '(*foo*/)#' matches a path consisting of zero or more directories matching the pattern *foo*.

As a shorthand, '**/' is equivalent to '(*/)#'; note that this therefore matches files in the current directory as well as subdirectories. Thus:

        ls (*/)#bar

or

        ls **/bar

does a recursive directory search for files named 'bar' (potentially including the file 'bar' in the current directory). This form does not follow symbolic links; the alternative form '***/' does, but is otherwise identical. Neither of these can be combined with other forms of globbing within the same path segment; in that case, the '*' operators revert to their usual effect.

Even shorter forms are available when the option GLOB_STAR_SHORT is set. In that case if no / immediately follows a ** or *** they are treated as if both a / plus a further * are present. Hence:

        setopt GLOBSTARSHORT
        ls **.c

is equivalent to

        ls **/*.c

14.8.7 Glob Qualifiers

Patterns used for filename generation may end in a list of qualifiers enclosed in parentheses. The qualifiers specify which filenames that otherwise match the given pattern will be inserted in the argument list.

If the option BARE_GLOB_QUAL is set, then a trailing set of parentheses containing no '|' or '(' characters (or '~' if it is special) is taken as a set of glob qualifiers. A glob subexpression that would normally be taken as glob qualifiers, for example '(^x)', can be forced to be treated as part of the glob pattern by doubling the parentheses, in this case producing '((^x))'.

If the option EXTENDED_GLOB is set, a different syntax for glob qualifiers is available, namely '(#q*x*)' where *x* is any of the same glob qualifiers used in the other format. The qualifiers must still appear at the end of the pattern. However, with this syntax multiple glob qualifiers may be chained together. They are treated as a logical AND of the individual sets of flags. Also, as the syntax is unambiguous, the expression will be treated as glob qualifiers just as long any parentheses contained within it are balanced; appearance of '|', '(' or '~' does not negate the effect. Note that qualifiers will be recognised in this form even if a bare glob qualifier exists at the end of the pattern, for example '*(#q*)(.)' will recognise executable regular files if both options are set; however, mixed syntax should probably be avoided for the sake of clarity. Note that within conditions using the '[[' form the presence of a parenthesised expression (#q...) at the end of a string indicates that globbing should be performed; the expression may include glob qualifiers, but it is also valid if it is simply (#q). This does not apply to the right hand side of pattern match operators as the syntax already has special significance.

A qualifier may be any one of the following:

/	directories
F	'full' (i.e. non-empty) directories. Note that the opposite sense (^F) expands to empty directories and all non-directories. Use (/^F) for empty directories.
.	plain files
@	symbolic links
=	sockets
p	named pipes (FIFOs)
*	executable plain files (0100 or 0010 or 0001)
%	device files (character or block special)
%b	block special files
%c	character special files
r	owner-readable files (0400)
w	owner-writable files (0200)
x	owner-executable files (0100)
A	group-readable files (0040)
I	group-writable files (0020)
E	group-executable files (0010)
R	world-readable files (0004)
W	world-writable files (0002)
X	world-executable files (0001)
s	setuid files (04000)
S	setgid files (02000)
t	files with the sticky bit (01000)
f*spec*	files with access rights matching *spec*. This *spec* may be a octal number optionally preceded by a '=', a '+', or a '-'. If none of these characters is given, the behavior is the same as for '='. The octal number describes the mode bits to be expected, if combined with a '=', the value given must match the file-modes exactly, with a '+', at least the bits in the given number must be set in the file-modes, and with a '-', the bits in the number must not be set. Giving a '?' instead of a octal digit anywhere in the number ensures that the corresponding bits in the file-modes are not checked, this is only useful in combination with '='.

If the qualifier 'f' is followed by any other character anything up to the next matching character ('[', '{', and '<' match ']', '}', and '>' respectively, any other character matches itself) is taken as a list of comma-separated *sub-specs*.

Each *sub-spec* may be either an octal number as described above or a list of any of the characters 'u', 'g', 'o', and 'a', followed by a '=', a '+', or a '-', followed by a list of any of the characters 'r', 'w', 'x', 's', and 't', or an octal digit. The first list of characters specify which access rights are to be checked. If a 'u' is given, those for the owner of the file are used, if a 'g' is given, those of the group are checked, a 'o' means to test those of other users, and the 'a' says to test all three groups. The '=', '+', and '-' again says how the modes are to be checked and have the same meaning as described for the first form above. The second list of characters finally says which access rights are to be expected: 'r' for read access, 'w' for write access, 'x' for the right to execute the file (or to search a directory), 's' for the setuid and setgid bits, and 't' for the sticky bit.

Thus, '*(f70?)' gives the files for which the owner has read, write, and execute permission, and for which other group members have no rights, independent of the permissions for other users. The pattern '*(f-100)' gives all files for which the owner does not have execute permission, and '*(f:gu+w,o-rx:)' gives the files for which the owner and the other members of the group have at least write permission, and for which other users don't have read or execute permission.

e*string*

+*cmd*   The *string* will be executed as shell code. The filename will be included in the list if and only if the code returns a zero status (usually the status of the last command).

In the first form, the first character after the 'e' will be used as a separator and anything up to the next matching separator will be taken as the *string*; '[', '{', and '<' match ']', '}', and '>', respectively, while any other character matches itself. Note that expansions must be quoted in the *string* to prevent them from being expanded before globbing is done. *string* is then executed as shell code. The string globqual is appended to the array zsh_eval_context the duration of execution.

During the execution of *string* the filename currently being tested is available in the parameter REPLY; the parameter may be altered to a string to be inserted into the list instead of the original filename. In addition, the parameter reply may be set to an array or a string, which overrides the value of REPLY. If set to an array, the latter is inserted into the command line word by word.

For example, suppose a directory contains a single file 'lonely'. Then the expression '*(e:'reply=(${REPLY}{1,2})':)' will cause the words 'lonely1' and 'lonely2' to be inserted into the command line. Note the quoting of *string*.

The form +*cmd* has the same effect, but no delimiters appear around *cmd*. Instead, *cmd* is taken as the longest sequence of characters following the + that are alphanumeric or underscore. Typically *cmd* will be the name of a shell function that contains the appropriate test. For example,

```
nt() { [[ $REPLY -nt $NTREF ]] }
NTREF=reffile
ls -l *(+nt)
```

lists all files in the directory that have been modified more recently than reffile.

d*dev*   files on the device *dev*

l[-|+]*ct* files having a link count less than *ct* (-), greater than *ct* (+), or equal to *ct*

U   files owned by the effective user ID

G   files owned by the effective group ID

u*id*   files owned by user ID *id* if that is a number. Otherwise, *id* specifies a user name: the character after the 'u' will be taken as a separator and the string between it and the next matching separator will be taken as a user name. The starting separators '[', '{', and '<' match the final separators ']', '}', and '>', respectively; any other character matches itself. The selected files are those owned by this user. For example, 'u:foo:' or 'u[foo]' selects files owned by user 'foo'.

g*id*   like u*id* but with group IDs or names

a[Mwhms][-|+]*n*

    files accessed exactly *n* days ago. Files accessed within the last *n* days are selected using a negative value for *n* (-*n*). Files accessed more than *n* days ago are selected by a positive *n* value (+*n*). Optional unit specifiers 'M', 'w', 'h', 'm' or 's' (e.g. 'ah5') cause the check to be performed with months (of 30 days), weeks, hours, minutes or seconds instead of days, respectively. An explicit 'd' for days is also allowed.

    Any fractional part of the difference between the access time and the current part in the appropriate units is ignored in the comparison. For instance, 'echo *(ah-5)' would echo files accessed within the last five hours, while 'echo *(ah+5)' would echo files accessed at least six hours ago, as times strictly between five and six hours are treated as five hours.

m[Mwhms][-|+]*n*

    like the file access qualifier, except that it uses the file modification time.

c[Mwhms][-|+]*n*

    like the file access qualifier, except that it uses the file inode change time.

L[+|-]*n*   files less than *n* bytes (-), more than *n* bytes (+), or exactly *n* bytes in length.

    If this flag is directly followed by a *size specifier* 'k' ('K'), 'm' ('M'), or 'p' ('P') (e.g. 'Lk-50') the check is performed with kilobytes, megabytes, or blocks (of 512 bytes) instead. (On some systems additional specifiers are available for gigabytes, 'g' or 'G', and terabytes, 't' or 'T'.) If a size specifier is used a file is regarded as "exactly" the size if the file size rounded up to the next unit is equal to the test size. Hence '*(Lm1)' matches files from 1 byte up to 1 Megabyte inclusive. Note also that the set of files "less than" the test size only includes files that would not match the equality test; hence '*(Lm-1)' only matches files of zero size.

^   negates all qualifiers following it

-     toggles between making the qualifiers work on symbolic links (the default) and the files they point to

M   sets the `MARK_DIRS` option for the current pattern

T   appends a trailing qualifier mark to the filenames, analogous to the `LIST_TYPES` option, for the current pattern (overrides M)

N   sets the `NULL_GLOB` option for the current pattern

D   sets the `GLOB_DOTS` option for the current pattern

n   sets the `NUMERIC_GLOB_SORT` option for the current pattern

Y*n*   enables short-circuit mode: the pattern will expand to at most *n* filenames. If more than *n* matches exist, only the first *n* matches in directory traversal order will be considered.

           Implies oN when no o*c* qualifier is used.

o*c*   specifies how the names of the files should be sorted. If *c* is n they are sorted by name; if it is L they are sorted depending on the size (length) of the files; if l they are sorted by the number of links; if a, m, or c they are sorted by the time of the last access, modification, or inode change respectively; if d, files in subdirectories appear before those in the current directory at each level of the search — this is best combined with other criteria, for example 'odon' to sort on names for files within the same directory; if N, no sorting is performed. Note that a, m, and c compare the age against the current time, hence the first name in the list is the youngest file. Also note that the modifiers ^ and - are used, so '*(^-oL)' gives a list of all files sorted by file size in descending order, following any symbolic links. Unless oN is used, multiple order specifiers may occur to resolve ties.

           The default sorting is n (by name) unless the Y glob qualifier is used, in which case it is N (unsorted).

           oe and o+ are special cases; they are each followed by shell code, delimited as for the e glob qualifier and the + glob qualifier respectively (see above). The code is executed for each matched file with the parameter `REPLY` set to the name of the file on entry and `globsort` appended to `zsh_eval_context`. The code should modify the parameter `REPLY` in some fashion. On return, the value of the parameter is used instead of the file name as the string on which to sort. Unlike other sort operators, oe and o+ may be repeated, but note that the maximum number of sort operators of any kind that may appear in any glob expression is 12.

O*c*   like 'o', but sorts in descending order; i.e. '*(^oc)' is the same as '*(Oc)' and '*(^Oc)' is the same as '*(oc)'; 'Od' puts files in the current directory before those in subdirectories at each level of the search.

[*beg*[,*end*]]
           specifies which of the matched filenames should be included in the returned list. The syntax is the same as for array subscripts. *beg* and the optional *end* may be mathematical expressions. As in parameter subscripting they may be negative to make them count from the last match backward. E.g.: '*(-OL[1,3])' gives a list of the names of the three largest files.

P*string*   The *string* will be prepended to each glob match as a separate word. *string* is delimited in the same way as arguments to the e glob qualifier described above. The qualifier can be repeated; the words are prepended separately so that the resulting command line contains the words in the same order they were given in the list of glob qualifiers.

A typical use for this is to prepend an option before all occurrences of a file name; for example, the pattern '*(P:-f:)' produces the command line arguments '-f *file1* -f *file2* ...'

If the modifier ^ is active, then *string* will be appended instead of prepended. Prepending and appending is done independently so both can be used on the same glob expression; for example by writing '*(P:foo:^P:bar:^P:baz:)' which produces the command line arguments 'foo baz *file1* bar ...'

More than one of these lists can be combined, separated by commas. The whole list matches if at least one of the sublists matches (they are 'or'ed, the qualifiers in the sublists are 'and'ed). Some qualifiers, however, affect all matches generated, independent of the sublist in which they are given. These are the qualifiers 'M', 'T', 'N', 'D', 'n', 'o', 'O' and the subscripts given in brackets ('[...]').

If a ':' appears in a qualifier list, the remainder of the expression in parenthesis is interpreted as a modifier (see Section 14.1.4 [Modifiers], page 47, in Section 14.1 [History Expansion], page 45). Each modifier must be introduced by a separate ':'. Note also that the result after modification does not have to be an existing file. The name of any existing file can be followed by a modifier of the form '(:...)' even if no actual filename generation is performed, although note that the presence of the parentheses causes the entire expression to be subjected to any global pattern matching options such as NULL_GLOB. Thus:

        ls *(-/)

lists all directories and symbolic links that point to directories, and

        ls *(-@)

lists all broken symbolic links, and

        ls *(%W)

lists all world-writable device files in the current directory, and

        ls *(W,X)

lists all files in the current directory that are world-writable or world-executable, and

        echo /tmp/foo*(u0^@:t)

outputs the basename of all root-owned files beginning with the string 'foo' in /tmp, ignoring symlinks, and

        ls *.*~(lex|parse).[ch](^D^l1)

lists all files having a link count of one whose names contain a dot (but not those starting with a dot, since GLOB_DOTS is explicitly switched off) except for lex.c, lex.h, parse.c and parse.h.

        print b*.pro(#q:s/pro/shmo/)(#q.:s/builtin/shmiltin/)

demonstrates how colon modifiers and other qualifiers may be chained together. The ordinary qualifier '.' is applied first, then the colon modifiers in order from left to right. So if EXTENDED_GLOB is set and the base pattern matches the regular file builtin.pro, the shell will print 'shmiltin.shmo'.

15 Parameters

15.1 Description

A parameter has a name, a value, and a number of attributes. A name may be any sequence of alphanumeric characters and underscores, or the single characters '*', '@', '#', '?', '-', '$', or '!'. A parameter whose name begins with an alphanumeric or underscore is also referred to as a *variable*.

The attributes of a parameter determine the *type* of its value, often referred to as the parameter type or variable type, and also control other processing that may be applied to the value when it is referenced. The value type may be a *scalar* (a string, an integer, or a floating point number), an array (indexed numerically), or an *associative* array (an unordered set of name-value pairs, indexed by name, also referred to as a *hash*).

Named scalar parameters may have the *exported*, -x, attribute, to copy them into the process environment, which is then passed from the shell to any new processes that it starts. Exported parameters are called *environment variables*. The shell also *imports* environment variables at startup time and automatically marks the corresponding parameters as exported. Some environment variables are not imported for reasons of security or because they would interfere with the correct operation of other shell features.

Parameters may also be *special*, that is, they have a predetermined meaning to the shell. Special parameters cannot have their type changed or their readonly attribute turned off, and if a special parameter is unset, then later recreated, the special properties will be retained.

To declare the type of a parameter, or to assign a string or numeric value to a scalar parameter, use the `typeset` builtin.

The value of a scalar parameter may also be assigned by writing:

name=value

In scalar assignment, *value* is expanded as a single string, in which the elements of arrays are joined together; filename expansion is not performed unless the option `GLOB_ASSIGN` is set.

When the integer attribute, -i, or a floating point attribute, -E or -F, is set for *name*, the *value* is subject to arithmetic evaluation. Furthermore, by replacing '=' with '+=', a parameter can be incremented or appended to. See Section 15.2 [Array Parameters], page 86, and Chapter 11 [Arithmetic Evaluation], page 31, for additional forms of assignment.

Note that assignment may implicitly change the attributes of a parameter. For example, assigning a number to a variable in arithmetic evaluation may change its type to integer or float, and with `GLOB_ASSIGN` assigning a pattern to a variable may change its type to an array.

To reference the value of a parameter, write '$*name*' or '${*name*}'. See Section 14.3 [Parameter Expansion], page 52, for complete details. That section also explains the effect of the difference between scalar and array assignment on parameter expansion.

15.2 Array Parameters

To assign an array value, write one of:

> set -A *name value ...*
>
> *name*=(*value ...*)
>
> *name*=([*key*]=*value ...*)

If no parameter *name* exists, an ordinary array parameter is created. If the parameter *name* exists and is a scalar, it is replaced by a new array.

In the third form, *key* is an expression that will be evaluated in arithmetic context (in its simplest form, an integer) that gives the index of the element to be assigned with *value*. In this form any elements not explicitly mentioned that come before the largest index to which a value is assigned are assigned an empty string. The indices may be in any order. Note that this syntax is strict: [and]= must not be quoted, and *key* may not consist of the unquoted string]=, but is otherwise treated as a simple string. The enhanced forms of subscript expression that may be used when directly subscripting a variable name, described in the section Array Subscripts below, are not available.

The syntaxes with and without the explicit key may be mixed. An implicit *key* is deduced by incrementing the index from the previously assigned element. Note that it is not treated as an error if latter assignments in this form overwrite earlier assignments.

For example, assuming the option KSH_ARRAYS is not set, the following:

> array=(one [3]=three four)

causes the array variable **array** to contain four elements **one**, an empty string, **three** and **four**, in that order.

In the forms where only *value* is specified, full command line expansion is performed.

In the [*key*]=*value* form, both *key* and *value* undergo all forms of expansion allowed for single word shell expansions (this does not include filename generation); these are as performed by the parameter expansion flag (e) as described in Section 14.3 [Parameter Expansion], page 52. Nested parentheses may surround *value* and are included as part of the value, which is joined into a plain string; this differs from ksh which allows the values themselves to be arrays. A future version of zsh may support that. To cause the brackets to be interpreted as a character class for filename generation, and therefore to treat the resulting list of files as a set of values, quote the equal sign using any form of quoting. Example:

> *name*=([a-z]'='*)

To append to an array without changing the existing values, use one of the following:

> *name*+=(*value ...*)
>
> *name*+=([*key*]=*value ...*)

In the second form *key* may specify an existing index as well as an index off the end of the old array; any existing value is overwritten by *value*. Also, it is possible to use [*key*]+=*value* to append to the existing value at that index.

Within the parentheses on the right hand side of either form of the assignment, newlines and semicolons are treated the same as white space, separating individual *values*. Any consecutive sequence of such characters has the same effect.

Ordinary array parameters may also be explicitly declared with:

```
typeset -a name
```

Associative arrays *must* be declared before assignment, by using:

```
typeset -A name
```

When *name* refers to an associative array, the list in an assignment is interpreted as alternating keys and values:

> `set -A` *name key value ...*
>
> *name*=(*key value ...*)
>
> *name*=([*key*]=*value ...*)

Note that only one of the two syntaxes above may be used in any given assignment; the forms may not be mixed. This is unlike the case of numerically indexed arrays.

Every *key* must have a *value* in this case. Note that this assigns to the entire array, deleting any elements that do not appear in the list. The append syntax may also be used with an associative array:

> *name*+=(*key value ...*)
>
> *name*+=([*key*]=*value ...*)

This adds a new key/value pair if the key is not already present, and replaces the value for the existing key if it is. In the second form it is also possible to use [*key*]+=*value* to append to the existing value at that key. Expansion is performed identically to the corresponding forms for normal arrays, as described above.

To create an empty array (including associative arrays), use one of:

> `set -A` *name*
>
> *name*=()

15.2.1 Array Subscripts

Individual elements of an array may be selected using a subscript. A subscript of the form '[*exp*]' selects the single element *exp*, where *exp* is an arithmetic expression which will be subject to arithmetic expansion as if it were surrounded by '$((...))'. The elements are numbered beginning with 1, unless the KSH_ARRAYS option is set in which case they are numbered from zero.

Subscripts may be used inside braces used to delimit a parameter name, thus '${foo[2]}' is equivalent to '$foo[2]'. If the KSH_ARRAYS option is set, the braced form is the only one that works, as bracketed expressions otherwise are not treated as subscripts.

If the KSH_ARRAYS option is not set, then by default accesses to an array element with a subscript that evaluates to zero return an empty string, while an attempt to write such an element is treated as an error. For backward compatibility the KSH_ZERO_SUBSCRIPT option can be set to cause subscript values 0 and 1 to be equivalent; see the description of the option in Section 16.2 [Description of Options], page 110.

The same subscripting syntax is used for associative arrays, except that no arithmetic expansion is applied to *exp*. However, the parsing rules for arithmetic expressions still apply, which affects the way that certain special characters must be protected from interpretation. See *Subscript Parsing* below for details.

A subscript of the form '[*]' or '[@]' evaluates to all elements of an array; there is no difference between the two except when they appear within double quotes. '"$foo[*]"' evaluates to '"$foo[1] $foo[2] ..."', whereas '"$foo[@]"' evaluates to '"$foo[1]" "$foo[2]" ...'. For associative arrays, '[*]' or '[@]' evaluate to all the values, in no particular order. Note that this does not substitute the keys; see the documentation for the 'k' flag under Section 14.3 [Parameter Expansion], page 52, for complete details. When an array parameter is referenced as '$name' (with no subscript) it evaluates to '$name[*]', unless the KSH_ARRAYS option is set in which case it evaluates to '${name[0]}' (for an associative array, this means the value of the key '0', which may not exist even if there are values for other keys).

A subscript of the form '[exp1,exp2]' selects all elements in the range exp1 to exp2, inclusive. (Associative arrays are unordered, and so do not support ranges.) If one of the subscripts evaluates to a negative number, say -n, then the nth element from the end of the array is used. Thus '$foo[-3]' is the third element from the end of the array foo, and '$foo[1,-1]' is the same as '$foo[*]'.

Subscripting may also be performed on non-array values, in which case the subscripts specify a substring to be extracted. For example, if FOO is set to 'foobar', then 'echo $FOO[2,5]' prints 'ooba'. Note that some forms of subscripting described below perform pattern matching, and in that case the substring extends from the start of the match of the first subscript to the end of the match of the second subscript. For example,

```
string="abcdefghijklm"
print ${string[(r)d?,(r)h?]}
```

prints 'defghi'. This is an obvious generalisation of the rule for single-character matches. For a single subscript, only a single character is referenced (not the range of characters covered by the match).

Note that in substring operations the second subscript is handled differently by the r and R subscript flags: the former takes the shortest match as the length and the latter the longest match. Hence in the former case a * at the end is redundant while in the latter case it matches the whole remainder of the string. This does not affect the result of the single subscript case as here the length of the match is irrelevant.

15.2.2 Array Element Assignment

A subscript may be used on the left side of an assignment like so:

    name[exp]=value

In this form of assignment the element or range specified by exp is replaced by the expression on the right side. An array (but not an associative array) may be created by assignment to a range or element. Arrays do not nest, so assigning a parenthesized list of values to an element or range changes the number of elements in the array, shifting the other elements to accommodate the new values. (This is not supported for associative arrays.)

This syntax also works as an argument to the typeset command:

    typeset "name[exp]"=value

The value may not be a parenthesized list in this case; only single-element assignments may be made with typeset. Note that quotes are necessary in this case to prevent the brackets from being interpreted as filename generation operators. The noglob precommand modifier could be used instead.

To delete an element of an ordinary array, assign '()' to that element. To delete an element of an associative array, use the unset command:

```
unset "name[exp]"
```

15.2.3 Subscript Flags

If the opening bracket, or the comma in a range, in any subscript expression is directly followed by an opening parenthesis, the string up to the matching closing one is considered to be a list of flags, as in 'name[(flags)exp]'.

The flags s, n and b take an argument; the delimiter is shown below as ':', but any character, or the matching pairs '(...)', '{...}', '[...]', or '<...>', may be used, but note that '<...>' can only be used if the subscript is inside a double quoted expression or a parameter substitution enclosed in braces as otherwise the expression is interpreted as a redirection.

The flags currently understood are:

w   If the parameter subscripted is a scalar then this flag makes subscripting work on words instead of characters. The default word separator is whitespace. When combined with the i or I flag, the effect is to produce the index of the first character of the first/last word which matches the given pattern; note that a failed match in this case always yields 0.

s:string: This gives the *string* that separates words (for use with the w flag). The delimiter character : is arbitrary; see above.

p   Recognize the same escape sequences as the **print** builtin in the string argument of a subsequent 's' flag.

f   If the parameter subscripted is a scalar then this flag makes subscripting work on lines instead of characters, i.e. with elements separated by newlines. This is a shorthand for 'pws:\n:'.

r   Reverse subscripting: if this flag is given, the *exp* is taken as a pattern and the result is the first matching array element, substring or word (if the parameter is an array, if it is a scalar, or if it is a scalar and the 'w' flag is given, respectively). The subscript used is the number of the matching element, so that pairs of subscripts such as '$foo[(r)??,3]' and '$foo[(r)??,(r)f*]' are possible if the parameter is not an associative array. If the parameter is an associative array, only the value part of each pair is compared to the pattern, and the result is that value.

             If a search through an ordinary array failed, the search sets the subscript to one past the end of the array, and hence ${array[(r)pattern]} will substitute the empty string. Thus the success of a search can be tested by using the (i) flag, for example (assuming the option KSH_ARRAYS is not in effect):

                 [[${array[(i)pattern]} -le ${#array}]]

             If KSH_ARRAYS is in effect, the -le should be replaced by -lt.

R   Like 'r', but gives the last match. For associative arrays, gives all possible matches. May be used for assigning to ordinary array elements, but not for assigning to associative arrays. On failure, for normal arrays this has the effect of returning the element corresponding to subscript 0; this is empty unless one of the options KSH_ARRAYS or KSH_ZERO_SUBSCRIPT is in effect.

Note that in subscripts with both 'r' and 'R' pattern characters are active even if they were substituted for a parameter (regardless of the setting of GLOB_SUBST which controls this feature in normal pattern matching). The flag 'e' can be added to inhibit pattern matching. As this flag does not inhibit other forms of substitution, care is still required; using a parameter to hold the key has the desired effect:

```
key2='original key'
print ${array[(Re)$key2]}
```

i   Like 'r', but gives the index of the match instead; this may not be combined with a second argument. On the left side of an assignment, behaves like 'r'. For associative arrays, the key part of each pair is compared to the pattern, and the first matching key found is the result. On failure substitutes the length of the array plus one, as discussed under the description of 'r', or the empty string for an associative array.

I   Like 'i', but gives the index of the last match, or all possible matching keys in an associative array. On failure substitutes 0, or the empty string for an associative array. This flag is best when testing for values or keys that do not exist.

k   If used in a subscript on an associative array, this flag causes the keys to be interpreted as patterns, and returns the value for the first key found where *exp* is matched by the key. Note this could be any such key as no ordering of associative arrays is defined. This flag does not work on the left side of an assignment to an associative array element. If used on another type of parameter, this behaves like 'r'.

K   On an associative array this is like 'k' but returns all values where *exp* is matched by the keys. On other types of parameters this has the same effect as 'R'.

n:*expr*:   If combined with 'r', 'R', 'i' or 'I', makes them give the *n*th or *n*th last match (if *expr* evaluates to *n*). This flag is ignored when the array is associative. The delimiter character : is arbitrary; see above.

b:*expr*:   If combined with 'r', 'R', 'i' or 'I', makes them begin at the *n*th or *n*th last element, word, or character (if *expr* evaluates to *n*). This flag is ignored when the array is associative. The delimiter character : is arbitrary; see above.

e   This flag causes any pattern matching that would be performed on the subscript to use plain string matching instead. Hence '${array[(re)*]}' matches only the array element whose value is *. Note that other forms of substitution such as parameter substitution are not inhibited.

     This flag can also be used to force * or @ to be interpreted as a single key rather than as a reference to all values. It may be used for either purpose on the left side of an assignment.

See *Parameter Expansion Flags* (Section 14.3 [Parameter Expansion], page 52) for additional ways to manipulate the results of array subscripting.

15.2.4 Subscript Parsing

This discussion applies mainly to associative array key strings and to patterns used for reverse subscripting (the 'r', 'R', 'i', etc. flags), but it may also affect parameter substitutions that appear as part of an arithmetic expression in an ordinary subscript.

To avoid subscript parsing limitations in assignments to associative array elements, use the append syntax:

```
aa+=('key with "*strange*" characters' 'value string')
```

The basic rule to remember when writing a subscript expression is that all text between the opening '[' and the closing ']' is interpreted *as if* it were in double quotes (Section 6.9 [Quoting], page 18). However, unlike double quotes which normally cannot nest, subscript expressions may appear inside double-quoted strings or inside other subscript expressions (or both!), so the rules have two important differences.

The first difference is that brackets ('[' and ']') must appear as balanced pairs in a subscript expression unless they are preceded by a backslash ('\'). Therefore, within a subscript expression (and unlike true double-quoting) the sequence '\[' becomes '[', and similarly '\]' becomes ']'. This applies even in cases where a backslash is not normally required; for example, the pattern '[^[]' (to match any character other than an open bracket) should be written '[^\[]' in a reverse-subscript pattern. However, note that '\[^\[\]' and even '\[^[]' mean the *same* thing, because backslashes are always stripped when they appear before brackets!

The same rule applies to parentheses ('(' and ')') and braces ('{' and '}'): they must appear either in balanced pairs or preceded by a backslash, and backslashes that protect parentheses or braces are removed during parsing. This is because parameter expansions may be surrounded by balanced braces, and subscript flags are introduced by balanced parentheses.

The second difference is that a double-quote ('"') may appear as part of a subscript expression without being preceded by a backslash, and therefore that the two characters '\"' remain as two characters in the subscript (in true double-quoting, '\"' becomes '"'). However, because of the standard shell quoting rules, any double-quotes that appear must occur in balanced pairs unless preceded by a backslash. This makes it more difficult to write a subscript expression that contains an odd number of double-quote characters, but the reason for this difference is so that when a subscript expression appears inside true double-quotes, one can still write '\"' (rather than '\\\"') for '"'.

To use an odd number of double quotes as a key in an assignment, use the **typeset** builtin and an enclosing pair of double quotes; to refer to the value of that key, again use double quotes:

```
typeset -A aa
typeset "aa[one\"two\"three\"quotes]"=QQQ
print "$aa[one\"two\"three\"quotes]"
```

It is important to note that the quoting rules do not change when a parameter expansion with a subscript is nested inside another subscript expression. That is, it is not necessary to use additional backslashes within the inner subscript expression; they are removed only once, from the innermost subscript outwards. Parameters are also expanded from the innermost subscript first, as each expansion is encountered left to right in the outer expression.

A further complication arises from a way in which subscript parsing is *not* different from double quote parsing. As in true double-quoting, the sequences '*', and '\@' remain as two characters when they appear in a subscript expression. To use a literal '*' or '@' as an associative array key, the 'e' flag must be used:

```
typeset -A aa
aa[(e)*]=star
print $aa[(e)*]
```

A last detail must be considered when reverse subscripting is performed. Parameters appearing in the subscript expression are first expanded and then the complete expression is interpreted as a pattern. This has two effects: first, parameters behave as if GLOB_SUBST were on (and it cannot be turned off); second, backslashes are interpreted twice, once when parsing the array subscript and again when parsing the pattern. In a reverse subscript, it's necessary to use *four* backslashes to cause a single backslash to match literally in the pattern. For complex patterns, it is often easiest to assign the desired pattern to a parameter and then refer to that parameter in the subscript, because then the backslashes, brackets, parentheses, etc., are seen only when the complete expression is converted to a pattern. To match the value of a parameter literally in a reverse subscript, rather than as a pattern, use '${(q)name}' (Section 14.3 [Parameter Expansion], page 52) to quote the expanded value.

Note that the 'k' and 'K' flags are reverse subscripting for an ordinary array, but are *not* reverse subscripting for an associative array! (For an associative array, the keys in the array itself are interpreted as patterns by those flags; the subscript is a plain string in that case.)

One final note, not directly related to subscripting: the numeric names of positional parameters (Section 15.3 [Positional Parameters], page 92) are parsed specially, so for example '$2foo' is equivalent to '${2}foo'. Therefore, to use subscript syntax to extract a substring from a positional parameter, the expansion must be surrounded by braces; for example, '${2[3,5]}' evaluates to the third through fifth characters of the second positional parameter, but '$2[3,5]' is the entire second parameter concatenated with the filename generation pattern '[3,5]'.

15.3 Positional Parameters

The positional parameters provide access to the command-line arguments of a shell function, shell script, or the shell itself; see Chapter 4 [Invocation], page 6, and also Chapter 9 [Functions], page 24. The parameter *n*, where *n* is a number, is the *n*th positional parameter. The parameter '$0' is a special case, see Section 15.5 [Parameters Set By The Shell], page 93.

The parameters *, @ and argv are arrays containing all the positional parameters; thus '$argv[n]', etc., is equivalent to simply '$n'. Note that the options KSH_ARRAYS or KSH_ZERO_SUBSCRIPT apply to these arrays as well, so with either of those options set, '${argv[0]}' is equivalent to '$1' and so on.

Positional parameters may be changed after the shell or function starts by using the set builtin, by assigning to the argv array, or by direct assignment of the form '*n*=*value*' where *n* is the number of the positional parameter to be changed. This also creates (with empty values) any of the positions from 1 to *n* that do not already have values. Note that, because the positional parameters form an array, an array assignment of the form '*n*=(*value* ...)' is allowed, and has the effect of shifting all the values at positions greater than *n* by as many positions as necessary to accommodate the new values.

15.4 Local Parameters

Shell function executions delimit scopes for shell parameters. (Parameters are dynamically scoped.) The `typeset` builtin, and its alternative forms `declare`, `integer`, `local` and `readonly` (but not `export`), can be used to declare a parameter as being local to the innermost scope.

When a parameter is read or assigned to, the innermost existing parameter of that name is used. (That is, the local parameter hides any less-local parameter.) However, assigning to a non-existent parameter, or declaring a new parameter with `export`, causes it to be created in the *outer*most scope.

Local parameters disappear when their scope ends. `unset` can be used to delete a parameter while it is still in scope; any outer parameter of the same name remains hidden.

Special parameters may also be made local; they retain their special attributes unless either the existing or the newly-created parameter has the `-h` (hide) attribute. This may have unexpected effects: there is no default value, so if there is no assignment at the point the variable is made local, it will be set to an empty value (or zero in the case of integers). The following:

```
typeset PATH=/new/directory:$PATH
```

is valid for temporarily allowing the shell or programmes called from it to find the programs in `/new/directory` inside a function.

Note that the restriction in older versions of zsh that local parameters were never exported has been removed.

15.5 Parameters Set By The Shell

In the parameter lists that follow, the mark '<S>' indicates that the parameter is special. '<Z>' indicates that the parameter does not exist when the shell initializes in `sh` or `ksh` emulation mode.

The following parameters are automatically set by the shell:

! <S> The process ID of the last command started in the background with &, or put into the background with the `bg` builtin.

<S> The number of positional parameters in decimal. Note that some confusion may occur with the syntax $#*param* which substitutes the length of *param*. Use `${#}` to resolve ambiguities. In particular, the sequence '$#-...' in an arithmetic expression is interpreted as the length of the parameter -, q.v.

ARGC <S> <Z>

  Same as #.

$ <S> The process ID of this shell. Note that this indicates the original shell started by invoking `zsh`; all processes forked from the shells without executing a new program, such as subshells started by (...), substitute the same value.

- <S> Flags supplied to the shell on invocation or by the `set` or `setopt` commands.

* <S> An array containing the positional parameters.

argv <S> <Z>

    Same as `*`. Assigning to `argv` changes the local positional parameters, but `argv` is *not* itself a local parameter. Deleting `argv` with `unset` in any function deletes it everywhere, although only the innermost positional parameter array is deleted (so `*` and `@` in other scopes are not affected).

@ <S>   Same as `argv[@]`, even when `argv` is not set.

? <S>   The exit status returned by the last command.

0 <S>   The name used to invoke the current shell, or as set by the `-c` command line option upon invocation. If the `FUNCTION_ARGZERO` option is set, `$0` is set upon entry to a shell function to the name of the function, and upon entry to a sourced script to the name of the script, and reset to its previous value when the function or script returns.

status <S> <Z>

    Same as `?`.

pipestatus <S> <Z>

    An array containing the exit statuses returned by all commands in the last pipeline.

_ <S>   The last argument of the previous command. Also, this parameter is set in the environment of every command executed to the full pathname of the command.

CPUTYPE   The machine type (microprocessor class or machine model), as determined at run time.

EGID <S>   The effective group ID of the shell process. If you have sufficient privileges, you may change the effective group ID of the shell process by assigning to this parameter. Also (assuming sufficient privileges), you may start a single command with a different effective group ID by '`(EGID=gid; command)`'

    If this is made local, it is not implicitly set to 0, but may be explicitly set locally.

EUID <S>   The effective user ID of the shell process. If you have sufficient privileges, you may change the effective user ID of the shell process by assigning to this parameter. Also (assuming sufficient privileges), you may start a single command with a different effective user ID by '`(EUID=uid; command)`'

    If this is made local, it is not implicitly set to 0, but may be explicitly set locally.

ERRNO <S>   The value of errno (see man page errno(3)) as set by the most recently failed system call. This value is system dependent and is intended for debugging purposes. It is also useful with the `zsh/system` module which allows the number to be turned into a name or message.

FUNCNEST <S>

    Integer. If greater than or equal to zero, the maximum nesting depth of shell functions. When it is exceeded, an error is raised at the point where a function is called. The default value is determined when the shell is configured, but is typically 500. Increasing the value increases the danger of a runaway function recursion causing the shell to crash. Setting a negative value turns off the check.

GID <S>   The real group ID of the shell process. If you have sufficient privileges, you may change the group ID of the shell process by assigning to this parameter. Also (assuming sufficient privileges), you may start a single command under a different group ID by '(GID=*gid*; command)'

If this is made local, it is not implicitly set to 0, but may be explicitly set locally.

HISTCMD   The current history event number in an interactive shell, in other words the event number for the command that caused $HISTCMD to be read. If the current history event modifies the history, HISTCMD changes to the new maximum history event number.

HOST   The current hostname.

LINENO <S>

The line number of the current line within the current script, sourced file, or shell function being executed, whichever was started most recently. Note that in the case of shell functions the line number refers to the function as it appeared in the original definition, not necessarily as displayed by the **functions** builtin.

LOGNAME   If the corresponding variable is not set in the environment of the shell, it is initialized to the login name corresponding to the current login session. This parameter is exported by default but this can be disabled using the **typeset** builtin. The value is set to the string returned by the man page getlogin(3) system call if that is available.

MACHTYPE   The machine type (microprocessor class or machine model), as determined at compile time.

OLDPWD   The previous working directory. This is set when the shell initializes and whenever the directory changes.

OPTARG <S>

The value of the last option argument processed by the **getopts** command.

OPTIND <S>

The index of the last option argument processed by the **getopts** command.

OSTYPE   The operating system, as determined at compile time.

PPID <S>   The process ID of the parent of the shell. As for $$, the value indicates the parent of the original shell and does not change in subshells.

PWD   The present working directory. This is set when the shell initializes and whenever the directory changes.

RANDOM <S>

A pseudo-random integer from 0 to 32767, newly generated each time this parameter is referenced. The random number generator can be seeded by assigning a numeric value to RANDOM.

The values of RANDOM form an intentionally-repeatable pseudo-random sequence; subshells that reference RANDOM will result in identical pseudo-random values unless the value of RANDOM is referenced or seeded in the parent shell in between subshell invocations.

SECONDS <S>
> The number of seconds since shell invocation. If this parameter is assigned a value, then the value returned upon reference will be the value that was assigned plus the number of seconds since the assignment.
>
> Unlike other special parameters, the type of the SECONDS parameter can be changed using the typeset command. Only integer and one of the floating point types are allowed. For example, 'typeset -F SECONDS' causes the value to be reported as a floating point number. The value is available to microsecond accuracy, although the shell may show more or fewer digits depending on the use of typeset. See the documentation for the builtin typeset in Chapter 17 [Shell Builtin Commands], page 139, for more details.

SHLVL <S>   Incremented by one each time a new shell is started.

signals
> An array containing the names of the signals. Note that with the standard zsh numbering of array indices, where the first element has index 1, the signals are offset by 1 from the signal number used by the operating system. For example, on typical Unix-like systems HUP is signal number 1, but is referred to as $signals[2]. This is because of EXIT at position 1 in the array, which is used internally by zsh but is not known to the operating system.

TRY_BLOCK_ERROR <S>
> In an always block, indicates whether the preceding list of code caused an error. The value is 1 to indicate an error, 0 otherwise. It may be reset, clearing the error condition. See Section 6.3 [Complex Commands], page 11,

TRY_BLOCK_INTERRUPT <S>
> This variable works in a similar way to TRY_BLOCK_ERROR, but represents the status of an interrupt from the signal SIGINT, which typically comes from the keyboard when the user types ^C. If set to 0, any such interrupt will be reset; otherwise, the interrupt is propagated after the always block.
>
> Note that it is possible that an interrupt arrives during the execution of the always block; this interrupt is also propagated.

TTY   The name of the tty associated with the shell, if any.

TTYIDLE <S>
> The idle time of the tty associated with the shell in seconds or -1 if there is no such tty.

UID <S>
> The real user ID of the shell process. If you have sufficient privileges, you may change the user ID of the shell by assigning to this parameter. Also (assuming sufficient privileges), you may start a single command under a different user ID by '(UID=uid; command)'
>
> If this is made local, it is not implicitly set to 0, but may be explicitly set locally.

USERNAME <S>
> The username corresponding to the real user ID of the shell process. If you have sufficient privileges, you may change the username (and also the user ID and group ID) of the shell by assigning to this parameter. Also (assuming sufficient

privileges), you may start a single command under a different username (and user ID and group ID) by '(USERNAME=*username*; command)'

VENDOR   The vendor, as determined at compile time.

zsh_eval_context <S> <Z> (ZSH_EVAL_CONTEXT <S>)

An array (colon-separated list) indicating the context of shell code that is being run. Each time a piece of shell code that is stored within the shell is executed a string is temporarily appended to the array to indicate the type of operation that is being performed. Read in order the array gives an indication of the stack of operations being performed with the most immediate context last.

Note that the variable does not give information on syntactic context such as pipelines or subshells. Use $ZSH_SUBSHELL to detect subshells.

The context is one of the following:

cmdarg   Code specified by the -c option to the command line that invoked the shell.

cmdsubst   Command substitution using the '...' or $(...) construct.

equalsubst
          File substitution using the =(...) construct.

eval   Code executed by the eval builtin.

evalautofunc
          Code executed with the KSH_AUTOLOAD mechanism in order to define an autoloaded function.

fc   Code from the shell history executed by the -e option to the fc builtin.

file   Lines of code being read directly from a file, for example by the source builtin.

filecode   Lines of code being read from a .zwc file instead of directly from the source file.

globqual   Code executed by the e or + glob qualifier.

globsort   Code executed to order files by the o glob qualifier.

insubst   File substitution using the <(...) construct.

loadautofunc
          Code read directly from a file to define an autoloaded function.

outsubst   File substitution using the >(...) construct.

sched   Code executed by the sched builtin.

shfunc   A shell function.

stty   Code passed to stty by the STTY environment variable. Normally this is passed directly to the system's stty command, so this value is unlikely to be seen in practice.

style   Code executed as part of a style retrieved by the **zstyle** builtin from the **zsh/zutil** module.

toplevel   The highest execution level of a script or interactive shell.

trap   Code executed as a trap defined by the **trap** builtin. Traps defined as functions have the context **shfunc**. As traps are asynchronous they may have a different hierarchy from other code.

zpty   Code executed by the **zpty** builtin from the **zsh/zpty** module.

zregexparse-guard

> Code executed as a guard by the **zregexparse** command from the **zsh/zutil** module.

zregexparse-action

> Code executed as an action by the **zregexparse** command from the **zsh/zutil** module.

ZSH_ARGZERO

> If zsh was invoked to run a script, this is the name of the script. Otherwise, it is the name used to invoke the current shell. This is the same as the value of **$0** when the **POSIX_ARGZERO** option is set, but is always available.

ZSH_EXECUTION_STRING

> If the shell was started with the option -c, this contains the argument passed to the option. Otherwise it is not set.

ZSH_NAME   Expands to the basename of the command used to invoke this instance of zsh.

ZSH_PATCHLEVEL

> The output of 'git describe --tags --long' for the zsh repository used to build the shell. This is most useful in order to keep track of versions of the shell during development between releases; hence most users should not use it and should instead rely on **$ZSH_VERSION**.

zsh_scheduled_events

> See Section 22.24 [The zsh/sched Module], page 360.

ZSH_SCRIPT

> If zsh was invoked to run a script, this is the name of the script, otherwise it is unset.

ZSH_SUBSHELL

> Readonly integer. Initially zero, incremented each time the shell forks to create a subshell for executing code. Hence '(print $ZSH_SUBSHELL)' and 'print $(print $ZSH_SUBSHELL)' output 1, while '((print $ZSH_SUBSHELL))' outputs 2.

ZSH_VERSION

> The version number of the release of zsh.

15.6 Parameters Used By The Shell

The following parameters are used by the shell. Again, '<S>' indicates that the parameter is special and '<Z>' indicates that the parameter does not exist when the shell initializes in `sh` or `ksh` emulation mode.

In cases where there are two parameters with an upper- and lowercase form of the same name, such as `path` and `PATH`, the lowercase form is an array and the uppercase form is a scalar with the elements of the array joined together by colons. These are similar to tied parameters created via '`typeset -T`'. The normal use for the colon-separated form is for exporting to the environment, while the array form is easier to manipulate within the shell. Note that unsetting either of the pair will unset the other; they retain their special properties when recreated, and recreating one of the pair will recreate the other.

ARGV0
: If exported, its value is used as the `argv[0]` of external commands. Usually used in constructs like '`ARGV0=emacs nethack`'.

BAUD
: The rate in bits per second at which data reaches the terminal. The line editor will use this value in order to compensate for a slow terminal by delaying updates to the display until necessary. If the parameter is unset or the value is zero the compensation mechanism is turned off. The parameter is not set by default.

: This parameter may be profitably set in some circumstances, e.g. for slow modems dialing into a communications server, or on a slow wide area network. It should be set to the baud rate of the slowest part of the link for best performance.

cdpath <S> <Z> (CDPATH <S>)
: An array (colon-separated list) of directories specifying the search path for the `cd` command.

COLUMNS <S>
: The number of columns for this terminal session. Used for printing select lists and for the line editor.

CORRECT_IGNORE
: If set, is treated as a pattern during spelling correction. Any potential correction that matches the pattern is ignored. For example, if the value is '`_*`' then completion functions (which, by convention, have names beginning with '`_`') will never be offered as spelling corrections. The pattern does not apply to the correction of file names, as applied by the `CORRECT_ALL` option (so with the example just given files beginning with '`_`' in the current directory would still be completed).

CORRECT_IGNORE_FILE
: If set, is treated as a pattern during spelling correction of file names. Any file name that matches the pattern is never offered as a correction. For example, if the value is '`.*`' then dot file names will never be offered as spelling corrections. This is useful with the `CORRECT_ALL` option.

DIRSTACKSIZE

> The maximum size of the directory stack, by default there is no limit. If the stack gets larger than this, it will be truncated automatically. This is useful with the `AUTO_PUSHD` option.

ENV

> If the `ENV` environment variable is set when zsh is invoked as `sh` or `ksh`, `$ENV` is sourced after the profile scripts. The value of `ENV` is subjected to parameter expansion, command substitution, and arithmetic expansion before being interpreted as a pathname. Note that `ENV` is *not* used unless the shell is interactive and zsh is emulating *sh* or *ksh*.

FCEDIT

> The default editor for the `fc` builtin. If `FCEDIT` is not set, the parameter `EDITOR` is used; if that is not set either, a builtin default, usually `vi`, is used.

fignore <S> <Z> (FIGNORE <S>)

> An array (colon separated list) containing the suffixes of files to be ignored during filename completion. However, if completion only generates files with suffixes in this list, then these files are completed anyway.

fpath <S> <Z> (FPATH <S>)

> An array (colon separated list) of directories specifying the search path for function definitions. This path is searched when a function with the `-u` attribute is referenced. If an executable file is found, then it is read and executed in the current environment.

histchars <S>

> Three characters used by the shell's history and lexical analysis mechanism. The first character signals the start of a history expansion (default '`!`'). The second character signals the start of a quick history substitution (default '`^`'). The third character is the comment character (default '`#`').
>
> The characters must be in the ASCII character set; any attempt to set **histchars** to characters with a locale-dependent meaning will be rejected with an error message.

HISTCHARS <S> <Z>

> Same as **histchars**. (Deprecated.)

HISTFILE

> The file to save the history in when an interactive shell exits. If unset, the history is not saved.

HISTORY_IGNORE

> If set, is treated as a pattern at the time history files are written. Any potential history entry that matches the pattern is skipped. For example, if the value is '`fc *`' then commands that invoke the interactive history editor are never written to the history file.
>
> Note that `HISTORY_IGNORE` defines a single pattern: to specify alternatives use the '(*first*|*second*|...)' syntax.
>
> Compare the `HIST_NO_STORE` option or the **zshaddhistory** hook, either of which would prevent such commands from being added to the interactive history at all. If you wish to use `HISTORY_IGNORE` to stop history being added in the first place, you can define the following hook:

```
zshaddhistory() {
  emulate -L zsh
  ## uncomment if HISTORY_IGNORE
  ## should use EXTENDED_GLOB syntax
  # setopt extendedglob
  [[ $1 != ${~HISTORY_IGNORE} ]]
}
```

HISTSIZE <S>

> The maximum number of events stored in the internal history list. If you use the HIST_EXPIRE_DUPS_FIRST option, setting this value larger than the SAVEHIST size will give you the difference as a cushion for saving duplicated history events.
>
> If this is made local, it is not implicitly set to 0, but may be explicitly set locally.

HOME <S>   The default argument for the cd command. This is not set automatically by the shell in sh, ksh or csh emulation, but it is typically present in the environment anyway, and if it becomes set it has its usual special behaviour.

IFS <S>   Internal field separators (by default space, tab, newline and NUL), that are used to separate words which result from command or parameter expansion and words read by the **read** builtin. Any characters from the set space, tab and newline that appear in the IFS are called *IFS white space*. One or more IFS white space characters or one non-IFS white space character together with any adjacent IFS white space character delimit a field. If an IFS white space character appears twice consecutively in the IFS, this character is treated as if it were not an IFS white space character.

> If the parameter is unset, the default is used. Note this has a different effect from setting the parameter to an empty string.

KEYBOARD_HACK

> This variable defines a character to be removed from the end of the command line before interpreting it (interactive shells only). It is intended to fix the problem with keys placed annoyingly close to return and replaces the SUNKEYBOARDHACK option which did this for backquotes only. Should the chosen character be one of singlequote, doublequote or backquote, there must also be an odd number of them on the command line for the last one to be removed.
>
> For backward compatibility, if the SUNKEYBOARDHACK option is explicitly set, the value of KEYBOARD_HACK reverts to backquote. If the option is explicitly unset, this variable is set to empty.

KEYTIMEOUT

> The time the shell waits, in hundredths of seconds, for another key to be pressed when reading bound multi-character sequences.

LANG <S>   This variable determines the locale category for any category not specifically selected via a variable starting with 'LC_'.

LC_ALL <S>

> This variable overrides the value of the 'LANG' variable and the value of any of the other variables starting with 'LC_'.

LC_COLLATE <S>

> This variable determines the locale category for character collation information within ranges in glob brackets and for sorting.

LC_CTYPE <S>

> This variable determines the locale category for character handling functions. If the MULTIBYTE option is in effect this variable or LANG should contain a value that reflects the character set in use, even if it is a single-byte character set, unless only the 7-bit subset (ASCII) is used. For example, if the character set is ISO-8859-1, a suitable value might be en_US.iso88591 (certain Linux distributions) or en_US.ISO8859-1 (MacOS).

LC_MESSAGES <S>

> This variable determines the language in which messages should be written. Note that zsh does not use message catalogs.

LC_NUMERIC <S>

> This variable affects the decimal point character and thousands separator character for the formatted input/output functions and string conversion functions. Note that zsh ignores this setting when parsing floating point mathematical expressions.

LC_TIME <S>

> This variable determines the locale category for date and time formatting in prompt escape sequences.

LINES <S>   The number of lines for this terminal session. Used for printing select lists and for the line editor.

LISTMAX   In the line editor, the number of matches to list without asking first. If the value is negative, the list will be shown if it spans at most as many lines as given by the absolute value. If set to zero, the shell asks only if the top of the listing would scroll off the screen.

LOGCHECK   The interval in seconds between checks for login/logout activity using the watch parameter.

MAIL   If this parameter is set and mailpath is not set, the shell looks for mail in the specified file.

MAILCHECK

> The interval in seconds between checks for new mail.

mailpath <S> <Z> (MAILPATH <S>)

> An array (colon-separated list) of filenames to check for new mail. Each filename can be followed by a '?' and a message that will be printed. The message will undergo parameter expansion, command substitution and arithmetic expansion with the variable $_ defined as the name of the file that has changed. The default message is 'You have new mail'. If an element is a directory instead of a file the shell will recursively check every file in every subdirectory of the element.

manpath <S> <Z> (MANPATH <S> <Z>)

> An array (colon-separated list) whose value is not used by the shell. The manpath array can be useful, however, since setting it also sets MANPATH, and vice versa.

match
mbegin
mend

> Arrays set by the shell when the b globbing flag is used in pattern matches. See the subsection *Globbing flags* in Section 14.8 [Filename Generation], page 72.

MATCH
MBEGIN
MEND

> Set by the shell when the m globbing flag is used in pattern matches. See the subsection *Globbing flags* in Section 14.8 [Filename Generation], page 72.

module_path <S> <Z> (MODULE_PATH <S>)

> An array (colon-separated list) of directories that zmodload searches for dynamically loadable modules. This is initialized to a standard pathname, usually '/usr/local/lib/zsh/$ZSH_VERSION'. (The '/usr/local/lib' part varies from installation to installation.) For security reasons, any value set in the environment when the shell is started will be ignored.
>
> These parameters only exist if the installation supports dynamic module loading.

NULLCMD <S>

> The command name to assume if a redirection is specified with no command. Defaults to cat. For *sh/ksh* behavior, change this to :. For *csh*-like behavior, unset this parameter; the shell will print an error message if null commands are entered.

path <S> <Z> (PATH <S>)

> An array (colon-separated list) of directories to search for commands. When this parameter is set, each directory is scanned and all files found are put in a hash table.

POSTEDIT <S>

> This string is output whenever the line editor exits. It usually contains termcap strings to reset the terminal.

PROMPT <S> <Z>
PROMPT2 <S> <Z>
PROMPT3 <S> <Z>
PROMPT4 <S> <Z>

> Same as PS1, PS2, PS3 and PS4, respectively.

prompt <S> <Z>

> Same as PS1.

PROMPT_EOL_MARK

> When the PROMPT_CR and PROMPT_SP options are set, the PROMPT_EOL_MARK parameter can be used to customize how the end of partial lines are shown.

This parameter undergoes prompt expansion, with the `PROMPT_PERCENT` option set. If not set, the default behavior is equivalent to the value '`%B%S%#%s%b`'.

PS1 \<S\>   The primary prompt string, printed before a command is read. It undergoes a special form of expansion before being displayed; see Chapter 13 [Prompt Expansion], page 39. The default is '`%m%# `'.

PS2 \<S\>   The secondary prompt, printed when the shell needs more information to complete a command. It is expanded in the same way as `PS1`. The default is '`%_> `', which displays any shell constructs or quotation marks which are currently being processed.

PS3 \<S\>   Selection prompt used within a `select` loop. It is expanded in the same way as `PS1`. The default is '`?# `'.

PS4 \<S\>   The execution trace prompt. Default is '`+%N:%i> `', which displays the name of the current shell structure and the line number within it. In sh or ksh emulation, the default is '`+ `'.

psvar \<S\> \<Z\> (PSVAR \<S\>)
        An array (colon-separated list) whose elements can be used in `PROMPT` strings. Setting `psvar` also sets `PSVAR`, and vice versa.

READNULLCMD \<S\>
        The command name to assume if a single input redirection is specified with no command. Defaults to `more`.

REPORTMEMORY
        If nonnegative, commands whose maximum resident set size (roughly speaking, main memory usage) in kilobytes is greater than this value have timing statistics reported. The format used to output statistics is the value of the `TIMEFMT` parameter, which is the same as for the `REPORTTIME` variable and the `time` builtin; note that by default this does not output memory usage. Appending "` max RSS %M`" to the value of `TIMEFMT` causes it to output the value that triggered the report. If `REPORTTIME` is also in use, at most a single report is printed for both triggers. This feature requires the `getrusage()` system call, commonly supported by modern Unix-like systems.

REPORTTIME
        If nonnegative, commands whose combined user and system execution times (measured in seconds) are greater than this value have timing statistics printed for them. Output is suppressed for commands executed within the line editor, including completion; commands explicitly marked with the `time` keyword still cause the summary to be printed in this case.

REPLY   This parameter is reserved by convention to pass string values between shell scripts and shell builtins in situations where a function call or redirection are impossible or undesirable. The `read` builtin and the `select` complex command may set `REPLY`, and filename generation both sets and examines its value when evaluating certain expressions. Some modules also employ `REPLY` for similar purposes.

reply   As `REPLY`, but for array values rather than strings.

RPROMPT <S>

RPS1 <S>   This prompt is displayed on the right-hand side of the screen when the primary prompt is being displayed on the left. This does not work if the SINGLE_LINE_ZLE option is set. It is expanded in the same way as PS1.

RPROMPT2 <S>

RPS2 <S>   This prompt is displayed on the right-hand side of the screen when the secondary prompt is being displayed on the left. This does not work if the SINGLE_LINE_ZLE option is set. It is expanded in the same way as PS2.

SAVEHIST   The maximum number of history events to save in the history file.

If this is made local, it is not implicitly set to 0, but may be explicitly set locally.

SPROMPT <S>

The prompt used for spelling correction. The sequence '%R' expands to the string which presumably needs spelling correction, and '%r' expands to the proposed correction. All other prompt escapes are also allowed.

The actions available at the prompt are [nyae]:

n ('no') (default)
Discard the correction and run the command.

y ('yes')   Make the correction and run the command.

a ('abort') Discard the entire command line without running it.

e ('edit')   Resume editing the command line.

STTY   If this parameter is set in a command's environment, the shell runs the stty command with the value of this parameter as arguments in order to set up the terminal before executing the command. The modes apply only to the command, and are reset when it finishes or is suspended. If the command is suspended and continued later with the fg or wait builtins it will see the modes specified by STTY, as if it were not suspended. This (intentionally) does not apply if the command is continued via 'kill -CONT'. STTY is ignored if the command is run in the background, or if it is in the environment of the shell but not explicitly assigned to in the input line. This avoids running stty at every external command by accidentally exporting it. Also note that STTY should not be used for window size specifications; these will not be local to the command.

TERM <S>   The type of terminal in use. This is used when looking up termcap sequences. An assignment to TERM causes zsh to re-initialize the terminal, even if the value does not change (e.g., 'TERM=$TERM'). It is necessary to make such an assignment upon any change to the terminal definition database or terminal type in order for the new settings to take effect.

TERMINFO <S>

A reference to your terminfo database, used by the 'terminfo' library when the system has it; see man page terminfo(5). If set, this causes the shell to reinitialise the terminal, making the workaround 'TERM=$TERM' unnecessary.

TERMINFO_DIRS <S>
> A colon-seprarated list of terminfo databases, used by the 'terminfo' library when the system has it; see man page terminfo(5). This variable is only used by certain terminal libraries, in particular ncurses; see man page terminfo(5) to check support on your system. If set, this causes the shell to reinitialise the terminal, making the workaround 'TERM=$TERM' unnecessary. Note that unlike other colon-separated arrays this is not tied to a zsh array.

TIMEFMT
> The format of process time reports with the **time** keyword. The default is '%J %U user %S system %P cpu %*E total'. Recognizes the following escape sequences, although not all may be available on all systems, and some that are available may not be useful:

%%	A '%'.
%U	CPU seconds spent in user mode.
%S	CPU seconds spent in kernel mode.
%E	Elapsed time in seconds.
%P	The CPU percentage, computed as 100*(%U+%S)/%E.
%W	Number of times the process was swapped.
%X	The average amount in (shared) text space used in kilobytes.
%D	The average amount in (unshared) data/stack space used in kilobytes.
%K	The total space used (%X+%D) in kilobytes.
%M	The maximum memory the process had in use at any time in kilobytes.
%F	The number of major page faults (page needed to be brought from disk).
%R	The number of minor page faults.
%I	The number of input operations.
%O	The number of output operations.
%r	The number of socket messages received.
%s	The number of socket messages sent.
%k	The number of signals received.
%w	Number of voluntary context switches (waits).
%c	Number of involuntary context switches.
%J	The name of this job.

> A star may be inserted between the percent sign and flags printing time (e.g., '%*E'); this causes the time to be printed in 'hh:mm:ss.ttt' format (hours and minutes are only printed if they are not zero). Alternatively, 'm' or 'u' may be used (e.g., '%mE') to produce time output in milliseconds or microseconds, respectively.

TMOUT   If this parameter is nonzero, the shell will receive an ALRM signal if a command is not entered within the specified number of seconds after issuing a prompt. If there is a trap on SIGALRM, it will be executed and a new alarm is scheduled using the value of the TMOUT parameter after executing the trap. If no trap is set, and the idle time of the terminal is not less than the value of the TMOUT parameter, zsh terminates. Otherwise a new alarm is scheduled to TMOUT seconds after the last keypress.

TMPPREFIX
                A pathname prefix which the shell will use for all temporary files. Note that this should include an initial part for the file name as well as any directory names. The default is '/tmp/zsh'.

TMPSUFFIX
                A filename suffix which the shell will use for temporary files created by process substitutions (e.g., '=(list)'). Note that the value should include a leading dot '.' if intended to be interpreted as a file extension. The default is not to append any suffix, thus this parameter should be assigned only when needed and then unset again.

watch <S> <Z> (WATCH <S>)
                An array (colon-separated list) of login/logout events to report.

                If it contains the single word 'all', then all login/logout events are reported. If it contains the single word 'notme', then all events are reported as with 'all' except $USERNAME.

                An entry in this list may consist of a username, an '@' followed by a remote hostname, and a '%' followed by a line (tty). Any of these may be a pattern (be sure to quote this during the assignment to watch so that it does not immediately perform file generation); the setting of the EXTENDED_GLOB option is respected. Any or all of these components may be present in an entry; if a login/logout event matches all of them, it is reported.

                For example, with the EXTENDED_GLOB option set, the following:

                    watch=('^(pws|barts)')

                causes reports for activity assoicated with any user other than pws or barts.

WATCHFMT   The format of login/logout reports if the watch parameter is set. Default is '%n has %a %l from %m'. Recognizes the following escape sequences:

                %n   The name of the user that logged in/out.

                %a   The observed action, i.e. "logged on" or "logged off".

                %l   The line (tty) the user is logged in on.

                %M   The full hostname of the remote host.

                %m   The hostname up to the first '.'. If only the IP address is available or the utmp field contains the name of an X-windows display, the whole name is printed.

                            NOTE: The '%m' and '%M' escapes will work only if there is a host name field in the utmp on your machine. Otherwise they are treated as ordinary strings.

%S (%s)	Start (stop) standout mode.
%U (%u)	Start (stop) underline mode.
%B (%b)	Start (stop) boldface mode.
%t	
%@	The time, in 12-hour, am/pm format.
%T	The time, in 24-hour format.
%w	The date in '*day-dd*' format.
%W	The date in '*mm/dd/yy*' format.
%D	The date in '*yy-mm-dd*' format.

%D{*string*}

> The date formatted as *string* using the **strftime** function, with zsh extensions as described by Chapter 13 [Prompt Expansion], page 39.

%(*x*:*true-text*:*false-text*)

> Specifies a ternary expression. The character following the *x* is arbitrary; the same character is used to separate the text for the "true" result from that for the "false" result. Both the separator and the right parenthesis may be escaped with a backslash. Ternary expressions may be nested.
>
> The test character *x* may be any one of '1', 'n', 'm' or 'M', which indicate a 'true' result if the corresponding escape sequence would return a non-empty value; or it may be 'a', which indicates a 'true' result if the watched user has logged in, or 'false' if he has logged out. Other characters evaluate to neither true nor false; the entire expression is omitted in this case.
>
> If the result is 'true', then the *true-text* is formatted according to the rules above and printed, and the *false-text* is skipped. If 'false', the *true-text* is skipped and the *false-text* is formatted and printed. Either or both of the branches may be empty, but both separators must be present in any case.

WORDCHARS <S>

> A list of non-alphanumeric characters considered part of a word by the line editor.

ZBEEP

> If set, this gives a string of characters, which can use all the same codes as the **bindkey** command as described in Section 22.32 [The zsh/zle Module], page 378, that will be output to the terminal instead of beeping. This may have a visible instead of an audible effect; for example, the string '\e[?5h\e[?5l' on a vt100 or xterm will have the effect of flashing reverse video on and off (if you usually use reverse video, you should use the string '\e[?5l\e[?5h' instead). This takes precedence over the NOBEEP option.

ZDOTDIR

> The directory to search for shell startup files (.zshrc, etc), if not $HOME.

`zle_bracketed_paste`

> Many terminal emulators have a feature that allows applications to identify when text is pasted into the terminal rather than being typed normally. For ZLE, this means that special characters such as tabs and newlines can be inserted instead of invoking editor commands. Furthermore, pasted text forms a single undo event and if the region is active, pasted text will replace the region.
>
> This two-element array contains the terminal escape sequences for enabling and disabling the feature. These escape sequences are used to enable bracketed paste when ZLE is active and disable it at other times. Unsetting the parameter has the effect of ensuring that bracketed paste remains disabled.

`zle_highlight`

> An array describing contexts in which ZLE should highlight the input text. See Section 18.7 [Character Highlighting], page 221.

`ZLE_LINE_ABORTED`

> This parameter is set by the line editor when an error occurs. It contains the line that was being edited at the point of the error. 'print -zr -- $ZLE_LINE_ABORTED' can be used to recover the line. Only the most recent line of this kind is remembered.

`ZLE_REMOVE_SUFFIX_CHARS`
`ZLE_SPACE_SUFFIX_CHARS`

> These parameters are used by the line editor. In certain circumstances suffixes (typically space or slash) added by the completion system will be removed automatically, either because the next editing command was not an insertable character, or because the character was marked as requiring the suffix to be removed.
>
> These variables can contain the sets of characters that will cause the suffix to be removed. If `ZLE_REMOVE_SUFFIX_CHARS` is set, those characters will cause the suffix to be removed; if `ZLE_SPACE_SUFFIX_CHARS` is set, those characters will cause the suffix to be removed and replaced by a space.
>
> If `ZLE_REMOVE_SUFFIX_CHARS` is not set, the default behaviour is equivalent to:
>
>   ZLE_REMOVE_SUFFIX_CHARS=$' \t\n;&|'
>
> If `ZLE_REMOVE_SUFFIX_CHARS` is set but is empty, no characters have this behaviour. `ZLE_SPACE_SUFFIX_CHARS` takes precedence, so that the following:
>
>   ZLE_SPACE_SUFFIX_CHARS=$'&|'
>
> causes the characters '&' and '|' to remove the suffix but to replace it with a space.
>
> To illustrate the difference, suppose that the option `AUTO_REMOVE_SLASH` is in effect and the directory `DIR` has just been completed, with an appended /, following which the user types '&'. The default result is 'DIR&'. With `ZLE_REMOVE_SUFFIX_CHARS` set but without including '&' the result is 'DIR/&'. With `ZLE_SPACE_SUFFIX_CHARS` set to include '&' the result is 'DIR &'.
>
> Note that certain completions may provide their own suffix removal or replacement behaviour which overrides the values described here. See the completion system documentation in Chapter 20 [Completion System], page 242.

`ZLE_RPROMPT_INDENT <S>`

>If set, used to give the indentation between the right hand side of the right prompt in the line editor as given by `RPS1` or `RPROMPT` and the right hand side of the screen. If not set, the value 1 is used.

>Typically this will be used to set the value to 0 so that the prompt appears flush with the right hand side of the screen. This is not the default as many terminals do not handle this correctly, in particular when the prompt appears at the extreme bottom right of the screen. Recent virtual terminals are more likely to handle this case correctly. Some experimentation is necessary.

16 Options

16.1 Specifying Options

Options are primarily referred to by name. These names are case insensitive and underscores are ignored. For example, 'allexport' is equivalent to 'A__lleXP_ort'.

The sense of an option name may be inverted by preceding it with 'no', so 'setopt No_Beep' is equivalent to 'unsetopt beep'. This inversion can only be done once, so 'nonobeep' is *not* a synonym for 'beep'. Similarly, 'tify' is not a synonym for 'nonotify' (the inversion of 'notify').

Some options also have one or more single letter names. There are two sets of single letter options: one used by default, and another used to emulate *sh/ksh* (used when the `SH_OPTION_LETTERS` option is set). The single letter options can be used on the shell command line, or with the `set`, `setopt` and `unsetopt` builtins, as normal Unix options preceded by '-'.

The sense of the single letter options may be inverted by using '+' instead of '-'. Some of the single letter option names refer to an option being off, in which case the inversion of that name refers to the option being on. For example, '+n' is the short name of 'exec', and '-n' is the short name of its inversion, 'noexec'.

In strings of single letter options supplied to the shell at startup, trailing whitespace will be ignored; for example the string '-f ' will be treated just as '-f', but the string '-f i' is an error. This is because many systems which implement the '#!' mechanism for calling scripts do not strip trailing whitespace.

16.2 Description of Options

In the following list, options set by default in all emulations are marked <D>; those set by default only in csh, ksh, sh, or zsh emulations are marked <C>, <K>, <S>, <Z> as appropriate. When listing options (by 'setopt', 'unsetopt', 'set -o' or 'set +o'), those turned on by default appear in the list prefixed with 'no'. Hence (unless `KSH_OPTION_PRINT` is set), 'setopt' shows all options whose settings are changed from the default.

16.2.1 Changing Directories

AUTO_CD (-J)

> If a command is issued that can't be executed as a normal command, and the command is the name of a directory, perform the `cd` command to that directory. This option is only applicable if the option `SHIN_STDIN` is set, i.e. if commands are being read from standard input. The option is designed for interactive use; it is recommended that `cd` be used explicitly in scripts to avoid ambiguity.

AUTO_PUSHD (-N)

> Make `cd` push the old directory onto the directory stack.

CDABLE_VARS (-T)

> If the argument to a `cd` command (or an implied `cd` with the `AUTO_CD` option set) is not a directory, and does not begin with a slash, try to expand the expression as if it were preceded by a '~' (see Section 14.7 [Filename Expansion], page 69).

CHASE_DOTS

> When changing to a directory containing a path segment '..' which would otherwise be treated as canceling the previous segment in the path (in other words, 'foo/..' would be removed from the path, or if '..' is the first part of the path, the last part of the current working directory would be removed), instead resolve the path to the physical directory. This option is overridden by `CHASE_LINKS`.
>
> For example, suppose /foo/bar is a link to the directory /alt/rod. Without this option set, 'cd /foo/bar/..' changes to /foo; with it set, it changes to /alt. The same applies if the current directory is /foo/bar and 'cd ..' is used. Note that all other symbolic links in the path will also be resolved.

CHASE_LINKS (-w)

> Resolve symbolic links to their true values when changing directory. This also has the effect of `CHASE_DOTS`, i.e. a '..' path segment will be treated as referring to the physical parent, even if the preceding path segment is a symbolic link.

POSIX_CD <K> <S>

> Modifies the behaviour of `cd`, `chdir` and `pushd` commands to make them more compatible with the POSIX standard. The behaviour with the option unset is described in the documentation for the `cd` builtin in Chapter 17 [Shell Builtin Commands], page 139. If the option is set, the shell does not test for directories beneath the local directory ('.') until after all directories in `cdpath` have been tested.
>
> Also, if the option is set, the conditions under which the shell prints the new directory after changing to it are modified. It is no longer restricted to interactive shells (although printing of the directory stack with `pushd` is still limited to interactive shells); and any use of a component of `CDPATH`, including a '.' but excluding an empty component that is otherwise treated as '.', causes the directory to be printed.

PUSHD_IGNORE_DUPS

> Don't push multiple copies of the same directory onto the directory stack.

PUSHD_MINUS

        Exchanges the meanings of '+' and '-' when used with a number to specify a directory in the stack.

PUSHD_SILENT (-E)

        Do not print the directory stack after `pushd` or `popd`.

PUSHD_TO_HOME (-D)

        Have `pushd` with no arguments act like 'pushd $HOME'.

16.2.2 Completion

ALWAYS_LAST_PROMPT <D>

        If unset, key functions that list completions try to return to the last prompt if given a numeric argument. If set these functions try to return to the last prompt if given *no* numeric argument.

ALWAYS_TO_END

        If a completion is performed with the cursor within a word, and a full completion is inserted, the cursor is moved to the end of the word. That is, the cursor is moved to the end of the word if either a single match is inserted or menu completion is performed.

AUTO_LIST (-9) <D>

        Automatically list choices on an ambiguous completion.

AUTO_MENU <D>

        Automatically use menu completion after the second consecutive request for completion, for example by pressing the tab key repeatedly. This option is overridden by `MENU_COMPLETE`.

AUTO_NAME_DIRS

        Any parameter that is set to the absolute name of a directory immediately becomes a name for that directory, that will be used by the '%~' and related prompt sequences, and will be available when completion is performed on a word starting with '~'. (Otherwise, the parameter must be used in the form '~*param*' first.)

AUTO_PARAM_KEYS <D>

        If a parameter name was completed and a following character (normally a space) automatically inserted, and the next character typed is one of those that have to come directly after the name (like '}', ':', etc.), the automatically added character is deleted, so that the character typed comes immediately after the parameter name. Completion in a brace expansion is affected similarly: the added character is a ',', which will be removed if '}' is typed next.

AUTO_PARAM_SLASH <D>

        If a parameter is completed whose content is the name of a directory, then add a trailing slash instead of a space.

AUTO_REMOVE_SLASH <D>

> When the last character resulting from a completion is a slash and the next character typed is a word delimiter, a slash, or a character that ends a command (such as a semicolon or an ampersand), remove the slash.

BASH_AUTO_LIST

> On an ambiguous completion, automatically list choices when the completion function is called twice in succession. This takes precedence over AUTO_LIST. The setting of LIST_AMBIGUOUS is respected. If AUTO_MENU is set, the menu behaviour will then start with the third press. Note that this will not work with MENU_COMPLETE, since repeated completion calls immediately cycle through the list in that case.

COMPLETE_ALIASES

> Prevents aliases on the command line from being internally substituted before completion is attempted. The effect is to make the alias a distinct command for completion purposes.

COMPLETE_IN_WORD

> If unset, the cursor is set to the end of the word if completion is started. Otherwise it stays there and completion is done from both ends.

GLOB_COMPLETE

> When the current word has a glob pattern, do not insert all the words resulting from the expansion but generate matches as for completion and cycle through them like MENU_COMPLETE. The matches are generated as if a '*' was added to the end of the word, or inserted at the cursor when COMPLETE_IN_WORD is set. This actually uses pattern matching, not globbing, so it works not only for files but for any completion, such as options, user names, etc.

> Note that when the pattern matcher is used, matching control (for example, case-insensitive or anchored matching) cannot be used. This limitation only applies when the current word contains a pattern; simply turning on the GLOB_COMPLETE option does not have this effect.

HASH_LIST_ALL <D>

> Whenever a command completion or spelling correction is attempted, make sure the entire command path is hashed first. This makes the first completion slower but avoids false reports of spelling errors.

LIST_AMBIGUOUS <D>

> This option works when AUTO_LIST or BASH_AUTO_LIST is also set. If there is an unambiguous prefix to insert on the command line, that is done without a completion list being displayed; in other words, auto-listing behaviour only takes place when nothing would be inserted. In the case of BASH_AUTO_LIST, this means that the list will be delayed to the third call of the function.

LIST_BEEP <D>

> Beep on an ambiguous completion. More accurately, this forces the completion widgets to return status 1 on an ambiguous completion, which causes the shell to beep if the option BEEP is also set; this may be modified if completion is called from a user-defined widget.

LIST_PACKED

> Try to make the completion list smaller (occupying less lines) by printing the matches in columns with different widths.

LIST_ROWS_FIRST

> Lay out the matches in completion lists sorted horizontally, that is, the second match is to the right of the first one, not under it as usual.

LIST_TYPES (-X) <D>

> When listing files that are possible completions, show the type of each file with a trailing identifying mark.

MENU_COMPLETE (-Y)

> On an ambiguous completion, instead of listing possibilities or beeping, insert the first match immediately. Then when completion is requested again, remove the first match and insert the second match, etc. When there are no more matches, go back to the first one again. `reverse-menu-complete` may be used to loop through the list in the other direction. This option overrides `AUTO_MENU`.

REC_EXACT (-S)

> If the string on the command line exactly matches one of the possible completions, it is accepted, even if there is another completion (i.e. that string with something else added) that also matches.

16.2.3 Expansion and Globbing

BAD_PATTERN (+2) <C> <Z>

> If a pattern for filename generation is badly formed, print an error message. (If this option is unset, the pattern will be left unchanged.)

BARE_GLOB_QUAL <Z>

> In a glob pattern, treat a trailing set of parentheses as a qualifier list, if it contains no '|', '(' or (if special) '~' characters. See Section 14.8 [Filename Generation], page 72.

BRACE_CCL

> Expand expressions in braces which would not otherwise undergo brace expansion to a lexically ordered list of all the characters. See Section 14.6 [Brace Expansion], page 68.

CASE_GLOB <D>

> Make globbing (filename generation) sensitive to case. Note that other uses of patterns are always sensitive to case. If the option is unset, the presence of any character which is special to filename generation will cause case-insensitive matching. For example, `cvs(/)` can match the directory `CVS` owing to the presence of the globbing flag (unless the option `BARE_GLOB_QUAL` is unset).

CASE_MATCH <D>

> Make regular expressions using the `zsh/regex` module (including matches with `=~`) sensitive to case.

CSH_NULL_GLOB <C>

> If a pattern for filename generation has no matches, delete the pattern from the argument list; do not report an error unless all the patterns in a command have no matches. Overrides NOMATCH.

EQUALS <Z>

> Perform = filename expansion. (See Section 14.7 [Filename Expansion], page 69.)

EXTENDED_GLOB

> Treat the '#', '~' and '^' characters as part of patterns for filename generation, etc. (An initial unquoted '~' always produces named directory expansion.)

FORCE_FLOAT

> Constants in arithmetic evaluation will be treated as floating point even without the use of a decimal point; the values of integer variables will be converted to floating point when used in arithmetic expressions. Integers in any base will be converted.

GLOB (+F, ksh: +f) <D>

> Perform filename generation (globbing). (See Section 14.8 [Filename Generation], page 72.)

GLOB_ASSIGN <C>

> If this option is set, filename generation (globbing) is performed on the right hand side of scalar parameter assignments of the form 'name=pattern (e.g. 'foo=*'). If the result has more than one word the parameter will become an array with those words as arguments. This option is provided for backwards compatibility only: globbing is always performed on the right hand side of array assignments of the form 'name=(value)' (e.g. 'foo=(*)') and this form is recommended for clarity; with this option set, it is not possible to predict whether the result will be an array or a scalar.

GLOB_DOTS (-4)

> Do not require a leading '.' in a filename to be matched explicitly.

GLOB_STAR_SHORT

> When this option is set and the default zsh-style globbing is in effect, the pattern '**/*' can be abbreviated to '**' and the pattern '***/*' can be abbreviated to ***. Hence '**.c' finds a file ending in .c in any subdirectory, and '***.c' does the same while also following symbolic links. A / immediately after the '**' or '***' forces the pattern to be treated as the unabbreviated form.

GLOB_SUBST <C> <K> <S>

> Treat any characters resulting from parameter expansion as being eligible for filename expansion and filename generation, and any characters resulting from command substitution as being eligible for filename generation. Braces (and commas in between) do not become eligible for expansion.

HIST_SUBST_PATTERN

> Substitutions using the :s and :& history modifiers are performed with pattern matching instead of string matching. This occurs wherever history modifiers are

valid, including glob qualifiers and parameters. See Section 14.1.4 [Modifiers], page 47.

IGNORE_BRACES (-I) <S>

> Do not perform brace expansion. For historical reasons this also includes the effect of the IGNORE_CLOSE_BRACES option.

IGNORE_CLOSE_BRACES

> When neither this option nor IGNORE_BRACES is set, a sole close brace character '}' is syntactically significant at any point on a command line. This has the effect that no semicolon or newline is necessary before the brace terminating a function or current shell construct. When either option is set, a closing brace is syntactically significant only in command position. Unlike IGNORE_BRACES, this option does not disable brace expansion.

> For example, with both options unset a function may be defined in the following fashion:

```
args() { echo $# }
```

> while if either option is set, this does not work and something equivalent to the following is required:

```
args() { echo $#; }
```

KSH_GLOB <K>

> In pattern matching, the interpretation of parentheses is affected by a preceding '@', '*', '+', '?' or '!'. See Section 14.8 [Filename Generation], page 72.

MAGIC_EQUAL_SUBST

> All unquoted arguments of the form 'anything=expression' appearing after the command name have filename expansion (that is, where expression has a leading '~' or '=') performed on expression as if it were a parameter assignment. The argument is not otherwise treated specially; it is passed to the command as a single argument, and not used as an actual parameter assignment. For example, in echo foo=~/bar:~/rod, both occurrences of ~ would be replaced. Note that this happens anyway with typeset and similar statements.

> This option respects the setting of the KSH_TYPESET option. In other words, if both options are in effect, arguments looking like assignments will not undergo word splitting.

MARK_DIRS (-8, ksh: -X)

> Append a trailing '/' to all directory names resulting from filename generation (globbing).

MULTIBYTE <D>

> Respect multibyte characters when found in strings. When this option is set, strings are examined using the system library to determine how many bytes form a character, depending on the current locale. This affects the way characters are counted in pattern matching, parameter values and various delimiters.

> The option is on by default if the shell was compiled with MULTIBYTE_SUPPORT; otherwise it is off by default and has no effect if turned on.

If the option is off a single byte is always treated as a single character. This setting is designed purely for examining strings known to contain raw bytes or other values that may not be characters in the current locale. It is not necessary to unset the option merely because the character set for the current locale does not contain multibyte characters.

The option does not affect the shell's editor, which always uses the locale to determine multibyte characters. This is because the character set displayed by the terminal emulator is independent of shell settings.

NOMATCH (+3) <C> <Z>

If a pattern for filename generation has no matches, print an error, instead of leaving it unchanged in the argument list. This also applies to file expansion of an initial '~' or '='.

NULL_GLOB (-G)

If a pattern for filename generation has no matches, delete the pattern from the argument list instead of reporting an error. Overrides NOMATCH.

NUMERIC_GLOB_SORT

If numeric filenames are matched by a filename generation pattern, sort the filenames numerically rather than lexicographically.

RC_EXPAND_PARAM (-P)

Array expansions of the form '*foo*${*xx*}*bar*', where the parameter *xx* is set to (*a b c*), are substituted with '*fooabar foobbar foocbar*' instead of the default '*fooa b cbar*'. Note that an empty array will therefore cause all arguments to be removed.

REMATCH_PCRE

If set, regular expression matching with the =~ operator will use Perl-Compatible Regular Expressions from the PCRE library. (The zsh/pcre module must be available.) If not set, regular expressions will use the extended regexp syntax provided by the system libraries.

SH_GLOB <K> <S>

Disables the special meaning of '(', '|', ')' and '<' for globbing the result of parameter and command substitutions, and in some other places where the shell accepts patterns. If SH_GLOB is set but KSH_GLOB is not, the shell allows the interpretation of subshell expressions enclosed in parentheses in some cases where there is no space before the opening parenthesis, e.g. !(true) is interpreted as if there were a space after the !. This option is set by default if zsh is invoked as **sh** or **ksh**.

UNSET (+u, ksh: +u) <K> <S> <Z>

Treat unset parameters as if they were empty when substituting, and as if they were zero when reading their values in arithmetic expansion and arithmetic commands. Otherwise they are treated as an error.

WARN_CREATE_GLOBAL

Print a warning message when a global parameter is created in a function by an assignment or in math context. This often indicates that a parameter has not been declared local when it should have been. Parameters explicitly declared global from within a function using `typeset -g` do not cause a warning. Note that there is no warning when a local parameter is assigned to in a nested function, which may also indicate an error.

WARN_NESTED_VAR

Print a warning message when an existing parameter from an enclosing function scope, or global, is set in a function by an assignment or in math context. Assignment to shell special parameters does not cause a warning. This is the companion to `WARN_CREATE_GLOBAL` as in this case the warning is only printed when a parameter is *not* created. Where possible, use of `typeset -g` to set the parameter suppresses the error, but note that this needs to be used every time the parameter is set. To restrict the effect of this option to a single function scope, use '`functions -W`'.

For example, the following code produces a warning for the assignment inside the function `nested` as that overrides the value within `toplevel`

```
toplevel() {
  local foo="in fn"
  nested
}
nested() {
    foo="in nested"
}
setopt warn_nested_var
toplevel
```

16.2.4 History

APPEND_HISTORY <D>

If this is set, zsh sessions will append their history list to the history file, rather than replace it. Thus, multiple parallel zsh sessions will all have the new entries from their history lists added to the history file, in the order that they exit. The file will still be periodically re-written to trim it when the number of lines grows 20% beyond the value specified by `$SAVEHIST` (see also the `HIST_SAVE_BY_COPY` option).

BANG_HIST (+K) <C> <Z>

Perform textual history expansion, *csh*-style, treating the character '`!`' specially.

EXTENDED_HISTORY <C>

Save each command's beginning timestamp (in seconds since the epoch) and the duration (in seconds) to the history file. The format of this prefixed data is:

'`: `<*beginning time*>`:`<*elapsed seconds*>`;`<*command*>'.

HIST_ALLOW_CLOBBER

Add '`|`' to output redirections in the history. This allows history references to clobber files even when `CLOBBER` is unset.

HIST_BEEP <D>
> Beep in ZLE when a widget attempts to access a history entry which isn't there.

HIST_EXPIRE_DUPS_FIRST
> If the internal history needs to be trimmed to add the current command line, setting this option will cause the oldest history event that has a duplicate to be lost before losing a unique event from the list. You should be sure to set the value of HISTSIZE to a larger number than SAVEHIST in order to give you some room for the duplicated events, otherwise this option will behave just like HIST_IGNORE_ALL_DUPS once the history fills up with unique events.

HIST_FCNTL_LOCK
> When writing out the history file, by default zsh uses ad-hoc file locking to avoid known problems with locking on some operating systems. With this option locking is done by means of the system's fcntl call, where this method is available. On recent operating systems this may provide better performance, in particular avoiding history corruption when files are stored on NFS.

HIST_FIND_NO_DUPS
> When searching for history entries in the line editor, do not display duplicates of a line previously found, even if the duplicates are not contiguous.

HIST_IGNORE_ALL_DUPS
> If a new command line being added to the history list duplicates an older one, the older command is removed from the list (even if it is not the previous event).

HIST_IGNORE_DUPS (-h)
> Do not enter command lines into the history list if they are duplicates of the previous event.

HIST_IGNORE_SPACE (-g)
> Remove command lines from the history list when the first character on the line is a space, or when one of the expanded aliases contains a leading space. Only normal aliases (not global or suffix aliases) have this behaviour. Note that the command lingers in the internal history until the next command is entered before it vanishes, allowing you to briefly reuse or edit the line. If you want to make it vanish right away without entering another command, type a space and press return.

HIST_LEX_WORDS
> By default, shell history that is read in from files is split into words on all white space. This means that arguments with quoted whitespace are not correctly handled, with the consequence that references to words in history lines that have been read from a file may be inaccurate. When this option is set, words read in from a history file are divided up in a similar fashion to normal shell command line handling. Although this produces more accurately delimited words, if the size of the history file is large this can be slow. Trial and error is necessary to decide.

HIST_NO_FUNCTIONS

Remove function definitions from the history list. Note that the function lingers in the internal history until the next command is entered before it vanishes, allowing you to briefly reuse or edit the definition.

HIST_NO_STORE

Remove the `history` (`fc -l`) command from the history list when invoked. Note that the command lingers in the internal history until the next command is entered before it vanishes, allowing you to briefly reuse or edit the line.

HIST_REDUCE_BLANKS

Remove superfluous blanks from each command line being added to the history list.

HIST_SAVE_BY_COPY <D>

When the history file is re-written, we normally write out a copy of the file named `$HISTFILE.new` and then rename it over the old one. However, if this option is unset, we instead truncate the old history file and write out the new version in-place. If one of the history-appending options is enabled, this option only has an effect when the enlarged history file needs to be re-written to trim it down to size. Disable this only if you have special needs, as doing so makes it possible to lose history entries if zsh gets interrupted during the save.

When writing out a copy of the history file, zsh preserves the old file's permissions and group information, but will refuse to write out a new file if it would change the history file's owner.

HIST_SAVE_NO_DUPS

When writing out the history file, older commands that duplicate newer ones are omitted.

HIST_VERIFY

Whenever the user enters a line with history expansion, don't execute the line directly; instead, perform history expansion and reload the line into the editing buffer.

INC_APPEND_HISTORY

This option works like **APPEND_HISTORY** except that new history lines are added to the `$HISTFILE` incrementally (as soon as they are entered), rather than waiting until the shell exits. The file will still be periodically re-written to trim it when the number of lines grows 20% beyond the value specified by `$SAVEHIST` (see also the **HIST_SAVE_BY_COPY** option).

INC_APPEND_HISTORY_TIME

This option is a variant of **INC_APPEND_HISTORY** in which, where possible, the history entry is written out to the file after the command is finished, so that the time taken by the command is recorded correctly in the history file in **EXTENDED_HISTORY** format. This means that the history entry will not be available immediately from other instances of the shell that are using the same history file.

This option is only useful if **INC_APPEND_HISTORY** and **SHARE_HISTORY** are turned off. The three options should be considered mutually exclusive.

SHARE_HISTORY <K>

> This option both imports new commands from the history file, and also causes your typed commands to be appended to the history file (the latter is like specifying INC_APPEND_HISTORY, which should be turned off if this option is in effect). The history lines are also output with timestamps ala EXTENDED_HISTORY (which makes it easier to find the spot where we left off reading the file after it gets re-written).
>
> By default, history movement commands visit the imported lines as well as the local lines, but you can toggle this on and off with the set-local-history zle binding. It is also possible to create a zle widget that will make some commands ignore imported commands, and some include them.
>
> If you find that you want more control over when commands get imported, you may wish to turn SHARE_HISTORY off, INC_APPEND_HISTORY or INC_APPEND_HISTORY_TIME (see above) on, and then manually import commands whenever you need them using 'fc -RI'.

16.2.5 Initialisation

ALL_EXPORT (-a, ksh: -a)

> All parameters subsequently defined are automatically exported.

GLOBAL_EXPORT <Z>

> If this option is set, passing the -x flag to the builtins declare, float, integer, readonly and typeset (but not local) will also set the -g flag; hence parameters exported to the environment will not be made local to the enclosing function, unless they were already or the flag +g is given explicitly. If the option is unset, exported parameters will be made local in just the same way as any other parameter.
>
> This option is set by default for backward compatibility; it is not recommended that its behaviour be relied upon. Note that the builtin export always sets both the -x and -g flags, and hence its effect extends beyond the scope of the enclosing function; this is the most portable way to achieve this behaviour.

GLOBAL_RCS (-d) <D>

> If this option is unset, the startup files /etc/zprofile, /etc/zshrc, /etc/zlogin and /etc/zlogout will not be run. It can be disabled and re-enabled at any time, including inside local startup files (.zshrc, etc.).

RCS (+f) <D>

> After /etc/zshenv is sourced on startup, source the .zshenv, /etc/zprofile, .zprofile, /etc/zshrc, .zshrc, /etc/zlogin, .zlogin, and .zlogout files, as described in Chapter 5 [Files], page 8. If this option is unset, the /etc/zshenv file is still sourced, but any of the others will not be; it can be set at any time to prevent the remaining startup files after the currently executing one from being sourced.

16.2.6 Input/Output

ALIASES <D>

> Expand aliases.

CLOBBER (+C, ksh: +C) <D>

> Allows '>' redirection to truncate existing files. Otherwise '>!' or '>|' must be used to truncate a file.
>
> If the option is not set, and the option APPEND_CREATE is also not set, '>>!' or '>>|' must be used to create a file. If either option is set, '>>' may be used.

CORRECT (-0)

> Try to correct the spelling of commands. Note that, when the HASH_LIST_ALL option is not set or when some directories in the path are not readable, this may falsely report spelling errors the first time some commands are used.
>
> The shell variable CORRECT_IGNORE may be set to a pattern to match words that will never be offered as corrections.

CORRECT_ALL (-0)

> Try to correct the spelling of all arguments in a line.
>
> The shell variable CORRECT_IGNORE_FILE may be set to a pattern to match file names that will never be offered as corrections.

DVORAK

> Use the Dvorak keyboard instead of the standard qwerty keyboard as a basis for examining spelling mistakes for the CORRECT and CORRECT_ALL options and the spell-word editor command.

FLOW_CONTROL <D>

> If this option is unset, output flow control via start/stop characters (usually assigned to ^S/^Q) is disabled in the shell's editor.

IGNORE_EOF (-7)

> Do not exit on end-of-file. Require the use of exit or logout instead. However, ten consecutive EOFs will cause the shell to exit anyway, to avoid the shell hanging if its tty goes away.
>
> Also, if this option is set and the Zsh Line Editor is used, widgets implemented by shell functions can be bound to EOF (normally Control-D) without printing the normal warning message. This works only for normal widgets, not for completion widgets.

INTERACTIVE_COMMENTS (-k) <K> <S>

> Allow comments even in interactive shells.

HASH_CMDS <D>

> Note the location of each command the first time it is executed. Subsequent invocations of the same command will use the saved location, avoiding a path search. If this option is unset, no path hashing is done at all. However, when CORRECT is set, commands whose names do not appear in the functions or aliases hash tables are hashed in order to avoid reporting them as spelling errors.

HASH_DIRS <D>

> Whenever a command name is hashed, hash the directory containing it, as well as all directories that occur earlier in the path. Has no effect if neither HASH_CMDS nor CORRECT is set.

HASH_EXECUTABLES_ONLY

When hashing commands because of **HASH_CMDS**, check that the file to be hashed is actually an executable. This option is unset by default as if the path contains a large number of commands, or consists of many remote files, the additional tests can take a long time. Trial and error is needed to show if this option is beneficial.

MAIL_WARNING (-U)

Print a warning message if a mail file has been accessed since the shell last checked.

PATH_DIRS (-Q)

Perform a path search even on command names with slashes in them. Thus if '/usr/local/bin' is in the user's path, and he or she types 'X11/xinit', the command '/usr/local/bin/X11/xinit' will be executed (assuming it exists). Commands explicitly beginning with '/', './' or '../' are not subject to the path search. This also applies to the '.' and **source** builtins.

Note that subdirectories of the current directory are always searched for executables specified in this form. This takes place before any search indicated by this option, and regardless of whether '.' or the current directory appear in the command search path.

PATH_SCRIPT'<K> <S>

If this option is not set, a script passed as the first non-option argument to the shell must contain the name of the file to open. If this option is set, and the script does not specify a directory path, the script is looked for first in the current directory, then in the command path. See Chapter 4 [Invocation], page 6.

PRINT_EIGHT_BIT

Print eight bit characters literally in completion lists, etc. This option is not necessary if your system correctly returns the printability of eight bit characters (see man page ctype(3)).

PRINT_EXIT_VALUE (-1)

Print the exit value of programs with non-zero exit status. This is only available at the command line in interactive shells.

RC_QUOTES

Allow the character sequence '' '' to signify a single quote within singly quoted strings. Note this does not apply in quoted strings using the format $'...', where a backslashed single quote can be used.

RM_STAR_SILENT (-H) <K> <S>

Do not query the user before executing 'rm *' or 'rm path/*'.

RM_STAR_WAIT

If querying the user before executing 'rm *' or 'rm path/*', first wait ten seconds and ignore anything typed in that time. This avoids the problem of reflexively answering 'yes' to the query when one didn't really mean it. The wait and query can always be avoided by expanding the '*' in ZLE (with tab).

SHORT_LOOPS <C> <Z>

> Allow the short forms of **for**, **repeat**, **select**, **if**, and **function** constructs.

SUN_KEYBOARD_HACK (-L)

> If a line ends with a backquote, and there are an odd number of backquotes on the line, ignore the trailing backquote. This is useful on some keyboards where the return key is too small, and the backquote key lies annoyingly close to it. As an alternative the variable KEYBOARD_HACK lets you choose the character to be removed.

16.2.7 Job Control

AUTO_CONTINUE

> With this option set, stopped jobs that are removed from the job table with the **disown** builtin command are automatically sent a CONT signal to make them running.

AUTO_RESUME (-W)

> Treat single word simple commands without redirection as candidates for resumption of an existing job.

BG_NICE (-6) <C> <Z>

> Run all background jobs at a lower priority. This option is set by default.

CHECK_JOBS <Z>

> Report the status of background and suspended jobs before exiting a shell with job control; a second attempt to exit the shell will succeed. NO_CHECK_JOBS is best used only in combination with NO_HUP, else such jobs will be killed automatically.
>
> The check is omitted if the commands run from the previous command line included a 'jobs' command, since it is assumed the user is aware that there are background or suspended jobs. A 'jobs' command run from one of the hook functions defined in the section Special Functions in Chapter 9 [Functions], page 24, is not counted for this purpose.

CHECK_RUNNING_JOBS <Z>

> Check for both running and suspended jobs when CHECK_JOBS is enabled. When this option is disabled, zsh checks only for suspended jobs, which matches the default behavior of bash.
>
> This option has no effect unless CHECK_JOBS is set.

HUP <Z>   Send the HUP signal to running jobs when the shell exits.

LONG_LIST_JOBS (-R)

> Print job notifications in the long format by default.

MONITOR (-m, ksh: -m)

> Allow job control. Set by default in interactive shells.

NOTIFY (-5, ksh: -b) <Z>

> Report the status of background jobs immediately, rather than waiting until just before printing a prompt.

POSIX_JOBS <K> <S>

>   This option makes job control more compliant with the POSIX standard.

>   When the option is not set, the MONITOR option is unset on entry to subshells, so that job control is no longer active. When the option is set, the MONITOR option and job control remain active in the subshell, but note that the subshell has no access to jobs in the parent shell.

>   When the option is not set, jobs put in the background or foreground with bg or fg are displayed with the same information that would be reported by jobs. When the option is set, only the text is printed. The output from jobs itself is not affected by the option.

>   When the option is not set, job information from the parent shell is saved for output within a subshell (for example, within a pipeline). When the option is set, the output of jobs is empty until a job is started within the subshell.

>   In previous versions of the shell, it was necessary to enable POSIX_JOBS in order for the builtin command wait to return the status of background jobs that had already exited. This is no longer the case.

16.2.8 Prompting

PROMPT_BANG <K>

>   If set, '!' is treated specially in prompt expansion. See Chapter 13 [Prompt Expansion], page 39.

PROMPT_CR (+V) <D>

>   Print a carriage return just before printing a prompt in the line editor. This is on by default as multi-line editing is only possible if the editor knows where the start of the line appears.

PROMPT_SP <D>

>   Attempt to preserve a partial line (i.e. a line that did not end with a newline) that would otherwise be covered up by the command prompt due to the PROMPT_CR option. This works by outputting some cursor-control characters, including a series of spaces, that should make the terminal wrap to the next line when a partial line is present (note that this is only successful if your terminal has automatic margins, which is typical).

>   When a partial line is preserved, by default you will see an inverse+bold character at the end of the partial line: a '%' for a normal user or a '#' for root. If set, the shell parameter PROMPT_EOL_MARK can be used to customize how the end of partial lines are shown.

>   NOTE: if the PROMPT_CR option is not set, enabling this option will have no effect. This option is on by default.

PROMPT_PERCENT <C> <Z>

>   If set, '%' is treated specially in prompt expansion. See Chapter 13 [Prompt Expansion], page 39.

PROMPT_SUBST <K> <S>

> If set, *parameter expansion*, *command substitution* and *arithmetic expansion* are performed in prompts. Substitutions within prompts do not affect the command status.

TRANSIENT_RPROMPT

> Remove any right prompt from display when accepting a command line. This may be useful with terminals with other cut/paste methods.

16.2.9 Scripts and Functions

ALIAS_FUNC_DEF <S>

> By default, zsh does not allow the definition of functions using the '*name* ()' syntax if *name* was expanded as an alias: this causes an error. This is usually the desired behaviour, as otherwise the combination of an alias and a function based on the same definition can easily cause problems.
>
> When this option is set, aliases can be used for defining functions.
>
> For example, consider the following definitions as they might occur in a startup file.
>
> ```
> alias foo=bar
> foo() {
>     print This probably does not do what you expect.
> }
> ```
>
> Here, `foo` is expanded as an alias to `bar` before the () is encountered, so the function defined would be named `bar`. By default this is instead an error in native mode. Note that quoting any part of the function name, or using the keyword `function`, avoids the problem, so is recommended when the function name can also be an alias.

C_BASES

> Output hexadecimal numbers in the standard C format, for example '0xFF' instead of the usual '16#FF'. If the option OCTAL_ZEROES is also set (it is not by default), octal numbers will be treated similarly and hence appear as '077' instead of '8#77'. This option has no effect on the choice of the output base, nor on the output of bases other than hexadecimal and octal. Note that these formats will be understood on input irrespective of the setting of C_BASES.

C_PRECEDENCES

> This alters the precedence of arithmetic operators to be more like C and other programming languages; Chapter 11 [Arithmetic Evaluation], page 31, has an explicit list.

DEBUG_BEFORE_CMD <D>

> Run the DEBUG trap before each command; otherwise it is run after each command. Setting this option mimics the behaviour of ksh 93; with the option unset the behaviour is that of ksh 88.

ERR_EXIT (-e, ksh: -e)

> If a command has a non-zero exit status, execute the ZERR trap, if set, and exit. This is disabled while running initialization scripts.

The behaviour is also disabled inside `DEBUG` traps. In this case the option is handled specially: it is unset on entry to the trap. If the option `DEBUG_BEFORE_CMD` is set, as it is by default, and the option `ERR_EXIT` is found to have been set on exit, then the command for which the `DEBUG` trap is being executed is skipped. The option is restored after the trap exits.

Non-zero status in a command list containing `&&` or `||` is ignored for commands not at the end of the list. Hence

```
false && true
```

does not trigger exit.

Exiting due to `ERR_EXIT` has certain interactions with asynchronous jobs noted in Chapter 10 [Jobs & Signals], page 30.

ERR_RETURN

> If a command has a non-zero exit status, return immediately from the enclosing function. The logic is similar to that for `ERR_EXIT`, except that an implicit **return** statement is executed instead of an **exit**. This will trigger an exit at the outermost level of a non-interactive script.
>
> Normally this option inherits the behaviour of `ERR_EXIT` that code followed by '`&&`' '`||`' does not trigger a return. Hence in the following:
>
> ```
> summit || true
> ```
>
> no return is forced as the combined effect always has a zero return status.
>
> Note. however, that if **summit** in the above example is itself a function, code inside it is considered separately: it may force a return from **summit** (assuming the option remains set within **summit**), but not from the enclosing context. This behaviour is different from `ERR_EXIT` which is unaffected by function scope.

EVAL_LINENO <Z>

> If set, line numbers of expressions evaluated using the builtin **eval** are tracked separately of the enclosing environment. This applies both to the parameter `LINENO` and the line number output by the prompt escape `%i`. If the option is set, the prompt escape `%N` will output the string '`(eval)`' instead of the script or function name as an indication. (The two prompt escapes are typically used in the parameter `PS4` to be output when the option `XTRACE` is set.) If `EVAL_LINENO` is unset, the line number of the surrounding script or function is retained during the evaluation.

EXEC (+n, ksh: +n) <D>

> Do execute commands. Without this option, commands are read and checked for syntax errors, but not executed. This option cannot be turned off in an interactive shell, except when '`-n`' is supplied to the shell at startup.

FUNCTION_ARGZERO <C> <Z>

> When executing a shell function or sourcing a script, set `$0` temporarily to the name of the function/script. Note that toggling `FUNCTION_ARGZERO` from on to off (or off to on) does not change the current value of `$0`. Only the state upon entry to the function or script has an effect. Compare `POSIX_ARGZERO`.

LOCAL_LOOPS

> When this option is not set, the effect of **break** and **continue** commands may propagate outside function scope, affecting loops in calling functions. When the option is set in a calling function, a **break** or a **continue** that is not caught within a called function (regardless of the setting of the option within that function) produces a warning and the effect is cancelled.

LOCAL_OPTIONS <K>

> If this option is set at the point of return from a shell function, most options (including this one) which were in force upon entry to the function are restored; options that are not restored are **PRIVILEGED** and **RESTRICTED**. Otherwise, only this option, and the **LOCAL_LOOPS**, **XTRACE** and **PRINT_EXIT_VALUE** options are restored. Hence if this is explicitly unset by a shell function the other options in force at the point of return will remain so. A shell function can also guarantee itself a known shell configuration with a formulation like 'emulate -L zsh'; the -L activates **LOCAL_OPTIONS**.

LOCAL_PATTERNS

> If this option is set at the point of return from a shell function, the state of pattern disables, as set with the builtin command 'disable -p', is restored to what it was when the function was entered. The behaviour of this option is similar to the effect of **LOCAL_OPTIONS** on options; hence 'emulate -L sh' (or indeed any other emulation with the -L option) activates **LOCAL_PATTERNS**.

LOCAL_TRAPS <K>

> If this option is set when a signal trap is set inside a function, then the previous status of the trap for that signal will be restored when the function exits. Note that this option must be set *prior* to altering the trap behaviour in a function; unlike **LOCAL_OPTIONS**, the value on exit from the function is irrelevant. However, it does not need to be set before any global trap for that to be correctly restored by a function. For example,
>
> ```
>         unsetopt localtraps
>         trap - INT
>         fn() { setopt localtraps; trap '' INT; sleep 3; }
> ```
>
> will restore normal handling of **SIGINT** after the function exits.

MULTI_FUNC_DEF <Z>

> Allow definitions of multiple functions at once in the form 'fn1 fn2...()'; if the option is not set, this causes a parse error. Definition of multiple functions with the **function** keyword is always allowed. Multiple function definitions are not often used and can cause obscure errors.

MULTIOS <Z>

> Perform implicit *tees* or *cats* when multiple redirections are attempted (see Chapter 7 [Redirection], page 19).

OCTAL_ZEROES <S>

> Interpret any integer constant beginning with a 0 as octal, per IEEE Std 1003.2-1992 (ISO 9945-2:1993). This is not enabled by default as it causes problems with parsing of, for example, date and time strings with leading zeroes.

Sequences of digits indicating a numeric base such as the '08' component in '08#77' are always interpreted as decimal, regardless of leading zeroes.

PIPE_FAIL

By default, when a pipeline exits the exit status recorded by the shell and returned by the shell variable $? reflects that of the rightmost element of a pipeline. If this option is set, the exit status instead reflects the status of the rightmost element of the pipeline that was non-zero, or zero if all elements exited with zero status.

SOURCE_TRACE

If set, zsh will print an informational message announcing the name of each file it loads. The format of the output is similar to that for the XTRACE option, with the message <sourcetrace>. A file may be loaded by the shell itself when it starts up and shuts down (Startup/Shutdown Files) or by the use of the 'source' and 'dot' builtin commands.

TYPESET_SILENT

If this is unset, executing any of the 'typeset' family of commands with no options and a list of parameters that have no values to be assigned but already exist will display the value of the parameter. If the option is set, they will only be shown when parameters are selected with the '-m' option. The option '-p' is available whether or not the option is set.

VERBOSE (-v, ksh: -v)

Print shell input lines as they are read.

XTRACE (-x, ksh: -x)

Print commands and their arguments as they are executed. The output is preceded by the value of $PS4, formatted as described in Chapter 13 [Prompt Expansion], page 39.

16.2.10 Shell Emulation

APPEND_CREATE <K> <S>

This option only applies when NO_CLOBBER (-C) is in effect.

If this option is not set, the shell will report an error when a append redirection (>>) is used on a file that does not already exists (the traditional zsh behaviour of NO_CLOBBER). If the option is set, no error is reported (POSIX behaviour).

BASH_REMATCH

When set, matches performed with the =~ operator will set the BASH_REMATCH array variable, instead of the default MATCH and match variables. The first element of the BASH_REMATCH array will contain the entire matched text and subsequent elements will contain extracted substrings. This option makes more sense when KSH_ARRAYS is also set, so that the entire matched portion is stored at index 0 and the first substring is at index 1. Without this option, the MATCH variable contains the entire matched text and the match array variable contains substrings.

BSD_ECHO <S>

> Make the `echo` builtin compatible with the BSD man page echo(1) command. This disables backslashed escape sequences in echo strings unless the `-e` option is specified.

CONTINUE_ON_ERROR

> If a fatal error is encountered (see Section 6.6 [Errors], page 16), and the code is running in a script, the shell will resume execution at the next statement in the script at the top level, in other words outside all functions or shell constructs such as loops and conditions. This mimics the behaviour of interactive shells, where the shell returns to the line editor to read a new command; it was the normal behaviour in versions of zsh before 5.0.1.

CSH_JUNKIE_HISTORY <C>

> A history reference without an event specifier will always refer to the previous command. Without this option, such a history reference refers to the same event as the previous history reference on the current command line, defaulting to the previous command.

CSH_JUNKIE_LOOPS <C>

> Allow loop bodies to take the form '*list*; `end`' instead of '`do` *list*; `done`'.

CSH_JUNKIE_QUOTES <C>

> Changes the rules for single- and double-quoted text to match that of *csh*. These require that embedded newlines be preceded by a backslash; unescaped newlines will cause an error message. In double-quoted strings, it is made impossible to escape '$', ''' or '"' (and '\' itself no longer needs escaping). Command substitutions are only expanded once, and cannot be nested.

CSH_NULLCMD <C>

> Do not use the values of `NULLCMD` and `READNULLCMD` when running redirections with no command. This make such redirections fail (see Chapter 7 [Redirection], page 19).

KSH_ARRAYS <K> <S>

> Emulate *ksh* array handling as closely as possible. If this option is set, array elements are numbered from zero, an array parameter without subscript refers to the first element instead of the whole array, and braces are required to delimit a subscript ('`${path[2]}`' rather than just '`$path[2]`') or to apply modifiers to any parameter ('`${PWD:h}`' rather than '`$PWD:h`').

KSH_AUTOLOAD <K> <S>

> Emulate *ksh* function autoloading. This means that when a function is autoloaded, the corresponding file is merely executed, and must define the function itself. (By default, the function is defined to the contents of the file. However, the most common *ksh*-style case - of the file containing only a simple definition of the function - is always handled in the *ksh*-compatible manner.)

KSH_OPTION_PRINT <K>

> Alters the way options settings are printed: instead of separate lists of set and unset options, all options are shown, marked 'on' if they are in the non-default state, 'off' otherwise.

KSH_TYPESET

>This option is now obsolete: a better appropximation to the behaviour of other shells is obtained with the reserved word interface to `declare`, `export`, `float`, `integer`, `local`, `readonly` and `typeset`. Note that the option is only applied when the reserved word interface is *not* in use.

>Alters the way arguments to the `typeset` family of commands, including `declare`, `export`, `float`, `integer`, `local` and `readonly`, are processed. Without this option, zsh will perform normal word splitting after command and parameter expansion in arguments of an assignment; with it, word splitting does not take place in those cases.

KSH_ZERO_SUBSCRIPT

>Treat use of a subscript of value zero in array or string expressions as a reference to the first element, i.e. the element that usually has the subscript 1. Ignored if `KSH_ARRAYS` is also set.

>If neither this option nor `KSH_ARRAYS` is set, accesses to an element of an array or string with subscript zero return an empty element or string, while attempts to set element zero of an array or string are treated as an error. However, attempts to set an otherwise valid subscript range that includes zero will succeed. For example, if `KSH_ZERO_SUBSCRIPT` is not set,

>>`array[0]=(element)`

>is an error, while

>>`array[0,1]=(element)`

>is not and will replace the first element of the array.

>This option is for compatibility with older versions of the shell and is not recommended in new code.

POSIX_ALIASES <K> <S>

>When this option is set, reserved words are not candidates for alias expansion: it is still possible to declare any of them as an alias, but the alias will never be expanded. Reserved words are described in Section 6.5 [Reserved Words], page 16.

>Alias expansion takes place while text is being read; hence when this option is set it does not take effect until the end of any function or other piece of shell code parsed as one unit. Note this may cause differences from other shells even when the option is in effect. For example, when running a command with 'zsh -c', or even 'zsh -o posixaliases -c', the entire command argument is parsed as one unit, so aliases defined within the argument are not available even in later lines. If in doubt, avoid use of aliases in non-interactive code.

POSIX_ARGZERO

>This option may be used to temporarily disable `FUNCTION_ARGZERO` and thereby restore the value of `$0` to the name used to invoke the shell (or as set by the `-c` command line option). For compatibility with previous versions of the shell, emulations use `NO_FUNCTION_ARGZERO` instead of `POSIX_ARGZERO`, which may result in unexpected scoping of `$0` if the emulation mode is changed inside

a function or script. To avoid this, explicitly enable POSIX_ARGZERO in the emulate command:

    emulate sh -o POSIX_ARGZERO

Note that NO_POSIX_ARGZERO has no effect unless FUNCTION_ARGZERO was already enabled upon entry to the function or script.

POSIX_BUILTINS <K> <S>

When this option is set the command builtin can be used to execute shell builtin commands. Parameter assignments specified before shell functions and special builtins are kept after the command completes unless the special builtin is prefixed with the command builtin. Special builtins are ., :, break, continue, declare, eval, exit, export, integer, local, readonly, return, set, shift, source, times, trap and unset.

In addition, various error conditions associated with the above builtins or exec cause a non-interactive shell to exit and an interactive shell to return to its top-level processing.

Furthermore, functions and shell builtins are not executed after an exec prefix; the command to be executed must be an external command found in the path.

Furthermore, the getopts builtin behaves in a POSIX-compatible fashion in that the associated variable OPTIND is not made local to functions.

Moreover, the warning and special exit code from [[-o non_existent_option]] are suppressed.

POSIX_IDENTIFIERS <K> <S>

When this option is set, only the ASCII characters a to z, A to Z, 0 to 9 and _ may be used in identifiers (names of shell parameters and modules).

In addition, setting this option limits the effect of parameter substitution with no braces, so that the expression $# is treated as the parameter $# even if followed by a valid parameter name. When it is unset, zsh allows expressions of the form $#name to refer to the length of $name, even for special variables, for example in expressions such as $#- and $#*.

Another difference is that with the option set assignment to an unset variable in arithmetic context causes the variable to be created as a scalar rather than a numeric type. So after 'unset t; ((t = 3))'. without POSIX_IDENTIFIERS set t has integer type, while with it set it has scalar type.

When the option is unset and multibyte character support is enabled (i.e. it is compiled in and the option MULTIBYTE is set), then additionally any alphanumeric characters in the local character set may be used in identifiers. Note that scripts and functions written with this feature are not portable, and also that both options must be set before the script or function is parsed; setting them during execution is not sufficient as the syntax variable=value has already been parsed as a command rather than an assignment.

If multibyte character support is not compiled into the shell this option is ignored; all octets with the top bit set may be used in identifiers. This is non-standard but is the traditional zsh behaviour.

POSIX_STRINGS <K> <S>

> This option affects processing of quoted strings. Currently it only affects the behaviour of null characters, i.e. character 0 in the portable character set corresponding to US ASCII.
>
> When this option is not set, null characters embedded within strings of the form `$'...'` are treated as ordinary characters. The entire string is maintained within the shell and output to files where necessary, although owing to restrictions of the library interface the string is truncated at the null character in file names, environment variables, or in arguments to external programs.
>
> When this option is set, the `$'...'` expression is truncated at the null character. Note that remaining parts of the same string beyond the termination of the quotes are not truncated.
>
> For example, the command line argument `a$'b\0c'd` is treated with the option off as the characters `a`, `b`, null, `c`, `d`, and with the option on as the characters `a`, `b`, `d`.

POSIX_TRAPS <K> <S>

> When this option is set, the usual zsh behaviour of executing traps for `EXIT` on exit from shell functions is suppressed. In that case, manipulating `EXIT` traps always alters the global trap for exiting the shell; the `LOCAL_TRAPS` option is ignored for the `EXIT` trap. Furthermore, a `return` statement executed in a trap with no argument passes back from the function the value from the surrounding context, not from code executed within the trap.

SH_FILE_EXPANSION <K> <S>

> Perform filename expansion (e.g., ~ expansion) *before* parameter expansion, command substitution, arithmetic expansion and brace expansion. If this option is unset, it is performed *after* brace expansion, so things like '`~$USERNAME`' and '`~{pfalstad,rc}`' will work.

SH_NULLCMD <K> <S>

> Do not use the values of `NULLCMD` and `READNULLCMD` when doing redirections, use '`:`' instead (see Chapter 7 [Redirection], page 19).

SH_OPTION_LETTERS <K> <S>

> If this option is set the shell tries to interpret single letter options (which are used with `set` and `setopt`) like *ksh* does. This also affects the value of the - special parameter.

SH_WORD_SPLIT (-y) <K> <S>

> Causes field splitting to be performed on unquoted parameter expansions. Note that this option has nothing to do with word splitting. (See Section 14.3 [Parameter Expansion], page 52.)

TRAPS_ASYNC

> While waiting for a program to exit, handle signals and run traps immediately. Otherwise the trap is run after a child process has exited. Note this does not affect the point at which traps are run for any case other than when the shell is waiting for a child process.

16.2.11 Shell State

INTERACTIVE (-i, ksh: -i)

>This is an interactive shell. This option is set upon initialisation if the standard input is a tty and commands are being read from standard input. (See the discussion of SHIN_STDIN.) This heuristic may be overridden by specifying a state for this option on the command line. The value of this option can only be changed via flags supplied at invocation of the shell. It cannot be changed once zsh is running.

LOGIN (-l, ksh: -l)

>This is a login shell. If this option is not explicitly set, the shell becomes a login shell if the first character of the argv[0] passed to the shell is a '-'.

PRIVILEGED (-p, ksh: -p)

>Turn on privileged mode. Typically this is used when script is to be run with elevated privileges. This should be done as follows directly with the -p option to zsh so that it takes effect during startup.

>```
>#!/bin/zsh -p
>```

>The option is enabled automatically on startup if the effective user (group) ID is not equal to the real user (group) ID. In this case, turning the option off causes the effective user and group IDs to be set to the real user and group IDs. Be aware that if that fails the shell may be running with different IDs than was intended so a script should check for failure and act accordingly, for example:

>```
>unsetopt privileged || exit
>```

>The PRIVILEGED option disables sourcing user startup files. If zsh is invoked as 'sh' or 'ksh' with this option set, /etc/suid_profile is sourced (after /etc/profile on interactive shells). Sourcing ~/.profile is disabled and the contents of the ENV variable is ignored. This option cannot be changed using the -m option of setopt and unsetopt, and changing it inside a function always changes it globally regardless of the LOCAL_OPTIONS option.

RESTRICTED (-r)

>Enables restricted mode. This option cannot be changed using unsetopt, and setting it inside a function always changes it globally regardless of the LOCAL_OPTIONS option. See Section 4.3 [Restricted Shell], page 8.

SHIN_STDIN (-s, ksh: -s)

>Commands are being read from the standard input. Commands are read from standard input if no command is specified with -c and no file of commands is specified. If SHIN_STDIN is set explicitly on the command line, any argument that would otherwise have been taken as a file to run will instead be treated as a normal positional parameter. Note that setting or unsetting this option on the command line does not necessarily affect the state the option will have while the shell is running - that is purely an indicator of whether or not commands are *actually* being read from standard input. The value of this option can only be changed via flags supplied at invocation of the shell. It cannot be changed once zsh is running.

SINGLE_COMMAND (-t, ksh: -t)

> If the shell is reading from standard input, it exits after a single command has been executed. This also makes the shell non-interactive, unless the **INTERACTIVE** option is explicitly set on the command line. The value of this option can only be changed via flags supplied at invocation of the shell. It cannot be changed once zsh is running.

16.2.12 Zle

BEEP (+B) <D>

> Beep on error in ZLE.

COMBINING_CHARS

> Assume that the terminal displays combining characters correctly. Specifically, if a base alphanumeric character is followed by one or more zero-width punctuation characters, assume that the zero-width characters will be displayed as modifications to the base character within the same width. Not all terminals handle this. If this option is not set, zero-width characters are displayed separately with special mark-up.
>
> If this option is set, the pattern test [[:WORD:]] matches a zero-width punctuation character on the assumption that it will be used as part of a word in combination with a word character. Otherwise the base shell does not handle combining characters specially.

EMACS

> If ZLE is loaded, turning on this option has the equivalent effect of 'bindkey -e'. In addition, the VI option is unset. Turning it off has no effect. The option setting is not guaranteed to reflect the current keymap. This option is provided for compatibility; bindkey is the recommended interface.

OVERSTRIKE

> Start up the line editor in overstrike mode.

SINGLE_LINE_ZLE (-M) <K>

> Use single-line command line editing instead of multi-line.
>
> Note that although this is on by default in ksh emulation it only provides superficial compatibility with the ksh line editor and reduces the effectiveness of the zsh line editor. As it has no effect on shell syntax, many users may wish to disable this option when using ksh emulation interactively.

VI

> If ZLE is loaded, turning on this option has the equivalent effect of 'bindkey -v'. In addition, the EMACS option is unset. Turning it off has no effect. The option setting is not guaranteed to reflect the current keymap. This option is provided for compatibility; bindkey is the recommended interface.

ZLE (-Z)

> Use the zsh line editor. Set by default in interactive shells connected to a terminal.

16.3 Option Aliases

Some options have alternative names. These aliases are never used for output, but can be used just like normal option names when specifying options to the shell.

```
BRACE_EXPAND
            NO_IGNORE_BRACES (ksh and bash compatibility)
DOT_GLOB   GLOB_DOTS (bash compatibility)
HASH_ALL   HASH_CMDS (bash compatibility)
HIST_APPEND
            APPEND_HISTORY (bash compatibility)
HIST_EXPAND
            BANG_HIST (bash compatibility)
LOG        NO_HIST_NO_FUNCTIONS (ksh compatibility)
MAIL_WARN
            MAIL_WARNING (bash compatibility)
ONE_CMD    SINGLE_COMMAND (bash compatibility)
PHYSICAL   CHASE_LINKS (ksh and bash compatibility)
PROMPT_VARS
            PROMPT_SUBST (bash compatibility)
STDIN      SHIN_STDIN (ksh compatibility)
TRACK_ALL
            HASH_CMDS (ksh compatibility)
```

16.4 Single Letter Options

16.4.1 Default set

-0	CORRECT
-1	PRINT_EXIT_VALUE
-2	NO_BAD_PATTERN
-3	NO_NOMATCH
-4	GLOB_DOTS
-5	NOTIFY
-6	BG_NICE
-7	IGNORE_EOF
-8	MARK_DIRS
-9	AUTO_LIST
-B	NO_BEEP
-C	NO_CLOBBER
-D	PUSHD_TO_HOME

-E	PUSHD_SILENT
-F	*NO*_GLOB
-G	NULL_GLOB
-H	RM_STAR_SILENT
-I	IGNORE_BRACES
-J	AUTO_CD
-K	*NO*_BANG_HIST
-L	SUN_KEYBOARD_HACK
-M	SINGLE_LINE_ZLE
-N	AUTO_PUSHD
-O	CORRECT_ALL
-P	RC_EXPAND_PARAM
-Q	PATH_DIRS
-R	LONG_LIST_JOBS
-S	REC_EXACT
-T	CDABLE_VARS
-U	MAIL_WARNING
-V	*NO*_PROMPT_CR
-W	AUTO_RESUME
-X	LIST_TYPES
-Y	MENU_COMPLETE
-Z	ZLE
-a	ALL_EXPORT
-e	ERR_EXIT
-f	*NO*_RCS
-g	HIST_IGNORE_SPACE
-h	HIST_IGNORE_DUPS
-i	INTERACTIVE
-k	INTERACTIVE_COMMENTS
-l	LOGIN
-m	MONITOR
-n	*NO*_EXEC
-p	PRIVILEGED

`-r`	RESTRICTED
`-s`	SHIN_STDIN
`-t`	SINGLE_COMMAND
`-u`	*NO*_UNSET
`-v`	VERBOSE
`-w`	CHASE_LINKS
`-x`	XTRACE
`-y`	SH_WORD_SPLIT

16.4.2 sh/ksh emulation set

`-C`	*NO*_CLOBBER
`-T`	TRAPS_ASYNC
`-X`	MARK_DIRS
`-a`	ALL_EXPORT
`-b`	NOTIFY
`-e`	ERR_EXIT
`-f`	*NO*_GLOB
`-i`	INTERACTIVE
`-l`	LOGIN
`-m`	MONITOR
`-n`	*NO*_EXEC
`-p`	PRIVILEGED
`-r`	RESTRICTED
`-s`	SHIN_STDIN
`-t`	SINGLE_COMMAND
`-u`	*NO*_UNSET
`-v`	VERBOSE
`-x`	XTRACE

16.4.3 Also note

`-A`	Used by **set** for setting arrays
`-b`	Used on the command line to specify end of option processing
`-c`	Used on the command line to specify a single command
`-m`	Used by **setopt** for pattern-matching option setting
`-o`	Used in all places to allow use of long option names
`-s`	Used by **set** to sort positional parameters

17 Shell Builtin Commands

Some shell builtin commands take options as described in individual entries; these are often referred to in the list below as '`flags`' to avoid confusion with shell options, which may also have an effect on the behaviour of builtin commands. In this introductory section, '`option`' always has the meaning of an option to a command that should be familiar to most command line users.

Typically, options are single letters preceded by a hyphen (-). Options that take an argument accept it either immediately following the option letter or after white space, for example '`print -C3 *`' or '`print -C 3 *`' are equivalent. Arguments to options are not the same as arguments to the command; the documentation indicates which is which. Options that do not take an argument may be combined in a single word, for example '`print -ca *`' and '`print -c -a *`' are equivalent.

Some shell builtin commands also take options that begin with '+' instead of '-'. The list below makes clear which commands these are.

Options (together with their individual arguments, if any) must appear in a group before any non-option arguments; once the first non-option argument has been found, option processing is terminated.

All builtin commands other than precommand modifiers, even those that have no options, can be given the argument '--' to terminate option processing. This indicates that the following words are non-option arguments, but is otherwise ignored. This is useful in cases where arguments to the command may begin with '-'. For historical reasons, most builtin commands also recognize a single '-' in a separate word for this purpose; note that this is less standard and use of '--' is recommended.

- *simple command*

> See Section 6.2 [Precommand Modifiers], page 11.

. *file* [*arg ...*]

> Read commands from *file* and execute them in the current shell environment.
>
> If *file* does not contain a slash, or if `PATH_DIRS` is set, the shell looks in the components of `$path` to find the directory containing *file*. Files in the current directory are not read unless '.' appears somewhere in `$path`. If a file named '*file*`.zwc`' is found, is newer than *file*, and is the compiled form (created with the `zcompile` builtin) of *file*, then commands are read from that file instead of *file*.
>
> If any arguments *arg* are given, they become the positional parameters; the old positional parameters are restored when the *file* is done executing. However, if no arguments are given, the positional parameters remain those of the calling context, and no restoring is done.
>
> If *file* was not found the return status is 127; if *file* was found but contained a syntax error the return status is 126; else the return status is the exit status of the last command executed.

: [*arg ...*]

> This command does nothing, although normal argument expansions is performed which may have effects on shell parameters. A zero exit status is returned.

alias [{+|-}gmrsL] [*name*[=*value*] ...]

> For each *name* with a corresponding *value*, define an alias with that value. A
> trailing space in *value* causes the next word to be checked for alias expansion.
> If the **-g** flag is present, define a global alias; global aliases are expanded even
> if they do not occur in command position.
>
> If the **-s** flag is present, define a suffix alias: if the command word on a command
> line is in the form '*text*.*name*', where *text* is any non-empty string, it is replaced
> by the text '*value text*.*name*'. Note that *name* is treated as a literal string,
> not a pattern. A trailing space in *value* is not special in this case. For example,
>
>> **alias -s ps=gv**
>
> will cause the command '***.ps**' to be expanded to '**gv *.ps**'. As alias expansion
> is carried out earlier than globbing, the '***.ps**' will then be expanded. Suffix
> aliases constitute a different name space from other aliases (so in the above
> example it is still possible to create an alias for the command **ps**) and the two
> sets are never listed together.
>
> For each *name* with no *value*, print the value of *name*, if any. With no argu-
> ments, print all currently defined aliases other than suffix aliases. If the **-m** flag
> is given the arguments are taken as patterns (they should be quoted to preserve
> them from being interpreted as glob patterns), and the aliases matching these
> patterns are printed. When printing aliases and one of the **-g**, **-r** or **-s** flags is
> present, restrict the printing to global, regular or suffix aliases, respectively; a
> regular alias is one which is neither a global nor a suffix alias. Using '**+**' instead
> of '**-**', or ending the option list with a single '**+**', prevents the values of the
> aliases from being printed.
>
> If the **-L** flag is present, then print each alias in a manner suitable for putting
> in a startup script. The exit status is nonzero if a *name* (with no *value*) is given
> for which no alias has been defined.
>
> For more on aliases, include common problems, see Section 6.8 [Aliasing],
> page 17.

autoload [{+|-}RTUXdkmrtWz] [-w] [*name* ...]

> See the section 'Autoloading Functions' in Chapter 9 [Functions], page 24, for
> full details. The **fpath** parameter will be searched to find the function definition
> when the function is first referenced.
>
> If *name* consists of an absolute path, the function is defined to load from the
> file given (searching as usual for dump files in the given location). The name of
> the function is the basename (non-directory part) of the file. It is normally an
> error if the function is not found in the given location; however, if the option **-d**
> is given, searching for the function defaults to **$fpath**. If a function is loaded
> by absolute path, any functions loaded from it that are marked for **autoload**
> without an absolute path have the load path of the parent function temporarily
> prepended to **$fpath**.
>
> If the option **-r** or **-R** is given, the function is searched for immediately and the
> location is recorded internally for use when the function is executed; a relative
> path is expanded using the value of **$PWD**. This protects against a change to
> **$fpath** after the call to **autoload**. With **-r**, if the function is not found, it is

silently left unresolved until execution; with -R, an error message is printed and command processing aborted immediately the search fails, i.e. at the `autoload` command rather than at function execution..

The flag -X may be used only inside a shell function. It causes the calling function to be marked for autoloading and then immediately loaded and executed, with the current array of positional parameters as arguments. This replaces the previous definition of the function. If no function definition is found, an error is printed and the function remains undefined and marked for autoloading. If an argument is given, it is used as a directory (i.e. it does not include the name of the function) in which the function is to be found; this may be combined with the -d option to allow the function search to default to `$fpath` if it is not in the given location.

The flag +X attempts to load each *name* as an autoloaded function, but does *not* execute it. The exit status is zero (success) if the function was not previously defined *and* a definition for it was found. This does *not* replace any existing definition of the function. The exit status is nonzero (failure) if the function was already defined or when no definition was found. In the latter case the function remains undefined and marked for autoloading. If ksh-style autoloading is enabled, the function created will contain the contents of the file plus a call to the function itself appended to it, thus giving normal ksh autoloading behaviour on the first call to the function. If the -m flag is also given each *name* is treated as a pattern and all functions already marked for autoload that match the pattern are loaded.

With the -t flag, turn on execution tracing; with -T, turn on execution tracing only for the current function, turning it off on entry to any called functions that do not also have tracing enabled.

With the -U flag, alias expansion is suppressed when the function is loaded.

With the -w flag, the *names* are taken as names of files compiled with the `zcompile` builtin, and all functions defined in them are marked for autoloading.

The flags -z and -k mark the function to be autoloaded using the zsh or ksh style, as if the option `KSH_AUTOLOAD` were unset or were set, respectively. The flags override the setting of the option at the time the function is loaded.

Note that the `autoload` command makes no attempt to ensure the shell options set during the loading or execution of the file have any particular value. For this, the `emulate` command can be used:

```
emulate zsh -c 'autoload -Uz func'
```

arranges that when *func* is loaded the shell is in native `zsh` emulation, and this emulation is also applied when *func* is run.

Some of the functions of `autoload` are also provided by `functions -u` or `functions -U`, but `autoload` is a more comprehensive interface.

bg [*job* ...]
job ... &   Put each specified *job* in the background, or the current job if none is specified.

bindkey   See Section 18.3 [Zle Builtins], page 185.

break [*n*]

> Exit from an enclosing **for**, **while**, **until**, **select** or **repeat** loop. If an arithmetic expression *n* is specified, then break *n* levels instead of just one.

builtin *name* [*args* ...]

> Executes the builtin *name*, with the given *args*.

bye   Same as **exit**.

cap   See Section 22.3 [The zsh/cap Module], page 332.

cd [-qsLP] [*arg*]
cd [-qsLP] *old new*
cd [-qsLP] {+|-}*n*

> Change the current directory. In the first form, change the current directory to *arg*, or to the value of **$HOME** if *arg* is not specified. If *arg* is '-', change to the previous directory.
>
> Otherwise, if *arg* begins with a slash, attempt to change to the directory given by *arg*.
>
> If *arg* does not begin with a slash, the behaviour depends on whether the current directory '.' occurs in the list of directories contained in the shell parameter **cdpath**. If it does not, first attempt to change to the directory *arg* under the current directory, and if that fails but **cdpath** is set and contains at least one element attempt to change to the directory *arg* under each component of **cdpath** in turn until successful. If '.' occurs in **cdpath**, then **cdpath** is searched strictly in order so that '.' is only tried at the appropriate point.
>
> The order of testing **cdpath** is modified if the option **POSIX_CD** is set, as described in the documentation for the option.
>
> If no directory is found, the option **CDABLE_VARS** is set, and a parameter named *arg* exists whose value begins with a slash, treat its value as the directory. In that case, the parameter is added to the named directory hash table.
>
> The second form of **cd** substitutes the string *new* for the string *old* in the name of the current directory, and tries to change to this new directory.
>
> The third form of **cd** extracts an entry from the directory stack, and changes to that directory. An argument of the form '+*n*' identifies a stack entry by counting from the left of the list shown by the **dirs** command, starting with zero. An argument of the form '-*n*' counts from the right. If the **PUSHD_MINUS** option is set, the meanings of '+' and '-' in this context are swapped.
>
> If the -q (quiet) option is specified, the hook function **chpwd** and the functions in the array **chpwd_functions** are not called. This is useful for calls to **cd** that do not change the environment seen by an interactive user.
>
> If the -s option is specified, **cd** refuses to change the current directory if the given pathname contains symlinks. If the -P option is given or the **CHASE_LINKS** option is set, symbolic links are resolved to their true values. If the -L option is given symbolic links are retained in the directory (and not resolved) regardless of the state of the **CHASE_LINKS** option.

chdir   Same as **cd**.

clone　　See Section 22.4 [The zsh/clone Module], page 332.

command [-pvV] *simple command*

　　　　　The simple command argument is taken as an external command instead of a function or builtin and is executed. If the POSIX_BUILTINS option is set, builtins will also be executed but certain special properties of them are suppressed. The -p flag causes a default path to be searched instead of that in $path. With the -v flag, command is similar to whence and with -V, it is equivalent to whence -v.

　　　　　See also Section 6.2 [Precommand Modifiers], page 11.

comparguments

　　　　　See Section 22.8 [The zsh/computil Module], page 339.

compcall　See Section 22.5 [The zsh/compctl Module], page 333.

compctl　　See Section 22.5 [The zsh/compctl Module], page 333.

compdescribe

　　　　　See Section 22.8 [The zsh/computil Module], page 339.

compfiles

　　　　　See Section 22.8 [The zsh/computil Module], page 339.

compgroups

　　　　　See Section 22.8 [The zsh/computil Module], page 339.

compquote

　　　　　See Section 22.8 [The zsh/computil Module], page 339.

comptags　See Section 22.8 [The zsh/computil Module], page 339.

comptry　　See Section 22.8 [The zsh/computil Module], page 339.

compvalues

　　　　　See Section 22.8 [The zsh/computil Module], page 339.

continue [*n*]

　　　　　Resume the next iteration of the enclosing for, while, until, select or repeat loop. If an arithmetic expression *n* is specified, break out of *n*-1 loops and resume at the *n*th enclosing loop.

declare　　Same as typeset.

dirs [-c] [*arg* ...]
dirs [-lpv]

　　　　　With no arguments, print the contents of the directory stack. Directories are added to this stack with the pushd command, and removed with the cd or popd commands. If arguments are specified, load them onto the directory stack, replacing anything that was there, and push the current directory onto the stack.

　　　　　-c　　　　clear the directory stack.

　　　　　-l　　　　print directory names in full instead of using of using ~ expressions (Section 14.7 [Filename Expansion], page 69).

<dl>
<dt>-p</dt>
<dd>print directory entries one per line.</dd>
<dt>-v</dt>
<dd>number the directories in the stack when printing.</dd>
</dl>

disable [-afmprs] *name* ...

Temporarily disable the *named* hash table elements or patterns. The default is to disable builtin commands. This allows you to use an external command with the same name as a builtin command. The -a option causes **disable** to act on regular or global aliases. The -s option causes **disable** to act on suffix aliases. The -f option causes **disable** to act on shell functions. The -r options causes **disable** to act on reserved words. Without arguments all disabled hash table elements from the corresponding hash table are printed. With the -m flag the arguments are taken as patterns (which should be quoted to prevent them from undergoing filename expansion), and all hash table elements from the corresponding hash table matching these patterns are disabled. Disabled objects can be enabled with the **enable** command.

With the option -p, *name* ... refer to elements of the shell's pattern syntax as described in Section 14.8 [Filename Generation], page 72. Certain elements can be disabled separately, as given below.

Note that patterns not allowed by the current settings for the options **EXTENDED_GLOB**, **KSH_GLOB** and **SH_GLOB** are never enabled, regardless of the setting here. For example, if **EXTENDED_GLOB** is not active, the pattern ^ is ineffective even if 'disable -p "^"' has not been issued. The list below indicates any option settings that restrict the use of the pattern. It should be noted that setting **SH_GLOB** has a wider effect than merely disabling patterns as certain expressions, in particular those involving parentheses, are parsed differently.

The following patterns may be disabled; all the strings need quoting on the command line to prevent them from being interpreted immediately as patterns and the patterns are shown below in single quotes as a reminder.

<dl>
<dt>'?'</dt>
<dd>The pattern character ? wherever it occurs, including when preceding a parenthesis with **KSH_GLOB**.</dd>
<dt>'*'</dt>
<dd>The pattern character * wherever it occurs, including recursive globbing and when preceding a parenthesis with **KSH_GLOB**.</dd>
<dt>'['</dt>
<dd>Character classes.</dd>
<dt>'<' (NO_SH_GLOB)</dt>
<dd>Numeric ranges.</dd>
<dt>'|' (NO_SH_GLOB)</dt>
<dd>Alternation in grouped patterns, case statements, or KSH_GLOB parenthesised expressions.</dd>
<dt>'(' (NO_SH_GLOB)</dt>
<dd>Grouping using single parentheses. Disabling this does not disable the use of parentheses for **KSH_GLOB** where they are introduced by a special character, nor for glob qualifiers (use '**setopt**</dd>
</dl>

NO_BARE_GLOB_QUAL' to disable glob qualifiers that use parentheses only).

'~' (EXTENDED_GLOB)
:   Exclusion in the form A~B.

'^' (EXTENDED_GLOB)
:   Exclusion in the form A^B.

'#' (EXTENDED_GLOB)
:   The pattern character # wherever it occurs, both for repetition of a previous pattern and for indicating globbing flags.

'?(' (KSH_GLOB)
:   The grouping form ?(...). Note this is also disabled if '?' is disabled.

'*(' (KSH_GLOB)
:   The grouping form *(...). Note this is also disabled if '*' is disabled.

'+(' (KSH_GLOB)
:   The grouping form +(...).

'!(' (KSH_GLOB)
:   The grouping form !(...).

'@(' (KSH_GLOB)
:   The grouping form @(...).

disown [*job* ...]
job ... &|
job ... &!
:   Remove the specified *job*s from the job table; the shell will no longer report their status, and will not complain if you try to exit an interactive shell with them running or stopped. If no *job* is specified, disown the current job.

    If the *job*s are currently stopped and the AUTO_CONTINUE option is not set, a warning is printed containing information about how to make them running after they have been disowned. If one of the latter two forms is used, the *job*s will automatically be made running, independent of the setting of the AUTO_CONTINUE option.

echo [-neE] [*arg* ...]
:   Write each *arg* on the standard output, with a space separating each one. If the -n flag is not present, print a newline at the end. **echo** recognizes the following escape sequences:

\a	bell character
\b	backspace
\c	suppress subsequent characters and final newline
\e	escape
\f	form feed

\n	linefeed (newline)
\r	carriage return
\t	horizontal tab
\v	vertical tab
\\	backslash
\o*NNN*	character code in octal
\x*NN*	character code in hexadecimal
\u*NNNN*	unicode character code in hexadecimal

\U*NNNNNNNN*
       unicode character code in hexadecimal

The -E flag, or the BSD_ECHO option, can be used to disable these escape sequences. In the latter case, -e flag can be used to enable them.

Note that for standards compliance a double dash does not terminate option processing; instead, it is printed directly. However, a single dash does terminate option processing, so the first dash, possibly following options, is not printed, but everything following it is printed as an argument. The single dash behaviour is different from other shells. For a more portable way of printing text, see **printf**, and for a more controllable way of printing text within zsh, see **print**.

echotc   See Section 22.29 [The zsh/termcap Module], page 370.

echoti   See Section 22.30 [The zsh/terminfo Module], page 370.

emulate [-lLR] [{zsh|sh|ksh|csh} [*flags* ...]]

Without any argument print current emulation mode.

With single argument set up zsh options to emulate the specified shell as much as possible. *csh* will never be fully emulated. If the argument is not one of the shells listed above, **zsh** will be used as a default; more precisely, the tests performed on the argument are the same as those used to determine the emulation at startup based on the shell name, see Section 4.2 [Compatibility], page 7, . In addition to setting shell options, the command also restores the pristine state of pattern enables, as if all patterns had been enabled using **enable -p**.

If the **emulate** command occurs inside a function that has been marked for execution tracing with **functions -t** then the **xtrace** option will be turned on regardless of emulation mode or other options. Note that code executed inside the function by the ., **source**, or **eval** commands is not considered to be running directly from the function, hence does not provoke this behaviour.

If the -R switch is given, all settable options are reset to their default value corresponding to the specified emulation mode, except for certain options describing the interactive environment; otherwise, only those options likely to cause portability problems in scripts and functions are altered. If the -L switch is given, the options LOCAL_OPTIONS, LOCAL_PATTERNS and LOCAL_TRAPS will be set as well, causing the effects of the **emulate** command and any **setopt**, disable -p or enable -p, and trap commands to be local to the immediately surrounding shell function, if any; normally these options are turned off in all emulation modes except ksh. The -L switch is mutually exclusive with the use of -c in *flags*.

If there is a single argument and the -l switch is given, the options that would be set or unset (the latter indicated with the prefix 'no') are listed. -l can be combined with -L or -R and the list will be modified in the appropriate way. Note the list does not depend on the current setting of options, i.e. it includes all options that may in principle change, not just those that would actually change.

The *flags* may be any of the invocation-time flags described in Chapter 4 [Invocation], page 6, except that '-o EMACS' and '-o VI' may not be used. Flags such as '+r'/'+o RESTRICTED' may be prohibited in some circumstances.

If -c *arg* appears in *flags*, *arg* is evaluated while the requested emulation is temporarily in effect. In this case the emulation mode and all options are restored to their previous values before emulate returns. The -R switch may precede the name of the shell to emulate; note this has a meaning distinct from including -R in *flags*.

Use of -c enables 'sticky' emulation mode for functions defined within the evaluated expression: the emulation mode is associated thereafter with the function so that whenever the function is executed the emulation (respecting the -R switch, if present) and all options are set (and pattern disables cleared) before entry to the function, and the state is restored after exit. If the function is called when the sticky emulation is already in effect, either within an 'emulate *shell* -c' expression or within another function with the same sticky emulation, entry and exit from the function do not cause options to be altered (except due to standard processing such as the LOCAL_OPTIONS option). This also applies to functions marked for autoload within the sticky emulation; the appropriate set of options will be applied at the point the function is loaded as well as when it is run.

For example:

```
emulate sh -c 'fni() { setopt cshnullglob; }
fno() { fni; }'
fno
```

The two functions fni and fno are defined with sticky sh emulation. fno is then executed, causing options associated with emulations to be set to their values in sh. fno then calls fni; because fni is also marked for sticky sh emulation, no option changes take place on entry to or exit from it. Hence the option cshnullglob, turned off by sh emulation, will be turned on within fni and remain on return to fno. On exit from fno, the emulation mode and all options will be restored to the state they were in before entry to the temporary emulation.

The documentation above is typically sufficient for the intended purpose of executing code designed for other shells in a suitable environment. More detailed rules follow.

· 1.   The sticky emulation environment provided by 'emulate *shell* -c' is identical to that provided by entry to a function marked for sticky emulation as a consequence of being defined in such an environment. Hence, for example, the sticky emulation is inherited by subfunctions defined within functions with sticky emulation.

2.   No change of options takes place on entry to or exit from functions that are not marked for sticky emulation, other than those that would normally take place, even if those functions are called within sticky emulation.

3.   No special handling is provided for functions marked for `autoload` nor for functions present in wordcode created by the `zcompile` command.

4.   The presence or absence of the -R switch to `emulate` corresponds to different sticky emulation modes, so for example 'emulate sh -c', 'emulate -R sh -c' and 'emulate csh -c' are treated as three distinct sticky emulations.

5.   Difference in shell options supplied in addition to the basic emulation also mean the sticky emulations are different, so for example 'emulate zsh -c' and 'emulate zsh -o cbases -c' are treated as distinct sticky emulations.

enable [-afmprs] *name* ...

Enable the *named* hash table elements, presumably disabled earlier with `disable`. The default is to enable builtin commands. The -a option causes `enable` to act on regular or global aliases. The -s option causes `enable` to act on suffix aliases. The -f option causes `enable` to act on shell functions. The -r option causes `enable` to act on reserved words. Without arguments all enabled hash table elements from the corresponding hash table are printed. With the -m flag the arguments are taken as patterns (should be quoted) and all hash table elements from the corresponding hash table matching these patterns are enabled. Enabled objects can be disabled with the `disable` builtin command.

`enable -p` reenables patterns disabled with `disable -p`. Note that it does not override globbing options; for example, 'enable -p "~"' does not cause the pattern character ~ to be active unless the EXTENDED_GLOB option is also set. To enable all possible patterns (so that they may be individually disabled with `disable -p`), use 'setopt EXTENDED_GLOB KSH_GLOB NO_SH_GLOB'.

eval [*arg* ...]

Read the arguments as input to the shell and execute the resulting command(s) in the current shell process. The return status is the same as if the commands had been executed directly by the shell; if there are no *args* or they contain no commands (i.e. are an empty string or whitespace) the return status is zero.

exec [-cl] [-a *argv0*] [*command* [*arg* ...]]

> Replace the current shell with *command* rather than forking. If *command* is a shell builtin command or a shell function, the shell executes it, and exits when the command is complete.
>
> With -c clear the environment; with -l prepend - to the argv[0] string of the command executed (to simulate a login shell); with -a *argv0* set the argv[0] string of the command executed. See Section 6.2 [Precommand Modifiers], page 11.
>
> If the option POSIX_BUILTINS is set, *command* is never interpreted as a shell builtin command or shell function. This means further precommand modifiers such as builtin and noglob are also not interpreted within the shell. Hence *command* is always found by searching the command path.
>
> If *command* is omitted but any redirections are specified, then the redirections will take effect in the current shell.

exit [*n*] Exit the shell with the exit status specified by an arithmetic expression *n*; if none is specified, use the exit status from the last command executed. An EOF condition will also cause the shell to exit, unless the IGNORE_EOF option is set.

> See notes at the end of Chapter 10 [Jobs & Signals], page 30, for some possibly unexpected interactions of the exit command with jobs.

export [*name*[=*value*] ...]

> The specified *names* are marked for automatic export to the environment of subsequently executed commands. Equivalent to typeset -gx. If a parameter specified does not already exist, it is created in the global scope.

false [*arg* ...]

> Do nothing and return an exit status of 1.

fc [-e *ename*] [-LI] [-m *match*] [*old*=*new* ...] [*first* [*last*]]
fc -l [-LI] [-nrdfEiD] [-t *timefmt*] [-m *match*]
    [*old*=*new* ...] [*first* [*last*]]
fc -p [-a] [*filename* [*histsize* [*savehistsize*]]]
fc -P
fc -ARWI [*filename*]

> The fc command controls the interactive history mechanism. Note that reading and writing of history options is only performed if the shell is interactive. Usually this is detected automatically, but it can be forced by setting the interactive option when starting the shell.
>
> The first two forms of this command select a range of events from *first* to *last* from the history list. The arguments *first* and *last* may be specified as a number or as a string. A negative number is used as an offset to the current history event number. A string specifies the most recent event beginning with the given string. All substitutions *old*=*new*, if any, are then performed on the text of the events.
>
> In addition to the number range,
>
> -I   restricts to only internal events (not from $HISTFILE)

-L	restricts to only local events (not from other shells, see **SHARE_HISTORY** in Section 16.2 [Description of Options], page 110, – note that $HISTFILE is considered local when read at startup)
-m	takes the first argument as a pattern (should be quoted) and only the history events matching this pattern are considered

If *first* is not specified, it will be set to -1 (the most recent event), or to -16 if the -1 flag is given. If *last* is not specified, it will be set to *first*, or to -1 if the -1 flag is given. However, if the current event has added entries to the history with 'print -s' or 'fc -R', then the default *last* for -1 includes all new history entries since the current event began.

When the -1 flag is given, the resulting events are listed on standard output. Otherwise the editor program *ename* is invoked on a file containing these history events. If *ename* is not given, the value of the parameter **FCEDIT** is used; if that is not set the value of the parameter **EDITOR** is used; if that is not set a builtin default, usually 'vi' is used. If *ename* is '-', no editor is invoked. When editing is complete, the edited command is executed.

The flag -r reverses the order of the events and the flag -n suppresses event numbers when listing.

Also when listing,

-d	prints timestamps for each event
-f	prints full time-date stamps in the US '*MM/DD/YY hh:mm*' format
-E	prints full time-date stamps in the European '*dd.mm.yyyy hh:mm*' format
-i	prints full time-date stamps in ISO8601 '*yyyy-mm-dd hh:mm*' format
-t *fmt*	prints time and date stamps in the given format; *fmt* is formatted with the strftime function with the zsh extensions described for the %D{*string*} prompt format in Chapter 13 [Prompt Expansion], page 39. The resulting formatted string must be no more than 256 characters or will not be printed
-D	prints elapsed times; may be combined with one of the options above

'fc -p' pushes the current history list onto a stack and switches to a new history list. If the -a option is also specified, this history list will be automatically popped when the current function scope is exited, which is a much better solution than creating a trap function to call 'fc -P' manually. If no arguments are specified, the history list is left empty, $HISTFILE is unset, and $HISTSIZE & $SAVEHIST are set to their default values. If one argument is given, $HISTFILE is set to that filename, $HISTSIZE & $SAVEHIST are left unchanged, and the history file is read in (if it exists) to initialize the new list. If a second argument is specified, $HISTSIZE & $SAVEHIST are instead set to the single specified numeric value. Finally, if a third argument is specified, $SAVEHIST is set to a separate value from $HISTSIZE. You are free to change these environment values for the new history list however you desire in order to manipulate the new history list.

'fc -P' pops the history list back to an older list saved by 'fc -p'. The current list is saved to its $HISTFILE before it is destroyed (assuming that $HISTFILE and $SAVEHIST are set appropriately, of course). The values of $HISTFILE, $HISTSIZE, and $SAVEHIST are restored to the values they had when 'fc -p' was called. Note that this restoration can conflict with making these variables "local", so your best bet is to avoid local declarations for these variables in functions that use 'fc -p'. The one other guaranteed-safe combination is declaring these variables to be local at the top of your function and using the automatic option (-a) with 'fc -p'. Finally, note that it is legal to manually pop a push marked for automatic popping if you need to do so before the function exits.

'fc -R' reads the history from the given file, 'fc -W' writes the history out to the given file, and 'fc -A' appends the history out to the given file. If no filename is specified, the $HISTFILE is assumed. If the -I option is added to -R, only those events that are not already contained within the internal history list are added. If the -I option is added to -A or -W, only those events that are new since last incremental append/write to the history file are appended/written. In any case, the created file will have no more than $SAVEHIST entries.

fg [*job* ...]

job ...   Bring each specified *job* in turn to the foreground. If no *job* is specified, resume the current job.

float [{+|-}Hghlprtux] [{+|-}EFLRZ [*n*]] [*name*[=*value*] ...]

Equivalent to typeset -E, except that options irrelevant to floating point numbers are not permitted.

functions [{+|-}UkmtTuWz] [-x *num*] [*name* ...]
functions -M [-s] *mathfn* [*min* [*max* [*shellfn*]]]
functions -M [-m *pattern* ...]
functions +M [-m] *mathfn* ...

Equivalent to typeset -f, with the exception of the -x, -M and -W options. For functions -u and functions -U, see autoload, which provides additional options.

The -x option indicates that any functions output will have each leading tab for indentation, added by the shell to show syntactic structure, expanded to the given number *num* of spaces. *num* can also be 0 to suppress all indentation.

The -W option turns on the option WARN_NESTED_VAR for the named function or functions only. The option is turned off at the start of nested functions (apart from anonoymous functions) unless the called function also has the -W attribute.

Use of the -M option may not be combined with any of the options handled by typeset -f.

functions -M *mathfn* defines *mathfn* as the name of a mathematical function recognised in all forms of arithmetical expressions; see Chapter 11 [Arithmetic

Evaluation], page 31. By default *mathfn* may take any number of comma-separated arguments. If *min* is given, it must have exactly *min* args; if *min* and *max* are both given, it must have at least *min* and at most *max* args. *max* may be -1 to indicate that there is no upper limit.

By default the function is implemented by a shell function of the same name; if *shellfn* is specified it gives the name of the corresponding shell function while *mathfn* remains the name used in arithmetical expressions. The name of the function in $0 is *mathfn* (not *shellfn* as would usually be the case), provided the option FUNCTION_ARGZERO is in effect. The positional parameters in the shell function correspond to the arguments of the mathematical function call. The result of the last arithmetical expression evaluated inside the shell function (even if it is a form that normally only returns a status) gives the result of the mathematical function.

If the additional option -s is given to functions -M, the argument to the function is a single string: anything between the opening and matching closing parenthesis is passed to the function as a single argument, even if it includes commas or white space. The minimum and maximum argument specifiers must therefore be 1 if given. An empty argument list is passed as a zero-length string.

functions -M with no arguments lists all such user-defined functions in the same form as a definition. With the additional option -m and a list of arguments, all functions whose *mathfn* matches one of the pattern arguments are listed.

function +M removes the list of mathematical functions; with the additional option -m the arguments are treated as patterns and all functions whose *mathfn* matches the pattern are removed. Note that the shell function implementing the behaviour is not removed (regardless of whether its name coincides with *mathfn*).

For example, the following prints the cube of 3:

```
zmath_cube() { (( $1 * $1 * $1 )) }
functions -M cube 1 1 zmath_cube
print $(( cube(3) ))
```

The following string function takes a single argument, including the commas, so prints 11:

```
stringfn() { (( $#1 )) }
functions -Ms stringfn
print $(( stringfn(foo,bar,rod) ))
```

getcap   See Section 22.3 [The zsh/cap Module], page 332.

getln [-AclneE] *name* ...
         Read the top value from the buffer stack and put it in the shell parameter *name*. Equivalent to **read -zr**.

getopts *optstring name* [*arg* ...]
         Checks the *args* for legal options. If the *args* are omitted, use the positional parameters. A valid option argument begins with a '+' or a '−'. An argument not beginning with a '+' or a '−', or the argument '−−', ends the options. Note that a single '−' is not considered a valid option argument. *optstring* contains

the letters that `getopts` recognizes. If a letter is followed by a ':', that option requires an argument. The options can be separated from the argument by blanks.

Each time it is invoked, `getopts` places the option letter it finds in the shell parameter *name*, prepended with a '+' when *arg* begins with a '+'. The index of the next *arg* is stored in `OPTIND`. The option argument, if any, is stored in `OPTARG`.

The first option to be examined may be changed by explicitly assigning to `OPTIND`. `OPTIND` has an initial value of `1`, and is normally set to `1` upon entry to a shell function and restored upon exit (this is disabled by the `POSIX_BUILTINS` option). `OPTARG` is not reset and retains its value from the most recent call to `getopts`. If either of `OPTIND` or `OPTARG` is explicitly unset, it remains unset, and the index or option argument is not stored. The option itself is still stored in *name* in this case.

A leading ':' in *optstring* causes `getopts` to store the letter of any invalid option in `OPTARG`, and to set *name* to '?' for an unknown option and to ':' when a required argument is missing. Otherwise, `getopts` sets *name* to '?' and prints an error message when an option is invalid. The exit status is nonzero when there are no more options.

`hash` [`-Ldfmrv`] [*name*[=*value*]] ...

> `hash` can be used to directly modify the contents of the command hash table, and the named directory hash table. Normally one would modify these tables by modifying one's `PATH` (for the command hash table) or by creating appropriate shell parameters (for the named directory hash table). The choice of hash table to work on is determined by the `-d` option; without the option the command hash table is used, and with the option the named directory hash table is used.
>
> Given no arguments, and neither the `-r` or `-f` options, the selected hash table will be listed in full.
>
> The `-r` option causes the selected hash table to be emptied. It will be subsequently rebuilt in the normal fashion. The `-f` option causes the selected hash table to be fully rebuilt immediately. For the command hash table this hashes all the absolute directories in the `PATH`, and for the named directory hash table this adds all users' home directories. These two options cannot be used with any arguments.
>
> The `-m` option causes the arguments to be taken as patterns (which should be quoted) and the elements of the hash table matching those patterns are printed. This is the only way to display a limited selection of hash table elements.
>
> For each *name* with a corresponding *value*, put '*name*' in the selected hash table, associating it with the pathname '*value*'. In the command hash table, this means that whenever '*name*' is used as a command argument, the shell will try to execute the file given by '*value*'. In the named directory hash table, this means that '*value*' may be referred to as '~*name*'.
>
> For each *name* with no corresponding *value*, attempt to add *name* to the hash table, checking what the appropriate `value` is in the normal manner for that

hash table. If an appropriate `value` can't be found, then the hash table will be unchanged.

The `-v` option causes hash table entries to be listed as they are added by explicit specification. If has no effect if used with `-f`.

If the `-L` flag is present, then each hash table entry is printed in the form of a call to hash.

`history`   Same as `fc -l`.

`integer [ {+|-}Hghlprtux ] [ {+|-}LRZi [ n ] ] [ name[=value] ... ]`
Equivalent to `typeset -i`, except that options irrelevant to integers are not permitted.

`jobs [ -dlprs ] [ job ... ]`
`jobs -Z string`
Lists information about each given job, or all jobs if *job* is omitted. The `-l` flag lists process IDs, and the `-p` flag lists process groups. If the `-r` flag is specified only running jobs will be listed and if the `-s` flag is given only stopped jobs are shown. If the `-d` flag is given, the directory from which the job was started (which may not be the current directory of the job) will also be shown.

The `-Z` option replaces the shell's argument and environment space with the given string, truncated if necessary to fit. This will normally be visible in `ps` (man page ps(1)) listings. This feature is typically used by daemons, to indicate their state.

`kill [ -s signal_name | -n signal_number | -sig ] job ...`
`kill -l [ sig ... ]`
Sends either `SIGTERM` or the specified signal to the given jobs or processes. Signals are given by number or by names, with or without the 'SIG' prefix. If the signal being sent is not 'KILL' or 'CONT', then the job will be sent a 'CONT' signal if it is stopped. The argument *job* can be the process ID of a job not in the job list. In the second form, `kill -l`, if *sig* is not specified the signal names are listed. Otherwise, for each *sig* that is a name, the corresponding signal number is listed. For each *sig* that is a signal number or a number representing the exit status of a process which was terminated or stopped by a signal the name of the signal is printed.

On some systems, alternative signal names are allowed for a few signals. Typical examples are `SIGCHLD` and `SIGCLD` or `SIGPOLL` and `SIGIO`, assuming they correspond to the same signal number. `kill -l` will only list the preferred form, however `kill -l` *alt* will show if the alternative form corresponds to a signal number. For example, under Linux `kill -l IO` and `kill -l POLL` both output 29, hence `kill -IO` and `kill -POLL` have the same effect.

Many systems will allow process IDs to be negative to kill a process group or zero to kill the current process group.

`let arg ...` Evaluate each *arg* as an arithmetic expression. See Chapter 11 [Arithmetic Evaluation], page 31, for a description of arithmetic expressions. The exit status is 0 if the value of the last expression is nonzero, 1 if it is zero, and 2 if an error occurred.

limit [-hs] [*resource* [*limit*]] ...

Set or display resource limits. Unless the -s flag is given, the limit applies only the children of the shell. If -s is given without other arguments, the resource limits of the current shell is set to the previously set resource limits of the children.

If *limit* is not specified, print the current limit placed on *resource*, otherwise set the limit to the specified value. If the -h flag is given, use hard limits instead of soft limits. If no *resource* is given, print all limits.

When looping over multiple resources, the shell will abort immediately if it detects a badly formed argument. However, if it fails to set a limit for some other reason it will continue trying to set the remaining limits.

resource can be one of:

addressspace

Maximum amount of address space used.

aiomemorylocked

Maximum amount of memory locked in RAM for AIO operations.

aiooperations

Maximum number of AIO operations.

cachedthreads

Maximum number of cached threads.

coredumpsize

Maximum size of a core dump.

cputime   Maximum CPU seconds per process.

datasize   Maximum data size (including stack) for each process.

descriptors

Maximum value for a file descriptor.

filesize   Largest single file allowed.

kqueues   Maximum number of kqueues allocated.

maxproc   Maximum number of processes.

maxpthreads

Maximum number of threads per process.

memorylocked

Maximum amount of memory locked in RAM.

memoryuse

Maximum resident set size.

msgqueue   Maximum number of bytes in POSIX message queues.

posixlocks

Maximum number of POSIX locks per user.

pseudoterminals
> Maximum number of pseudo-terminals.

resident   Maximum resident set size.

sigpending
> Maximum number of pending signals.

sockbufsize
> Maximum size of all socket buffers.

stacksize
> Maximum stack size for each process.

swapsize   Maximum amount of swap used.

vmemorysize
> Maximum amount of virtual memory.

Which of these resource limits are available depends on the system. *resource* can be abbreviated to any unambiguous prefix. It can also be an integer, which corresponds to the integer defined for the resource by the operating system.

If argument corresponds to a number which is out of the range of the resources configured into the shell, the shell will try to read or write the limit anyway, and will report an error if this fails. As the shell does not store such resources internally, an attempt to set the limit will fail unless the **-s** option is present.

limit is a number, with an optional scaling factor, as follows:

*n*h	hours
*n*k	kilobytes (default)
*n*m	megabytes or minutes
*n*g	gigabytes
[*mm*:]*ss*	minutes and seconds

The **limit** command is not made available by default when the shell starts in a mode emulating another shell. It can be made available with the command '**zmodload -F zsh/rlimits b:limit**'.

local [{+|-}AHUahlprtux] [{+|-}EFLRZi [*n*]] [*name*[=*value*] ...]
> Same as **typeset**, except that the options **-g**, and **-f** are not permitted. In this case the **-x** option does not force the use of **-g**, i.e. exported variables will be local to functions.

log   List all users currently logged in who are affected by the current setting of the **watch** parameter.

logout [*n*]
> Same as **exit**, except that it only works in a login shell.

noglob *simple command*
> See Section 6.2 [Precommand Modifiers], page 11.

popd [-q] [{+|-}n]

> Remove an entry from the directory stack, and perform a cd to the new top directory. With no argument, the current top entry is removed. An argument of the form '+n' identifies a stack entry by counting from the left of the list shown by the **dirs** command, starting with zero. An argument of the form −n counts from the right. If the PUSHD_MINUS option is set, the meanings of '+' and '−' in this context are swapped.
>
> If the -q (quiet) option is specified, the hook function **chpwd** and the functions in the array $chpwd_functions are not called, and the new directory stack is not printed. This is useful for calls to **popd** that do not change the environment seen by an interactive user.

print [-abcDilmnNoOpPrsSz] [-u n] [-f format] [-C cols]
  [-v name] [-xX tabstop] [-R [-en]] [arg ...]

> With the '-f' option the arguments are printed as described by **printf**. With no flags or with the flag '−', the arguments are printed on the standard output as described by **echo**, with the following differences: the escape sequence '\M-x' (or '\Mx') metafies the character x (sets the highest bit), '\C-x' (or '\Cx') produces a control character ('\C-@' and '\C-?' give the characters NULL and delete), a character code in octal is represented by '\NNN' (instead of '\0NNN'), and '\E' is a synonym for '\e'. Finally, if not in an escape sequence, '\' escapes the following character and is not printed.

-a	Print arguments with the column incrementing first. Only useful with the -c and -C options.
-b	Recognize all the escape sequences defined for the **bindkey** command, see Section 18.3 [Zle Builtins], page 185.
-c	Print the arguments in columns. Unless -a is also given, arguments are printed with the row incrementing first.
-C cols	Print the arguments in *cols* columns. Unless -a is also given, arguments are printed with the row incrementing first.
-D	Treat the arguments as paths, replacing directory prefixes with ~ expressions corresponding to directory names, as appropriate.
-i	If given together with -o or -O, sorting is performed case-independently.
-l	Print the arguments separated by newlines instead of spaces.
-m	Take the first argument as a pattern (should be quoted), and remove it from the argument list together with subsequent arguments that do not match this pattern.
-n	Do not add a newline to the output.
-N	Print the arguments separated and terminated by nulls.
-o	Print the arguments sorted in ascending order.
-O	Print the arguments sorted in descending order.

-p   Print the arguments to the input of the coprocess.

-P   Perform prompt expansion (see Chapter 13 [Prompt Expansion], page 39). In combination with '-f', prompt escape sequences are parsed only within interpolated arguments, not within the format string.

-r   Ignore the escape conventions of echo.

-R   Emulate the BSD echo command, which does not process escape sequences unless the -e flag is given. The -n flag suppresses the trailing newline. Only the -e and -n flags are recognized after -R; all other arguments and options are printed.

-s   Place the results in the history list instead of on the standard output. Each argument to the print command is treated as a single word in the history, regardless of its content.

-S   Place the results in the history list instead of on the standard output. In this case only a single argument is allowed; it will be split into words as if it were a full shell command line. The effect is similar to reading the line from a history file with the HIST_LEX_WORDS option active.

-u *n*   Print the arguments to file descriptor *n*.

-v *name* Store the printed arguments as the value of the parameter *name*.

-x *tab-stop*

   Expand leading tabs on each line of output in the printed string assuming a tab stop every *tab-stop* characters. This is appropriate for formatting code that may be indented with tabs. Note that leading tabs of any argument to print, not just the first, are expanded, even if print is using spaces to separate arguments (the column count is maintained across arguments but may be incorrect on output owing to previous unexpanded tabs).

   The start of the output of each print command is assumed to be aligned with a tab stop. Widths of multibyte characters are handled if the option MULTIBYTE is in effect. This option is ignored if other formatting options are in effect, namely column alignment or printf style, or if output is to a special location such as shell history or the command line editor.

-X *tab-stop*

   This is similar to -x, except that all tabs in the printed string are expanded. This is appropriate if tabs in the arguments are being used to produce a table format.

-z   Push the arguments onto the editing buffer stack, separated by spaces.

If any of '-m', '-o' or '-O' are used in combination with '-f' and there are no arguments (after the removal process in the case of '-m') then nothing is printed.

`printf` [`-v` *name*] *format* [*arg* ...]

Print the arguments according to the format specification. Formatting rules are the same as used in C. The same escape sequences as for `echo` are recognised in the format. All C conversion specifications ending in one of `csdiouxXeEfgGn` are handled. In addition to this, '%b' can be used instead of '%s' to cause escape sequences in the argument to be recognised and '%q' can be used to quote the argument in such a way that allows it to be reused as shell input. With the numeric format specifiers, if the corresponding argument starts with a quote character, the numeric value of the following character is used as the number to print; otherwise the argument is evaluated as an arithmetic expression. See Chapter 11 [Arithmetic Evaluation], page 31, for a description of arithmetic expressions. With '%n', the corresponding argument is taken as an identifier which is created as an integer parameter.

Normally, conversion specifications are applied to each argument in order but they can explicitly specify the *n*th argument is to be used by replacing '%' by '%*n*$' and '*' by '**n*$'. It is recommended that you do not mix references of this explicit style with the normal style and the handling of such mixed styles may be subject to future change.

If arguments remain unused after formatting, the format string is reused until all arguments have been consumed. With the `print` builtin, this can be suppressed by using the `-r` option. If more arguments are required by the format than have been specified, the behaviour is as if zero or an empty string had been specified as the argument.

The `-v` option causes the output to be stored as the value of the parameter *name*, instead of printed. If *name* is an array and the format string is reused when consuming arguments then one array element will be used for each use of the format string.

`pushd` [`-qsLP`] [*arg*]
`pushd` [`-qsLP`] *old new*
`pushd` [`-qsLP`] {+|-}*n*

Change the current directory, and push the old current directory onto the directory stack. In the first form, change the current directory to *arg*. If *arg* is not specified, change to the second directory on the stack (that is, exchange the top two entries), or change to `$HOME` if the `PUSHD_TO_HOME` option is set or if there is only one entry on the stack. Otherwise, *arg* is interpreted as it would be by `cd`. The meaning of *old* and *new* in the second form is also the same as for `cd`.

The third form of `pushd` changes directory by rotating the directory list. An argument of the form '+*n*' identifies a stack entry by counting from the left of the list shown by the `dirs` command, starting with zero. An argument of the form '-*n*' counts from the right. If the `PUSHD_MINUS` option is set, the meanings of '+' and '-' in this context are swapped.

If the `-q` (quiet) option is specified, the hook function `chpwd` and the functions in the array `$chpwd_functions` are not called, and the new directory stack is not printed. This is useful for calls to **pushd** that do not change the environment seen by an interactive user.

If the option **-q** is not specified and the shell option **PUSHD_SILENT** is not set, the directory stack will be printed after a **pushd** is performed.

The options **-s**, **-L** and **-P** have the same meanings as for the **cd** builtin.

pushln [*arg ...*]

Equivalent to **print -nz**.

pwd [**-rLP**]

Print the absolute pathname of the current working directory. If the **-r** or the **-P** flag is specified, or the **CHASE_LINKS** option is set and the **-L** flag is not given, the printed path will not contain symbolic links.

r   Same as **fc -e -**.

read [**-rszpqAclneE**] [**-t** [*num*]] [**-k** [*num*]] [**-d** *delim*]
      [**-u** *n*] [*name*[?*prompt*]] [*name ...*]

Read one line and break it into fields using the characters in **$IFS** as separators, except as noted below. The first field is assigned to the first *name*, the second field to the second *name*, etc., with leftover fields assigned to the last *name*. If *name* is omitted then **REPLY** is used for scalars and **reply** for arrays.

-r   Raw mode: a '\' at the end of a line does not signify line continuation and backslashes in the line don't quote the following character and are not removed.

-s   Don't echo back characters if reading from the terminal.

-q   Read only one character from the terminal and set *name* to 'y' if this character was 'y' or 'Y' and to 'n' otherwise. With this flag set the return status is zero only if the character was 'y' or 'Y'. This option may be used with a timeout (see **-t**); if the read times out, or encounters end of file, status 2 is returned. Input is read from the terminal unless one of **-u** or **-p** is present. This option may also be used within zle widgets.

-k [*num*] Read only one (or *num*) characters. All are assigned to the first *name*, without word splitting. This flag is ignored when **-q** is present. Input is read from the terminal unless one of **-u** or **-p** is present. This option may also be used within zle widgets.

Note that despite the mnemonic 'key' this option does read full characters, which may consist of multiple bytes if the option **MULTIBYTE** is set.

-z   Read one entry from the editor buffer stack and assign it to the first *name*, without word splitting. Text is pushed onto the stack with 'print -z' or with **push-line** from the line editor (see Chapter 18 [Zsh Line Editor], page 183). This flag is ignored when the **-k** or **-q** flags are present.

-e
-E   The input read is printed (echoed) to the standard output. If the
            -e flag is used, no input is assigned to the parameters.

-A   The first *name* is taken as the name of an array and all words are
            assigned to it.

-c
-l   These flags are allowed only if called inside a function used for
            completion (specified with the -K flag to `compctl`). If the -c flag
            is given, the words of the current command are read. If the -l flag
            is given, the whole line is assigned as a scalar. If both flags are
            present, -l is used and -c is ignored.

-n   Together with -c, the number of the word the cursor is on is read.
            With -l, the index of the character the cursor is on is read. Note
            that the command name is word number 1, not word 0, and that
            when the cursor is at the end of the line, its character index is the
            length of the line plus one.

-u *n*   Input is read from file descriptor *n*.

-p   Input is read from the coprocess.

-d *delim* Input is terminated by the first character of *delim* instead of by
            newline.

-t [*num*] Test if input is available before attempting to read. If *num* is
            present, it must begin with a digit and will be evaluated to give a
            number of seconds, which may be a floating point number; in this
            case the read times out if input is not available within this time.
            If *num* is not present, it is taken to be zero, so that **read** returns
            immediately if no input is available. If no input is available, return
            status 1 and do not set any variables.

            This option is not available when reading from the editor buffer
            with -z, when called from within completion with -c or -l, with
            -q which clears the input queue before reading, or within zle where
            other mechanisms should be used to test for input.

            Note that read does not attempt to alter the input processing mode.
            The default mode is canonical input, in which an entire line is read
            at a time, so usually '**read** -t' will not read anything until an entire
            line has been typed. However, when reading from the terminal with
            -k input is processed one key at a time; in this case, only availability
            of the first character is tested, so that e.g. '**read** -t -k 2' can still
            block on the second character. Use two instances of '**read** -t -k'
            if this is not what is wanted.

If the first argument contains a '?', the remainder of this word is used as a
prompt on standard error when the shell is interactive.

The value (exit status) of **read** is 1 when an end-of-file is encountered, or when
-c or -l is present and the command is not called from a `compctl` function, or
as described for -q. Otherwise the value is 0.

The behavior of some combinations of the -k, -p, -q, -u and -z flags is undefined. Presently -q cancels all the others, -p cancels -u, -k cancels -z, and otherwise -z cancels both -p and -u.

The -c or -l flags cancel any and all of -kpquz.

readonly   Same as `typeset -r`. With the `POSIX_BUILTINS` option set, same as `typeset -gr`.

rehash   Same as `hash -r`.

return [*n*]

Causes a shell function or '.' script to return to the invoking script with the return status specified by an arithmetic expression *n*. If *n* is omitted, the return status is that of the last command executed.

If `return` was executed from a trap in a TRAP*NAL* function, the effect is different for zero and non-zero return status. With zero status (or after an implicit return at the end of the trap), the shell will return to whatever it was previously processing; with a non-zero status, the shell will behave as interrupted except that the return status of the trap is retained. Note that the numeric value of the signal which caused the trap is passed as the first argument, so the statement 'return $((128+$1))' will return the same status as if the signal had not been trapped.

sched   See Section 22.24 [The zsh/sched Module], page 360.

set [{+|-}*options* | {+|-}o [*option_name*]] ... [{+|-}A [*name*]]
    [*arg* ...]

Set the options for the shell and/or set the positional parameters, or declare and set an array. If the -s option is given, it causes the specified arguments to be sorted before assigning them to the positional parameters (or to the array *name* if -A is used). With +s sort arguments in descending order. For the meaning of the other flags, see Chapter 16 [Options], page 110. Flags may be specified by name using the -o option. If no option name is supplied with -o, the current option states are printed: see the description of `setopt` below for more information on the format. With +o they are printed in a form that can be used as input to the shell.

If the -A flag is specified, *name* is set to an array containing the given *args*; if no *name* is specified, all arrays are printed together with their values.

If +A is used and *name* is an array, the given arguments will replace the initial elements of that array; if no *name* is specified, all arrays are printed without their values.

The behaviour of arguments after -A *name* or +A *name* depends on whether the option `KSH_ARRAYS` is set. If it is not set, all arguments following *name* are treated as values for the array, regardless of their form. If the option is set, normal option processing continues at that point; only regular arguments are treated as values for the array. This means that

```
set -A array -x -- foo
```

sets `array` to '-x -- foo' if `KSH_ARRAYS` is not set, but sets the array to `foo` and turns on the option '-x' if it is set.

If the −A flag is not present, but there are arguments beyond the options, the positional parameters are set. If the option list (if any) is terminated by '−−', and there are no further arguments, the positional parameters will be unset.

If no arguments and no '−−' are given, then the names and values of all parameters are printed on the standard output. If the only argument is '+', the names of all parameters are printed.

For historical reasons, 'set −' is treated as 'set +xv' and 'set − *args*' as 'set +xv −− *args*' when in any other emulation mode than zsh's native mode.

setcap   See Section 22.3 [The zsh/cap Module], page 332.

setopt [{+|−}*options* | {+|−}o *option_name*] [−m] [*name* ...]

Set the options for the shell. All options specified either with flags or by name are set.

If no arguments are supplied, the names of all options currently set are printed. The form is chosen so as to minimize the differences from the default options for the current emulation (the default emulation being native **zsh**, shown as <Z> in Section 16.2 [Description of Options], page 110). Options that are on by default for the emulation are shown with the prefix **no** only if they are off, while other options are shown without the prefix **no** and only if they are on. In addition to options changed from the default state by the user, any options activated automatically by the shell (for example, SHIN_STDIN or INTERACTIVE) will be shown in the list. The format is further modified by the option KSH_OPTION_PRINT, however the rationale for choosing options with or without the **no** prefix remains the same in this case.

If the −m flag is given the arguments are taken as patterns (which should be quoted to protect them from filename expansion), and all options with names matching these patterns are set.

Note that a bad option name does not cause execution of subsequent shell code to be aborted; this is behaviour is different from that of 'set −o'. This is because **set** is regarded as a special builtin by the POSIX standard, but **setopt** is not.

shift [−p] [*n*] [*name* ...]

The positional parameters ${*n*+1} ... are renamed to $1 ..., where *n* is an arithmetic expression that defaults to 1. If any *names* are given then the arrays with these names are shifted instead of the positional parameters.

If the option −p is given arguments are instead removed (popped) from the end rather than the start of the array.

source *file* [*arg* ...]

Same as '.', except that the current directory is always searched and is always searched first, before directories in $path.

stat   See Section 22.26 [The zsh/stat Module], page 362.

suspend [−f]

Suspend the execution of the shell (send it a SIGTSTP) until it receives a SIGCONT. Unless the −f option is given, this will refuse to suspend a login shell.

test [arg ...]
[[arg ...]]

Like the system version of test. Added for compatibility; use conditional expressions instead (see Chapter 12 [Conditional Expressions], page 36). The main differences between the conditional expression syntax and the test and [builtins are: these commands are not handled syntactically, so for example an empty variable expansion may cause an argument to be omitted; syntax errors cause status 2 to be returned instead of a shell error; and arithmetic operators expect integer arguments rather than arithmetic expressions.

The command attempts to implement POSIX and its extensions where these are specified. Unfortunately there are intrinsic ambiguities in the syntax; in particular there is no distinction between test operators and strings that resemble them. The standard attempts to resolve these for small numbers of arguments (up to four); for five or more arguments compatibility cannot be relied on. Users are urged wherever possible to use the '[[' test syntax which does not have these ambiguities.

times
Print the accumulated user and system times for the shell and for processes run from the shell.

trap [arg] [sig ...]

arg is a series of commands (usually quoted to protect it from immediate evaluation by the shell) to be read and executed when the shell receives any of the signals specified by one or more sig args. Each sig can be given as a number, or as the name of a signal either with or without the string SIG in front (e.g. 1, HUP, and SIGHUP are all the same signal).

If arg is '−', then the specified signals are reset to their defaults, or, if no sig args are present, all traps are reset.

If arg is an empty string, then the specified signals are ignored by the shell (and by the commands it invokes).

If arg is omitted but one or more sig args are provided (i.e. the first argument is a valid signal number or name), the effect is the same as if arg had been specified as '−'.

The trap command with no arguments prints a list of commands associated with each signal.

If sig is ZERR then arg will be executed after each command with a nonzero exit status. ERR is an alias for ZERR on systems that have no SIGERR signal (this is the usual case).

If sig is DEBUG then arg will be executed before each command if the option DEBUG_BEFORE_CMD is set (as it is by default), else after each command. Here, a 'command' is what is described as a 'sublist' in the shell grammar, see Section 6.1 [Simple Commands & Pipelines], page 10. If DEBUG_BEFORE_CMD is set various additional features are available. First, it is possible to skip the next command by setting the option ERR_EXIT; see the description of the ERR_EXIT option in Section 16.2 [Description of Options], page 110. Also, the shell parameter ZSH_DEBUG_CMD is set to the string corresponding to the command to be executed following the trap. Note that this string is reconstructed from the internal format and may not be formatted the same way as the original text. The parameter is unset after the trap is executed.

If *sig* is 0 or `EXIT` and the `trap` statement is executed inside the body of a function, then the command *arg* is executed after the function completes. The value of `$?` at the start of execution is the exit status of the shell or the return status of the function exiting. If *sig* is 0 or `EXIT` and the `trap` statement is not executed inside the body of a function, then the command *arg* is executed when the shell terminates; the trap runs before any `zshexit` hook functions.

`ZERR`, `DEBUG`, and `EXIT` traps are not executed inside other traps. `ZERR` and `DEBUG` traps are kept within subshells, while other traps are reset.

Note that traps defined with the `trap` builtin are slightly different from those defined as 'TRAP*NAL* () { ... }', as the latter have their own function environment (line numbers, local variables, etc.) while the former use the environment of the command in which they were called. For example,

        trap 'print $LINENO' DEBUG

will print the line number of a command executed after it has run, while

        TRAPDEBUG() { print $LINENO; }

will always print the number zero.

Alternative signal names are allowed as described under `kill` above. Defining a trap under either name causes any trap under an alternative name to be removed. However, it is recommended that for consistency users stick exclusively to one name or another.

`true` [*arg* ...]

Do nothing and return an exit status of 0.

`ttyctl` [`-fu`]

The `-f` option freezes the tty (i.e. terminal or terminal emulator), and `-u` unfreezes it. When the tty is frozen, no changes made to the tty settings by external programs will be honored by the shell, except for changes in the size of the screen; the shell will simply reset the settings to their previous values as soon as each command exits or is suspended. Thus, `stty` and similar programs have no effect when the tty is frozen. Freezing the tty does not cause the current state to be remembered: instead, it causes future changes to the state to be blocked.

Without options it reports whether the terminal is frozen or not.

Note that, regardless of whether the tty is frozen or not, the shell needs to change the settings when the line editor starts, so unfreezing the tty does not guarantee settings made on the command line are preserved. Strings of commands run between editing the command line will see a consistent tty state. See also the shell variable `STTY` for a means of initialising the tty before running external commands.

`type` [`-wfpamsS`] *name* ...

Equivalent to `whence -v`.

```
typeset [ {+|-}AHUaghlmrtux ] [ {+|-}EFLRZip [ n ] ]
         [ + ] [ name[=value] ... ]
typeset -T [ {+|-}Uglrux ] [ {+|-}LRZp [ n ] ]
         [ + | SCALAR[=value] array[=(value ...)] [ sep ] ]
typeset -f [ {+|-}TUkmtuz ] [ + ] [ name ... ]
```
Set or display attributes and values for shell parameters.

Except as noted below for control flags that change the behavior, a parameter is created for each *name* that does not already refer to one. When inside a function, a new parameter is created for every *name* (even those that already exist), and is unset again when the function completes. See Section 15.4 [Local Parameters], page 93. The same rules apply to special shell parameters, which retain their special attributes when made local.

For each *name=value* assignment, the parameter *name* is set to *value*.

If the shell option TYPESET_SILENT is not set, for each remaining *name* that refers to a parameter that is already set, the name and value of the parameter are printed in the form of an assignment. Nothing is printed for newly-created parameters, or when any attribute flags listed below are given along with the *name*. Using '+' instead of minus to introduce an attribute turns it off.

If no *name* is present, the names and values of all parameters are printed. In this case the attribute flags restrict the display to only those parameters that have the specified attributes, and using '+' rather than '-' to introduce the flag suppresses printing of the values of parameters when there is no parameter name.

All forms of the command handle scalar assignment. Array assignment is possible if any of the reserved words declare, export, float, integer, local, readonly or typeset is matched when the line is parsed (N.B. not when it is executed). In this case the arguments are parsed as assignments, except that the '+=' syntax and the GLOB_ASSIGN option are not supported, and scalar values after = are *not* split further into words, even if expanded (regardless of the setting of the KSH_TYPESET option; this option is obsolete).

Examples of the differences between command and reserved word parsing:

```
# Reserved word parsing
typeset svar=$(echo one word) avar=(several words)
```

The above creates a scalar parameter **svar** and an array parameter **avar** as if the assignments had been

```
svar="one word"
avar=(several words)
```

On the other hand:

```
# Normal builtin interface
builtin typeset svar=$(echo two words)
```

The **builtin** keyword causes the above to use the standard builtin interface to **typeset** in which argument parsing is performed in the same way as for other commands. This example creates a scalar **svar** containing the value **two** and another scalar parameter **words** with no value. An array value in this case would either cause an error or be treated as an obscure set of glob qualifiers.

Arbitrary arguments are allowed if they take the form of assignments after command line expansion; however, these only perform scalar assignment:

```
var='svar=val'
typeset $var
```

The above sets the scalar parameter `svar` to the value `val`. Parentheses around the value within `var` would not cause array assignment as they will be treated as ordinary characters when `$var` is substituted. Any non-trivial expansion in the name part of the assignment causes the argument to be treated in this fashion:

```
typeset {var1,var2,var3}=name
```

The above syntax is valid, and has the expected effect of setting the three parameters to the same value, but the command line is parsed as a set of three normal command line arguments to `typeset` after expansion. Hence it is not possible to assign to multiple arrays by this means.

Note that each interface to any of the commands my be disabled separately. For example, 'disable -r typeset' disables the reserved word interface to `typeset`, exposing the builtin interface, while 'disable typeset' disables the builtin. Note that disabling the reserved word interface for `typeset` may cause problems with the output of 'typeset -p', which assumes the reserved word interface is available in order to restore array and associative array values.

Unlike parameter assignment statements, `typeset`'s exit status on an assignment that involves a command substitution does not reflect the exit status of the command substitution. Therefore, to test for an error in a command substitution, separate the declaration of the parameter from its initialization:

```
# WRONG
typeset var1=$(exit 1) || echo "Trouble with var1"

# RIGHT
typeset var1 && var1=$(exit 1) || echo "Trouble with var1"
```

To initialize a parameter *param* to a command output and mark it readonly, use `typeset -r` *param* or `readonly` *param* after the parameter assignment statement.

If no attribute flags are given, and either no *name* arguments are present or the flag +m is used, then each parameter name printed is preceded by a list of the attributes of that parameter (`array`, `association`, `exported`, `float`, `integer`, `readonly`, or `undefined` for autoloaded parameters not yet loaded). If +m is used with attribute flags, and all those flags are introduced with +, the matching parameter names are printed but their values are not.

The following control flags change the behavior of `typeset`:

+   If '+' appears by itself in a separate word as the last option, then the names of all parameters (functions with -f) are printed, but the values (function bodies) are not. No *name* arguments may appear, and it is an error for any other options to follow '+'. The effect of '+' is as if all attribute flags which precede it were given with a '+' prefix. For example, 'typeset -U +' is equivalent to 'typeset +U' and displays the names of all arrays having the uniqueness attribute, whereas 'typeset -f -U +' displays the names of all autoloadable functions. If + is the only option, then type information (array, readonly, etc.) is also printed for each parameter, in the same manner as 'typeset +m "*"'.

-g The -g (global) means that any resulting parameter will not be restricted to local scope. Note that this does not necessarily mean that the parameter will be global, as the flag will apply to any existing parameter (even if unset) from an enclosing function. This flag does not affect the parameter after creation, hence it has no effect when listing existing parameters, nor does the flag +g have any effect except in combination with -m (see below).

-m If the -m flag is given the *name* arguments are taken as patterns (use quoting to prevent these from being interpreted as file patterns). With no attribute flags, all parameters (or functions with the -f flag) with matching names are printed (the shell option TYPESET_SILENT is not used in this case).

If the +g flag is combined with -m, a new local parameter is created for every matching parameter that is not already local. Otherwise -m applies all other flags or assignments to the existing parameters.

Except when assignments are made with *name=value*, using +m forces the matching parameters and their attributes to be printed, even inside a function. Note that -m is ignored if no patterns are given, so 'typeset -m' displays attributes but 'typeset -a +m' does not.

-p [*n*] If the -p option is given, parameters and values are printed in the form of a typeset command with an assignment, regardless of other flags and options. Note that the -H flag on parameters is respected; no value will be shown for these parameters.

-p may be followed by an optional integer argument. Currently only the value 1 is supported. In this case arrays and associative arrays are printed with newlines between indented elements for readability.

-T [*scalar*[=*value*] *array*[=(*value* ...)] [*sep*]]
 This flag has a different meaning when used with -f; see below. Otherwise the -T option requires zero, two, or three arguments to be present. With no arguments, the list of parameters created in this fashion is shown. With two or three arguments, the first two are the name of a scalar and of an array parameter (in that order) that will be tied together in the manner of $PATH and $path. The optional third argument is a single-character separator which will be used to join the elements of the array to form the scalar; if absent, a colon is used, as with $PATH. Only the first character of

the separator is significant; any remaining characters are ignored. Multibyte characters are not yet supported.

Only one of the scalar and array parameters may be assigned an initial value (the restrictions on assignment forms described above also apply).

Both the scalar and the array may be manipulated as normal. If one is unset, the other will automatically be unset too. There is no way of untying the variables without unsetting them, nor of converting the type of one of them with another **typeset** command; +T does not work, assigning an array to *scalar* is an error, and assigning a scalar to *array* sets it to be a single-element array.

Note that both '**typeset -xT** ...' and '**export -T** ...' work, but only the scalar will be marked for export. Setting the value using the scalar version causes a split on all separators (which cannot be quoted). It is possible to apply **-T** to two previously tied variables but with a different separator character, in which case the variables remain joined as before but the separator is changed.

When an existing scalar is tied to a new array, the value of the scalar is preserved but no attribute other than export will be preserved.

Attribute flags that transform the final value (-L, -R, -Z, -l, -u) are only applied to the expanded value at the point of a parameter expansion expression using '$'. They are not applied when a parameter is retrieved internally by the shell for any purpose.

The following attribute flags may be specified:

-A   The names refer to associative array parameters; see Section 15.2 [Array Parameters], page 86.

-L [*n*]   Left justify and remove leading blanks from the value when the parameter is expanded. If *n* is nonzero, it defines the width of the field. If *n* is zero, the width is determined by the width of the value of the first assignment. In the case of numeric parameters, the length of the complete value assigned to the parameter is used to determine the width, not the value that would be output.

The width is the count of characters, which may be multibyte characters if the **MULTIBYTE** option is in effect. Note that the screen width of the character is not taken into account; if this is required, use padding with parameter expansion flags $\{(ml...)...\}$ as described in 'Parameter Expansion Flags' in Section 14.3 [Parameter Expansion], page 52.

When the parameter is expanded, it is filled on the right with blanks or truncated if necessary to fit the field. Note truncation can lead to unexpected results with numeric parameters. Leading zeros are removed if the -Z flag is also set.

-R [n]   Similar to -L, except that right justification is used; when the parameter is expanded, the field is left filled with blanks or truncated from the end. May not be combined with the -Z flag.

-U   For arrays (but not for associative arrays), keep only the first occurrence of each duplicated value. This may also be set for tied parameters (see -T) or colon-separated special parameters like PATH or FIGNORE, etc. Note the flag takes effect on assignment, and the type of the variable being assigned to is determinative; for variables with shared values it is therefore recommended to set the flag for all interfaces, e.g. 'typeset -U PATH path'.

This flag has a different meaning when used with -f; see below.

-Z [n]   Specially handled if set along with the -L flag. Otherwise, similar to -R, except that leading zeros are used for padding instead of blanks if the first non-blank character is a digit. Numeric parameters are specially handled: they are always eligible for padding with zeroes, and the zeroes are inserted at an appropriate place in the output.

-a   The names refer to array parameters. An array parameter may be created this way, but it may be assigned to in the **typeset** statement only if the reserved word form of **typeset** is enabled (as it is by default). When displaying, both normal and associative arrays are shown.

-f   The names refer to functions rather than parameters. No assignments can be made, and the only other valid flags are -t, -T, -k, -u, -U and -z. The flag -t turns on execution tracing for this function; the flag -T does the same, but turns off tracing for any named (not anonymous) function called from the present one, unless that function also has the -t or -T flag. The -u and -U flags cause the function to be marked for autoloading; -U also causes alias expansion to be suppressed when the function is loaded. See the description of the 'autoload' builtin for details.

Note that the builtin **functions** provides the same basic capabilities as **typeset** -f but gives access to a few extra options; **autoload** gives further additional options for the case **typeset** -fu and **typeset** -fU.

-h   Hide: only useful for special parameters (those marked '<S>' in the table in Section 15.5 [Parameters Set By The Shell], page 93), and for local parameters with the same name as a special parameter, though harmless for others. A special parameter with this attribute will not retain its special effect when made local. Thus after 'typeset -h PATH', a function containing 'typeset PATH' will create an ordinary local parameter without the usual behaviour of PATH. Alternatively, the local parameter may itself be given this attribute; hence inside a function 'typeset -h PATH' creates an ordinary local parameter and the special PATH parameter is not altered in any way. It is also possible to create a local parameter using 'typeset +h *special*', where the local copy of *special* will retain its special properties regardless of having the -h attribute. Global special parameters loaded from shell modules (currently those in zsh/mapfile and zsh/parameter) are automatically given the -h attribute to avoid name clashes.

-H Hide value: specifies that typeset will not display the value of the parameter when listing parameters; the display for such parameters is always as if the '+' flag had been given. Use of the parameter is in other respects normal, and the option does not apply if the parameter is specified by name, or by pattern with the -m option. This is on by default for the parameters in the zsh/parameter and zsh/mapfile modules. Note, however, that unlike the -h flag this is also useful for non-special parameters.

-i [*n*] Use an internal integer representation. If *n* is nonzero it defines the output arithmetic base, otherwise it is determined by the first assignment. Bases from 2 to 36 inclusive are allowed.

-E [*n*] Use an internal double-precision floating point representation. On output the variable will be converted to scientific notation. If *n* is nonzero it defines the number of significant figures to display; the default is ten.

-F [*n*] Use an internal double-precision floating point representation. On output the variable will be converted to fixed-point decimal notation. If *n* is nonzero it defines the number of digits to display after the decimal point; the default is ten.

-l Convert the result to lower case whenever the parameter is expanded. The value is *not* converted when assigned.

-r The given *names* are marked readonly. Note that if *name* is a special parameter, the readonly attribute can be turned on, but cannot then be turned off.

If the POSIX_BUILTINS option is set, the readonly attribute is more restrictive: unset variables can be marked readonly and cannot then be set; furthermore, the readonly attribute cannot be removed from any variable.

It is still possible to change other attributes of the variable though, some of which like -U or -Z would affect the value. More generally, the readonly attribute should not be relied on as a security mechanism.

Note that in zsh (like in pdksh but unlike most other shells) it is still possible to create a local variable of the same name as this is considered a different variable (though this variable, too, can be marked readonly). Special variables that have been made readonly retain their value and readonly attribute when made local.

-t	Tags the named parameters. Tags have no special meaning to the shell. This flag has a different meaning when used with -f; see above.
-u	Convert the result to upper case whenever the parameter is expanded. The value is *not* converted when assigned. This flag has a different meaning when used with -f; see above.
-x	Mark for automatic export to the environment of subsequently executed commands. If the option GLOBAL_EXPORT is set, this implies the option -g, unless +g is also explicitly given; in other words the parameter is not made local to the enclosing function. This is for compatibility with previous versions of zsh.

ulimit [-HSa] [{ -bcdfiklmnpqrsTtvwx | -N *resource* } [*limit*] ...]

Set or display resource limits of the shell and the processes started by the shell. The value of *limit* can be a number in the unit specified below or one of the values 'unlimited', which removes the limit on the resource, or 'hard', which uses the current value of the hard limit on the resource.

By default, only soft limits are manipulated. If the -H flag is given use hard limits instead of soft limits. If the -S flag is given together with the -H flag set both hard and soft limits.

If no options are used, the file size limit (-f) is assumed.

If *limit* is omitted the current value of the specified resources are printed. When more than one resource value is printed, the limit name and unit is printed before each value.

When looping over multiple resources, the shell will abort immediately if it detects a badly formed argument. However, if it fails to set a limit for some other reason it will continue trying to set the remaining limits.

Not all the following resources are supported on all systems. Running ulimit -a will show which are supported.

-a	Lists all of the current resource limits.
-b	Socket buffer size in bytes (N.B. not kilobytes)
-c	512-byte blocks on the size of core dumps.
-d	Kilobytes on the size of the data segment.
-f	512-byte blocks on the size of files written.
-i	The number of pending signals.
-k	The number of kqueues allocated.
-l	Kilobytes on the size of locked-in memory.
-m	Kilobytes on the size of physical memory.
-n	open file descriptors.
-p	The number of pseudo-terminals.

-q   Bytes in POSIX message queues.

-r   Maximum real time priority. On some systems where this is not available, such as NetBSD, this has the same effect as -T for compatibility with **sh**.

-s   Kilobytes on the size of the stack.

-T   The number of simultaneous threads available to the user.

-t   CPU seconds to be used.

-u   The number of processes available to the user.

-v   Kilobytes on the size of virtual memory. On some systems this refers to the limit called 'address space'.

-w   Kilobytes on the size of swapped out memory.

-x   The number of locks on files.

A resource may also be specified by integer in the form '-N *resource*', where *resource* corresponds to the integer defined for the resource by the operating system. This may be used to set the limits for resources known to the shell which do not correspond to option letters. Such limits will be shown by number in the output of '**ulimit -a**'.

The number may alternatively be out of the range of limits compiled into the shell. The shell will try to read or write the limit anyway, and will report an error if this fails.

umask [-S] [*mask*]

      The umask is set to *mask*. *mask* can be either an octal number or a symbolic value as described in man page chmod(1). If *mask* is omitted, the current value is printed. The -S option causes the mask to be printed as a symbolic value. Otherwise, the mask is printed as an octal number. Note that in the symbolic form the permissions you specify are those which are to be allowed (not denied) to the users specified.

unalias [-ams] *name* ...

      Removes aliases. This command works the same as **unhash -a**, except that the -a option removes all regular or global aliases, or with -s all suffix aliases: in this case no *name* arguments may appear. The options -m (remove by pattern) and -s without -a (remove listed suffix aliases) behave as for **unhash -a**. Note that the meaning of -a is different between **unalias** and **unhash**.

unfunction

      Same as **unhash -f**.

unhash [-adfms] *name* ...

      Remove the element named *name* from an internal hash table. The default is remove elements from the command hash table. The -a option causes **unhash** to remove regular or global aliases; note when removing a global aliases that the argument must be quoted to prevent it from being expanded before being passed to the command. The -s option causes **unhash** to remove suffix aliases.

The -f option causes **unhash** to remove shell functions. The -d options causes **unhash** to remove named directories. If the -m flag is given the arguments are taken as patterns (should be quoted) and all elements of the corresponding hash table with matching names will be removed.

unlimit [-hs] *resource* ...

The resource limit for each *resource* is set to the hard limit. If the -h flag is given and the shell has appropriate privileges, the hard resource limit for each *resource* is removed. The resources of the shell process are only changed if the -s flag is given.

The **unlimit** command is not made available by default when the shell starts in a mode emulating another shell. It can be made available with the command 'zmodload -F zsh/rlimits b:unlimit'.

unset [-fmv] *name* ...

Each named parameter is unset. Local parameters remain local even if unset; they appear unset within scope, but the previous value will still reappear when the scope ends.

Individual elements of associative array parameters may be unset by using subscript syntax on *name*, which should be quoted (or the entire command prefixed with **noglob**) to protect the subscript from filename generation.

If the -m flag is specified the arguments are taken as patterns (should be quoted) and all parameters with matching names are unset. Note that this cannot be used when unsetting associative array elements, as the subscript will be treated as part of the pattern.

The -v flag specifies that *name* refers to parameters. This is the default behaviour.

unset -f is equivalent to **unfunction**.

unsetopt [{+|-}*options* | {+|-}o *option_name*] [*name* ...]

Unset the options for the shell. All options specified either with flags or by name are unset. If no arguments are supplied, the names of all options currently unset are printed. If the -m flag is given the arguments are taken as patterns (which should be quoted to preserve them from being interpreted as glob patterns), and all options with names matching these patterns are unset.

vared   See Section 18.3 [Zle Builtins], page 185.

wait [*job* ...]

Wait for the specified jobs or processes. If *job* is not given then all currently active child processes are waited for. Each *job* can be either a job specification or the process ID of a job in the job table. The exit status from this command is that of the job waited for. If *job* represents an unknown job or process ID, a warning is printed (unless the **POSIX_BUILTINS** option is set) and the exit status is 127.

It is possible to wait for recent processes (specified by process ID, not by job) that were running in the background even if the process has exited. Typically the process ID will be recorded by capturing the value of the variable $! immediately after the process has been started. There is a limit on the number of process IDs remembered by the shell; this is given by the value of the system configuration parameter `CHILD_MAX`. When this limit is reached, older process IDs are discarded, least recently started processes first.

Note there is no protection against the process ID wrapping, i.e. if the wait is not executed soon enough there is a chance the process waited for is the wrong one. A conflict implies both process IDs have been generated by the shell, as other processes are not recorded, and that the user is potentially interested in both, so this problem is intrinsic to process IDs.

whence [-vcwfpamsS] [-x num] name ...
> For each *name*, indicate how it would be interpreted if used as a command name.
>
> If *name* is not an alias, built-in command, external command, shell function, hashed command, or a reserved word, the exit status shall be non-zero, and — if -v, -c, or -w was passed — a message will be written to standard output. (This is different from other shells that write that message to standard error.)
>
> whence is most useful when *name* is only the last path component of a command, i.e. does not include a '/'; in particular, pattern matching only succeeds if just the non-directory component of the command is passed.
>
> | | |
> |---|---|
> | -v | Produce a more verbose report. |
> | -c | Print the results in a *csh*-like format. This takes precedence over -v. |
> | -w | For each *name*, print '*name*: *word*' where *word* is one of **alias**, **builtin**, **command**, **function**, **hashed**, **reserved** or **none**, according as *name* corresponds to an alias, a built-in command, an external command, a shell function, a command defined with the **hash** builtin, a reserved word, or is not recognised. This takes precedence over -v and -c. |
> | -f | Causes the contents of a shell function to be displayed, which would otherwise not happen unless the -c flag were used. |
> | -p | Do a path search for *name* even if it is an alias, reserved word, shell function or builtin. |
> | -a | Do a search for all occurrences of *name* throughout the command path. Normally only the first occurrence is printed. |
> | -m | The arguments are taken as patterns (pattern characters should be quoted), and the information is displayed for each command matching one of these patterns. |
> | -s | If a pathname contains symlinks, print the symlink-free pathname as well. |
> | -S | As -s, but if the pathname had to be resolved by following multiple symlinks, the intermediate steps are printed, too. The symlink resolved at each step might be anywhere in the path. |

-x *num*   Expand tabs when outputting shell functions using the -c option. This has the same effect as the -x option to the **functions** builtin.

where [-wpmsS] [-x *num*] *name* ...
    Equivalent to **whence** -ca.

which [-wpamsS] [-x *num*] *name* ...
    Equivalent to **whence** -c.

zcompile [-U] [-z | -k] [-R | -M] *file* [*name* ...]
zcompile -ca [-m] [-R | -M] *file* [*name* ...]
zcompile -t *file* [*name* ...]

This builtin command can be used to compile functions or scripts, storing the compiled form in a file, and to examine files containing the compiled form. This allows faster autoloading of functions and sourcing of scripts by avoiding parsing of the text when the files are read.

The first form (without the -c, -a or -t options) creates a compiled file. If only the *file* argument is given, the output file has the name '*file*.zwc' and will be placed in the same directory as the *file*. The shell will load the compiled file instead of the normal function file when the function is autoloaded; see Chapter 9 [Functions], page 24, for a description of how autoloaded functions are searched. The extension .zwc stands for 'zsh word code'.

If there is at least one *name* argument, all the named files are compiled into the output *file* given as the first argument. If *file* does not end in .zwc, this extension is automatically appended. Files containing multiple compiled functions are called 'digest' files, and are intended to be used as elements of the FPATH/fpath special array.

The second form, with the -c or -a options, writes the compiled definitions for all the named functions into *file*. For -c, the names must be functions currently defined in the shell, not those marked for autoloading. Undefined functions that are marked for autoloading may be written by using the -a option, in which case the **fpath** is searched and the contents of the definition files for those functions, if found, are compiled into *file*. If both -c and -a are given, names of both defined functions and functions marked for autoloading may be given. In either case, the functions in files written with the -c or -a option will be autoloaded as if the KSH_AUTOLOAD option were unset.

The reason for handling loaded and not-yet-loaded functions with different options is that some definition files for autoloading define multiple functions, including the function with the same name as the file, and, at the end, call that function. In such cases the output of 'zcompile -c' does not include the additional functions defined in the file, and any other initialization code in the file is lost. Using 'zcompile -a' captures all this extra information.

If the -m option is combined with -c or -a, the *names* are used as patterns and all functions whose names match one of these patterns will be written. If no *name* is given, the definitions of all functions currently defined or marked as autoloaded will be written.

Note the second form cannot be used for compiling functions that include redirections as part of the definition rather than within the body of the function; for example

```
fn1() { { ... } >~/logfile }
```

can be compiled but

```
fn1() { ... } >~/logfile
```

cannot. It is possible to use the first form of **zcompile** to compile autoloadable functions that include the full function definition instead of just the body of the function.

The third form, with the **-t** option, examines an existing compiled file. Without further arguments, the names of the original files compiled into it are listed. The first line of output shows the version of the shell which compiled the file and how the file will be used (i.e. by reading it directly or by mapping it into memory). With arguments, nothing is output and the return status is set to zero if definitions for *all names* were found in the compiled file, and non-zero if the definition for at least one *name* was not found.

Other options:

-U   Aliases are not expanded when compiling the *named* files.

-R   When the compiled file is read, its contents are copied into the shell's memory, rather than memory-mapped (see -M). This happens automatically on systems that do not support memory mapping.

              When compiling scripts instead of autoloadable functions, it is often desirable to use this option; otherwise the whole file, including the code to define functions which have already been defined, will remain mapped, consequently wasting memory.

-M   The compiled file is mapped into the shell's memory when read. This is done in such a way that multiple instances of the shell running on the same host will share this mapped file. If neither -R nor -M is given, the **zcompile** builtin decides what to do based on the size of the compiled file.

-k
-z   These options are used when the compiled file contains functions which are to be autoloaded. If -z is given, the function will be autoloaded as if the KSH_AUTOLOAD option is *not* set, even if it is set at the time the compiled file is read, while if the -k is given, the function will be loaded as if KSH_AUTOLOAD *is* set. These options also take precedence over any -k or -z options specified to the **autoload** builtin. If neither of these options is given, the function will be loaded as determined by the setting of the KSH_AUTOLOAD option at the time the compiled file is read.

              These options may also appear as many times as necessary between the listed *names* to specify the loading style of all following functions, up to the next -k or -z.

The created file always contains two versions of the compiled format, one for big-endian machines and one for small-endian machines. The upshot of this is that the compiled file is machine independent and if it is read or mapped, only one half of the file is actually used (and mapped).

zformat   See Section 22.37 [The zsh/zutil Module], page 382.

zftp   See Section 22.31 [The zsh/zftp Module], page 371.

zle   See Section 18.3 [Zle Builtins], page 185.

zmodload [-dL] [-s] [...]
zmodload -F [-alLme -P *param*] *module* [[+-]*feature* ...]
zmodload -e [-A] [...]
zmodload [-a [-bcpf [-I]]] [-iL] ...
zmodload -u [-abcdpf [-I]] [-iL] ...
zmodload -A [-L] [*modalias*[=*module*] ...]
zmodload -R *modalias* ...

Performs operations relating to zsh's loadable modules. Loading of modules while the shell is running ('dynamical loading') is not available on all operating systems, or on all installations on a particular operating system, although the zmodload command itself is always available and can be used to manipulate modules built into versions of the shell executable without dynamical loading.

Without arguments the names of all currently loaded binary modules are printed. The -L option causes this list to be in the form of a series of zmodload commands. Forms with arguments are:

zmodload [-is] *name* ...
zmodload -u [-i] *name* ...

In the simplest case, zmodload loads a binary module. The module must be in a file with a name consisting of the specified *name* followed by a standard suffix, usually '.so' ('.sl' on HPUX). If the module to be loaded is already loaded the duplicate module is ignored. If zmodload detects an inconsistency, such as an invalid module name or circular dependency list, the current code block is aborted. If it is available, the module is loaded if necessary, while if it is not available, non-zero status is silently returned. The option -i is accepted for compatibility but has no effect.

The *named* module is searched for in the same way a command is, using $module_path instead of $path. However, the path search is performed even when the module name contains a '/', which it usually does. There is no way to prevent the path search.

If the module supports features (see below), zmodload tries to enable all features when loading a module. If the module was successfully loaded but not all features could be enabled, zmodload returns status 2.

If the option -s is given, no error is printed if the module was not available (though other errors indicating a problem with the module are printed). The return status indicates if the module was loaded. This is appropriate if the caller considers the module optional.

With -u, zmodload unloads modules. The same *name* must be given that was given when the module was loaded, but it is not necessary for the module to exist in the file system. The -i option suppresses the error if the module is already unloaded (or was never loaded).

Each module has a boot and a cleanup function. The module will not be loaded if its boot function fails. Similarly a module can only be unloaded if its cleanup function runs successfully.

zmodload -F [-almLe -P *param*] *module* [[+-]*feature* ...]

zmodload -F allows more selective control over the features provided by modules. With no options apart from -F, the module named *module* is loaded, if it was not already loaded, and the list of *features* is set to the required state. If no *features* are specified, the module is loaded, if it was not already loaded, but the state of features is unchanged. Each feature may be preceded by a + to turn the feature on, or - to turn it off; the + is assumed if neither character is present. Any feature not explicitly mentioned is left in its current state; if the module was not previously loaded this means any such features will remain disabled. The return status is zero if all features were set, 1 if the module failed to load, and 2 if some features could not be set (for example, a parameter couldn't be added because there was a different parameter of the same name) but the module was loaded.

The standard features are builtins, conditions, parameters and math functions; these are indicated by the prefix 'b:', 'c:' ('C:' for an infix condition), 'p:' and 'f:', respectively, followed by the name that the corresponding feature would have in the shell. For example, 'b:strftime' indicates a builtin named strftime and p:EPOCHSECONDS indicates a parameter named EPOCHSECONDS. The module may provide other ('abstract') features of its own as indicated by its documentation; these have no prefix.

With -l or -L, features provided by the module are listed. With -l alone, a list of features together with their states is shown, one feature per line. With -L alone, a zmodload -F command that would cause enabled features of the module to be turned on is shown. With -lL, a zmodload -F command that would cause all the features to be set to their current state is shown. If one of these combinations is given with the option -P *param* then the parameter *param* is set to an array of features, either features together with their state or (if -L alone is given) enabled features.

With the option -L the module name may be omitted; then a list of all enabled features for all modules providing features is printed in the form of `zmodload -F` commands. If `-l` is also given, the state of both enabled and disabled features is output in that form.

A set of features may be provided together with `-l` or `-L` and a module name; in that case only the state of those features is considered. Each feature may be preceded by `+` or `-` but the character has no effect. If no set of features is provided, all features are considered.

With `-e`, the command first tests that the module is loaded; if it is not, status 1 is returned. If the module is loaded, the list of features given as an argument is examined. Any feature given with no prefix is simply tested to see if the module provides it; any feature given with a prefix `+` or `-` is tested to see if is provided and in the given state. If the tests on all features in the list succeed, status 0 is returned, else status 1.

With `-m`, each entry in the given list of features is taken as a pattern to be matched against the list of features provided by the module. An initial `+` or `-` must be given explicitly. This may not be combined with the `-a` option as autoloads must be specified explicitly.

With `-a`, the given list of features is marked for autoload from the specified module, which may not yet be loaded. An optional `+` may appear before the feature name. If the feature is prefixed with `-`, any existing autoload is removed. The options `-l` and `-L` may be used to list autoloads. Autoloading is specific to individual features; when the module is loaded only the requested feature is enabled. Autoload requests are preserved if the module is subsequently unloaded until an explicit '`zmodload -Fa` module `-feature`' is issued. It is not an error to request an autoload for a feature of a module that is already loaded.

When the module is loaded each autoload is checked against the features actually provided by the module; if the feature is not provided the autoload request is deleted. A warning message is output; if the module is being loaded to provide a different feature, and that autoload is successful, there is no effect on the status of the current command. If the module is already loaded at the time when `zmodload -Fa` is run, an error message is printed and status 1 returned.

`zmodload -Fa` can be used with the `-l`, `-L`, `-e` and `-P` options for listing and testing the existence of autoloadable features. In this case `-l` is ignored if `-L` is specified. `zmodload -FaL` with no module name lists autoloads for all modules.

Note that only standard features as described above can be autoloaded; other features require the module to be loaded before enabling.

`zmodload -d` [`-L`] [*name*]
`zmodload -d` *name dep ...*
`zmodload -ud` *name* [*dep ...*]

>The `-d` option can be used to specify module dependencies. The modules named in the second and subsequent arguments will be loaded before the module named in the first argument.

>With `-d` and one argument, all dependencies for that module are listed. With `-d` and no arguments, all module dependencies are listed. This listing is by default in a Makefile-like format. The `-L` option changes this format to a list of **zmodload -d** commands.

>If `-d` and `-u` are both used, dependencies are removed. If only one argument is given, all dependencies for that module are removed.

`zmodload -ab` [`-L`]
`zmodload -ab` [`-i`] *name* [*builtin ...*]
`zmodload -ub` [`-i`] *builtin ...*

>The `-ab` option defines autoloaded builtins. It defines the specified *builtins*. When any of those builtins is called, the module specified in the first argument is loaded and all its features are enabled (for selective control of features use 'zmodload -F -a' as described above). If only the *name* is given, one builtin is defined, with the same name as the module. `-i` suppresses the error if the builtin is already defined or autoloaded, but not if another builtin of the same name is already defined.

>With `-ab` and no arguments, all autoloaded builtins are listed, with the module name (if different) shown in parentheses after the builtin name. The `-L` option changes this format to a list of **zmodload -a** commands.

>If `-b` is used together with the `-u` option, it removes builtins previously defined with `-ab`. This is only possible if the builtin is not yet loaded. `-i` suppresses the error if the builtin is already removed (or never existed).

>Autoload requests are retained if the module is subsequently unloaded until an explicit 'zmodload -ub *builtin*' is issued.

`zmodload -ac` [`-IL`]
`zmodload -ac` [`-iI`] *name* [*cond ...*]
`zmodload -uc` [`-iI`] *cond ...*

>The `-ac` option is used to define autoloaded condition codes. The *cond* strings give the names of the conditions defined by the module. The optional `-I` option is used to define infix condition names. Without this option prefix condition names are defined.

>If given no condition names, all defined names are listed (as a series of **zmodload** commands if the `-L` option is given).

>The `-uc` option removes definitions for autoloaded conditions.

```
zmodload -ap [ -L ]
zmodload -ap [ -i ] name [ parameter ... ]
zmodload -up [ -i ] parameter ...
```
> The -p option is like the -b and -c options, but makes zmodload work on autoloaded parameters instead.

```
zmodload -af [ -L ]
zmodload -af [ -i ] name [ function ... ]
zmodload -uf [ -i ] function ...
```
> The -f option is like the -b, -p, and -c options, but makes zmodload work on autoloaded math functions instead.

```
zmodload -a [ -L ]
zmodload -a [ -i ] name [ builtin ... ]
zmodload -ua [ -i ] builtin ...
```
> Equivalent to -ab and -ub.

```
zmodload -e [ -A ] [ string ... ]
```
> The -e option without arguments lists all loaded modules; if the -A option is also given, module aliases corresponding to loaded modules are also shown. If arguments are provided, nothing is printed; the return status is set to zero if all *strings* given as arguments are names of loaded modules and to one if at least on *string* is not the name of a loaded module. This can be used to test for the availability of things implemented by modules. In this case, any aliases are automatically resolved and the -A flag is not used.

```
zmodload -A [ -L ] [ modalias[=module] ... ]
```
> For each argument, if both *modalias* and *module* are given, define *modalias* to be an alias for the module *module*. If the module *modalias* is ever subsequently requested, either via a call to zmodload or implicitly, the shell will attempt to load *module* instead. If *module* is not given, show the definition of *modalias*. If no arguments are given, list all defined module aliases. When listing, if the -L flag was also given, list the definition as a zmodload command to recreate the alias.
>
> The existence of aliases for modules is completely independent of whether the name resolved is actually loaded as a module: while the alias exists, loading and unloading the module under any alias has exactly the same effect as using the resolved name, and does not affect the connection between the alias and the resolved name which can be removed either by zmodload -R or by redefining the alias. Chains of aliases (i.e. where the first resolved name is itself an alias) are valid so long as these are not circular. As the aliases take the same format as module names, they may include path separators: in this case, there is no requirement for any part of the path named to exist as the alias will be resolved first. For example, 'any/old/alias' is always a valid alias.

Dependencies added to aliased modules are actually added to the resolved module; these remain if the alias is removed. It is valid to create an alias whose name is one of the standard shell modules and which resolves to a different module. However, if a module has dependencies, it will not be possible to use the module name as an alias as the module will already be marked as a loadable module in its own right.

Apart from the above, aliases can be used in the `zmodload` command anywhere module names are required. However, aliases will not be shown in lists of loaded modules with a bare 'zmodload'.

`zmodload -R` *modalias* ...

For each *modalias* argument that was previously defined as a module alias via `zmodload -A`, delete the alias. If any was not defined, an error is caused and the remainder of the line is ignored.

Note that **zsh** makes no distinction between modules that were linked into the shell and modules that are loaded dynamically. In both cases this builtin command has to be used to make available the builtins and other things defined by modules (unless the module is autoloaded on these definitions). This is true even for systems that don't support dynamic loading of modules.

`zparseopts`
See Section 22.37 [The zsh/zutil Module], page 382.

`zprof`   See Section 22.34 [The zsh/zprof Module], page 378.

`zpty`   See Section 22.35 [The zsh/zpty Module], page 379.

`zregexparse`
See Section 22.37 [The zsh/zutil Module], page 382.

`zsocket`   See Section 22.25 [The zsh/net/socket Module], page 361.

`zstyle`   See Section 22.37 [The zsh/zutil Module], page 382.

`ztcp`   See Section 22.28 [The zsh/net/tcp Module], page 368.

18 Zsh Line Editor

18.1 Description

If the `ZLE` option is set (which it is by default in interactive shells) and the shell input is attached to the terminal, the user is able to edit command lines.

There are two display modes. The first, multiline mode, is the default. It only works if the `TERM` parameter is set to a valid terminal type that can move the cursor up. The second, single line mode, is used if `TERM` is invalid or incapable of moving the cursor up, or if the `SINGLE_LINE_ZLE` option is set. This mode is similar to *ksh*, and uses no termcap sequences. If `TERM` is "emacs", the `ZLE` option will be unset by default.

The parameters BAUD, COLUMNS, and LINES are also used by the line editor. See Section 15.6 [Parameters Used By The Shell], page 99.

The parameter zle_highlight is also used by the line editor; see Section 18.7 [Character Highlighting], page 221. Highlighting of special characters and the region between the cursor and the mark (as set with set-mark-command in Emacs mode, or by visual-mode in Vi mode) is enabled by default; consult this reference for more information. Irascible conservatives will wish to know that all highlighting may be disabled by the following setting:

```
zle_highlight=(none)
```

In many places, references are made to the **numeric argument**. This can by default be entered in emacs mode by holding the alt key and typing a number, or pressing escape before each digit, and in vi command mode by typing the number before entering a command. Generally the numeric argument causes the next command entered to be repeated the specified number of times, unless otherwise noted below; this is implemented by the digit-argument widget. See also Section 18.6.4 [Arguments], page 213, for some other ways the numeric argument can be modified.

18.2 Keymaps

A keymap in ZLE contains a set of bindings between key sequences and ZLE commands. The empty key sequence cannot be bound.

There can be any number of keymaps at any time, and each keymap has one or more names. If all of a keymap's names are deleted, it disappears. bindkey can be used to manipulate keymap names.

Initially, there are eight keymaps:

emacs	EMACS emulation
viins	vi emulation - insert mode
vicmd	vi emulation - command mode
viopp	vi emulation - operator pending
visual	vi emulation - selection active
isearch	incremental search mode
command	read a command name
.safe	fallback keymap

The '.safe' keymap is special. It can never be altered, and the name can never be removed. However, it can be linked to other names, which can be removed. In the future other special keymaps may be added; users should avoid using names beginning with '.' for their own keymaps.

In addition to these names, either 'emacs' or 'viins' is also linked to the name 'main'. If one of the VISUAL or EDITOR environment variables contain the string 'vi' when the shell starts up then it will be 'viins', otherwise it will be 'emacs'. bindkey's -e and -v options provide a convenient way to override this default choice.

When the editor starts up, it will select the 'main' keymap. If that keymap doesn't exist, it will use '.safe' instead.

In the '.safe' keymap, each single key is bound to **self-insert**, except for ^J (line feed) and ^M (return) which are bound to **accept-line**. This is deliberately not pleasant to use; if you are using it, it means you deleted the main keymap, and you should put it back.

18.2.1 Reading Commands

When ZLE is reading a command from the terminal, it may read a sequence that is bound to some command and is also a prefix of a longer bound string. In this case ZLE will wait a certain time to see if more characters are typed, and if not (or they don't match any longer string) it will execute the binding. This timeout is defined by the KEYTIMEOUT parameter; its default is 0.4 sec. There is no timeout if the prefix string is not itself bound to a command.

The key timeout is also applied when ZLE is reading the bytes from a multibyte character string when it is in the appropriate mode. (This requires that the shell was compiled with multibyte mode enabled; typically also the locale has characters with the UTF-8 encoding, although any multibyte encoding known to the operating system is supported.) If the second or a subsequent byte is not read within the timeout period, the shell acts as if ? were typed and resets the input state.

As well as ZLE commands, key sequences can be bound to other strings, by using 'bindkey -s'. When such a sequence is read, the replacement string is pushed back as input, and the command reading process starts again using these fake keystrokes. This input can itself invoke further replacement strings, but in order to detect loops the process will be stopped if there are twenty such replacements without a real command being read.

A key sequence typed by the user can be turned into a command name for use in user-defined widgets with the **read-command** widget, described in Section 18.6.6 [Miscellaneous], page 215, below.

18.2.2 Local Keymaps

While for normal editing a single keymap is used exclusively, in many modes a local keymap allows for some keys to be customised. For example, in an incremental search mode, a binding in the **isearch** keymap will override a binding in the **main** keymap but all keys that are not overridden can still be used.

If a key sequence is defined in a local keymap, it will hide a key sequence in the global keymap that is a prefix of that sequence. An example of this occurs with the binding of iw in **viopp** as this hides the binding of i in **vicmd**. However, a longer sequence in the global keymap that shares the same prefix can still apply so for example the binding of ^Xa in the global keymap will be unaffected by the binding of ^Xb in the local keymap.

18.3 Zle Builtins

The ZLE module contains three related builtin commands. The **bindkey** command manipulates keymaps and key bindings; the **vared** command invokes ZLE on the value of a shell parameter; and the **zle** command manipulates editing widgets and allows command line access to ZLE commands from within shell functions.

```
bindkey [ options ] -l [ -L ] [ keymap ... ]
bindkey [ options ] -d
bindkey [ options ] -D keymap ...
bindkey [ options ] -A old-keymap new-keymap
bindkey [ options ] -N new-keymap [ old-keymap ]
bindkey [ options ] -m
bindkey [ options ] -r in-string ...
bindkey [ options ] -s in-string out-string ...
bindkey [ options ] in-string command ...
bindkey [ options ] [ in-string ]
```

bindkey's options can be divided into three categories: keymap selection for the current command, operation selection, and others. The keymap selection options are:

-e   Selects keymap 'emacs' for any operations by the current command, and also links 'emacs' to 'main' so that it is selected by default the next time the editor starts.

-v   Selects keymap 'viins' for any operations by the current command, and also links 'viins' to 'main' so that it is selected by default the next time the editor starts.

-a   Selects keymap 'vicmd' for any operations by the current command.

-M keymap

The *keymap* specifies a keymap name that is selected for any operations by the current command.

If a keymap selection is required and none of the options above are used, the 'main' keymap is used. Some operations do not permit a keymap to be selected, namely:

-l   List all existing keymap names; if any arguments are given, list just those keymaps.

If the -L option is also used, list in the form of bindkey commands to create or link the keymaps. 'bindkey -1L main' shows which keymap is linked to 'main', if any, and hence if the standard emacs or vi emulation is in effect. This option does not show the .safe keymap because it cannot be created in that fashion; however, neither is 'bindkey -1L .safe' reported as an error, it simply outputs nothing.

-d   Delete all existing keymaps and reset to the default state.

-D keymap ...

Delete the named *keymaps*.

-A old-keymap new-keymap

Make the *new-keymap* name an alias for *old-keymap*, so that both names refer to the same keymap. The names have equal standing; if either is deleted, the other remains. If there is already a keymap with the *new-keymap* name, it is deleted.

-N *new-keymap* [*old-keymap*]

> Create a new keymap, named *new-keymap*. If a keymap already has that name, it is deleted. If an *old-keymap* name is given, the new keymap is initialized to be a duplicate of it, otherwise the new keymap will be empty.

To use a newly created keymap, it should be linked to `main`. Hence the sequence of commands to create and use a new keymap 'mymap' initialized from the `emacs` keymap (which remains unchanged) is:

```
bindkey -N mymap emacs
bindkey -A mymap main
```

Note that while 'bindkey -A *newmap* main' will work when *newmap* is `emacs` or `viins`, it will not work for `vicmd`, as switching from vi insert to command mode becomes impossible.

The following operations act on the 'main' keymap if no keymap selection option was given:

-m

> Add the built-in set of meta-key bindings to the selected keymap. Only keys that are unbound or bound to `self-insert` are affected.

-r *in-string* ...

> Unbind the specified *in-string*s in the selected keymap. This is exactly equivalent to binding the strings to `undefined-key`.
>
> When -R is also used, interpret the *in-string*s as ranges.
>
> When -p is also used, the *in-string*s specify prefixes. Any binding that has the given *in-string* as a prefix, not including the binding for the *in-string* itself, if any, will be removed. For example,
>
> ```
> bindkey -rpM viins '^['
> ```
>
> will remove all bindings in the vi-insert keymap beginning with an escape character (probably cursor keys), but leave the binding for the escape character itself (probably `vi-cmd-mode`). This is incompatible with the option -R.

-s *in-string* *out-string* ...

> Bind each *in-string* to each *out-string*. When *in-string* is typed, *out-string* will be pushed back and treated as input to the line editor. When -R is also used, interpret the *in-string*s as ranges.
>
> Note that both *in-string* and *out-string* are subject to the same form of interpretation, as described below.

in-string *command* ...

> Bind each *in-string* to each *command*. When -R is used, interpret the *in-string*s as ranges.

[*in-string*]

> List key bindings. If an *in-string* is specified, the binding of that string in the selected keymap is displayed. Otherwise, all key bindings in the selected keymap are displayed. (As a special case, if the

-e or -v option is used alone, the keymap is *not* displayed - the implicit linking of keymaps is the only thing that happens.)

When the option -p is used, the *in-string* must be present. The listing shows all bindings which have the given key sequence as a prefix, not including any bindings for the key sequence itself.

When the -L option is used, the list is in the form of bindkey commands to create the key bindings.

When the -R option is used as noted above, a valid range consists of two characters, with an optional '-' between them. All characters between the two specified, inclusive, are bound as specified.

For either *in-string* or *out-string*, the following escape sequences are recognised:

\a	bell character
\b	backspace
\e, \E	escape
\f	form feed
\n	linefeed (newline)
\r	carriage return
\t	horizontal tab
\v	vertical tab
NNN	character code in octal
\x*NN*	character code in hexadecimal
\u*NNNN*	unicode character code in hexadecimal
\U*NNNNNNNN*	unicode character code in hexadecimal
\M[-]*X*	character with meta bit set
\C[-]*X*	control character
^*X*	control character

In all other cases, '\' escapes the following character. Delete is written as '^?'. Note that '\M^?' and '^\M?' are not the same, and that (unlike emacs), the bindings '\M-*X*' and '\e*X*' are entirely distinct, although they are initialized to the same bindings by 'bindkey -m'.

vared [-Aacghe] [-p *prompt*] [-r *rprompt*]
    [-M *main-keymap*] [-m *vicmd-keymap*]
    [-i *init-widget*] [-f *finish-widget*]
    [-t *tty*] name

        The value of the parameter *name* is loaded into the edit buffer, and the line editor is invoked. When the editor exits, *name* is set to the string value returned by the editor. When the -c flag is given, the parameter is created if it doesn't already exist. The **-a** flag may be given with **-c** to create an array parameter, or the **-A** flag to create an associative array. If the type of an existing parameter does not match the type to be created, the parameter is unset and recreated. The **-g** flag may be given to suppress warnings from the WARN_CREATE_GLOBAL and WARN_NESTED_VAR options.

If an array or array slice is being edited, separator characters as defined in **$IFS** will be shown quoted with a backslash, as will backslashes themselves. Conversely, when the edited text is split into an array, a backslash quotes an immediately following separator character or backslash; no other special handling of backslashes, or any handling of quotes, is performed.

Individual elements of existing array or associative array parameters may be edited by using subscript syntax on *name*. New elements are created automatically, even without **-c**.

If the **-p** flag is given, the following string will be taken as the prompt to display at the left. If the **-r** flag is given, the following string gives the prompt to display at the right. If the **-h** flag is specified, the history can be accessed from ZLE. If the **-e** flag is given, typing ^D (Control-D) on an empty line causes **vared** to exit immediately with a non-zero return value.

The **-M** option gives a keymap to link to the **main** keymap during editing, and the **-m** option gives a keymap to link to the **vicmd** keymap during editing. For vi-style editing, this allows a pair of keymaps to override **viins** and **vicmd**. For emacs-style editing, only **-M** is normally needed but the **-m** option may still be used. On exit, the previous keymaps will be restored.

Vared calls the usual 'zle-line-init' and 'zle-line-finish' hooks before and after it takes control. Using the **-i** and **-f** options, it is possible to replace these with other custom widgets.

If '**-t** *tty*' is given, *tty* is the name of a terminal device to be used instead of the default **/dev/tty**. If *tty* does not refer to a terminal an error is reported.

zle
zle -l [**-L** | **-a**] [*string ...*]
zle -D *widget ...*
zle -A *old-widget new-widget*
zle -N *widget* [*function*]
zle -f *flag* [*flag...*]
zle -C *widget completion-widget function*
zle -R [**-c**] [*display-string*] [*string ...*]
zle -M *string*
zle -U *string*
zle -K *keymap*
zle -F [**-L** | **-w**] [*fd* [*handler*]]
zle -I
zle -T [*tc function* | **-r** *tc* | **-L**]
zle *widget* [**-n** *num*] [**-Nw**] [**-K** *keymap*] *args ...*
     The **zle** builtin performs a number of different actions concerning ZLE.

With no options and no arguments, only the return status will be set. It is zero if ZLE is currently active and widgets could be invoked using this builtin command and non-zero otherwise. Note that even if non-zero status is returned, zle may still be active as part of the completion system; this does not allow direct calls to ZLE widgets.

Otherwise, which operation it performs depends on its options:

-l [-L | -a] [*string*]

> List all existing user-defined widgets. If the −L option is used, list in the form of `zle` commands to create the widgets.
>
> When combined with the −a option, all widget names are listed, including the builtin ones. In this case the −L option is ignored.
>
> If at least one *string* is given, and −a is present or −L is not used, nothing will be printed. The return status will be zero if all *string*s are names of existing widgets and non-zero if at least one *string* is not a name of a defined widget. If −a is also present, all widget names are used for the comparison including builtin widgets, else only user-defined widgets are used.
>
> If at least one *string* is present and the −L option is used, user-defined widgets matching any *string* are listed in the form of `zle` commands to create the widgets.

-D *widget* ...

> Delete the named *widget*s.

-A *old-widget new-widget*

> Make the *new-widget* name an alias for *old-widget*, so that both names refer to the same widget. The names have equal standing; if either is deleted, the other remains. If there is already a widget with the *new-widget* name, it is deleted.

-N *widget* [*function*]

> Create a user-defined widget. If there is already a widget with the specified name, it is overwritten. When the new widget is invoked from within the editor, the specified shell *function* is called. If no function name is specified, it defaults to the same name as the widget. For further information, see Section 18.4 [Zle Widgets], page 195.

-f *flag* [*flag...*]

> Set various flags on the running widget. Possible values for *flag* are:
>
> **yank** for indicating that the widget has yanked text into the buffer. If the widget is wrapping an existing internal widget, no further action is necessary, but if it has inserted the text manually, then it should also take care to set `YANK_START` and `YANK_END` correctly. **yankbefore** does the same but is used when the yanked text appears after the cursor.

kill for indicating that text has been killed into the cutbuffer. When repeatedly invoking a kill widget, text is appended to the cutbuffer instead of replacing it, but when wrapping such widgets, it is necessary to call 'zle -f kill' to retain this effect.

vichange for indicating that the widget represents a vi change that can be repeated as a whole with 'vi-repeat-change'. The flag should be set early in the function before inspecting the value of NUMERIC or invoking other widgets. This has no effect for a widget invoked from insert mode. If insert mode is active when the widget finishes, the change extends until next returning to command mode.

-C *widget completion-widget function*

Create a user-defined completion widget named *widget*. The completion widget will behave like the built-in completion-widget whose name is given as *completion-widget*. To generate the completions, the shell function *function* will be called. For further information, see Chapter 19 [Completion Widgets], page 225.

-R [-c] [*display-string*] [*string* ...]

Redisplay the command line; this is to be called from within a user-defined widget to allow changes to become visible. If a *display-string* is given and not empty, this is shown in the status line (immediately below the line being edited).

If the optional *string*s are given they are listed below the prompt in the same way as completion lists are printed. If no *string*s are given but the -c option is used such a list is cleared.

Note that this option is only useful for widgets that do not exit immediately after using it because the strings displayed will be erased immediately after return from the widget.

This command can safely be called outside user defined widgets; if zle is active, the display will be refreshed, while if zle is not active, the command has no effect. In this case there will usually be no other arguments.

The status is zero if zle was active, else one.

-M *string*   As with the -R option, the *string* will be displayed below the command line; unlike the -R option, the string will not be put into the status line but will instead be printed normally below the prompt. This means that the *string* will still be displayed after the widget returns (until it is overwritten by subsequent commands).

-U *string*   This pushes the characters in the *string* onto the input stack of ZLE. After the widget currently executed finishes ZLE will behave as if the characters in the *string* were typed by the user.

As ZLE uses a stack, if this option is used repeatedly the last string pushed onto the stack will be processed first. However, the characters in each *string* will be processed in the order in which they appear in the string.

-K *keymap*

> Selects the keymap named *keymap*. An error message will be displayed if there is no such keymap.
>
> This keymap selection affects the interpretation of following keystrokes within this invocation of ZLE. Any following invocation (e.g., the next command line) will start as usual with the 'main' keymap selected.

-F [-L | -w] [*fd* [*handler*]]

> Only available if your system supports one of the 'poll' or 'select' system calls; most modern systems do.
>
> Installs *handler* (the name of a shell function) to handle input from file descriptor *fd*. Installing a handler for an *fd* which is already handled causes the existing handler to be replaced. Any number of handlers for any number of readable file descriptors may be installed. Note that zle makes no attempt to check whether this *fd* is actually readable when installing the handler. The user must make their own arrangements for handling the file descriptor when zle is not active.
>
> When zle is attempting to read data, it will examine both the terminal and the list of handled *fd*'s. If data becomes available on a handled *fd*, zle calls *handler* with the fd which is ready for reading as the first argument. Under normal circumstances this is the only argument, but if an error was detected, a second argument provides details: 'hup' for a disconnect, 'nval' for a closed or otherwise invalid descriptor, or 'err' for any other condition. Systems that support only the 'select' system call always use 'err'.
>
> If the option -w is also given, the *handler* is instead a line editor widget, typically a shell function made into a widget using 'zle -N'. In that case *handler* can use all the facilities of zle to update the current editing line. Note, however, that as handling *fd* takes place at a low level changes to the display will not automatically appear; the widget should call 'zle -R' to force redisplay. As of this writing, widget handlers only support a single argument and thus are never passed a string for error state, so widgets must be prepared to test the descriptor themselves.
>
> If either type of handler produces output to the terminal, it should call 'zle -I' before doing so (see below). Handlers should not attempt to read from the terminal.
>
> If no *handler* is given, but an *fd* is present, any handler for that *fd* is removed. If there is none, an error message is printed and status 1 is returned.
>
> If no arguments are given, or the -L option is supplied, a list of handlers is printed in a form which can be stored for later execution.

An *fd* (but not a *handler*) may optionally be given with the -L option; in this case, the function will list the handler if any, else silently return status 1.

Note that this feature should be used with care. Activity on one of the *fd*'s which is not properly handled can cause the terminal to become unusable. Removing an *fd* handler from within a signal trap may cause unpredictable behavior.

Here is a simple example of using this feature. A connection to a remote TCP port is created using the ztcp command; see Section 22.28 [The zsh/net/tcp Module], page 368. Then a handler is installed which simply prints out any data which arrives on this connection. Note that 'select' will indicate that the file descriptor needs handling if the remote side has closed the connection; we handle that by testing for a failed read.

```
if ztcp pwspc 2811; then
  tcpfd=$REPLY
  handler() {
    zle -I
    local line
    if ! read -r line <&$1; then
      # select marks this fd if we reach EOF,
      # so handle this specially.
      print "[Read on fd $1 failed, removing.]" >&2
      zle -F $1
      return 1
    fi
    print -r - $line
  }
  zle -F $tcpfd handler
fi
```

-I   Unusually, this option is most useful outside ordinary widget functions, though it may be used within if normal output to the terminal is required. It invalidates the current zle display in preparation for output; typically this will be from a trap function. It has no effect if zle is not active. When a trap exits, the shell checks to see if the display needs restoring, hence the following will print output in such a way as not to disturb the line being edited:

```
TRAPUSR1() {
  # Invalidate zle display
  [[ -o zle ]] && zle -I
  # Show output
  print Hello
}
```

In general, the trap function may need to test whether zle is active before using this method (as shown in the example), since the zsh/zle module may not even be loaded; if it is not, the command can be skipped.

It is possible to call 'zle -I' several times before control is returned to the editor; the display will only be invalidated the first time to minimise disruption.

Note that there are normally better ways of manipulating the display from within zle widgets; see, for example, 'zle -R' above.

The returned status is zero if zle was invalidated, even though this may have been by a previous call to 'zle -I' or by a system notification. To test if a zle widget may be called at this point, execute zle with no arguments and examine the return status.

-T   This is used to add, list or remove internal transformations on the processing performed by the line editor. It is typically used only for debugging or testing and is therefore of little interest to the general user.

'zle -T *transformation func*' specifies that the given *transformation* (see below) is effected by shell function *func*.

'zle -Tr *transformation*' removes the given *transformation* if it was present (it is not an error if none was).

'zle -TL' can be used to list all transformations currently in operation.

Currently the only transformation is tc. This is used instead of outputting termcap codes to the terminal. When the transformation is in operation the shell function is passed the termcap code that would be output as its first argument; if the operation required a numeric argument, that is passed as a second argument. The function should set the shell variable REPLY to the transformed termcap code. Typically this is used to produce some simply formatted version of the code and optional argument for debugging or testing. Note that this transformation is not applied to other non-printing characters such as carriage returns and newlines.

widget [-n *num*] [-Nw] [-K *keymap*] *args* ...
Invoke the specified *widget*. This can only be done when ZLE is active; normally this will be within a user-defined widget.

With the options -n and -N, the current numeric argument will be saved and then restored after the call to *widget*; '-n *num*' sets the numeric argument temporarily to *num*, while '-N' sets it to the default, i.e. as if there were none.

With the option -K, *keymap* will be used as the current keymap during the execution of the widget. The previous keymap will be restored when the widget exits.

Normally, calling a widget in this way does not set the special parameter WIDGET and related parameters, so that the environment appears as if the top-level widget called by the user were still active.

With the option -w, WIDGET and related parameters are set to reflect the widget being executed by the zle call.

Any further arguments will be passed to the widget; note that as standard argument handling is performed, any general argument list should be preceded by --. If it is a shell function, these are passed down as positional parameters; for builtin widgets it is up to the widget in question what it does with them. Currently arguments are only handled by the incremental-search commands, the history-search-forward and -backward and the corresponding functions prefixed by vi-, and by universal-argument. No error is flagged if the command does not use the arguments, or only uses some of them.

The return status reflects the success or failure of the operation carried out by the widget, or if it is a user-defined widget the return status of the shell function.

A non-zero return status causes the shell to beep when the widget exits, unless the BEEP options was unset or the widget was called via the zle command. Thus if a user defined widget requires an immediate beep, it should call the beep widget directly.

18.4 Widgets

All actions in the editor are performed by 'widgets'. A widget's job is simply to perform some small action. The ZLE commands that key sequences in keymaps are bound to are in fact widgets. Widgets can be user-defined or built in.

The standard widgets built into ZLE are listed in Standard Widgets below. Other built-in widgets can be defined by other modules (see Chapter 22 [Zsh Modules], page 329). Each built-in widget has two names: its normal canonical name, and the same name preceded by a '.'. The '.' name is special: it can't be rebound to a different widget. This makes the widget available even when its usual name has been redefined.

User-defined widgets are defined using 'zle -N', and implemented as shell functions. When the widget is executed, the corresponding shell function is executed, and can perform editing (or other) actions. It is recommended that user-defined widgets should not have names starting with '.'.

18.5 User-Defined Widgets

User-defined widgets, being implemented as shell functions, can execute any normal shell command. They can also run other widgets (whether built-in or user-defined) using the zle builtin command. The standard input of the function is redirected from /dev/null to prevent external commands from unintentionally blocking ZLE by reading from the terminal, but read -k or read -q can be used to read characters. Finally, they can examine and edit the ZLE buffer being edited by reading and setting the special parameters described below.

These special parameters are always available in widget functions, but are not in any way special outside ZLE. If they have some normal value outside ZLE, that value is temporarily inaccessible, but will return when the widget function exits. These special parameters in fact have local scope, like parameters created in a function using `local`.

Inside completion widgets and traps called while ZLE is active, these parameters are available read-only.

Note that the parameters appear as local to any ZLE widget in which they appear. Hence if it is desired to override them this needs to be done within a nested function:

```
widget-function() {
    # $WIDGET here refers to the special variable
    # that is local inside widget-function
    () {
        # This anonymous nested function allows WIDGET
        # to be used as a local variable.  The -h
        # removes the special status of the variable.
        local -h WIDGET
    }
}
```

BUFFER (scalar)

> The entire contents of the edit buffer. If it is written to, the cursor remains at the same offset, unless that would put it outside the buffer.

BUFFERLINES (integer)

> The number of screen lines needed for the edit buffer currently displayed on screen (i.e. without any changes to the preceding parameters done after the last redisplay); read-only.

CONTEXT (scalar)

> The context in which zle was called to read a line; read-only. One of the values:
>
> | | |
> |---|---|
> | start | The start of a command line (at prompt PS1). |
> | cont | A continuation to a command line (at prompt PS2). |
> | select | In a select loop (at prompt PS3). |
> | vared | Editing a variable in vared. |

CURSOR (integer)

> The offset of the cursor, within the edit buffer. This is in the range 0 to `$#BUFFER`, and is by definition equal to `$#LBUFFER`. Attempts to move the cursor outside the buffer will result in the cursor being moved to the appropriate end of the buffer.

CUTBUFFER (scalar)

> The last item cut using one of the 'kill-' commands; the string which the next yank would insert in the line. Later entries in the kill ring are in the array `killring`. Note that the command 'zle copy-region-as-kill *string*' can be used to set the text of the cut buffer from a shell function and cycle the kill ring in the same way as interactively killing text.

HISTNO (integer)

> The current history number. Setting this has the same effect as moving up or down in the history to the corresponding history line. An attempt to set it is

ignored if the line is not stored in the history. Note this is not the same as the parameter HISTCMD, which always gives the number of the history line being added to the main shell's history. HISTNO refers to the line being retrieved within zle.

ISEARCHMATCH_ACTIVE (integer)
ISEARCHMATCH_START (integer)
ISEARCHMATCH_END (integer)

ISEARCHMATCH_ACTIVE indicates whether a part of the BUFFER is currently matched by an incremental search pattern. ISEARCHMATCH_START and ISEARCHMATCH_END give the location of the matched part and are in the same units as CURSOR. They are only valid for reading when ISEARCHMATCH_ACTIVE is non-zero.

All parameters are read-only.

KEYMAP (scalar)

The name of the currently selected keymap; read-only.

KEYS (scalar)

The keys typed to invoke this widget, as a literal string; read-only.

KEYS_QUEUED_COUNT (integer)

The number of bytes pushed back to the input queue and therefore available for reading immediately before any I/O is done; read-only. See also PENDING; the two values are distinct.

killring (array)

The array of previously killed items, with the most recently killed first. This gives the items that would be retrieved by a yank-pop in the same order. Note, however, that the most recently killed item is in $CUTBUFFER; $killring shows the array of previous entries.

The default size for the kill ring is eight, however the length may be changed by normal array operations. Any empty string in the kill ring is ignored by the yank-pop command, hence the size of the array effectively sets the maximum length of the kill ring, while the number of non-zero strings gives the current length, both as seen by the user at the command line.

LASTABORTEDSEARCH (scalar)

The last search string used by an interactive search that was aborted by the user (status 3 returned by the search widget).

LASTSEARCH (scalar)

The last search string used by an interactive search; read-only. This is set even if the search failed (status 0, 1 or 2 returned by the search widget), but not if it was aborted by the user.

LASTWIDGET (scalar)

The name of the last widget that was executed; read-only.

LBUFFER (scalar)

> The part of the buffer that lies to the left of the cursor position. If it is assigned to, only that part of the buffer is replaced, and the cursor remains between the new $LBUFFER and the old $RBUFFER.

MARK (integer)

> Like CURSOR, but for the mark. With vi-mode operators that wait for a movement command to select a region of text, setting MARK allows the selection to extend in both directions from the initial cursor position.

NUMERIC (integer)

> The numeric argument. If no numeric argument was given, this parameter is unset. When this is set inside a widget function, builtin widgets called with the zle builtin command will use the value assigned. If it is unset inside a widget function, builtin widgets called behave as if no numeric argument was given.

PENDING (integer)

> The number of bytes pending for input, i.e. the number of bytes which have already been typed and can immediately be read. On systems where the shell is not able to get this information, this parameter will always have a value of zero. Read-only. See also KEYS_QUEUED_COUNT; the two values are distinct.

PREBUFFER (scalar)

> In a multi-line input at the secondary prompt, this read-only parameter contains the contents of the lines before the one the cursor is currently in.

PREDISPLAY (scalar)

> Text to be displayed before the start of the editable text buffer. This does not have to be a complete line; to display a complete line, a newline must be appended explicitly. The text is reset on each new invocation (but not recursive invocation) of zle.

POSTDISPLAY (scalar)

> Text to be displayed after the end of the editable text buffer. This does not have to be a complete line; to display a complete line, a newline must be prepended explicitly. The text is reset on each new invocation (but not recursive invocation) of zle.

RBUFFER (scalar)

> The part of the buffer that lies to the right of the cursor position. If it is assigned to, only that part of the buffer is replaced, and the cursor remains between the old $LBUFFER and the new $RBUFFER.

REGION_ACTIVE (integer)

> Indicates if the region is currently active. It can be assigned 0 or 1 to deactivate and activate the region respectively. A value of 2 activates the region in line-wise mode with the highlighted text extending for whole lines only; see Section 18.7 [Character Highlighting], page 221.

region_highlight (array)

> Each element of this array may be set to a string that describes highlighting for an arbitrary region of the command line that will take effect the next time

the command line is redisplayed. Highlighting of the non-editable parts of the command line in PREDISPLAY and POSTDISPLAY are possible, but note that the P flag is needed for character indexing to include PREDISPLAY.

Each string consists of the following parts:

- Optionally, a 'P' to signify that the start and end offset that follow include any string set by the PREDISPLAY special parameter; this is needed if the predisplay string itself is to be highlighted. Whitespace may follow the 'P'.
- A start offset in the same units as CURSOR, terminated by whitespace.
- An end offset in the same units as CURSOR, terminated by whitespace.
- A highlight specification in the same format as used for contexts in the parameter zle_highlight, see Section 18.7 [Character Highlighting], page 221; for example, standout or fg=red,bold.

For example,

```
region_highlight=("P0 20 bold")
```

specifies that the first twenty characters of the text including any predisplay string should be highlighted in bold.

Note that the effect of region_highlight is not saved and disappears as soon as the line is accepted.

The final highlighting on the command line depends on both region_highlight and zle_highlight; see Section 18.7 [Character Highlighting], page 221, for details.

registers (associative array)

The contents of each of the vi register buffers. These are typically set using vi-set-buffer followed by a delete, change or yank command.

SUFFIX_ACTIVE (integer)
SUFFIX_START (integer)
SUFFIX_END (integer)

SUFFIX_ACTIVE indicates whether an auto-removable completion suffix is currently active. SUFFIX_START and SUFFIX_END give the location of the suffix and are in the same units as CURSOR. They are only valid for reading when SUFFIX_ACTIVE is non-zero.

All parameters are read-only.

UNDO_CHANGE_NO (integer)

A number representing the state of the undo history. The only use of this is passing as an argument to the undo widget in order to undo back to the recorded point. Read-only.

UNDO_LIMIT_NO (integer)

A number corresponding to an existing change in the undo history; compare UNDO_CHANGE_NO. If this is set to a value greater than zero, the undo command will not allow the line to be undone beyond the given change number. It is still possible to use 'zle undo *change*' in a widget to undo beyond that point; in that case, it will not be possible to undo at all until UNDO_LIMIT_NO is reduced. Set to 0 to disable the limit.

A typical use of this variable in a widget function is as follows (note the additional function scope is required):

```
() {
    local UNDO_LIMIT_NO=$UNDO_CHANGE_NO
    # Perform some form of recursive edit.
}
```

WIDGET (scalar)

> The name of the widget currently being executed; read-only.

WIDGETFUNC (scalar)

> The name of the shell function that implements a widget defined with either `zle -N` or `zle -C`. In the former case, this is the second argument to the `zle -N` command that defined the widget, or the first argument if there was no second argument. In the latter case this is the third argument to the `zle -C` command that defined the widget. Read-only.

WIDGETSTYLE (scalar)

> Describes the implementation behind the completion widget currently being executed; the second argument that followed `zle -C` when the widget was defined. This is the name of a builtin completion widget. For widgets defined with `zle -N` this is set to the empty string. Read-only.

YANK_ACTIVE (integer)
YANK_START (integer)
YANK_END (integer)

> YANK_ACTIVE indicates whether text has just been yanked (pasted) into the buffer. YANK_START and YANK_END give the location of the pasted text and are in the same units as CURSOR. They are only valid for reading when YANK_ACTIVE is non-zero. They can also be assigned by widgets that insert text in a yank-like fashion, for example wrappers of `bracketed-paste`. See also `zle -f`.
>
> YANK_ACTIVE is read-only.

ZLE_RECURSIVE (integer)

> Usually zero, but incremented inside any instance of `recursive-edit`. Hence indicates the current recursion level.
>
> ZLE_RECURSIVE is read-only.

ZLE_STATE (scalar)

> Contains a set of space-separated words that describe the current `zle` state.
>
> Currently, the states shown are the insert mode as set by the `overwrite-mode` or `vi-replace` widgets and whether history commands will visit imported entries as controlled by the set-local-history widget. The string contains '`insert`' if characters to be inserted on the command line move existing characters to the right or '`overwrite`' if characters to be inserted overwrite existing characters. It contains '`localhistory`' if only local history commands will be visited or '`globalhistory`' if imported history commands will also be visited.
>
> The substrings are sorted in alphabetical order so that if you want to test for two specific substrings in a future-proof way, you can do match by doing:

```
if [[ $ZLE_STATE == *globalhistory*insert* ]]; then ...; fi
```

18.5.1 Special Widgets

There are a few user-defined widgets which are special to the shell. If they do not exist, no special action is taken. The environment provided is identical to that for any other editing widget.

zle-isearch-exit

> Executed at the end of incremental search at the point where the isearch prompt is removed from the display. See zle-isearch-update for an example.

zle-isearch-update

> Executed within incremental search when the display is about to be redrawn. Additional output below the incremental search prompt can be generated by using 'zle -M' within the widget. For example,

> > zle-isearch-update() { zle -M "Line $HISTNO"; }
> > zle -N zle-isearch-update

> Note the line output by 'zle -M' is not deleted on exit from incremental search. This can be done from a zle-isearch-exit widget:

> > zle-isearch-exit() { zle -M ""; }
> > zle -N zle-isearch-exit

zle-line-pre-redraw

> Executed whenever the input line is about to be redrawn, providing an opportunity to update the region_highlight array.

zle-line-init

> Executed every time the line editor is started to read a new line of input. The following example puts the line editor into vi command mode when it starts up.

> > zle-line-init() { zle -K vicmd; }
> > zle -N zle-line-init

> (The command inside the function sets the keymap directly; it is equivalent to zle vi-cmd-mode.)

zle-line-finish

> This is similar to zle-line-init but is executed every time the line editor has finished reading a line of input.

zle-history-line-set

> Executed when the history line changes.

zle-keymap-select

> Executed every time the keymap changes, i.e. the special parameter KEYMAP is set to a different value, while the line editor is active. Initialising the keymap when the line editor starts does not cause the widget to be called.

> The value $KEYMAP within the function reflects the new keymap. The old keymap is passed as the sole argument.

> This can be used for detecting switches between the vi command (vicmd) and insert (usually main) keymaps.

18.6 Standard Widgets

The following is a list of all the standard widgets, and their default bindings in emacs mode, vi command mode and vi insert mode (the 'emacs', 'vicmd' and 'viins' keymaps, respectively).

Note that cursor keys are bound to movement keys in all three keymaps; the shell assumes that the cursor keys send the key sequences reported by the terminal-handling library (termcap or terminfo). The key sequences shown in the list are those based on the VT100, common on many modern terminals, but in fact these are not necessarily bound. In the case of the viins keymap, the initial escape character of the sequences serves also to return to the vicmd keymap: whether this happens is determined by the KEYTIMEOUT parameter, see Chapter 15 [Parameters], page 85.

18.6.1 Movement

vi-backward-blank-word (unbound) (B) (unbound)
> Move backward one word, where a word is defined as a series of non-blank characters.

vi-backward-blank-word-end (unbound) (gE) (unbound)
> Move to the end of the previous word, where a word is defined as a series of non-blank characters.

backward-char (^B ESC-[D) (unbound) (unbound)
> Move backward one character.

vi-backward-char (unbound) (^H h ^?) (ESC-[D)
> Move backward one character, without changing lines.

backward-word (ESC-B ESC-b) (unbound) (unbound)
> Move to the beginning of the previous word.

emacs-backward-word
> Move to the beginning of the previous word.

vi-backward-word (unbound) (b) (unbound)
> Move to the beginning of the previous word, vi-style.

vi-backward-word-end (unbound) (ge) (unbound)
> Move to the end of the previous word, vi-style.

beginning-of-line (^A) (unbound) (unbound)
> Move to the beginning of the line. If already at the beginning of the line, move to the beginning of the previous line, if any.

vi-beginning-of-line
> Move to the beginning of the line, without changing lines.

down-line (unbound) (unbound) (unbound)
> Move down a line in the buffer.

end-of-line (^E) (unbound) (unbound)
> Move to the end of the line. If already at the end of the line, move to the end of the next line, if any.

`vi-end-of-line` (unbound) (`$`) (unbound)

> Move to the end of the line. If an argument is given to this command, the cursor will be moved to the end of the line (argument - 1) lines down.

`vi-forward-blank-word` (unbound) (`W`) (unbound)

> Move forward one word, where a word is defined as a series of non-blank characters.

`vi-forward-blank-word-end` (unbound) (`E`) (unbound)

> Move to the end of the current word, or, if at the end of the current word, to the end of the next word, where a word is defined as a series of non-blank characters.

`forward-char` (`^F ESC-[C`) (unbound) (unbound)

> Move forward one character.

`vi-forward-char` (unbound) (`space l`) (`ESC-[C`)

> Move forward one character.

`vi-find-next-char` (`^X^F`) (`f`) (unbound)

> Read a character from the keyboard, and move to the next occurrence of it in the line.

`vi-find-next-char-skip` (unbound) (`t`) (unbound)

> Read a character from the keyboard, and move to the position just before the next occurrence of it in the line.

`vi-find-prev-char` (unbound) (`F`) (unbound)

> Read a character from the keyboard, and move to the previous occurrence of it in the line.

`vi-find-prev-char-skip` (unbound) (`T`) (unbound)

> Read a character from the keyboard, and move to the position just after the previous occurrence of it in the line.

`vi-first-non-blank` (unbound) (`^`) (unbound)

> Move to the first non-blank character in the line.

`vi-forward-word` (unbound) (`w`) (unbound)

> Move forward one word, vi-style.

`forward-word` (`ESC-F ESC-f`) (unbound) (unbound)

> Move to the beginning of the next word. The editor's idea of a word is specified with the `WORDCHARS` parameter.

`emacs-forward-word`

> Move to the end of the next word.

`vi-forward-word-end` (unbound) (`e`) (unbound)

> Move to the end of the next word.

`vi-goto-column` (`ESC-|`) (`|`) (unbound)

> Move to the column specified by the numeric argument.

`vi-goto-mark` (unbound) (`'`) (unbound)

> Move to the specified mark.

`vi-goto-mark-line` (unbound) (') (unbound)
> Move to beginning of the line containing the specified mark.

`vi-repeat-find` (unbound) (;) (unbound)
> Repeat the last `vi-find` command.

`vi-rev-repeat-find` (unbound) (,) (unbound)
> Repeat the last `vi-find` command in the opposite direction.

`up-line` (unbound) (unbound) (unbound)
> Move up a line in the buffer.

18.6.2 History Control

`beginning-of-buffer-or-history` (ESC-<) (**gg**) (unbound)
> Move to the beginning of the buffer, or if already there, move to the first event in the history list.

`beginning-of-line-hist`
> Move to the beginning of the line. If already at the beginning of the buffer, move to the previous history line.

`beginning-of-history`
> Move to the first event in the history list.

`down-line-or-history` (^N ESC-[B) (j) (ESC-[B)
> Move down a line in the buffer, or if already at the bottom line, move to the next event in the history list.

`vi-down-line-or-history` (unbound) (+) (unbound)
> Move down a line in the buffer, or if already at the bottom line, move to the next event in the history list. Then move to the first non-blank character on the line.

`down-line-or-search`
> Move down a line in the buffer, or if already at the bottom line, search forward in the history for a line beginning with the first word in the buffer.
>
> If called from a function by the `zle` command with arguments, the first argument is taken as the string for which to search, rather than the first word in the buffer.

`down-history` (unbound) (^N) (unbound)
> Move to the next event in the history list.

`history-beginning-search-backward`
> Search backward in the history for a line beginning with the current line up to the cursor. This leaves the cursor in its original position.

`end-of-buffer-or-history` (ESC->) (unbound) (unbound)
> Move to the end of the buffer, or if already there, move to the last event in the history list.

`end-of-line-hist`
> Move to the end of the line. If already at the end of the buffer, move to the next history line.

end-of-history

> Move to the last event in the history list.

vi-fetch-history (unbound) (**G**) (unbound)

> Fetch the history line specified by the numeric argument. This defaults to the current history line (i.e. the one that isn't history yet).

history-incremental-search-backward (**^R ^Xr**) (unbound) (unbound)

> Search backward incrementally for a specified string. The search is case-insensitive if the search string does not have uppercase letters and no numeric argument was given. The string may begin with '^' to anchor the search to the beginning of the line. When called from a user-defined function returns the following statuses: 0, if the search succeeded; 1, if the search failed; 2, if the search term was a bad pattern; 3, if the search was aborted by the **send-break** command.
>
> A restricted set of editing functions is available in the mini-buffer. Keys are looked up in the special **isearch** keymap, and if not found there in the main keymap (note that by default the **isearch** keymap is empty). An interrupt signal, as defined by the stty setting, will stop the search and go back to the original line. An undefined key will have the same effect. Note that the following always perform the same task within incremental searches and cannot be replaced by user defined widgets, nor can the set of functions be extended. The supported functions are:

accept-and-hold
accept-and-infer-next-history
accept-line
accept-line-and-down-history

> Perform the usual function after exiting incremental search. The command line displayed is executed.

backward-delete-char
vi-backward-delete-char

> Back up one place in the search history. If the search has been repeated this does not immediately erase a character in the mini-buffer.

accept-search

> Exit incremental search, retaining the command line but performing no further action. Note that this function is not bound by default and has no effect outside incremental search.

backward-delete-word
backward-kill-word
vi-backward-kill-word

> Back up one character in the minibuffer; if multiple searches have been performed since the character was inserted the search history is rewound to the point just before the character was entered. Hence this has the effect of repeating **backward-delete-char**.

clear-screen

> Clear the screen, remaining in incremental search mode.

history-incremental-search-backward

> Find the next occurrence of the contents of the mini-buffer. If the mini-buffer is empty, the most recent previously used search string is reinstated.

history-incremental-search-forward

> Invert the sense of the search.

magic-space

> Inserts a non-magical space.

quoted-insert
vi-quoted-insert

> Quote the character to insert into the minibuffer.

redisplay

> Redisplay the command line, remaining in incremental search mode.

vi-cmd-mode

> Select the 'vicmd' keymap; the 'main' keymap (insert mode) will be selected initially.
>
> In addition, the modifications that were made while in vi insert mode are merged to form a single undo event.

vi-repeat-search
vi-rev-repeat-search

> Repeat the search. The direction of the search is indicated in the mini-buffer.

Any character that is not bound to one of the above functions, or **self-insert** or **self-insert-unmeta**, will cause the mode to be exited. The character is then looked up and executed in the keymap in effect at that point.

When called from a widget function by the **zle** command, the incremental search commands can take a string argument. This will be treated as a string of keys, as for arguments to the **bindkey** command, and used as initial input for the command. Any characters in the string which are unused by the incremental search will be silently ignored. For example,

> **zle history-incremental-search-backward forceps**

will search backwards for **forceps**, leaving the minibuffer containing the string 'forceps'.

history-incremental-search-forward (^S ^Xs) (unbound) (unbound)

> Search forward incrementally for a specified string. The search is case-insensitive if the search string does not have uppercase letters and no numeric argument was given. The string may begin with '^' to anchor the search to the beginning of the line. The functions available in the mini-buffer are the same as for **history-incremental-search-backward**.

`history-incremental-pattern-search-backward`
`history-incremental-pattern-search-forward`

These widgets behave similarly to the corresponding widgets with no `-pattern`, but the search string typed by the user is treated as a pattern, respecting the current settings of the various options affecting pattern matching. See Section 14.8 [Filename Generation], page 72, for a description of patterns. If no numeric argument was given lowercase letters in the search string may match uppercase letters in the history. The string may begin with '^' to anchor the search to the beginning of the line.

The prompt changes to indicate an invalid pattern; this may simply indicate the pattern is not yet complete.

Note that only non-overlapping matches are reported, so an expression with wildcards may return fewer matches on a line than are visible by inspection.

`history-search-backward` (ESC-P ESC-p) (unbound) (unbound)

Search backward in the history for a line beginning with the first word in the buffer.

If called from a function by the `zle` command with arguments, the first argument is taken as the string for which to search, rather than the first word in the buffer.

`vi-history-search-backward` (unbound) (/) (unbound)

Search backward in the history for a specified string. The string may begin with '^' to anchor the search to the beginning of the line.

A restricted set of editing functions is available in the mini-buffer. An interrupt signal, as defined by the stty setting, will stop the search. The functions available in the mini-buffer are: `accept-line`, `backward-delete-char`, `vi-backward-delete-char`, `backward-kill-word`, `vi-backward-kill-word`, `clear-screen`, `redisplay`, `quoted-insert` and `vi-quoted-insert`.

`vi-cmd-mode` is treated the same as accept-line, and `magic-space` is treated as a space. Any other character that is not bound to self-insert or self-insert-unmeta will beep and be ignored. If the function is called from vi command mode, the bindings of the current insert mode will be used.

If called from a function by the `zle` command with arguments, the first argument is taken as the string for which to search, rather than the first word in the buffer.

`history-search-forward` (ESC-N ESC-n) (unbound) (unbound)

Search forward in the history for a line beginning with the first word in the buffer.

If called from a function by the `zle` command with arguments, the first argument is taken as the string for which to search, rather than the first word in the buffer.

`vi-history-search-forward` (unbound) (?) (unbound)

Search forward in the history for a specified string. The string may begin with '^' to anchor the search to the beginning of the line. The functions available in the mini-buffer are the same as for `vi-history-search-backward`. Argument handling is also the same as for that command.

`infer-next-history` (`^X^N`) (unbound) (unbound)
> Search in the history list for a line matching the current one and fetch the event following it.

`insert-last-word` (`ESC-_` `ESC-.`) (unbound) (unbound)
> Insert the last word from the previous history event at the cursor position. If a positive numeric argument is given, insert that word from the end of the previous history event. If the argument is zero or negative insert that word from the left (zero inserts the previous command word). Repeating this command replaces the word just inserted with the last word from the history event prior to the one just used; numeric arguments can be used in the same way to pick a word from that event.
>
> When called from a shell function invoked from a user-defined widget, the command can take one to three arguments. The first argument specifies a history offset which applies to successive calls to this widget: if it is -1, the default behaviour is used, while if it is 1, successive calls will move forwards through the history. The value 0 can be used to indicate that the history line examined by the previous execution of the command will be reexamined. Note that negative numbers should be preceded by a '`--`' argument to avoid confusing them with options.
>
> If two arguments are given, the second specifies the word on the command line in normal array index notation (as a more natural alternative to the numeric argument). Hence 1 is the first word, and -1 (the default) is the last word.
>
> If a third argument is given, its value is ignored, but it is used to signify that the history offset is relative to the current history line, rather than the one remembered after the previous invocations of `insert-last-word`.
>
> For example, the default behaviour of the command corresponds to
>
>   zle insert-last-word -- -1 -1
>
> while the command
>
>   zle insert-last-word -- -1 1 -
>
> always copies the first word of the line in the history immediately before the line being edited. This has the side effect that later invocations of the widget will be relative to that line.

`vi-repeat-search` (unbound) (`n`) (unbound)
> Repeat the last vi history search.

`vi-rev-repeat-search` (unbound) (`N`) (unbound)
> Repeat the last vi history search, but in reverse.

`up-line-or-history` (`^P` `ESC-[A`) (`k`) (`ESC-[A`)
> Move up a line in the buffer, or if already at the top line, move to the previous event in the history list.

`vi-up-line-or-history` (unbound) (-) (unbound)
> Move up a line in the buffer, or if already at the top line, move to the previous event in the history list. Then move to the first non-blank character on the line.

`up-line-or-search`
> Move up a line in the buffer, or if already at the top line, search backward in the history for a line beginning with the first word in the buffer.
>
> If called from a function by the `zle` command with arguments, the first argument is taken as the string for which to search, rather than the first word in the buffer.

`up-history` (unbound) (^P) (unbound)
> Move to the previous event in the history list.

`history-beginning-search-forward`
> Search forward in the history for a line beginning with the current line up to the cursor. This leaves the cursor in its original position.

`set-local-history`
> By default, history movement commands visit the imported lines as well as the local lines. This widget lets you toggle this on and off, or set it with the numeric argument. Zero for both local and imported lines and nonzero for only local lines.

18.6.3 Modifying Text

`vi-add-eol` (unbound) (A) (unbound)
> Move to the end of the line and enter insert mode.

`vi-add-next` (unbound) (a) (unbound)
> Enter insert mode after the current cursor position, without changing lines.

`backward-delete-char` (^H ^?) (unbound) (unbound)
> Delete the character behind the cursor.

`vi-backward-delete-char` (unbound) (X) (^H)
> Delete the character behind the cursor, without changing lines. If in insert mode, this won't delete past the point where insert mode was last entered.

`backward-delete-word`
> Delete the word behind the cursor.

`backward-kill-line`
> Kill from the beginning of the line to the cursor position.

`backward-kill-word` (^W ESC-^H ESC-^?) (unbound) (unbound)
> Kill the word behind the cursor.

`vi-backward-kill-word` (unbound) (unbound) (^W)
> Kill the word behind the cursor, without going past the point where insert mode was last entered.

`capitalize-word` (ESC-C ESC-c) (unbound) (unbound)
> Capitalize the current word and move past it.

`vi-change` (unbound) (c) (unbound)

> Read a movement command from the keyboard, and kill from the cursor position to the endpoint of the movement. Then enter insert mode. If the command is `vi-change`, change the current line.
>
> For compatibility with vi, if the command is `vi-forward-word` or `vi-forward-blank-word`, the whitespace after the word is not included. If you prefer the more consistent behaviour with the whitespace included use the following key binding:
>
> ```
> bindkey -a -s cw dwi
> ```

`vi-change-eol` (unbound) (C) (unbound)

> Kill to the end of the line and enter insert mode.

`vi-change-whole-line` (unbound) (S) (unbound)

> Kill the current line and enter insert mode.

`copy-region-as-kill` (ESC-W ESC-w) (unbound) (unbound)

> Copy the area from the cursor to the mark to the kill buffer.
>
> If called from a ZLE widget function in the form 'zle copy-region-as-kill *string*' then *string* will be taken as the text to copy to the kill buffer. The cursor, the mark and the text on the command line are not used in this case.

`copy-prev-word` (ESC-^_) (unbound) (unbound)

> Duplicate the word to the left of the cursor.

`copy-prev-shell-word`

> Like `copy-prev-word`, but the word is found by using shell parsing, whereas `copy-prev-word` looks for blanks. This makes a difference when the word is quoted and contains spaces.

`vi-delete` (unbound) (d) (unbound)

> Read a movement command from the keyboard, and kill from the cursor position to the endpoint of the movement. If the command is `vi-delete`, kill the current line.

`delete-char`

> Delete the character under the cursor.

`vi-delete-char` (unbound) (x) (unbound)

> Delete the character under the cursor, without going past the end of the line.

`delete-word`

> Delete the current word.

`down-case-word` (ESC-L ESC-l) (unbound) (unbound)

> Convert the current word to all lowercase and move past it.

`vi-down-case` (unbound) (gu) (unbound)

> Read a movement command from the keyboard, and convert all characters from the cursor position to the endpoint of the movement to lowercase. If the movement command is `vi-down-case`, swap the case of all characters on the current line.

`kill-word` (ESC-D ESC-d) (unbound) (unbound)
> Kill the current word.

`gosmacs-transpose-chars`
> Exchange the two characters behind the cursor.

`vi-indent` (unbound) (>) (unbound)
> Indent a number of lines.

`vi-insert` (unbound) (i) (unbound)
> Enter insert mode.

`vi-insert-bol` (unbound) (I) (unbound)
> Move to the first non-blank character on the line and enter insert mode.

`vi-join` (^X^J) (J) (unbound)
> Join the current line with the next one.

`kill-line` (^K) (unbound) (unbound)
> Kill from the cursor to the end of the line. If already on the end of the line, kill the newline character.

`vi-kill-line` (unbound) (unbound) (^U)
> Kill from the cursor back to wherever insert mode was last entered.

`vi-kill-eol` (unbound) (D) (unbound)
> Kill from the cursor to the end of the line.

`kill-region`
> Kill from the cursor to the mark.

`kill-buffer` (^X^K) (unbound) (unbound)
> Kill the entire buffer.

`kill-whole-line` (^U) (unbound) (unbound)
> Kill the current line.

`vi-match-bracket` (^X^B) (%) (unbound)
> Move to the bracket character (one of {}, () or []) that matches the one under the cursor. If the cursor is not on a bracket character, move forward without going past the end of the line to find one, and then go to the matching bracket.

`vi-open-line-above` (unbound) (O) (unbound)
> Open a line above the cursor and enter insert mode.

`vi-open-line-below` (unbound) (o) (unbound)
> Open a line below the cursor and enter insert mode.

`vi-oper-swap-case` (unbound) (g~) (unbound)
> Read a movement command from the keyboard, and swap the case of all characters from the cursor position to the endpoint of the movement. If the movement command is `vi-oper-swap-case`, swap the case of all characters on the current line.

`overwrite-mode` (^X^O) (unbound) (unbound)
> Toggle between overwrite mode and insert mode.

vi-put-before (unbound) (P) (unbound)

> Insert the contents of the kill buffer before the cursor. If the kill buffer contains a sequence of lines (as opposed to characters), paste it above the current line.

vi-put-after (unbound) (p) (unbound)

> Insert the contents of the kill buffer after the cursor. If the kill buffer contains a sequence of lines (as opposed to characters), paste it below the current line.

put-replace-selection (unbound) (unbound) (unbound)

> Replace the contents of the current region or selection with the contents of the kill buffer. If the kill buffer contains a sequence of lines (as opposed to characters), the current line will be split by the pasted lines.

quoted-insert (^V) (unbound) (unbound)

> Insert the next character typed into the buffer literally. An interrupt character will not be inserted.

vi-quoted-insert (unbound) (unbound) (^Q ^V)

> Display a '^' at the cursor position, and insert the next character typed into the buffer literally. An interrupt character will not be inserted.

quote-line (ESC-') (unbound) (unbound)

> Quote the current line; that is, put a '' character at the beginning and the end, and convert all '' characters to ''\'''.

quote-region (ESC-") (unbound) (unbound)

> Quote the region from the cursor to the mark.

vi-replace (unbound) (R) (unbound)

> Enter overwrite mode.

vi-repeat-change (unbound) (.) (unbound)

> Repeat the last vi mode text modification. If a count was used with the modification, it is remembered. If a count is given to this command, it overrides the remembered count, and is remembered for future uses of this command. The cut buffer specification is similarly remembered.

vi-replace-chars (unbound) (r) (unbound)

> Replace the character under the cursor with a character read from the keyboard.

self-insert (printable characters) (unbound) (printable characters and some control characters)

> Insert a character into the buffer at the cursor position.

self-insert-unmeta (ESC-^I ESC-^J ESC-^M) (unbound) (unbound)

> Insert a character into the buffer after stripping the meta bit and converting ^M to ^J.

vi-substitute (unbound) (s) (unbound)

> Substitute the next character(s).

vi-swap-case (unbound) (~) (unbound)

> Swap the case of the character under the cursor and move past it.

transpose-chars (^T) (unbound) (unbound)

> Exchange the two characters to the left of the cursor if at end of line, else exchange the character under the cursor with the character to the left.

transpose-words (ESC-T ESC-t) (unbound) (unbound)

> Exchange the current word with the one before it.
>
> With a positive numeric argument N, the word around the cursor, or following it if the cursor is between words, is transposed with the preceding N words. The cursor is put at the end of the resulting group of words.
>
> With a negative numeric argument $-N$, the effect is the same as using a positive argument N except that the original cursor position is retained, regardless of how the words are rearranged.

vi-unindent (unbound) (<) (unbound)

> Unindent a number of lines.

vi-up-case (unbound) (gU) (unbound)

> Read a movement command from the keyboard, and convert all characters from the cursor position to the endpoint of the movement to lowercase. If the movement command is **vi-up-case**, swap the case of all characters on the current line.

up-case-word (ESC-U ESC-u) (unbound) (unbound)

> Convert the current word to all caps and move past it.

yank (^Y) (unbound) (unbound)

> Insert the contents of the kill buffer at the cursor position.

yank-pop (ESC-y) (unbound) (unbound)

> Remove the text just yanked, rotate the kill-ring (the history of previously killed text) and yank the new top. Only works following **yank**, **vi-put-before**, **vi-put-after** or **yank-pop**.

vi-yank (unbound) (y) (unbound)

> Read a movement command from the keyboard, and copy the region from the cursor position to the endpoint of the movement into the kill buffer. If the command is **vi-yank**, copy the current line.

vi-yank-whole-line (unbound) (Y) (unbound)

> Copy the current line into the kill buffer.

vi-yank-eol

> Copy the region from the cursor position to the end of the line into the kill buffer. Arguably, this is what Y should do in vi, but it isn't what it actually does.

18.6.4 Arguments

digit-argument (ESC-0..ESC-9) (1-9) (unbound)

> Start a new numeric argument, or add to the current one. See also **vi-digit-or-beginning-of-line**. This only works if bound to a key sequence ending in a decimal digit.

Inside a widget function, a call to this function treats the last key of the key sequence which called the widget as the digit.

neg-argument (ESC--) (unbound) (unbound)
Changes the sign of the following argument.

universal-argument
Multiply the argument of the next command by 4. Alternatively, if this command is followed by an integer (positive or negative), use that as the argument for the next command. Thus digits cannot be repeated using this command. For example, if this command occurs twice, followed immediately by `forward-char`, move forward sixteen spaces; if instead it is followed by -2, then `forward-char`, move backward two spaces.

Inside a widget function, if passed an argument, i.e. 'zle universal-argument num', the numeric argument will be set to *num*; this is equivalent to 'NUMERIC=*num*'.

argument-base
Use the existing numeric argument as a numeric base, which must be in the range 2 to 36 inclusive. Subsequent use of `digit-argument` and `universal-argument` will input a new numeric argument in the given base. The usual hexadecimal convention is used: the letter `a` or `A` corresponds to 10, and so on. Arguments in bases requiring digits from 10 upwards are more conveniently input with `universal-argument`, since `ESC-a` etc. are not usually bound to `digit-argument`.

The function can be used with a command argument inside a user-defined widget. The following code sets the base to 16 and lets the user input a hexadecimal argument until a key out of the digit range is typed:

```
zle argument-base 16
zle universal-argument
```

18.6.5 Completion

accept-and-menu-complete
In a menu completion, insert the current completion into the buffer, and advance to the next possible completion.

complete-word
Attempt completion on the current word.

delete-char-or-list (^D) (unbound) (unbound)
Delete the character under the cursor. If the cursor is at the end of the line, list possible completions for the current word.

expand-cmd-path
Expand the current command to its full pathname.

expand-or-complete (TAB) (unbound) (TAB)
Attempt shell expansion on the current word. If that fails, attempt completion.

expand-or-complete-prefix
Attempt shell expansion on the current word up to cursor.

`expand-history` (ESC-space ESC-!) (unbound) (unbound)

> Perform history expansion on the edit buffer.

`expand-word` (^X*) (unbound) (unbound)

> Attempt shell expansion on the current word.

`list-choices` (ESC-^D) (^D =) (^D)

> List possible completions for the current word.

`list-expand` (^Xg ^XG) (^G) (^G)

> List the expansion of the current word.

`magic-space`

> Perform history expansion and insert a space into the buffer. This is intended to be bound to space.

`menu-complete`

> Like `complete-word`, except that menu completion is used. See the `MENU_COMPLETE` option.

`menu-expand-or-complete`

> Like `expand-or-complete`, except that menu completion is used.

`reverse-menu-complete`

> Perform menu completion, like `menu-complete`, except that if a menu completion is already in progress, move to the *previous* completion rather than the next.

`end-of-list`

> When a previous completion displayed a list below the prompt, this widget can be used to move the prompt below the list.

18.6.6 Miscellaneous

`accept-and-hold` (ESC-A ESC-a) (unbound) (unbound)

> Push the contents of the buffer on the buffer stack and execute it.

`accept-and-infer-next-history`

> Execute the contents of the buffer. Then search the history list for a line matching the current one and push the event following onto the buffer stack.

`accept-line` (^J ^M) (^J ^M) (^J ^M)

> Finish editing the buffer. Normally this causes the buffer to be executed as a shell command.

`accept-line-and-down-history` (^O) (unbound) (unbound)

> Execute the current line, and push the next history event on the buffer stack.

`auto-suffix-remove`

> If the previous action added a suffix (space, slash, etc.) to the word on the command line, remove it. Otherwise do nothing. Removing the suffix ends any active menu completion or menu selection.
>
> This widget is intended to be called from user-defined widgets to enforce a desired suffix-removal behavior.

auto-suffix-retain

> If the previous action added a suffix (space, slash, etc.) to the word on the command line, force it to be preserved. Otherwise do nothing. Retaining the suffix ends any active menu completion or menu selection.
>
> This widget is intended to be called from user-defined widgets to enforce a desired suffix-preservation behavior.

beep   Beep, unless the `BEEP` option is unset.

bracketed-paste

> This widget is invoked when text is pasted to the terminal emulator. It is not intended to be bound to actual keys but instead to the special sequence generated by the terminal emulator when text is pasted.
>
> When invoked interactively, the pasted text is inserted to the buffer and placed in the cutbuffer. If a numeric argument is given, shell quoting will be applied to the pasted text before it is inserted.
>
> When a named buffer is specified with `vi-set-buffer` (`"x`), the pasted text is stored in that named buffer but not inserted.
>
> When called from a widget function as '`bracketed-paste` *name*', the pasted text is assigned to the variable *name* and no other processing is done.
>
> See also the `zle_bracketed_paste` parameter.

vi-cmd-mode (^X^V) (unbound) (^[)

> Enter command mode; that is, select the 'vicmd' keymap. Yes, this is bound by default in emacs mode.

vi-caps-lock-panic

> Hang until any lowercase key is pressed. This is for vi users without the mental capacity to keep track of their caps lock key (like the author).

clear-screen (^L ESC-^L) (^L) (^L)

> Clear the screen and redraw the prompt.

deactivate-region

> Make the current region inactive. This disables vim-style visual selection mode if it is active.

describe-key-briefly

> Reads a key sequence, then prints the function bound to that sequence.

exchange-point-and-mark (^X^X) (unbound) (unbound)

> Exchange the cursor position (point) with the position of the mark. Unless a negative numeric argument is given, the region between point and mark is activated so that it can be highlighted. If a zero numeric argument is given, the region is activated but point and mark are not swapped.

execute-named-cmd (ESC-x) (:) (unbound)

> Read the name of an editor command and execute it. Aliasing this widget with '`zle -A`' or replacing it with '`zle -N`' has no effect when interpreting key bindings, but '`zle execute-named-cmd`' will invoke such an alias or replacement.

A restricted set of editing functions is available in the mini-buffer. Keys are looked up in the special `command` keymap, and if not found there in the main keymap. An interrupt signal, as defined by the stty setting, will abort the function. Note that the following always perform the same task within the `executed-named-cmd` environment and cannot be replaced by user defined widgets, nor can the set of functions be extended. The allowed functions are: `backward-delete-char`, `vi-backward-delete-char`, `clear-screen`, `redisplay`, `quoted-insert`, `vi-quoted-insert`, `backward-kill-word`, `vi-backward-kill-word`, `kill-whole-line`, `vi-kill-line`, `backward-kill-line`, `list-choices`, `delete-char-or-list`, `complete-word`, `accept-line`, `expand-or-complete` and `expand-or-complete-prefix`.

`kill-region` kills the last word, and vi-cmd-mode is treated the same as accept-line. The space and tab characters, if not bound to one of these functions, will complete the name and then list the possibilities if the `AUTO_LIST` option is set. Any other character that is not bound to `self-insert` or `self-insert-unmeta` will beep and be ignored. The bindings of the current insert mode will be used.

Currently this command may not be redefined or called by name.

execute-last-named-cmd (ESC-z) (unbound) (unbound)

Redo the last function executed with `execute-named-cmd`.

Like `execute-named-cmd`, this command may not be redefined, but it may be called by name.

get-line (ESC-G ESC-g) (unbound) (unbound)

Pop the top line off the buffer stack and insert it at the cursor position.

pound-insert (unbound) (#) (unbound)

If there is no # character at the beginning of the buffer, add one to the beginning of each line. If there is one, remove a # from each line that has one. In either case, accept the current line. The `INTERACTIVE_COMMENTS` option must be set for this to have any usefulness.

vi-pound-insert

If there is no # character at the beginning of the current line, add one. If there is one, remove it. The `INTERACTIVE_COMMENTS` option must be set for this to have any usefulness.

push-input

Push the entire current multiline construct onto the buffer stack and return to the top-level (`PS1`) prompt. If the current parser construct is only a single line, this is exactly like `push-line`. Next time the editor starts up or is popped with `get-line`, the construct will be popped off the top of the buffer stack and loaded into the editing buffer.

push-line (^Q ESC-Q ESC-q) (unbound) (unbound)

Push the current buffer onto the buffer stack and clear the buffer. Next time the editor starts up, the buffer will be popped off the top of the buffer stack and loaded into the editing buffer.

push-line-or-edit

At the top-level (PS1) prompt, equivalent to push-line. At a secondary (PS2) prompt, move the entire current multiline construct into the editor buffer. The latter is equivalent to push-input followed by get-line.

read-command

Only useful from a user-defined widget. A keystroke is read just as in normal operation, but instead of the command being executed the name of the command that would be executed is stored in the shell parameter REPLY. This can be used as the argument of a future zle command. If the key sequence is not bound, status 1 is returned; typically, however, REPLY is set to undefined-key to indicate a useless key sequence.

recursive-edit

Only useful from a user-defined widget. At this point in the function, the editor regains control until one of the standard widgets which would normally cause zle to exit (typically an accept-line caused by hitting the return key) is executed. Instead, control returns to the user-defined widget. The status returned is non-zero if the return was caused by an error, but the function still continues executing and hence may tidy up. This makes it safe for the user-defined widget to alter the command line or key bindings temporarily.

The following widget, caps-lock, serves as an example.

```
self-insert-ucase() {
  LBUFFER+=${(U)KEYS[-1]}
}

integer stat

zle -N self-insert self-insert-ucase
zle -A caps-lock save-caps-lock
zle -A accept-line caps-lock

zle recursive-edit
stat=$?

zle -A .self-insert self-insert
zle -A save-caps-lock caps-lock
zle -D save-caps-lock

(( stat )) && zle send-break

return $stat
```

This causes typed letters to be inserted capitalised until either accept-line (i.e. typically the return key) is typed or the caps-lock widget is invoked again; the later is handled by saving the old definition of caps-lock as save-caps-lock and then rebinding it to invoke accept-line. Note that an error from the recursive edit is detected as a non-zero return status and propagated by using the **send-break** widget.

redisplay (unbound) (^R) (^R)

Redisplays the edit buffer.

reset-prompt (unbound) (unbound) (unbound)

Force the prompts on both the left and right of the screen to be re-expanded, then redisplay the edit buffer. This reflects changes both to the prompt variables themselves and changes in the expansion of the values (for example, changes in time or directory, or changes to the value of variables referred to by the prompt).

Otherwise, the prompt is only expanded each time zle starts, and when the display as been interrupted by output from another part of the shell (such as a job notification) which causes the command line to be reprinted.

send-break (^G ESC-^G) (unbound) (unbound)

Abort the current editor function, e.g. **execute-named-command**, or the editor itself, e.g. if you are in **vared**. Otherwise abort the parsing of the current line; in this case the aborted line is available in the shell variable **ZLE_LINE_ABORTED**. If the editor is aborted from within **vared**, the variable **ZLE_VARED_ABORTED** is set.

run-help (ESC-H ESC-h) (unbound) (unbound)

Push the buffer onto the buffer stack, and execute the command 'run-help *cmd*', where *cmd* is the current command. **run-help** is normally aliased to **man**.

vi-set-buffer (unbound) (") (unbound)

Specify a buffer to be used in the following command. There are 37 buffers that can be specified: the 26 'named' buffers "a to "z, the 'yank' buffer "0, the nine 'queued' buffers "1 to "9 and the 'black hole' buffer "_. The named buffers can also be specified as "A to "Z.

When a buffer is specified for a cut, change or yank command, the text concerned replaces the previous contents of the specified buffer. If a named buffer is specified using a capital, the newly cut text is appended to the buffer instead of overwriting it. When using the "_ buffer, nothing happens. This can be useful for deleting text without affecting any buffers.

If no buffer is specified for a cut or change command, "1 is used, and the contents of "1 to "8 are each shifted along one buffer; the contents of "9 is lost. If no buffer is specified for a yank command, "0 is used. Finally, a paste command without a specified buffer will paste the text from the most recent command regardless of any buffer that might have been used with that command.

When called from a widget function by the **zle** command, the buffer can optionally be specified with an argument. For example,

```
zle vi-set-buffer A
```

vi-set-mark (unbound) (m) (unbound)

Set the specified mark at the cursor position.

set-mark-command (^@) (unbound) (unbound)
>Set the mark at the cursor position. If called with a negative numeric argument, do not set the mark but deactivate the region so that it is no longer highlighted (it is still usable for other purposes). Otherwise the region is marked as active.

spell-word (ESC-$ ESC-S ESC-s) (unbound) (unbound)
>Attempt spelling correction on the current word.

split-undo
>Breaks the undo sequence at the current change. This is useful in vi mode as changes made in insert mode are coalesced on entering command mode. Similarly, undo will normally revert as one all the changes made by a user-defined widget.

undefined-key
>This command is executed when a key sequence that is not bound to any command is typed. By default it beeps.

undo (^_ ^Xu ^X^U) (u) (unbound)
>Incrementally undo the last text modification. When called from a user-defined widget, takes an optional argument indicating a previous state of the undo history as returned by the UNDO_CHANGE_NO variable; modifications are undone until that state is reached, subject to any limit imposed by the UNDO_LIMIT_NO variable.

>Note that when invoked from vi command mode, the full prior change made in insert mode is reverted, the changes having been merged when command mode was selected.

redo (unbound) (^R) (unbound)
>Incrementally redo undone text modifications.

vi-undo-change (unbound) (unbound) (unbound)
>Undo the last text modification. If repeated, redo the modification.

visual-mode (unbound) (v) (unbound)
>Toggle vim-style visual selection mode. If line-wise visual mode is currently enabled then it is changed to being character-wise. If used following an operator, it forces the subsequent movement command to be treated as a character-wise movement.

visual-line-mode (unbound) (V) (unbound)
>Toggle vim-style line-wise visual selection mode. If character-wise visual mode is currently enabled then it is changed to being line-wise. If used following an operator, it forces the subsequent movement command to be treated as a line-wise movement.

what-cursor-position (^X=) (ga) (unbound)
>Print the character under the cursor, its code as an octal, decimal and hexadecimal number, the current cursor position within the buffer and the column of the cursor in the current line.

where-is Read the name of an editor command and print the listing of key sequences that invoke the specified command. A restricted set of editing functions is available in the mini-buffer. Keys are looked up in the special `command` keymap, and if not found there in the main keymap.

which-command (ESC-?) (unbound) (unbound)
> Push the buffer onto the buffer stack, and execute the command 'which-command *cmd*'. where *cmd* is the current command. `which-command` is normally aliased to `whence`.

vi-digit-or-beginning-of-line (unbound) (0) (unbound)
> If the last command executed was a digit as part of an argument, continue the argument. Otherwise, execute vi-beginning-of-line.

18.6.7 Text Objects

Text objects are commands that can be used to select a block of text according to some criteria. They are a feature of the vim text editor and so are primarily intended for use with vi operators or from visual selection mode. However, they can also be used from vi-insert or emacs mode. Key bindings listed below apply to the `viopp` and `visual` keymaps.

select-a-blank-word (aW)
> Select a word including adjacent blanks, where a word is defined as a series of non-blank characters. With a numeric argument, multiple words will be selected.

select-a-shell-word (aa)
> Select the current command argument applying the normal rules for quoting.

select-a-word (aw)
> Select a word including adjacent blanks, using the normal vi-style word definition. With a numeric argument, multiple words will be selected.

select-in-blank-word (iW)
> Select a word, where a word is defined as a series of non-blank characters. With a numeric argument, multiple words will be selected.

select-in-shell-word (ia)
> Select the current command argument applying the normal rules for quoting. If the argument begins and ends with matching quote characters, these are not included in the selection.

select-in-word (iw)
> Select a word, using the normal vi-style word definition. With a numeric argument, multiple words will be selected.

18.7 Character Highlighting

The line editor has the ability to highlight characters or regions of the line that have a particular significance. This is controlled by the array parameter `zle_highlight`, if it has been set by the user.

If the parameter contains the single entry `none` all highlighting is turned off. Note the parameter is still expected to be an array.

Otherwise each entry of the array should consist of a word indicating a context for highlighting, then a colon, then a comma-separated list of the types of highlighting to apply in that context.

The contexts available for highlighting are the following:

default   Any text within the command line not affected by any other highlighting. Text outside the editable area of the command line is not affected.

isearch   When one of the incremental history search widgets is active, the area of the command line matched by the search string or pattern.

region   The currently selected text. In emacs terminology, this is referred to as the region and is bounded by the cursor (point) and the mark. The region is only highlighted if it is active, which is the case after the mark is modified with **set-mark-command** or **exchange-point-and-mark**. Note that whether or not the region is active has no effect on its use within emacs style widgets, it simply determines whether it is highlighted. In vi mode, the region corresponds to selected text in visual mode.

special   Individual characters that have no direct printable representation but are shown in a special manner by the line editor. These characters are described below.

suffix   This context is used in completion for characters that are marked as suffixes that will be removed if the completion ends at that point, the most obvious example being a slash (/) after a directory name. Note that suffix removal is configurable; the circumstances under which the suffix will be removed may differ for different completions.

paste   Following a command to paste text, the characters that were inserted.

When **region_highlight** is set, the contexts that describe a region — **isearch**, **region**, **suffix**, and **paste** — are applied first, then **region_highlight** is applied, then the remaining **zle_highlight** contexts are applied. If a particular character is affected by multiple specifications, the last specification wins.

zle_highlight may contain additional fields for controlling how terminal sequences to change colours are output. Each of the following is followed by a colon and a string in the same form as for key bindings. This will not be necessary for the vast majority of terminals as the defaults shown in parentheses are widely used.

fg_start_code (\e[3)
> The start of the escape sequence for the foreground colour. This is followed by one to three ASCII digits representing the colour. Only used for palette colors, i.e. not 24-bit colors specified via a color triplet.

fg_default_code (9)
> The number to use instead of the colour to reset the default foreground colour.

fg_end_code (m)
> The end of the escape sequence for the foreground colour.

bg_start_code (\e[4)
> The start of the escape sequence for the background colour. See **fg_start_code** above.

bg_default_code (9)

> The number to use instead of the colour to reset the default background colour.

bg_end_code (m)

> The end of the escape sequence for the background colour.

The available types of highlighting are the following. Note that not all types of highlighting are available on all terminals:

> No highlighting is applied to the given context. It is not useful for this to appear with other types of highlighting; it is used to override a default.

fg=*colour*

> The foreground colour should be set to *colour*, a decimal integer, the name of one of the eight most widely-supported colours or as a '#' followed by an RGB triplet in hexadecimal format.

> Not all terminals support this and, of those that do, not all provide facilities to test the support, hence the user should decide based on the terminal type. Most terminals support the colours black, red, green, yellow, blue, magenta, cyan and white, which can be set by name. In addition. default may be used to set the terminal's default foreground colour. Abbreviations are allowed; b or bl selects black. Some terminals may generate additional colours if the bold attribute is also present.

> On recent terminals and on systems with an up-to-date terminal database the number of colours supported may be tested by the command 'echotc Co'; if this succeeds, it indicates a limit on the number of colours which will be enforced by the line editor. The number of colours is in any case limited to 256 (i.e. the range 0 to 255).

> Some modern terminal emulators have support for 24-bit true colour (16 million colours). In this case, the hex triplet format can be used. This consists of either a three or six digit hexadecimal number describing the red, green and blue components of the colour. Hex triplets can also be used with 88 and 256 colour terminals via the zsh/nearcolor module (see Section 22.18 [The zsh/nearcolor Module], page 353).

> Colour is also known as color.

bg=*colour*

> The background colour should be set to *colour*. This works similarly to the foreground colour, except the background is not usually affected by the bold attribute.

bold

> The characters in the given context are shown in a bold font. Not all terminals distinguish bold fonts.

standout

> The characters in the given context are shown in the terminal's standout mode. The actual effect is specific to the terminal; on many terminals it is inverse video. On some such terminals, where the cursor does not blink it appears with standout mode negated, making it less than clear where the cursor actually is. On such terminals one of the other effects may be preferable for highlighting the region and matched search string.

`underline`

> The characters in the given context are shown underlined. Some terminals show the foreground in a different colour instead; in this case whitespace will not be highlighted.

The characters described above as 'special' are as follows. The formatting described here is used irrespective of whether the characters are highlighted:

ASCII control characters

> Control characters in the ASCII range are shown as '^' followed by the base character.

Unprintable multibyte characters

> This item applies to control characters not in the ASCII range, plus other characters as follows. If the `MULTIBYTE` option is in effect, multibyte characters not in the ASCII character set that are reported as having zero width are treated as combining characters when the option `COMBINING_CHARS` is on. If the option is off, or if a character appears where a combining character is not valid, the character is treated as unprintable.

> Unprintable multibyte characters are shown as a hexadecimal number between angle brackets. The number is the code point of the character in the wide character set; this may or may not be Unicode, depending on the operating system.

Invalid multibyte characters

> If the `MULTIBYTE` option is in effect, any sequence of one or more bytes that does not form a valid character in the current character set is treated as a series of bytes each shown as a special character. This case can be distinguished from other unprintable characters as the bytes are represented as two hexadecimal digits between angle brackets, as distinct from the four or eight digits that are used for unprintable characters that are nonetheless valid in the current character set.

> Not all systems support this: for it to work, the system's representation of wide characters must be code values from the Universal Character Set, as defined by ISO 10646 (also known as Unicode).

Wrapped double-width characters

> When a double-width character appears in the final column of a line, it is instead shown on the next line. The empty space left in the original position is highlighted as a special character.

If `zle_highlight` is not set or no value applies to a particular context, the defaults applied are equivalent to

```
zle_highlight=(region:standout special:standout
suffix:bold isearch:underline paste:standout)
```

i.e. both the region and special characters are shown in standout mode.

Within widgets, arbitrary regions may be highlighted by setting the special array parameter `region_highlight`; see Section 18.4 [Zle Widgets], page 195.

19 Completion Widgets

19.1 Description

The shell's programmable completion mechanism can be manipulated in two ways; here the low-level features supporting the newer, function-based mechanism are defined. A complete set of shell functions based on these features is described in the next chapter, Chapter 20 [Completion System], page 242, and users with no interest in adding to that system (or, potentially, writing their own — see dictionary entry for 'hubris') should skip the current section. The older system based on the `compctl` builtin command is described in Chapter 21 [Completion Using compctl], page 319.

Completion widgets are defined by the `-C` option to the `zle` builtin command provided by the `zsh/zle` module (see Section 22.32 [The zsh/zle Module], page 378). For example,

        zle -C complete expand-or-complete completer

defines a widget named 'complete'. The second argument is the name of any of the builtin widgets that handle completions: `complete-word`, `expand-or-complete`, `expand-or-complete-prefix`, `menu-complete`, `menu-expand-or-complete`, `reverse-menu-complete`, `list-choices`, or `delete-char-or-list`. Note that this will still work even if the widget in question has been re-bound.

When this newly defined widget is bound to a key using the `bindkey` builtin command defined in the `zsh/zle` module (Chapter 18 [Zsh Line Editor], page 183), typing that key will call the shell function 'completer'. This function is responsible for generating the possible matches using the builtins described below. As with other ZLE widgets, the function is called with its standard input closed.

Once the function returns, the completion code takes over control again and treats the matches in the same manner as the specified builtin widget, in this case `expand-or-complete`.

19.2 Completion Special Parameters

The parameters `ZLE_REMOVE_SUFFIX_CHARS` and `ZLE_SPACE_SUFFIX_CHARS` are used by the completion mechanism, but are not special. See Section 15.6 [Parameters Used By The Shell], page 99.

Inside completion widgets, and any functions called from them, some parameters have special meaning; outside these functions they are not special to the shell in any way. These parameters are used to pass information between the completion code and the completion widget. Some of the builtin commands and the condition codes use or change the current values of these parameters. Any existing values will be hidden during execution of completion widgets; except for `compstate`, the parameters are reset on each function exit (including nested function calls from within the completion widget) to the values they had when the function was entered.

CURRENT   This is the number of the current word, i.e. the word the cursor is currently on in the `words` array. Note that this value is only correct if the `ksharrays` option is not set.

IPREFIX Initially this will be set to the empty string. This parameter functions like PREFIX; it contains a string which precedes the one in PREFIX and is not considered part of the list of matches. Typically, a string is transferred from the beginning of PREFIX to the end of IPREFIX, for example:

```
IPREFIX=${PREFIX%%\=*}=
PREFIX=${PREFIX#*=}
```

causes the part of the prefix up to and including the first equal sign not to be treated as part of a matched string. This can be done automatically by the compset builtin, see below.

ISUFFIX As IPREFIX, but for a suffix that should not be considered part of the matches; note that the ISUFFIX string follows the SUFFIX string.

PREFIX Initially this will be set to the part of the current word from the beginning of the word up to the position of the cursor; it may be altered to give a common prefix for all matches.

QIPREFIX This parameter is read-only and contains the quoted string up to the word being completed. E.g. when completing '"foo', this parameter contains the double quote. If the -q option of compset is used (see below), and the original string was '"foo bar' with the cursor on the 'bar', this parameter contains '"foo '.

QISUFFIX Like QIPREFIX, but containing the suffix.

SUFFIX Initially this will be set to the part of the current word from the cursor position to the end; it may be altered to give a common suffix for all matches. It is most useful when the option COMPLETE_IN_WORD is set, as otherwise the whole word on the command line is treated as a prefix.

compstate

This is an associative array with various keys and values that the completion code uses to exchange information with the completion widget. The keys are:

all_quotes

The -q option of the compset builtin command (see below) allows a quoted string to be broken into separate words; if the cursor is on one of those words, that word will be completed, possibly invoking 'compset -q' recursively. With this key it is possible to test the types of quoted strings which are currently broken into parts in this fashion. Its value contains one character for each quoting level. The characters are a single quote or a double quote for strings quoted with these characters, a dollars sign for strings quoted with $'...' and a backslash for strings not starting with a quote character. The first character in the value always corresponds to the innermost quoting level.

context This will be set by the completion code to the overall context in which completion is attempted. Possible values are:

array_value
> when completing inside the value of an array parameter assignment; in this case the **words** array contains the words inside the parentheses.

brace_parameter
> when completing the name of a parameter in a parameter expansion beginning with ${. This context will also be set when completing parameter flags following ${(; the full command line argument is presented and the handler must test the value to be completed to ascertain that this is the case.

assign_parameter
> when completing the name of a parameter in a parameter assignment.

command
> when completing for a normal command (either in command position or for an argument of the command).

condition
> when completing inside a '[[...]]' conditional expression; in this case the **words** array contains only the words inside the conditional expression.

math
> when completing in a mathematical environment such as a '((...))' construct.

parameter
> when completing the name of a parameter in a parameter expansion beginning with $ but not ${.

redirect
> when completing after a redirection operator.

subscript
> when completing inside a parameter subscript.

value
> when completing the value of a parameter assignment.

exact
Controls the behaviour when the **REC_EXACT** option is set. It will be set to **accept** if an exact match would be accepted, and will be unset otherwise.

If it was set when at least one match equal to the string on the line was generated, the match is accepted.

exact_string
The string of an exact match if one was found, otherwise unset.

ignored
The number of words that were ignored because they matched one of the patterns given with the **-F** option to the **compadd** builtin command.

insert
This controls the manner in which a match is inserted into the command line. On entry to the widget function, if it is unset the

command line is not to be changed; if set to unambiguous, any prefix common to all matches is to be inserted; if set to automenu-unambiguous, the common prefix is to be inserted and the next invocation of the completion code may start menu completion (due to the AUTO_MENU option being set); if set to menu or automenu menu completion will be started for the matches currently generated (in the latter case this will happen because the AUTO_MENU is set). The value may also contain the string 'tab' when the completion code would normally not really do completion, but only insert the TAB character.

On exit it may be set to any of the values above (where setting it to the empty string is the same as unsetting it), or to a number, in which case the match whose number is given will be inserted into the command line. Negative numbers count backward from the last match (with '-1' selecting the last match) and out-of-range values are wrapped around, so that a value of zero selects the last match and a value one more than the maximum selects the first. Unless the value of this key ends in a space, the match is inserted as in a menu completion, i.e. without automatically appending a space.

Both menu and automenu may also specify the number of the match to insert, given after a colon. For example, 'menu:2' says to start menu completion, beginning with the second match.

Note that a value containing the substring 'tab' makes the matches generated be ignored and only the TAB be inserted.

Finally, it may also be set to all, which makes all matches generated be inserted into the line.

insert_positions
> When the completion system inserts an unambiguous string into the line, there may be multiple places where characters are missing or where the character inserted differs from at least one match. The value of this key contains a colon separated list of all these positions, as indexes into the command line.

last_prompt
> If this is set to a non-empty string for every match added, the completion code will move the cursor back to the previous prompt after the list of completions has been displayed. Initially this is set or unset according to the ALWAYS_LAST_PROMPT option.

list
> This controls whether or how the list of matches will be displayed. If it is unset or empty they will never be listed; if its value begins with list, they will always be listed; if it begins with autolist or ambiguous, they will be listed when the AUTO_LIST or LIST_AMBIGUOUS options respectively would normally cause them to be.

If the substring **force** appears in the value, this makes the list be shown even if there is only one match. Normally, the list would be shown only if there are at least two matches.

The value contains the substring **packed** if the **LIST_PACKED** option is set. If this substring is given for all matches added to a group, this group will show the **LIST_PACKED** behavior. The same is done for the **LIST_ROWS_FIRST** option with the substring **rows**.

Finally, if the value contains the string **explanations**, only the explanation strings, if any, will be listed and if it contains **messages**, only the messages (added with the -x option of **compadd**) will be listed. If it contains both **explanations** and **messages** both kinds of explanation strings will be listed. It will be set appropriately on entry to a completion widget and may be changed there.

list_lines

This gives the number of lines that are needed to display the full list of completions. Note that to calculate the total number of lines to display you need to add the number of lines needed for the command line to this value, this is available as the value of the **BUFFERLINES** special parameter.

list_max   Initially this is set to the value of the **LISTMAX** parameter. It may be set to any other value; when the widget exits this value will be used in the same way as the value of **LISTMAX**.

nmatches   The number of matches generated and accepted by the completion code so far.

old_insert

On entry to the widget this will be set to the number of the match of an old list of completions that is currently inserted into the command line. If no match has been inserted, this is unset.

As with **old_list**, the value of this key will only be used if it is the string **keep**. If it was set to this value by the widget and there was an old match inserted into the command line, this match will be kept and if the value of the **insert** key specifies that another match should be inserted, this will be inserted after the old one.

old_list   This is set to **yes** if there is still a valid list of completions from a previous completion at the time the widget is invoked. This will usually be the case if and only if the previous editing operation was a completion widget or one of the builtin completion functions. If there is a valid list and it is also currently shown on the screen, the value of this key is **shown**.

After the widget has exited the value of this key is only used if it was set to **keep**. In this case the completion code will continue to use this old list. If the widget generated new matches, they will not be used.

parameter

The name of the parameter when completing in a subscript or in the value of a parameter assignment.

pattern_insert

Normally this is set to **menu**, which specifies that menu completion will be used whenever a set of matches was generated using pattern matching. If it is set to any other non-empty string by the user and menu completion is not selected by other option settings, the code will instead insert any common prefix for the generated matches as with normal completion.

pattern_match

Locally controls the behaviour given by the GLOB_COMPLETE option. Initially it is set to '*' if and only if the option is set. The completion widget may set it to this value, to an empty string (which has the same effect as unsetting it), or to any other non-empty string. If it is non-empty, unquoted metacharacters on the command line will be treated as patterns; if it is '*', then additionally a wildcard '*' is assumed at the cursor position; if it is empty or unset, metacharacters will be treated literally.

Note that the matcher specifications given to the **compadd** builtin command are not used if this is set to a non-empty string.

quote

When completing inside quotes, this contains the quotation character (i.e. either a single quote, a double quote, or a backtick). Otherwise it is unset.

quoting

When completing inside single quotes, this is set to the string **single**; inside double quotes, the string **double**; inside backticks, the string **backtick**. Otherwise it is unset.

redirect

The redirection operator when completing in a redirection position, i.e. one of <, >, etc.

restore

This is set to **auto** before a function is entered, which forces the special parameters mentioned above (**words**, CURRENT, PREFIX, IPREFIX, SUFFIX, and ISUFFIX) to be restored to their previous values when the function exits. If a function unsets it or sets it to any other string, they will not be restored.

to_end

Specifies the occasions on which the cursor is moved to the end of a string when a match is inserted. On entry to a widget function, it may be **single** if this will happen when a single unambiguous match was inserted or **match** if it will happen any time a match is inserted (for example, by menu completion; this is likely to be the effect of the ALWAYS_TO_END option).

On exit, it may be set to **single** as above. It may also be set to **always**, or to the empty string or unset; in those cases the cursor will be moved to the end of the string always or never respectively. Any other string is treated as **match**.

unambiguous

> This key is read-only and will always be set to the common (unambiguous) prefix the completion code has generated for all matches added so far.

unambiguous_cursor

> This gives the position the cursor would be placed at if the common prefix in the **unambiguous** key were inserted, relative to the value of that key. The cursor would be placed before the character whose index is given by this key.

unambiguous_positions

> This contains all positions where characters in the unambiguous string are missing or where the character inserted differs from at least one of the matches. The positions are given as indexes into the string given by the value of the **unambiguous** key.

vared

> If completion is called while editing a line using the **vared** builtin, the value of this key is set to the name of the parameter given as an argument to **vared**. This key is only set while a **vared** command is active.

words   This array contains the words present on the command line currently being edited.

19.3 Completion Builtin Commands

compadd [-akqQfenUlo12C] [-F *array*]
        [-P *prefix*] [-S *suffix*]
        [-p *hidden-prefix*] [-s *hidden-suffix*]
        [-i *ignored-prefix*] [-I *ignored-suffix*]
        [-W *file-prefix*] [-d *array*]
        [-J *name*] [-V *name*] [-X *explanation*] [-x *message*]
        [-r *remove-chars*] [-R *remove-func*]
        [-D *array*] [-O *array*] [-A *array*]
        [-E *number*]
        [-M *match-spec*] [--] [*words* ...]

> This builtin command can be used to add matches directly and control all the information the completion code stores with each possible match. The return status is zero if at least one match was added and non-zero if no matches were added.

> The completion code breaks the string to complete into seven fields in the order:

> > *<ipre><apre><hpre><word><hsuf><asuf><isuf>*

> The first field is an ignored prefix taken from the command line, the contents of the **IPREFIX** parameter plus the string given with the **-i** option. With the **-U** option, only the string from the **-i** option is used. The field *<apre>* is an optional prefix string given with the **-P** option. The *<hpre>* field is a string that is considered part of the match but that should not be shown when listing

completions, given with the -p option; for example, functions that do filename generation might specify a common path prefix this way. <word> is the part of the match that should appear in the list of completions, i.e. one of the *words* given at the end of the compadd command line. The suffixes <hsuf>, <asuf> and <isuf> correspond to the prefixes <hpre>, <apre> and <ipre> and are given by the options -s, -S and -I, respectively.

The supported flags are:

-P *prefix* This gives a string to be inserted before the given *words*. The string given is not considered as part of the match and any shell metacharacters in it will not be quoted when the string is inserted.

-S *suffix* Like -P, but gives a string to be inserted after the match.

-p *hidden-prefix*
This gives a string that should be inserted into the command line before the match but that should not appear in the list of matches. Unless the -U option is given, this string must be matched as part of the string on the command line.

-s *hidden-suffix*
Like '-p', but gives a string to insert after the match.

-i *ignored-prefix*
This gives a string to insert into the command line just before any string given with the '-P' option. Without '-P' the string is inserted before the string given with '-p' or directly before the match.

-I *ignored-suffix*
Like -i, but gives an ignored suffix.

-a With this flag the *words* are taken as names of arrays and the possible matches are their values. If only some elements of the arrays are needed, the *words* may also contain subscripts, as in 'foo[2,-1]'.

-k With this flag the *words* are taken as names of associative arrays and the possible matches are their keys. As for -a, the *words* may also contain subscripts, as in 'foo[(R)*bar*]'.

-d *array* This adds per-match display strings. The *array* should contain one element per *word* given. The completion code will then display the first element instead of the first *word*, and so on. The *array* may be given as the name of an array parameter or directly as a space-separated list of words in parentheses.

If there are fewer display strings than *words*, the leftover *words* will be displayed unchanged and if there are more display strings than *words*, the leftover display strings will be silently ignored.

-1 This option only has an effect if used together with the -d option. If it is given, the display strings are listed one per line, not arrayed in columns.

-o This option only has an effect if used together with the **-d** option. If it is given, the order of the output is determined by the match strings; otherwise it is determined by the display strings (i.e. the strings given by the **-d** option).

-J *name* Gives the name of the group of matches the words should be stored in.

-V *name* Like **-J** but naming an unsorted group. These are in a different name space than groups created with the **-J** flag.

-1 If given together with the **-V** option, makes only consecutive duplicates in the group be removed. If combined with the **-J** option, this has no visible effect. Note that groups with and without this flag are in different name spaces.

-2 If given together with the **-J** or **-V** option, makes all duplicates be kept. Again, groups with and without this flag are in different name spaces.

-X *explanation*

The *explanation* string will be printed with the list of matches, above the group currently selected.

-x *message*

Like **-X**, but the *message* will be printed even if there are no matches in the group.

-q The suffix given with **-S** will be automatically removed if the next character typed is a blank or does not insert anything, or if the suffix consists of only one character and the next character typed is the same character.

-r *remove-chars*

This is a more versatile form of the **-q** option. The suffix given with **-S** or the slash automatically added after completing directories will be automatically removed if the next character typed inserts one of the characters given in the *remove-chars*. This string is parsed as a characters class and understands the backslash sequences used by the **print** command. For example, '**-r "a-z\t"**' removes the suffix if the next character typed inserts a lower case character or a TAB, and '**-r "^0-9"**' removes the suffix if the next character typed inserts anything but a digit. One extra backslash sequence is understood in this string: '**\-**' stands for all characters that insert nothing. Thus '**-S "=" -q**' is the same as '**-S "=" -r "= \t\n\-"**'.

This option may also be used without the **-S** option; then any automatically added space will be removed when one of the characters in the list is typed.

-R *remove-func*

This is another form of the **-r** option. When a suffix has been inserted and the completion accepted, the function *remove-func* will be called after the next character typed. It is passed the length of the suffix as an argument and can use the special parameters available in ordinary (non-completion) zle widgets (see Chapter 18 [Zsh Line Editor], page 183) to analyse and modify the command line.

-f   If this flag is given, all of the matches built from *words* are marked as being the names of files. They are not required to be actual filenames, but if they are, and the option LIST_TYPES is set, the characters describing the types of the files in the completion lists will be shown. This also forces a slash to be added when the name of a directory is completed.

-e   This flag can be used to tell the completion code that the matches added are parameter names for a parameter expansion. This will make the AUTO_PARAM_SLASH and AUTO_PARAM_KEYS options be used for the matches.

-W *file-prefix*

This string is a pathname that will be prepended to each of the matches formed by the given *words* together with any prefix specified by the -p option to form a complete filename for testing. Hence it is only useful if combined with the -f flag, as the tests will not otherwise be performed.

-F *array*   Specifies an array containing patterns. Words matching one of these patterns are ignored, i.e. not considered to be possible matches.

The *array* may be the name of an array parameter or a list of literal patterns enclosed in parentheses and quoted, as in '-F "(*?.o *?.h)"'. If the name of an array is given, the elements of the array are taken as the patterns.

-Q   This flag instructs the completion code not to quote any metacharacters in the words when inserting them into the command line.

-M *match-spec*

This gives local match specifications as described below in Section 19.5 [Completion Matching Control], page 238. This option may be given more than once. In this case all *match-specs* given are concatenated with spaces between them to form the specification string to use. Note that they will only be used if the -U option is not given.

-n   Specifies that the words added are to be used as possible matches, but are not to appear in the completion listing.

-U   If this flag is given, all words given will be accepted and no matching will be done by the completion code. Normally this is used in functions that do the matching themselves.

-O *array*   If this option is given, the *words* are *not* added to the set of possible completions. Instead, matching is done as usual and all of the *words* given as arguments that match the string on the command line will be stored in the array parameter whose name is given as *array*.

-A *array*   As the -O option, except that instead of those of the *words* which match being stored in *array*, the strings generated internally by the completion code are stored. For example, with a matching specification of '-M "L:|no="', the string 'nof' on the command line and the string 'foo' as one of the *words*, this option stores the string 'nofoo' in the array, whereas the -O option stores the 'foo' originally given.

-D *array*   As with -O, the *words* are not added to the set of possible completions. Instead, the completion code tests whether each *word* in turn matches what is on the line. If the *n*th *word* does not match, the *n*th element of the *array* is removed. Elements for which the corresponding *word* is matched are retained.

-C   This option adds a special match which expands to all other matches when inserted into the line, even those that are added after this option is used. Together with the -d option it is possible to specify a string that should be displayed in the list for this special match. If no string is given, it will be shown as a string containing the strings that would be inserted for the other matches, truncated to the width of the screen.

-E *number*

This option adds *number* empty matches after the *words* have been added. An empty match takes up space in completion listings but will never be inserted in the line and can't be selected with menu completion or menu selection. This makes empty matches only useful to format completion lists and to make explanatory string be shown in completion lists (since empty matches can be given display strings with the -d option). And because all but one empty string would otherwise be removed, this option implies the -V and -2 options (even if an explicit -J option is given). This can be important to note as it affects the name space into which matches are added.

-

--   This flag ends the list of flags and options. All arguments after it will be taken as the words to use as matches even if they begin with hyphens.

Except for the -M flag, if any of these flags is given more than once, the first one (and its argument) will be used.

```
compset -p number
compset -P [ number ] pattern
compset -s number
compset -S [ number ] pattern
compset -n begin [ end ]
compset -N beg-pat [ end-pat ]
compset -q
```

This command simplifies modification of the special parameters, while its return status allows tests on them to be carried out.

The options are:

-p *number*

> If the contents of the PREFIX parameter is longer than *number* characters, the first *number* characters are removed from it and appended to the contents of the IPREFIX parameter.

-P [*number*] *pattern*

> If the value of the PREFIX parameter begins with anything that matches the *pattern*, the matched portion is removed from PREFIX and appended to IPREFIX.

> Without the optional *number*, the longest match is taken, but if *number* is given, anything up to the *number*th match is moved. If the *number* is negative, the *number*th longest match is moved. For example, if PREFIX contains the string 'a=b=c', then compset -P '*\=' will move the string 'a=b=' into the IPREFIX parameter, but compset -P 1 '*\=' will move only the string 'a='.

-s *number*

> As -p, but transfer the last *number* characters from the value of SUFFIX to the front of the value of ISUFFIX.

-S [*number*] *pattern*

> As -P, but match the last portion of SUFFIX and transfer the matched portion to the front of the value of ISUFFIX.

-n *begin* [*end*]

> If the current word position as specified by the parameter CURRENT is greater than or equal to *begin*, anything up to the *begin*th word is removed from the words array and the value of the parameter CURRENT is decremented by *begin*.

> If the optional *end* is given, the modification is done only if the current word position is also less than or equal to *end*. In this case, the words from position *end* onwards are also removed from the words array.

> Both *begin* and *end* may be negative to count backwards from the last element of the words array.

-N *beg-pat* [*end-pat*]

> If one of the elements of the words array before the one at the index given by the value of the parameter CURRENT matches the pattern

beg-pat, all elements up to and including the matching one are removed from the **words** array and the value of **CURRENT** is changed to point to the same word in the changed array.

If the optional pattern *end-pat* is also given, and there is an element in the **words** array matching this pattern, the parameters are modified only if the index of this word is higher than the one given by the **CURRENT** parameter (so that the matching word has to be after the cursor). In this case, the words starting with the one matching **end-pat** are also removed from the **words** array. If **words** contains no word matching *end-pat*, the testing and modification is performed as if it were not given.

-q   The word currently being completed is split on spaces into separate words, respecting the usual shell quoting conventions. The resulting words are stored in the **words** array, and **CURRENT**, **PREFIX**, **SUFFIX**, **QIPREFIX**, and **QISUFFIX** are modified to reflect the word part that is completed.

In all the above cases the return status is zero if the test succeeded and the parameters were modified and non-zero otherwise. This allows one to use this builtin in tests such as:

```
if compset -P '*\='; then ...
```

This forces anything up to and including the last equal sign to be ignored by the completion code.

compcall [**-TD**]

This allows the use of completions defined with the **compctl** builtin from within completion widgets. The list of matches will be generated as if one of the non-widget completion functions (**complete-word**, etc.) had been called, except that only **compctls** given for specific commands are used. To force the code to try completions defined with the **-T** option of **compctl** and/or the default completion (whether defined by **compctl -D** or the builtin default) in the appropriate places, the **-T** and/or **-D** flags can be passed to **compcall**.

The return status can be used to test if a matching **compctl** definition was found. It is non-zero if a **compctl** was found and zero otherwise.

Note that this builtin is defined by the **zsh/compctl** module.

19.4 Completion Condition Codes

The following additional condition codes for use within the [[...]] construct are available in completion widgets. These work on the special parameters. All of these tests can also be performed by the **compset** builtin, but in the case of the condition codes the contents of the special parameters are not modified.

-prefix [*number*] *pattern*

true if the test for the **-P** option of **compset** would succeed.

-suffix [*number*] *pattern*

        true if the test for the -S option of `compset` would succeed.

-after *beg-pat*

        true if the test of the -N option with only the *beg-pat* given would succeed.

-between *beg-pat end-pat*

        true if the test for the -N option with both patterns would succeed.

19.5 Completion Matching Control

It is possible by use of the -M option of the `compadd` builtin command to specify how the characters in the string to be completed (referred to here as the command line) map onto the characters in the list of matches produced by the completion code (referred to here as the trial completions). Note that this is not used if the command line contains a glob pattern and the GLOB_COMPLETE option is set or the `pattern_match` of the `compstate` special association is set to a non-empty string.

The *match-spec* given as the argument to the -M option (see Section 19.3 [Completion Builtin Commands], page 231) consists of one or more matching descriptions separated by whitespace. Each description consists of a letter followed by a colon and then the patterns describing which character sequences on the line match which character sequences in the trial completion. Any sequence of characters not handled in this fashion must match exactly, as usual.

The forms of *match-spec* understood are as follows. In each case, the form with an upper case initial character retains the string already typed on the command line as the final result of completion, while with a lower case initial character the string on the command line is changed into the corresponding part of the trial completion.

m:*lpat*=*tpat*
M:*lpat*=*tpat*

        Here, *lpat* is a pattern that matches on the command line, corresponding to *tpat* which matches in the trial completion.

l:*lanchor*|*lpat*=*tpat*
L:*lanchor*|*lpat*=*tpat*
l:*lanchor*||*ranchor*=*tpat*
L:*lanchor*||*ranchor*=*tpat*
b:*lpat*=*tpat*
B:*lpat*=*tpat*

        These letters are for patterns that are anchored by another pattern on the left side. Matching for *lpat* and *tpat* is as for m and M, but the pattern *lpat* matched on the command line must be preceded by the pattern *lanchor*. The *lanchor* can be blank to anchor the match to the start of the command line string; otherwise the anchor can occur anywhere, but must match in both the command line and trial completion strings.

        If no *lpat* is given but a *ranchor* is, this matches the gap between substrings matched by *lanchor* and *ranchor*. Unlike *lanchor*, the *ranchor* only needs to match the trial completion string.

The b and B forms are similar to l and L with an empty anchor, but need to match only the beginning of the word on the command line or trial completion, respectively.

r:*lpat*|*ranchor*=*tpat*
R:*lpat*|*ranchor*=*tpat*
r:*lanchor*||*ranchor*=*tpat*
R:*lanchor*||*ranchor*=*tpat*
e:*lpat*=*tpat*
E:*lpat*=*tpat*

As l, L, b and B, with the difference that the command line and trial completion patterns are anchored on the right side. Here an empty *ranchor* and the e and E forms force the match to the end of the command line or trial completion string.

x: This form is used to mark the end of matching specifications: subsequent specifications are ignored. In a single standalone list of specifications this has no use but where matching specifications are accumulated, such as from nested function calls, it can allow one function to override another.

Each *lpat*, *tpat* or *anchor* is either an empty string or consists of a sequence of literal characters (which may be quoted with a backslash), question marks, character classes, and correspondence classes; ordinary shell patterns are not used. Literal characters match only themselves, question marks match any character, and character classes are formed as for globbing and match any character in the given set.

Correspondence classes are defined like character classes, but with two differences: they are delimited by a pair of braces, and negated classes are not allowed, so the characters ! and ^ have no special meaning directly after the opening brace. They indicate that a range of characters on the line match a range of characters in the trial completion, but (unlike ordinary character classes) paired according to the corresponding position in the sequence. For example, to make any ASCII lower case letter on the line match the corresponding upper case letter in the trial completion, you can use 'm:{a-z}={A-Z}' (however, see below for the recommended form for this). More than one pair of classes can occur, in which case the first class before the = corresponds to the first after it, and so on. If one side has more such classes than the other side, the superfluous classes behave like normal character classes. In anchor patterns correspondence classes also behave like normal character classes.

The standard '[:*name*:]' forms described for standard shell patterns (see Section 14.8 [Filename Generation], page 72) may appear in correspondence classes as well as normal character classes. The only special behaviour in correspondence classes is if the form on the left and the form on the right are each one of [:upper:], [:lower:]. In these cases the character in the word and the character on the line must be the same up to a difference in case. Hence to make any lower case character on the line match the corresponding upper case character in the trial completion you can use 'm:{[:lower:]}={[:upper:]}'. Although the matching system does not yet handle multibyte characters, this is likely to be a future extension, at which point this syntax will handle arbitrary alphabets; hence this form, rather than the use of explicit ranges, is the recommended form. In other cases '[:*name*:]' forms are allowed. If the two forms on the left and right are the same, the characters must match exactly. In remaining cases, the corresponding tests are applied to both characters, but they are not otherwise constrained; any matching character in one set goes with any matching character in the other set: this is equivalent to the behaviour of ordinary character classes.

The pattern *tpat* may also be one or two stars, '*' or '**'. This means that the pattern on the command line can match any number of characters in the trial completion. In this case the pattern must be anchored (on either side); in the case of a single star, the *anchor* then determines how much of the trial completion is to be included — only the characters up to the next appearance of the anchor will be matched. With two stars, substrings matched by the anchor can be matched, too.

Examples:

The keys of the **options** association defined by the **parameter** module are the option names in all-lower-case form, without underscores, and without the optional **no** at the beginning even though the builtins **setopt** and **unsetopt** understand option names with upper case letters, underscores, and the optional **no**. The following alters the matching rules so that the prefix **no** and any underscore are ignored when trying to match the trial completions generated and upper case letters on the line match the corresponding lower case letters in the words:

```
compadd -M 'L:|[nN][oO]= M:_= M:{[:upper:]}={[:lower:]}' - \
    ${(k)options}
```

The first part says that the pattern '[nN][oO]' at the beginning (the empty anchor before the pipe symbol) of the string on the line matches the empty string in the list of words generated by completion, so it will be ignored if present. The second part does the same for an underscore anywhere in the command line string, and the third part uses correspondence classes so that any upper case letter on the line matches the corresponding lower case letter in the word. The use of the upper case forms of the specification characters (L and M) guarantees that what has already been typed on the command line (in particular the prefix **no**) will not be deleted.

Note that the use of L in the first part means that it matches only when at the beginning of both the command line string and the trial completion. I.e., the string '_NO_f' would not be completed to '_NO_foo', nor would 'NONO_f' be completed to 'NONO_foo' because of the leading underscore or the second 'NO' on the line which makes the pattern fail even though they are otherwise ignored. To fix this, one would use 'B:[nN][oO]=' instead of the first part. As described above, this matches at the beginning of the trial completion, independent of other characters or substrings at the beginning of the command line word which are ignored by the same or other *match-specs*.

The second example makes completion case insensitive. This is just the same as in the option example, except here we wish to retain the characters in the list of completions:

```
compadd -M 'm:{[:lower:]}={[:upper:]}' ...
```

This makes lower case letters match their upper case counterparts. To make upper case letters match the lower case forms as well:

```
compadd -M 'm:{[:lower:][:upper:]}={[:upper:][:lower:]}' ...
```

A nice example for the use of * patterns is partial word completion. Sometimes you would like to make strings like 'c.s.u' complete to strings like '**comp.source.unix**', i.e. the word on the command line consists of multiple parts, separated by a dot in this example, where each part should be completed separately — note, however, that the case where each part of the word, i.e. 'comp', 'source' and 'unix' in this example, is to be completed from separate sets of matches is a different problem to be solved by the implementation of the completion widget. The example can be handled by:

```
compadd -M 'r:|.=* r:|=*' \
    - comp.sources.unix comp.sources.misc ...
```

The first specification says that *lpat* is the empty string, while *anchor* is a dot; *tpat* is *, so this can match anything except for the '.' from the anchor in the trial completion word. So in 'c.s.u', the matcher sees 'c', followed by the empty string, followed by the anchor '.', and likewise for the second dot, and replaces the empty strings before the anchors, giving 'c[omp].s[ources].u[nix]', where the last part of the completion is just as normal.

With the pattern shown above, the string 'c.u' could not be completed to 'comp.sources.unix' because the single star means that no dot (matched by the anchor) can be skipped. By using two stars as in 'r:|.=**', however, 'c.u' could be completed to 'comp.sources.unix'. This also shows that in some cases, especially if the anchor is a real pattern, like a character class, the form with two stars may result in more matches than one would like.

The second specification is needed to make this work when the cursor is in the middle of the string on the command line and the option COMPLETE_IN_WORD is set. In this case the completion code would normally try to match trial completions that end with the string as typed so far, i.e. it will only insert new characters at the cursor position rather than at the end. However in our example we would like the code to recognise matches which contain extra characters after the string on the line (the 'nix' in the example). Hence we say that the empty string at the end of the string on the line matches any characters at the end of the trial completion.

More generally, the specification

```
compadd -M 'r:|[.,_-]=* r:|=*' ...
```

allows one to complete words with abbreviations before any of the characters in the square brackets. For example, to complete veryverylongfile.c rather than veryverylongheader.h with the above in effect, you can just type very.c before attempting completion.

The specifications with both a left and a right anchor are useful to complete partial words whose parts are not separated by some special character. For example, in some places strings have to be completed that are formed 'LikeThis' (i.e. the separate parts are determined by a leading upper case letter) or maybe one has to complete strings with trailing numbers. Here one could use the simple form with only one anchor as in:

```
compadd -M 'r:|[[:upper:]0-9]=* r:|=*' LikeTHIS FooHoo 5foo123 5bar234
```

But with this, the string 'H' would neither complete to 'FooHoo' nor to 'LikeTHIS' because in each case there is an upper case letter before the 'H' and that is matched by the anchor. Likewise, a '2' would not be completed. In both cases this could be changed by using 'r:|[[:upper:]0-9]=**', but then 'H' completes to both 'LikeTHIS' and 'FooHoo' and a '2' matches the other strings because characters can be inserted before every upper case letter and digit. To avoid this one would use:

```
compadd -M 'r:[^[:upper:]0-9]||[[:upper:]0-9]=** r:|=*' \
```

```
LikeTHIS FooHoo foo123 bar234
```

By using these two anchors, a 'H' matches only upper case 'H's that are immediately preceded by something matching the left anchor '[^[:upper:]0-9]'. The effect is, of course, that 'H' matches only the string 'FooHoo', a '2' matches only 'bar234' and so on.

When using the completion system (see Chapter 20 [Completion System], page 242), users can define match specifications that are to be used for specific contexts by using the `matcher` and `matcher-list` styles. The values for the latter will be used everywhere.

19.6 Completion Widget Example

The first step is to define the widget:

```
zle -C complete complete-word complete-files
```

Then the widget can be bound to a key using the `bindkey` builtin command:

```
bindkey '^X\t' complete
```

After that the shell function `complete-files` will be invoked after typing control-X and TAB. The function should then generate the matches, e.g.:

```
complete-files () { compadd - * }
```

This function will complete files in the current directory matching the current word.

20 Completion System

20.1 Description

This describes the shell code for the 'new' completion system, referred to as `compsys`. It is written in shell functions based on the features described in the previous chapter, Chapter 19 [Completion Widgets], page 225.

The features are contextual, sensitive to the point at which completion is started. Many completions are already provided. For this reason, a user can perform a great many tasks without knowing any details beyond how to initialize the system, which is described in Section 20.2 [Initialization], page 243.

The context that decides what completion is to be performed may be

- an argument or option position: these describe the position on the command line at which completion is requested. For example 'first argument to rmdir, the word being completed names a directory';

- a special context, denoting an element in the shell's syntax. For example 'a word in command position' or 'an array subscript'.

A full context specification contains other elements, as we shall describe.

Besides commands names and contexts, the system employs two more concepts, *styles* and *tags*. These provide ways for the user to configure the system's behaviour.

Tags play a dual role. They serve as a classification system for the matches, typically indicating a class of object that the user may need to distinguish. For example, when completing arguments of the `ls` command the user may prefer to try **files** before **directories**, so both of these are tags. They also appear as the rightmost element in a context specification.

Styles modify various operations of the completion system, such as output formatting, but also what kinds of completers are used (and in what order), or which tags are examined. Styles may accept arguments and are manipulated using the `zstyle` command described in Section 22.37 [The zsh/zutil Module], page 382.

In summary, tags describe *what* the completion objects are, and style **how** they are to be completed. At various points of execution, the completion system checks what styles and/or tags are defined for the current context, and uses that to modify its behavior. The full description of context handling, which determines how tags and other elements of the context influence the behaviour of styles, is described in Section 20.3 [Completion System Configuration], page 249.

When a completion is requested, a dispatcher function is called; see the description of `_main_complete` in the list of control functions below. This dispatcher decides which function should be called to produce the completions, and calls it. The result is passed to one or more *completers*, functions that implement individual completion strategies: simple completion, error correction, completion with error correction, menu selection, etc.

More generally, the shell functions contained in the completion system are of two types:

- those beginning 'comp' are to be called directly; there are only a few of these;
- those beginning '_' are called by the completion code. The shell functions of this set, which implement completion behaviour and may be bound to keystrokes, are referred to as 'widgets'. These proliferate as new completions are required.

20.2 Initialization

If the system was installed completely, it should be enough to call the shell function `compinit` from your initialization file; see the next section. However, the function `compinstall` can be run by a user to configure various aspects of the completion system.

Usually, `compinstall` will insert code into `.zshrc`, although if that is not writable it will save it in another file and tell you that file's location. Note that it is up to you to make sure that the lines added to `.zshrc` are actually run; you may, for example, need to move them to an earlier place in the file if `.zshrc` usually returns early. So long as you keep them all together (including the comment lines at the start and finish), you can rerun `compinstall` and it will correctly locate and modify these lines. Note, however, that any code you add to this section by hand is likely to be lost if you rerun `compinstall`, although lines using the command 'zstyle' should be gracefully handled.

The new code will take effect next time you start the shell, or run `.zshrc` by hand; there is also an option to make them take effect immediately. However, if `compinstall` has removed definitions, you will need to restart the shell to see the changes.

To run `compinstall` you will need to make sure it is in a directory mentioned in your `fpath` parameter, which should already be the case if zsh was properly configured as long as your startup files do not remove the appropriate directories from `fpath`. Then it must be autoloaded ('`autoload -U compinstall`' is recommended). You can abort the installation any time you are being prompted for information, and your `.zshrc` will not be altered at all; changes only take place right at the end, where you are specifically asked for confirmation.

20.2.1 Use of compinit

This section describes the use of `compinit` to initialize completion for the current session when called directly; if you have run `compinstall` it will be called automatically from your `.zshrc`.

To initialize the system, the function `compinit` should be in a directory mentioned in the `fpath` parameter, and should be autoloaded ('`autoload -U compinit`' is recommended), and then run simply as '`compinit`'. This will define a few utility functions, arrange for all the necessary shell functions to be autoloaded, and will then re-define all widgets that do completion to use the new system. If you use the **menu-select** widget, which is part of the **zsh/complist** module, you should make sure that that module is loaded before the call to `compinit` so that that widget is also re-defined. If completion styles (see below) are set up to perform expansion as well as completion by default, and the TAB key is bound to **expand-or-complete**, compinit will rebind it to **complete-word**; this is necessary to use the correct form of expansion.

Should you need to use the original completion commands, you can still bind keys to the old widgets by putting a '`.`' in front of the widget name, e.g. '`.expand-or-complete`'.

To speed up the running of `compinit`, it can be made to produce a dumped configuration that will be read in on future invocations; this is the default, but can be turned off by calling `compinit` with the option `-D`. The dumped file is `.zcompdump` in the same directory as the startup files (i.e. `$ZDOTDIR` or `$HOME`); alternatively, an explicit file name can be given by '`compinit -d` *dumpfile*'. The next invocation of `compinit` will read the dumped file instead of performing a full initialization.

If the number of completion files changes, `compinit` will recognise this and produce a new dump file. However, if the name of a function or the arguments in the first line of a `#compdef` function (as described below) change, it is easiest to delete the dump file by hand so that `compinit` will re-create it the next time it is run. The check performed to see if there are new functions can be omitted by giving the option `-C`. In this case the dump file will only be created if there isn't one already.

The dumping is actually done by another function, `compdump`, but you will only need to run this yourself if you change the configuration (e.g. using `compdef`) and then want to dump the new one. The name of the old dumped file will be remembered for this purpose.

If the parameter `_compdir` is set, `compinit` uses it as a directory where completion functions can be found; this is only necessary if they are not already in the function search path.

For security reasons `compinit` also checks if the completion system would use files not owned by root or by the current user, or files in directories that are world- or group-writable or that are not owned by root or by the current user. If such files or directories are found, `compinit` will ask if the completion system should really be used. To avoid these tests and make all files found be used without asking, use the option `-u`, and to make `compinit` silently ignore all insecure files and directories use the option -i. This security check is skipped entirely when the -C option is given.

The security check can be retried at any time by running the function compaudit. This is the same check used by compinit, but when it is executed directly any changes to fpath are made local to the function so they do not persist. The directories to be checked may be passed as arguments; if none are given, compaudit uses fpath and _compdir to find completion system directories, adding missing ones to fpath as necessary. To force a check of exactly the directories currently named in fpath, set _compdir to an empty string before calling compaudit or compinit.

The function bashcompinit provides compatibility with bash's programmable completion system. When run it will define the functions, compgen and complete which correspond to the bash builtins with the same names. It will then be possible to use completion specifications and functions written for bash.

20.2.2 Autoloaded files

The convention for autoloaded functions used in completion is that they start with an underscore; as already mentioned, the fpath/FPATH parameter must contain the directory in which they are stored. If zsh was properly installed on your system, then fpath/FPATH automatically contains the required directories for the standard functions.

For incomplete installations, if compinit does not find enough files beginning with an underscore (fewer than twenty) in the search path, it will try to find more by adding the directory _compdir to the search path. If that directory has a subdirectory named Base, all subdirectories will be added to the path. Furthermore, if the subdirectory Base has a subdirectory named Core, compinit will add all subdirectories of the subdirectories to the path: this allows the functions to be in the same format as in the zsh source distribution.

When compinit is run, it searches all such files accessible via fpath/FPATH and reads the first line of each of them. This line should contain one of the tags described below. Files whose first line does not start with one of these tags are not considered to be part of the completion system and will not be treated specially.

The tags are:

#compdef name ... [-{p|P} pattern ... [-N name ...]]

> The file will be made autoloadable and the function defined in it will be called when completing names, each of which is either the name of a command whose arguments are to be completed or one of a number of special contexts in the form -context- described below.

> Each name may also be of the form 'cmd=service'. When completing the command cmd, the function typically behaves as if the command (or special context) service was being completed instead. This provides a way of altering the behaviour of functions that can perform many different completions. It is implemented by setting the parameter $service when calling the function; the function may choose to interpret this how it wishes, and simpler functions will probably ignore it.

> If the #compdef line contains one of the options -p or -P, the words following are taken to be patterns. The function will be called when completion is attempted

for a command or context that matches one of the patterns. The options -p and -P are used to specify patterns to be tried before or after other completions respectively. Hence -P may be used to specify default actions.

The option -N is used after a list following -p or -P; it specifies that remaining words no longer define patterns. It is possible to toggle between the three options as many times as necessary.

#compdef -k *style key-sequence* ...

> This option creates a widget behaving like the builtin widget *style* and binds it to the given *key-sequences*, if any. The *style* must be one of the builtin widgets that perform completion, namely complete-word, delete-char-or-list, expand-or-complete, expand-or-complete-prefix, list-choices, menu-complete, menu-expand-or-complete, or reverse-menu-complete. If the zsh/complist module is loaded (see Section 22.7 [The zsh/complist Module], page 333) the widget menu-select is also available.

> When one of the *key-sequences* is typed, the function in the file will be invoked to generate the matches. Note that a key will not be re-bound if it already was (that is, was bound to something other than undefined-key). The widget created has the same name as the file and can be bound to any other keys using bindkey as usual.

#compdef -K *widget-name style key-sequence* [*name style seq* ...]

> This is similar to -k except that only one *key-sequence* argument may be given for each *widget-name style* pair. However, the entire set of three arguments may be repeated with a different set of arguments. Note in particular that the *widget-name* must be distinct in each set. If it does not begin with '_' this will be added. The *widget-name* should not clash with the name of any existing widget: names based on the name of the function are most useful. For example,

> > #compdef -K _foo_complete complete-word "^X^C" \
> >   _foo_list list-choices "^X^D"

> (all on one line) defines a widget _foo_complete for completion, bound to '^X^C', and a widget _foo_list for listing, bound to '^X^D'.

#autoload [*options*]

> Functions with the #autoload tag are marked for autoloading but are not otherwise treated specially. Typically they are to be called from within one of the completion functions. Any *options* supplied will be passed to the autoload builtin; a typical use is +X to force the function to be loaded immediately. Note that the -U and -z flags are always added implicitly.

The # is part of the tag name and no white space is allowed after it. The #compdef tags use the compdef function described below; the main difference is that the name of the function is supplied implicitly.

The special contexts for which completion functions can be defined are:

-array-value-

> The right hand side of an array-assignment ('*name*=(...)')

-brace-parameter-

> The name of a parameter expansion within braces ('${...}')

`-assign-parameter-`

> The name of a parameter in an assignment, i.e. on the left hand side of an '='

`-command-`

> A word in command position

`-condition-`

> A word inside a condition ('`[[...]]`')

`-default-`

> Any word for which no other completion is defined

`-equal-`   A word beginning with an equals sign

`-first-`   This is tried before any other completion function. The function called may set the `_compskip` parameter to one of various values: `all`: no further completion is attempted; a string containing the substring `patterns`: no pattern completion functions will be called; a string containing `default`: the function for the '`-default-`' context will not be called, but functions defined for commands will be.

`-math-`   Inside mathematical contexts, such as '`((...))`'

`-parameter-`

> The name of a parameter expansion ('`$...`')

`-redirect-`

> The word after a redirection operator.

`-subscript-`

> The contents of a parameter subscript.

`-tilde-`   After an initial tilde ('`~`'), but before the first slash in the word.

`-value-`   On the right hand side of an assignment.

Default implementations are supplied for each of these contexts. In most cases the context *-context-* is implemented by a corresponding function *_context*, for example the context '`-tilde-`' and the function '`_tilde`').

The contexts `-redirect-` and `-value-` allow extra context-specific information. (Internally, this is handled by the functions for each context calling the function `_dispatch`.) The extra information is added separated by commas.

For the `-redirect-` context, the extra information is in the form '`-redirect-,op,command`', where *op* is the redirection operator and *command* is the name of the command on the line. If there is no command on the line yet, the *command* field will be empty.

For the `-value-` context, the form is '`-value-,name,command`', where *name* is the name of the parameter on the left hand side of the assignment. In the case of elements of an associative array, for example '`assoc=(key <TAB>`', *name* is expanded to '*name-key*'. In certain special contexts, such as completing after '`make CFLAGS=`', the *command* part gives the name of the command, here `make`; otherwise it is empty.

It is not necessary to define fully specific completions as the functions provided will try to generate completions by progressively replacing the elements with '`-default-`'. For example, when completing after 'foo=<TAB>', `_value` will try the names '-value-,foo,' (note the empty *command* part), '-value-,foo,-default-' and'-value-,-default-,-default-', in that order, until it finds a function to handle the context.

As an example:

```
compdef '_files -g "*.log"' '-redirect-,2>,-default-'
```

completes files matching '*.log' after '2> <TAB>' for any command with no more specific handler defined.

Also:

```
compdef _foo -value-,-default-,-default-
```

specifies that `_foo` provides completions for the values of parameters for which no special function has been defined. This is usually handled by the function `_value` itself.

The same lookup rules are used when looking up styles (as described below); for example

```
zstyle ':completion:*:*:-redirect-,2>,*:*' file-patterns '*.log'
```

is another way to make completion after '2> <TAB>' complete files matching '*.log'.

20.2.3 Functions

The following function is defined by `compinit` and may be called directly.

compdef [-ane] *function name* ... [-{p|P} *pattern* ... [-N *name* ...]]
compdef -d *name* ...
compdef -k [-an] *function style key-sequence* [*key-sequence* ...]
compdef -K [-an] *function name style key-seq* [*name style seq* ...]

> The first form defines the *function* to call for completion in the given contexts as described for the `#compdef` tag above.
>
> Alternatively, all the arguments may have the form '*cmd=service*'. Here *service* should already have been defined by '*cmd1=service*' lines in `#compdef` files, as described above. The argument for *cmd* will be completed in the same way as *service*.
>
> The *function* argument may alternatively be a string containing almost any shell code. If the string contains an equal sign, the above will take precedence. The option −e may be used to specify the first argument is to be evaluated as shell code even if it contains an equal sign. The string will be executed using the `eval` builtin command to generate completions. This provides a way of avoiding having to define a new completion function. For example, to complete files ending in '.h' as arguments to the command `foo`:
>
> ```
> compdef '_files -g "*.h"' foo
> ```
>
> The option −n prevents any completions already defined for the command or context from being overwritten.
>
> The option −d deletes any completion defined for the command or contexts listed.
>
> The *names* may also contain −p, −P and −N options as described for the `#compdef` tag. The effect on the argument list is identical, switching between

definitions of patterns tried initially, patterns tried finally, and normal commands and contexts.

The parameter `$_compskip` may be set by any function defined for a pattern context. If it is set to a value containing the substring 'patterns' none of the pattern-functions will be called; if it is set to a value containing the substring 'all', no other function will be called. Setting `$_compskip` in this manner is of particular utility when using the -p option, as otherwise the dispatcher will move on to additional functions (likely the default one) after calling the pattern-context one, which can mangle the display of completion possibilities if not handled properly.

The form with -k defines a widget with the same name as the *function* that will be called for each of the *key-sequences*; this is like the #compdef -k tag. The function should generate the completions needed and will otherwise behave like the builtin widget whose name is given as the *style* argument. The widgets usable for this are: complete-word, delete-char-or-list, expand-or-complete, expand-or-complete-prefix, list-choices, menu-complete, menu-expand-or-complete, and reverse-menu-complete, as well as menu-select if the zsh/complist module is loaded. The option -n prevents the key being bound if it is already to bound to something other than undefined-key.

The form with -K is similar and defines multiple widgets based on the same *function*, each of which requires the set of three arguments *name*, *style* and *key-sequence*, where the latter two are as for -k and the first must be a unique widget name beginning with an underscore.

Wherever applicable, the -a option makes the *function* autoloadable, equivalent to autoload -U *function*.

The function compdef can be used to associate existing completion functions with new commands. For example,

```
compdef _pids foo
```

uses the function _pids to complete process IDs for the command foo.

Note also the _gnu_generic function described below, which can be used to complete options for commands that understand the '--help' option.

20.3 Completion System Configuration

This section gives a short overview of how the completion system works, and then more detail on how users can configure how and when matches are generated.

20.3.1 Overview

When completion is attempted somewhere on the command line the completion system begins building the context. The context represents everything that the shell knows about the meaning of the command line and the significance of the cursor position. This takes account of a number of things including the command word (such as 'grep' or 'zsh') and options to which the current word may be an argument (such as the '-o' option to zsh which takes a shell option as an argument).

The context starts out very generic ("we are beginning a completion") and becomes more specific as more is learned ("the current word is in a position that is usually a command name" or "the current word might be a variable name" and so on). Therefore the context will vary during the same call to the completion system.

This context information is condensed into a string consisting of multiple fields separated by colons, referred to simply as 'the context' in the remainder of the documentation. Note that a user of the completion system rarely needs to compose a context string, unless for example a new function is being written to perform completion for a new command. What a user may need to do is compose a *style* pattern, which is matched against a context when needed to look up context-sensitive options that configure the completion system.

The next few paragraphs explain how a context is composed within the completion function suite. Following that is discussion of how *styles* are defined. Styles determine such things as how the matches are generated, similarly to shell options but with much more control. They are defined with the **zstyle** builtin command (Section 22.37 [The zsh/zutil Module], page 382).

The context string always consists of a fixed set of fields, separated by colons and with a leading colon before the first. Fields which are not yet known are left empty, but the surrounding colons appear anyway. The fields are always in the order `:completion:`*function*`:`*completer*`:`*command*`:`*argument*`:`*tag*. These have the following meaning:

- The literal string **completion**, saying that this style is used by the completion system. This distinguishes the context from those used by, for example, zle widgets and ZFTP functions.

- The *function*, if completion is called from a named widget rather than through the normal completion system. Typically this is blank, but it is set by special widgets such as **predict-on** and the various functions in the **Widget** directory of the distribution to the name of that function, often in an abbreviated form.

- The *completer* currently active, the name of the function without the leading underscore and with other underscores converted to hyphens. A 'completer' is in overall control of how completion is to be performed; '**complete**' is the simplest, but other completers exist to perform related tasks such as correction, or to modify the behaviour of a later completer. See Section 20.4 [Control Functions], page 282, for more information.

- The *command* or a special *-context-*, just at it appears following the **#compdef** tag or the **compdef** function. Completion functions for commands that have sub-commands usually modify this field to contain the name of the command followed by a minus sign and the sub-command. For example, the completion function for the **cvs** command sets this field to **cvs-add** when completing arguments to the **add** subcommand.

- The *argument*; this indicates which command line or option argument we are completing. For command arguments this generally takes the form **argument-**n, where n is the number of the argument, and for arguments to options the form **option-**opt**-**n where n is the number of the argument to option opt. However, this is only the case if the command line is parsed with standard UNIX-style options and arguments, so many completions do not set this.

- The *tag*. As described previously, tags are used to discriminate between the types of matches a completion function can generate in a certain context. Any completion function may use any tag name it likes, but a list of the more common ones is given below.

The context is gradually put together as the functions are executed, starting with the main entry point, which adds `:completion:` and the *function* element if necessary. The completer then adds the *completer* element. The contextual completion adds the *command* and *argument* options. Finally, the *tag* is added when the types of completion are known. For example, the context name

```
:completion::complete:dvips:option-o-1:files
```

says that normal completion was attempted as the first argument to the option `-o` of the command `dvips`:

```
dvips -o ...
```

and the completion function will generate filenames.

Usually completion will be tried for all possible tags in an order given by the completion function. However, this can be altered by using the **tag-order** style. Completion is then restricted to the list of given tags in the given order.

The **_complete_help** bindable command shows all the contexts and tags available for completion at a particular point. This provides an easy way of finding information for **tag-order** and other styles. It is described in Section 20.5 [Bindable Commands], page 289.

When looking up styles the completion system uses full context names, including the tag. Looking up the value of a style therefore consists of two things: the context, which is matched to the most specific (best fitting) style pattern, and the name of the style itself, which must be matched exactly. The following examples demonstrate that style patterns may be loosely defined for styles that apply broadly, or as tightly defined as desired for styles that apply in narrower circumstances.

For example, many completion functions can generate matches in a simple and a verbose form and use the **verbose** style to decide which form should be used. To make all such functions use the verbose form, put

```
zstyle ':completion:*' verbose yes
```

in a startup file (probably `.zshrc`). This gives the **verbose** style the value **yes** in every context inside the completion system, unless that context has a more specific definition. It is best to avoid giving the context as '*' in case the style has some meaning outside the completion system.

Many such general purpose styles can be configured simply by using the **compinstall** function.

A more specific example of the use of the **verbose** style is by the completion for the **kill** builtin. If the style is set, the builtin lists full job texts and process command lines; otherwise it shows the bare job numbers and PIDs. To turn the style off for this use only:

```
zstyle ':completion:*:*:kill:*:*' verbose no
```

For even more control, the style can use one of the tags 'jobs' or 'processes'. To turn off verbose display only for jobs:

```
zstyle ':completion:*:*:kill:*:jobs' verbose no
```

The `-e` option to **zstyle** even allows completion function code to appear as the argument to a style; this requires some understanding of the internals of completion functions (see Chapter 19 [Completion Widgets], page 225)). For example,

```
zstyle -e ':completion:*' hosts 'reply=($myhosts)'
```
This forces the value of the **hosts** style to be read from the variable **myhosts** each time a host name is needed; this is useful if the value of **myhosts** can change dynamically. For another useful example, see the example in the description of the **file-list** style below. This form can be slow and should be avoided for commonly examined styles such as **menu** and **list-rows-first**.

Note that the order in which styles are *defined* does not matter; the style mechanism uses the most specific possible match for a particular style to determine the set of values. More precisely, strings are preferred over patterns (for example, ':completion::complete:::foo' is more specific than ':completion::complete:::*'), and longer patterns are preferred over shorter patterns.

A good rule of thumb is that any completion style pattern that needs to include more than one wildcard (*) and that does not end in a tag name, should include all six colons (:), possibly surrounding additional wildcards.

Style names like those of tags are arbitrary and depend on the completion function. However, the following two sections list some of the most common tags and styles.

20.3.2 Standard Tags

Some of the following are only used when looking up particular styles and do not refer to a type of match.

accounts   used to look up the **users-hosts** style

all-expansions
> used by the **_expand** completer when adding the single string containing all possible expansions

all-files
> for the names of all files (as distinct from a particular subset, see the **globbed-files** tag).

arguments
> for arguments to a command

arrays   for names of array parameters

association-keys
> for keys of associative arrays; used when completing inside a subscript to a parameter of this type

bookmarks
> when completing bookmarks (e.g. for URLs and the **zftp** function suite)

builtins   for names of builtin commands

characters
> for single characters in arguments of commands such as **stty**. Also used when completing character classes after an opening bracket

colormapids
> for X colormap ids

colors   for color names

commands   for names of external commands. Also used by complex commands such as **cvs** when completing names subcommands.

contexts   for contexts in arguments to the **zstyle** builtin command

corrections
            used by the **_approximate** and **_correct** completers for possible corrections

cursors   for cursor names used by X programs

default   used in some contexts to provide a way of supplying a default when more specific tags are also valid. Note that this tag is used when only the *function* field of the context name is set

descriptions
            used when looking up the value of the **format** style to generate descriptions for types of matches

devices   for names of device special files

directories
            for names of directories — **local-directories** is used instead when completing arguments of **cd** and related builtin commands when the **cdpath** array is set

directory-stack
            for entries in the directory stack

displays   for X display names

domains   for network domains

email-*plugin*
            for email addresses from the '**_email-***plugin*' backend of **_email_addresses**

expansions
            used by the **_expand** completer for individual words (as opposed to the complete set of expansions) resulting from the expansion of a word on the command line

extensions
            for X server extensions

file-descriptors
            for numbers of open file descriptors

files   the generic file-matching tag used by functions completing filenames

fonts   for X font names

fstypes   for file system types (e.g. for the **mount** command)

functions
            names of functions — normally shell functions, although certain commands may understand other kinds of function

globbed-files
            for filenames when the name has been generated by pattern matching

groups   for names of user groups

history-words
            for words from the history

hosts   for hostnames

indexes   for array indexes

jobs   for jobs (as listed by the 'jobs' builtin)

interfaces
            for network interfaces

keymaps   for names of zsh keymaps

keysyms   for names of X keysyms

libraries
            for names of system libraries

limits   for system limits

local-directories
            for names of directories that are subdirectories of the current working direc-
            tory when completing arguments of **cd** and related builtin commands (compare
            path-directories) — when the **cdpath** array is unset, **directories** is used
            instead

manuals   for names of manual pages

mailboxes
            for e-mail folders

maps   for map names (e.g. NIS maps)

messages   used to look up the **format** style for messages

modifiers
            for names of X modifiers

modules   for modules (e.g. **zsh** modules)

my-accounts
            used to look up the **users-hosts** style

named-directories
            for named directories (you wouldn't have guessed that, would you?)

names   for all kinds of names

newsgroups
            for USENET groups

nicknames
            for nicknames of NIS maps

options   for command options

original   used by the `_approximate`, `_correct` and `_expand` completers when offering the original string as a match

other-accounts
            used to look up the **users-hosts** style

other-files
            for the names of any non-directory files. This is used instead of **all-files** when the **list-dirs-first** style is in effect.

packages   for packages (e.g. **rpm** or installed **Debian** packages)

parameters
            for names of parameters

path-directories
            for names of directories found by searching the **cdpath** array when completing arguments of **cd** and related builtin commands (compare **local-directories**)

paths   used to look up the values of the **expand**, **ambiguous** and **special-dirs** styles

pods   for perl pods (documentation files)

ports   for communication ports

prefixes   for prefixes (like those of a URL)

printers   for print queue names

processes
            for process identifiers

processes-names
            used to look up the **command** style when generating the names of processes for **killall**

sequences
            for sequences (e.g. **mh** sequences)

sessions   for sessions in the **zftp** function suite

signals   for signal names

strings   for strings (e.g. the replacement strings for the **cd** builtin command)

styles   for styles used by the zstyle builtin command

suffixes   for filename extensions

tags   for tags (e.g. **rpm** tags)

targets   for makefile targets

time-zones
            for time zones (e.g. when setting the **TZ** parameter)

types   for types of whatever (e.g. address types for the **xhost** command)

urls   used to look up the **urls** and **local** styles when completing URLs users   for usernames

values   for one of a set of values in certain lists

variant   used by `_pick_variant` to look up the command to run when determining what program is installed for a particular command name.

visuals   for X visuals

warnings   used to look up the **format** style for warnings

widgets   for zsh widget names

windows   for IDs of X windows

zsh-options
     for shell options

20.3.3 Standard Styles

Note that the values of several of these styles represent boolean values. Any of the strings 'true', 'on', 'yes', and '1' can be used for the value 'true' and any of the strings '**false**', '**off**', 'no', and '0' for the value 'false'. The behavior for any other value is undefined except where explicitly mentioned. The default value may be either 'true' or 'false' if the style is not set.

Some of these styles are tested first for every possible tag corresponding to a type of match, and if no style was found, for the **default** tag. The most notable styles of this type are **menu**, **list-colors** and styles controlling completion listing such as **list-packed** and **last-prompt**. When tested for the **default** tag, only the *function* field of the context will be set so that a style using the **default** tag will normally be defined along the lines of:

        zstyle ':completion:*:default' menu ...

accept-exact

     This is tested for the **default** tag in addition to the tags valid for the current context. If it is set to 'true' and any of the trial matches is the same as the string on the command line, this match will immediately be accepted (even if it would otherwise be considered ambiguous).

     When completing pathnames (where the tag used is '**paths**') this style accepts any number of patterns as the value in addition to the boolean values. Pathnames matching one of these patterns will be accepted immediately even if the command line contains some more partially typed pathname components and these match no file under the directory accepted.

     This style is also used by the **_expand** completer to decide if words beginning with a tilde or parameter expansion should be expanded. For example, if there are parameters **foo** and **foobar**, the string '**$foo**' will only be expanded if **accept-exact** is set to 'true'; otherwise the completion system will be allowed to complete $foo to $foobar. If the style is set to 'continue', **_expand** will add the expansion as a match and the completion system will also be allowed to continue.

accept-exact-dirs

This is used by filename completion. Unlike **accept-exact** it is a boolean. By default, filename completion examines all components of a path to see if there are completions of that component, even if the component matches an existing directory. For example, when completion after **/usr/bin/**, the function examines possible completions to **/usr**.

When this style is 'true', any prefix of a path that matches an existing directory is accepted without any attempt to complete it further. Hence, in the given example, the path **/usr/bin/** is accepted immediately and completion tried in that directory.

This style is also useful when completing after directories that magically appear when referenced, such as ZFS **.zfs** directories or NetApp **.snapshot** directories. When the style is set the shell does not check for the existence of the directory within the parent directory.

If you wish to inhibit this behaviour entirely, set the **path-completion** style (see below) to 'false'.

add-space

This style is used by the **_expand** completer. If it is 'true' (the default), a space will be inserted after all words resulting from the expansion, or a slash in the case of directory names. If the value is '**file**', the completer will only add a space to names of existing files. Either a boolean 'true' or the value '**file**' may be combined with '**subst**', in which case the completer will not add a space to words generated from the expansion of a substitution of the form '$(...)' or '${...}'.

The **_prefix** completer uses this style as a simple boolean value to decide if a space should be inserted before the suffix.

ambiguous

This applies when completing non-final components of filename paths, in other words those with a trailing slash. If it is set, the cursor is left after the first ambiguous component, even if menu completion is in use. The style is always tested with the **paths** tag.

assign-list

When completing after an equals sign that is being treated as an assignment, the completion system normally completes only one filename. In some cases the value may be a list of filenames separated by colons, as with **PATH** and similar parameters. This style can be set to a list of patterns matching the names of such parameters.

The default is to complete lists when the word on the line already contains a colon.

auto-description

If set, this style's value will be used as the description for options that are not described by the completion functions, but that have exactly one argument. The sequence '%d' in the value will be replaced by the description for this argument. Depending on personal preferences, it may be useful to set this style to something like 'specify: %d'. Note that this may not work for some commands.

avoid-completer

This is used by the _all_matches completer to decide if the string consisting of all matches should be added to the list currently being generated. Its value is a list of names of completers. If any of these is the name of the completer that generated the matches in this completion, the string will not be added.

The default value for this style is '_expand _old_list _correct _approximate', i.e. it contains the completers for which a string with all matches will almost never be wanted.

cache-path

This style defines the path where any cache files containing dumped completion data are stored. It defaults to '$ZDOTDIR/.zcompcache', or '$HOME/.zcompcache' if $ZDOTDIR is not defined. The completion cache will not be used unless the **use-cache** style is set.

cache-policy

This style defines the function that will be used to determine whether a cache needs rebuilding. See the section on the _cache_invalid function below.

call-command

This style is used in the function for commands such as **make** and **ant** where calling the command directly to generate matches suffers problems such as being slow or, as in the case of **make** can potentially cause actions in the makefile to be executed. If it is set to 'true' the command is called to generate matches. The default value of this style is 'false'.

command   In many places, completion functions need to call external commands to generate the list of completions. This style can be used to override the command that is called in some such cases. The elements of the value are joined with spaces to form a command line to execute. The value can also start with a hyphen, in which case the usual command will be added to the end; this is most useful for putting 'builtin' or 'command' in front to make sure the appropriate version of a command is called, for example to avoid calling a shell function with the same name as an external command.

As an example, the completion function for process IDs uses this style with the **processes** tag to generate the IDs to complete and the list of processes to display (if the **verbose** style is 'true'). The list produced by the command should look like the output of the **ps** command. The first line is not displayed, but is searched for the string 'PID' (or 'pid') to find the position of the process IDs in the following lines. If the line does not contain 'PID', the first numbers in each of the other lines are taken as the process IDs to complete.

Note that the completion function generally has to call the specified command for each attempt to generate the completion list. Hence care should be taken to specify only commands that take a short time to run, and in particular to avoid any that may never terminate.

command-path

> This is a list of directories to search for commands to complete. The default for this style is the value of the special parameter `path`.

commands This is used by the function completing sub-commands for the system initialisation scripts (residing in `/etc/init.d` or somewhere not too far away from that). Its values give the default commands to complete for those commands for which the completion function isn't able to find them out automatically. The default for this style are the two strings '`start`' and '`stop`'.

complete This is used by the `_expand_alias` function when invoked as a bindable command. If set to 'true' and the word on the command line is not the name of an alias, matching alias names will be completed.

complete-options

> This is used by the completer for `cd`, `chdir` and `pushd`. For these commands a - is used to introduce a directory stack entry and completion of these is far more common than completing options. Hence unless the value of this style is 'true' options will not be completed, even after an initial -. If it is 'true', options will be completed after an initial - unless there is a preceding -- on the command line.

completer

> The strings given as the value of this style provide the names of the completer functions to use. The available completer functions are described in Section 20.4 [Control Functions], page 282.
>
> Each string may be either the name of a completer function or a string of the form '*function*:*name*'. In the first case the *completer* field of the context will contain the name of the completer without the leading underscore and with all other underscores replaced by hyphens. In the second case the *function* is the name of the completer to call, but the context will contain the user-defined *name* in the *completer* field of the context. If the *name* starts with a hyphen, the string for the context will be build from the name of the completer function as in the first case with the *name* appended to it. For example:
>
> ```
> zstyle ':completion:*' completer _complete _complete:-foo
> ```
>
> Here, completion will call the `_complete` completer twice, once using '`complete`' and once using '`complete-foo`' in the *completer* field of the context. Normally, using the same completer more than once only makes sense when used with the '*functions*:*name*' form, because otherwise the context name will be the same in all calls to the completer; possible exceptions to this rule are the `_ignored` and `_prefix` completers.
>
> The default value for this style is '`_complete _ignored`': only completion will be done, first using the `ignored-patterns` style and the `$fignore` array and then without ignoring matches.

condition

> This style is used by the `_list` completer function to decide if insertion of matches should be delayed unconditionally. The default is 'true'.

delimiters

This style is used when adding a delimiter for use with history modifiers or glob qualifiers that have delimited arguments. It is an array of preferred delimiters to add. Non-special characters are preferred as the completion system may otherwise become confused. The default list is :, +, /, -, %. The list may be empty to force a delimiter to be typed.

disabled If this is set to 'true', the `_expand_alias` completer and bindable command will try to expand disabled aliases, too. The default is 'false'.

domains A list of names of network domains for completion. If this is not set, domain names will be taken from the file `/etc/resolv.conf`.

environ The environ style is used when completing for 'sudo'. It is set to an array of '*VAR=value*' assignments to be exported into the local environment before the completion for the target command is invoked.

```
zstyle ':completion:*:sudo::' environ \
    PATH="/sbin:/usr/sbin:$PATH" HOME="/root"
```

expand This style is used when completing strings consisting of multiple parts, such as path names.

If one of its values is the string '**prefix**', the partially typed word from the line will be expanded as far as possible even if trailing parts cannot be completed.

If one of its values is the string '**suffix**', matching names for components after the first ambiguous one will also be added. This means that the resulting string is the longest unambiguous string possible. However, menu completion can be used to cycle through all matches.

fake This style may be set for any completion context. It specifies additional strings that will always be completed in that context. The form of each string is '*value*: *description*'; the colon and description may be omitted, but any literal colons in *value* must be quoted with a backslash. Any *description* provided is shown alongside the value in completion listings.

It is important to use a sufficiently restrictive context when specifying fake strings. Note that the styles **fake-files** and **fake-parameters** provide additional features when completing files or parameters.

fake-always

This works identically to the **fake** style except that the **ignored-patterns** style is not applied to it. This makes it possible to override a set of matches completely by setting the ignored patterns to '*'.

The following shows a way of supplementing any tag with arbitrary data, but having it behave for display purposes like a separate tag. In this example we use the features of the **tag-order** style to divide the **named-directories** tag into two when performing completion with the standard completer **complete** for arguments of **cd**. The tag **named-directories-normal** behaves as normal, but the tag **named-directories-mine** contains a fixed set of directories. This has the effect of adding the match group 'extra directories' with the given completions.

```
zstyle ':completion::complete:cd:*' tag-order \
  'named-directories:-mine:extra\ directories
  named-directories:-normal:named\ directories *'
zstyle ':completion::complete:cd:*:named-directories-mine' \
  fake-always mydir1 mydir2
zstyle ':completion::complete:cd:*:named-directories-mine' \
  ignored-patterns '*'
```

fake-files

> This style is used when completing files and looked up without a tag. Its values are of the form '*dir*:*names*...'. This will add the *names* (strings separated by spaces) as possible matches when completing in the directory *dir*, even if no such files really exist. The dir may be a pattern; pattern characters or colons in *dir* should be quoted with a backslash to be treated literally.
>
> This can be useful on systems that support special file systems whose top-level pathnames can not be listed or generated with glob patterns (but see **accept-exact-dirs** for a more general way of dealing with this problem). It can also be used for directories for which one does not have read permission.
>
> The pattern form can be used to add a certain 'magic' entry to all directories on a particular file system.

fake-parameters

> This is used by the completion function for parameter names. Its values are names of parameters that might not yet be set but should be completed nonetheless. Each name may also be followed by a colon and a string specifying the type of the parameter (like '**scalar**', '**array**' or '**integer**'). If the type is given, the name will only be completed if parameters of that type are required in the particular context. Names for which no type is specified will always be completed.

file-list

> This style controls whether files completed using the standard builtin mechanism are to be listed with a long list similar to **ls -l**. Note that this feature uses the shell module **zsh/stat** for file information; this loads the builtin **stat** which will replace any external **stat** executable. To avoid this the following code can be included in an initialization file:
>
> ```
> zmodload -i zsh/stat
> disable stat
> ```
>
> The style may either be set to a 'true' value (or '**all**'), or one of the values '**insert**' or '**list**', indicating that files are to be listed in long format in all circumstances, or when attempting to insert a file name, or when listing file names without attempting to insert one.
>
> More generally, the value may be an array of any of the above values, optionally followed by =*num*. If *num* is present it gives the maximum number of matches for which long listing style will be used. For example,
>
> ```
> zstyle ':completion:*' file-list list=20 insert=10
> ```

specifies that long format will be used when listing up to 20 files or inserting a file with up to 10 matches (assuming a listing is to be shown at all, for example on an ambiguous completion), else short format will be used.

```
zstyle -e ':completion:*' file-list \
        '(( ${+NUMERIC} )) && reply=(true)'
```

specifies that long format will be used any time a numeric argument is supplied, else short format.

file-patterns

This is used by the standard function for completing filenames, `_files`. If the style is unset up to three tags are offered, 'globbed-files','directories' and 'all-files', depending on the types of files expected by the caller of `_files`. The first two ('globbed-files' and 'directories') are normally offered together to make it easier to complete files in sub-directories.

The `file-patterns` style provides alternatives to the default tags, which are not used. Its value consists of elements of the form '*pattern*:*tag*'; each string may contain any number of such specifications separated by spaces.

The *pattern* is a pattern that is to be used to generate filenames. Any occurrence of the sequence '%p' is replaced by any pattern(s) passed by the function calling `_files`. Colons in the pattern must be preceded by a backslash to make them distinguishable from the colon before the *tag*. If more than one pattern is needed, the patterns can be given inside braces, separated by commas.

The *tag*s of all strings in the value will be offered by `_files` and used when looking up other styles. Any *tag*s in the same word will be offered at the same time and before later words. If no ':*tag*' is given the 'files' tag will be used.

The *tag* may also be followed by an optional second colon and a description, which will be used for the '%d' in the value of the `format` style (if that is set) instead of the default description supplied by the completion function. If the description given here contains itself a '%d', that is replaced with the description supplied by the completion function.

For example, to make the `rm` command first complete only names of object files and then the names of all files if there is no matching object file:

```
zstyle ':completion:*:*:rm:*:*' file-patterns \
        '*.o:object-files' '%p:all-files'
```

To alter the default behaviour of file completion — offer files matching a pattern and directories on the first attempt, then all files — to offer only matching files on the first attempt, then directories, and finally all files:

```
zstyle ':completion:*' file-patterns \
        '%p:globbed-files' '*(-/):directories' '*:all-files'
```

This works even where there is no special pattern: `_files` matches all files using the pattern '*' at the first step and stops when it sees this pattern. Note also it will never try a pattern more than once for a single completion attempt.

During the execution of completion functions, the `EXTENDED_GLOB` option is in effect, so the characters '#', '~' and '^' have special meanings in the patterns.

file-sort

> The standard filename completion function uses this style without a tag to determine in which order the names should be listed; menu completion will cycle through them in the same order. The possible values are: 'size' to sort by the size of the file; 'links' to sort by the number of links to the file; 'modification' (or 'time' or 'date') to sort by the last modification time; 'access' to sort by the last access time; and 'inode' (or 'change') to sort by the last inode change time. If the style is set to any other value, or is unset, files will be sorted alphabetically by name. If the value contains the string 'reverse', sorting is done in the opposite order. If the value contains the string 'follow', timestamps are associated with the targets of symbolic links; the default is to use the timestamps of the links themselves.

file-split-chars

> A set of characters that will cause *all* file completions for the given context to be split at the point where any of the characters occurs. A typical use is to set the style to :; then everything up to and including the last : in the string so far is ignored when completing files. As this is quite heavy-handed, it is usually preferable to update completion functions for contexts where this behaviour is useful.

filter

> The ldap plugin of email address completion (see _email_addresses) uses this style to specify the attributes to match against when filtering entries. So for example, if the style is set to 'sn', matching is done against surnames. Standard LDAP filtering is used so normal completion matching is bypassed. If this style is not set, the LDAP plugin is skipped. You may also need to set the command style to specify how to connect to your LDAP server.

force-list

> This forces a list of completions to be shown at any point where listing is done, even in cases where the list would usually be suppressed. For example, normally the list is only shown if there are at least two different matches. By setting this style to 'always', the list will always be shown, even if there is only a single match that will immediately be accepted. The style may also be set to a number. In this case the list will be shown if there are at least that many matches, even if they would all insert the same string.

> This style is tested for the default tag as well as for each tag valid for the current completion. Hence the listing can be forced only for certain types of match.

format

> If this is set for the descriptions tag, its value is used as a string to display above matches in completion lists. The sequence '%d' in this string will be replaced with a short description of what these matches are. This string may also contain the following sequences to specify output attributes (see Chapter 13 [Prompt Expansion], page 39): '%B', '%S', '%U', '%F', '%K' and their lower case counterparts, as well as '%{...%}'. '%F', '%K' and '%{...%}' take arguments in the same form as prompt expansion. Note that the sequence '%G' is not available; an argument to '%{' should be used instead.

The style is tested with each tag valid for the current completion before it is tested for the **descriptions** tag. Hence different format strings can be defined for different types of match.

Note also that some completer functions define additional '%'-sequences. These are described for the completer functions that make use of them.

Some completion functions display messages that may be customised by setting this style for the **messages** tag. Here, the '%d' is replaced with a message given by the completion function.

Finally, the format string is looked up with the **warnings** tag, for use when no matches could be generated at all. In this case the '%d' is replaced with the descriptions for the matches that were expected separated by spaces. The sequence '%D' is replaced with the same descriptions separated by newlines.

It is possible to use printf-style field width specifiers with '%d' and similar escape sequences. This is handled by the **zformat** builtin command from the **zsh/zutil** module, see Section 22.37 [The zsh/zutil Module], page 382.

glob
: This is used by the **_expand** completer. If it is set to 'true' (the default), globbing will be attempted on the words resulting from a previous substitution (see the **substitute** style) or else the original string from the line.

global
: If this is set to 'true' (the default), the **_expand_alias** completer and bindable command will try to expand global aliases.

group-name
: The completion system can group different types of matches, which appear in separate lists. This style can be used to give the names of groups for particular tags. For example, in command position the completion system generates names of builtin and external commands, names of aliases, shell functions and parameters and reserved words as possible completions. To have the external commands and shell functions listed separately:

```
zstyle ':completion:*:*:-command-:*:commands' \
        group-name commands
zstyle ':completion:*:*:-command-:*:functions' \
        group-name functions
```

As a consequence, any match with the same tag will be displayed in the same group.

If the name given is the empty string the name of the tag for the matches will be used as the name of the group. So, to have all different types of matches displayed separately, one can just set:

```
zstyle ':completion:*' group-name ''
```

All matches for which no group name is defined will be put in a group named **-default-**.

group-order
: This style is additional to the **group-name** style to specify the order for display of the groups defined by that style (compare **tag-order**, which determines which completions appear at all). The groups named are shown in the given order; any other groups are shown in the order defined by the completion function.

For example, to have names of builtin commands, shell functions and external commands appear in that order when completing in command position:

```
zstyle ':completion:*:*:-command-:*:*' group-order \
        builtins functions commands
```

groups   A list of names of UNIX groups. If this is not set, group names are taken from the YP database or the file '/etc/group'.

hidden   If this is set to 'true', matches for the given context will not be listed, although any description for the matches set with the `format` style will be shown. If it is set to 'all', not even the description will be displayed.

Note that the matches will still be completed; they are just not shown in the list. To avoid having matches considered as possible completions at all, the `tag-order` style can be modified as described below.

hosts   A list of names of hosts that should be completed. If this is not set, hostnames are taken from the file '/etc/hosts'.

hosts-ports

This style is used by commands that need or accept hostnames and network ports. The strings in the value should be of the form '*host*:*port*'. Valid ports are determined by the presence of hostnames; multiple ports for the same host may appear.

ignore-line

This is tested for each tag valid for the current completion. If it is set to 'true', none of the words that are already on the line will be considered as possible completions. If it is set to 'current', the word the cursor is on will not be considered as a possible completion. The value 'current-shown' is similar but only applies if the list of completions is currently shown on the screen. Finally, if the style is set to 'other', all words on the line except for the current one will be excluded from the possible completions.

The values 'current' and 'current-shown' are a bit like the opposite of the `accept-exact` style: only strings with missing characters will be completed.

Note that you almost certainly don't want to set this to 'true' or 'other' for a general context such as ':completion:*'. This is because it would disallow completion of, for example, options multiple times even if the command in question accepts the option more than once.

ignore-parents

The style is tested without a tag by the function completing pathnames in order to determine whether to ignore the names of directories already mentioned in the current word, or the name of the current working directory. The value must include one or both of the following strings:

parent   The name of any directory whose path is already contained in the word on the line is ignored. For example, when completing after `foo/../`, the directory `foo` will not be considered a valid completion.

pwd The name of the current working directory will not be completed; hence, for example, completion after ../ will not use the name of the current directory.

In addition, the value may include one or both of:

.. Ignore the specified directories only when the word on the line contains the substring '../'.

directory

  Ignore the specified directories only when names of directories are completed, not when completing names of files.

Excluded values act in a similar fashion to values of the **ignored-patterns** style, so they can be restored to consideration by the **_ignored** completer.

extra-verbose

  If set, the completion listing is more verbose at the cost of a probable decrease in completion speed. Completion performance will suffer if this style is set to 'true'.

ignored-patterns

  A list of patterns; any trial completion matching one of the patterns will be excluded from consideration. The **_ignored** completer can appear in the list of completers to restore the ignored matches. This is a more configurable version of the shell parameter **$fignore**.

  Note that the **EXTENDED_GLOB** option is set during the execution of completion functions, so the characters '#', '~' and '^' have special meanings in the patterns.

insert This style is used by the **_all_matches** completer to decide whether to insert the list of all matches unconditionally instead of adding the list as another match.

insert-ids

  When completing process IDs, for example as arguments to the **kill** and **wait** builtins the name of a command may be converted to the appropriate process ID. A problem arises when the process name typed is not unique. By default (or if this style is set explicitly to 'menu') the name will be converted immediately to a set of possible IDs, and menu completion will be started to cycle through them.

  If the value of the style is '**single**', the shell will wait until the user has typed enough to make the command unique before converting the name to an ID; attempts at completion will be unsuccessful until that point. If the value is any other string, menu completion will be started when the string typed by the user is longer than the common prefix to the corresponding IDs.

insert-tab

  If this is set to 'true', the completion system will insert a TAB character (assuming that was used to start completion) instead of performing completion when there is no non-blank character to the left of the cursor. If it is set to 'false', completion will be done even there.

The value may also contain the substrings 'pending' or 'pending=*val*'. In this case, the typed character will be inserted instead of starting completion when there is unprocessed input pending. If a *val* is given, completion will not be done if there are at least that many characters of unprocessed input. This is often useful when pasting characters into a terminal. Note however, that it relies on the $PENDING special parameter from the zsh/zle module being set properly which is not guaranteed on all platforms.

The default value of this style is 'true' except for completion within vared builtin command where it is 'false'.

insert-unambiguous

> This is used by the _match and _approximate completers. These completers are often used with menu completion since the word typed may bear little resemblance to the final completion. However, if this style is 'true', the completer will start menu completion only if it could find no unambiguous initial string at least as long as the original string typed by the user.
>
> In the case of the _approximate completer, the completer field in the context will already have been set to one of correct-*num* or approximate-*num*, where *num* is the number of errors that were accepted.
>
> In the case of the _match completer, the style may also be set to the string 'pattern'. Then the pattern on the line is left unchanged if it does not match unambiguously.

gain-privileges

> If set to true, this style enables the use of commands like sudo or doas to gain extra privileges when retrieving information for completion. This is only done when a command such as sudo appears on the command-line. To force the use of, e.g. sudo or to override any prefix that might be added due to gain-privileges, the command style can be used with a value that begins with a hyphen.

keep-prefix

> This style is used by the _expand completer. If it is 'true', the completer will try to keep a prefix containing a tilde or parameter expansion. Hence, for example, the string '~/f*' would be expanded to '~/foo' instead of '/home/user/foo'. If the style is set to 'changed' (the default), the prefix will only be left unchanged if there were other changes between the expanded words and the original word from the command line. Any other value forces the prefix to be expanded unconditionally.
>
> The behaviour of _expand when this style is 'true' is to cause _expand to give up when a single expansion with the restored prefix is the same as the original; hence any remaining completers may be called.

last-prompt

> This is a more flexible form of the ALWAYS_LAST_PROMPT option. If it is 'true', the completion system will try to return the cursor to the previous command line after displaying a completion list. It is tested for all tags valid for the current completion, then the default tag. The cursor will be moved back to

the previous line if this style is 'true' for all types of match. Note that unlike the `ALWAYS_LAST_PROMPT` option this is independent of the numeric argument.

`known-hosts-files`

> This style should contain a list of files to search for host names and (if the `use-ip` style is set) IP addresses in a format compatible with ssh `known_hosts` files. If it is not set, the files `/etc/ssh/ssh_known_hosts` and `~/.ssh/known_hosts` are used.

`list`

> This style is used by the `_history_complete_word` bindable command. If it is set to 'true' it has no effect. If it is set to 'false' matches will not be listed. This overrides the setting of the options controlling listing behaviour, in particular `AUTO_LIST`. The context always starts with ':completion:history-words'.

`list-colors`

> If the `zsh/complist` module is loaded, this style can be used to set color specifications. This mechanism replaces the use of the `ZLS_COLORS` and `ZLS_COLOURS` parameters described in Section 22.7 [The zsh/complist Module], page 333, but the syntax is the same.

> If this style is set for the `default` tag, the strings in the value are taken as specifications that are to be used everywhere. If it is set for other tags, the specifications are used only for matches of the type described by the tag. For this to work best, the `group-name` style must be set to an empty string.

> In addition to setting styles for specific tags, it is also possible to use group names specified explicitly by the `group-name` tag together with the '(group)' syntax allowed by the `ZLS_COLORS` and `ZLS_COLOURS` parameters and simply using the `default` tag.

> It is possible to use any color specifications already set up for the GNU version of the `ls` command:

> ```
> zstyle ':completion:*:default' list-colors \
>       ${(s.:.)LS_COLORS}
> ```

> The default colors are the same as for the GNU `ls` command and can be obtained by setting the style to an empty string (i.e. '').

`list-dirs-first`

> This is used by file completion. If set, directories to be completed are listed separately from and before completion for other files, regardless of tag ordering. In addition, the tag `other-files` is used in place of `all-files` for the remaining files, to indicate that no directories are presented with that tag.

`list-grouped`

> If this style is 'true' (the default), the completion system will try to make certain completion listings more compact by grouping matches. For example, options for commands that have the same description (shown when the `verbose` style is set to 'true') will appear as a single entry. However, menu selection can be used to cycle through all the matches.

list-packed

> This is tested for each tag valid in the current context as well as the **default** tag. If it is set to 'true', the corresponding matches appear in listings as if the **LIST_PACKED** option were set. If it is set to 'false', they are listed normally.

list-prompt

> If this style is set for the **default** tag, completion lists that don't fit on the screen can be scrolled (see Section 22.7 [The zsh/complist Module], page 333). The value, if not the empty string, will be displayed after every screenful and the shell will prompt for a key press; if the style is set to the empty string, a default prompt will be used.
>
> The value may contain the escape sequences: '%l' or '%L', which will be replaced by the number of the last line displayed and the total number of lines; '%m' or '%M', the number of the last match shown and the total number of matches; and '%p' and '%P', 'Top' when at the beginning of the list, 'Bottom' when at the end and the position shown as a percentage of the total length otherwise. In each case the form with the uppercase letter will be replaced by a string of fixed width, padded to the right with spaces, while the lowercase form will be replaced by a variable width string. As in other prompt strings, the escape sequences '%S', '%s', '%B', '%b', '%U', '%u' for entering and leaving the display modes standout, bold and underline, and '%F', '%f', '%K', '%k' for changing the foreground background colour, are also available, as is the form '%{...%}' for enclosing escape sequences which display with zero (or, with a numeric argument, some other) width.
>
> After deleting this prompt the variable **LISTPROMPT** should be unset for the removal to take effect.

list-rows-first

> This style is tested in the same way as the **list-packed** style and determines whether matches are to be listed in a rows-first fashion as if the **LIST_ROWS_FIRST** option were set.

list-suffixes

> This style is used by the function that completes filenames. If it is 'true', and completion is attempted on a string containing multiple partially typed pathname components, all ambiguous components will be shown. Otherwise, completion stops at the first ambiguous component.

list-separator

> The value of this style is used in completion listing to separate the string to complete from a description when possible (e.g. when completing options). It defaults to '--' (two hyphens).

local   This is for use with functions that complete URLs for which the corresponding files are available directly from the file system. Its value should consist of three strings: a hostname, the path to the default web pages for the server, and the directory name used by a user placing web pages within their home area.

> For example:

```
zstyle ':completion:*' local toast \
```

```
            /var/http/public/toast public_html
```

Completion after 'http://toast/stuff/' will look for files in the directory /var/http/public/toast/stuff, while completion after 'http://toast/~yousir/' will look for files in the directory ~yousir/public_html.

mail-directory

If set, zsh will assume that mailbox files can be found in the directory specified. It defaults to '~/Mail'.

match-original

This is used by the _match completer. If it is set to **only**, _match will try to generate matches without inserting a '*' at the cursor position. If set to any other non-empty value, it will first try to generate matches without inserting the '*' and if that yields no matches, it will try again with the '*' inserted. If it is unset or set to the empty string, matching will only be performed with the '*' inserted.

matcher This style is tested separately for each tag valid in the current context. Its value is placed before any match specifications given by the **matcher-list** style so can override them via the use of an **x:** specification. The value should be in the form described in Section 19.5 [Completion Matching Control], page 238. For examples of this, see the description of the **tag-order** style.

matcher-list

This style can be set to a list of match specifications that are to be applied everywhere. Match specifications are described in Section 19.5 [Completion Matching Control], page 238. The completion system will try them one after another for each completer selected. For example, to try first simple completion and, if that generates no matches, case-insensitive completion:

```
    zstyle ':completion:*' matcher-list '' 'm:{a-zA-Z}={A-Za-z}'
```

By default each specification replaces the previous one; however, if a specification is prefixed with +, it is added to the existing list. Hence it is possible to create increasingly general specifications without repetition:

```
    zstyle ':completion:*' matcher-list \
        '' '+m:{a-z}={A-Z}' '+m:{A-Z}={a-z}'
```

It is possible to create match specifications valid for particular completers by using the third field of the context. This applies only to completers that override the global matcher-list, which as of this writing includes only **_prefix** and **_ignored**. For example, to use the completers **_complete** and **_prefix** but allow case-insensitive completion only with **_complete**:

```
    zstyle ':completion:*' completer _complete _prefix
    zstyle ':completion:*:complete:*:*:*' matcher-list \
        '' 'm:{a-zA-Z}={A-Za-z}'
```

User-defined names, as explained for the **completer** style, are available. This makes it possible to try the same completer more than once with different match specifications each time. For example, to try normal completion without a match specification, then normal completion with case-insensitive matching, then correction, and finally partial-word completion:

```
zstyle ':completion:*' completer \
    _complete _correct _complete:foo
zstyle ':completion:*:complete:*:*:*' matcher-list \
    '' 'm:{a-zA-Z}={A-Za-z}'
zstyle ':completion:*:foo:*:*:*' matcher-list \
    'm:{a-zA-Z}={A-Za-z} r:|[-_./]=* r:|=*'
```

If the style is unset in any context no match specification is applied. Note also that some completers such as _correct and _approximate do not use the match specifications at all, though these completers will only ever be called once even if the matcher-list contains more than one element.

Where multiple specifications are useful, note that the *entire* completion is done for each element of matcher-list, which can quickly reduce the shell's performance. As a rough rule of thumb, one to three strings will give acceptable performance. On the other hand, putting multiple space-separated values into the same string does not have an appreciable impact on performance.

If there is no current matcher or it is empty, and the option NO_CASE_GLOB is in effect, the matching for files is performed case-insensitively in any case. However, any matcher must explicitly specify case-insensitive matching if that is required.

max-errors

This is used by the _approximate and _correct completer functions to determine the maximum number of errors to allow. The completer will try to generate completions by first allowing one error, then two errors, and so on, until either a match or matches were found or the maximum number of errors given by this style has been reached.

If the value for this style contains the string 'numeric', the completer function will take any numeric argument as the maximum number of errors allowed. For example, with

```
zstyle ':completion:*:approximate:::' max-errors 2 numeric
```

two errors are allowed if no numeric argument is given, but with a numeric argument of six (as in 'ESC-6 TAB'), up to six errors are accepted. Hence with a value of '0 numeric', no correcting completion will be attempted unless a numeric argument is given.

If the value contains the string 'not-numeric', the completer will *not* try to generate corrected completions when given a numeric argument, so in this case the number given should be greater than zero. For example, '2 not-numeric' specifies that correcting completion with two errors will usually be performed, but if a numeric argument is given, correcting completion will not be performed.

The default value for this style is '2 numeric'.

max-matches-width

This style is used to determine the trade off between the width of the display used for matches and the width used for their descriptions when the verbose style is in effect. The value gives the number of display columns to reserve for the matches. The default is half the width of the screen.

This has the most impact when several matches have the same description and so will be grouped together. Increasing the style will allow more matches to be grouped together; decreasing it will allow more of the description to be visible.

menu   If this is 'true' in the context of any of the tags defined for the current completion menu completion will be used. The value for a specific tag will take precedence over that for the 'default' tag.

If none of the values found in this way is 'true' but at least one is set to 'auto', the shell behaves as if the AUTO_MENU option is set.

If one of the values is explicitly set to 'false', menu completion will be explicitly turned off, overriding the MENU_COMPLETE option and other settings.

In the form 'yes=num', where 'yes' may be any of the 'true' values ('yes', 'true', 'on' and '1'), menu completion will be turned on if there are at least num matches. In the form 'yes=long', menu completion will be turned on if the list does not fit on the screen. This does not activate menu completion if the widget normally only lists completions, but menu completion can be activated in that case with the value 'yes=long-list' (Typically, the value 'select=long-list' described later is more useful as it provides control over scrolling.)

Similarly, with any of the 'false' values (as in 'no=10'), menu completion will not be used if there are num or more matches.

The value of this widget also controls menu selection, as implemented by the zsh/complist module. The following values may appear either alongside or instead of the values above.

If the value contains the string 'select', menu selection will be started unconditionally.

In the form 'select=num', menu selection will only be started if there are at least num matches. If the values for more than one tag provide a number, the smallest number is taken.

Menu selection can be turned off explicitly by defining a value containing the string 'no-select'.

It is also possible to start menu selection only if the list of matches does not fit on the screen by using the value 'select=long'. To start menu selection even if the current widget only performs listing, use the value 'select=long-list'.

To turn on menu completion or menu selection when there are a certain number of matches or the list of matches does not fit on the screen, both of 'yes=' and 'select=' may be given twice, once with a number and once with 'long' or 'long-list'.

Finally, it is possible to activate two special modes of menu selection. The word 'interactive' in the value causes interactive mode to be entered immediately when menu selection is started; see Section 22.7 [The zsh/complist Module], page 333, for a description of interactive mode. Including the string 'search' does the same for incremental search mode. To select backward incremental search, include the string 'search-backward'.

muttrc   If set, gives the location of the mutt configuration file. It defaults to '~/.muttrc'.

numbers   This is used with the jobs tag. If it is 'true', the shell will complete job numbers instead of the shortest unambiguous prefix of the job command text. If the value is a number, job numbers will only be used if that many words from the job descriptions are required to resolve ambiguities. For example, if the value is '1', strings will only be used if all jobs differ in the first word on their command lines.

old-list This is used by the _oldlist completer. If it is set to 'always', then standard widgets which perform listing will retain the current list of matches, however they were generated; this can be turned off explicitly with the value 'never', giving the behaviour without the _oldlist completer. If the style is unset, or any other value, then the existing list of completions is displayed if it is not already; otherwise, the standard completion list is generated; this is the default behaviour of _oldlist. However, if there is an old list and this style contains the name of the completer function that generated the list, then the old list will be used even if it was generated by a widget which does not do listing.

For example, suppose you type ^Xc to use the _correct_word widget, which generates a list of corrections for the word under the cursor. Usually, typing ^D would generate a standard list of completions for the word on the command line, and show that. With _oldlist, it will instead show the list of corrections already generated.

As another example consider the _match completer: with the insert-unambiguous style set to 'true' it inserts only a common prefix string, if there is any. However, this may remove parts of the original pattern, so that further completion could produce more matches than on the first attempt. By using the _oldlist completer and setting this style to _match, the list of matches generated on the first attempt will be used again.

old-matches

This is used by the _all_matches completer to decide if an old list of matches should be used if one exists. This is selected by one of the 'true' values or by the string 'only'. If the value is 'only', _all_matches will only use an old list and won't have any effect on the list of matches currently being generated.

If this style is set it is generally unwise to call the _all_matches completer unconditionally. One possible use is for either this style or the completer style to be defined with the -e option to zstyle to make the style conditional.

old-menu This is used by the _oldlist completer. It controls how menu completion behaves when a completion has already been inserted and the user types a standard completion key such as TAB. The default behaviour of _oldlist is that menu completion always continues with the existing list of completions. If this style is set to 'false', however, a new completion is started if the old list was generated by a different completion command; this is the behaviour without the _oldlist completer.

For example, suppose you type ^Xc to generate a list of corrections, and menu completion is started in one of the usual ways. Usually, or with this style set to 'false', typing TAB at this point would start trying to complete the line as it now appears. With _oldlist, it instead continues to cycle through the list of corrections.

original This is used by the _approximate and _correct completers to decide if the original string should be added as a possible completion. Normally, this is done only if there are at least two possible corrections, but if this style is set to 'true', it is always added. Note that the style will be examined with the completer field in the context name set to correct-*num* or approximate-*num*, where *num* is the number of errors that were accepted.

packageset

This style is used when completing arguments of the Debian 'dpkg' program. It contains an override for the default package set for a given context. For example,

```
zstyle ':completion:*:complete:dpkg:option--status-1:*' \
              packageset avail
```

causes available packages, rather than only installed packages, to be completed for 'dpkg --status'.

path The function that completes color names uses this style with the colors tag. The value should be the pathname of a file containing color names in the format of an X11 rgb.txt file. If the style is not set but this file is found in one of various standard locations it will be used as the default.

path-completion

This is used by filename completion. By default, filename completion examines all components of a path to see if there are completions of that component. For example, /u/b/z can be completed to /usr/bin/zsh. Explicitly setting this style to 'false' inhibits this behaviour for path components up to the / before the cursor; this overrides the setting of accept-exact-dirs.

Even with the style set to 'false', it is still possible to complete multiple paths by setting the option COMPLETE_IN_WORD and moving the cursor back to the first component in the path to be completed. For example, /u/b/z can be completed to /usr/bin/zsh if the cursor is after the /u.

pine-directory

If set, specifies the directory containing PINE mailbox files. There is no default, since recursively searching this directory is inconvenient for anyone who doesn't use PINE.

ports A list of Internet service names (network ports) to complete. If this is not set, service names are taken from the file '/etc/services'.

prefix-hidden

This is used for certain completions which share a common prefix, for example command options beginning with dashes. If it is 'true', the prefix will not be shown in the list of matches.

The default value for this style is 'false'.

prefix-needed

This style is also relevant for matches with a common prefix. If it is set to 'true' this common prefix must be typed by the user to generate the matches.

The style is applicable to the **options**, **signals**, **jobs**, **functions**, and **parameters** completion tags.

For command options, this means that the initial '-', '+', or '--' must be typed explicitly before option names will be completed.

For signals, an initial '-' is required before signal names will be completed.

For jobs, an initial '%' is required before job names will be completed.

For function and parameter names, an initial '_' or '.' is required before function or parameter names starting with those characters will be completed.

The default value for this style is 'false' for **function** and **parameter** completions, and 'true' otherwise.

preserve-prefix

This style is used when completing path names. Its value should be a pattern matching an initial prefix of the word to complete that should be left unchanged under all circumstances. For example, on some Unices an initial '//' (double slash) has a special meaning; setting this style to the string '//' will preserve it. As another example, setting this style to '?:/' under Cygwin would allow completion after 'a:/...' and so on.

range

This is used by the **_history** completer and the **_history_complete_word** bindable command to decide which words should be completed.

If it is a single number, only the last N words from the history will be completed.

If it is a range of the form '*max*:*slice*', the last *slice* words will be completed; then if that yields no matches, the *slice* words before those will be tried and so on. This process stops either when at least one match has been found, or *max* words have been tried.

The default is to complete all words from the history at once.

recursive-files

If this style is set, its value is an array of patterns to be tested against '$PWD/': note the trailing slash, which allows directories in the pattern to be delimited unambiguously by including slashes on both sides. If an ordinary file completion fails and the word on the command line does not yet have a directory part to its name, the style is retrieved using the same tag as for the completion just attempted, then the elements tested against $PWD/ in turn. If one matches, then the shell reattempts completion by prepending the word on the command line with each directory in the expansion of **/*(/) in turn. Typically the elements of the style will be set to restrict the number of directories beneath the current one to a manageable number, for example '*/.git/*'.

For example,

```
zstyle ':completion:*' recursive-files '*/zsh/*'
```

If the current directory is /home/pws/zsh/Src, then zle_tr*TAB* can be completed to Zle/zle_tricky.c.

regular   This style is used by the _expand_alias completer and bindable command. If set to 'true' (the default), regular aliases will be expanded but only in command position. If it is set to 'false', regular aliases will never be expanded. If it is set to 'always', regular aliases will be expanded even if not in command position.

rehash   If this is set when completing external commands, the internal list (hash) of commands will be updated for each search by issuing the rehash command. There is a speed penalty for this which is only likely to be noticeable when directories in the path have slow file access.

remote-access

If set to 'false', certain commands will be prevented from making Internet connections to retrieve remote information. This includes the completion for the CVS command.

It is not always possible to know if connections are in fact to a remote site, so some may be prevented unnecessarily.

remove-all-dups

The _history_complete_word bindable command and the _history completer use this to decide if all duplicate matches should be removed, rather than just consecutive duplicates.

select-prompt

If this is set for the default tag, its value will be displayed during menu selection (see the menu style above) when the completion list does not fit on the screen as a whole. The same escapes as for the list-prompt style are understood, except that the numbers refer to the match or line the mark is on. A default prompt is used when the value is the empty string.

select-scroll

This style is tested for the default tag and determines how a completion list is scrolled during a menu selection (see the menu style above) when the completion list does not fit on the screen as a whole. If the value is '0' (zero), the list is scrolled by half-screenfuls; if it is a positive integer, the list is scrolled by the given number of lines; if it is a negative number, the list is scrolled by a screenful minus the absolute value of the given number of lines. The default is to scroll by single lines.

separate-sections

This style is used with the manuals tag when completing names of manual pages. If it is 'true', entries for different sections are added separately using tag names of the form 'manual.X', where X is the section number. When the group-name style is also in effect, pages from different sections will appear separately. This style is also used similarly with the words style when completing words for the dict command. It allows words from different dictionary databases to be added separately. The default for this style is 'false'.

show-ambiguity

If the **zsh/complist** module is loaded, this style can be used to highlight the first ambiguous character in completion lists. The value is either a color indication such as those supported by the **list-colors** style or, with a value of 'true', a default of underlining is selected. The highlighting is only applied if the completion display strings correspond to the actual matches.

show-completer

Tested whenever a new completer is tried. If it is 'true', the completion system outputs a progress message in the listing area showing what completer is being tried. The message will be overwritten by any output when completions are found and is removed after completion is finished.

single-ignored

This is used by the **_ignored** completer when there is only one match. If its value is '**show**', the single match will be displayed but not inserted. If the value is '**menu**', then the single match and the original string are both added as matches and menu completion is started, making it easy to select either of them.

sort

Many completion widgets call **_description** at some point which decides whether the matches are added sorted or unsorted (often indirectly via **_wanted** or **_requested**). This style can be set explicitly to one of the usual 'true' or 'false' values as an override. If it is not set for the context, the standard behaviour of the calling widget is used.

The style is tested first against the full context including the tag, and if that fails to produce a value against the context without the tag.

If the calling widget explicitly requests unsorted matches, this is usually honoured. However, the default (unsorted) behaviour of completion for the command history may be overridden by setting the style to 'true'.

In the **_expand** completer, if it is set to 'true', the expansions generated will always be sorted. If it is set to '**menu**', then the expansions are only sorted when they are offered as single strings but not in the string containing all possible expansions.

special-dirs

Normally, the completion code will not produce the directory names '.' and '..' as possible completions. If this style is set to 'true', it will add both '.' and '..' as possible completions; if it is set to '..', only '..' will be added.

The following example sets **special-dirs** to '..' when the current prefix is empty, is a single '.', or consists only of a path beginning with '../'. Otherwise the value is 'false'.

```
zstyle -e ':completion:*' special-dirs \
    '[[ $PREFIX = (../)#(|.|..) ]] && reply=(..)'
```

squeeze-slashes

If set to 'true', sequences of slashes in filename paths (for example in '**foo//bar**') will be treated as a single slash. This is the usual behaviour of UNIX paths.

However, by default the file completion function behaves as if there were a '*' between the slashes.

stop   If set to 'true', the `_history_complete_word` bindable command will stop once when reaching the beginning or end of the history. Invoking `_history_complete_word` will then wrap around to the opposite end of the history. If this style is set to 'false' (the default), `_history_complete_word` will loop immediately as in a menu completion.

strip-comments

If set to 'true', this style causes non-essential comment text to be removed from completion matches. Currently it is only used when completing e-mail addresses where it removes any display name from the addresses, cutting them down to plain *user@host* form.

subst-globs-only

This is used by the `_expand` completer. If it is set to 'true', the expansion will only be used if it resulted from globbing; hence, if expansions resulted from the use of the **substitute** style described below, but these were not further changed by globbing, the expansions will be rejected.

The default for this style is 'false'.

substitute

This boolean style controls whether the `_expand` completer will first try to expand all substitutions in the string (such as '$(...)' and '${...}').

The default is 'true'.

suffix This is used by the `_expand` completer if the word starts with a tilde or contains a parameter expansion. If it is set to 'true', the word will only be expanded if it doesn't have a suffix, i.e. if it is something like '~foo' or '$foo' rather than '~foo/' or '$foo/bar', unless that suffix itself contains characters eligible for expansion. The default for this style is 'true'.

tag-order

This provides a mechanism for sorting how the tags available in a particular context will be used.

The values for the style are sets of space-separated lists of tags. The tags in each value will be tried at the same time; if no match is found, the next value is used. (See the **file-patterns** style for an exception to this behavior.)

For example:

```
zstyle ':completion:*:complete:-command-:*:*' tag-order \
    'commands functions'
```

specifies that completion in command position first offers external commands and shell functions. Remaining tags will be tried if no completions are found.

In addition to tag names, each string in the value may take one of the following forms:

–   If any value consists of only a hyphen, then *only* the tags specified in the other values are generated. Normally all tags not explicitly selected are tried last if the specified tags fail to generate any matches. This means that a single value consisting only of a single hyphen turns off completion.

! *tags...*   A string starting with an exclamation mark specifies names of tags that are *not* to be used. The effect is the same as if all other possible tags for the context had been listed.

tag:*label* ...

Here, *tag* is one of the standard tags and *label* is an arbitrary name. Matches are generated as normal but the name *label* is used in contexts instead of *tag*. This is not useful in words starting with !.

If the *label* starts with a hyphen, the *tag* is prepended to the *label* to form the name used for lookup. This can be used to make the completion system try a certain tag more than once, supplying different style settings for each attempt; see below for an example.

tag:*label*:*description*

As before, but **description** will replace the '%d' in the value of the **format** style instead of the default description supplied by the completion function. Spaces in the description must be quoted with a backslash. A '%d' appearing in *description* is replaced with the description given by the completion function.

In any of the forms above the tag may be a pattern or several patterns in the form '{*pat1*,*pat2*...}'. In this case all matching tags will be used except for any given explicitly in the same string.

One use of these features is to try one tag more than once, setting other styles differently on each attempt, but still to use all the other tags without having to repeat them all. For example, to make completion of function names in command position ignore all the completion functions starting with an underscore the first time completion is tried:

```
zstyle ':completion:*:*:-command-:*:*' tag-order \
    'functions:-non-comp *' functions
zstyle ':completion:*:functions-non-comp' \
    ignored-patterns '_*'
```

On the first attempt, all tags will be offered but the **functions** tag will be replaced by **functions-non-comp**. The **ignored-patterns** style is set for this tag to exclude functions starting with an underscore. If there are no matches, the second value of the **tag-order** style is used which completes functions using the default tag, this time presumably including all function names.

The matches for one tag can be split into different groups. For example:

```
zstyle ':completion:*' tag-order \
    'options:-long:long\ options
    options:-short:short\ options
    options:-single-letter:single\ letter\ options'
zstyle ':completion:*:options-long' \
    ignored-patterns '[-+](|-|[^-]*)'
```

```
zstyle ':completion:*:options-short' \
    ignored-patterns '--*' '[-+]?'
zstyle ':completion:*:options-single-letter' \
    ignored-patterns '???*'
```

With the **group-names** style set, options beginning with '--', options beginning with a single '-' or '+' but containing multiple characters, and single-letter options will be displayed in separate groups with different descriptions.

Another use of patterns is to try multiple match specifications one after another. The **matcher-list** style offers something similar, but it is tested very early in the completion system and hence can't be set for single commands nor for more specific contexts. Here is how to try normal completion without any match specification and, if that generates no matches, try again with case-insensitive matching, restricting the effect to arguments of the command **foo**:

```
zstyle ':completion:*:*:foo:*:*' tag-order '*' '*:-case'
zstyle ':completion:*-case' matcher 'm:{a-z}={A-Z}'
```

First, all the tags offered when completing after **foo** are tried using the normal tag name. If that generates no matches, the second value of **tag-order** is used, which tries all tags again except that this time each has **-case** appended to its name for lookup of styles. Hence this time the value for the **matcher** style from the second call to **zstyle** in the example is used to make completion case-insensitive.

It is possible to use the **-e** option of the **zstyle** builtin command to specify conditions for the use of particular tags. For example:

```
zstyle -e '*:-command-:*' tag-order '
    if [[ -n $PREFIX$SUFFIX ]]; then
      reply=( )
    else
      reply=( - )
    fi'
```

Completion in command position will be attempted only if the string typed so far is not empty. This is tested using the **PREFIX** special parameter; see Chapter 19 [Completion Widgets], page 225, for a description of parameters which are special inside completion widgets. Setting **reply** to an empty array provides the default behaviour of trying all tags at once; setting it to an array containing only a hyphen disables the use of all tags and hence of all completions.

If no **tag-order** style has been defined for a context, the strings '(|*-)argument-* (|*-)option-* values' and 'options' plus all tags offered by the completion function will be used to provide a sensible default behavior that causes arguments (whether normal command arguments or arguments of options) to be completed before option names for most commands.

urls   This is used together with the **urls** tag by functions completing URLs.

If the value consists of more than one string, or if the only string does not name a file or directory, the strings are used as the URLs to complete.

If the value contains only one string which is the name of a normal file the URLs are taken from that file (where the URLs may be separated by white space or newlines).

Finally, if the only string in the value names a directory, the directory hierarchy rooted at this directory gives the completions. The top level directory should be the file access method, such as 'http', 'ftp', 'bookmark' and so on. In many cases the next level of directories will be a filename. The directory hierarchy can descend as deep as necessary.

For example,

```
zstyle ':completion:*' urls ~/.urls
mkdir -p ~/.urls/ftp/ftp.zsh.org/pub
```

allows completion of all the components of the URL `ftp://ftp.zsh.org/pub` after suitable commands such as 'netscape' or 'lynx'. Note, however, that access methods and files are completed separately, so if the **hosts** style is set hosts can be completed without reference to the **urls** style.

See the description in the function **_urls** itself for more information (e.g. 'more `$^fpath/_urls(N)`').

use-cache

If this is set, the completion caching layer is activated for any completions which use it (via the **_store_cache**, **_retrieve_cache**, and **_cache_invalid** functions). The directory containing the cache files can be changed with the **cache-path** style.

use-compctl

If this style is set to a string *not* equal to **false**, 0, **no**, and **off**, the completion system may use any completion specifications defined with the **compctl** builtin command. If the style is unset, this is done only if the **zsh/compctl** module is loaded. The string may also contain the substring 'first' to use completions defined with 'compctl -T', and the substring 'default' to use the completion defined with 'compctl -D'.

Note that this is only intended to smooth the transition from **compctl** to the new completion system and may disappear in the future.

Note also that the definitions from **compctl** will only be used if there is no specific completion function for the command in question. For example, if there is a function **_foo** to complete arguments to the command **foo**, **compctl** will never be invoked for **foo**. However, the **compctl** version will be tried if **foo** only uses default completion.

use-ip

By default, the function **_hosts** that completes host names strips IP addresses from entries read from host databases such as NIS and ssh files. If this style is 'true', the corresponding IP addresses can be completed as well. This style is not use in any context where the **hosts** style is set; note also it must be set before the cache of host names is generated (typically the first completion attempt).

users   This may be set to a list of usernames to be completed. If it is not set all usernames will be completed. Note that if it is set only that list of users will be completed; this is because on some systems querying all users can take a prohibitive amount of time.

users-hosts
         The values of this style should be of the form '*user@host*' or '*user*:*host*'. It is used for commands that need pairs of user- and hostnames. These commands will complete usernames from this style (only), and will restrict subsequent hostname completion to hosts paired with that user in one of the values of the style.

         It is possible to group values for sets of commands which allow a remote login, such as **rlogin** and **ssh**, by using the **my-accounts** tag. Similarly, values for sets of commands which usually refer to the accounts of other people, such as **talk** and **finger**, can be grouped by using the **other-accounts** tag. More ambivalent commands may use the **accounts** tag.

users-hosts-ports
         Like **users-hosts** but used for commands like **telnet** and containing strings of the form '*user@host*:*port*'.

verbose If set, as it is by default, the completion listing is more verbose. In particular many commands show descriptions for options if this style is 'true'.

word   This is used by the **_list** completer, which prevents the insertion of completions until a second completion attempt when the line has not changed. The normal way of finding out if the line has changed is to compare its entire contents between the two occasions. If this style is 'true', the comparison is instead performed only on the current word. Hence if completion is performed on another word with the same contents, completion will not be delayed.

20.4 Control Functions

The initialization script **compinit** redefines all the widgets which perform completion to call the supplied widget function **_main_complete**. This function acts as a wrapper calling the so-called 'completer' functions that generate matches. If **_main_complete** is called with arguments, these are taken as the names of completer functions to be called in the order given. If no arguments are given, the set of functions to try is taken from the **completer** style. For example, to use normal completion and correction if that doesn't generate any matches:

```
zstyle ':completion:*' completer _complete _correct
```

after calling **compinit**. The default value for this style is '**_complete _ignored**', i.e. normally only ordinary completion is tried, first with the effect of the **ignored-patterns** style and then without it. The **_main_complete** function uses the return status of the completer functions to decide if other completers should be called. If the return status is zero, no other completers are tried and the **_main_complete** function returns.

If the first argument to **_main_complete** is a single hyphen, the arguments will not be taken as names of completers. Instead, the second argument gives a name to use in the *completer* field of the context and the other arguments give a command name and arguments to call to generate the matches.

The following completer functions are contained in the distribution, although users may write their own. Note that in contexts the leading underscore is stripped, for example basic completion is performed in the context ':completion::complete:...'.

_all_matches

This completer can be used to add a string consisting of all other matches. As it influences later completers it must appear as the first completer in the list. The list of all matches is affected by the **avoid-completer** and **old-matches** styles described above.

It may be useful to use the **_generic** function described below to bind **_all_matches** to its own keystroke, for example:

```
zle -C all-matches complete-word _generic
bindkey '^Xa' all-matches
zstyle ':completion:all-matches:*' old-matches only
zstyle ':completion:all-matches::::' completer _all_matches
```

Note that this does not generate completions by itself: first use any of the standard ways of generating a list of completions, then use ^Xa to show all matches. It is possible instead to add a standard completer to the list and request that the list of all matches should be directly inserted:

```
zstyle ':completion:all-matches::::' completer \
        _all_matches _complete
zstyle ':completion:all-matches:*' insert true
```

In this case the **old-matches** style should not be set.

_approximate

This is similar to the basic **_complete** completer but allows the completions to undergo corrections. The maximum number of errors can be specified by the **max-errors** style; see the description of approximate matching in Section 14.8 [Filename Generation], page 72, for how errors are counted. Normally this completer will only be tried after the normal **_complete** completer:

```
zstyle ':completion:*' completer _complete _approximate
```

This will give correcting completion if and only if normal completion yields no possible completions. When corrected completions are found, the completer will normally start menu completion allowing you to cycle through these strings.

This completer uses the tags **corrections** and **original** when generating the possible corrections and the original string. The **format** style for the former may contain the additional sequences '%e' and '%o' which will be replaced by the number of errors accepted to generate the corrections and the original string, respectively.

The completer progressively increases the number of errors allowed up to the limit by the **max-errors** style, hence if a completion is found with one error, no completions with two errors will be shown, and so on. It modifies the completer name in the context to indicate the number of errors being tried: on the first try the completer field contains 'approximate-1', on the second try 'approximate-2', and so on.

When _approximate is called from another function, the number of errors to accept may be passed with the -a option. The argument is in the same format as the max-errors style, all in one string.

Note that this completer (and the _correct completer mentioned below) can be quite expensive to call, especially when a large number of errors are allowed. One way to avoid this is to set up the completer style using the -e option to zstyle so that some completers are only used when completion is attempted a second time on the same string, e.g.:

```
zstyle -e ':completion:*' completer '
  if [[ $_last_try != "$HISTNO$BUFFER$CURSOR" ]]; then
    _last_try="$HISTNO$BUFFER$CURSOR"
    reply=(_complete _match _prefix)
  else
    reply=(_ignored _correct _approximate)
  fi'
```

This uses the HISTNO parameter and the BUFFER and CURSOR special parameters that are available inside zle and completion widgets to find out if the command line hasn't changed since the last time completion was tried. Only then are the _ignored, _correct and _approximate completers called.

_canonical_paths [-A var] [-N] [-MJV12nfX] tag descr [paths ...]

This completion function completes all paths given to it, and also tries to offer completions which point to the same file as one of the paths given (relative path when an absolute path is given, and vice versa; when ..'s are present in the word to be completed; and some paths got from symlinks).

-A, if specified, takes the paths from the array variable specified. Paths can also be specified on the command line as shown above. -N, if specified, prevents canonicalizing the paths given before using them for completion, in case they are already so. The options -M, -J, -V, -1, -2, -n, -F, -X are passed to compadd.

See _description for a description of tag and descr.

_cmdambivalent

Completes the remaining positional arguments as an external command. The external command and its arguments are completed as separate arguments (in a manner appropriate for completing /usr/bin/env) if there are two or more remaining positional arguments on the command line, and as a quoted command string (in the manner of system(...)) otherwise. See also _cmdstring and _precommand.

This function takes no arguments.

_cmdstring

Completes an external command as a single argument, as for system(...).

_complete

This completer generates all possible completions in a context-sensitive manner, i.e. using the settings defined with the compdef function explained above and the current settings of all special parameters. This gives the normal completion behaviour.

To complete arguments of commands, _complete uses the utility function _normal, which is in turn responsible for finding the particular function; it is described below. Various contexts of the form -context- are handled specifically. These are all mentioned above as possible arguments to the #compdef tag.

Before trying to find a function for a specific context, _complete checks if the parameter 'compcontext' is set. Setting 'compcontext' allows the usual completion dispatching to be overridden which is useful in places such as a function that uses **vared** for input. If it is set to an array, the elements are taken to be the possible matches which will be completed using the tag 'values' and the description 'value'. If it is set to an associative array, the keys are used as the possible completions and the values (if non-empty) are used as descriptions for the matches. If 'compcontext' is set to a string containing colons, it should be of the form '*tag*:*descr*:*action*'. In this case the *tag* and *descr* give the tag and description to use and the *action* indicates what should be completed in one of the forms accepted by the **_arguments** utility function described below.

Finally, if 'compcontext' is set to a string without colons, the value is taken as the name of the context to use and the function defined for that context will be called. For this purpose, there is a special context named -command-line- that completes whole command lines (commands and their arguments). This is not used by the completion system itself but is nonetheless handled when explicitly called.

_correct   Generate corrections, but not completions, for the current word; this is similar to _approximate but will not allow any number of extra characters at the cursor as that completer does. The effect is similar to spell-checking. It is based on _approximate, but the completer field in the context name is **correct**.

For example, with:

```
zstyle ':completion:::::' completer \
        _complete _correct _approximate
zstyle ':completion:*:correct:::' max-errors 2 not-numeric
zstyle ':completion:*:approximate:::' max-errors 3 numeric
```

correction will accept up to two errors. If a numeric argument is given, correction will not be performed, but correcting completion will be, and will accept as many errors as given by the numeric argument. Without a numeric argument, first correction and then correcting completion will be tried, with the first one accepting two errors and the second one accepting three errors.

When _correct is called as a function, the number of errors to accept may be given following the -a option. The argument is in the same form a values to the **accept** style, all in one string.

This completer function is intended to be used without the _approximate completer or, as in the example, just before it. Using it after the _approximate completer is useless since _approximate will at least generate the corrected strings generated by the _correct completer — and probably more.

_expand   This completer function does not really perform completion, but instead checks if the word on the command line is eligible for expansion and, if it is, gives detailed control over how this expansion is done. For this to happen, the completion system needs to be invoked with **complete-word**, not **expand-or-complete** (the default binding for **TAB**), as otherwise the string will be expanded by the shell's internal mechanism before the completion system is started. Note also this completer should be called before the **_complete** completer function.

The tags used when generating expansions are **all-expansions** for the string containing all possible expansions, **expansions** when adding the possible expansions as single matches and **original** when adding the original string from the line. The order in which these strings are generated, if at all, can be controlled by the **group-order** and **tag-order** styles, as usual.

The format string for **all-expansions** and for **expansions** may contain the sequence '%o' which will be replaced by the original string from the line.

The kind of expansion to be tried is controlled by the **substitute**, **glob** and **subst-globs-only** styles.

It is also possible to call **_expand** as a function, in which case the different modes may be selected with options: **-s** for **substitute**, **-g** for **glob** and **-o** for **subst-globs-only**.

_expand_alias
    If the word the cursor is on is an alias, it is expanded and no other completers are called. The types of aliases which are to be expanded can be controlled with the styles **regular**, **global** and **disabled**.

This function is also a bindable command, see Section 20.5 [Bindable Commands], page 289.

_extensions
    If the cursor follows the string '*.', filename extensions are completed. The extensions are taken from files in current directory or a directory specified at the beginning of the current word. For exact matches, completion continues to allow other completers such as **_expand** to expand the pattern. The standard **add-space** and **prefix-hidden** styles are observed.

_external_pwds
    Completes current directories of other zsh processes belonging to the current user.

This is intended to be used via **_generic**, bound to a custom key combination. Note that pattern matching is enabled so matching is performed similar to how it works with the **_match** completer.

_history   Complete words from the shell's command history. This completer can be controlled by the **remove-all-dups**, and **sort** styles as for the **_history_complete_word** bindable command, see Section 20.5 [Bindable Commands], page 289, and Section 20.3 [Completion System Configuration], page 249.

_ignored   The **ignored-patterns** style can be set to a list of patterns which are compared against possible completions; matching ones are removed. With this completer those matches can be reinstated, as if no `ignored-patterns` style were set. The completer actually generates its own list of matches; which completers are invoked is determined in the same way as for the `_prefix` completer. The `single-ignored` style is also available as described above.

_list   This completer allows the insertion of matches to be delayed until completion is attempted a second time without the word on the line being changed. On the first attempt, only the list of matches will be shown. It is affected by the styles `condition` and `word`, see Section 20.3 [Completion System Configuration], page 249.

_match   This completer is intended to be used after the `_complete` completer. It behaves similarly but the string on the command line may be a pattern to match against trial completions. This gives the effect of the `GLOB_COMPLETE` option.

Normally completion will be performed by taking the pattern from the line, inserting a '`*`' at the cursor position and comparing the resulting pattern with the possible completions generated. This can be modified with the `match-original` style described above.

The generated matches will be offered in a menu completion unless the `insert-unambiguous` style is set to 'true'; see the description above for other options for this style.

Note that matcher specifications defined globally or used by the completion functions (the styles `matcher-list` and `matcher`) will not be used.

_menu   This completer was written as simple example function to show how menu completion can be enabled in shell code. However, it has the notable effect of disabling menu selection which can be useful with `_generic` based widgets. It should be used as the first completer in the list. Note that this is independent of the setting of the `MENU_COMPLETE` option and does not work with the other menu completion widgets such as `reverse-menu-complete`, or `accept-and-menu-complete`.

_oldlist This completer controls how the standard completion widgets behave when there is an existing list of completions which may have been generated by a special completion (i.e. a separately-bound completion command). It allows the ordinary completion keys to continue to use the list of completions thus generated, instead of producing a new list of ordinary contextual completions. It should appear in the list of completers before any of the widgets which generate matches. It uses two styles: `old-list` and `old-menu`, see Section 20.3 [Completion System Configuration], page 249.

_precommand
         Complete an external command in word-separated arguments, as for `exec` and `/usr/bin/env`.

_prefix This completer can be used to try completion with the suffix (everything after the cursor) ignored. In other words, the suffix will not be considered to be part of the word to complete. The effect is similar to the `expand-or-complete-prefix` command.

The `completer` style is used to decide which other completers are to be called to generate matches. If this style is unset, the list of completers set for the current context is used — except, of course, the `_prefix` completer itself. Furthermore, if this completer appears more than once in the list of completers only those completers not already tried by the last invocation of `_prefix` will be called.

For example, consider this global `completer` style:

```
zstyle ':completion:*' completer \
    _complete _prefix _correct _prefix:foo
```

Here, the `_prefix` completer tries normal completion but ignoring the suffix. If that doesn't generate any matches, and neither does the call to the `_correct` completer after it, `_prefix` will be called a second time and, now only trying correction with the suffix ignored. On the second invocation the completer part of the context appears as 'foo'.

To use `_prefix` as the last resort and try only normal completion when it is invoked:

```
zstyle ':completion:*' completer _complete ... _prefix
zstyle ':completion::prefix:*' completer _complete
```

The `add-space` style is also respected. If it is set to 'true' then `_prefix` will insert a space between the matches generated (if any) and the suffix.

Note that this completer is only useful if the `COMPLETE_IN_WORD` option is set; otherwise, the cursor will be moved to the end of the current word before the completion code is called and hence there will be no suffix.

`_user_expand`

This completer behaves similarly to the `_expand` completer but instead performs expansions defined by users. The styles `add-space` and `sort` styles specific to the `_expand` completer are usable with `_user_expand` in addition to other styles handled more generally by the completion system. The tag `all-expansions` is also available.

The expansion depends on the array style `user-expand` being defined for the current context; remember that the context for completers is less specific than that for contextual completion as the full context has not yet been determined. Elements of the array may have one of the following forms:

`$hash`

hash is the name of an associative array. Note this is not a full parameter expression, merely a $, suitably quoted to prevent immediate expansion, followed by the name of an associative array. If the trial expansion word matches a key in hash, the resulting expansion is the corresponding value.

`_func`

_func is the name of a shell function whose name must begin with _ but is not otherwise special to the completion system. The function is called with the trial word as an argument. If the word is to be expanded, the function should set the array `reply` to a list of expansions. Optionally, it can set REPLY to a word that will be used as a description for the set of expansions. The return status of the function is irrelevant.

20.5 Bindable Commands

In addition to the context-dependent completions provided, which are expected to work in an intuitively obvious way, there are a few widgets implementing special behaviour which can be bound separately to keys. The following is a list of these and their default bindings.

_bash_completions

> This function is used by two widgets, _bash_complete-word and _bash_list-choices. It exists to provide compatibility with completion bindings in bash. The last character of the binding determines what is completed: '!', command names; '$', environment variables; '@', host names; '/', file names; '~' user names. In bash, the binding preceded by '\e' gives completion, and preceded by '^X' lists options. As some of these bindings clash with standard zsh bindings, only '\e~' and '^X~' are bound by default. To add the rest, the following should be added to .zshrc after compinit has been run:

```
for key in '!' '$' '@' '/' '~'; do
    bindkey "\e$key" _bash_complete-word
    bindkey "^X$key" _bash_list-choices
done
```

> This includes the bindings for '~' in case they were already bound to something else; the completion code does not override user bindings.

_correct_filename (^XC)

> Correct the filename path at the cursor position. Allows up to six errors in the name. Can also be called with an argument to correct a filename path, independently of zle; the correction is printed on standard output.

_correct_word (^Xc)

> Performs correction of the current argument using the usual contextual completions as possible choices. This stores the string 'correct-word' in the *function* field of the context name and then calls the _correct completer.

_expand_alias (^Xa)

> This function can be used as a completer and as a bindable command. It expands the word the cursor is on if it is an alias. The types of alias expanded can be controlled with the styles regular, global and disabled.

> When used as a bindable command there is one additional feature that can be selected by setting the complete style to 'true'. In this case, if the word is not the name of an alias, _expand_alias tries to complete the word to a full alias name without expanding it. It leaves the cursor directly after the completed word so that invoking _expand_alias once more will expand the now-complete alias name.

_expand_word (^Xe)

>Performs expansion on the current word: equivalent to the standard **expand-word** command, but using the **_expand** completer. Before calling it, the *function* field of the context is set to '**expand-word**'.

_generic   This function is not defined as a widget and not bound by default. However, it can be used to define a widget and will then store the name of the widget in the *function* field of the context and call the completion system. This allows custom completion widgets with their own set of style settings to be defined easily. For example, to define a widget that performs normal completion and starts menu selection:

```
zle -C foo complete-word _generic
bindkey '...' foo
zstyle ':completion:foo:*' menu yes select=1
```

>Note in particular that the **completer** style may be set for the context in order to change the set of functions used to generate possible matches. If **_generic** is called with arguments, those are passed through to **_main_complete** as the list of completers in place of those defined by the **completer** style.

_history_complete_word (\e/)

>Complete words from the shell's command history. This uses the **list**, **remove-all-dups**, **sort**, and **stop** styles.

_most_recent_file (^Xm)

>Complete the name of the most recently modified file matching the pattern on the command line (which may be blank). If given a numeric argument N, complete the Nth most recently modified file. Note the completion, if any, is always unique.

_next_tags (^Xn)

>This command alters the set of matches used to that for the next tag, or set of tags, either as given by the **tag-order** style or as set by default; these matches would otherwise not be available. Successive invocations of the command cycle through all possible sets of tags.

_read_comp (^X^R)

>Prompt the user for a string, and use that to perform completion on the current word. There are two possibilities for the string. First, it can be a set of words beginning '_', for example '**_files -/**', in which case the function with any arguments will be called to generate the completions. Unambiguous parts of the function name will be completed automatically (normal completion is not available at this point) until a space is typed.

>Second, any other string will be passed as a set of arguments to **compadd** and should hence be an expression specifying what should be completed.

>A very restricted set of editing commands is available when reading the string: '**DEL**' and '**^H**' delete the last character; '**^U**' deletes the line, and '**^C**' and '**^G**' abort the function, while '**RET**' accepts the completion. Note the string is used verbatim as a command line, so arguments must be quoted in accordance with standard shell rules.

Once a string has been read, the next call to `_read_comp` will use the existing string instead of reading a new one. To force a new string to be read, call `_read_comp` with a numeric argument.

`_complete_debug` (^X?)

This widget performs ordinary completion, but captures in a temporary file a trace of the shell commands executed by the completion system. Each completion attempt gets its own file. A command to view each of these files is pushed onto the editor buffer stack.

`_complete_help` (^Xh)

This widget displays information about the context names, the tags, and the completion functions used when completing at the current cursor position. If given a numeric argument other than 1 (as in 'ESC-2 ^Xh'), then the styles used and the contexts for which they are used will be shown, too.

Note that the information about styles may be incomplete; it depends on the information available from the completion functions called, which in turn is determined by the user's own styles and other settings.

`_complete_help_generic`

Unlike other commands listed here, this must be created as a normal ZLE widget rather than a completion widget (i.e. with `zle -N`). It is used for generating help with a widget bound to the `_generic` widget that is described above.

If this widget is created using the name of the function, as it is by default, then when executed it will read a key sequence. This is expected to be bound to a call to a completion function that uses the `_generic` widget. That widget will be executed, and information provided in the same format that the `_complete_help` widget displays for contextual completion.

If the widget's name contains `debug`, for example if it is created as 'zle -N `_complete_debug_generic` `_complete_help_generic`', it will read and execute the keystring for a generic widget as before, but then generate debugging information as done by `_complete_debug` for contextual completion.

If the widget's name contains `noread`, it will not read a keystring but instead arrange that the next use of a generic widget run in the same shell will have the effect as described above.

The widget works by setting the shell parameter `ZSH_TRACE_GENERIC_WIDGET` which is read by `_generic`. Unsetting the parameter cancels any pending effect of the `noread` form.

For example, after executing the following:

```
zle -N _complete_debug_generic _complete_help_generic
bindkey '^x:' _complete_debug_generic
```

typing 'C-x :' followed by the key sequence for a generic widget will cause trace output for that widget to be saved to a file.

`_complete_tag` (^Xt)

This widget completes symbol tags created by the **etags** or **ctags** programmes (note there is no connection with the completion system's tags) stored in a file

TAGS, in the format used by **etags**, or **tags**, in the format created by **ctags**. It will look back up the path hierarchy for the first occurrence of either file; if both exist, the file **TAGS** is preferred. You can specify the full path to a **TAGS** or **tags** file by setting the parameter **$TAGSFILE** or **$tagsfile** respectively. The corresponding completion tags used are **etags** and **vtags**, after emacs and vi respectively.

20.6 Utility Functions

Descriptions follow for utility functions that may be useful when writing completion functions. If functions are installed in subdirectories, most of these reside in the **Base** subdirectory. Like the example functions for commands in the distribution, the utility functions generating matches all follow the convention of returning status zero if they generated completions and non-zero if no matching completions could be added.

_absolute_command_paths

> This function completes external commands as absolute paths (unlike **_command_names -e** which completes their basenames). It takes no arguments.

_all_labels [-x] [-12VJ] *tag name descr* [*command arg ...*]

> This is a convenient interface to the **_next_label** function below, implementing the loop shown in the **_next_label** example. The *command* and its arguments are called to generate the matches. The options stored in the parameter *name* will automatically be inserted into the *args* passed to the *command*. Normally, they are put directly after the *command*, but if one of the *args* is a single hyphen, they are inserted directly before that. If the hyphen is the last argument, it will be removed from the argument list before the *command* is called. This allows **_all_labels** to be used in almost all cases where the matches can be generated by a single call to the **compadd** builtin command or by a call to one of the utility functions.

> For example:

```
local expl
...
if _requested foo; then
  ...
  _all_labels foo expl '...' compadd ... - $matches
fi
```

> Will complete the strings from the **matches** parameter, using **compadd** with additional options which will take precedence over those generated by **_all_labels**.

_alternative [-O *name*] [-C *name*] *spec ...*

> This function is useful in simple cases where multiple tags are available. Essentially it implements a loop like the one described for the **_tags** function below.

> The tags to use and the action to perform if a tag is requested are described using the *specs* which are of the form: '*tag*:*descr*:*action*'. The *tags* are offered

using _tags and if the tag is requested, the *action* is executed with the given description *descr*. The *action*s are those accepted by the _arguments function (described below), excluding the '->*state*' and '=...' forms.

For example, the *action* may be a simple function call:

```
_alternative \
    'users:user:_users' \
    'hosts:host:_hosts'
```

offers usernames and hostnames as possible matches, generated by the _users and _hosts functions respectively.

Like _arguments, this function uses _all_labels to execute the actions, which will loop over all sets of tags. Special handling is only required if there is an additional valid tag, for example inside a function called from _alternative.

The option '-O *name*' is used in the same way as by the _arguments function. In other words, the elements of the *name* array will be passed to compadd when executing an action.

Like _tags this function supports the -C option to give a different name for the argument context field.

_arguments [-nswWCRS] [-A *pat*] [-O *name*] [-M *matchspec*]
        [:] *spec* ...
_arguments [*opt* ...] -- [-l] [-i *pats*] [-s *pair*]
        [*helpspec* ...]

This function can be used to give a complete specification for completion for a command whose arguments follow standard UNIX option and argument conventions.

Options Overview

Options to _arguments itself must be in separate words, i.e. -s -w, not -sw. The options are followed by *specs* that describe options and arguments of the analyzed command. To avoid ambiguity, all options to _arguments itself may be separated from the *spec* forms by a single colon.

The '--' form is used to intuit *spec* forms from the help output of the command being analyzed, and is described in detail below. The *opts* for the '--' form are otherwise the same options as the first form. Note that '-s' following '--' has a distinct meaning from '-s' preceding '--', and both may appear.

The option switches -s, -S, -A, -w, and -W affect how _arguments parses the analyzed command line's options. These switches are useful for commands with standard argument parsing.

The options of _arguments have the following meanings:

-n   With this option, _arguments sets the parameter NORMARG to the position of the first normal argument in the $words array, i.e. the position after the end of the options. If that argument has not been reached, NORMARG is set to -1. The caller should declare 'integer NORMARG' if the -n option is passed; otherwise the parameter is not used.

-s   Enable *option stacking* for single-letter options, whereby multiple single-letter options may be combined into a single word. For example, the two options '-x' and '-y' may be combined into a single word '-xy'. By default, every word corresponds to a single option name ('-xy' is a single option named 'xy').

Options beginning with a single hyphen or plus sign are eligible for stacking; words beginning with two hyphens are not.

Note that -s after -- has a different meaning, which is documented in the segment entitled 'Deriving *spec* forms from the help output'.

-w   In combination with -s, allow option stacking even if one or more of the options take arguments. For example, if -x takes an argument, with no -s, '-xy' is considered as a single (unhandled) option; with -s, -xy is an option with the argument 'y'; with both -s and -w, -xy is the option -x and the option -y with arguments to -x (and to -y, if it takes arguments) still to come in subsequent words.

-W   This option takes -w a stage further: it is possible to complete single-letter options even after an argument that occurs in the same word. However, it depends on the action performed whether options will really be completed at this point. For more control, use a utility function like _guard as part of the action.

-C   Modify the curcontext parameter for an action of the form '->state'. This is discussed in detail below.

-R   Return status 300 instead of zero when a $state is to be handled, in the '->string' syntax.

-S   Do not complete options after a '--' appearing on the line, and ignore the '--'. For example, with -S, in the line

              foobar -x -- -y

          the '-x' is considered an option, the '-y' is considered an argument, and the '--' is considered to be neither.

-A *pat*   Do not complete options after the first non-option argument on the line. *pat* is a pattern matching all strings which are not to be taken as arguments. For example, to make _arguments stop completing options after the first normal argument, but ignoring all strings starting with a hyphen even if they are not described by one of the *optspecs*, the form is '-A "-*"'.

-O *name*   Pass the elements of the array *name* as arguments to functions called to execute *actions*. This is discussed in detail below.

-M *matchspec*
          Use the match specification *matchspec* for completing option names and values. The default *matchspec* allows partial word completion after '_' and '-', such as completing '-f-b' to '-foo-bar'. The default *matchspec* is:

              r:|[_-]=* r:|=*

specs: overview

Each of the following forms is a *spec* describing individual sets of options or arguments on the command line being analyzed.

n: message: action

n: : message: action

> This describes the *n*'th normal argument. The *message* will be printed above the matches generated and the *action* indicates what can be completed in this position (see below). If there are two colons before the *message* the argument is optional. If the *message* contains only white space, nothing will be printed above the matches unless the action adds an explanation string itself.

: message: action

: : message: action

> Similar, but describes the *next* argument, whatever number that happens to be. If all arguments are specified in this form in the correct order the numbers are unnecessary.

*: message: action

*: : message: action

*: : : message: action

> This describes how arguments (usually non-option arguments, those not beginning with - or +) are to be completed when neither of the first two forms was provided. Any number of arguments can be completed in this fashion.

> With two colons before the *message*, the **words** special array and the **CURRENT** special parameter are modified to refer only to the normal arguments when the *action* is executed or evaluated. With three colons before the *message* they are modified to refer only to the normal arguments covered by this description.

optspec

optspec: ...

> This describes an option. The colon indicates handling for one or more arguments to the option; if it is not present, the option is assumed to take no arguments.

> The following forms are available for the initial *optspec*, whether or not the option has arguments.

> **optspec*   Here *optspec* is one of the remaining forms below. This indicates the following *optspec* may be repeated. Otherwise if the corresponding option is already present on the command line to the left of the cursor it will not be offered again.

> *-optname*
> *+optname*   In the simplest form the *optspec* is just the option name beginning with a minus or a plus sign, such as '**-foo**'.

The first argument for the option (if any) must follow as a *separate* word directly after the option.

Either of '-+*optname*' and '+-*optname*' can be used to specify that -*optname* and +*optname* are both valid.

In all the remaining forms, the leading '-' may be replaced by or paired with '+' in this way.

-*optname*-

The first argument of the option must come directly after the option name *in the same word*. For example, '-foo-:...' specifies that the completed option and argument will look like '-foo*arg*'.

-*optname*+

The first argument may appear immediately after *optname* in the same word, or may appear as a separate word after the option. For example, '-foo+:...' specifies that the completed option and argument will look like either '-foo*arg*' or '-foo *arg*'.

-*optname*=

The argument may appear as the next word, or in same word as the option name provided that it is separated from it by an equals sign, for example '-foo=*arg*' or '-foo *arg*'.

-*optname*=-

The argument to the option must appear after an equals sign in the same word, and may not be given in the next argument.

optspec [*explanation*]

An explanation string may be appended to any of the preceding forms of *optspec* by enclosing it in brackets, as in '-q[query operation]'.

The **verbose** style is used to decide whether the explanation strings are displayed with the option in a completion listing.

If no bracketed explanation string is given but the **auto-description** style is set and only one argument is described for this *optspec*, the value of the style is displayed, with any appearance of the sequence '%d' in it replaced by the *message* of the first *optarg* that follows the *optspec*; see below.

It is possible for options with a literal '+' or '=' to appear, but that character must be quoted, for example '-\+'.

Each *optarg* following an *optspec* must take one of the following forms:

:*message*:*action*

::*message*:*action*

> An argument to the option; *message* and *action* are treated as for ordinary arguments. In the first form, the argument is mandatory, and in the second form it is optional.
>
> This group may be repeated for options which take multiple arguments. In other words, :*message1*:*action1*:*message2*:*action2* specifies that the option takes two arguments.

:**pattern*:*message*:*action*

:**pattern*::*message*:*action*

:**pattern*:::*message*:*action*

> This describes multiple arguments. Only the last *optarg* for an option taking multiple arguments may be given in this form. If the *pattern* is empty (i.e. :*:), all the remaining words on the line are to be completed as described by the *action*; otherwise, all the words up to and including a word matching the *pattern* are to be completed using the *action*.
>
> Multiple colons are treated as for the '*:...' forms for ordinary arguments: when the *message* is preceded by two colons, the words special array and the CURRENT special parameter are modified during the execution or evaluation of the *action* to refer only to the words after the option. When preceded by three colons, they are modified to refer only to the words covered by this description.

Any literal colon in an *optname*, *message*, or *action* must be preceded by a backslash, '\:'.

Each of the forms above may be preceded by a list in parentheses of option names and argument numbers. If the given option is on the command line, the options and arguments indicated in parentheses will not be offered. For example, '(-two -three 1)-one:...' completes the option '-one'; if this appears on the command line, the options -two and -three and the first ordinary argument will not be completed after it. '(-foo):...' specifies an ordinary argument completion; -foo will not be completed if that argument is already present.

Other items may appear in the list of excluded options to indicate various other items that should not be applied when the current specification is matched: a single star (*) for the rest arguments (i.e. a specification of the form '*:...'); a colon (:) for all normal (non-option-) arguments; and a hyphen (-) for all options. For example, if '(*)' appears before an option and the option appears on the command line, the list of remaining arguments (those shown in the above table beginning with '*:') will not be completed.

To aid in reuse of specifications, it is possible to precede any of the forms above with '!'; then the form will no longer be completed, although if the option or argument appears on the command line they will be skipped as normal. The main use for this is when the arguments are given by an array, and _arguments is called repeatedly for more specific contexts: on the first call '_arguments $global_options' is used, and on subsequent calls '_arguments !$^global_options'.

specs: actions

In each of the forms above the *action* determines how completions should be generated. Except for the '->*string*' form below, the *action* will be executed by calling the _all_labels function to process all tag labels. No special handling of tags is needed unless a function call introduces a new one.

The functions called to execute *actions* will be called with the elements of the array named by the '-O *name*' option as arguments. This can be used, for example, to pass the same set of options for the compadd builtin to all *actions*. The forms for *action* are as follows.

(single unquoted space)

> This is useful where an argument is required but it is not possible or desirable to generate matches for it. The *message* will be displayed but no completions listed. Note that even in this case the colon at the end of the *message* is needed; it may only be omitted when neither a *message* nor an *action* is given.

(*item1 item2 ...*)

> One of a list of possible matches, for example:
>
> :foo:(foo bar baz)

((*item1*\:*desc1* ...))

> Similar to the above, but with descriptions for each possible match. Note the backslash before the colon. For example,
>
> :foo:((a\:bar b\:baz))
>
> The matches will be listed together with their descriptions if the description style is set with the values tag in the context.

->*string*   In this form, _arguments processes the arguments and options and then returns control to the calling function with parameters set to indicate the state of processing; the calling function then makes its own arrangements for generating completions. For example, functions that implement a state machine can use this type of action.

Where _arguments encounters *action* in the '->*string*' format, it will strip all leading and trailing whitespace from *string* and set the array state to the set of all *strings* for which an action is to be performed. The elements of the array state_descr are assigned the corresponding *message* field from each *optarg* containing such an *action*.

By default and in common with all other well behaved completion functions, _arguments returns status zero if it was able to add matches and non-zero otherwise. However, if the -R option is given, _arguments will instead return a status of 300 to indicate that $state is to be handled.

In addition to $state and $state_descr, _arguments also sets the global parameters 'context', 'line' and 'opt_args' as described below, and does not reset any changes made to the special parameters such as PREFIX and words. This gives the calling function the choice of resetting these parameters or propagating changes in them.

A function calling _arguments with at least one action containing a '->string' must therefore declare appropriate local parameters:

```
local context state state_descr line
typeset -A opt_args
```

to prevent _arguments from altering the global environment.

{eval-string}

A string in braces is evaluated as shell code to generate matches. If the eval-string itself does not begin with an opening parenthesis or brace it is split into separate words before execution.

= action

If the action starts with '= ' (an equals sign followed by a space), _arguments will insert the contents of the argument field of the current context as the new first element in the words special array and increment the value of the CURRENT special parameter. This has the effect of inserting a dummy word onto the completion command line while not changing the point at which completion is taking place.

This is most useful with one of the specifiers that restrict the words on the command line on which the action is to operate (the two- and three-colon forms above). One particular use is when an action itself causes _arguments on a restricted range; it is necessary to use this trick to insert an appropriate command name into the range for the second call to _arguments to be able to parse the line.

word...
word...

This covers all forms other than those above. If the action starts with a space, the remaining list of words will be invoked unchanged.

Otherwise it will be invoked with some extra strings placed after the first word; these are to be passed down as options to the compadd builtin. They ensure that the state specified by _arguments, in particular the descriptions of options and arguments, is correctly passed to the completion command. These additional arguments are taken from the array parameter 'expl'; this will be set up before executing the action and hence may be referred to inside it, typically in an expansion of the form '$expl[@]' which preserves empty elements of the array.

During the performance of the action the array 'line' will be set to the normal arguments from the command line, i.e. the words from the command line after the command name excluding all options and their arguments. Options are stored in the associative array 'opt_args' with option names as keys and their arguments as the values. For options that have more than one argument these are given as one string, separated by colons. All colons and backslashes in the original arguments are preceded with backslashes.

The parameter 'context' is set when returning to the calling function to perform an action of the form '->*string*'. It is set to an array of elements corresponding to the elements of $state. Each element is a suitable name for the argument field of the context: either a string of the form 'option-*opt-n*' for the *n*'th argument of the option *-opt*, or a string of the form 'argument-*n*' for the *n*'th argument. For 'rest' arguments, that is those in the list at the end not handled by position, *n* is the string 'rest'. For example, when completing the argument of the -o option, the name is 'option-o-1', while for the second normal (non-option-) argument it is 'argument-2'.

Furthermore, during the evaluation of the *action* the context name in the curcontext parameter is altered to append the same string that is stored in the context parameter.

The option -C tells _arguments to modify the curcontext parameter for an action of the form '->*state*'. This is the standard parameter used to keep track of the current context. Here it (and not the context array) should be made local to the calling function to avoid passing back the modified value and should be initialised to the current value at the start of the function:

```
local curcontext="$curcontext"
```

This is useful where it is not possible for multiple states to be valid together.

Grouping Options

Options can be grouped to simplify exclusion lists. A group is introduced with '+' followed by a name for the group in the subsequent word. Whole groups can then be referenced in an exclusion list or a group name can be used to disambiguate between two forms of the same option. For example:

```
_arguments \
    '(group2--x)-a' \
  + group1 \
    -m \
    '(group2)-n' \
  + group2 \
    -x -y
```

If the name of a group is specified in the form '(*name*)' then only one value from that group will ever be completed; more formally, all specifications are mutually exclusive to all other specifications in that group. This is useful for defining options that are aliases for each other. For example:

```
_arguments \
    -a -b \
  + '(operation)' \
```

```
{-c,--compress}'[compress]' \
{-d,--decompress}'[decompress]' \
{-l,--list}'[list]'
```

If an option in a group appears on the command line, it is stored in the associative array 'opt_args' with 'group-option' as a key. In the example above, a key 'operation--c' is used if the option '-c' is present on the command line.

Specifying Multiple Sets of Arguments

It is possible to specify multiple sets of options and arguments with the sets separated by single hyphens. This differs from groups in that sets are considered to be mutually exclusive of each other.

Specifications before the first set and from any group are common to all sets. For example:

```
_arguments \
    -a \
  - set1 \
    -c \
  - set2 \
    -d \
    ':arg:(x2 y2)'
```

This defines two sets. When the command line contains the option '-c', the '-d' option and the argument will not be considered possible completions. When it contains '-d' or an argument, the option '-c' will not be considered. However, after '-a' both sets will still be considered valid.

As for groups, the name of a set may appear in exclusion lists, either alone or preceding a normal option or argument specification.

The completion code has to parse the command line separately for each set. This can be slow so sets should only be used when necessary. A useful alternative is often an option specification with rest-arguments (as in '-foo:*:...'); here the option **-foo** swallows up all remaining arguments as described by the *optarg* definitions.

Deriving spec forms from the help output

The option '--' allows **_arguments** to work out the names of long options that support the '--help' option which is standard in many GNU commands. The command word is called with the argument '--help' and the output examined for option names. Clearly, it can be dangerous to pass this to commands which may not support this option as the behaviour of the command is unspecified.

In addition to options, '**_arguments** --' will try to deduce the types of arguments available for options when the form '--*opt*=*val*' is valid. It is also possible to provide hints by examining the help text of the command and adding *help-spec* of the form '*pattern*:*message*:*action*'; note that other **_arguments** *spec* forms are not used. The *pattern* is matched against the help text for an option, and if it matches the *message* and *action* are used as for other argument specifiers. The special case of '*:' means both *message* and *action* are empty, which has the effect of causing options having no description in the help output to be ordered in listings ahead of options that have a description.

For example:

```
_arguments -- '*\*:toggle:(yes no)' \
              '*=FILE*:file:_files' \
              '*=DIR*:directory:_files -/' \
              '*=PATH*:directory:_files -/'
```

Here, 'yes' and 'no' will be completed as the argument of options whose description ends in a star; file names will be completed for options that contain the substring '=FILE' in the description; and directories will be completed for options whose description contains '=DIR' or '=PATH'. The last three are in fact the default and so need not be given explicitly, although it is possible to override the use of these patterns. A typical help text which uses this feature is:

```
    -C, --directory=DIR          change to directory DIR
```

so that the above specifications will cause directories to be completed after '--directory', though not after '-C'.

Note also that `_arguments` tries to find out automatically if the argument for an option is optional. This can be specified explicitly by doubling the colon before the *message*.

If the *pattern* ends in '(-)', this will be removed from the pattern and the *action* will be used only directly after the '=', not in the next word. This is the behaviour of a normal specification defined with the form '=-'.

By default, the command (with the option '--help') is run after resetting all the locale categories (except for `LC_CTYPE`) to 'C'. If the localized help output is known to work, the option '-l' can be specified after the '`_arguments --`' so that the command is run in the current locale.

The '`_arguments --`' can be followed by the option '`-i` *patterns*' to give patterns for options which are not to be completed. The patterns can be given as the name of an array parameter or as a literal list in parentheses. For example,

```
_arguments -- -i \
    "(--(en|dis)able-FEATURE*)"
```

will cause completion to ignore the options '`--enable-FEATURE`' and '`--disable-FEATURE`' (this example is useful with GNU `configure`).

The '`_arguments --`' form can also be followed by the option '`-s` *pair*' to describe option aliases. The *pair* consists of a list of alternating patterns and corresponding replacements, enclosed in parens and quoted so that it forms a single argument word in the `_arguments` call.

For example, some `configure`-script help output describes options only as '`--enable-foo`', but the script also accepts the negated form '`--disable-foo`'. To allow completion of the second form:

```
_arguments -- -s "((#s)--enable- --disable-)"
```

Miscellaneous notes

Finally, note that `_arguments` generally expects to be the primary function handling any completion for which it is used. It may have side effects which change the treatment of any matches added by other functions called after it. To combine `_arguments` with other functions, those functions should be called either before `_arguments`, as an *action* within a *spec*, or in handlers for '`->state`' actions.

Here is a more general example of the use of `_arguments`:

```
_arguments '-l+:left border:' \
           '-format:paper size:(letter A4)' \
           '*-copy:output file:_files::resolution:(300 600)' \
           ':postscript file:_files -g \*.\(ps\|eps\)' \
           '*:page number:'
```

This describes three options: '`-l`', '`-format`', and '`-copy`'. The first takes one argument described as '*left border*' for which no completion will be offered because of the empty action. Its argument may come directly after the '`-l`' or it may be given as the next word on the line.

The '`-format`' option takes one argument in the next word, described as '*paper size*' for which only the strings '`letter`' and '`A4`' will be completed.

The '`-copy`' option may appear more than once on the command line and takes two arguments. The first is mandatory and will be completed as a filename. The second is optional (because of the second colon before the description '*resolution*') and will be completed from the strings '300' and '600'.

The last two descriptions say what should be completed as arguments. The first describes the first argument as a '*postscript file*' and makes files ending in '`ps`' or '`eps`' be completed. The last description gives all other arguments the description '*page numbers*' but does not offer completions.

`_cache_invalid` *cache_identifier*

This function returns status zero if the completions cache corresponding to the given cache identifier needs rebuilding. It determines this by looking up the `cache-policy` style for the current context. This should provide a function name which is run with the full path to the relevant cache file as the only argument.

Example:

```
_example_caching_policy () {
    # rebuild if cache is more than a week old
    local -a oldp
    oldp=( "$1"(Nm+7) )
    (( $#oldp ))
}
```

`_call_function` *return name* [*arg* ...]

If a function *name* exists, it is called with the arguments *args*. The *return* argument gives the name of a parameter in which the return status from the function *name* should be stored; if *return* is empty or a single hyphen it is ignored.

The return status of `_call_function` itself is zero if the function *name* exists and was called and non-zero otherwise.

_call_program [-l] [-p] *tag string* ...

> This function provides a mechanism for the user to override the use of an external command. It looks up the **command** style with the supplied *tag*. If the style is set, its value is used as the command to execute. The *strings* from the call to **_call_program**, or from the style if set, are concatenated with spaces between them and the resulting string is evaluated. The return status is the return status of the command called.
>
> By default, the command is run in an environment where all the locale categories (except for **LC_CTYPE**) are reset to 'C' by calling the utility function **_comp_locale** (see below). If the option '-l' is given, the command is run with the current locale.
>
> If the option '-p' is supplied it indicates that the command output is influenced by the permissions it is run with. If the **gain-privileges** style is set to true, **_call_program** will make use of commands such as **sudo**, if present on the command-line, to match the permissions to whatever the final command is likely to run under. When looking up the **gain-privileges** and **command** styles, the command component of the zstyle context will end with a slash ('/') followed by the command that would be used to gain privileges.

_combination [-s *pattern*] *tag style spec* ... *field opts* ...

> This function is used to complete combinations of values, for example pairs of hostnames and usernames. The *style* argument gives the style which defines the pairs; it is looked up in a context with the *tag* specified.
>
> The style name consists of field names separated by hyphens, for example 'users-hosts-ports'. For each field for a value is already known, a *spec* of the form 'field=pattern' is given. For example, if the command line so far specifies a user 'pws', the argument 'users=pws' should appear.
>
> The next argument with no equals sign is taken as the name of the field for which completions should be generated (presumably not one of the *fields* for which the value is known).
>
> The matches generated will be taken from the value of the style. These should contain the possible values for the combinations in the appropriate order (users, hosts, ports in the example above). The values for the different fields are separated by colons. This can be altered with the option -s to **_combination** which specifies a pattern. Typically this is a character class, as for example '-s "[:@]"' in the case of the **users-hosts** style. Each 'field=pattern' specification restricts the completions which apply to elements of the style with appropriately matching fields.
>
> If no style with the given name is defined for the given tag, or if none of the strings in style's value match, but a function name of the required field preceded by an underscore is defined, that function will be called to generate the matches. For example, if there is no 'users-hosts-ports' or no matching hostname when a host is required, the function '_hosts' will automatically be called.
>
> If the same name is used for more than one field, in both the 'field=pattern' and the argument that gives the name of the field to be completed, the number of

the field (starting with one) may be given after the fieldname, separated from it by a colon.

All arguments after the required field name are passed to `compadd` when generating matches from the style value, or to the functions for the fields if they are called.

`_command_names` [-e | -]

This function completes words that are valid at command position: names of aliases, builtins, hashed commands, functions, and so on. With the `-e` flag, only hashed commands are completed. The `-` flag is ignored.

`_comp_locale`

This function resets all the locale categories other than `LC_CTYPE` to 'C' so that the output from external commands can be easily analyzed by the completion system. `LC_CTYPE` retains the current value (taking `LC_ALL` and `LANG` into account), ensuring that non-ASCII characters in file names are still handled properly.

This function should normally be run only in a subshell, because the new locale is exported to the environment. Typical usage would be '$(`_comp_locale`; *command* ...)'.

`_completers` [-p]

This function completes names of completers.

-p   Include the leading underscore ('_') in the matches.

`_describe` [-12JVx] [-oO | -t *tag*] *descr name1* [*name2*] [*opt* ...]
[-- *name1* [*name2*] [*opt* ...] ...]

This function associates completions with descriptions. Multiple groups separated by `--` can be supplied, potentially with different completion options *opts*.

The *descr* is taken as a string to display above the matches if the **format** style for the **descriptions** tag is set. This is followed by one or two names of arrays followed by options to pass to `compadd`. The array *name1* contains the possible completions with their descriptions in the form '*completion*:*description*'. Any literal colons in *completion* must be quoted with a backslash. If a *name2* is given, it should have the same number of elements as *name1*; in this case the corresponding elements are added as possible completions instead of the *completion* strings from *name1*. The completion list will retain the descriptions from *name1*. Finally, a set of completion options can appear.

If the option '-o' appears before the first argument, the matches added will be treated as names of command options (N.B. not shell options), typically following a '-', '--' or '+' on the command line. In this case `_describe` uses the **prefix-hidden**, **prefix-needed** and **verbose** styles to find out if the strings should be added as completions and if the descriptions should be shown. Without the '-o' option, only the **verbose** style is used to decide how descriptions are shown. If '-O' is used instead of '-o', command options are completed as above but `_describe` will not handle the **prefix-needed** style.

With the `-t` option a *tag* can be specified. The default is '**values**' or, if the `-o` option is given, '**options**'.

The options -1, -2, -J, -V, -x are passed to _next_label.

If selected by the list-grouped style, strings with the same description will appear together in the list.

_describe uses the _all_labels function to generate the matches, so it does not need to appear inside a loop over tag labels.

_description [-x] [-12VJ] *tag name descr* [*spec ...*]

This function is not to be confused with the previous one; it is used as a helper function for creating options to compadd. It is buried inside many of the higher level completion functions and so often does not need to be called directly.

The styles listed below are tested in the current context using the given *tag*. The resulting options for compadd are put into the array named *name* (this is traditionally 'expl', but this convention is not enforced). The description for the corresponding set of matches is passed to the function in *descr*.

The styles tested are: format, hidden, matcher, ignored-patterns and group-name. The format style is first tested for the given *tag* and then for the descriptions tag if no value was found, while the remainder are only tested for the tag given as the first argument. The function also calls _setup which tests some more styles.

The string returned by the format style (if any) will be modified so that the sequence '%d' is replaced by the *descr* given as the third argument without any leading or trailing white space. If, after removing the white space, the *descr* is the empty string, the format style will not be used and the options put into the *name* array will not contain an explanation string to be displayed above the matches.

If _description is called with more than three arguments, the additional *specs* should be of the form 'char:str'. These supply escape sequence replacements for the format style: every appearance of '%char' will be replaced by *string*.

If the -x option is given, the description will be passed to compadd using the -x option instead of the default -X. This means that the description will be displayed even if there are no corresponding matches.

The options placed in the array *name* take account of the group-name style, so matches are placed in a separate group where necessary. The group normally has its elements sorted (by passing the option -J to compadd), but if an option starting with '-V', '-J', '-1', or '-2' is passed to _description, that option will be included in the array. Hence it is possible for the completion group to be unsorted by giving the option '-V', '-1V', or '-2V'.

In most cases, the function will be used like this:

```
local expl
_description files expl file
compadd "$expl[@]" - "$files[@]"
```

Note the use of the parameter expl, the hyphen, and the list of matches. Almost all calls to compadd within the completion system use a similar format; this ensures that user-specified styles are correctly passed down to the builtins which implement the internals of completion.

_dir_list [-s *sep*] [-S]

> Complete a list of directory names separated by colons (the same format as $PATH).
>
> -s *sep*   Use *sep* as separator between items. *sep* defaults to a colon (':').
>
> -S   Add *sep* instead of slash ('/') as an autoremoveable suffix.

_dispatch *context string ...*

> This sets the current context to *context* and looks for completion functions to handle this context by hunting through the list of command names or special contexts (as described above for **compdef**) given as *string*s. The first completion function to be defined for one of the contexts in the list is used to generate matches. Typically, the last *string* is **-default-** to cause the function for default completion to be used as a fallback.
>
> The function sets the parameter **$service** to the *string* being tried, and sets the *context/command* field (the fourth) of the **$curcontext** parameter to the *context* given as the first argument.

_email_addresses [-c] [-n *plugin*]

> Complete email addresses. Addresses are provided by plugins.
>
> -c   Complete bare **localhost@domain.tld** addresses, without a name part or a comment. Without this option, RFC822 '*Firstname Lastname <address>*' strings are completed.
>
> -n *plugin*   Complete aliases from *plugin*.
>
> The following plugins are available by default: **_email-ldap** (see the **filter** style), **_email-local** (completes *user@hostname* Unix addresses), **_email-mail** (completes aliases from ~/.mailrc), **_email-mush**, **_email-mutt**, and **_email-pine**.
>
> Addresses from the **_email-***foo* plugin are added under the tag 'email-*foo*'.
>
> *Writing plugins*
>
> Plugins are written as separate functions with names starting with '**_email-**'. They are invoked with the **-c** option and **compadd** options. They should either do their own completion or set the **$reply** array to a list of '*alias: address*' elements and return 300. New plugins will be picked up and run automatically.

_files   The function **_files** calls **_path_files** with all the arguments it was passed except for -g and -/. The use of these two options depends on the setting of the **file-patterns** style.

> This function accepts the full set of options allowed by **_path_files**, described below.

_gnu_generic

> This function is a simple wrapper around the **_arguments** function described above. It can be used to determine automatically the long options understood by commands that produce a list when passed the option '**--help**'. It is intended to be used as a top-level completion function in its own right. For example, to enable option completion for the commands **foo** and **bar**, use

```
        compdef _gnu_generic foo bar
```
after the call to `compinit`.

The completion system as supplied is conservative in its use of this function, since it is important to be sure the command understands the option '`--help`'.

`_guard` [*options*] *pattern descr*

This function displays *descr* if *pattern* matches the string to be completed. It is intended to be used in the *action* for the specifications passed to `_arguments` and similar functions.

The return status is zero if the message was displayed and the word to complete is not empty, and non-zero otherwise.

The *pattern* may be preceded by any of the options understood by `compadd` that are passed down from `_description`, namely -M, -J, -V, -1, -2, -n, -F and -X. All of these options will be ignored. This fits in conveniently with the argument-passing conventions of actions for `_arguments`.

As an example, consider a command taking the options -n and -none, where -n must be followed by a numeric value in the same word. By using:

```
        _arguments '-n-: :_guard "[0-9]#" "numeric value"' '-none'
```

`_arguments` can be made to both display the message '`numeric value`' and complete options after '`-n<TAB>`'. If the '`-n`' is already followed by one or more digits (the pattern passed to `_guard`) only the message will be displayed; if the '`-n`' is followed by another character, only options are completed.

`_message` [-r12] [-VJ *group*] *descr*
`_message` -e [*tag*] *descr*

The *descr* is used in the same way as the third argument to the `_description` function, except that the resulting string will always be shown whether or not matches were generated. This is useful for displaying a help message in places where no completions can be generated.

The `format` style is examined with the `messages` tag to find a message; the usual tag, `descriptions`, is used only if the style is not set with the former.

If the -r option is given, no style is used; the *descr* is taken literally as the string to display. This is most useful when the *descr* comes from a pre-processed argument list which already contains an expanded description.

The -12VJ options and the *group* are passed to `compadd` and hence determine the group the message string is added to.

The second -e form gives a description for completions with the tag *tag* to be shown even if there are no matches for that tag. This form is called by `_arguments` in the event that there is no action for an option specification. The tag can be omitted and if so the tag is taken from the parameter `$curtag`; this is maintained by the completion system and so is usually correct. Note that if there are no matches at the time this function is called, `compstate[insert]` is cleared, so additional matches generated later are not inserted on the command line.

_multi_parts [-i] *sep array*

    The argument *sep* is a separator character. The *array* may be either the name of an array parameter or a literal array in the form '(`foo bar`)', a parenthesised list of words separated by whitespace. The possible completions are the strings from the array. However, each chunk delimited by *sep* will be completed separately. For example, the **_tar** function uses '**_multi_parts** / *patharray*' to complete partial file paths from the given array of complete file paths.

    The -i option causes **_multi_parts** to insert a unique match even if that requires multiple separators to be inserted. This is not usually the expected behaviour with filenames, but certain other types of completion, for example those with a fixed set of possibilities, may be more suited to this form.

    Like other utility functions, this function accepts the '-V', '-J', '-1', '-2', '-n', '-f', '-X', '-M', '-P', '-S', '-r', '-R', and '-q' options and passes them to the **compadd** builtin.

_next_label [-x] [-12VJ] *tag name descr* [*option ...*]

    This function is used to implement the loop over different tag labels for a particular tag as described above for the **tag-order** style. On each call it checks to see if there are any more tag labels; if there is it returns status zero, otherwise non-zero. As this function requires a current tag to be set, it must always follow a call to **_tags** or **_requested**.

    The -x12VJ options and the first three arguments are passed to the **_description** function. Where appropriate the *tag* will be replaced by a tag label in this call. Any description given in the **tag-order** style is preferred to the *descr* passed to **_next_label**.

    The *options* given after the *descr* are set in the parameter given by *name*, and hence are to be passed to **compadd** or whatever function is called to add the matches.

    Here is a typical use of this function for the tag **foo**. The call to **_requested** determines if tag **foo** is required at all; the loop over **_next_label** handles any labels defined for the tag in the **tag-order** style.

```
local expl ret=1
...
if _requested foo; then
  ...
  while _next_label foo expl '...'; do
    compadd "$expl[@]" ... && ret=0
  done
  ...
fi
return ret
```

_normal   This is the standard function called to handle completion outside any special -*context*-. It is called both to complete the command word and also the arguments for a command. In the second case, **_normal** looks for a special completion for that command, and if there is none it uses the completion for the -**default**- context.

A second use is to reexamine the command line specified by the $words array and the $CURRENT parameter after those have been modified. For example, the function _precommand, which completes after pre-command specifiers such as nohup, removes the first word from the words array, decrements the CURRENT parameter, then calls _normal again. The effect is that 'nohup *cmd* ...' is treated in the same way as '*cmd* ...'.

If the command name matches one of the patterns given by one of the options -p or -P to compdef, the corresponding completion function is called and then the parameter _compskip is checked. If it is set completion is terminated at that point even if no matches have been found. This is the same effect as in the -first- context.

_options   This can be used to complete the names of shell options. It provides a matcher specification that ignores a leading 'no', ignores underscores and allows upper-case letters to match their lower-case counterparts (for example, 'glob', 'noglob', 'NO_GLOB' are all completed). Any arguments are propagated to the compadd builtin.

_options_set and _options_unset

These functions complete only set or unset options, with the same matching specification used in the _options function.

Note that you need to uncomment a few lines in the _main_complete function for these functions to work properly. The lines in question are used to store the option settings in effect before the completion widget locally sets the options it needs. Hence these functions are not generally used by the completion system.

_parameters

This is used to complete the names of shell parameters.

The option '-g *pattern*' limits the completion to parameters whose type matches the *pattern*. The type of a parameter is that shown by 'print ${(t)*param*}', hence judicious use of '*' in *pattern* is probably necessary.

All other arguments are passed to the compadd builtin.

_path_files

This function is used throughout the completion system to complete filenames. It allows completion of partial paths. For example, the string '/u/i/s/sig' may be completed to '/usr/include/sys/signal.h'.

The options accepted by both _path_files and _files are:

-f   Complete all filenames. This is the default.

-/   Specifies that only directories should be completed.

-g *pattern* Specifies that only files matching the *pattern* should be completed.

-W *paths*   Specifies path prefixes that are to be prepended to the string from the command line to generate the filenames but that should not be inserted as completions nor shown in completion listings. Here, *paths* may be the name of an array parameter, a literal list of paths enclosed in parentheses or an absolute pathname.

-F *ignored-files*

This behaves as for the corresponding option to the `compadd` builtin. It gives direct control over which filenames should be ignored. If the option is not present, the `ignored-patterns` style is used.

Both `_path_files` and `_files` also accept the following options which are passed to `compadd`: '-J', '-V', '-1', '-2', '-n', '-X', '-M', '-P', '-S', '-q', '-r', and '-R'.

Finally, the `_path_files` function uses the styles `expand`, `ambiguous`, `special-dirs`, `list-suffixes` and `file-sort` described above.

`_pick_variant` [-b *builtin-label*] [-c *command*] [-r *name*]

       label=*pattern* ... *label* [*arg* ...]

This function is used to resolve situations where a single command name requires more than one type of handling, either because it has more than one variant or because there is a name clash between two different commands.

The command to run is taken from the first element of the array `words` unless this is overridden by the option `-c`. This command is run and its output is compared with a series of patterns. Arguments to be passed to the command can be specified at the end after all the other arguments. The patterns to try in order are given by the arguments *label*=*pattern*; if the output of '*command arg* ...' contains *pattern*, then *label* is selected as the label for the command variant. If none of the patterns match, the final command label is selected and status 1 is returned.

If the '-b *builtin-label*' is given, the command is tested to see if it is provided as a shell builtin, possibly autoloaded; if so, the label *builtin-label* is selected as the label for the variant.

If the '-r *name*' is given, the *label* picked is stored in the parameter named *name*.

The results are also cached in the `_cmd_variant` associative array indexed by the name of the command run.

`_regex_arguments` *name spec* ...

This function generates a completion function *name* which matches the specifications *specs*, a set of regular expressions as described below. After running `_regex_arguments`, the function *name* should be called as a normal completion function. The pattern to be matched is given by the contents of the `words` array up to the current cursor position joined together with null characters; no quotation is applied.

The arguments are grouped as sets of alternatives separated by '|', which are tried one after the other until one matches. Each alternative consists of a one or more specifications which are tried left to right, with each pattern matched being stripped in turn from the command line being tested, until all of the group succeeds or until one fails; in the latter case, the next alternative is tried. This structure can be repeated to arbitrary depth by using parentheses; matching proceeds from inside to outside.

A special procedure is applied if no test succeeds but the remaining command line string contains no null character (implying the remaining word is the one for which completions are to be generated). The completion target is restricted to the remaining word and any *actions* for the corresponding patterns are executed. In this case, nothing is stripped from the command line string. The order of evaluation of the *actions* can be determined by the `tag-order` style; the various formats supported by `_alternative` can be used in *action*. The *descr* is used for setting up the array parameter `expl`.

Specification arguments take one of following forms, in which metacharacters such as '(', ')', '#' and '|' should be quoted.

/*pattern*/ [%*lookahead*%] [−*guard*] [:*tag*:*descr*:*action*]

> This is a single primitive component. The function tests whether the combined pattern '(#b)((#B)*pattern*)*lookahead**' matches the command line string. If so, '*guard*' is evaluated and its return status is examined to determine if the test has succeeded. The *pattern* string '[]' is guaranteed never to match. The *lookahead* is not stripped from the command line before the next pattern is examined.
>
> The argument starting with : is used in the same manner as an argument to `_alternative`.
>
> A component is used as follows: *pattern* is tested to see if the component already exists on the command line. If it does, any following specifications are examined to find something to complete. If a component is reached but no such pattern exists yet on the command line, the string containing the *action* is used to generate matches to insert at that point.

/*pattern*/+ [%*lookahead*%] [−*guard*] [:*tag*:*descr*:*action*]

> This is similar to '/*pattern*/ ...' but the left part of the command line string (i.e. the part already matched by previous patterns) is also considered part of the completion target.

/*pattern*/− [%*lookahead*%] [−*guard*] [:*tag*:*descr*:*action*]

> This is similar to '/*pattern*/ ...' but the *actions* of the current and previously matched patterns are ignored even if the following '*pattern*' matches the empty string.

(*spec*) Parentheses may be used to groups *specs*; note each parenthesis is a single argument to `_regex_arguments`.

spec # This allows any number of repetitions of *spec*.

spec spec The two *specs* are to be matched one after the other as described above.

spec | *spec*

> Either of the two *specs* can be matched.

The function `_regex_words` can be used as a helper function to generate matches for a set of alternative words possibly with their own arguments as a command line argument.

Examples:

```
_regex_arguments _tst /$'[^\0]#\0'/ \
     /$'[^\0]#\0'/ :'compadd aaa'
```

This generates a function _tst that completes aaa as its only argument. The *tag* and *description* for the action have been omitted for brevity (this works but is not recommended in normal use). The first component matches the command word, which is arbitrary; the second matches any argument. As the argument is also arbitrary, any following component would not depend on aaa being present.

```
_regex_arguments _tst /$'[^\0]#\0'/ \
     /$'aaa\0'/ :'compadd aaa'
```

This is a more typical use; it is similar, but any following patterns would only match if aaa was present as the first argument.

```
_regex_arguments _tst /$'[^\0]#\0'/ \( \
     /$'aaa\0'/ :'compadd aaa' \
     /$'bbb\0'/ :'compadd bbb' \) \#
```

In this example, an indefinite number of command arguments may be completed. Odd arguments are completed as aaa and even arguments as bbb. Completion fails unless the set of aaa and bbb arguments before the current one is matched correctly.

```
_regex_arguments _tst /$'[^\0]#\0'/ \
     \( /$'aaa\0'/ :'compadd aaa' \| \
     /$'bbb\0'/ :'compadd bbb' \) \#
```

This is similar, but either aaa or bbb may be completed for any argument. In this case _regex_words could be used to generate a suitable expression for the arguments.

_regex_words *tag description spec ...*

This function can be used to generate arguments for the **_regex_arguments** command which may be inserted at any point where a set of rules is expected. The *tag* and *description* give a standard tag and description pertaining to the current context. Each *spec* contains two or three arguments separated by a colon: note that there is no leading colon in this case.

Each *spec* gives one of a set of words that may be completed at this point, together with arguments. It is thus roughly equivalent to the **_arguments** function when used in normal (non-regex) completion.

The part of the *spec* before the first colon is the word to be completed. This may contain a *; the entire word, before and after the * is completed, but only the text before the * is required for the context to be matched, so that further arguments may be completed after the abbreviated form.

The second part of *spec* is a description for the word being completed.

The optional third part of the *spec* describes how words following the one being completed are themselves to be completed. It will be evaluated in order to avoid problems with quoting. This means that typically it contains a reference to an array containing previously generated regex arguments.

The option -t *term* specifies a terminator for the word instead of the usual space. This is handled as an auto-removable suffix in the manner of the option -s *sep* to _values.

The result of the processing by _regex_words is placed in the array reply, which should be made local to the calling function. If the set of words and arguments may be matched repeatedly, a # should be appended to the generated array at that point.

For example:

```
local -a reply
_regex_words mydb-commands 'mydb commands' \
  'add:add an entry to mydb:$mydb_add_cmds' \
  'show:show entries in mydb'
_regex_arguments _mydb "$reply[@]"
_mydb "$@"
```

This shows a completion function for a command mydb which takes two command arguments, add and show. show takes no arguments, while the arguments for add have already been prepared in an array mydb_add_cmds, quite possibly by a previous call to _regex_words.

_requested [-x] [-12VJ] *tag* [*name descr* [*command* [*arg* ...]]]

This function is called to decide whether a tag already registered by a call to _tags (see below) has been requested by the user and hence completion should be performed for it. It returns status zero if the tag is requested and non-zero otherwise. The function is typically used as part of a loop over different tags as follows:

```
_tags foo bar baz
while _tags; do
  if _requested foo; then
    ... # perform completion for foo
  fi
  ... # test the tags bar and baz in the same way
  ... # exit loop if matches were generated
done
```

Note that the test for whether matches were generated is not performed until the end of the _tags loop. This is so that the user can set the tag-order style to specify a set of tags to be completed at the same time.

If *name* and *descr* are given, _requested calls the _description function with these arguments together with the options passed to _requested.

If *command* is given, the _all_labels function will be called immediately with the same arguments. In simple cases this makes it possible to perform the test for the tag and the matching in one go. For example:

```
local expl ret=1
_tags foo bar baz
while _tags; do
  _requested foo expl 'description' \
      compadd foobar foobaz && ret=0
```

```
      ...
      (( ret )) || break
done
```

If the *command* is not `compadd`, it must nevertheless be prepared to handle the same options.

`_retrieve_cache` *cache_identifier*

> This function retrieves completion information from the file given by *cache_identifier*, stored in a directory specified by the `cache-path` style which defaults to `~/.zcompcache`. The return status is zero if retrieval was successful. It will only attempt retrieval if the `use-cache` style is set, so you can call this function without worrying about whether the user wanted to use the caching layer.
>
> See `_store_cache` below for more details.

`_sep_parts`

> This function is passed alternating arrays and separators as arguments. The arrays specify completions for parts of strings to be separated by the separators. The arrays may be the names of array parameters or a quoted list of words in parentheses. For example, with the array 'hosts=(ftp news)' the call '`_sep_parts '(foo bar)' @ hosts`' will complete the string 'f' to 'foo' and the string 'b@n' to 'bar@news'.
>
> This function accepts the `compadd` options '-V', '-J', '-1', '-2', '-n', '-X', '-M', '-P', '-S', '-r', '-R', and '-q' and passes them on to the `compadd` builtin used to add the matches.

`_sequence` [-s *sep*] [-n *max*] [-d] *function* [-] ...

> This function is a wrapper to other functions for completing items in a separated list. The same function is used to complete each item in the list. The separator is specified with the -s option. If -s is omitted it will use ','. Duplicate values are not matched unless -d is specified. If there is a fixed or maximum number of items in the list, this can be specified with the -n option.
>
> Common `compadd` options are passed on to the function. It is possible to use `compadd` directly with `_sequence`, though `_values` may be more appropriate in this situation.

`_setup` *tag* [*group*]

> This function sets up the special parameters used by the completion system appropriately for the *tag* given as the first argument. It uses the styles `list-colors`, `list-packed`, `list-rows-first`, `last-prompt`, `accept-exact`, `menu` and `force-list`.
>
> The optional *group* supplies the name of the group in which the matches will be placed. If it is not given, the *tag* is used as the group name.
>
> This function is called automatically from `_description` and hence is not normally called explicitly.

`_store_cache` *cache_identifier* *param* ...

> This function, together with `_retrieve_cache` and `_cache_invalid`, implements a caching layer which can be used in any completion function. Data ob-

tained by costly operations are stored in parameters; this function then dumps the values of those parameters to a file. The data can then be retrieved quickly from that file via `_retrieve_cache`, even in different instances of the shell.

The *cache_identifier* specifies the file which the data should be dumped to. The file is stored in a directory specified by the **cache-path** style which defaults to `~/.zcompcache`. The remaining *params* arguments are the parameters to dump to the file.

The return status is zero if storage was successful. The function will only attempt storage if the **use-cache** style is set, so you can call this function without worrying about whether the user wanted to use the caching layer.

The completion function may avoid calling `_retrieve_cache` when it already has the completion data available as parameters. However, in that case it should call `_cache_invalid` to check whether the data in the parameters and in the cache are still valid.

See the _perl_modules completion function for a simple example of the usage of the caching layer.

`_tags` [[`-C` *name*] *tag* ...]

If called with arguments, these are taken to be the names of tags valid for completions in the current context. These tags are stored internally and sorted by using the **tag-order** style.

Next, `_tags` is called repeatedly without arguments from the same completion function. This successively selects the first, second, etc. set of tags requested by the user. The return status is zero if at least one of the tags is requested and non-zero otherwise. To test if a particular tag is to be tried, the `_requested` function should be called (see above).

If '`-C` *name*' is given, *name* is temporarily stored in the *argument* field (the fifth) of the context in the **curcontext** parameter during the call to `_tags`; the field is restored on exit. This allows `_tags` to use a more specific context without having to change and reset the **curcontext** parameter (which has the same effect).

`_tilde_files`

Like `_files`, but resolve leading tildes according to the rules of filename expansion, so the suggested completions don't start with a '`~`' even if the filename on the command-line does.

`_values` [`-O` *name*] [`-s` *sep*] [`-S` *sep*] [`-wC`] *desc spec* ...

This is used to complete arbitrary keywords (values) and their arguments, or lists of such combinations.

If the first argument is the option '`-O` *name*', it will be used in the same way as by the `_arguments` function. In other words, the elements of the *name* array will be passed to **compadd** when executing an action.

If the first argument (or the first argument after '`-O` *name*') is '`-s`', the next argument is used as the character that separates multiple values. This character is automatically added after each value in an auto-removable fashion (see below); all values completed by '`_values -s`' appear in the same word on the command line, unlike completion using _arguments. If this option is not present, only a single value will be completed per word.

Normally, _values will only use the current word to determine which values are already present on the command line and hence are not to be completed again. If the -w option is given, other arguments are examined as well.

The first non-option argument is used as a string to print as a description before listing the values.

All other arguments describe the possible values and their arguments in the same format used for the description of options by the _arguments function (see above). The only differences are that no minus or plus sign is required at the beginning, values can have only one argument, and the forms of action beginning with an equal sign are not supported.

The character separating a value from its argument can be set using the option -S (like -s, followed by the character to use as the separator in the next argument). By default the equals sign will be used as the separator between values and arguments.

Example:

```
_values -s , 'description' \
        '*foo[bar]' \
        '(two)*one[number]:first count:' \
        'two[another number]::second count:(1 2 3)'
```

This describes three possible values: 'foo', 'one', and 'two'. The first is described as 'bar', takes no argument and may appear more than once. The second is described as 'number', may appear more than once, and takes one mandatory argument described as 'first count'; no action is specified, so it will not be completed. The '(two)' at the beginning says that if the value 'one' is on the line, the value 'two' will no longer be considered a possible completion. Finally, the last value ('two') is described as 'another number' and takes an optional argument described as 'second count' for which the completions (to appear after an '=') are '1', '2', and '3'. The _values function will complete lists of these values separated by commas.

Like _arguments, this function temporarily adds another context name component to the arguments element (the fifth) of the current context while executing the action. Here this name is just the name of the value for which the argument is completed.

The style verbose is used to decide if the descriptions for the values (but not those for the arguments) should be printed.

The associative array val_args is used to report values and their arguments; this works similarly to the opt_args associative array used by _arguments. Hence the function calling _values should declare the local parameters state, state_descr, line, context and val_args:

```
local context state state_descr line
typeset -A val_args
```

when using an action of the form '->string'. With this function the context parameter will be set to the name of the value whose argument is to be completed. Note that for _values, the state and state_descr are scalars rather than arrays. Only a single matching state is returned.

Note also that _values normally adds the character used as the separator between values as an auto-removable suffix (similar to a '/' after a directory). However, this is not possible for a '->*string*' action as the matches for the argument are generated by the calling function. To get the usual behaviour, the calling function can add the separator *x* as a suffix by passing the options '-qS *x*' either directly or indirectly to compadd.

The option -C is treated in the same way as it is by _arguments. In that case the parameter curcontext should be made local instead of context (as described above).

_wanted [-x] [-C *name*] [-12VJ] *tag name descr command* [*arg* ...]

In many contexts, completion can only generate one particular set of matches, usually corresponding to a single tag. However, it is still necessary to decide whether the user requires matches of this type. This function is useful in such a case.

The arguments to _wanted are the same as those to _requested, i.e. arguments to be passed to _description. However, in this case the *command* is not optional; all the processing of tags, including the loop over both tags and tag labels and the generation of matches, is carried out automatically by _wanted.

Hence to offer only one tag and immediately add the corresponding matches with the given description:

```
local expl
_wanted tag expl 'description' \
    compadd matches...
```

Note that, as for _requested, the *command* must be able to accept options to be passed down to compadd.

Like _tags this function supports the -C option to give a different name for the argument context field. The -x option has the same meaning as for _description.

_widgets [-g *pattern*]

This function completes names of zle widgets (see Section 18.4 [Zle Widgets], page 195). The *pattern*, if present, is matched against values of the $widgets special parameter, documented in Section 22.33 [The zsh/zleparameter Module], page 378.

20.7 Completion System Variables

There are some standard variables, initialised by the _main_complete function and then used from other functions.

The standard variables are:

_comp_caller_options

The completion system uses setopt to set a number of options. This allows functions to be written without concern for compatibility with every possible combination of user options. However, sometimes completion needs to know what the user's option preferences are. These are saved in the `_comp_caller_options` associative array. Option names, spelled in lowercase without underscores, are mapped to one or other of the strings 'on' and 'off'.

`_comp_priv_prefix`

> Completion functions such as `_sudo` can set the `_comp_priv_prefix` array to a command prefix that may then be used by `_call_program` to match the privileges when calling programs to generate matches.

Two more features are offered by the `_main_complete` function. The arrays `compprefuncs` and `comppostfuncs` may contain names of functions that are to be called immediately before or after completion has been tried. A function will only be called once unless it explicitly reinserts itself into the array.

20.8 Completion Directories

In the source distribution, the files are contained in various subdirectories of the `Completion` directory. They may have been installed in the same structure, or into one single function directory. The following is a description of the files found in the original directory structure. If you wish to alter an installed file, you will need to copy it to some directory which appears earlier in your `fpath` than the standard directory where it appears.

`Base`   The core functions and special completion widgets automatically bound to keys. You will certainly need most of these, though will probably not need to alter them. Many of these are documented above.

`Zsh`   Functions for completing arguments of shell builtin commands and utility functions for this. Some of these are also used by functions from the `Unix` directory.

`Unix`   Functions for completing arguments of external commands and suites of commands. They may need modifying for your system, although in many cases some attempt is made to decide which version of a command is present. For example, completion for the `mount` command tries to determine the system it is running on, while completion for many other utilities try to decide whether the GNU version of the command is in use, and hence whether the `--help` option is supported.

`X, AIX, BSD, ...`

> Completion and utility function for commands available only on some systems. These are not arranged hierarchically, so, for example, both the `Linux` and `Debian` directories, as well as the `X` directory, may be useful on your system.

21 Completion Using compctl

21.1 Types of completion

This version of zsh has two ways of performing completion of words on the command line. New users of the shell may prefer to use the newer and more powerful system based on shell functions; this is described in Chapter 20 [Completion System], page 242, and the basic shell mechanisms which support it are described in Chapter 19 [Completion Widgets], page 225. This chapter describes the older `compctl` command.

21.2 Description

```
compctl [ -CDT ] options [ command ... ]
compctl [ -CDT ] options [ -x pattern options - ... -- ]
        [ + options [ -x ... -- ] ... [+] ] [ command ... ]
compctl -M match-specs ...
compctl -L [ -CDTM ] [ command ... ]
compctl + command ...
```

Control the editor's completion behavior according to the supplied set of *options*. Various editing commands, notably `expand-or-complete-word`, usually bound to tab, will attempt to complete a word typed by the user, while others, notably `delete-char-or-list`, usually bound to ^D in EMACS editing mode, list the possibilities; `compctl` controls what those possibilities are. They may for example be filenames (the most common case, and hence the default), shell variables, or words from a user-specified list.

21.3 Command Flags

Completion of the arguments of a command may be different for each command or may use the default. The behavior when completing the command word itself may also be separately specified. These correspond to the following flags and arguments, all of which (except for -L) may be combined with any combination of the *options* described subsequently in Section 21.4 [Option Flags], page 322:

command ...

> controls completion for the named commands, which must be listed last on the command line. If completion is attempted for a command with a pathname containing slashes and no completion definition is found, the search is retried with the last pathname component. If the command starts with a =, completion is tried with the pathname of the command.

> Any of the *command* strings may be patterns of the form normally used for filename generation. These should be quoted to protect them from immediate expansion; for example the command string `'foo*'` arranges for completion of the words of any command beginning with `foo`. When completion is attempted, all pattern completions are tried in the reverse order of their definition until one matches. By default, completion then proceeds as normal, i.e. the shell will try to generate more matches for the specific command on the command line; this can be overridden by including `-tn` in the flags for the pattern completion.

Note that aliases are expanded before the command name is determined unless the COMPLETE_ALIASES option is set. Commands may not be combined with the -C, -D or -T flags.

-C   controls completion when the command word itself is being completed. If no
            compctl -C command has been issued, the names of any executable command
            (whether in the path or specific to the shell, such as aliases or functions) are
            completed.

-D   controls default completion behavior for the arguments of commands not as-
            signed any special behavior. If no compctl -D command has been issued, file-
            names are completed.

-T   supplies completion flags to be used before any other processing is done, even
            before processing for compctls defined for specific commands. This is especially
            useful when combined with extended completion (the -x flag, see Section 21.6
            [Extended Completion], page 327, below). Using this flag you can define default
            behavior which will apply to all commands without exception, or you can alter
            the standard behavior for all commands. For example, if your access to the user
            database is too slow and/or it contains too many users (so that completion after
            '~' is too slow to be usable), you can use

```
compctl -T -x 's[~] C[0,[^/]#]' -k friends -S/ -tn
```

            to complete the strings in the array friends after a '~'. The C[...] argument
            is necessary so that this form of ~-completion is not tried after the directory
            name is finished.

-L   lists the existing completion behavior in a manner suitable for putting into a
            start-up script; the existing behavior is not changed. Any combination of the
            above forms, or the -M flag (which must follow the -L flag), may be speci-
            fied, otherwise all defined completions are listed. Any other flags supplied are
            ignored.

no argument

            If no argument is given, compctl lists all defined completions in an abbreviated
            form; with a list of *options*, all completions with those flags set (not counting
            extended completion) are listed.

If the + flag is alone and followed immediately by the *command* list, the completion behavior for all the commands in the list is reset to the default. In other words, completion will subsequently use the options specified by the -D flag.

The form with -M as the first and only option defines global matching specifications (see Section 19.5 [Completion Matching Control], page 238). The match specifications given will be used for every completion attempt (only when using compctl, not with the new completion system) and are tried in the order in which they are defined until one generates at least one match. E.g.:

```
compctl -M '' 'm:{a-zA-Z}={A-Za-z}'
```

This will first try completion without any global match specifications (the empty string) and, if that generates no matches, will try case insensitive completion.

21.4 Option Flags

[-fcFBdeaRGovNAIOPZEnbjrzu/12]
[-k *array*] [-g *globstring*] [-s *substring*]
[-K *function*]
[-Q] [-P *prefix*] [-S *suffix*]
[-W *file-prefix*] [-H *num pattern*]
[-q] [-X *explanation*] [-Y *explanation*]
[-y *func-or-var*] [-l *cmd*] [-h *cmd*] [-U]
[-t *continue*] [-J *name*] [-V *name*]
[-M *match-spec*]

The remaining *options* specify the type of command arguments to look for during completion. Any combination of these flags may be specified; the result is a sorted list of all the possibilities. The options are as follows.

21.4.1 Simple Flags

These produce completion lists made up by the shell itself:

-f	Filenames and file system paths.
-/	Just file system paths.
-c	Command names, including aliases, shell functions, builtins and reserved words.
-F	Function names.
-B	Names of builtin commands.
-m	Names of external commands.
-w	Reserved words.
-a	Alias names.
-R	Names of regular (non-global) aliases.
-G	Names of global aliases.
-d	This can be combined with -F, -B, -w, -a, -R and -G to get names of disabled functions, builtins, reserved words or aliases.
-e	This option (to show enabled commands) is in effect by default, but may be combined with -d; -de in combination with -F, -B, -w, -a, -R and -G will complete names of functions, builtins, reserved words or aliases whether or not they are disabled.
-o	Names of shell options (see Chapter 16 [Options], page 110).
-v	Names of any variable defined in the shell.
-N	Names of scalar (non-array) parameters.
-A	Array names.
-I	Names of integer variables.

-O	Names of read-only variables.
-p	Names of parameters used by the shell (including special parameters).
-Z	Names of shell special parameters.
-E	Names of environment variables.
-n	Named directories.
-b	Key binding names.
-j	Job names: the first word of the job leader's command line. This is useful with the **kill** builtin.
-r	Names of running jobs.
-z	Names of suspended jobs.
-u	User names.

21.4.2 Flags with Arguments

These have user supplied arguments to determine how the list of completions is to be made up:

-k *array*   Names taken from the elements of $*array* (note that the '$' does not appear on the command line). Alternatively, the argument *array* itself may be a set of space- or comma-separated values in parentheses, in which any delimiter may be escaped with a backslash; in this case the argument should be quoted. For example,

```
compctl -k "(cputime filesize datasize stacksize
          coredumpsize resident descriptors)" limit
```

-g *globstring*

> The *globstring* is expanded using filename globbing; it should be quoted to protect it from immediate expansion. The resulting filenames are taken as the possible completions. Use '*(/)' instead of '*/' for directories. The **fignore** special parameter is not applied to the resulting files. More than one pattern may be given separated by blanks. (Note that brace expansion is *not* part of globbing. Use the syntax '(either|or)' to match alternatives.)

-s *substring*

> The *substring* is split into words and these words are than expanded using all shell expansion mechanisms (see Chapter 14 [Expansion], page 45). The resulting words are taken as possible completions. The **fignore** special parameter is not applied to the resulting files. Note that -g is faster for filenames.

-K *function*

> Call the given function to get the completions. Unless the name starts with an underscore, the function is passed two arguments: the prefix and the suffix of the word on which completion is to be attempted, in other words those characters before the cursor position, and those from the cursor position onwards. The whole command line can be accessed with the -c and -l flags of the **read** builtin. The function should set the variable **reply** to an array containing the

completions (one completion per element); note that `reply` should not be made local to the function. From such a function the command line can be accessed with the `-c` and `-l` flags to the `read` builtin. For example,

```
function whoson { reply=('users'); }
compctl -K whoson talk
```

completes only logged-on users after 'talk'. Note that 'whoson' must return an array, so 'reply='users'' would be incorrect.

-H *num pattern*

The possible completions are taken from the last *num* history lines. Only words matching *pattern* are taken. If *num* is zero or negative the whole history is searched and if *pattern* is the empty string all words are taken (as with '*'). A typical use is

```
compctl -D -f + -H 0 ''
```

which forces completion to look back in the history list for a word if no filename matches.

21.4.3 Control Flags

These do not directly specify types of name to be completed, but manipulate the options that do:

-Q   This instructs the shell not to quote any metacharacters in the possible completions. Normally the results of a completion are inserted into the command line with any metacharacters quoted so that they are interpreted as normal characters. This is appropriate for filenames and ordinary strings. However, for special effects, such as inserting a backquoted expression from a completion array (`-k`) so that the expression will not be evaluated until the complete line is executed, this option must be used.

-P *prefix*   The *prefix* is inserted just before the completed string; any initial part already typed will be completed and the whole *prefix* ignored for completion purposes. For example,

```
compctl -j -P "%" kill
```

inserts a '%' after the kill command and then completes job names.

-S *suffix*   When a completion is found the *suffix* is inserted after the completed string. In the case of menu completion the suffix is inserted immediately, but it is still possible to cycle through the list of completions by repeatedly hitting the same key.

-W *file-prefix*

With directory *file-prefix*: for command, file, directory and globbing completion (options `-c`, `-f`, `-/`, `-g`), the file prefix is implicitly added in front of the completion. For example,

```
compctl -/ -W ~/Mail maildirs
```

completes any subdirectories to any depth beneath the directory `~/Mail`, although that prefix does not appear on the command line. The *file-prefix* may also be of the form accepted by the `-k` flag, i.e. the name of an array or a literal list in parenthesis. In this case all the directories in the list will be searched for possible completions.

-q   If used with a suffix as specified by the -S option, this causes the suffix to be removed if the next character typed is a blank or does not insert anything or if the suffix consists of only one character and the next character typed is the same character; this the same rule used for the AUTO_REMOVE_SLASH option. The option is most useful for list separators (comma, colon, etc.).

-l *cmd*   This option restricts the range of command line words that are considered to be arguments. If combined with one of the extended completion patterns 'p[...]', 'r[...]', or 'R[...]' (see Section 21.6 [Extended Completion], page 327, below) the range is restricted to the range of arguments specified in the brackets. Completion is then performed as if these had been given as arguments to the *cmd* supplied with the option. If the *cmd* string is empty the first word in the range is instead taken as the command name, and command name completion performed on the first word in the range. For example,

    compctl -x 'r[-exec,;]' -l '' -- find

completes arguments between '-exec' and the following ';' (or the end of the command line if there is no such string) as if they were a separate command line.

-h *cmd*   Normally zsh completes quoted strings as a whole. With this option, completion can be done separately on different parts of such strings. It works like the -l option but makes the completion code work on the parts of the current word that are separated by spaces. These parts are completed as if they were arguments to the given *cmd*. If *cmd* is the empty string, the first part is completed as a command name, as with -l.

-U   Use the whole list of possible completions, whether or not they actually match the word on the command line. The word typed so far will be deleted. This is most useful with a function (given by the -K option) which can examine the word components passed to it (or via the **read** builtin's -c and -l flags) and use its own criteria to decide what matches. If there is no completion, the original word is retained. Since the produced possible completions seldom have interesting common prefixes and suffixes, menu completion is started immediately if AUTO_MENU is set and this flag is used.

-y *func-or-var*
         The list provided by *func-or-var* is displayed instead of the list of completions whenever a listing is required; the actual completions to be inserted are not affected. It can be provided in two ways. Firstly, if *func-or-var* begins with a **$** it defines a variable, or if it begins with a left parenthesis a literal array, which contains the list. A variable may have been set by a call to a function using the -K option. Otherwise it contains the name of a function which will be executed to create the list. The function will be passed as an argument list all matching completions, including prefixes and suffixes expanded in full, and should set the array **reply** to the result. In both cases, the display list will only be retrieved after a complete list of matches has been created.

Note that the returned list does not have to correspond, even in length, to the original set of matches, and may be passed as a scalar instead of an array. No special formatting of characters is performed on the output in this case; in particular, newlines are printed literally and if they appear output in columns is suppressed.

-X *explanation*

Print *explanation* when trying completion on the current set of options. A '%n' in this string is replaced by the number of matches that were added for this explanation string. The explanation only appears if completion was tried and there was no unique match, or when listing completions. Explanation strings will be listed together with the matches of the group specified together with the **-X** option (using the **-J** or **-V** option). If the same explanation string is given to multiple **-X** options, the string appears only once (for each group) and the number of matches shown for the '%n' is the total number of all matches for each of these uses. In any case, the explanation string will only be shown if there was at least one match added for the explanation string.

The sequences %B, %b, %S, %s, %U, and %u specify output attributes (bold, standout, and underline), %F, %f, %K, %k specify foreground and background colours, and %{...%} can be used to include literal escape sequences as in prompts.

-Y *explanation*

Identical to **-X**, except that the *explanation* first undergoes expansion following the usual rules for strings in double quotes. The expansion will be carried out after any functions are called for the **-K** or **-y** options, allowing them to set variables.

-t *continue*

The *continue*-string contains a character that specifies which set of completion flags should be used next. It is useful:

(i) With **-T**, or when trying a list of pattern completions, when **compctl** would usually continue with ordinary processing after finding matches; this can be suppressed with '**-tn**'.

(ii) With a list of alternatives separated by +, when **compctl** would normally stop when one of the alternatives generates matches. It can be forced to consider the next set of completions by adding '**-t+**' to the flags of the alternative before the '+'.

(iii) In an extended completion list (see below), when **compctl** would normally continue until a set of conditions succeeded, then use only the immediately following flags. With '**-t-**', **compctl** will continue trying extended completions after the next '−'; with '**-tx**' it will attempt completion with the default flags, in other words those before the '**-x**'.

-J *name*   This gives the name of the group the matches should be placed in. Groups are listed and sorted separately; likewise, menu completion will offer the matches in the groups in the order in which the groups were defined. If no group name is explicitly given, the matches are stored in a group named **default**. The first time a group name is encountered, a group with that name is created. After that all matches with the same group name are stored in that group.

This can be useful with non-exclusive alternative completions. For example, in

```
compctl -f -J files -t+ + -v -J variables foo
```

both files and variables are possible completions, as the -t+ forces both sets of alternatives before and after the + to be considered at once. Because of the -J options, however, all files are listed before all variables.

-V *name* Like -J, but matches within the group will not be sorted in listings nor in menu completion. These unsorted groups are in a different name space from the sorted ones, so groups defined as -J files and -V files are distinct.

-1 If given together with the -V option, makes only consecutive duplicates in the group be removed. Note that groups with and without this flag are in different name spaces.

-2 If given together with the -J or -V option, makes all duplicates be kept. Again, groups with and without this flag are in different name spaces.

-M *match-spec*

This defines additional matching control specifications that should be used only when testing words for the list of flags this flag appears in. The format of the *match-spec* string is described in Section 19.5 [Completion Matching Control], page 238.

21.5 Alternative Completion

compctl [-CDT] *options* + *options* [+ ...] [+] *command* ...

The form with '+' specifies alternative options. Completion is tried with the options before the first '+'. If this produces no matches completion is tried with the flags after the '+' and so on. If there are no flags after the last '+' and a match has not been found up to that point, default completion is tried. If the list of flags contains a -t with a + character, the next list of flags is used even if the current list produced matches.

Additional options are available that restrict completion to some part of the command line; this is referred to as 'extended completion'.

21.6 Extended Completion

compctl [-CDT] *options* -x *pattern options* - ... --
      [*command* ...]
compctl [-CDT] *options* [-x *pattern options* - ... --]
      [+ *options* [-x ... --] ... [+]] [*command* ...]

The form with '-x' specifies extended completion for the commands given; as shown, it may be combined with alternative completion using '+'. Each *pattern* is examined in turn; when a match is found, the corresponding *options*, as described in Section 21.4 [Option Flags], page 322, above, are used to generate possible completions. If no *pattern* matches, the *options* given before the -x are used.

Note that each pattern should be supplied as a single argument and should be quoted to prevent expansion of metacharacters by the shell.

A *pattern* is built of sub-patterns separated by commas; it matches if at least one of these sub-patterns matches (they are 'or'ed). These sub-patterns are in turn composed of other sub-patterns separated by white spaces which match if all of the sub-patterns match (they are 'and'ed). An element of the sub-patterns is of the form 'c [...] [...]', where the pairs of brackets may be repeated as often as necessary, and matches if any of the sets of brackets match (an 'or'). The example below makes this clearer.

The elements may be any of the following:

s [*string*] ...

> Matches if the current word on the command line starts with one of the strings given in brackets. The *string* is not removed and is not part of the completion.

S [*string*] ...

> Like s [*string*] except that the *string* is part of the completion.

p [*from*, *to*] ...

> Matches if the number of the current word is between one of the *from* and *to* pairs inclusive. The comma and *to* are optional; *to* defaults to the same value as *from*. The numbers may be negative: -*n* refers to the *n*'th last word on the line.

c [*offset*, *string*] ...

> Matches if the *string* matches the word offset by *offset* from the current word position. Usually *offset* will be negative.

C [*offset*, *pattern*] ...

> Like c but using pattern matching instead.

w [*index*, *string*] ...

> Matches if the word in position *index* is equal to the corresponding *string*. Note that the word count is made after any alias expansion.

W [*index*, *pattern*] ...

> Like w but using pattern matching instead.

n [*index*, *string*] ...

> Matches if the current word contains *string*. Anything up to and including the *index*th occurrence of this string will not be considered part of the completion, but the rest will. *index* may be negative to count from the end: in most cases, *index* will be 1 or -1. For example,
>
>   compctl -s ''users'' -x 'n[1,@]' -k hosts -- talk
>
> will usually complete usernames, but if you insert an @ after the name, names from the array *hosts* (assumed to contain hostnames, though you must make the array yourself) will be completed. Other commands such as rcp can be handled similarly.

N [*index*, *string*] ...

> Like n except that the string will be taken as a character class. Anything up to and including the *index*th occurrence of any of the characters in *string* will not be considered part of the completion.

m[*min*,*max*]...
> Matches if the total number of words lies between *min* and *max* inclusive.

r[*str1*,*str2*]...
> Matches if the cursor is after a word with prefix *str1*. If there is also a word with prefix *str2* on the command line after the one matched by *str1* it matches only if the cursor is before this word. If the comma and *str2* are omitted, it matches if the cursor is after a word with prefix *str1*.

R[*str1*,*str2*]...
> Like r but using pattern matching instead.

q[*str*]...   Matches the word currently being completed is in single quotes and the *str* begins with the letter 's', or if completion is done in double quotes and *str* starts with the letter 'd', or if completion is done in backticks and *str* starts with a 'b'.

21.7 Example

```
compctl -u -x 's[+] c[-1,-f],s[-f+]' \
    -g '~/Mail/*(:t)' - 's[-f],c[-1,-f]' -f -- mail
```

This is to be interpreted as follows:

If the current command is `mail`, then

> if ((the current word begins with + and the previous word is -f) or (the current word begins with -f+)), then complete the non-directory part (the ':t' glob modifier) of files in the directory ~/Mail; else

> if the current word begins with -f or the previous word was -f, then complete any file; else

> complete user names.

22 Zsh Modules

22.1 Description

Some optional parts of zsh are in modules, separate from the core of the shell. Each of these modules may be linked in to the shell at build time, or can be dynamically linked while the shell is running if the installation supports this feature. Modules are linked at runtime with the `zmodload` command, see Chapter 17 [Shell Builtin Commands], page 139.

The modules that are bundled with the zsh distribution are:

zsh/attr   Builtins for manipulating extended attributes (xattr).

zsh/cap   Builtins for manipulating POSIX.1e (POSIX.6) capability (privilege) sets.

zsh/clone
> A builtin that can clone a running shell onto another terminal.

`zsh/compctl`

> The `compctl` builtin for controlling completion.

`zsh/complete`

> The basic completion code.

`zsh/complist`

> Completion listing extensions.

`zsh/computil`

> A module with utility builtins needed for the shell function based completion system.

`zsh/curses`

> curses windowing commands

`zsh/datetime`

> Some date/time commands and parameters.

`zsh/db/gdbm`

> Builtins for managing associative array parameters tied to GDBM databases.

`zsh/deltochar`

> A ZLE function duplicating EMACS' `zap-to-char`.

`zsh/example`

> An example of how to write a module.

`zsh/files`

> Some basic file manipulation commands as builtins.

`zsh/langinfo`

> Interface to locale information.

`zsh/mapfile`

> Access to external files via a special associative array.

`zsh/mathfunc`

> Standard scientific functions for use in mathematical evaluations.

`zsh/nearcolor`

> Map colours to the nearest colour in the available palette.

`zsh/newuser`

> Arrange for files for new users to be installed.

`zsh/parameter`

> Access to internal hash tables via special associative arrays.

`zsh/pcre`   Interface to the PCRE library.

`zsh/param/private`

> Builtins for managing private-scoped parameters in function context.

`zsh/regex`

> Interface to the POSIX regex library.

`zsh/sched`

A builtin that provides a timed execution facility within the shell.

`zsh/net/socket`

Manipulation of Unix domain sockets

`zsh/stat`   A builtin command interface to the **stat** system call.

`zsh/system`

A builtin interface to various low-level system features.

`zsh/net/tcp`

Manipulation of TCP sockets

`zsh/termcap`

Interface to the termcap database.

`zsh/terminfo`

Interface to the terminfo database.

`zsh/zftp`   A builtin FTP client.

`zsh/zle`   The Zsh Line Editor, including the **bindkey** and **vared** builtins.

`zsh/zleparameter`

Access to internals of the Zsh Line Editor via parameters.

`zsh/zprof`

A module allowing profiling for shell functions.

`zsh/zpty`   A builtin for starting a command in a pseudo-terminal.

`zsh/zselect`

Block and return when file descriptors are ready.

`zsh/zutil`

Some utility builtins, e.g. the one for supporting configuration via styles.

22.2 The zsh/attr Module

The **zsh/attr** module is used for manipulating extended attributes. The **-h** option causes all commands to operate on symbolic links instead of their targets. The builtins in this module are:

zgetattr [**-h**] *filename attribute* [*parameter*]

Get the extended attribute *attribute* from the specified *filename*. If the optional argument *parameter* is given, the attribute is set on that parameter instead of being printed to stdout.

zsetattr [**-h**] *filename attribute value*

Set the extended attribute *attribute* on the specified *filename* to *value*.

zdelattr [**-h**] *filename attribute*

Remove the extended attribute *attribute* from the specified *filename*.

zlistattr [-h] *filename* [*parameter*]

>   List the extended attributes currently set on the specified *filename*. If the optional argument *parameter* is given, the list of attributes is set on that parameter instead of being printed to stdout.

zgetattr and zlistattr allocate memory dynamically. If the attribute or list of attributes grows between the allocation and the call to get them, they return 2. On all other errors, 1 is returned. This allows the calling function to check for this case and retry.

22.3 The zsh/cap Module

The zsh/cap module is used for manipulating POSIX.1e (POSIX.6) capability sets. If the operating system does not support this interface, the builtins defined by this module will do nothing. The builtins in this module are:

cap [*capabilities*]

>   Change the shell's process capability sets to the specified *capabilities*, otherwise display the shell's current capabilities.

getcap *filename* ...

>   This is a built-in implementation of the POSIX standard utility. It displays the capability sets on each specified *filename*.

setcap *capabilities filename* ...

>   This is a built-in implementation of the POSIX standard utility. It sets the capability sets on each specified *filename* to the specified *capabilities*.

22.4 The zsh/clone Module

The zsh/clone module makes available one builtin command:

clone *tty*   Creates a forked instance of the current shell, attached to the specified *tty*. In the new shell, the PID, PPID and TTY special parameters are changed appropriately. $! is set to zero in the new shell, and to the new shell's PID in the original shell.

>   The return status of the builtin is zero in both shells if successful, and non-zero on error.

>   The target of clone should be an unused terminal, such as an unused virtual console or a virtual terminal created by

>   ```
>   xterm -e sh -c 'trap : INT QUIT TSTP; tty;
>           while :; do sleep 100000000; done'
>   ```

>   Some words of explanation are warranted about this long xterm command line: when doing clone on a pseudo-terminal, some other session ("session" meant as a unix session group, or SID) is already owning the terminal. Hence the cloned zsh cannot acquire the pseudo-terminal as a controlling tty. That means two things:

>   - the job control signals will go to the sh-started-by-xterm process group (that's why we disable INT QUIT and TSTP with trap; otherwise the while loop could get suspended or killed)

- the cloned shell will have job control disabled, and the job control keys (control-C, control-\ and control-Z) will not work.

This does not apply when cloning to an *unused* vc.

Cloning to a used (and unprepared) terminal will result in two processes reading simultaneously from the same terminal, with input bytes going randomly to either process.

`clone` is mostly useful as a shell built-in replacement for openvt.

22.5 The zsh/compctl Module

The `zsh/compctl` module makes available two builtin commands. `compctl`, is the old, deprecated way to control completions for ZLE. See Chapter 21 [Completion Using compctl], page 319. The other builtin command, `compcall` can be used in user-defined completion widgets, see Chapter 19 [Completion Widgets], page 225.

22.6 The zsh/complete Module

The `zsh/complete` module makes available several builtin commands which can be used in user-defined completion widgets, see Chapter 19 [Completion Widgets], page 225.

22.7 The zsh/complist Module

The `zsh/complist` module offers three extensions to completion listings: the ability to highlight matches in such a list, the ability to scroll through long lists and a different style of menu completion.

22.7.1 Colored completion listings

Whenever one of the parameters ZLS_COLORS or ZLS_COLOURS is set and the `zsh/complist` module is loaded or linked into the shell, completion lists will be colored. Note, however, that `complist` will not automatically be loaded if it is not linked in: on systems with dynamic loading, 'zmodload zsh/complist' is required.

The parameters ZLS_COLORS and ZLS_COLOURS describe how matches are highlighted. To turn on highlighting an empty value suffices, in which case all the default values given below will be used. The format of the value of these parameters is the same as used by the GNU version of the `ls` command: a colon-separated list of specifications of the form 'name=value'. The *name* may be one of the following strings, most of which specify file types for which the *value* will be used. The strings and their default values are:

no 0   for normal text (i.e. when displaying something other than a matched file)

fi 0   for regular files

di 32   for directories

ln 36   for symbolic links. If this has the special value `target`, symbolic links are dereferenced and the target file used to determine the display format.

pi 31   for named pipes (FIFOs)

so 33   for sockets

bd 44;37   for block devices

cd 44;37   for character devices

or *none*   for a symlink to nonexistent file (default is the value defined for `ln`)

mi *none*   for a non-existent file (default is the value defined for `fi`); this code is currently not used

su 37;41   for files with setuid bit set

sg 30;43   for files with setgid bit set

tw 30;42   for world writable directories with sticky bit set

ow 34;43   for world writable directories without sticky bit set

sa *none*   for files with an associated suffix alias; this is only tested after specific suffixes, as described below

st 37;44   for directories with sticky bit set but not world writable

ex 35   for executable files

lc \e[for the left code (see below)

rc m   for the right code

tc 0   for the character indicating the file type printed after filenames if the `LIST_TYPES` option is set

sp 0   for the spaces printed after matches to align the next column

ec *none*   for the end code

Apart from these strings, the *name* may also be an asterisk ('`*`') followed by any string. The *value* given for such a string will be used for all files whose name ends with the string. The *name* may also be an equals sign ('`=`') followed by a pattern; the `EXTENDED_GLOB` option will be turned on for evaluation of the pattern. The *value* given for this pattern will be used for all matches (not just filenames) whose display string are matched by the pattern. Definitions for the form with the leading equal sign take precedence over the values defined for file types, which in turn take precedence over the form with the leading asterisk (file extensions).

The leading-equals form also allows different parts of the displayed strings to be colored differently. For this, the pattern has to use the '`(#b)`' globbing flag and pairs of parentheses surrounding the parts of the strings that are to be colored differently. In this case the *value* may consist of more than one color code separated by equal signs. The first code will be used for all parts for which no explicit code is specified and the following codes will be used for the parts matched by the sub-patterns in parentheses. For example, the specification '`=(#b)(?)*(?)=0=3=7`' will be used for all matches which are at least two characters long and will use the code '3' for the first character, '7' for the last character and '0' for the rest.

All three forms of *name* may be preceded by a pattern in parentheses. If this is given, the *value* will be used only for matches in groups whose names are matched by the pattern given in the parentheses. For example, '`(g*)m*=43`' highlights all matches beginning with 'm' in groups whose names begin with 'g' using the color code '43'. In case of the '`lc`', '`rc`', and '`ec`' codes, the group pattern is ignored.

Note also that all patterns are tried in the order in which they appear in the parameter value until the first one matches which is then used. Patterns may be matched against completions, descriptions (possibly with spaces appended for padding), or lines consisting of a completion followed by a description. For consistent coloring it may be necessary to use more than one pattern or a pattern with backreferences.

When printing a match, the code prints the value of `lc`, the value for the file-type or the last matching specification with a '*', the value of `rc`, the string to display for the match itself, and then the value of `ec` if that is defined or the values of `lc`, `no`, and `rc` if `ec` is not defined.

The default values are ISO 6429 (ANSI) compliant and can be used on vt100 compatible terminals such as `xterms`. On monochrome terminals the default values will have no visible effect. The `colors` function from the contribution can be used to get associative arrays containing the codes for ANSI terminals (see Section 26.12 [Other Functions], page 489). For example, after loading `colors`, one could use '`$color[red]`' to get the code for foreground color red and '`$color[bg-green]`' for the code for background color green.

If the completion system invoked by compinit is used, these parameters should not be set directly because the system controls them itself. Instead, the `list-colors` style should be used (see Section 20.3 [Completion System Configuration], page 249).

22.7.2 Scrolling in completion listings

To enable scrolling through a completion list, the `LISTPROMPT` parameter must be set. Its value will be used as the prompt; if it is the empty string, a default prompt will be used. The value may contain escapes of the form '%x'. It supports the escapes '%B', '%b', '%S', '%s', '%U', '%u', '%F', '%f', '%K', '%k' and '%{...%}' used also in shell prompts as well as three pairs of additional sequences: a '%l' or '%L' is replaced by the number of the last line shown and the total number of lines in the form '*number/total*'; a '%m' or '%M' is replaced with the number of the last match shown and the total number of matches; and '%p' or '%P' is replaced with 'Top', 'Bottom' or the position of the first line shown in percent of the total number of lines, respectively. In each of these cases the form with the uppercase letter will be replaced with a string of fixed width, padded to the right with spaces, while the lowercase form will not be padded.

If the parameter `LISTPROMPT` is set, the completion code will not ask if the list should be shown. Instead it immediately starts displaying the list, stopping after the first screenful, showing the prompt at the bottom, waiting for a keypress after temporarily switching to the `listscroll` keymap. Some of the zle functions have a special meaning while scrolling lists:

`send-break`
> stops listing discarding the key pressed

`accept-line, down-history, down-line-or-history`
`down-line-or-search, vi-down-line-or-history`
> scrolls forward one line

`complete-word, menu-complete, expand-or-complete`
`expand-or-complete-prefix, menu-complete-or-expand`
> scrolls forward one screenful

`accept-search`
>   stop listing but take no other action

Every other character stops listing and immediately processes the key as usual. Any key that is not bound in the `listscroll` keymap or that is bound to `undefined-key` is looked up in the keymap currently selected.

As for the `ZLS_COLORS` and `ZLS_COLOURS` parameters, `LISTPROMPT` should not be set directly when using the shell function based completion system. Instead, the `list-prompt` style should be used.

22.7.3 Menu selection

The `zsh/complist` module also offers an alternative style of selecting matches from a list, called menu selection, which can be used if the shell is set up to return to the last prompt after showing a completion list (see the `ALWAYS_LAST_PROMPT` option in Chapter 16 [Options], page 110).

Menu selection can be invoked directly by the widget `menu-select` defined by this module. This is a standard ZLE widget that can be bound to a key in the usual way as described in Chapter 18 [Zsh Line Editor], page 183.

Alternatively, the parameter `MENUSELECT` can be set to an integer, which gives the minimum number of matches that must be present before menu selection is automatically turned on. This second method requires that menu completion be started, either directly from a widget such as `menu-complete`, or due to one of the options `MENU_COMPLETE` or `AUTO_MENU` being set. If `MENUSELECT` is set, but is 0, 1 or empty, menu selection will always be started during an ambiguous menu completion.

When using the completion system based on shell functions, the `MENUSELECT` parameter should not be used (like the `ZLS_COLORS` and `ZLS_COLOURS` parameters described above). Instead, the `menu` style should be used with the `select=...` keyword.

After menu selection is started, the matches will be listed. If there are more matches than fit on the screen, only the first screenful is shown. The matches to insert into the command line can be selected from this list. In the list one match is highlighted using the value for `ma` from the `ZLS_COLORS` or `ZLS_COLOURS` parameter. The default value for this is '7' which forces the selected match to be highlighted using standout mode on a vt100-compatible terminal. If neither `ZLS_COLORS` nor `ZLS_COLOURS` is set, the same terminal control sequence as for the '%S' escape in prompts is used.

If there are more matches than fit on the screen and the parameter `MENUPROMPT` is set, its value will be shown below the matches. It supports the same escape sequences as `LISTPROMPT`, but the number of the match or line shown will be that of the one where the mark is placed. If its value is the empty string, a default prompt will be used.

The `MENUSCROLL` parameter can be used to specify how the list is scrolled. If the parameter is unset, this is done line by line, if it is set to '0' (zero), the list will scroll half the number of lines of the screen. If the value is positive, it gives the number of lines to scroll and if it is negative, the list will be scrolled the number of lines of the screen minus the (absolute) value.

As for the `ZLS_COLORS`, `ZLS_COLOURS` and `LISTPROMPT` parameters, neither `MENUPROMPT` nor `MENUSCROLL` should be set directly when using the shell function based completion system. Instead, the `select-prompt` and `select-scroll` styles should be used.

The completion code sometimes decides not to show all of the matches in the list. These hidden matches are either matches for which the completion function which added them explicitly requested that they not appear in the list (using the -n option of the `compadd` builtin command) or they are matches which duplicate a string already in the list (because they differ only in things like prefixes or suffixes that are not displayed). In the list used for menu selection, however, even these matches are shown so that it is possible to select them. To highlight such matches the `hi` and `du` capabilities in the `ZLS_COLORS` and `ZLS_COLOURS` parameters are supported for hidden matches of the first and second kind, respectively.

Selecting matches is done by moving the mark around using the zle movement functions. When not all matches can be shown on the screen at the same time, the list will scroll up and down when crossing the top or bottom line. The following zle functions have special meaning during menu selection. Note that the following always perform the same task within the menu selection map and cannot be replaced by user defined widgets, nor can the set of functions be extended:

`accept-line, accept-search`
> accept the current match and leave menu selection (but do not cause the command line to be accepted)

`send-break`
> leaves menu selection and restores the previous contents of the command line

`redisplay, clear-screen`
> execute their normal function without leaving menu selection

`accept-and-hold, accept-and-menu-complete`
> accept the currently inserted match and continue selection allowing to select the next match to insert into the line

`accept-and-infer-next-history`
> accepts the current match and then tries completion with menu selection again; in the case of files this allows one to select a directory and immediately attempt to complete files in it; if there are no matches, a message is shown and one can use **undo** to go back to completion on the previous level, every other key leaves menu selection (including the other zle functions which are otherwise special during menu selection)

`undo`
> removes matches inserted during the menu selection by one of the three functions before

`down-history, down-line-or-history`
`vi-down-line-or-history, down-line-or-search`
> moves the mark one line down

`up-history, up-line-or-history`
`vi-up-line-or-history, up-line-or-search`
> moves the mark one line up

`forward-char, vi-forward-char`
> moves the mark one column right

`backward-char, vi-backward-char`
> moves the mark one column left

`forward-word`, `vi-forward-word`
`vi-forward-word-end`, `emacs-forward-word`
>   moves the mark one screenful down

`backward-word`, `vi-backward-word`, `emacs-backward-word`
>   moves the mark one screenful up

`vi-forward-blank-word`, `vi-forward-blank-word-end`
>   moves the mark to the first line of the next group of matches

`vi-backward-blank-word`
>   moves the mark to the last line of the previous group of matches

`beginning-of-history`
>   moves the mark to the first line

`end-of-history`
>   moves the mark to the last line

`beginning-of-buffer-or-history`, `beginning-of-line`
`beginning-of-line-hist`, `vi-beginning-of-line`
>   moves the mark to the leftmost column

`end-of-buffer-or-history`, `end-of-line`
`end-of-line-hist`, `vi-end-of-line`
>   moves the mark to the rightmost column

`complete-word`, `menu-complete`, `expand-or-complete`
`expand-or-complete-prefix`, `menu-expand-or-complete`
>   moves the mark to the next match

`reverse-menu-complete`
>   moves the mark to the previous match

`vi-insert`
>   this toggles between normal and interactive mode; in interactive mode the keys bound to **self-insert** and **self-insert-unmeta** insert into the command line as in normal editing mode but without leaving menu selection; after each character completion is tried again and the list changes to contain only the new matches; the completion widgets make the longest unambiguous string be inserted in the command line and **undo** and **backward-delete-char** go back to the previous set of matches

`history-incremental-search-forward`
`history-incremental-search-backward`
>   this starts incremental searches in the list of completions displayed; in this mode, **accept-line** only leaves incremental search, going back to the normal menu selection mode

All movement functions wrap around at the edges; any other zle function not listed leaves menu selection and executes that function. It is possible to make widgets in the above list do the same by using the form of the widget with a '.' in front. For example, the widget '.accept-line' has the effect of leaving menu selection and accepting the entire command line.

During this selection the widget uses the keymap `menuselect`. Any key that is not defined in this keymap or that is bound to `undefined-key` is looked up in the keymap currently selected. This is used to ensure that the most important keys used during selection (namely the cursor keys, return, and TAB) have sensible defaults. However, keys in the `menuselect` keymap can be modified directly using the `bindkey` builtin command (see Section 22.32 [The zsh/zle Module], page 378). For example, to make the return key leave menu selection without accepting the match currently selected one could call

```
bindkey -M menuselect '^M' send-break
```

after loading the `zsh/complist` module.

22.8 The zsh/computil Module

The `zsh/computil` module adds several builtin commands that are used by some of the completion functions in the completion system based on shell functions (see Chapter 20 [Completion System], page 242,). Except for `compquote` these builtin commands are very specialised and thus not very interesting when writing your own completion functions. In summary, these builtin commands are:

`comparguments`

> This is used by the `_arguments` function to do the argument and command line parsing. Like `compdescribe` it has an option `-i` to do the parsing and initialize some internal state and various options to access the state information to decide what should be completed.

`compdescribe`

> This is used by the `_describe` function to build the displays for the matches and to get the strings to add as matches with their options. On the first call one of the options `-i` or `-I` should be supplied as the first argument. In the first case, display strings without the descriptions will be generated, in the second case, the string used to separate the matches from their descriptions must be given as the second argument and the descriptions (if any) will be shown. All other arguments are like the definition arguments to `_describe` itself.

> Once `compdescribe` has been called with either the `-i` or the `-I` option, it can be repeatedly called with the `-g` option and the names of four parameters as its arguments. This will step through the different sets of matches and store the value of `compstate[list]` in the first scalar, the options for `compadd` in the second array, the matches in the third array, and the strings to be displayed in the completion listing in the fourth array. The arrays may then be directly given to `compadd` to register the matches with the completion code.

`compfiles`

> Used by the `_path_files` function to optimize complex recursive filename generation (globbing). It does three things. With the `-p` and `-P` options it builds the glob patterns to use, including the paths already handled and trying to optimize the patterns with respect to the prefix and suffix from the line and the match specification currently used. The `-i` option does the directory tests for the `ignore-parents` style and the `-r` option tests if a component for some of

the matches are equal to the string on the line and removes all other matches if that is true.

compgroups

Used by the **_tags** function to implement the internals of the **group-order** style. This only takes its arguments as names of completion groups and creates the groups for it (all six types: sorted and unsorted, both without removing duplicates, with removing all duplicates and with removing consecutive duplicates).

compquote [**-p**] *names* ...

There may be reasons to write completion functions that have to add the matches using the **-Q** option to **compadd** and perform quoting themselves. Instead of interpreting the first character of the **all_quotes** key of the **compstate** special association and using the **q** flag for parameter expansions, one can use this builtin command. The arguments are the names of scalar or array parameters and the values of these parameters are quoted as needed for the innermost quoting level. If the **-p** option is given, quoting is done as if there is some prefix before the values of the parameters, so that a leading equal sign will not be quoted.

The return status is non-zero in case of an error and zero otherwise.

comptags
comptry   These implement the internals of the tags mechanism.

compvalues

Like **comparguments**, but for the **_values** function.

22.9 The zsh/curses Module

The **zsh/curses** module makes available one builtin command and various parameters.

22.9.1 Builtin

```
zcurses init
zcurses end
zcurses addwin targetwin nlines ncols begin_y begin_x [ parentwin ]
zcurses delwin targetwin
zcurses refresh [ targetwin ... ]
zcurses touch targetwin ...
zcurses move targetwin new_y new_x
zcurses clear targetwin [ redraw | eol | bot ]
zcurses position targetwin array
zcurses char targetwin character
zcurses string targetwin string
zcurses border targetwin border
zcurses attr targetwin [ [+|-]attribute | fg_col/bg_col ] [...]
zcurses bg targetwin [ [+|-]attribute | fg_col/bg_col | @char ] [...]
zcurses scroll targetwin [ on | off | [+|-]lines ]
zcurses input targetwin [ param [ kparam [ mparam ] ] ]
zcurses mouse [ delay num | [+|-]motion ]
zcurses timeout targetwin intval
zcurses querychar targetwin [ param ]
zcurses resize height width [ endwin | nosave | endwin_nosave ]
```

Manipulate curses windows. All uses of this command should be bracketed by 'zcurses init' to initialise use of curses, and 'zcurses end' to end it; omitting 'zcurses end' can cause the terminal to be in an unwanted state.

The subcommand **addwin** creates a window with *nlines* lines and *ncols* columns. Its upper left corner will be placed at row *begin_y* and column *begin_x* of the screen. *targetwin* is a string and refers to the name of a window that is not currently assigned. Note in particular the curses convention that vertical values appear before horizontal values.

If **addwin** is given an existing window as the final argument, the new window is created as a subwindow of *parentwin*. This differs from an ordinary new window in that the memory of the window contents is shared with the parent's memory. Subwindows must be deleted before their parent. Note that the coordinates of subwindows are relative to the screen, not the parent, as with other windows.

Use the subcommand **delwin** to delete a window created with **addwin**. Note that **end** does *not* implicitly delete windows, and that **delwin** does not erase the screen image of the window.

The window corresponding to the full visible screen is called **stdscr**; it always exists after 'zcurses init' and cannot be delete with **delwin**.

The subcommand **refresh** will refresh window *targetwin*; this is necessary to make any pending changes (such as characters you have prepared for output with **char**) visible on the screen. **refresh** without an argument causes the screen to be cleared and redrawn. If multiple windows are given, the screen is updated once at the end.

The subcommand **touch** marks the *targetwin*s listed as changed. This is necessary before **refresh**ing windows if a window that was in front of another window (which may be **stdscr**) is deleted.

The subcommand **move** moves the cursor position in *targetwin* to new coordinates *new_y* and *new_x*. Note that the subcommand **string** (but not the subcommand **char**) advances the cursor position over the characters added.

The subcommand **clear** erases the contents of *targetwin*. One (and no more than one) of three options may be specified. With the option **redraw**, in addition the next **refresh** of *targetwin* will cause the screen to be cleared and repainted. With the option **eol**, *targetwin* is only cleared to the end of the current cursor line. With the option **bot**, *targetwin* is cleared to the end of the window, i.e everything to the right and below the cursor is cleared.

The subcommand **position** writes various positions associated with *targetwin* into the array named *array*. These are, in order:

-     The y and x coordinates of the cursor relative to the top left of *targetwin*

-     The y and x coordinates of the top left of *targetwin* on the screen

-     The size of *targetwin* in y and x dimensions.

Outputting characters and strings are achieved by **char** and **string** respectively.

To draw a border around window *targetwin*, use **border**. Note that the border is not subsequently handled specially: in other words, the border is simply a set of characters output at the edge of the window. Hence it can be overwritten, can scroll off the window, etc.

The subcommand **attr** will set *targetwin*'s attributes or foreground/background color pair for any successive character output. Each *attribute* given on the line may be prepended by a **+** to set or a **-** to unset that attribute; **+** is assumed if absent. The attributes supported are **blink**, **bold**, **dim**, **reverse**, **standout**, and **underline**.

Each *fg_col/bg_col* attribute (to be read as '*fg_col* on *bg_col*') sets the foreground and background color for character output. The color **default** is sometimes available (in particular if the library is ncurses), specifying the foreground or background color with which the terminal started. The color pair **default/default** is always available. To use more than the 8 named colors (red, green, etc.) construct the *fg_col/bg_col* pairs where *fg_col* and *bg_col* are decimal integers, e.g **128/200**. The maximum color value is 254 if the terminal supports 256 colors.

bg overrides the color and other attributes of all characters in the window. Its usual use is to set the background initially, but it will overwrite the attributes of any characters at the time when it is called. In addition to the arguments allowed with **attr**, an argument **@***char* specifies a character to be shown in otherwise blank areas of the window. Owing to limitations of curses this cannot be a multibyte character (use of ASCII characters only is recommended). As the specified set of attributes override the existing background, turning attributes off in the arguments is not useful, though this does not cause an error.

The subcommand `scroll` can be used with `on` or `off` to enabled or disable scrolling of a window when the cursor would otherwise move below the window due to typing or output. It can also be used with a positive or negative integer to scroll the window up or down the given number of lines without changing the current cursor position (which therefore appears to move in the opposite direction relative to the window). In the second case, if scrolling is `off` it is temporarily turned `on` to allow the window to be scrolled.

The subcommand `input` reads a single character from the window without echoing it back. If *param* is supplied the character is assigned to the parameter *param*, else it is assigned to the parameter `REPLY`.

If both *param* and *kparam* are supplied, the key is read in 'keypad' mode. In this mode special keys such as function keys and arrow keys return the name of the key in the parameter *kparam*. The key names are the macros defined in the `curses.h` or `ncurses.h` with the prefix 'KEY_' removed; see also the description of the parameter `zcurses_keycodes` below. Other keys cause a value to be set in *param* as before. On a successful return only one of *param* or *kparam* contains a non-empty string; the other is set to an empty string.

If *mparam* is also supplied, `input` attempts to handle mouse input. This is only available with the ncurses library; mouse handling can be detected by checking for the exit status of 'zcurses mouse' with no arguments. If a mouse button is clicked (or double- or triple-clicked, or pressed or released with a configurable delay from being clicked) then `kparam` is set to the string `MOUSE`, and *mparam* is set to an array consisting of the following elements:

- An identifier to discriminate different input devices; this is only rarely useful.

- The x, y and z coordinates of the mouse click relative to the full screen, as three elements in that order (i.e. the y coordinate is, unusually, after the x coordinate). The z coordinate is only available for a few unusual input devices and is otherwise set to zero.

- Any events that occurred as separate items; usually there will be just one. An event consists of `PRESSED`, `RELEASED`, `CLICKED`, `DOUBLE_CLICKED` or `TRIPLE_CLICKED` followed immediately (in the same element) by the number of the button.

- If the shift key was pressed, the string `SHIFT`.

- If the control key was pressed, the string `CTRL`.

- If the alt key was pressed, the string `ALT`.

Not all mouse events may be passed through to the terminal window; most terminal emulators handle some mouse events themselves. Note that the ncurses manual implies that using input both with and without mouse handling may cause the mouse cursor to appear and disappear.

The subcommand `mouse` can be used to configure the use of the mouse. There is no window argument; mouse options are global. 'zcurses mouse' with no arguments returns status 0 if mouse handling is possible, else status 1. Otherwise, the possible arguments (which may be combined on the same command line) are as follows. `delay` *num* sets the maximum delay in milliseconds between press and release events to be considered as a click; the value 0 disables click resolution, and the default is one sixth of a second. `motion` proceeded by an optional '+' (the default) or − turns on or off reporting of mouse motion in addition to clicks, presses and releases, which are always reported. However, it appears reports for mouse motion are not currently implemented.

The subcommand `timeout` specifies a timeout value for input from *targetwin*. If *intval* is negative, 'zcurses input' waits indefinitely for a character to be typed; this is the default. If *intval* is zero, 'zcurses input' returns immediately; if there is typeahead it is returned, else no input is done and status 1 is returned. If *intval* is positive, 'zcurses input' waits *intval* milliseconds for input and if there is none at the end of that period returns status 1.

The subcommand `querychar` queries the character at the current cursor position. The return values are stored in the array named *param* if supplied, else in the array `reply`. The first value is the character (which may be a multibyte character if the system supports them); the second is the color pair in the usual *fg_col*/*bg_col* notation, or 0 if color is not supported. Any attributes other than color that apply to the character, as set with the subcommand `attr`, appear as additional elements.

The subcommand `resize` resizes `stdscr` and all windows to given dimensions (windows that stick out from the new dimensions are resized down). The underlying curses extension (`resize_term call`) can be unavailable. To verify, zeroes can be used for *height* and *width*. If the result of the subcommand is 0, resize_term is available (2 otherwise). Tests show that resizing can be normally accomplished by calling `zcurses end` and `zcurses refresh`. The `resize` subcommand is provided for versatility. Multiple system configurations have been checked and `zcurses end` and `zcurses refresh` are still needed for correct terminal state after resize. To invoke them with `resize`, use *endwin* argument. Using *nosave* argument will cause new terminal state to not be saved internally by `zcurses`. This is also provided for versatility and should normally be not needed.

22.9.2 Parameters

ZCURSES_COLORS

> Readonly integer. The maximum number of colors the terminal supports. This value is initialised by the curses library and is not available until the first time `zcurses init` is run.

ZCURSES_COLOR_PAIRS

> Readonly integer. The maximum number of color pairs *fg_col*/*bg_col* that may be defined in 'zcurses attr' commands; note this limit applies to all color pairs that have been used whether or not they are currently active. This value

is initialised by the curses library and is not available until the first time `zcurses init` is run.

`zcurses_attrs`

Readonly array. The attributes supported by `zsh/curses`; available as soon as the module is loaded.

`zcurses_colors`

Readonly array. The colors supported by `zsh/curses`; available as soon as the module is loaded.

`zcurses_keycodes`

Readonly array. The values that may be returned in the second parameter supplied to 'zcurses input' in the order in which they are defined internally by curses. Not all function keys are listed, only `F0`; curses reserves space for `F0` up to `F63`.

`zcurses_windows`

Readonly array. The current list of windows, i.e. all windows that have been created with 'zcurses addwin' and not removed with 'zcurses delwin'.

22.10 The zsh/datetime Module

The `zsh/datetime` module makes available one builtin command:

`strftime` [`-s` scalar] format [epochtime [nanoseconds]]
`strftime -r` [`-q`] [`-s` scalar] format timestring

Output the date in the format specified. With no epochtime, the current system date/time is used; optionally, epochtime may be used to specify the number of seconds since the epoch, and nanoseconds may additionally be used to specify the number of nanoseconds past the second (otherwise that number is assumed to be 0). See man page strftime(3) for details. The zsh extensions described in Chapter 13 [Prompt Expansion], page 39, are also available.

`-q`　　Run quietly; suppress printing of all error messages described below. Errors for invalid epochtime values are always printed.

`-r`　　With the option `-r` (reverse), use format to parse the input string timestring and output the number of seconds since the epoch at which the time occurred. The parsing is implemented by the system function `strptime`; see man page strptime(3). This means that zsh format extensions are not available, but for reverse lookup they are not required.

In most implementations of `strftime` any timezone in the timestring is ignored and the local timezone declared by the `TZ` environment variable is used; other parameters are set to zero if not present.

If timestring does not match format the command returns status 1 and prints an error message. If timestring matches format but not all characters in timestring were used, the conversion succeeds but also prints an error message.

> If either of the system functions `strptime` or `mktime` is not available, status 2 is returned and an error message is printed.

-s *scalar*   Assign the date string (or epoch time in seconds if -r is given) to *scalar* instead of printing it.

> Note that depending on the system's declared integral time type, `strftime` may produce incorrect results for epoch times greater than 2147483647 which corresponds to 2038-01-19 03:14:07 +0000.

The `zsh/datetime` module makes available several parameters; all are readonly:

EPOCHREALTIME

> A floating point value representing the number of seconds since the epoch. The notional accuracy is to nanoseconds if the `clock_gettime` call is available and to microseconds otherwise, but in practice the range of double precision floating point and shell scheduling latencies may be significant effects.

EPOCHSECONDS

> An integer value representing the number of seconds since the epoch.

epochtime

> An array value containing the number of seconds since the epoch in the first element and the remainder of the time since the epoch in nanoseconds in the second element. To ensure the two elements are consistent the array should be copied or otherwise referenced as a single substitution before the values are used. The following idiom may be used:
>
> ```
> for secs nsecs in $epochtime; do
>     ...
> done
> ```

22.11 The zsh/db/gdbm Module

The `zsh/db/gdbm` module is used to create "tied" associative arrays that interface to database files. If the GDBM interface is not available, the builtins defined by this module will report an error. This module is also intended as a prototype for creating additional database interfaces, so the `ztie` builtin may move to a more generic module in the future.

The builtins in this module are:

ztie -d db/gdbm -f *filename* [-r] *arrayname*

> Open the GDBM database identified by *filename* and, if successful, create the associative array *arrayname* linked to the file. To create a local tied array, the parameter must first be declared, so commands similar to the following would be executed inside a function scope:
>
> ```
> local -A sampledb
> ztie -d db/gdbm -f sample.gdbm sampledb
> ```
>
> The -r option opens the database file for reading only, creating a parameter with the readonly attribute. Without this option, using 'ztie' on a file for which the user does not have write permission is an error. If writable, the database is

opened synchronously so fields changed in *arrayname* are immediately written to *filename*.

Changes to the file modes *filename* after it has been opened do not alter the state of *arrayname*, but 'typeset -r *arrayname*' works as expected.

zuntie [-u] *arrayname* ...
> Close the GDBM database associated with each *arrayname* and then unset the parameter. The -u option forces an unset of parameters made readonly with 'ztie -r'.
>
> This happens automatically if the parameter is explicitly unset or its local scope (function) ends. Note that a readonly parameter may not be explicitly unset, so the only way to unset a global parameter created with 'ztie -r' is to use 'zuntie -u'.

zgdbmpath *parametername*
> Put path to database file assigned to *parametername* into REPLY scalar.

zgdbm_tied
> Array holding names of all tied parameters.

The fields of an associative array tied to GDBM are neither cached nor otherwise stored in memory, they are read from or written to the database on each reference. Thus, for example, the values in a readonly array may be changed by a second writer of the same database file.

22.12 The zsh/deltochar Module

The zsh/deltochar module makes available two ZLE functions:

delete-to-char
> Read a character from the keyboard, and delete from the cursor position up to and including the next (or, with repeat count *n*, the *n*th) instance of that character. Negative repeat counts mean delete backwards.

zap-to-char
> This behaves like delete-to-char, except that the final occurrence of the character itself is not deleted.

22.13 The zsh/example Module

The zsh/example module makes available one builtin command:

example [-flags] [*args* ...]
> Displays the flags and arguments it is invoked with.

The purpose of the module is to serve as an example of how to write a module.

22.14 The zsh/files Module

The `zsh/files` module makes available some common commands for file manipulation as builtins; these commands are probably not needed for many normal situations but can be useful in emergency recovery situations with constrained resources. The commands do not implement all features now required by relevant standards committees.

For all commands, a variant beginning `zf_` is also available and loaded automatically. Using the features capability of zmodload will let you load only those names you want. Note that it's possible to load only the builtins with zsh-specific names using the following command:

```
zmodload -m -F zsh/files b:zf_\*
```

The commands loaded by default are:

chgrp [-hRs] *group filename* ...

> Changes group of files specified. This is equivalent to **chown** with a *user-spec* argument of ':*group*'.

chown [-hRs] *user-spec filename* ...

> Changes ownership and group of files specified.

> The *user-spec* can be in four forms:

> | | |
> |---|---|
> | *user* | change owner to *user*; do not change group |
> | *user*:: | change owner to *user*; do not change group |
> | *user*: | change owner to *user*; change group to *user*'s primary group |

> *user*:*group*
> > change owner to *user*; change group to *group*

> | | |
> |---|---|
> | :*group* | do not change owner; change group to *group* |

> In each case, the ':' may instead be a '.'. The rule is that if there is a ':' then the separator is ':', otherwise if there is a '.' then the separator is '.', otherwise there is no separator.

> Each of *user* and *group* may be either a username (or group name, as appropriate) or a decimal user ID (group ID). Interpretation as a name takes precedence, if there is an all-numeric username (or group name).

> If the target is a symbolic link, the **-h** option causes **chown** to set the ownership of the link instead of its target.

> The **-R** option causes **chown** to recursively descend into directories, changing the ownership of all files in the directory after changing the ownership of the directory itself.

> The **-s** option is a zsh extension to **chown** functionality. It enables paranoid behaviour, intended to avoid security problems involving a **chown** being tricked into affecting files other than the ones intended. It will refuse to follow symbolic links, so that (for example) "**chown luser /tmp/foo/passwd**" can't accidentally chown /etc/passwd if /tmp/foo happens to be a link to /etc. It will also check where it is after leaving directories, so that a recursive chown of a deep directory tree can't end up recursively chowning /usr as a result of directories being moved up the tree.

ln [-dfhins] *filename dest*
ln [-dfhins] *filename ... dir*

> Creates hard (or, with -s, symbolic) links. In the first form, the specified *destination* is created, as a link to the specified *filename*. In the second form, each of the *filenames* is taken in turn, and linked to a pathname in the specified *directory* that has the same last pathname component.
>
> Normally, ln will not attempt to create hard links to directories. This check can be overridden using the -d option. Typically only the super-user can actually succeed in creating hard links to directories. This does not apply to symbolic links in any case.
>
> By default, existing files cannot be replaced by links. The -i option causes the user to be queried about replacing existing files. The -f option causes existing files to be silently deleted, without querying. -f takes precedence.
>
> The -h and -n options are identical and both exist for compatibility; either one indicates that if the target is a symlink then it should not be dereferenced. Typically this is used in combination with -sf so that if an existing link points to a directory then it will be removed, instead of followed. If this option is used with multiple filenames and the target is a symbolic link pointing to a directory then the result is an error.

mkdir [-p] [-m *mode*] *dir ...*

> Creates directories. With the -p option, non-existing parent directories are first created if necessary, and there will be no complaint if the directory already exists. The -m option can be used to specify (in octal) a set of file permissions for the created directories, otherwise mode 777 modified by the current umask (see man page umask(2)) is used.

mv [-fi] *filename dest*
mv [-fi] *filename ... dir*

> Moves files. In the first form, the specified *filename* is moved to the specified *destination*. In the second form, each of the *filenames* is taken in turn, and moved to a pathname in the specified *directory* that has the same last pathname component.
>
> By default, the user will be queried before replacing any file that the user cannot write to, but writable files will be silently removed. The -i option causes the user to be queried about replacing any existing files. The -f option causes any existing files to be silently deleted, without querying. -f takes precedence.
>
> Note that this mv will not move files across devices. Historical versions of mv, when actual renaming is impossible, fall back on copying and removing files; if this behaviour is desired, use cp and rm manually. This may change in a future version.

rm [-dfirs] *filename ...*

> Removes files and directories specified.
>
> Normally, rm will not remove directories (except with the -r option). The -d option causes rm to try removing directories with unlink (see man page unlink(2)), the same method used for files. Typically only the super-user can

actually succeed in unlinking directories in this way. `-d` takes precedence over `-r`.

By default, the user will be queried before removing any file that the user cannot write to, but writable files will be silently removed. The `-i` option causes the user to be queried about removing any files. The `-f` option causes files to be silently deleted, without querying, and suppresses all error indications. `-f` takes precedence.

The `-r` option causes `rm` to recursively descend into directories, deleting all files in the directory before removing the directory with the `rmdir` system call (see man page rmdir(2)).

The `-s` option is a zsh extension to `rm` functionality. It enables paranoid behaviour, intended to avoid common security problems involving a root-run `rm` being tricked into removing files other than the ones intended. It will refuse to follow symbolic links, so that (for example) "`rm /tmp/foo/passwd`" can't accidentally remove `/etc/passwd` if `/tmp/foo` happens to be a link to `/etc`. It will also check where it is after leaving directories, so that a recursive removal of a deep directory tree can't end up recursively removing `/usr` as a result of directories being moved up the tree.

`rmdir` *dir* ...

Removes empty directories specified.

`sync`   Calls the system call of the same name (see man page sync(2)), which flushes dirty buffers to disk. It might return before the I/O has actually been completed.

22.15 The zsh/langinfo Module

The `zsh/langinfo` module makes available one parameter:

`langinfo` An associative array that maps langinfo elements to their values.

Your implementation may support a number of the following keys:

CODESET, D_T_FMT, D_FMT, T_FMT, RADIXCHAR, THOUSEP, YESEXPR, NOEXPR, CRNCYSTR, ABDAY_{1..7}, DAY_{1..7}, ABMON_{1..12}, MON_{1..12}, T_FMT_AMPM, AM_STR, PM_STR, ERA, ERA_D_FMT, ERA_D_T_FMT, ERA_T_FMT, ALT_DIGITS

22.16 The zsh/mapfile Module

The `zsh/mapfile` module provides one special associative array parameter of the same name.

`mapfile`   This associative array takes as keys the names of files; the resulting value is the content of the file. The value is treated identically to any other text coming from a parameter. The value may also be assigned to, in which case the file in question is written (whether or not it originally existed); or an element may be unset, which will delete the file in question. For example, '`vared mapfile[myfile]`' works as expected, editing the file '`myfile`'.

When the array is accessed as a whole, the keys are the names of files in the current directory, and the values are empty (to save a huge overhead in memory). Thus `${(k)mapfile}` has the same affect as the glob operator `*(D)`, since files beginning with a dot are not special. Care must be taken with expressions such as `rm ${(k)mapfile}`, which will delete every file in the current directory without the usual '`rm *`' test.

The parameter `mapfile` may be made read-only; in that case, files referenced may not be written or deleted.

A file may conveniently be read into an array as one line per element with the form '*array*=("${(f@)mapfile[*filename*]}")'. The double quotes and the '`@`' are necessary to prevent empty lines from being removed. Note that if the file ends with a newline, the shell will split on the final newline, generating an additional empty field; this can be suppressed by using '*array*=("${(f@)${mapfile[*filename*]%$'\n'}}")'.

22.16.1 Limitations

Although reading and writing of the file in question is efficiently handled, zsh's internal memory management may be arbitrarily baroque; however, `mapfile` is usually very much more efficient than anything involving a loop. Note in particular that the whole contents of the file will always reside physically in memory when accessed (possibly multiple times, due to standard parameter substitution operations). In particular, this means handling of sufficiently long files (greater than the machine's swap space, or than the range of the pointer type) will be incorrect.

No errors are printed or flagged for non-existent, unreadable, or unwritable files, as the parameter mechanism is too low in the shell execution hierarchy to make this convenient.

It is unfortunate that the mechanism for loading modules does not yet allow the user to specify the name of the shell parameter to be given the special behaviour.

22.17 The zsh/mathfunc Module

The `zsh/mathfunc` module provides standard mathematical functions for use when evaluating mathematical formulae. The syntax agrees with normal C and FORTRAN conventions, for example,

```
(( f = sin(0.3) ))
```

assigns the sine of 0.3 to the parameter f.

Most functions take floating point arguments and return a floating point value. However, any necessary conversions from or to integer type will be performed automatically by the shell. Apart from `atan` with a second argument and the `abs`, `int` and `float` functions, all functions behave as noted in the manual page for the corresponding C function, except that any arguments out of range for the function in question will be detected by the shell and an error reported.

The following functions take a single floating point argument: `acos`, `acosh`, `asin`, `asinh`, `atan`, `atanh`, `cbrt`, `ceil`, `cos`, `cosh`, `erf`, `erfc`, `exp`, `expm1`, `fabs`, `floor`, `gamma`, `j0`, `j1`, `lgamma`, `log`, `log10`, `log1p`, `log2`, `logb`, `sin`, `sinh`, `sqrt`, `tan`, `tanh`, `y0`, `y1`. The `atan` function can optionally take a second argument, in which case it behaves like the C function `atan2`. The `ilogb` function takes a single floating point argument, but returns an integer.

The function `signgam` takes no arguments, and returns an integer, which is the C variable of the same name, as described in man page gamma(3). Note that it is therefore only useful immediately after a call to `gamma` or `lgamma`. Note also that '`signgam()`' and '`signgam`' are distinct expressions.

The functions `min`, `max`, and `sum` are defined not in this module but in the `zmathfunc` autoloadable function, described in Section 26.10 [Mathematical Functions], page 485.

The following functions take two floating point arguments: `copysign`, `fmod`, `hypot`, `nextafter`.

The following take an integer first argument and a floating point second argument: `jn`, `yn`.

The following take a floating point first argument and an integer second argument: `ldexp`, `scalb`.

The function `abs` does not convert the type of its single argument; it returns the absolute value of either a floating point number or an integer. The functions `float` and `int` convert their arguments into a floating point or integer value (by truncation) respectively.

Note that the C `pow` function is available in ordinary math evaluation as the '`**`' operator and is not provided here.

The function `rand48` is available if your system's mathematical library has the function `erand48(3)`. It returns a pseudo-random floating point number between 0 and 1. It takes a single string optional argument.

If the argument is not present, the random number seed is initialised by three calls to the `rand(3)` function — this produces the same random numbers as the next three values of `$RANDOM`.

If the argument is present, it gives the name of a scalar parameter where the current random number seed will be stored. On the first call, the value must contain at least twelve hexadecimal digits (the remainder of the string is ignored), or the seed will be initialised in the same manner as for a call to `rand48` with no argument. Subsequent calls to `rand48`(*param*) will then maintain the seed in the parameter *param* as a string of twelve hexadecimal digits, with no base signifier. The random number sequences for different parameters are completely independent, and are also independent from that used by calls to `rand48` with no argument.

For example, consider

```
print $(( rand48(seed) ))
print $(( rand48() ))
print $(( rand48(seed) ))
```

Assuming `$seed` does not exist, it will be initialised by the first call. In the second call, the default seed is initialised; note, however, that because of the properties of `rand()` there is a correlation between the seeds used for the two initialisations, so for more secure uses, you should generate your own 12-byte seed. The third call returns to the same sequence of random numbers used in the first call, unaffected by the intervening `rand48()`.

22.18 The zsh/nearcolor Module

The **zsh/nearcolor** module replaces colours specified as hex triplets with the nearest colour in the 88 or 256 colour palettes that are widely used by terminal emulators. By default, 24-bit true colour escape codes are generated when colours are specified using hex triplets. These are not supported by all terminals. The purpose of this module is to make it easier to define colour preferences in a form that can work across a range of terminal emulators.

Aside from the default colour, the ANSI standard for terminal escape codes provides for eight colours. The bright attribute brings this to sixteen. These basic colours are commonly used in terminal applications due to being widely supported. Expanded 88 and 256 colour palettes are also common and, while the first sixteen colours vary somewhat between terminals and configurations, these add a generally consistent and predictable set of colours.

In order to use the **zsh/nearcolor** module, it only needs to be loaded. Thereafter, whenever a colour is specified using a hex triplet, it will be compared against each of the available colours and the closest will be selected. The first sixteen colours are never matched in this process due to being unpredictable.

It isn't possible to reliably detect support for true colour in the terminal emulator. It is therefore recommended to be selective in loading the **zsh/nearcolor** module. For example, the following checks the COLORTERM environment variable:

```
[[ $COLORTERM = *(24bit|truecolor)* ]] || zmodload zsh/nearcolor
```

Note that some terminals accept the true color escape codes but map them internally to a more limited palette in a similar manner to the **zsh/nearcolor** module.

22.19 The zsh/newuser Module

The **zsh/newuser** module is loaded at boot if it is available, the RCS option is set, and the PRIVILEGED option is not set (all three are true by default). This takes place immediately after commands in the global **zshenv** file (typically /etc/zshenv), if any, have been executed. If the module is not available it is silently ignored by the shell; the module may safely be removed from $MODULE_PATH by the administrator if it is not required.

On loading, the module tests if any of the start-up files .zshenv, .zprofile, .zshrc or .zlogin exist in the directory given by the environment variable ZDOTDIR, or the user's home directory if that is not set. The test is not performed and the module halts processing if the shell was in an emulation mode (i.e. had been invoked as some other shell than zsh).

If none of the start-up files were found, the module then looks for the file **newuser** first in a sitewide directory, usually the parent directory of the **site-functions** directory, and if that is not found the module searches in a version-specific directory, usually the parent of the **functions** directory containing version-specific functions. (These directories can be configured when zsh is built using the --enable-site-scriptdir=dir and --enable-scriptdir=dir flags to **configure**, respectively; the defaults are prefix/share/zsh and prefix/share/zsh/$ZSH_VERSION where the default prefix is /usr/local.)

If the file **newuser** is found, it is then sourced in the same manner as a start-up file. The file is expected to contain code to install start-up files for the user, however any valid shell code will be executed.

The `zsh/newuser` module is then unconditionally unloaded.

Note that it is possible to achieve exactly the same effect as the `zsh/newuser` module by adding code to `/etc/zshenv`. The module exists simply to allow the shell to make arrangements for new users without the need for intervention by package maintainers and system administrators.

The script supplied with the module invokes the shell function `zsh-newuser-install`. This may be invoked directly by the user even if the `zsh/newuser` module is disabled. Note, however, that if the module is not installed the function will not be installed either. The function is documented in Section 26.11 [User Configuration Functions], page 489.

22.20 The zsh/parameter Module

The `zsh/parameter` module gives access to some of the internal hash tables used by the shell by defining some special parameters.

options
: The keys for this associative array are the names of the options that can be set and unset using the **setopt** and **unsetopt** builtins. The value of each key is either the string **on** if the option is currently set, or the string **off** if the option is unset. Setting a key to one of these strings is like setting or unsetting the option, respectively. Unsetting a key in this array is like setting it to the value **off**.

commands
: This array gives access to the command hash table. The keys are the names of external commands, the values are the pathnames of the files that would be executed when the command would be invoked. Setting a key in this array defines a new entry in this table in the same way as with the **hash** builtin. Unsetting a key as in '`unset "commands[foo]"`' removes the entry for the given key from the command hash table.

functions
: This associative array maps names of enabled functions to their definitions. Setting a key in it is like defining a function with the name given by the key and the body given by the value. Unsetting a key removes the definition for the function named by the key.

dis_functions
: Like **functions** but for disabled functions.

functions_source
: This readonly associative array maps names of enabled functions to the name of the file containing the source of the function.

: For an autoloaded function that has already been loaded, or marked for autoload with an absolute path, or that has had its path resolved with '`functions -r`', this is the file found for autoloading, resolved to an absolute path.

: For a function defined within the body of a script or sourced file, this is the name of that file. In this case, this is the exact path originally used to that file, which may be a relative path.

: For any other function, including any defined at an interactive prompt or an autoload function whose path has not yet been resolved, this is the empty string.

However, the hash element is reported as defined just so long as the function is present: the keys to this hash are the same as those to `$funcions`.

dis_functions_source

> Like `functions_source` but for disabled functions.

builtins   This associative array gives information about the builtin commands currently enabled. The keys are the names of the builtin commands and the values are either 'undefined' for builtin commands that will automatically be loaded from a module if invoked or 'defined' for builtin commands that are already loaded.

dis_builtins

> Like `builtins` but for disabled builtin commands.

reswords   This array contains the enabled reserved words.

dis_reswords

> Like `reswords` but for disabled reserved words.

patchars   This array contains the enabled pattern characters.

dis_patchars

> Like `patchars` but for disabled pattern characters.

aliases   This maps the names of the regular aliases currently enabled to their expansions.

dis_aliases

> Like `aliases` but for disabled regular aliases.

galiases   Like `aliases`, but for global aliases.

dis_galiases

> Like `galiases` but for disabled global aliases.

saliases   Like `raliases`, but for suffix aliases.

dis_saliases

> Like `saliases` but for disabled suffix aliases.

parameters

> The keys in this associative array are the names of the parameters currently defined. The values are strings describing the type of the parameter, in the same format used by the t parameter flag, see Section 14.3 [Parameter Expansion], page 52, . Setting or unsetting keys in this array is not possible.

modules   An associative array giving information about modules. The keys are the names of the modules loaded, registered to be autoloaded, or aliased. The value says which state the named module is in and is one of the strings 'loaded', 'autoloaded', or 'alias:name', where name is the name the module is aliased to.

> Setting or unsetting keys in this array is not possible.

dirstack   A normal array holding the elements of the directory stack. Note that the output of the **dirs** builtin command includes one more directory, the current working directory.

history   This associative array maps history event numbers to the full history lines. Although it is presented as an associative array, the array of all values (`${history[@]}`) is guaranteed to be returned in order from most recent to oldest history event, that is, by decreasing history event number.

historywords

A special array containing the words stored in the history. These also appear in most to least recent order.

jobdirs   This associative array maps job numbers to the directories from which the job was started (which may not be the current directory of the job).

The keys of the associative arrays are usually valid job numbers, and these are the values output with, for example, `${(k)jobdirs}`. Non-numeric job references may be used when looking up a value; for example, `${jobdirs[%+]}` refers to the current job.

jobtexts   This associative array maps job numbers to the texts of the command lines that were used to start the jobs.

Handling of the keys of the associative array is as described for `jobdirs` above.

jobstates

This associative array gives information about the states of the jobs currently known. The keys are the job numbers and the values are strings of the form '*job-state*:*mark*:*pid*=*state*...'. The *job-state* gives the state the whole job is currently in, one of '**running**', '**suspended**', or '**done**'. The *mark* is '**+**' for the current job, '**-**' for the previous job and empty otherwise. This is followed by one '*:pid*=*state*' for every process in the job. The *pids* are, of course, the process IDs and the *state* describes the state of that process.

Handling of the keys of the associative array is as described for `jobdirs` above.

nameddirs

This associative array maps the names of named directories to the pathnames they stand for.

userdirs   This associative array maps user names to the pathnames of their home directories.

usergroups

This associative array maps names of system groups of which the current user is a member to the corresponding group identifiers. The contents are the same as the groups output by the `id` command.

funcfiletrace

This array contains the absolute line numbers and corresponding file names for the point where the current function, sourced file, or (if `EVAL_LINENO` is set) `eval` command was called. The array is of the same length as `funcsourcetrace` and `functrace`, but differs from `funcsourcetrace` in that the line and file are the point of call, not the point of definition, and differs from `functrace` in that all values are absolute line numbers in files, rather than relative to the start of a function, if any.

funcsourcetrace

This array contains the file names and line numbers of the points where the functions, sourced files, and (if `EVAL_LINENO` is set) `eval` commands currently being executed were defined. The line number is the line where the 'function name' or 'name ()' started. In the case of an autoloaded function the line number is reported as zero. The format of each element is *filename*:*lineno*.

For functions autoloaded from a file in native zsh format, where only the body of the function occurs in the file, or for files that have been executed by the `source` or '.' builtins, the trace information is shown as *filename*:*0*, since the entire file is the definition. The source file name is resolved to an absolute path when the function is loaded or the path to it otherwise resolved.

Most users will be interested in the information in the `funcfiletrace` array instead.

funcstack

This array contains the names of the functions, sourced files, and (if `EVAL_LINENO` is set) `eval` commands. currently being executed. The first element is the name of the function using the parameter.

The standard shell array `zsh_eval_context` can be used to determine the type of shell construct being executed at each depth: note, however, that is in the opposite order, with the most recent item last, and it is more detailed, for example including an entry for `toplevel`, the main shell code being executed either interactively or from a script, which is not present in `$funcstack`.

functrace

This array contains the names and line numbers of the callers corresponding to the functions currently being executed. The format of each element is *name*:*lineno*. Callers are also shown for sourced files; the caller is the point where the `source` or '.' command was executed.

22.21 The zsh/pcre Module

The `zsh/pcre` module makes some commands available as builtins:

pcre_compile [`-aimxs`] *PCRE*

Compiles a perl-compatible regular expression.

Option `-a` will force the pattern to be anchored. Option `-i` will compile a case-insensitive pattern. Option `-m` will compile a multi-line pattern; that is, ^ and $ will match newlines within the pattern. Option `-x` will compile an extended pattern, wherein whitespace and # comments are ignored. Option `-s` makes the dot metacharacter match all characters, including those that indicate newline.

pcre_study

Studies the previously-compiled PCRE which may result in faster matching.

pcre_match [`-v` *var*] [`-a` *arr*] [`-n` *offset*] [`-b`] *string*

Returns successfully if `string` matches the previously-compiled PCRE.

Upon successful match, if the expression captures substrings within parentheses, `pcre_match` will set the array `match` to those substrings, unless the `-a` option is given, in which case it will set the array *arr*. Similarly, the variable MATCH will be set to the entire matched portion of the string, unless the -v option is given, in which case the variable *var* will be set. No variables are altered if there is no successful match. A -n option starts searching for a match from the byte *offset* position in *string*. If the -b option is given, the variable ZPCRE_OP will be set to an offset pair string, representing the byte offset positions of the entire matched portion within the *string*. For example, a ZPCRE_OP set to "32 45" indicates that the matched portion began on byte offset 32 and ended on byte offset 44. Here, byte offset position 45 is the position directly after the matched portion. Keep in mind that the byte position isn't necessarily the same as the character position when UTF-8 characters are involved. Consequently, the byte offset positions are only to be relied on in the context of using them for subsequent searches on *string*, using an offset position as an argument to the -n option. This is mostly used to implement the "find all non-overlapping matches" functionality.

A simple example of "find all non-overlapping matches":

```
string="The following zip codes: 78884 90210 99513"
pcre_compile -m "\d{5}"
accum=()
pcre_match -b -- $string
while [[ $? -eq 0 ]] do
    b=($=ZPCRE_OP)
    accum+=$MATCH
    pcre_match -b -n $b[2] -- $string
done
print -l $accum
```

The **zsh/pcre** module makes available the following test condition:

expr -pcre-match *pcre*

> Matches a string against a perl-compatible regular expression.

> For example,

```
[[ "$text" -pcre-match ^d+$ ]] &&
print text variable contains only "d's".
```

> If the REMATCH_PCRE option is set, the =~ operator is equivalent to -pcre-match, and the NO_CASE_MATCH option may be used. Note that NO_CASE_MATCH never applies to the **pcre_match** builtin, instead use the -i switch of **pcre_compile**.

22.22 The zsh/param/private Module

The **zsh/param/private** module is used to create parameters whose scope is limited to the current function body, and *not* to other functions called by the current function.

This module provides a single autoloaded builtin:

private [{+|-}AHUahlprtux] [{+|-}EFLRZi [*n*]] [*name*[=*value*] ...]

> The **private** builtin accepts all the same options and arguments as **local** (Chapter 17 [Shell Builtin Commands], page 139) except for the '-T' option. Tied parameters may not be made private.

If used at the top level (outside a function scope), `private` creates a normal parameter in the same manner as `declare` or `typeset`. A warning about this is printed if `WARN_CREATE_GLOBAL` is set (Chapter 16 [Options], page 110). Used inside a function scope, `private` creates a local parameter similar to one declared with `local`, except having special properties noted below.

Special parameters which expose or manipulate internal shell state, such as `ARGC`, `argv`, `COLUMNS`, `LINES`, `UID`, `EUID`, `IFS`, `PROMPT`, `RANDOM`, `SECONDS`, etc., cannot be made private unless the '`-h`' option is used to hide the special meaning of the parameter. This may change in the future.

As with other `typeset` equivalents, `private` is both a builtin and a reserved word, so arrays may be assigned with parenthesized word list *name*=(*value*...) syntax. However, the reserved word '`private`' is not available until `zsh/param/private` is loaded, so care must be taken with order of execution and parsing for function definitions which use `private`. To compensate for this, the module also adds the option '`-P`' to the '`local`' builtin to declare private parameters.

For example, this construction fails if `zsh/param/private` has not yet been loaded when '`bad_declaration`' is defined:

```
bad_declaration() {
  zmodload zsh/param/private
  private array=( one two three )
}
```

This construction works because `local` is already a keyword, and the module is loaded before the statement is executed:

```
good_declaration() {
  zmodload zsh/param/private
  local -P array=( one two three )
}
```

The following is usable in scripts but may have trouble with `autoload`:

```
zmodload zsh/param/private
iffy_declaration() {
  private array=( one two three )
}
```

The `private` builtin may always be used with scalar assignments and for declarations without assignments.

Parameters declared with `private` have the following properties:

- Within the function body where it is declared, the parameter behaves as a local, except as noted above for tied or special parameters.

- The type of a parameter declared private cannot be changed in the scope where it was declared, even if the parameter is unset. Thus an array cannot be assigned to a private scalar, etc.

- Within any other function called by the declaring function, the private parameter does *NOT* hide other parameters of the same name, so for example a global parameter of the same name is visible and may be assigned or unset. This includes calls to anonymous functions, although that may also change in the future.

- An exported private remains in the environment of inner scopes but appears unset for the current shell in those scopes. Generally, exporting private parameters should be avoided.

Note that this differs from the static scope defined by compiled languages derived from C, in that the a new call to the same function creates a new scope, i.e., the parameter is still associated with the call stack rather than with the function definition. It differs from ksh 'typeset -S' because the syntax used to define the function has no bearing on whether the parameter scope is respected.

22.23 The zsh/regex Module

The **zsh/regex** module makes available the following test condition:

expr **-regex-match** *regex*

Matches a string against a POSIX extended regular expression. On successful match, matched portion of the string will normally be placed in the **MATCH** variable. If there are any capturing parentheses within the regex, then the **match** array variable will contain those. If the match is not successful, then the variables will not be altered.

For example,

```
[[ alphabetical -regex-match ^a([^a]+)a([^a]+)a ]] &&
print -l $MATCH X $match
```

If the option **REMATCH_PCRE** is not set, then the =~ operator will automatically load this module as needed and will invoke the **-regex-match** operator.

If **BASH_REMATCH** is set, then the array **BASH_REMATCH** will be set instead of **MATCH** and **match**.

22.24 The zsh/sched Module

The **zsh/sched** module makes available one builtin command and one parameter.

sched [-o] [+]*hh*:*mm*[:*ss*] *command* ...
sched [-o] [+]*seconds command* ...
sched [-*item*]

Make an entry in the scheduled list of commands to execute. The time may be specified in either absolute or relative time, and either as hours, minutes and (optionally) seconds separated by a colon, or seconds alone. An absolute number of seconds indicates the time since the epoch (1970/01/01 00:00); this is useful in combination with the features in the **zsh/datetime** module, see Section 22.10 [The zsh/datetime Module], page 345.

With no arguments, prints the list of scheduled commands. If the scheduled command has the -o flag set, this is shown at the start of the command.

With the argument '-*item*', removes the given item from the list. The numbering of the list is continuous and entries are in time order, so the numbering can change when entries are added or deleted.

Commands are executed either immediately before a prompt, or while the shell's line editor is waiting for input. In the latter case it is useful to be able to produce output that does not interfere with the line being edited. Providing the option -o causes the shell to clear the command line before the event and redraw it afterwards. This should be used with any scheduled event that produces visible output to the terminal; it is not needed, for example, with output that updates a terminal emulator's title bar.

To effect changes to the editor buffer when an event executes, use the 'zle' command with no arguments to test whether the editor is active, and if it is, then use 'zle *widget*' to access the editor via the named *widget*.

The **sched** builtin is not made available by default when the shell starts in a mode emulating another shell. It can be made available with the command 'zmodload -F zsh/sched b:sched'.

zsh_scheduled_events

A readonly array corresponding to the events scheduled by the **sched** builtin. The indices of the array correspond to the numbers shown when **sched** is run with no arguments (provided that the **KSH_ARRAYS** option is not set). The value of the array consists of the scheduled time in seconds since the epoch (see Section 22.10 [The zsh/datetime Module], page 345, for facilities for using this number), followed by a colon, followed by any options (which may be empty but will be preceded by a '-' otherwise), followed by a colon, followed by the command to be executed.

The **sched** builtin should be used for manipulating the events. Note that this will have an immediate effect on the contents of the array, so that indices may become invalid.

22.25 The zsh/net/socket Module

The **zsh/net/socket** module makes available one builtin command:

zsocket [-altv] [-d *fd*] [*args*]

zsocket is implemented as a builtin to allow full use of shell command line editing, file I/O, and job control mechanisms.

22.25.1 Outbound Connections

zsocket [-v] [-d *fd*] *filename*

Open a new Unix domain connection to *filename*. The shell parameter **REPLY** will be set to the file descriptor associated with that connection. Currently, only stream connections are supported.

If -d is specified, its argument will be taken as the target file descriptor for the connection.

In order to elicit more verbose output, use -v.

File descriptors can be closed with normal shell syntax when no longer needed, for example:

```
exec {REPLY}>&-
```

22.25.2 Inbound Connections

zsocket -l [-v] [-d *fd*] *filename*

> zsocket -l will open a socket listening on *filename*. The shell parameter REPLY will be set to the file descriptor associated with that listener.
>
> If -d is specified, its argument will be taken as the target file descriptor for the connection.
>
> In order to elicit more verbose output, use -v.

zsocket -a [-tv] [-d *targetfd*] *listenfd*

> zsocket -a will accept an incoming connection to the socket associated with *listenfd*. The shell parameter REPLY will be set to the file descriptor associated with the inbound connection.
>
> If -d is specified, its argument will be taken as the target file descriptor for the connection.
>
> If -t is specified, zsocket will return if no incoming connection is pending. Otherwise it will wait for one.
>
> In order to elicit more verbose output, use -v.

22.26 The zsh/stat Module

The zsh/stat module makes available one builtin command under two possible names:

zstat [-gnNolLtTrs] [-f *fd*] [-H *hash*] [-A *array*] [-F *fmt*]
    [+*element*] [*file ...*]

stat ...
> The command acts as a front end to the stat system call (see man page stat(2)). The same command is provided with two names; as the name stat is often used by an external command it is recommended that only the zstat form of the command is used. This can be arranged by loading the module with the command 'zmodload -F zsh/stat b:zstat'.
>
> If the stat call fails, the appropriate system error message printed and status 1 is returned. The fields of struct stat give information about the files provided as arguments to the command. In addition to those available from the stat call, an extra element 'link' is provided. These elements are:

> device
> > The number of the device on which the file resides.

> inode
> > The unique number of the file on this device (*'inode'* number).

> mode
> > The mode of the file; that is, the file's type and access permissions. With the -s option, this will be returned as a string corresponding to the first column in the display of the ls -l command.

> nlink
> > The number of hard links to the file.

> uid
> > The user ID of the owner of the file. With the -s option, this is displayed as a user name.

> gid
> > The group ID of the file. With the -s option, this is displayed as a group name.

rdev	The raw device number. This is only useful for special devices.
size	The size of the file in bytes.
atime	
mtime	
ctime	The last access, modification and inode change times of the file, respectively, as the number of seconds since midnight GMT on 1st January, 1970. With the -s option, these are printed as strings for the local time zone; the format can be altered with the -F option, and with the -g option the times are in GMT.
blksize	The number of bytes in one allocation block on the device on which the file resides.
block	The number of disk blocks used by the file.
link	If the file is a link and the -L option is in effect, this contains the name of the file linked to, otherwise it is empty. Note that if this element is selected ("zstat +link") then the -L option is automatically used.

A particular element may be selected by including its name preceded by a '+' in the option list; only one element is allowed. The element may be shortened to any unique set of leading characters. Otherwise, all elements will be shown for all files.

Options:

-A *array*	Instead of displaying the results on standard output, assign them to an *array*, one **struct stat** element per array element for each file in order. In this case neither the name of the element nor the name of the files appears in *array* unless the -t or -n options were given, respectively. If -t is given, the element name appears as a prefix to the appropriate array element; if -n is given, the file name appears as a separate array element preceding all the others. Other formatting options are respected.
-H *hash*	Similar to -A, but instead assign the values to *hash*. The keys are the elements listed above. If the -n option is provided then the name of the file is included in the hash with key **name**.
-f *fd*	Use the file on file descriptor *fd* instead of named files; no list of file names is allowed in this case.
-F *fmt*	Supplies a **strftime** (see man page strftime(3)) string for the formatting of the time elements. The format string supports all of the zsh extensions described in Chapter 13 [Prompt Expansion], page 39. The -s option is implied.
-g	Show the time elements in the GMT time zone. The -s option is implied.
-l	List the names of the type elements (to standard output or an array as appropriate) and return immediately; arguments, and options other than -A, are ignored.

-L   Perform an `lstat` (see man page lstat(2)) rather than a `stat` system call. In this case, if the file is a link, information about the link itself rather than the target file is returned. This option is required to make the `link` element useful. It's important to note that this is the exact opposite from man page ls(1), etc.

-n   Always show the names of files. Usually these are only shown when output is to standard output and there is more than one file in the list.

-N   Never show the names of files.

-o   If a raw file mode is printed, show it in octal, which is more useful for human consumption than the default of decimal. A leading zero will be printed in this case. Note that this does not affect whether a raw or formatted file mode is shown, which is controlled by the `-r` and `-s` options, nor whether a mode is shown at all.

-r   Print raw data (the default format) alongside string data (the `-s` format); the string data appears in parentheses after the raw data.

-s   Print `mode`, `uid`, `gid` and the three time elements as strings instead of numbers. In each case the format is like that of `ls -l`.

-t   Always show the type names for the elements of `struct stat`. Usually these are only shown when output is to standard output and no individual element has been selected.

-T   Never show the type names of the `struct stat` elements.

22.27 The zsh/system Module

The `zsh/system` module makes available various builtin commands and parameters.

22.27.1 Builtins

syserror [-e errvar] [-p prefix] [errno | errname]

This command prints out the error message associated with errno, a system error number, followed by a newline to standard error.

Instead of the error number, a name errname, for example ENOENT, may be used. The set of names is the same as the contents of the array `errnos`, see below.

If the string prefix is given, it is printed in front of the error message, with no intervening space.

If errvar is supplied, the entire message, without a newline, is assigned to the parameter names errvar and nothing is output.

A return status of 0 indicates the message was successfully printed (although it may not be useful if the error number was out of the system's range), a return status of 1 indicates an error in the parameters, and a return status of 2 indicates the error name was not recognised (no message is printed for this).

sysopen [-arw] [-m *permissions*] [-o *options*]
-u *fd file*

> This command opens a file. The -r, -w and -a flags indicate whether the file should be opened for reading, writing and appending, respectively. The -m option allows the initial permissions to use when creating a file to be specified in octal form. The file descriptor is specified with -u. Either an explicit file descriptor in the range 0 to 9 can be specified or a variable name can be given to which the file descriptor number will be assigned.
>
> The -o option allows various system specific options to be specified as a comma-separated list. The following is a list of possible options. Note that, depending on the system, some may not be available.

cloexec	mark file to be closed when other programs are executed
create	
creat	create file if it does not exist
excl	create file, error if it already exists
noatime	suppress updating of the file atime
nofollow	fail if *file* is a symbolic link
sync	request that writes wait until data has been physically written
truncate	
trunc	truncate file to size 0

> To close the file, use one of the following:

```
exec {fd}<&-
exec {fd}>&-
```

sysread [-c *countvar*] [-i *infd*] [-o *outfd*]
[-s *bufsize*] [-t *timeout*] [*param*]

> Perform a single system read from file descriptor *infd*, or zero if that is not given. The result of the read is stored in *param* or REPLY if that is not given. If *countvar* is given, the number of bytes read is assigned to the parameter named by *countvar*.
>
> The maximum number of bytes read is *bufsize* or 8192 if that is not given, however the command returns as soon as any number of bytes was successfully read.
>
> If *timeout* is given, it specifies a timeout in seconds, which may be zero to poll the file descriptor. This is handled by the poll system call if available, otherwise the select system call if available.
>
> If *outfd* is given, an attempt is made to write all the bytes just read to the file descriptor *outfd*. If this fails, because of a system error other than EINTR or because of an internal zsh error during an interrupt, the bytes read but not written are stored in the parameter named by *param* if supplied (no default is used in this case), and the number of bytes read but not written is stored in the parameter named by *countvar* if that is supplied. If it was successful, *countvar* contains the full number of bytes transferred, as usual, and *param* is not set.

The error **EINTR** (interrupted system call) is handled internally so that shell interrupts are transparent to the caller. Any other error causes a return.

The possible return statuses are

0	At least one byte of data was successfully read and, if appropriate, written.
1	There was an error in the parameters to the command. This is the only error for which a message is printed to standard error.
2	There was an error on the read, or on polling the input file descriptor for a timeout. The parameter **ERRNO** gives the error.
3	Data were successfully read, but there was an error writing them to *outfd*. The parameter **ERRNO** gives the error.
4	The attempt to read timed out. Note this does not set **ERRNO** as this is not a system error.
5	No system error occurred, but zero bytes were read. This usually indicates end of file. The parameters are set according to the usual rules; no write to *outfd* is attempted.

sysseek [-u *fd*] [-w start|end|current] *offset*

The current file position at which future reads and writes will take place is adjusted to the specified byte offset. The *offset* is evaluated as a math expression. The -u option allows the file descriptor to be specified. By default the offset is specified relative to the start or the file but, with the -w option, it is possible to specify that the offset should be relative to the current position or the end of the file.

syswrite [-c *countvar*] [-o *outfd*] *data*

The data (a single string of bytes) are written to the file descriptor *outfd*, or 1 if that is not given, using the **write** system call. Multiple write operations may be used if the first does not write all the data.

If *countvar* is given, the number of byte written is stored in the parameter named by *countvar*; this may not be the full length of *data* if an error occurred.

The error **EINTR** (interrupted system call) is handled internally by retrying; otherwise an error causes the command to return. For example, if the file descriptor is set to non-blocking output, an error **EAGAIN** (on some systems, **EWOULDBLOCK**) may result in the command returning early.

The return status may be 0 for success, 1 for an error in the parameters to the command, or 2 for an error on the write; no error message is printed in the last case, but the parameter **ERRNO** will reflect the error that occurred.

zsystem flock [-t *timeout*] [-f *var*] [-er] *file*
zsystem flock -u *fd_expr*

The builtin **zsystem**'s subcommand **flock** performs advisory file locking (via the man page fcntl(2) system call) over the entire contents of the given file. This form of locking requires the processes accessing the file to cooperate; its most obvious use is between two instances of the shell itself.

In the first form the named *file*, which must already exist, is locked by opening a file descriptor to the file and applying a lock to the file descriptor. The lock terminates when the shell process that created the lock exits; it is therefore often convenient to create file locks within subshells, since the lock is automatically released when the subshell exits. Status 0 is returned if the lock succeeds, else status 1.

In the second form the file descriptor given by the arithmetic expression *fd_expr* is closed, releasing a lock. The file descriptor can be queried by using the '-f *var*' form during the lock; on a successful lock, the shell variable *var* is set to the file descriptor used for locking. The lock will be released if the file descriptor is closed by any other means, for example using 'exec {*var*}>&-'; however, the form described here performs a safety check that the file descriptor is in use for file locking.

By default the shell waits indefinitely for the lock to succeed. The option -t *timeout* specifies a timeout for the lock in seconds; currently this must be an integer. The shell will attempt to lock the file once a second during this period. If the attempt times out, status 2 is returned.

If the option -e is given, the file descriptor for the lock is preserved when the shell uses exec to start a new process; otherwise it is closed at that point and the lock released.

If the option -r is given, the lock is only for reading, otherwise it is for reading and writing. The file descriptor is opened accordingly.

zsystem supports *subcommand*
> The builtin **zsystem**'s subcommand **supports** tests whether a given subcommand is supported. It returns status 0 if so, else status 1. It operates silently unless there was a syntax error (i.e. the wrong number of arguments), in which case status 255 is returned. Status 1 can indicate one of two things: *subcommand* is known but not supported by the current operating system, or *subcommand* is not known (possibly because this is an older version of the shell before it was implemented).

22.27.2 Math Functions

systell(fd**)**
> The systell math function returns the current file position for the file descriptor passed as an argument.

22.27.3 Parameters

errnos
> A readonly array of the names of errors defined on the system. These are typically macros defined in C by including the system header file **errno.h**. The index of each name (assuming the option **KSH_ARRAYS** is unset) corresponds to the error number. Error numbers *num* before the last known error which have no name are given the name E*num* in the array.
>
> Note that aliases for errors are not handled; only the canonical name is used.

sysparams

> A readonly associative array. The keys are:
>
> pid   Returns the process ID of the current process, even in subshells. Compare $$, which returns the process ID of the main shell process.
>
> ppid   Returns the process ID of the parent of the current process, even in subshells. Compare $PPID, which returns the process ID of the parent of the main shell process.
>
> **procsubstpid**
>
> > Returns the process ID of the last process started for process substitution, i.e. the <(...) and >(...) expansions.

22.28 The zsh/net/tcp Module

The zsh/net/tcp module makes available one builtin command:

ztcp [-acflLtv] [-d *fd*] [*args*]

> ztcp is implemented as a builtin to allow full use of shell command line editing, file I/O, and job control mechanisms.
>
> If ztcp is run with no options, it will output the contents of its session table.
>
> If it is run with only the option -L, it will output the contents of the session table in a format suitable for automatic parsing. The option is ignored if given with a command to open or close a session. The output consists of a set of lines, one per session, each containing the following elements separated by spaces:
>
> File descriptor
>
> > The file descriptor in use for the connection. For normal inbound (I) and outbound (O) connections this may be read and written by the usual shell mechanisms. However, it should only be close with 'ztcp -c'.
>
> Connection type
>
> > A letter indicating how the session was created:
> >
> > Z   A session created with the **zftp** command.
> >
> > L   A connection opened for listening with 'ztcp -l'.
> >
> > I   An inbound connection accepted with 'ztcp -a'.
> >
> > O   An outbound connection created with 'ztcp *host* ...'.
>
> The local host
>
> > This is usually set to an all-zero IP address as the address of the localhost is irrelevant.
>
> The local port
>
> > This is likely to be zero unless the connection is for listening.
>
> The remote host
>
> > This is the fully qualified domain name of the peer, if available, else an IP address. It is an all-zero IP address for a session opened for listening.

The remote port
        This is zero for a connection opened for listening.

22.28.1 Outbound Connections

`ztcp` [`-v`] [`-d` *fd*] *host* [*port*]
        Open a new TCP connection to *host*. If the *port* is omitted, it will default to
        port 23. The connection will be added to the session table and the shell param-
        eter `REPLY` will be set to the file descriptor associated with that connection.

        If `-d` is specified, its argument will be taken as the target file descriptor for the
        connection.

        In order to elicit more verbose output, use `-v`.

22.28.2 Inbound Connections

`ztcp -l` [`-v`] [`-d` *fd*] *port*
        `ztcp -l` will open a socket listening on TCP *port*. The socket will be added to
        the session table and the shell parameter `REPLY` will be set to the file descriptor
        associated with that listener.

        If `-d` is specified, its argument will be taken as the target file descriptor for the
        connection.

        In order to elicit more verbose output, use `-v`.

`ztcp -a` [`-tv`] [`-d` *targetfd*] *listenfd*
        `ztcp -a` will accept an incoming connection to the port associated with *listenfd*.
        The connection will be added to the session table and the shell parameter `REPLY`
        will be set to the file descriptor associated with the inbound connection.

        If `-d` is specified, its argument will be taken as the target file descriptor for the
        connection.

        If `-t` is specified, `ztcp` will return if no incoming connection is pending. Oth-
        erwise it will wait for one.

        In order to elicit more verbose output, use `-v`.

22.28.3 Closing Connections

`ztcp -cf` [`-v`] [*fd*]
`ztcp -c` [`-v`] [*fd*]
        `ztcp -c` will close the socket associated with *fd*. The socket will be removed
        from the session table. If *fd* is not specified, `ztcp` will close everything in the
        session table.

        Normally, sockets registered by zftp (see Section 22.31 [The zsh/zftp Module],
        page 371,) cannot be closed this way. In order to force such a socket closed,
        use `-f`.

        In order to elicit more verbose output, use `-v`.

22.28.4 Example

Here is how to create a TCP connection between two instances of zsh. We need to pick an unassigned port; here we use the randomly chosen 5123.

On `host1`,

```
zmodload zsh/net/tcp
ztcp -l 5123
listenfd=$REPLY
ztcp -a $listenfd
fd=$REPLY
```

The second from last command blocks until there is an incoming connection.

Now create a connection from `host2` (which may, of course, be the same machine):

```
zmodload zsh/net/tcp
ztcp host1 5123
fd=$REPLY
```

Now on each host, `$fd` contains a file descriptor for talking to the other. For example, on `host1`:

```
print This is a message >&$fd
```

and on `host2`:

```
read -r line <&$fd; print -r - $line
```

prints 'This is a message'.

To tidy up, on `host1`:

```
ztcp -c $listenfd
ztcp -c $fd
```

and on `host2`

```
ztcp -c $fd
```

22.29 The zsh/termcap Module

The `zsh/termcap` module makes available one builtin command:

echotc *cap* [*arg* ...]
> Output the termcap value corresponding to the capability *cap*, with optional arguments.

The `zsh/termcap` module makes available one parameter:

termcap An associative array that maps termcap capability codes to their values.

22.30 The zsh/terminfo Module

The `zsh/terminfo` module makes available one builtin command:

echoti *cap* [*arg*]
> Output the terminfo value corresponding to the capability *cap*, instantiated with *arg* if applicable.

The `zsh/terminfo` module makes available one parameter:

terminfo An associative array that maps terminfo capability names to their values.

22.31 The zsh/zftp Module

The **zsh/zftp** module makes available one builtin command:

zftp *subcommand* [*args*]

> The **zsh/zftp** module is a client for FTP (file transfer protocol). It is implemented as a builtin to allow full use of shell command line editing, file I/O, and job control mechanisms. Often, users will access it via shell functions providing a more powerful interface; a set is provided with the **zsh** distribution and is described in Chapter 25 [Zftp Function System], page 413. However, the **zftp** command is entirely usable in its own right.
>
> All commands consist of the command name **zftp** followed by the name of a subcommand. These are listed below. The return status of each subcommand is supposed to reflect the success or failure of the remote operation. See a description of the variable **ZFTP_VERBOSE** for more information on how responses from the server may be printed.

22.31.1 Subcommands

open *host*[:*port*] [*user* [*password* [*account*]]]

> Open a new FTP session to *host*, which may be the name of a TCP/IP connected host or an IP number in the standard dot notation. If the argument is in the form *host:port*, open a connection to TCP port *port* instead of the standard FTP port 21. This may be the name of a TCP service or a number: see the description of **ZFTP_PORT** below for more information.
>
> If IPv6 addresses in colon format are used, the *host* should be surrounded by quoted square brackets to distinguish it from the *port*, for example '[fe80::203:baff:fe02:8b56]'. For consistency this is allowed with all forms of *host*.
>
> Remaining arguments are passed to the **login** subcommand. Note that if no arguments beyond *host* are supplied, **open** will *not* automatically call **login**. If no arguments at all are supplied, **open** will use the parameters set by the **params** subcommand.
>
> After a successful open, the shell variables **ZFTP_HOST**, **ZFTP_PORT**, **ZFTP_IP** and **ZFTP_SYSTEM** are available; see 'Variables' below.

login [*name* [*password* [*account*]]]
user [*name* [*password* [*account*]]]

> Login the user *name* with parameters *password* and *account*. Any of the parameters can be omitted, and will be read from standard input if needed (*name* is always needed). If standard input is a terminal, a prompt for each one will be printed on standard error and *password* will not be echoed. If any of the parameters are not used, a warning message is printed.
>
> After a successful login, the shell variables **ZFTP_USER**, **ZFTP_ACCOUNT** and **ZFTP_PWD** are available; see 'Variables' below.
>
> This command may be re-issued when a user is already logged in, and the server will first be reinitialized for a new user.

`params` [*host* [*user* [*password* [*account*]]]]

`params -`   Store the given parameters for a later `open` command with no arguments. Only those given on the command line will be remembered. If no arguments are given, the parameters currently set are printed, although the password will appear as a line of stars; the return status is one if no parameters were set, zero otherwise.

Any of the parameters may be specified as a '?', which may need to be quoted to protect it from shell expansion. In this case, the appropriate parameter will be read from stdin as with the `login` subcommand, including special handling of *password*. If the '?' is followed by a string, that is used as the prompt for reading the parameter instead of the default message (any necessary punctuation and whitespace should be included at the end of the prompt). The first letter of the parameter (only) may be quoted with a '\'; hence an argument `"\\$word"` guarantees that the string from the shell parameter `$word` will be treated literally, whether or not it begins with a '?'.

If instead a single '-' is given, the existing parameters, if any, are deleted. In that case, calling `open` with no arguments will cause an error.

The list of parameters is not deleted after a `close`, however it will be deleted if the `zsh/zftp` module is unloaded.

For example,

        `zftp params ftp.elsewhere.xx juser '?Password for juser: '`

will store the host `ftp.elsewhere.xx` and the user `juser` and then prompt the user for the corresponding password with the given prompt.

`test`   Test the connection; if the server has reported that it has closed the connection (maybe due to a timeout), return status 2; if no connection was open anyway, return status 1; else return status 0. The `test` subcommand is silent, apart from messages printed by the `$ZFTP_VERBOSE` mechanism, or error messages if the connection closes. There is no network overhead for this test.

The test is only supported on systems with either the `select(2)` or `poll(2)` system calls; otherwise the message 'not supported on this system' is printed instead.

The `test` subcommand will automatically be called at the start of any other subcommand for the current session when a connection is open.

`cd` *directory*

    Change the remote directory to *directory*. Also alters the shell variable `ZFTP_PWD`.

`cdup`   Change the remote directory to the one higher in the directory tree. Note that `cd ..` will also work correctly on non-UNIX systems.

`dir` [*arg* ...]

    Give a (verbose) listing of the remote directory. The *args* are passed directly to the server. The command's behaviour is implementation dependent, but a UNIX server will typically interpret *args* as arguments to the `ls` command and with no arguments return the result of '`ls -l`'. The directory is listed to standard output.

ls [*arg* ...]

> Give a (short) listing of the remote directory. With no *arg*, produces a raw list of the files in the directory, one per line. Otherwise, up to vagaries of the server implementation, behaves similar to **dir**.

type [*type*]

> Change the type for the transfer to *type*, or print the current type if *type* is absent. The allowed values are 'A' (ASCII), 'I' (Image, i.e. binary), or 'B' (a synonym for 'I').

> The FTP default for a transfer is ASCII. However, if **zftp** finds that the remote host is a UNIX machine with 8-bit byes, it will automatically switch to using binary for file transfers upon **open**. This can subsequently be overridden.

> The transfer type is only passed to the remote host when a data connection is established; this command involves no network overhead.

ascii   The same as **type A**.

binary   The same as **type I**.

mode [S | B]

> Set the mode type to stream (S) or block (B). Stream mode is the default; block mode is not widely supported.

remote *file* ...
local [*file* ...]

> Print the size and last modification time of the remote or local files. If there is more than one item on the list, the name of the file is printed first. The first number is the file size, the second is the last modification time of the file in the format **CCYYMMDDhhmmSS** consisting of year, month, date, hour, minutes and seconds in GMT. Note that this format, including the length, is guaranteed, so that time strings can be directly compared via the **[[** builtin's **<** and **>** operators, even if they are too long to be represented as integers.

> Not all servers support the commands for retrieving this information. In that case, the **remote** command will print nothing and return status 2, compared with status 1 for a file not found.

> The **local** command (but not **remote**) may be used with no arguments, in which case the information comes from examining file descriptor zero. This is the same file as seen by a **put** command with no further redirection.

get *file* ...   Retrieve all *files* from the server, concatenating them and sending them to standard output.

put *file* ...   For each *file*, read a file from standard input and send that to the remote host with the given name.

append *file* ...

> As **put**, but if the remote *file* already exists, data is appended to it instead of overwriting it.

getat *file point*
putat *file point*
appendat *file point*

> Versions of get, put and append which will start the transfer at the given *point* in the remote *file*. This is useful for appending to an incomplete local file. However, note that this ability is not universally supported by servers (and is not quite the behaviour specified by the standard).

delete *file* ...

> Delete the list of files on the server.

mkdir *directory*

> Create a new directory *directory* on the server.

rmdir *directory*

> Delete the directory *directory* on the server.

rename *old-name new-name*

> Rename file *old-name* to *new-name* on the server.

site *arg* ...

> Send a host-specific command to the server. You will probably only need this if instructed by the server to use it.

quote *arg* ...

> Send the raw FTP command sequence to the server. You should be familiar with the FTP command set as defined in RFC959 before doing this. Useful commands may include STAT and HELP. Note also the mechanism for returning messages as described for the variable ZFTP_VERBOSE below, in particular that all messages from the control connection are sent to standard error.

close
quit   Close the current data connection. This unsets the shell parameters ZFTP_HOST, ZFTP_PORT, ZFTP_IP, ZFTP_SYSTEM, ZFTP_USER, ZFTP_ACCOUNT, ZFTP_PWD, ZFTP_TYPE and ZFTP_MODE.

session [*sessname*]

> Allows multiple FTP sessions to be used at once. The name of the session is an arbitrary string of characters; the default session is called 'default'. If this command is called without an argument, it will list all the current sessions; with an argument, it will either switch to the existing session called *sessname*, or create a new session of that name.
>
> Each session remembers the status of the connection, the set of connection-specific shell parameters (the same set as are unset when a connection closes, as given in the description of close), and any user parameters specified with the params subcommand. Changing to a previous session restores those values; changing to a new session initialises them in the same way as if zftp had just been loaded. The name of the current session is given by the parameter ZFTP_SESSION.

rmsession [*sessname*]

> Delete a session; if a name is not given, the current session is deleted. If the current session is deleted, the earliest existing session becomes the new

current session, otherwise the current session is not changed. If the session being deleted is the only one, a new session called 'default' is created and becomes the current session; note that this is a new session even if the session being deleted is also called 'default'. It is recommended that sessions not be deleted while background commands which use zftp are still active.

22.31.2 Parameters

The following shell parameters are used by zftp. Currently none of them are special.

ZFTP_TMOUT

> Integer. The time in seconds to wait for a network operation to complete before returning an error. If this is not set when the module is loaded, it will be given the default value 60. A value of zero turns off timeouts. If a timeout occurs on the control connection it will be closed. Use a larger value if this occurs too frequently.

ZFTP_IP   Readonly. The IP address of the current connection in dot notation.

ZFTP_HOST

> Readonly. The hostname of the current remote server. If the host was opened as an IP number, ZFTP_HOST contains that instead; this saves the overhead for a name lookup, as IP numbers are most commonly used when a nameserver is unavailable.

ZFTP_PORT

> Readonly. The number of the remote TCP port to which the connection is open (even if the port was originally specified as a named service). Usually this is the standard FTP port, 21.

> In the unlikely event that your system does not have the appropriate conversion functions, this appears in network byte order. If your system is little-endian, the port then consists of two swapped bytes and the standard port will be reported as 5376. In that case, numeric ports passed to zftp open will also need to be in this format.

ZFTP_SYSTEM

> Readonly. The system type string returned by the server in response to an FTP SYST request. The most interesting case is a string beginning "UNIX Type: L8", which ensures maximum compatibility with a local UNIX host.

ZFTP_TYPE

> Readonly. The type to be used for data transfers , either 'A' or 'I'. Use the type subcommand to change this.

ZFTP_USER

> Readonly. The username currently logged in, if any.

ZFTP_ACCOUNT

> Readonly. The account name of the current user, if any. Most servers do not require an account name.

ZFTP_PWD   Readonly. The current directory on the server.

ZFTP_CODE

> Readonly. The three digit code of the last FTP reply from the server as a string. This can still be read after the connection is closed, and is not changed when the current session changes.

ZFTP_REPLY

> Readonly. The last line of the last reply sent by the server. This can still be read after the connection is closed, and is not changed when the current session changes.

ZFTP_SESSION

> Readonly. The name of the current FTP session; see the description of the **session** subcommand.

ZFTP_PREFS

> A string of preferences for altering aspects of **zftp**'s behaviour. Each preference is a single character. The following are defined:
>
> | | |
> |---|---|
> | P | Passive: attempt to make the remote server initiate data transfers. This is slightly more efficient than sendport mode. If the letter S occurs later in the string, **zftp** will use sendport mode if passive mode is not available. |
> | S | Sendport: initiate transfers by the FTP PORT command. If this occurs before any P in the string, passive mode will never be attempted. |
> | D | Dumb: use only the bare minimum of FTP commands. This prevents the variables ZFTP_SYSTEM and ZFTP_PWD from being set, and will mean all connections default to ASCII type. It may prevent ZFTP_SIZE from being set during a transfer if the server does not send it anyway (many servers do). |
>
> If ZFTP_PREFS is not set when **zftp** is loaded, it will be set to a default of 'PS', i.e. use passive mode if available, otherwise fall back to sendport mode.

ZFTP_VERBOSE

> A string of digits between 0 and 5 inclusive, specifying which responses from the server should be printed. All responses go to standard error. If any of the numbers 1 to 5 appear in the string, raw responses from the server with reply codes beginning with that digit will be printed to standard error. The first digit of the three digit reply code is defined by RFC959 to correspond to:
>
> 1. A positive preliminary reply.
>
> 2. A positive completion reply.
>
> 3. A positive intermediate reply.
>
> 4. A transient negative completion reply.
>
> 5. A permanent negative completion reply.
>
> It should be noted that, for unknown reasons, the reply 'Service not available', which forces termination of a connection, is classified as 421, i.e. 'transient negative', an interesting interpretation of the word 'transient'.

The code 0 is special: it indicates that all but the last line of multiline replies read from the server will be printed to standard error in a processed format. By convention, servers use this mechanism for sending information for the user to read. The appropriate reply code, if it matches the same response, takes priority.

If ZFTP_VERBOSE is not set when zftp is loaded, it will be set to the default value 450, i.e., messages destined for the user and all errors will be printed. A null string is valid and specifies that no messages should be printed.

22.31.3 Functions

zftp_chpwd

If this function is set by the user, it is called every time the directory changes on the server, including when a user is logged in, or when a connection is closed. In the last case, $ZFTP_PWD will be unset; otherwise it will reflect the new directory.

zftp_progress

If this function is set by the user, it will be called during a get, put or append operation each time sufficient data has been received from the host. During a get, the data is sent to standard output, so it is vital that this function should write to standard error or directly to the terminal, *not* to standard output.

When it is called with a transfer in progress, the following additional shell parameters are set:

ZFTP_FILE

The name of the remote file being transferred from or to.

ZFTP_TRANSFER

A G for a get operation and a P for a put operation.

ZFTP_SIZE

The total size of the complete file being transferred: the same as the first value provided by the **remote** and **local** subcommands for a particular file. If the server cannot supply this value for a remote file being retrieved, it will not be set. If input is from a pipe the value may be incorrect and correspond simply to a full pipe buffer.

ZFTP_COUNT

The amount of data so far transferred; a number between zero and $ZFTP_SIZE, if that is set. This number is always available.

The function is initially called with ZFTP_TRANSFER set appropriately and ZFTP_COUNT set to zero. After the transfer is finished, the function will be called one more time with ZFTP_TRANSFER set to GF or PF, in case it wishes to tidy up. It is otherwise never called twice with the same value of ZFTP_COUNT.

Sometimes the progress meter may cause disruption. It is up to the user to decide whether the function should be defined and to use **unfunction** when necessary.

22.31.4 Problems

A connection may not be opened in the left hand side of a pipe as this occurs in a subshell and the file information is not updated in the main shell. In the case of type or mode changes or closing the connection in a subshell, the information is returned but variables are not updated until the next call to zftp. Other status changes in subshells will not be reflected by changes to the variables (but should be otherwise harmless).

Deleting sessions while a zftp command is active in the background can have unexpected effects, even if it does not use the session being deleted. This is because all shell subprocesses share information on the state of all connections, and deleting a session changes the ordering of that information.

On some operating systems, the control connection is not valid after a fork(), so that operations in subshells, on the left hand side of a pipeline, or in the background are not possible, as they should be. This is presumably a bug in the operating system.

22.32 The zsh/zle Module

The zsh/zle module contains the Zsh Line Editor. See Chapter 18 [Zsh Line Editor], page 183.

22.33 The zsh/zleparameter Module

The zsh/zleparameter module defines two special parameters that can be used to access internal information of the Zsh Line Editor (see Chapter 18 [Zsh Line Editor], page 183).

keymaps   This array contains the names of the keymaps currently defined.

widgets   This associative array contains one entry per widget. The name of the widget is the key and the value gives information about the widget. It is either the string 'builtin' for builtin widgets, a string of the form 'user:*name*' for user-defined widgets, where *name* is the name of the shell function implementing the widget, a string of the form 'completion:*type*:*name*' for completion widgets, or a null value if the widget is not yet fully defined. In the penultimate case, *type* is the name of the builtin widget the completion widget imitates in its behavior and *name* is the name of the shell function implementing the completion widget.

22.34 The zsh/zprof Module

When loaded, the zsh/zprof causes shell functions to be profiled. The profiling results can be obtained with the zprof builtin command made available by this module. There is no way to turn profiling off other than unloading the module.

zprof [-c]

Without the -c option, zprof lists profiling results to standard output. The format is comparable to that of commands like gprof.

At the top there is a summary listing all functions that were called at least once. This summary is sorted in decreasing order of the amount of time spent in each. The lines contain the number of the function in order, which is used in other parts of the list in suffixes of the form '[num]', then the number of calls made to the function. The next three columns list the time in milliseconds spent in the function and its descendants, the average time in milliseconds spent in the function and its descendants per call and the percentage of time spent in all shell functions used in this function and its descendants. The following three columns give the same information, but counting only the time spent in the function itself. The final column shows the name of the function.

After the summary, detailed information about every function that was invoked is listed, sorted in decreasing order of the amount of time spent in each function and its descendants. Each of these entries consists of descriptions for the functions that called the function described, the function itself, and the functions that were called from it. The description for the function itself has the same format as in the summary (and shows the same information). The other lines don't show the number of the function at the beginning and have their function named indented to make it easier to distinguish the line showing the function described in the section from the surrounding lines.

The information shown in this case is almost the same as in the summary, but only refers to the call hierarchy being displayed. For example, for a calling function the column showing the total running time lists the time spent in the described function and its descendants only for the times when it was called from that particular calling function. Likewise, for a called function, this columns lists the total time spent in the called function and its descendants only for the times when it was called from the function described.

Also in this case, the column showing the number of calls to a function also shows a slash and then the total number of invocations made to the called function.

As long as the zsh/zprof module is loaded, profiling will be done and multiple invocations of the zprof builtin command will show the times and numbers of calls since the module was loaded. With the -c option, the zprof builtin command will reset its internal counters and will not show the listing.

22.35 The zsh/zpty Module

The zsh/zpty module offers one builtin:

zpty [-e] [-b] name [arg ...]

> The arguments following name are concatenated with spaces between, then executed as a command, as if passed to the eval builtin. The command runs under a newly assigned pseudo-terminal; this is useful for running commands non-interactively which expect an interactive environment. The name is not part of the command, but is used to refer to this command in later calls to zpty.

> With the -e option, the pseudo-terminal is set up so that input characters are echoed.

> With the -b option, input to and output from the pseudo-terminal are made non-blocking.

The shell parameter `REPLY` is set to the file descriptor assigned to the master side of the pseudo-terminal. This allows the terminal to be monitored with ZLE descriptor handlers (see Section 18.3 [Zle Builtins], page 185) or manipulated with `sysread` and `syswrite` (see Section 22.27 [The zsh/system Module], page 364). *Warning*: Use of `sysread` and `syswrite` is *not* recommended, use `zpty -r` and `zpty -w` unless you know exactly what you are doing.

`zpty -d` [*name* ...]

The second form, with the `-d` option, is used to delete commands previously started, by supplying a list of their *names*. If no *name* is given, all commands are deleted. Deleting a command causes the HUP signal to be sent to the corresponding process.

`zpty -w` [`-n`] *name* [*string* ...]

The `-w` option can be used to send the to command *name* the given *string*s as input (separated by spaces). If the `-n` option is *not* given, a newline is added at the end.

If no *string* is provided, the standard input is copied to the pseudo-terminal; this may stop before copying the full input if the pseudo-terminal is non-blocking. The exact input is always copied: the `-n` option is not applied.

Note that the command under the pseudo-terminal sees this input as if it were typed, so beware when sending special tty driver characters such as word-erase, line-kill, and end-of-file.

`zpty -r` [`-mt`] *name* [*param* [*pattern*]]

The `-r` option can be used to read the output of the command *name*. With only a *name* argument, the output read is copied to the standard output. Unless the pseudo-terminal is non-blocking, copying continues until the command under the pseudo-terminal exits; when non-blocking, only as much output as is immediately available is copied. The return status is zero if any output is copied.

When also given a *param* argument, at most one line is read and stored in the parameter named *param*. Less than a full line may be read if the pseudo-terminal is non-blocking. The return status is zero if at least one character is stored in *param*.

If a *pattern* is given as well, output is read until the whole string read matches the *pattern*, even in the non-blocking case. The return status is zero if the string read matches the pattern, or if the command has exited but at least one character could still be read. If the option `-m` is present, the return status is zero only if the pattern matches. As of this writing, a maximum of one megabyte of output can be consumed this way; if a full megabyte is read without matching the pattern, the return status is non-zero.

In all cases, the return status is non-zero if nothing could be read, and is 2 if this is because the command has finished.

If the `-r` option is combined with the `-t` option, `zpty` tests whether output is available before trying to read. If no output is available, `zpty` immediately returns the status 1. When used with a *pattern*, the behaviour on a failed poll is similar to when the command has exited: the return value is zero if at least one character could still be read even if the pattern failed to match.

zpty -t *name*

The **-t** option without the **-r** option can be used to test whether the command *name* is still running. It returns a zero status if the command is running and a non-zero value otherwise.

zpty [**-L**]

The last form, without any arguments, is used to list the commands currently defined. If the **-L** option is given, this is done in the form of calls to the **zpty** builtin.

22.36 The zsh/zselect Module

The **zsh/zselect** module makes available one builtin command:

zselect [**-rwe**] [**-t** *timeout*] [**-a** *array*] [**-A** *assoc*] [*fd ...*]

The **zselect** builtin is a front-end to the 'select' system call, which blocks until a file descriptor is ready for reading or writing, or has an error condition, with an optional timeout. If this is not available on your system, the command prints an error message and returns status 2 (normal errors return status 1). For more information, see your systems documentation for man page select(3). Note there is no connection with the shell builtin of the same name.

Arguments and options may be intermingled in any order. Non-option arguments are file descriptors, which must be decimal integers. By default, file descriptors are to be tested for reading, i.e. **zselect** will return when data is available to be read from the file descriptor, or more precisely, when a read operation from the file descriptor will not block. After a **-r**, **-w** and **-e**, the given file descriptors are to be tested for reading, writing, or error conditions. These options and an arbitrary list of file descriptors may be given in any order.

(The presence of an 'error condition' is not well defined in the documentation for many implementations of the select system call. According to recent versions of the POSIX specification, it is really an *exception* condition, of which the only standard example is out-of-band data received on a socket. So zsh users are unlikely to find the **-e** option useful.)

The option '**-t** *timeout*' specifies a timeout in hundredths of a second. This may be zero, in which case the file descriptors will simply be polled and **zselect** will return immediately. It is possible to call zselect with no file descriptors and a non-zero timeout for use as a finer-grained replacement for 'sleep'; note, however, the return status is always 1 for a timeout.

The option '**-a** *array*' indicates that *array* should be set to indicate the file descriptor(s) which are ready. If the option is not given, the array **reply** will be used for this purpose. The array will contain a string similar to the arguments for **zselect**. For example,

```
zselect -t 0 -r 0 -w 1
```

might return immediately with status 0 and **$reply** containing '**-r 0 -w 1**' to show that both file descriptors are ready for the requested operations.

The option '-A *assoc*' indicates that the associative array *assoc* should be set to indicate the file descriptor(s) which are ready. This option overrides the option -a, nor will `reply` be modified. The keys of **assoc** are the file descriptors, and the corresponding values are any of the characters 'rwe' to indicate the condition.

The command returns status 0 if some file descriptors are ready for reading. If the operation timed out, or a timeout of 0 was given and no file descriptors were ready, or there was an error, it returns status 1 and the array will not be set (nor modified in any way). If there was an error in the select operation the appropriate error message is printed.

22.37 The zsh/zutil Module

The **zsh/zutil** module only adds some builtins:

```
zstyle [ -L [ pattern [ style ] ] ]
zstyle [ -e | - | -- ] pattern style string ...
zstyle -d [ pattern [ style ... ] ]
zstyle -g name [ pattern [ style ] ]
zstyle -{a|b|s} context style name [ sep ]
zstyle -{T|t} context style [ string ... ]
zstyle -m context style pattern
```

This builtin command is used to define and lookup styles. Styles are pairs of names and values, where the values consist of any number of strings. They are stored together with patterns and lookup is done by giving a string, called the 'context', which is compared to the patterns. The definition stored for the first matching pattern will be returned.

For ordering of comparisons, patterns are searched from most specific to least specific, and patterns that are equally specific keep the order in which they were defined. A pattern is considered to be more specific than another if it contains more components (substrings separated by colons) or if the patterns for the components are more specific, where simple strings are considered to be more specific than patterns and complex patterns are considered to be more specific than the pattern '*'.

The first form (without arguments) lists the definitions. Styles are shown in alphabetic order and patterns are shown in the order **zstyle** will test them.

If the -L option is given, listing is done in the form of calls to **zstyle**. The optional first argument is a pattern which will be matched against the string supplied as the pattern for the context; note that this means, for example, 'zstyle -L ":completion:*"' will match any supplied pattern beginning ':completion:', not just ":completion:*": use ":completion:*" to match that. The optional second argument limits the output to a specific *style* (not a pattern). -L is not compatible with any other options.

The other forms are the following:

zstyle [- | -- | -e] *pattern style string* ...

> Defines the given *style* for the *pattern* with the *string*s as the value. If the -e option is given, the *string*s will be concatenated (separated by spaces) and the resulting string will be evaluated (in the same way as it is done by the **eval** builtin command) when the style is looked up. In this case the parameter 'reply' must be assigned to set the strings returned after the evaluation. Before evaluating the value, **reply** is unset, and if it is still unset after the evaluation, the style is treated as if it were not set.

zstyle -d [*pattern* [*style* ...]]

> Delete style definitions. Without arguments all definitions are deleted, with a *pattern* all definitions for that pattern are deleted and if any *style*s are given, then only those styles are deleted for the *pattern*.

zstyle -g *name* [*pattern* [*style*]]

> Retrieve a style definition. The *name* is used as the name of an array in which the results are stored. Without any further arguments, all patterns defined are returned. With a *pattern* the styles defined for that pattern are returned and with both a *pattern* and a *style*, the value strings of that combination is returned.

The other forms can be used to look up or test patterns.

zstyle -s *context style name* [*sep*]

> The parameter *name* is set to the value of the style interpreted as a string. If the value contains several strings they are concatenated with spaces (or with the *sep* string if that is given) between them.

zstyle -b *context style name*

> The value is stored in *name* as a boolean, i.e. as the string 'yes' if the value has only one string and that string is equal to one of 'yes', 'true', 'on', or '1'. If the value is any other string or has more than one string, the parameter is set to 'no'.

zstyle -a *context style name*

> The value is stored in *name* as an array. If *name* is declared as an associative array, the first, third, etc. strings are used as the keys and the other strings are used as the values.

zstyle -t *context style* [*string* ...]
zstyle -T *context style* [*string* ...]

> Test the value of a style, i.e. the -t option only returns a status (sets $?). Without any *string* the return status is zero if the style is defined for at least one matching pattern, has only one string in its value, and that is equal to one of 'true', 'yes', 'on' or '1'. If any *string*s are given the status is zero if and only if at least one of the *string*s is equal to at least one of the strings in the value. If the style is defined but doesn't match, the return status is 1. If the style is not defined, the status is 2.

The **-T** option tests the values of the style like **-t**, but it returns status zero (rather than 2) if the style is not defined for any matching pattern.

zstyle -m *context style pattern*

Match a value. Returns status zero if the *pattern* matches at least one of the strings in the value.

zformat -f *param format spec ...*
zformat -a *array sep spec ...*

This builtin provides two different forms of formatting. The first form is selected with the **-f** option. In this case the *format* string will be modified by replacing sequences starting with a percent sign in it with strings from the *specs*. Each *spec* should be of the form '*char*:*string*' which will cause every appearance of the sequence '%*char*' in *format* to be replaced by the *string*. The '%' sequence may also contain optional minimum and maximum field width specifications between the '%' and the '*char*' in the form '%*min.maxc*', i.e. the minimum field width is given first and if the maximum field width is used, it has to be preceded by a dot. Specifying a minimum field width makes the result be padded with spaces to the right if the *string* is shorter than the requested width. Padding to the left can be achieved by giving a negative minimum field width. If a maximum field width is specified, the *string* will be truncated after that many characters. After all '%' sequences for the given *specs* have been processed, the resulting string is stored in the parameter *param*.

The %-escapes also understand ternary expressions in the form used by prompts. The % is followed by a '(' and then an ordinary format specifier character as described above. There may be a set of digits either before or after the '('; these specify a test number, which defaults to zero. Negative numbers are also allowed. An arbitrary delimiter character follows the format specifier, which is followed by a piece of 'true' text, the delimiter character again, a piece of 'false' text, and a closing parenthesis. The complete expression (without the digits) thus looks like '%(*X.text1.text2*)', except that the '.' character is arbitrary. The value given for the format specifier in the *char*:*string* expressions is evaluated as a mathematical expression, and compared with the test number. If they are the same, *text1* is output, else *text2* is output. A parenthesis may be escaped in *text2* as %). Either of *text1* or *text2* may contain nested %-escapes.

For example:

```
zformat -f REPLY "The answer is '%3(c.yes.no)'." c:3
```

outputs "The answer is 'yes'." to **REPLY** since the value for the format specifier c is 3, agreeing with the digit argument to the ternary expression.

The second form, using the **-a** option, can be used for aligning strings. Here, the *specs* are of the form '*left*:*right*' where '*left*' and '*right*' are arbitrary strings. These strings are modified by replacing the colons by the *sep* string and padding the *left* strings with spaces to the right so that the *sep* strings in the result (and hence the *right* strings after them) are all aligned if the strings are printed below each other. All strings without a colon are left unchanged and all strings with an empty *right* string have the trailing colon removed. In both cases the lengths of the strings are not used to determine how the other strings are to be aligned. A colon in the *left* string can be escaped with a backslash. The resulting strings are stored in the *array*.

zregexparse

This implements some internals of the `_regex_arguments` function.

zparseopts [-D -K -M -E] [-a *array*] [-A *assoc*] [-] *spec* ...

This builtin simplifies the parsing of options in positional parameters, i.e. the set of arguments given by `$*`. Each *spec* describes one option and must be of the form '*opt*[=*array*]'. If an option described by *opt* is found in the positional parameters it is copied into the *array* specified with the `-a` option; if the optional '=*array*' is given, it is instead copied into that array, which should be declared as a normal array and never as an associative array.

Note that it is an error to give any *spec* without an '=*array*' unless one of the `-a` or `-A` options is used.

Unless the `-E` option is given, parsing stops at the first string that isn't described by one of the *specs*. Even with `-E`, parsing always stops at a positional parameter equal to '-' or '--'.

The *opt* description must be one of the following. Any of the special characters can appear in the option name provided it is preceded by a backslash.

name

name+   The *name* is the name of the option without the leading '-'. To specify a GNU-style long option, one of the usual two leading '-' must be included in *name*; for example, a '--**file**' option is represented by a *name* of '-**file**'.

If a '+' appears after *name*, the option is appended to *array* each time it is found in the positional parameters; without the '+' only the *last* occurrence of the option is preserved.

If one of these forms is used, the option takes no argument, so parsing stops if the next positional parameter does not also begin with '-' (unless the `-E` option is used).

name:

name:-

name::   If one or two colons are given, the option takes an argument; with one colon, the argument is mandatory and with two colons it is optional. The argument is appended to the *array* after the option itself.

An optional argument is put into the same array element as the option name (note that this makes empty strings as arguments indistinguishable). A mandatory argument is added as a separate element unless the ':-' form is used, in which case the argument is put into the same element.

A '+' as described above may appear between the *name* and the first colon.

The options of **zparseopts** itself cannot be stacked because, for example, the stack '-DEK' is indistinguishable from a *spec* for the GNU-style long option '--DEK'. The options of **zparseopts** itself are:

-a *array*   As described above, this names the default array in which to store the recognised options.

-A *assoc*   If this is given, the options and their values are also put into an associative array with the option names as keys and the arguments (if any) as the values.

-D   If this option is given, all options found are removed from the positional parameters of the calling shell or shell function, up to but not including any not described by the *spec*s. This is similar to using the **shift** builtin.

-K   With this option, the arrays specified with the -a option and with the '=*array*' forms are kept unchanged when none of the *spec*s for them is used. Otherwise the entire array is replaced when any of the *spec*s is used. Individual elements of associative arrays specified with the -A option are preserved by -K. This allows assignment of default values to arrays before calling **zparseopts**.

-M   This changes the assignment rules to implement a map among equivalent option names. If any *spec* uses the '=*array*' form, the string *array* is interpreted as the name of another *spec*, which is used to choose where to store the values. If no other *spec* is found, the values are stored as usual. This changes only the way the values are stored, not the way $* is parsed, so results may be unpredictable if the '*name*+' specifier is used inconsistently.

-E   This changes the parsing rules to *not* stop at the first string that isn't described by one of the *spec*s. It can be used to test for or (if used together with -D) extract options and their arguments, ignoring all other options and arguments that may be in the positional parameters.

For example,

```
set -- -a -bx -c y -cz baz -cend
zparseopts a=foo b:=bar c+:=bar
```

will have the effect of

```
foo=(-a)
bar=(-b x -c y -c z)
```

The arguments from 'baz' on will not be used.

As an example for the -E option, consider:

```
set -- -a x -b y -c z arg1 arg2
zparseopts -E -D b:=bar
```

will have the effect of

```
bar=(-b y)
```

```
set -- -a x -c z arg1 arg2
```

I.e., the option -b and its arguments are taken from the positional parameters and put into the array `bar`.

The -M option can be used like this:

```
set -- -a -bx -c y -cz baz -cend
zparseopts -A bar -M a=foo b+: c:=b
```

to have the effect of

```
foo=(-a)
bar=(-a '' -b xyz)
```

23 Calendar Function System

23.1 Description

The shell is supplied with a series of functions to replace and enhance the traditional Unix `calendar` programme, which warns the user of imminent or future events, details of which are stored in a text file (typically `calendar` in the user's home directory). The version provided here includes a mechanism for alerting the user when an event is due.

In addition functions `age`, `before` and `after` are provided that can be used in a glob qualifier; they allow files to be selected based on their modification times.

The format of the `calendar` file and the dates used there in and in the `age` function are described first, then the functions that can be called to examine and modify the `calendar` file.

The functions here depend on the availability of the `zsh/datetime` module which is usually installed with the shell. The library function `strptime()` must be available; it is present on most recent operating systems.

23.2 File and Date Formats

23.2.1 Calendar File Format

The calendar file is by default `~/calendar`. This can be configured by the `calendar-file` style, see Section 23.4 [Calendar Styles], page 398. The basic format consists of a series of separate lines, with no indentation, each including a date and time specification followed by a description of the event.

Various enhancements to this format are supported, based on the syntax of Emacs calendar mode. An indented line indicates a continuation line that continues the description of the event from the preceding line (note the date may not be continued in this way). An initial ampersand (&) is ignored for compatibility.

An indented line on which the first non-whitespace character is # is not displayed with the calendar entry, but is still scanned for information. This can be used to hide information useful to the calendar system but not to the user, such as the unique identifier used by `calendar_add`.

The Emacs extension that a date with no description may refer to a number of succeeding events at different times is not supported.

Unless the `done-file` style has been altered, any events which have been processed are appended to the file with the same name as the calendar file with the suffix `.done`, hence `~/calendar.done` by default.

An example is shown below.

23.2.2 Date Format

The format of the date and time is designed to allow flexibility without admitting ambiguity. (The words 'date' and 'time' are both used in the documentation below; except where specifically noted this implies a string that may include both a date and a time specification.) Note that there is no localization support; month and day names must be in English and separator characters are fixed. Matching is case insensitive, and only the first three letters of the names are significant, although as a special case a form beginning "month" does not match "Monday". Furthermore, time zones are not handled; all times are assumed to be local.

It is recommended that, rather than exploring the intricacies of the system, users find a date format that is natural to them and stick to it. This will avoid unexpected effects. Various key facts should be noted.

- In particular, note the confusion between *month/day/year* and *day/month/year* when the month is numeric; these formats should be avoided if at all possible. Many alternatives are available.

- The year must be given in full to avoid confusion, and only years from 1900 to 2099 inclusive are matched.

The following give some obvious examples; users finding here a format they like and not subject to vagaries of style may skip the full description. As dates and times are matched separately (even though the time may be embedded in the date), any date format may be mixed with any format for the time of day provide the separators are clear (whitespace, colons, commas).

```
2007/04/03 13:13
2007/04/03:13:13
2007/04/03 1:13 pm
3rd April 2007, 13:13
April 3rd 2007 1:13 p.m.
Apr 3, 2007 13:13
Tue Apr 03 13:13:00 2007
13:13 2007/apr/3
```

More detailed rules follow.

Times are parsed and extracted before dates. They must use colons to separate hours and minutes, though a dot is allowed before seconds if they are present. This limits time formats to the following:

- HH:MM[:SS[.$FFFFF$]] [am|pm|a.m.|p.m.]

- $HH\!:\!MM.SS[.FFFFF]$ [am|pm|a.m.|p.m.]

Here, square brackets indicate optional elements, possibly with alternatives. Fractions of a second are recognised but ignored. For absolute times (the normal format require by the **calendar** file and the **age**, **before** and **after** functions) a date is mandatory but a time of day is not; the time returned is at the start of the date. One variation is allowed: if **a.m.** or **p.m.** or one of their variants is present, an hour without a minute is allowed, e.g. **3 p.m.**.

Time zones are not handled, though if one is matched following a time specification it will be removed to allow a surrounding date to be parsed. This only happens if the format of the timezone is not too unusual. The following are examples of forms that are understood:

```
+0100
GMT
GMT-7
CET+1CDT
```

Any part of the timezone that is not numeric must have exactly three capital letters in the name.

Dates suffer from the ambiguity between $DD/MM/YYYY$ and $MM/DD/YYYY$. It is recommended this form is avoided with purely numeric dates, but use of ordinals, eg. **3rd/04/2007**, will resolve the ambiguity as the ordinal is always parsed as the day of the month. Years must be four digits (and the first two must be **19** or **20**); **03/04/08** is not recognised. Other numbers may have leading zeroes, but they are not required. The following are handled:

- $YYYY/MM/DD$
- $YYYY\text{-}MM\text{-}DD$
- $YYYY/MNM/DD$
- $YYYY\text{-}MNM\text{-}DD$
- DD[th|st|rd] MNM[,] [$YYYY$]
- MNM DD[th|st|rd][,] [$YYYY$]
- DD[th|st|rd]$/MM$[,] $YYYY$
- DD[th|st|rd]$/MM/YYYY$
- MM/DD[th|st|rd][,] $YYYY$
- MM/DD[th|st|rd]$/YYYY$

Here, MNM is at least the first three letters of a month name, matched case-insensitively. The remainder of the month name may appear but its contents are irrelevant, so janissary, febrile, martial, apricot, maybe, junta, etc. are happily handled.

Where the year is shown as optional, the current year is assumed. There are only two such cases, the form **Jun 20** or **14 September** (the only two commonly occurring forms, apart from a "the" in some forms of English, which isn't currently supported). Such dates will of course become ambiguous in the future, so should ideally be avoided.

Times may follow dates with a colon, e.g. **1965/07/12:09:45**; this is in order to provide a format with no whitespace. A comma and whitespace are allowed, e.g. **1965/07/12, 09:45**. Currently the order of these separators is not checked, so illogical formats such as **1965/07/12, : ,09:45** will also be matched. For simplicity such variations are not shown in the list above. Otherwise, a time is only recognised as being associated with a date if there is only whitespace in between, or if the time was embedded in the date.

Days of the week are not normally scanned, but will be ignored if they occur at the start of the date pattern only. However, in contexts where it is useful to specify dates relative to today, days of the week with no other date specification may be given. The day is assumed to be either today or within the past week. Likewise, the words yesterday, today and tomorrow are handled. All matches are case-insensitive. Hence if today is Monday, then Sunday is equivalent to yesterday, Monday is equivalent to today, but Tuesday gives a date six days ago. This is not generally useful within the calendar file. Dates in this format may be combined with a time specification; for example Tomorrow, 8 p.m..

For example, the standard date format:

```
Fri Aug 18 17:00:48 BST 2006
```

is handled by matching $HH{:}MM{:}SS$ and removing it together with the matched (but unused) time zone. This leaves the following:

```
Fri Aug 18 2006
```

Fri is ignored and the rest is matched according to the standard rules.

23.2.3 Relative Time Format

In certain places relative times are handled. Here, a date is not allowed; instead a combination of various supported periods are allowed, together with an optional time. The periods must be in order from most to least significant.

In some cases, a more accurate calculation is possible when there is an anchor date: offsets of months or years pick the correct day, rather than being rounded, and it is possible to pick a particular day in a month as '(1st Friday)', etc., as described in more detail below.

Anchors are available in the following cases. If one or two times are passed to the function calendar, the start time acts an anchor for the end time when the end time is relative (even if the start time is implicit). When examining calendar files, the scheduled event being examined anchors the warning time when it is given explicitly by means of the WARN keyword; likewise, the scheduled event anchors a repetition period when given by the RPT keyword, so that specifications such as RPT 2 months, 3rd Thursday are handled properly. Finally, the -R argument to calendar_scandate directly provides an anchor for relative calculations.

The periods handled, with possible abbreviations are:

Years	years, yrs, ys, year, yr, y, yearly. A year is 365.25 days unless there is an anchor.
Months	months, mons, mnths, mths, month, mon, mnth, mth, monthly. Note that m, ms, mn, mns are ambiguous and are *not* handled. A month is a period of 30 days rather than a calendar month unless there is an anchor.
Weeks	weeks, wks, ws, week, wk, w, weekly
Days	days, dys, ds, day, dy, d, daily
Hours	hours, hrs, hs, hour, hr, h, hourly
Minutes	minutes, mins, minute, min, but *not* m, ms, mn or mns

Seconds   `seconds, secs, ss, second, sec, s`

Spaces between the numbers are optional, but are required between items, although a comma may be used (with or without spaces).

The forms `yearly` to `hourly` allow the number to be omitted; it is assumed to be 1. For example, `1 d` and `daily` are equivalent. Note that using those forms with plurals is confusing; `2 yearly` is the same as `2 years`, *not* twice yearly, so it is recommended they only be used without numbers.

When an anchor time is present, there is an extension to handle regular events in the form of the *n*th *someday* of the month. Such a specification must occur immediately after any year and month specification, but before any time of day, and must be in the form *n*(`th`|`st`|`rd`) *day*, for example `1st Tuesday` or `3rd Monday`. As in other places, days are matched case insensitively, must be in English, and only the first three letters are significant except that a form beginning 'month' does not match 'Monday'. No attempt is made to sanitize the resulting date; attempts to squeeze too many occurrences into a month will push the day into the next month (but in the obvious fashion, retaining the correct day of the week).

Here are some examples:

```
30 years 3 months 4 days 3:42:41
14 days 5 hours
Monthly, 3rd Thursday
4d,10hr
```

23.2.4 Example

Here is an example calendar file. It uses a consistent date format, as recommended above.

```
Feb 1, 2006 14:30 Pointless bureaucratic meeting
Mar 27, 2006 11:00 Mutual recrimination and finger pointing
  Bring water pistol and waterproofs
Mar 31, 2006 14:00 Very serious managerial pontification
  # UID 12C7878A9A50
Apr 10, 2006 13:30 Even more pointless blame assignment exercise WARN 30 mins
May 18, 2006 16:00 Regular moaning session RPT monthly, 3rd Thursday
```

The second entry has a continuation line. The third entry has a continuation line that will not be shown when the entry is displayed, but the unique identifier will be used by the `calendar_add` function when updating the event. The fourth entry will produce a warning 30 minutes before the event (to allow you to equip yourself appropriately). The fifth entry repeats after a month on the 3rd Thursday, i.e. June 15, 2006, at the same time.

23.3 User Functions

This section describes functions that are designed to be called directly by the user. The first part describes those functions associated with the user's calendar; the second part describes the use in glob qualifiers.

23.3.1 Calendar system functions

calendar [-abdDsv] [-C *calfile*] [-n *num*] [-S *showprog*]
      [[*start*] *end*]
calendar -r [-abdDrsv] [-C *calfile*] [-n *num*] [-S *showprog*]
      [*start*]

Show events in the calendar.

With no arguments, show events from the start of today until the end of the next working day after today. In other words, if today is Friday, Saturday, or Sunday, show up to the end of the following Monday, otherwise show today and tomorrow.

If *end* is given, show events from the start of today up to the time and date given, which is in the format described in the previous section. Note that if this is a date the time is assumed to be midnight at the start of the date, so that effectively this shows all events before the given date.

end may start with a +, in which case the remainder of the specification is a relative time format as described in the previous section indicating the range of time from the start time that is to be included.

If *start* is also given, show events starting from that time and date. The word now can be used to indicate the current time.

To implement an alert when events are due, include **calendar -s** in your ~/.zshrc file.

Options:

-a   Show all items in the calendar, regardless of the **start** and **end**.

-b   Brief: don't display continuation lines (i.e. indented lines following the line with the date/time), just the first line.

-B *lines*   Brief: display at most the first *lines* lines of the calendar entry. '-B 1' is equivalent to '-b'.

-C *calfile* Explicitly specify a calendar file instead of the value of the **calendar-file** style or the default ~/calendar.

-d   Move any events that have passed from the calendar file to the "done" file, as given by the **done-file** style or the default which is the calendar file with .done appended. This option is implied by the -s option.

-D   Turns off the option -d, even if the -s option is also present.

-n *num*, -*num*
        Show at least *num* events, if present in the calendar file, regardless of the **start** and **end**.

-r   Show all the remaining options in the calendar, ignoring the given *end* time. The *start* time is respected; any argument given is treated as a *start* time.

-s   Use the shell's `sched` command to schedule a timed event that will warn the user when an event is due. Note that the `sched` command only runs if the shell is at an interactive prompt; a foreground task blocks the scheduled task from running until it is finished.

The timed event usually runs the programme `calendar_show` to show the event, as described in Section 23.5 [Calendar Utility Functions], page 399.

By default, a warning of the event is shown five minutes before it is due. The warning period can be configured by the style `warn-time` or for a single calendar entry by including `WARN` *reltime* in the first line of the entry, where *reltime* is one of the usual relative time formats.

A repeated event may be indicated by including `RPT` *reldate* in the first line of the entry. After the scheduled event has been displayed it will be re-entered into the calendar file at a time *reldate* after the existing event. Note that this is currently the only use made of the repeat count, so that it is not possible to query the schedule for a recurrence of an event in the calendar until the previous event has passed.

If `RPT` is used, it is also possible to specify that certain recurrences of an event are rescheduled or cancelled. This is done with the `OCCURRENCE` keyword, followed by whitespace and the date and time of the occurrence in the regular sequence, followed by whitespace and either the date and time of the rescheduled event or the exact string `CANCELLED`. In this case the date and time must be in exactly the "date with local time" format used by the `text/calendar` MIME type (RFC 2445), *<YYYY><MM><DD>*T*<hh><mm><ss>* (note the presence of the literal character `T`). The first word (the regular recurrence) may be something other than a proper date/time to indicate that the event is additional to the normal sequence; a convention that retains the formatting appearance is `XXXXXXXTXXXXX`.

Furthermore, it is useful to record the next regular recurrence (as then the displayed date may be for a rescheduled event so cannot be used for calculating the regular sequence). This is specified by `RECURRENCE` and a time or date in the same format. `calendar_add` adds such an indication when it encounters a recurring event that does not include one, based on the headline date/time.

If `calendar_add` is used to update occurrences the `UID` keyword described there should be present in both the existing entry and the added occurrence in order to identify recurring event sequences.

For example,

```
Thu May 6, 2010 11:00 Informal chat RPT 1 week
  # RECURRENCE 20100506T110000
  # OCCURRENCE 20100513T110000 20100513T120000
```

```
# OCCURRENCE 20100520T110000 CANCELLED
```

The event that occurs at 11:00 on 13th May 2010 is rescheduled an hour later. The event that occurs a week later is cancelled. The occurrences are given on a continuation line starting with a # character so will not usually be displayed as part of the event. As elsewhere, no account of time zones is taken with the times. After the next event occurs the headline date/time will be 'Thu May 13, 2010 12:00' while the RECURRENCE date/time will be '20100513T110000' (note that cancelled and moved events are not taken account of in the RECURRENCE, which records what the next regular recurrence is, but they are accounted for in the headline date/time).

It is safe to run calendar -s to reschedule an existing event (if the calendar file has changed, for example), and also to have it running in multiples instances of the shell since the calendar file is locked when in use.

By default, expired events are moved to the "done" file; see the -d option. Use -D to prevent this.

-S *showprog*

    Explicitly specify a programme to be used for showing events instead of the value of the show-prog style or the default calendar_show.

-v   Verbose: show more information about stages of processing. This is useful for confirming that the function has successfully parsed the dates in the calendar file.

calendar_add [-BL] *event* ...

Adds a single event to the calendar in the appropriate location. The event can contain multiple lines, as described in Section 23.2 [Calendar File and Date Formats], page 387. Using this function ensures that the calendar file is sorted in date and time order. It also makes special arrangements for locking the file while it is altered. The old calendar is left in a file with the suffix .old.

The option -B indicates that backing up the calendar file will be handled by the caller and should not be performed by calendar_add. The option -L indicates that calendar_add does not need to lock the calendar file as it is already locked. These options will not usually be needed by users.

If the style reformat-date is true, the date and time of the new entry will be rewritten into the standard date format: see the descriptions of this style and the style date-format.

The function can use a unique identifier stored with each event to ensure that updates to existing events are treated correctly. The entry should contain the word UID, followed by whitespace, followed by a word consisting entirely of hexadecimal digits of arbitrary length (all digits are significant, including leading zeroes). As the UID is not directly useful to the user, it is convenient to hide it on an indented continuation line starting with a #, for example:

> ```
> Aug 31, 2007 09:30  Celebrate the end of the holidays
>  # UID 045B78A0
> ```

The second line will not be shown by the `calendar` function.

It is possible to specify the `RPT` keyword followed by `CANCELLED` instead of a relative time. This causes any matched event or series of events to be cancelled (the original event does not have to be marked as recurring in order to be cancelled by this method). A `UID` is required in order to match an existing event in the calendar.

`calendar_add` will attempt to manage recurrences and occurrences of repeating events as described for event scheduling by `calendar -s` above. To reschedule or cancel a single event `calendar_add` should be called with an entry that includes the correct `UID` but does *not* include the `RPT` keyword as this is taken to mean the entry applies to a series of repeating events and hence replaces all existing information. Each rescheduled or cancelled occurrence must have an `OCCURRENCE` keyword in the entry passed to `calendar_add` which will be merged into the calendar file. Any existing reference to the occurrence is replaced. An occurrence that does not refer to a valid existing event is added as a one-off occurrence to the same calendar entry.

`calendar_edit`

This calls the user's editor to edit the calendar file. If there are arguments, they are taken as the editor to use (the file name is appended to the commands); otherwise, the editor is given by the variable `VISUAL`, if set, else the variable `EDITOR`.

If the calendar scheduler was running, then after editing the file `calendar -s` is called to update it.

This function locks out the calendar system during the edit. Hence it should be used to edit the calendar file if there is any possibility of a calendar event occurring meanwhile. Note this can lead to another shell with calendar functions enabled hanging waiting for a lock, so it is necessary to quit the editor as soon as possible.

`calendar_parse` *calendar-entry*

This is the internal function that analyses the parts of a calendar entry, which is passed as the only argument. The function returns status 1 if the argument could not be parsed as a calendar entry and status 2 if the wrong number of arguments were passed; it also sets the parameter `reply` to an empty associative array. Otherwise, it returns status 0 and sets elements of the associative array `reply` as follows:

`time`   The time as a string of digits in the same units as `$EPOCHSECONDS`

`schedtime`

The regularly scheduled time. This may differ from the actual event time `time` if this is a recurring event and the next occurrence has been rescheduled. Then `time` gives the actual time and `schedtime` the time of the regular recurrence before modification.

text1   The text from the line not including the date and time of the event, but including any WARN or RPT keywords and values.

warntime   Any warning time given by the WARN keyword as a string of digits containing the time at which to warn in the same units as $EPOCHSECONDS. (Note this is an absolute time, not the relative time passed down.) Not set no WARN keyword and value were matched.

warnstr   The raw string matched after the WARN keyword, else unset.

rpttime   Any recurrence time given by the RPT keyword as a string of digits containing the time of the recurrence in the same units as $EPOCHSECONDS. (Note this is an absolute time.) Not set if no RPT keyword and value were matched.

schedrpttime
            The next regularly scheduled occurrence of a recurring event before modification. This may differ from rpttime, which is the actual time of the event that may have been rescheduled from the regular time.

rptstr   The raw string matched after the RPT keyword, else unset.

text2   The text from the line after removal of the date and any keywords and values.

calendar_showdate [-r] [-f fmt] date-spec ...
            The given date-spec is interpreted and the corresponding date and time printed. If the initial date-spec begins with a + or – it is treated as relative to the current time; date-specs after the first are treated as relative to the date calculated so far and a leading + is optional in that case. This allows one to use the system as a date calculator. For example, calendar_showdate '+1 month, 1st Friday' shows the date of the first Friday of next month.

            With the option -r nothing is printed but the value of the date and time in seconds since the epoch is stored in the parameter REPLY.

            With the option -f fmt the given date/time conversion format is passed to strftime; see notes on the date-format style below.

            In order to avoid ambiguity with negative relative date specifications, options must occur in separate words; in other words, -r and -f should not be combined in the same word.

calendar_sort
            Sorts the calendar file into date and time order. The old calendar is left in a file with the suffix .old.

23.3.2 Glob qualifiers

age   The function age can be autoloaded and use separately from the calendar system, although it uses the function calendar_scandate for date formatting. It requires the zsh/stat builtin, but uses only the builtin zstat.

`age` selects files having a given modification time for use as a glob qualifier. The format of the date is the same as that understood by the calendar system, described in Section 23.2 [Calendar File and Date Formats], page 387.

The function can take one or two arguments, which can be supplied either directly as command or arguments, or separately as shell parameters.

```
print *(e:age 2006/10/04 2006/10/09:)
```

The example above matches all files modified between the start of those dates. The second argument may alternatively be a relative time introduced by a +:

```
print *(e:age 2006/10/04 +5d:)
```

The example above is equivalent to the previous example.

In addition to the special use of days of the week, `today` and `yesterday`, times with no date may be specified; these apply to today. Obviously such uses become problematic around midnight.

```
print *(e-age 12:00 13:30-)
```

The example above shows files modified between 12:00 and 13:00 today.

```
print *(e:age 2006/10/04:)
```

The example above matches all files modified on that date. If the second argument is omitted it is taken to be exactly 24 hours after the first argument (even if the first argument contains a time).

```
print *(e-age 2006/10/04:10:15 2006/10/04:10:45-)
```

The example above supplies times. Note that whitespace within the time and date specification must be quoted to ensure `age` receives the correct arguments, hence the use of the additional colon to separate the date and time.

```
AGEREF=2006/10/04:10:15
AGEREF2=2006/10/04:10:45
print *(+age)
```

This shows the same example before using another form of argument passing. The dates and times in the parameters `AGEREF` and `AGEREF2` stay in effect until unset, but will be overridden if any argument is passed as an explicit argument to age. Any explicit argument causes both parameters to be ignored.

Instead of an explicit date and time, it's possible to use the modification time of a file as the date and time for either argument by introducing the file name with a colon:

```
print *(e-age :file1-)
```

matches all files created on the same day (24 hours starting from midnight) as `file1`.

```
print *(e-age :file1 :file2-)
```

matches all files modified no earlier than `file1` and no later than `file2`; precision here is to the nearest second.

after
before   The functions `after` and `before` are simpler versions of `age` that take just one argument. The argument is parsed similarly to an argument of `age`; if it

is not given the variable `AGEREF` is consulted. As the names of the functions suggest, a file matches if its modification time is after or before the time and date specified. If a time only is given the date is today.

The two following examples are therefore equivalent:

```
print *(e-after 12:00-)
print *(e-after today:12:00-)
```

23.4 Styles

The zsh style mechanism using the `zstyle` command is describe in Section 22.37 [The zsh/zutil Module], page 382. This is the same mechanism used in the completion system.

The styles below are all examined in the context `:datetime:`*function*`:`, for example `:datetime:calendar:`.

`calendar-file`

> The location of the main calendar. The default is `~/calendar`.

`date-format`

> A `strftime` format string (see man page strftime(3)) with the zsh extensions providing various numbers with no leading zero or space if the number is a single digit as described for the `%D{`*string*`}` prompt format in Chapter 13 [Prompt Expansion], page 39.

> This is used for outputting dates in `calendar`, both to support the `-v` option and when adding recurring events back to the calendar file, and in `calendar_showdate` as the final output format.

> If the style is not set, the default used is similar the standard system format as output by the `date` command (also known as 'ctime format'): '`%a %b %d %H:%M:%S %Z %Y`'.

`done-file`

> The location of the file to which events which have passed are appended. The default is the calendar file location with the suffix `.done`. The style may be set to an empty string in which case a "done" file will not be maintained.

`reformat-date`

> Boolean, used by `calendar_add`. If it is true, the date and time of new entries added to the calendar will be reformatted to the format given by the style `date-format` or its default. Only the date and time of the event itself is reformatted; any subsidiary dates and times such as those associated with repeat and warning times are left alone.

`show-prog`

> The programme run by `calendar` for showing events. It will be passed the start time and stop time of the events requested in seconds since the epoch followed by the event text. Note that `calendar -s` uses a start time and stop time equal to one another to indicate alerts for specific events.

> The default is the function `calendar_show`.

`warn-time`

> The time before an event at which a warning will be displayed, if the first line of the event does not include the text **EVENT** *reltime*. The default is 5 minutes.

23.5 Utility functions

`calendar_lockfiles`

> Attempt to lock the files given in the argument. To prevent problems with network file locking this is done in an ad hoc fashion by attempting to create a symbolic link to the file with the name *file*.`lockfile`. No other system level functions are used for locking, i.e. the file can be accessed and modified by any utility that does not use this mechanism. In particular, the user is not prevented from editing the calendar file at the same time unless `calendar_edit` is used.
>
> Three attempts are made to lock the file before giving up. If the module **zsh/zselect** is available, the times of the attempts are jittered so that multiple instances of the calling function are unlikely to retry at the same time.
>
> The files locked are appended to the array **lockfiles**, which should be local to the caller.
>
> If all files were successfully locked, status zero is returned, else status one.
>
> This function may be used as a general file locking function, although this will only work if only this mechanism is used to lock files.

`calendar_read`

> This is a backend used by various other functions to parse the calendar file, which is passed as the only argument. The array `calendar_entries` is set to the list of events in the file; no pruning is done except that ampersands are removed from the start of the line. Each entry may contain multiple lines.

`calendar_scandate`

> This is a generic function to parse dates and times that may be used separately from the calendar system. The argument is a date or time specification as described in Section 23.2 [Calendar File and Date Formats], page 387. The parameter **REPLY** is set to the number of seconds since the epoch corresponding to that date or time. By default, the date and time may occur anywhere within the given argument.
>
> Returns status zero if the date and time were successfully parsed, else one.
>
> Options:

> `-a` The date and time are anchored to the start of the argument; they will not be matched if there is preceding text.

> `-A` The date and time are anchored to both the start and end of the argument; they will not be matched if the is any other text in the argument.

> `-d` Enable additional debugging output.

> `-m` Minus. When `-R` *anchor_time* is also given the relative time is calculated backwards from *anchor_time*.

-r   The argument passed is to be parsed as a relative time.

-R *anchor_time*

The argument passed is to be parsed as a relative time. The time is relative to *anchor_time*, a time in seconds since the epoch, and the returned value is the absolute time corresponding to advancing *anchor_time* by the relative time given. This allows lengths of months to be correctly taken into account. If the final day does not exist in the given month, the last day of the final month is given. For example, if the anchor time is during 31st January 2007 and the relative time is 1 month, the final time is the same time of day during 28th February 2007.

-s   In addition to setting **REPLY**, set **REPLY2** to the remainder of the argument after the date and time have been stripped. This is empty if the option **-A** was given.

-t   Allow a time with no date specification. The date is assumed to be today. The behaviour is unspecified if the iron tongue of midnight is tolling twelve.

calendar_show

The function used by default to display events. It accepts a start time and end time for events, both in epoch seconds, and an event description.

The event is always printed to standard output. If the command line editor is active (which will usually be the case) the command line will be redisplayed after the output.

If the parameter **DISPLAY** is set and the start and end times are the same (indicating a scheduled event), the function uses the command **xmessage** to display a window with the event details.

23.6 Bugs

As the system is based entirely on shell functions (with a little support from the **zsh/datetime** module) the mechanisms used are not as robust as those provided by a dedicated calendar utility. Consequently the user should not rely on the shell for vital alerts.

There is no **calendar_delete** function.

There is no localization support for dates and times, nor any support for the use of time zones.

Relative periods of months and years do not take into account the variable number of days.

The **calendar_show** function is currently hardwired to use **xmessage** for displaying alerts on X Window System displays. This should be configurable and ideally integrate better with the desktop.

calendar_lockfiles hangs the shell while waiting for a lock on a file. If called from a scheduled task, it should instead reschedule the event that caused it.

24 TCP Function System

24.1 Description

A module `zsh/net/tcp` is provided to provide network I/O over TCP/IP from within the shell; see its description in Chapter 22 [Zsh Modules], page 329. This manual page describes a function suite based on the module. If the module is installed, the functions are usually installed at the same time, in which case they will be available for autoloading in the default function search path. In addition to the `zsh/net/tcp` module, the `zsh/zselect` module is used to implement timeouts on read operations. For troubleshooting tips, consult the corresponding advice for the `zftp` functions described in Chapter 25 [Zftp Function System], page 413.

There are functions corresponding to the basic I/O operations open, close, read and send, named `tcp_open` etc., as well as a function `tcp_expect` for pattern match analysis of data read as input. The system makes it easy to receive data from and send data to multiple named sessions at once. In addition, it can be linked with the shell's line editor in such a way that input data is automatically shown at the terminal. Other facilities available including logging, filtering and configurable output prompts.

To use the system where it is available, it should be enough to 'autoload -U tcp_open' and run `tcp_open` as documented below to start a session. The `tcp_open` function will autoload the remaining functions.

24.2 TCP User Functions

24.2.1 Basic I/O

`tcp_open` [-qz] *host port* [*sess*]
`tcp_open` [-qz] [-s *sess* | -l *sess*[,...]] ...
`tcp_open` [-qz] [-a *fd* | -f *fd*] [*sess*]

        Open a new session. In the first and simplest form, open a TCP connection to host *host* at port *port*; numeric and symbolic forms are understood for both.

        If *sess* is given, this becomes the name of the session which can be used to refer to multiple different TCP connections. If *sess* is not given, the function will invent a numeric name value (note this is *not* the same as the file descriptor to which the session is attached). It is recommended that session names not include 'funny' characters, where funny characters are not well-defined but certainly do not include alphanumerics or underscores, and certainly do include whitespace.

        In the second case, one or more sessions to be opened are given by name. A single session name is given after -s and a comma-separated list after -l; both options may be repeated as many times as necessary. A failure to open any session causes `tcp_open` to abort. The host and port are read from the file `.ztcp_sessions` in the same directory as the user's zsh initialisation files, i.e. usually the home directory, but `$ZDOTDIR` if that is set. The file consists of lines each giving a session name and the corresponding host and port, in that order (note the session name comes first, not last), separated by whitespace.

The third form allows passive and fake TCP connections. If the option -a is used, its argument is a file descriptor open for listening for connections. No function front-end is provided to open such a file descriptor, but a call to 'ztcp -l *port*' will create one with the file descriptor stored in the parameter $REPLY. The listening port can be closed with 'ztcp -c *fd*'. A call to 'tcp_open -a *fd*' will block until a remote TCP connection is made to *port* on the local machine. At this point, a session is created in the usual way and is largely indistinguishable from an active connection created with one of the first two forms.

If the option -f is used, its argument is a file descriptor which is used directly as if it were a TCP session. How well the remainder of the TCP function system copes with this depends on what actually underlies this file descriptor. A regular file is likely to be unusable; a FIFO (pipe) of some sort will work better, but note that it is not a good idea for two different sessions to attempt to read from the same FIFO at once.

If the option -q is given with any of the three forms, tcp_open will not print informational messages, although it will in any case exit with an appropriate status.

If the line editor (zle) is in use, which is typically the case if the shell is interactive, tcp_open installs a handler inside zle which will check for new data at the same time as it checks for keyboard input. This is convenient as the shell consumes no CPU time while waiting; the test is performed by the operating system. Giving the option -z to any of the forms of tcp_open prevents the handler from being installed, so data must be read explicitly. Note, however, this is not necessary for executing complete sets of send and read commands from a function, as zle is not active at this point. Generally speaking, the handler is only active when the shell is waiting for input at a command prompt or in the vared builtin. The option has no effect if zle is not active; '[[-o zle]]' will test for this.

The first session to be opened becomes the current session and subsequent calls to tcp_open do not change it. The current session is stored in the parameter $TCP_SESS; see below for more detail about the parameters used by the system.

The function tcp_on_open, if defined, is called when a session is opened. See the description below.

tcp_close [-qn] [-a | -l *sess*[,...] | *sess* ...]

Close the named sessions, or the current session if none is given, or all open sessions if -a is given. The options -l and -s are both handled for consistency with tcp_open, although the latter is redundant.

If the session being closed is the current one, $TCP_SESS is unset, leaving no current session, even if there are other sessions still open.

If the session was opened with tcp_open -f, the file descriptor is closed so long as it is in the range 0 to 9 accessible directly from the command line. If the option -n is given, no attempt will be made to close file descriptors in this case. The **-n** option is not used for genuine `ztcp` session; the file descriptors are always closed with the session.

If the option **-q** is given, no informational messages will be printed.

`tcp_read` [-bdq] [-t *TO*] [-T *TO*]
        [-a | -u *fd*[,...] | -l *sess*[,...] | -s *sess* ...]

Perform a read operation on the current session, or on a list of sessions if any are given with **-u**, **-l** or **-s**, or all open sessions if the option **-a** is given. Any of the **-u**, **-l** or **-s** options may be repeated or mixed together. The **-u** option specifies a file descriptor directly (only those managed by this system are useful), the other two specify sessions as described for `tcp_open` above.

The function checks for new data available on all the sessions listed. Unless the **-b** option is given, it will not block waiting for new data. Any one line of data from any of the available sessions will be read, stored in the parameter `$TCP_LINE`, and displayed to standard output unless `$TCP_SILENT` contains a non-empty string. When printed to standard output the string `$TCP_PROMPT` will be shown at the start of the line; the default form for this includes the name of the session being read. See below for more information on these parameters. In this mode, `tcp_read` can be called repeatedly until it returns status 2 which indicates all pending input from all specified sessions has been handled.

With the option **-b**, equivalent to an infinite timeout, the function will block until a line is available to read from one of the specified sessions. However, only a single line is returned.

The option **-d** indicates that all pending input should be drained. In this case `tcp_read` may process multiple lines in the manner given above; only the last is stored in `$TCP_LINE`, but the complete set is stored in the array `$tcp_lines`. This is cleared at the start of each call to `tcp_read`.

The options **-t** and **-T** specify a timeout in seconds, which may be a floating point number for increased accuracy. With **-t** the timeout is applied before each line read. With **-T**, the timeout applies to the overall operation, possibly including multiple read operations if the option **-d** is present; without this option, there is no distinction between **-t** and **-T**.

The function does not print informational messages, but if the option **-q** is given, no error message is printed for a non-existent session.

A return status of 2 indicates a timeout or no data to read. Any other non-zero return status indicates some error condition.

See `tcp_log` for how to control where data is sent by `tcp_read`.

`tcp_send` [-cnq] [-s *sess* | -l *sess*[,...]] *data* ...
`tcp_send` [-cnq] -a *data* ...

Send the supplied data strings to all the specified sessions in turn. The underlying operation differs little from a '`print -r`' to the session's file descriptor, although it attempts to prevent the shell from dying owing to a **SIGPIPE** caused by an attempt to write to a defunct session.

The option **-c** causes `tcp_send` to behave like `cat`. It reads lines from standard input until end of input and sends them in turn to the specified session(s) exactly as if they were given as *data* arguments to individual `tcp_send` commands.

The option -n prevents `tcp_send` from putting a newline at the end of the data strings.

The remaining options all behave as for `tcp_read`.

The data arguments are not further processed once they have been passed to `tcp_send`; they are simply passed down to `print -r`.

If the parameter `$TCP_OUTPUT` is a non-empty string and logging is enabled then the data sent to each session will be echoed to the log file(s) with `$TCP_OUTPUT` in front where appropriate, much in the manner of `$TCP_PROMPT`.

24.2.2 Session Management

tcp_alias [-q] *alias=sess* ...
tcp_alias [-q] [*alias* ...]
tcp_alias -d [-q] *alias* ...

This function is not particularly well tested.

The first form creates an alias for a session name; *alias* can then be used to refer to the existing session *sess*. As many aliases may be listed as required.

The second form lists any aliases specified, or all aliases if none.

The third form deletes all the aliases listed. The underlying sessions are not affected.

The option -q suppresses an inconsistently chosen subset of error messages.

tcp_log [-asc] [-n | -N] [*logfile*]

With an argument *logfile*, all future input from `tcp_read` will be logged to the named file. Unless -a (append) is given, this file will first be truncated or created empty. With no arguments, show the current status of logging.

With the option -s, per-session logging is enabled. Input from `tcp_read` is output to the file *logfile.sess*. As the session is automatically discriminated by the filename, the contents are raw (no `$TCP_PROMPT`). The option -a applies as above. Per-session logging and logging of all data in one file are not mutually exclusive.

The option -c closes all logging, both complete and per-session logs.

The options -n and -N respectively turn off or restore output of data read by `tcp_read` to standard output; hence '`tcp_log -cn`' turns off all output by `tcp_read`.

The function is purely a convenient front end to setting the parameters `$TCP_LOG`, `$TCP_LOG_SESS`, `$TCP_SILENT`, which are described below.

tcp_rename *old new*

Rename session *old* to session *new*. The old name becomes invalid.

tcp_sess [*sess* [*command* [*arg* ...]]]

With no arguments, list all the open sessions and associated file descriptors. The current session is marked with a star. For use in functions, direct access to the parameters `$tcp_by_name`, `$tcp_by_fd` and `$TCP_SESS` is probably more convenient; see below.

With a *sess* argument, set the current session to *sess*. This is equivalent to changing $TCP_SESS directly.

With additional arguments, temporarily set the current session while executing '*command arg ...*'. *command* is re-evaluated so as to expand aliases etc., but the remaining *args* are passed through as that appear to `tcp_sess`. The original session is restored when `tcp_sess` exits.

24.2.3 Advanced I/O

`tcp_command` *send-option ... send-argument ...*

This is a convenient front-end to `tcp_send`. All arguments are passed to `tcp_send`, then the function pauses waiting for data. While data is arriving at least every $TCP_TIMEOUT (default 0.3) seconds, data is handled and printed out according to the current settings. Status 0 is always returned.

This is generally only useful for interactive use, to prevent the display becoming fragmented by output returned from the connection. Within a programme or function it is generally better to handle reading data by a more explicit method.

`tcp_expect` [`-q`] [`-p` *var* | `-P` *var*] [`-t` *TO* | `-T` *TO*]
   [`-a` | `-s` *sess* | `-l` *sess*[,...]] *pattern ...*

Wait for input matching any of the given *patterns* from any of the specified sessions. Input is ignored until an input line matches one of the given patterns; at this point status zero is returned, the matching line is stored in $TCP_LINE, and the full set of lines read during the call to `tcp_expect` is stored in the array $tcp_expect_lines.

Sessions are specified in the same way as `tcp_read`: the default is to use the current session, otherwise the sessions specified by `-a`, `-s`, or `-l` are used.

Each *pattern* is a standard zsh extended-globbing pattern; note that it needs to be quoted to avoid it being expanded immediately by filename generation. It must match the full line, so to match a substring there must be a '`*`' at the start and end. The line matched against includes the $TCP_PROMPT added by `tcp_read`. It is possible to include the globbing flags '`#b`' or '`#m`' in the patterns to make backreferences available in the parameters $MATCH, $match, etc., as described in the base zsh documentation on pattern matching.

Unlike `tcp_read`, the default behaviour of `tcp_expect` is to block indefinitely until the required input is found. This can be modified by specifying a timeout with `-t` or `-T`; these function as in `tcp_read`, specifying a per-read or overall timeout, respectively, in seconds, as an integer or floating-point number. As `tcp_read`, the function returns status 2 if a timeout occurs.

The function returns as soon as any one of the patterns given match. If the caller needs to know which of the patterns matched, the option `-p` *var* can be used; on return, $var is set to the number of the pattern using ordinary zsh indexing, i.e. the first is 1, and so on. Note the absence of a '$' in front of *var*. To avoid clashes, the parameter cannot begin with '`_expect`'. The index -1 is used if there is a timeout and 0 if there is no match.

The option `-P` *var* works similarly to `-p`, but instead of numerical indexes the regular arguments must begin with a prefix followed by a colon: that prefix is then used as a tag to which *var* is set when the argument matches. The tag `timeout` is used if there is a timeout and the empty string if there is no match. Note it is acceptable for different arguments to start with the same prefix if the matches do not need to be distinguished.

The option `-q` is passed directly down to `tcp_read`.

As all input is done via `tcp_read`, all the usual rules about output of lines read apply. One exception is that the parameter `$tcp_lines` will only reflect the line actually matched by `tcp_expect`; use `$tcp_expect_lines` for the full set of lines read during the function call.

`tcp_proxy`

This is a simple-minded function to accept a TCP connection and execute a command with I/O redirected to the connection. Extreme caution should be taken as there is no security whatsoever and this can leave your computer open to the world. Ideally, it should only be used behind a firewall.

The first argument is a TCP port on which the function will listen.

The remaining arguments give a command and its arguments to execute with standard input, standard output and standard error redirected to the file descriptor on which the TCP session has been accepted. If no command is given, a new zsh is started. This gives everyone on your network direct access to your account, which in many cases will be a bad thing.

The command is run in the background, so `tcp_proxy` can then accept new connections. It continues to accept new connections until interrupted.

`tcp_spam [ -ertv ] [ -a | -s sess | -l sess[,...] ] cmd [ arg ... ]`
Execute '*cmd* [*arg* ...]' for each session in turn. Note this executes the command and arguments; it does not send the command line as data unless the `-t` (transmit) option is given.

The sessions may be selected explicitly with the standard `-a`, `-s` or `-l` options, or may be chosen implicitly. If none of the three options is given the rules are: first, if the array `$tcp_spam_list` is set, this is taken as the list of sessions, otherwise all sessions are taken. Second, any sessions given in the array `$tcp_no_spam_list` are removed from the list of sessions.

Normally, any sessions added by the '-a' flag or when all sessions are chosen implicitly are spammed in alphabetic order; sessions given by the `$tcp_spam_list` array or on the command line are spammed in the order given. The `-r` flag reverses the order however it was arrived it.

The `-v` flag specifies that a `$TCP_PROMPT` will be output before each session. This is output after any modification to `TCP_SESS` by the user-defined `tcp_on_spam` function described below. (Obviously that function is able to generate its own output.)

If the option `-e` is present, the line given as '*cmd* [*arg* ...]' is executed using `eval`, otherwise it is executed without any further processing.

`tcp_talk`   This is a fairly simple-minded attempt to force input to the line editor to go straight to the default `TCP_SESS`.

An escape string, `$TCP_TALK_ESCAPE`, default ':', is used to allow access to normal shell operation. If it is on its own at the start of the line, or followed only by whitespace, the line editor returns to normal operation. Otherwise, the string and any following whitespace are skipped and the remainder of the line executed as shell input without any change of the line editor's operating mode.

The current implementation is somewhat deficient in terms of use of the command history. For this reason, many users will prefer to use some form of alternative approach for sending data easily to the current session. One simple approach is to alias some special character (such as '%') to 'tcp_command --'.

`tcp_wait`   The sole argument is an integer or floating point number which gives the seconds to delay. The shell will do nothing for that period except wait for input on all TCP sessions by calling `tcp_read -a`. This is similar to the interactive behaviour at the command prompt when zle handlers are installed.

24.2.4 'One-shot' file transfer

`tcp_point` *port*
`tcp_shoot` *host port*

This pair of functions provide a simple way to transfer a file between two hosts within the shell. Note, however, that bulk data transfer is currently done using `cat`. `tcp_point` reads any data arriving at *port* and sends it to standard output; `tcp_shoot` connects to *port* on *host* and sends its standard input. Any unused *port* may be used; the standard mechanism for picking a port is to think of a random four-digit number above 1024 until one works.

To transfer a file from host `woodcock` to host `springes`, on `springes`:

```
tcp_point 8091 >output_file
```

and on `woodcock`:

```
tcp_shoot springes 8091 <input_file
```

As these two functions do not require `tcp_open` to set up a TCP connection first, they may need to be autoloaded separately.

24.3 TCP User-defined Functions

Certain functions, if defined by the user, will be called by the function system in certain contexts. This facility depends on the module **zsh/parameter**, which is usually available in interactive shells as the completion system depends on it. None of the functions need be defined; they simply provide convenient hooks when necessary.

Typically, these are called after the requested action has been taken, so that the various parameters will reflect the new state.

`tcp_on_alias` *alias fd*

When an alias is defined, this function will be called with two arguments: the name of the alias, and the file descriptor of the corresponding session.

`tcp_on_awol` *sess fd*

If the function `tcp_fd_handler` is handling input from the line editor and detects that the file descriptor is no longer reusable, by default it removes it from the list of file descriptors handled by this method and prints a message. If the function `tcp_on_awol` is defined it is called immediately before this point. It may return status 100, which indicates that the normal handling should still be performed; any other return status indicates that no further action should be taken and the `tcp_fd_handler` should return immediately with the given status. Typically the action of `tcp_on_awol` will be to close the session.

The variable `TCP_INVALIDATE_ZLE` will be a non-empty string if it is necessary to invalidate the line editor display using '`zle -I`' before printing output from the function.

('AWOL' is military jargon for 'absent without leave' or some variation. It has no pre-existing technical meaning known to the author.)

`tcp_on_close` *sess fd*

> This is called with the name of a session being closed and the file descriptor which corresponded to that session. Both will be invalid by the time the function is called.

`tcp_on_open` *sess fd*

> This is called after a new session has been defined with the session name and file descriptor as arguments. If it returns a non-zero status, opening the session is assumed to fail and the session is closed again; however, `tcp_open` will continue to attempt to open any remaining sessions given on the command line.

`tcp_on_rename` *oldsess fd newsess*

> This is called after a session has been renamed with the three arguments old session name, file descriptor, new session name.

`tcp_on_spam` *sess command ...*

> This is called once for each session spammed, just *before* a command is executed for a session by `tcp_spam`. The arguments are the session name followed by the command list to be executed. If `tcp_spam` was called with the option `-t`, the first command will be `tcp_send`.
>
> This function is called after `$TCP_SESS` is set to reflect the session to be spammed, but before any use of it is made. Hence it is possible to alter the value of `$TCP_SESS` within this function. For example, the session arguments to `tcp_spam` could include extra information to be stripped off and processed in `tcp_on_spam`.
>
> If the function sets the parameter `$REPLY` to 'done', the command line is not executed; in addition, no prompt is printed for the `-v` option to `tcp_spam`.

`tcp_on_unalias` *alias fd*

> This is called with the name of an alias and the corresponding session's file descriptor after an alias has been deleted.

24.4 TCP Utility Functions

The following functions are used by the TCP function system but will rarely if ever need to be called directly.

`tcp_fd_handler`

> This is the function installed by `tcp_open` for handling input from within the line editor, if that is required. It is in the format documented for the builtin '`zle -F`' in Section 18.3 [Zle Builtins], page 185, .
>
> While active, the function sets the parameter `TCP_HANDLER_ACTIVE` to 1. This allows shell code called internally (for example, by setting `tcp_on_read`) to tell if is being called when the shell is otherwise idle at the editor prompt.

`tcp_output` [`-q`] `-P` *prompt* `-F` *fd* `-S` *sess*

> This function is used for both logging and handling output to standard output, from within `tcp_read` and (if `$TCP_OUTPUT` is set) `tcp_send`.
>
> The *prompt* to use is specified by `-P`; the default is the empty string. It can contain:

> `%c`   Expands to 1 if the session is the current session, otherwise 0. Used with ternary expressions such as '`%(c.-.+)`' to output '+' for the current session and '-' otherwise.
>
> `%f`   Replaced by the session's file descriptor.
>
> `%s`   Replaced by the session name.
>
> `%%`   Replaced by a single '%'.

> The option `-q` suppresses output to standard output, but not to any log files which are configured.
>
> The `-S` and `-F` options are used to pass in the session name and file descriptor for possible replacement in the prompt.

24.5 TCP User Parameters

Parameters follow the usual convention that uppercase is used for scalars and integers, while lowercase is used for normal and associative array. It is always safe for user code to read these parameters. Some parameters may also be set; these are noted explicitly. Others are included in this group as they are set by the function system for the user's benefit, i.e. setting them is typically not useful but is benign.

It is often also useful to make settable parameters local to a function. For example, '`local TCP_SILENT=1`' specifies that data read during the function call will not be printed to standard output, regardless of the setting outside the function. Likewise, '`local TCP_SESS=`*sess*' sets a session for the duration of a function, and '`local TCP_PROMPT=`' specifies that no prompt is used for input during the function.

`tcp_expect_lines`

> Array. The set of lines read during the last call to `tcp_expect`, including the last (`$TCP_LINE`).

`tcp_filter`

> Array. May be set directly. A set of extended globbing patterns which, if matched in `tcp_output`, will cause the line not to be printed to standard output. The patterns should be defined as described for the arguments to `tcp_expect`. Output of line to log files is not affected.

TCP_HANDLER_ACTIVE

    Scalar. Set to 1 within `tcp_fd_handler` to indicate to functions called recursively that they have been called during an editor session. Otherwise unset.

TCP_LINE   The last line read by `tcp_read`, and hence also `tcp_expect`.

TCP_LINE_FD

    The file descriptor from which `$TCP_LINE` was read. `${tcp_by_fd[$TCP_LINE_FD]}` will give the corresponding session name.

tcp_lines

    Array. The set of lines read during the last call to `tcp_read`, including the last (`$TCP_LINE`).

TCP_LOG   May be set directly, although it is also controlled by `tcp_log`. The name of a file to which output from all sessions will be sent. The output is proceeded by the usual `$TCP_PROMPT`. If it is not an absolute path name, it will follow the user's current directory.

TCP_LOG_SESS

    May be set directly, although it is also controlled by `tcp_log`. The prefix for a set of files to which output from each session separately will be sent; the full filename is `${TCP_LOG_SESS}`.*sess*. Output to each file is raw; no prompt is added. If it is not an absolute path name, it will follow the user's current directory.

tcp_no_spam_list

    Array. May be set directly. See `tcp_spam` for how this is used.

TCP_OUTPUT

    May be set directly. If a non-empty string, any data sent to a session by `tcp_send` will be logged. This parameter gives the prompt to be used in a file specified by `$TCP_LOG` but not in a file generated from `$TCP_LOG_SESS`. The prompt string has the same format as `TCP_PROMPT` and the same rules for its use apply.

TCP_PROMPT

    May be set directly. Used as the prefix for data read by `tcp_read` which is printed to standard output or to the log file given by `$TCP_LOG`, if any. Any '`%s`', '`%f`' or '`%%`' occurring in the string will be replaced by the name of the session, the session's underlying file descriptor, or a single '`%`', respectively. The expression '`%c`' expands to 1 if the session being read is the current session, else 0; this is most useful in ternary expressions such as '`%(c.-.+)`' which outputs '+' if the session is the current one, else '-'.

    If the prompt starts with `%P`, this is stripped and the complete result of the previous stage is passed through standard prompt `%`-style formatting before being output.

TCP_READ_DEBUG

    May be set directly. If this has non-zero length, `tcp_read` will give some limited diagnostics about data being read.

TCP_SECONDS_START

This value is created and initialised to zero by tcp_open.

The functions tcp_read and tcp_expect use the shell's SECONDS parameter for their own timing purposes. If that parameter is not of floating point type on entry to one of the functions, it will create a local parameter SECONDS which is floating point and set the parameter TCP_SECONDS_START to the previous value of $SECONDS. If the parameter is already floating point, it is used without a local copy being created and TCP_SECONDS_START is not set. As the global value is zero, the shell elapsed time is guaranteed to be the sum of $SECONDS and $TCP_SECONDS_START.

This can be avoided by setting SECONDS globally to a floating point value using 'typeset -F SECONDS'; then the TCP functions will never make a local copy and never set TCP_SECONDS_START to a non-zero value.

TCP_SESS   May be set directly. The current session; must refer to one of the sessions established by tcp_open.

TCP_SILENT

May be set directly, although it is also controlled by tcp_log. If of non-zero length, data read by tcp_read will not be written to standard output, though may still be written to a log file.

tcp_spam_list

Array. May be set directly. See the description of the function tcp_spam for how this is used.

TCP_TALK_ESCAPE

May be set directly. See the description of the function tcp_talk for how this is used.

TCP_TIMEOUT

May be set directly. Currently this is only used by the function tcp_command, see above.

24.6 TCP User-defined Parameters

The following parameters are not set by the function system, but have a special effect if set by the user.

tcp_on_read

This should be an associative array; if it is not, the behaviour is undefined. Each key is the name of a shell function or other command, and the corresponding value is a shell pattern (using EXTENDED_GLOB). Every line read from a TCP session directly or indirectly using tcp_read (which includes lines read by tcp_expect) is compared against the pattern. If the line matches, the command given in the key is called with two arguments: the name of the session from which the line was read, and the line itself.

If any function called to handle a line returns a non-zero status, the line is not output. Thus a tcp_on_read handler containing only the instruction 'return

1' can be used to suppress output of particular lines (see, however, `tcp_filter` above). However, the line is still stored in `TCP_LINE` and `tcp_lines`; this occurs after all `tcp_on_read` processing.

24.7 TCP Utility Parameters

These parameters are controlled by the function system; they may be read directly, but should not usually be set by user code.

`tcp_aliases`

Associative array. The keys are the names of sessions established with `tcp_open`; each value is a space-separated list of aliases which refer to that session.

`tcp_by_fd`

Associative array. The keys are session file descriptors; each value is the name of that session.

`tcp_by_name`

Associative array. The keys are the names of sessions; each value is the file descriptor associated with that session.

24.8 TCP Examples

Here is a trivial example using a remote calculator.

To create a calculator server on port 7337 (see the `dc` manual page for quite how infuriating the underlying command is):

```
tcp_proxy 7337 dc
```

To connect to this from the same host with a session also named 'dc':

```
tcp_open localhost 7337 dc
```

To send a command to the remote session and wait a short while for output (assuming `dc` is the current session):

```
tcp_command 2 4 + p
```

To close the session:

```
tcp_close
```

The `tcp_proxy` needs to be killed to be stopped. Note this will not usually kill any connections which have already been accepted, and also that the port is not immediately available for reuse.

The following chunk of code puts a list of sessions into an xterm header, with the current session followed by a star.

```
print -n "\033]2;TCP:" ${(k)tcp_by_name:/$TCP_SESS/$TCP_SESS\*} "\a"
```

24.9 TCP Bugs

The function `tcp_read` uses the shell's normal `read` builtin. As this reads a complete line at once, data arriving without a terminating newline can cause the function to block indefinitely.

Though the function suite works well for interactive use and for data arriving in small amounts, the performance when large amounts of data are being exchanged is likely to be extremely poor.

25 Zftp Function System

25.1 Description

This describes the set of shell functions supplied with the source distribution as an interface to the `zftp` builtin command, allowing you to perform FTP operations from the shell command line or within functions or scripts. The interface is similar to a traditional FTP client (e.g. the `ftp` command itself, see man page ftp(1)), but as it is entirely done within the shell all the familiar completion, editing and globbing features, and so on, are present, and macros are particularly simple to write as they are just ordinary shell functions.

The prerequisite is that the `zftp` command, as described in Section 22.31 [The zsh/zftp Module], page 371, , must be available in the version of `zsh` installed at your site. If the shell is configured to load new commands at run time, it probably is: typing 'zmodload zsh/zftp' will make sure (if that runs silently, it has worked). If this is not the case, it is possible `zftp` was linked into the shell anyway: to test this, type 'which zftp' and if `zftp` is available you will get the message 'zftp: shell built-in command'.

Commands given directly with `zftp` builtin may be interspersed between the functions in this suite; in a few cases, using `zftp` directly may cause some of the status information stored in shell parameters to become invalid. Note in particular the description of the variables $ZFTP_TMOUT, $ZFTP_PREFS and $ZFTP_VERBOSE for `zftp`.

25.2 Installation

You should make sure all the functions from the `Functions/Zftp` directory of the source distribution are available; they all begin with the two letters 'zf'. They may already have been installed on your system; otherwise, you will need to find them and copy them. The directory should appear as one of the elements of the $fpath array (this should already be the case if they were installed), and at least the function `zfinit` should be autoloaded; it will autoload the rest. Finally, to initialize the use of the system you need to call the `zfinit` function. The following code in your `.zshrc` will arrange for this; assume the functions are stored in the directory ~/myfns:

```
fpath=(~/myfns $fpath)
autoload -U zfinit
zfinit
```

Note that **zfinit** assumes you are using the **zmodload** method to load the **zftp** command. If it is already built into the shell, change **zfinit** to **zfinit -n**. It is helpful (though not essential) if the call to **zfinit** appears after any code to initialize the new completion system, else unnecessary **compctl** commands will be given.

25.3 Functions

The sequence of operations in performing a file transfer is essentially the same as that in a standard FTP client. Note that, due to a quirk of the shell's **getopts** builtin, for those functions that handle options you must use '--' rather than '-' to ensure the remaining arguments are treated literally (a single '-' is treated as an argument).

25.3.1 Opening a connection

zfparams [*host* [*user* [*password* ...]]]

> Set or show the parameters for a future **zfopen** with no arguments. If no arguments are given, the current parameters are displayed (the password will be shown as a line of asterisks). If a *host* is given, and either the *user* or *password* is not, they will be prompted for; also, any parameter given as '?' will be prompted for, and if the '?' is followed by a string, that will be used as the prompt. As **zfopen** calls **zfparams** to store the parameters, this usually need not be called directly.

> A single argument '-' will delete the stored parameters. This will also cause the memory of the last directory (and so on) on the other host to be deleted.

zfopen [-1] [*host* [*user* [*password* [*account*]]]]

> If *host* is present, open a connection to that host under username *user* with password *password* (and, on the rare occasions when it is necessary, account *account*). If a necessary parameter is missing or given as '?' it will be prompted for. If *host* is not present, use a previously stored set of parameters.

> If the command was successful, and the terminal is compatible with **xterm** or is **sun-cmd**, a summary will appear in the title bar, giving the local **host:directory** and the remote **host:directory**; this is handled by the function **zftp_chpwd**, described below.

> Normally, the *host*, *user* and *password* are internally recorded for later re-opening, either by a **zfopen** with no arguments, or automatically (see below). With the option '-1', no information is stored. Also, if an open command with arguments failed, the parameters will not be retained (and any previous parameters will also be deleted). A **zfopen** on its own, or a **zfopen -1**, never alters the stored parameters.

> Both **zfopen** and **zfanon** (but not **zfparams**) understand URLs of the form **ftp://**host/path... as meaning to connect to the *host*, then change directory to *path* (which must be a directory, not a file). The '**ftp://**' can be omitted; the trailing '/' is enough to trigger recognition of the *path*. Note prefixes other than '**ftp:**' are not recognized, and that all characters after the first slash beyond *host* are significant in *path*.

`zfanon [ -1 ] ` *host*

> Open a connection *host* for anonymous FTP. The username used is 'anonymous'. The password (which will be reported the first time) is generated as *user@host*; this is then stored in the shell parameter `$EMAIL_ADDR` which can alternatively be set manually to a suitable string.

25.3.2 Directory management

`zfcd [ ` *dir* ` ]`
`zfcd -`
`zfcd ` *old new*

> Change the current directory on the remote server: this is implemented to have many of the features of the shell builtin `cd`.
>
> In the first form with *dir* present, change to the directory *dir*. The command 'zfcd ..' is treated specially, so is guaranteed to work on non-UNIX servers (note this is handled internally by `zftp`). If *dir* is omitted, has the effect of 'zfcd ~'.
>
> The second form changes to the directory previously current.
>
> The third form attempts to change the current directory by replacing the first occurrence of the string *old* with the string *new* in the current directory.
>
> Note that in this command, and indeed anywhere a remote filename is expected, the string which on the local host corresponds to '~' is converted back to a '~' before being passed to the remote machine. This is convenient because of the way expansion is performed on the command line before `zfcd` receives a string. For example, suppose the command is 'zfcd ~/foo'. The shell will expand this to a full path such as 'zfcd /home/user2/pws/foo'. At this stage, `zfcd` recognises the initial path as corresponding to '~' and will send the directory to the remote host as ~/foo, so that the '~' will be expanded by the server to the correct remote host directory. Other named directories of the form '~name' are not treated in this fashion.

`zfhere`   Change directory on the remote server to the one corresponding to the current local directory, with special handling of '~' as in `zfcd`. For example, if the current local directory is ~/foo/bar, then `zfhere` performs the effect of 'zfcd ~/foo/bar'.

`zfdir [ -rfd ] [ - ] [ ` *dir-options* ` ] [ ` *dir* ` ]`

> Produce a long directory listing. The arguments *dir-options* and *dir* are passed directly to the server and their effect is implementation dependent, but specifying a particular remote directory *dir* is usually possible. The output is passed through a pager given by the environment variable `$PAGER`, or 'more' if that is not set.
>
> The directory is usually cached for re-use. In fact, two caches are maintained. One is for use when there is no *dir-options* or *dir*, i.e. a full listing of the current remote directory; it is flushed when the current remote directory changes. The other is kept for repeated use of `zfdir` with the same arguments; for example, repeated use of 'zfdir /pub/gnu' will only require the directory to be retrieved

on the first call. Alternatively, this cache can be re-viewed with the -r option. As relative directories will confuse **zfdir**, the -f option can be used to force the cache to be flushed before the directory is listed. The option -d will delete both caches without showing a directory listing; it will also delete the cache of file names in the current remote directory, if any.

zfls [*ls-options*] [*dir*]

> List files on the remote server. With no arguments, this will produce a simple list of file names for the current remote directory. Any arguments are passed directly to the server. No pager and no caching is used.

25.3.3 Status commands

zftype [*type*]

> With no arguments, show the type of data to be transferred, usually ASCII or binary. With an argument, change the type: the types 'A' or 'ASCII' for ASCII data and 'B' or 'BINARY', 'I' or 'IMAGE' for binary data are understood case-insensitively.

zfstat [-v]

> Show the status of the current or last connection, as well as the status of some of **zftp**'s status variables. With the -v option, a more verbose listing is produced by querying the server for its version of events, too.

25.3.4 Retrieving files

The commands for retrieving files all take at least two options. -G suppresses remote filename expansion which would otherwise be performed (see below for a more detailed description of that). -t attempts to set the modification time of the local file to that of the remote file: see the description of the function **zfrtime** below for more information.

zfget [-Gtc] *file1* ...

> Retrieve all the listed files *file1* ... one at a time from the remote server. If a file contains a '/', the full name is passed to the remote server, but the file is stored locally under the name given by the part after the final '/'. The option -c (cat) forces all files to be sent as a single stream to standard output; in this case the -t option has no effect.

zfuget [-Gvst] *file1* ...

> As **zfget**, but only retrieve files where the version on the remote server is newer (has a later modification time), or where the local file does not exist. If the remote file is older but the files have different sizes, or if the sizes are the same but the remote file is newer, the user will usually be queried. With the option -s, the command runs silently and will always retrieve the file in either of those two cases. With the option -v, the command prints more information about the files while it is working out whether or not to transfer them.

zfcget [-Gt] *file1* ...

> As **zfget**, but if any of the local files exists, and is shorter than the corresponding remote file, the command assumes that it is the result of a partially

completed transfer and attempts to transfer the rest of the file. This is useful on a poor connection which keeps failing.

Note that this requires a commonly implemented, but non-standard, version of the FTP protocol, so is not guaranteed to work on all servers.

zfgcp [-Gt] *remote-file local-file*
zfgcp [-Gt] *rfile1 ... ldir*

This retrieves files from the remote server with arguments behaving similarly to the **cp** command.

In the first form, copy *remote-file* from the server to the local file *local-file*.

In the second form, copy all the remote files *rfile1 ...* into the local directory *ldir* retaining the same basenames. This assumes UNIX directory semantics.

25.3.5 Sending files

zfput [-r] *file1 ...*

Send all the *file1 ...* given separately to the remote server. If a filename contains a '/', the full filename is used locally to find the file, but only the basename is used for the remote file name.

With the option -r, if any of the *files* are directories they are sent recursively with all their subdirectories, including files beginning with '.'. This requires that the remote machine understand UNIX file semantics, since '/' is used as a directory separator.

zfuput [-vs] *file1 ...*

As **zfput**, but only send files which are newer than their remote equivalents, or if the remote file does not exist. The logic is the same as for **zfuget**, but reversed between local and remote files.

zfcput *file1 ...*

As **zfput**, but if any remote file already exists and is shorter than the local equivalent, assume it is the result of an incomplete transfer and send the rest of the file to append to the existing part. As the FTP append command is part of the standard set, this is in principle more likely to work than **zfcget**.

zfpcp *local-file remote-file*
zfpcp *lfile1 ... rdir*

This sends files to the remote server with arguments behaving similarly to the **cp** command.

With two arguments, copy *local-file* to the server as *remote-file*.

With more than two arguments, copy all the local files *lfile1 ...* into the existing remote directory *rdir* retaining the same basenames. This assumes UNIX directory semantics.

A problem arises if you attempt to use **zfpcp** *lfile1 rdir*, i.e. the second form of copying but with two arguments, as the command has no simple way of knowing if *rdir* corresponds to a directory or a filename. It attempts to resolve this in various ways. First, if the *rdir* argument is '.' or '..' or ends in a slash, it is assumed to be a directory. Secondly, if the operation of copying to a remote file in the first form failed, and the remote server sends back the expected failure code 553 and a reply including the string 'Is a directory', then zfpcp will retry using the second form.

25.3.6 Closing the connection

zfclose   Close the connection.

25.3.7 Session management

zfsession [-lvod] [*sessname*]

Allows you to manage multiple FTP sessions at once. By default, connections take place in a session called 'default'; by giving the command 'zfsession *sessname*' you can change to a new or existing session with a name of your choice. The new session remembers its own connection, as well as associated shell parameters, and also the host/user parameters set by zfparams. Hence you can have different sessions set up to connect to different hosts, each remembering the appropriate host, user and password.

With no arguments, zfsession prints the name of the current session; with the option -l it lists all sessions which currently exist, and with the option -v it gives a verbose list showing the host and directory for each session, where the current session is marked with an asterisk. With -o, it will switch to the most recent previous session.

With -d, the given session (or else the current one) is removed; everything to do with it is completely forgotten. If it was the only session, a new session called 'default' is created and made current. It is safest not to delete sessions while background commands using zftp are active.

zftransfer *sess1:file1 sess2:file2*

Transfer files between two sessions; no local copy is made. The file is read from the session *sess1* as *file1* and written to session *sess2* as file *file2*; *file1* and *file2* may be relative to the current directories of the session. Either *sess1* or *sess2* may be omitted (though the colon should be retained if there is a possibility of a colon appearing in the file name) and defaults to the current session; *file2* may be omitted or may end with a slash, in which case the basename of *file1* will be added. The sessions *sess1* and *sess2* must be distinct.

The operation is performed using pipes, so it is required that the connections still be valid in a subshell, which is not the case under versions of some operating systems, presumably due to a system bug.

25.3.8 Bookmarks

The two functions zfmark and zfgoto allow you to 'bookmark' the present location (host, user and directory) of the current FTP connection for later use. The file to be used for storing and retrieving bookmarks is given by the parameter $ZFTP_BMFILE; if not set when one of the two functions is called, it will be set to the file .zfbkmarks in the directory where your zsh startup files live (usually ~).

zfmark [*bookmark*]

> If given an argument, mark the current host, user and directory under the name *bookmark* for later use by **zfgoto**. If there is no connection open, use the values for the last connection immediately before it was closed; it is an error if there was none. Any existing bookmark under the same name will be silently replaced.
>
> If not given an argument, list the existing bookmarks and the points to which they refer in the form *user@host:directory*; this is the format in which they are stored, and the file may be edited directly.

zfgoto [**-n**] *bookmark*

> Return to the location given by *bookmark*, as previously set by **zfmark**. If the location has user 'ftp' or 'anonymous', open the connection with **zfanon**, so that no password is required. If the user and host parameters match those stored for the current session, if any, those will be used, and again no password is required. Otherwise a password will be prompted for.
>
> With the option **-n**, the bookmark is taken to be a nickname stored by the **ncftp** program in its bookmark file, which is assumed to be ~/.ncftp/bookmarks. The function works identically in other ways. Note that there is no mechanism for adding or modifying **ncftp** bookmarks from the zftp functions.

25.3.9 Other functions

Mostly, these functions will not be called directly (apart from **zfinit**), but are described here for completeness. You may wish to alter **zftp_chpwd** and **zftp_progress**, in particular.

zfinit [**-n**]

> As described above, this is used to initialize the zftp function system. The **-n** option should be used if the zftp command is already built into the shell.

zfautocheck [**-dn**]

> This function is called to implement automatic reopening behaviour, as described in more detail below. The options must appear in the first argument; **-n** prevents the command from changing to the old directory, while **-d** prevents it from setting the variable **do_close**, which it otherwise does as a flag for automatically closing the connection after a transfer. The host and directory for the last session are stored in the variable **$zflastsession**, but the internal host/user/password parameters must also be correctly set.

zfcd_match *prefix suffix*

> This performs matching for completion of remote directory names. If the remote server is UNIX, it will attempt to persuade the server to list the remote directory with subdirectories marked, which usually works but is not guaranteed. On other hosts it simply calls **zfget_match** and hence completes all files, not just directories. On some systems, directories may not even look like filenames.

zfget_match *prefix suffix*

> This performs matching for completion of remote filenames. It caches files for the current directory (only) in the shell parameter **$zftp_fcache**. It is in the

form to be called by the -K option of `compctl`, but also works when called from a widget-style completion function with *prefix* and *suffix* set appropriately.

`zfrglob` *varname*

Perform remote globbing, as describes in more detail below. *varname* is the name of a variable containing the pattern to be expanded; if there were any matches, the same variable will be set to the expanded set of filenames on return.

`zfrtime` *lfile rfile* [*time*]

Set the local file *lfile* to have the same modification time as the remote file *rfile*, or the explicit time *time* in FTP format `CCYYMMDDhhmmSS` for the GMT timezone. This uses the shell's `zsh/datetime` module to perform the conversion from GMT to local time.

`zftp_chpwd`

This function is called every time a connection is opened, or closed, or the remote directory changes. This version alters the title bar of an `xterm`-compatible or `sun-cmd` terminal emulator to reflect the local and remote hostnames and current directories. It works best when combined with the function `chpwd`. In particular, a function of the form

```
chpwd() {
  if [[ -n $ZFTP_USER ]]; then
    zftp_chpwd
  else
    # usual chpwd e.g put host:directory in title bar
  fi
}
```

fits in well.

`zftp_progress`

This function shows the status of the transfer. It will not write anything unless the output is going to a terminal; however, if you transfer files in the background, you should turn off progress reports by hand using '`zstyle ':zftp:*' progress none`'. Note also that if you alter it, any output *must* be to standard error, as standard output may be a file being received. The form of the progress meter, or whether it is used at all, can be configured without altering the function, as described in the next section.

`zffcache` This is used to implement caching of files in the current directory for each session separately. It is used by `zfget_match` and `zfrglob`.

25.4 Miscellaneous Features

25.4.1 Configuration

Various styles are available using the standard shell style mechanism, described in Section 22.37 [The zsh/zutil Module], page 382. Briefly, the command '`zstyle ':zftp:*'`

style value ...'. defines the *style* to have value *value*; more than one value may be given, although that is not useful in the cases described here. These values will then be used throughout the zftp function system. For more precise control, the first argument, which gives a context in which the style applies, can be modified to include a particular function, as for example ':`zftp:zfget`': the style will then have the given value only in the `zfget` function. Values for the same style in different contexts may be set; the most specific function will be used, where strings are held to be more specific than patterns, and longer patterns and shorter patterns. Note that only the top level function name, as called by the user, is used; calling of lower level functions is transparent to the user. Hence modifications to the title bar in `zftp_chpwd` use the contexts `:zftp:zfopen`, `:zftp:zfcd`, etc., depending where it was called from. The following styles are understood:

progress   Controls the way that `zftp_progress` reports on the progress of a transfer. If empty, unset, or '`none`', no progress report is made; if '`bar`' a growing bar of inverse video is shown; if '`percent`' (or any other string, though this may change in future), the percentage of the file transferred is shown. The bar meter requires that the width of the terminal be available via the `$COLUMNS` parameter (normally this is set automatically). If the size of the file being transferred is not available, `bar` and `percent` meters will simply show the number of bytes transferred so far.

When `zfinit` is run, if this style is not defined for the context `:zftp:*`, it will be set to '`bar`'.

update   Specifies the minimum time interval between updates of the progress meter in seconds. No update is made unless new data has been received, so the actual time interval is limited only by `$ZFTP_TIMEOUT`.

As described for `progress`, `zfinit` will force this to default to 1.

remote-glob
              If set to '`1`', '`yes`' or '`true`', filename generation (globbing) is performed on the remote machine instead of by zsh itself; see below.

titlebar   If set to '`1`', '`yes`' or '`true`', `zftp_chpwd` will put the remote host and remote directory into the titlebar of terminal emulators such as xterm or sun-cmd that allow this.

As described for `progress`, `zfinit` will force this to default to 1.

chpwd   If set to '`1`' '`yes`' or '`true`', `zftp_chpwd` will call the function `chpwd` when a connection is closed. This is useful if the remote host details were put into the terminal title bar by `zftp_chpwd` and your usual `chpwd` also modifies the title bar.

When `zfinit` is run, it will determine whether `chpwd` exists and if so it will set the default value for the style to 1 if none exists already.

Note that there is also an associative array `zfconfig` which contains values used by the function system. This should not be modified or overwritten.

25.4.2 Remote globbing

The commands for retrieving files usually perform filename generation (globbing) on their arguments; this can be turned off by passing the option -G to each of the commands. Normally this operates by retrieving a complete list of files for the directory in question, then matching these locally against the pattern supplied. This has the advantage that the full range of zsh patterns (respecting the setting of the option EXTENDED_GLOB) can be used. However, it means that the directory part of a filename will not be expanded and must be given exactly. If the remote server does not support the UNIX directory semantics, directory handling is problematic and it is recommended that globbing only be used within the current directory. The list of files in the current directory, if retrieved, will be cached, so that subsequent globs in the same directory without an intervening zfcd are much faster.

If the **remote-glob** style (see above) is set, globbing is instead performed on the remote host: the server is asked for a list of matching files. This is highly dependent on how the server is implemented, though typically UNIX servers will provide support for basic glob patterns. This may in some cases be faster, as it avoids retrieving the entire list of directory contents.

25.4.3 Automatic and temporary reopening

As described for the zfopen command, a subsequent zfopen with no parameters will reopen the connection to the last host (this includes connections made with the zfanon command). Opened in this fashion, the connection starts in the default remote directory and will remain open until explicitly closed.

Automatic re-opening is also available. If a connection is not currently open and a command requiring a connection is given, the last connection is implicitly reopened. In this case the directory which was current when the connection was closed again becomes the current directory (unless, of course, the command given changes it). Automatic reopening will also take place if the connection was close by the remote server for whatever reason (e.g. a timeout). It is not available if the -1 option to zfopen or zfanon was used.

Furthermore, if the command issued is a file transfer, the connection will be closed after the transfer is finished, hence providing a one-shot mode for transfers. This does not apply to directory changing or listing commands; for example a zfdir may reopen a connection but will leave it open. Also, automatic closure will only ever happen in the same command as automatic opening, i.e a zfdir directly followed by a zfget will never close the connection automatically.

Information about the previous connection is given by the zfstat function. So, for example, if that reports:

```
Session:        default
Not connected.
Last session:   ftp.bar.com:/pub/textfiles
```

then the command zfget file.txt will attempt to reopen a connection to ftp.bar.com, retrieve the file /pub/textfiles/file.txt, and immediately close the connection again. On the other hand, zfcd .. will open the connection in the directory /pub and leave it open.

Note that all the above is local to each session; if you return to a previous session, the connection for that session is the one which will be reopened.

25.4.4 Completion

Completion of local and remote files, directories, sessions and bookmarks is supported. The older, `compctl`-style completion is defined when `zfinit` is called; support for the new widget-based completion system is provided in the function `Completion/Zsh/Command/_zftp`, which should be installed with the other functions of the completion system and hence should automatically be available.

26 User Contributions

26.1 Description

The Zsh source distribution includes a number of items contributed by the user community. These are not inherently a part of the shell, and some may not be available in every zsh installation. The most significant of these are documented here. For documentation on other contributed items such as shell functions, look for comments in the function source files.

26.2 Utilities

26.2.1 Accessing On-Line Help

The key sequence `ESC h` is normally bound by ZLE to execute the `run-help` widget (see Chapter 18 [Zsh Line Editor], page 183). This invokes the `run-help` command with the command word from the current input line as its argument. By default, `run-help` is an alias for the `man` command, so this often fails when the command word is a shell builtin or a user-defined function. By redefining the `run-help` alias, one can improve the on-line help provided by the shell.

The `helpfiles` utility, found in the `Util` directory of the distribution, is a Perl program that can be used to process the zsh manual to produce a separate help file for each shell builtin and for many other shell features as well. The autoloadable `run-help` function, found in `Functions/Misc`, searches for these helpfiles and performs several other tests to produce the most complete help possible for the command.

Help files are installed by default to a subdirectory of `/usr/share/zsh` or `/usr/local/share/zsh`.

To create your own help files with `helpfiles`, choose or create a directory where the individual command help files will reside. For example, you might choose `~/zsh_help`. If you unpacked the zsh distribution in your home directory, you would use the commands:

```
mkdir ~/zsh_help
perl ~/zsh-5.7.1/Util/helpfiles ~/zsh_help
```

The `HELPDIR` parameter tells `run-help` where to look for the help files. When unset, it uses the default installation path. To use your own set of help files, set this to the appropriate path in one of your startup files:

```
HELPDIR=~/zsh_help
```

To use the **run-help** function, you need to add lines something like the following to your **.zshrc** or equivalent startup file:

```
unalias run-help
autoload run-help
```

Note that in order for 'autoload run-help' to work, the **run-help** file must be in one of the directories named in your **fpath** array (see Section 15.6 [Parameters Used By The Shell], page 99). This should already be the case if you have a standard zsh installation; if it is not, copy **Functions/Misc/run-help** to an appropriate directory.

26.2.2 Recompiling Functions

If you frequently edit your zsh functions, or periodically update your zsh installation to track the latest developments, you may find that function digests compiled with the **zcompile** builtin are frequently out of date with respect to the function source files. This is not usually a problem, because zsh always looks for the newest file when loading a function, but it may cause slower shell startup and function loading. Also, if a digest file is explicitly used as an element of **fpath**, zsh won't check whether any of its source files has changed.

The **zrecompile** autoloadable function, found in **Functions/Misc**, can be used to keep function digests up to date.

zrecompile [-qt] [*name* ...]
zrecompile [-qt] -p *arg* ... [-- *arg* ...]

> This tries to find ***.zwc** files and automatically re-compile them if at least one of the original files is newer than the compiled file. This works only if the names stored in the compiled files are full paths or are relative to the directory that contains the **.zwc** file.
>
> In the first form, each *name* is the name of a compiled file or a directory containing ***.zwc** files that should be checked. If no arguments are given, the directories and ***.zwc** files in **fpath** are used.
>
> When **-t** is given, no compilation is performed, but a return status of zero (true) is set if there are files that need to be re-compiled and non-zero (false) otherwise. The **-q** option quiets the chatty output that describes what **zrecompile** is doing.
>
> Without the **-t** option, the return status is zero if all files that needed re-compilation could be compiled and non-zero if compilation for at least one of the files failed.
>
> If the **-p** option is given, the *args* are interpreted as one or more sets of arguments for **zcompile**, separated by '--'. For example:
>
> ```
> zrecompile -p \
>         -R ~/.zshrc -- \
>         -M ~/.zcompdump -- \
>         ~/zsh/comp.zwc ~/zsh/Completion/*/_*
> ```
>
> This compiles ~/.zshrc into ~/.zshrc.zwc if that doesn't exist or if it is older than ~/.zshrc. The compiled file will be marked for reading instead

of mapping. The same is done for ~/.zcompdump and ~/.zcompdump.zwc, but this compiled file is marked for mapping. The last line re-creates the file ~/zsh/comp.zwc if any of the files matching the given pattern is newer than it.

Without the -p option, zrecompile does not create function digests that do not already exist, nor does it add new functions to the digest.

The following shell loop is an example of a method for creating function digests for all functions in your fpath, assuming that you have write permission to the directories:

```
for ((i=1; i <= $#fpath; ++i)); do
  dir=$fpath[i]
  zwc=${dir:t}.zwc
  if [[ $dir == (.|..) || $dir == (.|..)/* ]]; then
    continue
  fi
  files=($dir/*(N-.))
  if [[ -w $dir:h && -n $files ]]; then
    files=(${${(M)files%/*/*}#/})
    if ( cd $dir:h &&
         zrecompile -p -U -z $zwc $files ); then
      fpath[i]=$fpath[i].zwc
    fi
  fi
done
```

The -U and -z options are appropriate for functions in the default zsh installation fpath; you may need to use different options for your personal function directories.

Once the digests have been created and your fpath modified to refer to them, you can keep them up to date by running zrecompile with no arguments.

26.2.3 Keyboard Definition

The large number of possible combinations of keyboards, workstations, terminals, emulators, and window systems makes it impossible for zsh to have built-in key bindings for every situation. The zkbd utility, found in Functions/Misc, can help you quickly create key bindings for your configuration.

Run zkbd either as an autoloaded function, or as a shell script:

```
zsh -f ~/zsh-5.7.1/Functions/Misc/zkbd
```

When you run zkbd, it first asks you to enter your terminal type; if the default it offers is correct, just press return. It then asks you to press a number of different keys to determine characteristics of your keyboard and terminal; zkbd warns you if it finds anything out of the ordinary, such as a Delete key that sends neither ^H nor ^?.

The keystrokes read by zkbd are recorded as a definition for an associative array named key, written to a file in the subdirectory .zkbd within either your HOME or ZDOTDIR directory. The name of the file is composed from the TERM, VENDOR and OSTYPE parameters, joined by hyphens.

You may read this file into your `.zshrc` or another startup file with the 'source' or '.' commands, then reference the `key` parameter in bindkey commands, like this:

```
source ${ZDOTDIR:-$HOME}/.zkbd/$TERM-$VENDOR-$OSTYPE
[[ -n ${key[Left]} ]] && bindkey "${key[Left]}" backward-char
[[ -n ${key[Right]} ]] && bindkey "${key[Right]}" forward-char
# etc.
```

Note that in order for 'autoload zkbd' to work, the `zkdb` file must be in one of the directories named in your `fpath` array (see Section 15.6 [Parameters Used By The Shell], page 99). This should already be the case if you have a standard zsh installation; if it is not, copy `Functions/Misc/zkbd` to an appropriate directory.

26.2.4 Dumping Shell State

Occasionally you may encounter what appears to be a bug in the shell, particularly if you are using a beta version of zsh or a development release. Usually it is sufficient to send a description of the problem to one of the zsh mailing lists (see Section 2.3 [Mailing Lists], page 2), but sometimes one of the zsh developers will need to recreate your environment in order to track the problem down.

The script named `reporter`, found in the `Util` directory of the distribution, is provided for this purpose. (It is also possible to `autoload reporter`, but `reporter` is not installed in `fpath` by default.) This script outputs a detailed dump of the shell state, in the form of another script that can be read with 'zsh -f' to recreate that state.

To use `reporter`, read the script into your shell with the '.' command and redirect the output into a file:

```
. ~/zsh-5.7.1/Util/reporter > zsh.report
```

You should check the `zsh.report` file for any sensitive information such as passwords and delete them by hand before sending the script to the developers. Also, as the output can be voluminous, it's best to wait for the developers to ask for this information before sending it.

You can also use `reporter` to dump only a subset of the shell state. This is sometimes useful for creating startup files for the first time. Most of the output from reporter is far more detailed than usually is necessary for a startup file, but the `aliases`, `options`, and `zstyles` states may be useful because they include only changes from the defaults. The `bindings` state may be useful if you have created any of your own keymaps, because `reporter` arranges to dump the keymap creation commands as well as the bindings for every keymap.

As is usual with automated tools, if you create a startup file with `reporter`, you should edit the results to remove unnecessary commands. Note that if you're using the new completion system, you should *not* dump the `functions` state to your startup files with `reporter`; use the `compdump` function instead (see Chapter 20 [Completion System], page 242).

reporter [*state* ...]

        Print to standard output the indicated subset of the current shell state. The *state* arguments may be one or more of:

        all   Output everything listed below.

aliases   Output alias definitions.

bindings   Output ZLE key maps and bindings.

completion
>   Output old-style `compctl` commands. New completion is covered by `functions` and `zstyles`.

functions
>   Output autoloads and function definitions.

limits   Output `limit` commands.

options   Output `setopt` commands.

styles   Same as `zstyles`.

variables
>   Output shell parameter assignments, plus `export` commands for any environment variables.

zstyles   Output `zstyle` commands.

If the *state* is omitted, `all` is assumed.

With the exception of 'all', every *state* can be abbreviated by any prefix, even a single letter; thus `a` is the same as `aliases`, `z` is the same as `zstyles`, etc.

26.2.5 Manipulating Hook Functions

add-zsh-hook [-L | -dD] [-Uzk] *hook function*
>   Several functions are special to the shell, as described in the section Special Functions, Chapter 9 [Functions], page 24, in that they are automatically called at specific points during shell execution. Each has an associated array consisting of names of functions to be called at the same point; these are so-called 'hook functions'. The shell function `add-zsh-hook` provides a simple way of adding or removing functions from the array.
>
>   *hook* is one of `chpwd`, `periodic`, `precmd`, `preexec`, `zshaddhistory`, `zshexit`, or `zsh_directory_name`, the special functions in question. Note that `zsh_directory_name` is called in a different way from the other functions, but may still be manipulated as a hook.
>
>   *function* is name of an ordinary shell function. If no options are given this will be added to the array of functions to be executed in the given context. Functions are invoked in the order they were added.
>
>   If the option -L is given, the current values for the hook arrays are listed with `typeset`.
>
>   If the option -d is given, the *function* is removed from the array of functions to be executed.
>
>   If the option -D is given, the *function* is treated as a pattern and any matching names of functions are removed from the array of functions to be executed.
>
>   The options -U, -z and -k are passed as arguments to `autoload` for *function*. For functions contributed with zsh, the options -Uz are appropriate.

`add-zle-hook-widget` [`-L` | `-dD`] [`-Uzk`] *hook widgetname*

> Several widget names are special to the line editor, as described in the section Special Widgets, Section 18.4 [Zle Widgets], page 195, in that they are automatically called at specific points during editing. Unlike function hooks, these do not use a predefined array of other names to call at the same point; the shell function **add-zle-hook-widget** maintains a similar array and arranges for the special widget to invoke those additional widgets.
>
> *hook* is one of `isearch-exit`, `isearch-update`, `line-pre-redraw`, `line-init`, `line-finish`, `history-line-set`, or `keymap-select`, corresponding to each of the special widgets `zle-isearch-exit`, etc. The special widget names are also accepted as the *hook* argument.
>
> *widgetname* is the name of a ZLE widget. If no options are given this is added to the array of widgets to be invoked in the given hook context. Widgets are invoked in the order they were added, with
>
> > `zle widgetname -Nw -- "$@"`
>
> Note that this means that the 'WIDGET' special parameter tracks the *widgetname* when the widget function is called, rather than tracking the name of the corresponding special hook widget.
>
> If the option `-d` is given, the *widgetname* is removed from the array of widgets to be executed.
>
> If the option `-D` is given, the *widgetname* is treated as a pattern and any matching names of widgets are removed from the array.
>
> If *widgetname* does not name an existing widget when added to the array, it is assumed that a shell function also named *widgetname* is meant to provide the implementation of the widget. This name is therefore marked for autoloading, and the options `-U`, `-z` and `-k` are passed as arguments to **autoload** as with **add-zsh-hook**. The widget is also created with 'zle -N *widgetname*' to cause the corresponding function to be loaded the first time the hook is called.
>
> The arrays of *widgetname* are currently maintained in **zstyle** contexts, one for each *hook* context, with a style of '**widgets**'. If the `-L` option is given, this set of styles is listed with '**zstyle -L**'. This implementation may change, and the special widgets that refer to the styles are created only if **add-zle-hook-widget** is called to add at least one widget, so if this function is used for any hooks, then all hooks should be managed only via this function.

26.3 Remembering Recent Directories

The function **cdr** allows you to change the working directory to a previous working directory from a list maintained automatically. It is similar in concept to the directory stack controlled by the **pushd**, **popd** and **dirs** builtins, but is more configurable, and as it stores all entries in files it is maintained across sessions and (by default) between terminal emulators in the current session. Duplicates are automatically removed, so that the list reflects the single most recent use of each directory.

Note that the **pushd** directory stack is not actually modified or used by **cdr** unless you configure it to do so as described in the configuration section below.

26.3.1 Installation

The system works by means of a hook function that is called every time the directory changes. To install the system, autoload the required functions and use the **add-zsh-hook** function described above:

```
autoload -Uz chpwd_recent_dirs cdr add-zsh-hook
add-zsh-hook chpwd chpwd_recent_dirs
```

Now every time you change directly interactively, no matter which command you use, the directory to which you change will be remembered in most-recent-first order.

26.3.2 Use

All direct user interaction is via the **cdr** function.

The argument to cdr is a number N corresponding to the Nth most recently changed-to directory. 1 is the immediately preceding directory; the current directory is remembered but is not offered as a destination. Note that if you have multiple windows open 1 may refer to a directory changed to in another window; you can avoid this by having per-terminal files for storing directory as described for the **recent-dirs-file** style below.

If you set the **recent-dirs-default** style described below **cdr** will behave the same as **cd** if given a non-numeric argument, or more than one argument. The recent directory list is updated just the same however you change directory.

If the argument is omitted, 1 is assumed. This is similar to **pushd**'s behaviour of swapping the two most recent directories on the stack.

Completion for the argument to **cdr** is available if compinit has been run; menu selection is recommended, using:

```
zstyle ':completion:*:*:cdr:*:*' menu selection
```

to allow you to cycle through recent directories; the order is preserved, so the first choice is the most recent directory before the current one. The verbose style is also recommended to ensure the directory is shown; this style is on by default so no action is required unless you have changed it.

26.3.3 Options

The behaviour of **cdr** may be modified by the following options.

-l   lists the numbers and the corresponding directories in abbreviated form (i.e. with ~ substitution reapplied), one per line. The directories here are not quoted (this would only be an issue if a directory name contained a newline). This is used by the completion system.

-r   sets the variable **reply** to the current set of directories. Nothing is printed and the directory is not changed.

-e   allows you to edit the list of directories, one per line. The list can be edited to any extent you like; no sanity checking is performed. Completion is available. No quoting is necessary (except for newlines, where I have in any case no sympathy); directories are in unabbreviated from and contain an absolute path, i.e. they start with /. Usually the first entry should be left as the current directory.

-p 'pattern'

    Prunes any items in the directory list that match the given extended glob pattern; the pattern needs to be quoted from immediate expansion on the command line. The pattern is matched against each completely expanded file name in the list; the full string must match, so wildcards at the end (e.g. '*removeme*') are needed to remove entries with a given substring.

    If output is to a terminal, then the function will print the new list after pruning and prompt for confirmation by the user. This output and confirmation step can be skipped by using -P instead of -p.

26.3.4 Configuration

Configuration is by means of the styles mechanism that should be familiar from completion; if not, see the description of the **zstyle** command in Section 22.37 [The zsh/zutil Module], page 382. The context for setting styles should be ':chpwd:*' in case the meaning of the context is extended in future, for example:

    zstyle ':chpwd:*' recent-dirs-max 0

sets the value of the **recent-dirs-max** style to 0. In practice the style name is specific enough that a context of '*' should be fine.

An exception is **recent-dirs-insert**, which is used exclusively by the completion system and so has the usual completion system context (':completion:*' if nothing more specific is needed), though again '*' should be fine in practice.

recent-dirs-default

    If true, and the command is expecting a recent directory index, and either there is more than one argument or the argument is not an integer, then fall through to "cd". This allows the lazy to use only one command for directory changing. Completion recognises this, too; see recent-dirs-insert for how to control completion when this option is in use.

recent-dirs-file

    The file where the list of directories is saved. The default is ${ZDOTDIR:-$HOME}/.chpwd-recent-dirs, i.e. this is in your home directory unless you have set the variable ZDOTDIR to point somewhere else. Directory names are saved in $'...' quoted form, so each line in the file can be supplied directly to the shell as an argument.

    The value of this style may be an array. In this case, the first file in the list will always be used for saving directories while any other files are left untouched. When reading the recent directory list, if there are fewer than the maximum number of entries in the first file, the contents of later files in the array will be appended with duplicates removed from the list shown. The contents of the two files are not sorted together, i.e. all the entries in the first file are shown first. The special value + can appear in the list to indicate the default file should be read at that point. This allows effects like the following:

```
zstyle ':chpwd:*' recent-dirs-file \
~/.chpwd-recent-dirs-${TTY##*/} +
```

Recent directories are read from a file numbered according to the terminal. If there are insufficient entries the list is supplemented from the default file.

It is possible to use **zstyle -e** to make the directory configurable at run time:

```
zstyle -e ':chpwd:*' recent-dirs-file pick-recent-dirs-file
pick-recent-dirs-file() {
  if [[ $PWD = ~/text/writing(|/*) ]]; then
    reply=(~/.chpwd-recent-dirs-writing)
  else
    reply=(+)
  fi
}
```

In this example, if the current directory is **~/text/writing** or a directory under it, then use a special file for saving recent directories, else use the default.

recent-dirs-insert

Used by completion. If **recent-dirs-default** is true, then setting this to **true** causes the actual directory, rather than its index, to be inserted on the command line; this has the same effect as using the corresponding index, but makes the history clearer and the line easier to edit. With this setting, if part of an argument was already typed, normal directory completion rather than recent directory completion is done; this is because recent directory completion is expected to be done by cycling through entries menu fashion.

If the value of the style is **always**, then only recent directories will be completed; in that case, use the **cd** command when you want to complete other directories.

If the value is **fallback**, recent directories will be tried first, then normal directory completion is performed if recent directory completion failed to find a match.

Finally, if the value is **both** then both sets of completions are presented; the usual tag mechanism can be used to distinguish results, with recent directories tagged as **recent-dirs**. Note that the recent directories inserted are abbreviated with directory names where appropriate.

recent-dirs-max

The maximum number of directories to save to the file. If this is zero or negative there is no maximum. The default is 20. Note this includes the current directory, which isn't offered, so the highest number of directories you will be offered is one less than the maximum.

recent-dirs-prune

This style is an array determining what directories should (or should not) be added to the recent list. Elements of the array can include:

parent   Prune parents (more accurately, ancestors) from the recent list. If present, changing directly down by any number of directories causes the current directory to be overwritten. For example, changing from ~pws to ~pws/some/other/dir causes ~pws not to be left on the recent directory stack. This only applies to direct changes to descendant directories; earlier directories on the list are not pruned. For example, changing from ~pws/yet/another to ~pws/some/other/dir does not cause ~pws to be pruned.

pattern:*pattern*

Gives a zsh pattern for directories that should not be added to the recent list (if not already there). This element can be repeated to add different patterns. For example, 'pattern:/tmp(|/*)' stops /tmp or its descendants from being added. The EXTENDED_GLOB option is always turned on for these patterns.

recent-dirs-pushd

If set to true, cdr will use pushd instead of cd to change the directory, so the directory is saved on the directory stack. As the directory stack is completely separate from the list of files saved by the mechanism used in this file there is no obvious reason to do this.

26.3.5 Use with dynamic directory naming

It is possible to refer to recent directories using the dynamic directory name syntax by using the supplied function zsh_directory_name_cdr a hook:

```
autoload -Uz add-zsh-hook
add-zsh-hook -Uz zsh_directory_name zsh_directory_name_cdr
```

When this is done, ~[1] will refer to the most recent directory other than $PWD, and so on. Completion after ~[... also works.

26.3.6 Details of directory handling

This section is for the curious or confused; most users will not need to know this information.

Recent directories are saved to a file immediately and hence are preserved across sessions. Note currently no file locking is applied: the list is updated immediately on interactive commands and nowhere else (unlike history), and it is assumed you are only going to change directory in one window at once. This is not safe on shared accounts, but in any case the system has limited utility when someone else is changing to a different set of directories behind your back.

To make this a little safer, only directory changes instituted from the command line, either directly or indirectly through shell function calls (but not through subshells, evals, traps, completion functions and the like) are saved. Shell functions should use cd -q or pushd -q to avoid side effects if the change to the directory is to be invisible at the command line. See the contents of the function chpwd_recent_dirs for more details.

26.4 Abbreviated dynamic references to directories

The dynamic directory naming system is described in the subsection *Dynamic named directories* of Section 14.7 [Filename Expansion], page 69. In this, a reference to ~[...] is expanded by a function found by the hooks mechanism.

The contributed function `zsh_directory_name_generic` provides a system allowing the user to refer to directories with only a limited amount of new code. It supports all three of the standard interfaces for directory naming: converting from a name to a directory, converting in the reverse direction to find a short name, and completion of names.

The main feature of this function is a path-like syntax, combining abbreviations at multiple levels separated by ":". As an example, ~[g:p:s] might specify:

g   The top level directory for your git area. This first component has to match, or the function will retrun indicating another directory name hook function should be tried.

p   The name of a project within your git area.

s   The source area within that project.

This allows you to collapse references to long hierarchies to a very compact form, particularly if the hierarchies are similar across different areas of the disk.

Name components may be completed: if a description is shown at the top of the list of completions, it includes the path to which previous components expand, while the description for an individual completion shows the path segment it would add. No additional configuration is needed for this as the completion system is aware of the dynamic directory name mechanism.

26.4.1 Usage

To use the function, first define a wrapper function for your specific case. We'll assume it's to be autoloaded. This can have any name but we'll refer to it as zdn_mywrapper. This wrapper function will define various variables and then call this function with the same arguments that the wrapper function gets. This configuration is described below.

Then arrange for the wrapper to be run as a zsh_directory_name hook:

```
autoload -Uz add-zsh-hook zsh_diretory_name_generic zdn_mywrapper
add-zsh-hook -U zsh_directory_name zdn_mywrapper
```

26.4.2 Configuration

The wrapper function should define a local associative array zdn_top. Alternatively, this can be set with a style called **mapping**. The context for the style is :**zdn**:*wrapper-name* where *wrapper-name* is the function calling zsh_directory_name_generic; for example:

```
zstyle :zdn:zdn_mywrapper: mapping zdn_mywrapper_top
```

The keys in this associative array correspond to the first component of the name. The values are matching directories. They may have an optional suffix with a slash followed by a colon and the name of a variable in the same format to give the next component. (The slash before the colon is to disambiguate the case where a colon is needed in the path for a drive. There is otherwise no syntax for escaping this, so path components whose names start with a colon are not supported.) A special component :default: specifies a variable in the form /:*var* (the path section is ignored and so is usually empty) that will be used for the next component if no variable is given for the path. Variables referred to within **zdn_top** have the same format as **zdn_top** itself, but contain relative paths.

For example,

```
local -A zdn_top=(
  g   ~/git
  ga  ~/alternate/git
  gs  /scratch/$USER/git/:second2
  :default: /:second1
)
```

This specifies the behaviour of a directory referred to as ~[g:...] or ~[ga:...] or ~[gs:...]. Later path components are optional; in that case ~[g] expands to ~/git, and so on. gs expands to /scratch/$USER/git and uses the associative array second2 to match the second component; g and ga use the associative array second1 to match the second component.

When expanding a name to a directory, if the first component is not g or ga or gs, it is not an error; the function simply returns 1 so that a later hook function can be tried. However, matching the first component commits the function, so if a later component does not match, an error is printed (though this still does not stop later hooks from being executed).

For components after the first, a relative path is expected, but note that multiple levels may still appear. Here is an example of second1:

```
local -A second1=(
  p   myproject
  s   somproject
  os  otherproject/subproject/:third
)
```

The path as found from zdn_top is extended with the matching directory, so ~[g:p] becomes ~/git/myproject. The slash between is added automatically (it's not possible to have a later component modify the name of a directory already matched). Only os specifies a variable for a third component, and there's no :default:, so it's an error to use a name like ~[g:p:x] or ~[ga:s:y] because there's nowhere to look up the x or y.

The associative arrays need to be visible within this function; the generic function therefore uses internal variable names beginning _zdn_ in order to avoid clashes. Note that the variable reply needs to be passed back to the shell, so should not be local in the calling function.

The function does not test whether directories assembled by component actually exist; this allows the system to work across automounted file systems. The error from the command trying to use a non-existent directory should be sufficient to indicate the problem.

26.4.3 Complete example

Here is a full fictitious but usable autoloadable definition of the example function defined by the code above. So ~[gs:p:s] expands to /scratch/$USER/git/myscratchproject/top/srcdir (with $USER also expanded).

```
local -A zdn_top=(
  g   ~/git
  ga  ~/alternate/git
  gs  /scratch/$USER/git/:second2
  :default: /:second1
)
```

```
local -A second1=(
  p   myproject
  s   somproject
  os  otherproject/subproject/:third
)

local -A second2=(
  p   myscratchproject
  s   somescratchproject
)

local -A third=(
  s   top/srcdir
  d   top/documentation
)

# autoload not needed if you did this at initialisation...
autoload -Uz zsh_directory_name_generic
zsh_directory_name_generic "$@
```

It is also possible to use global associative arrays, suitably named, and set the style for the context of your wrapper function to refer to this. Then your set up code would contain the following:

```
typeset -A zdn_mywrapper_top=(...)
# ... and so on for other associative arrays ...
zstyle ':zdn:zdn_mywrapper:' mapping zdn_mywrapper_top
autoload -Uz add-zsh-hook zsh_directory_name_generic zdn_mywrapper
add-zsh-hook -U zsh_directory_name zdn_mywrapper
```

and the function `zdn_mywrapper` would contain only the following:

```
zsh_directory_name_generic "$@"
```

26.5 Gathering information from version control systems

In a lot of cases, it is nice to automatically retrieve information from version control systems (VCSs), such as subversion, CVS or git, to be able to provide it to the user; possibly in the user's prompt. So that you can instantly tell which branch you are currently on, for example.

In order to do that, you may use the `vcs_info` function.

The following VCSs are supported, showing the abbreviated name by which they are referred to within the system:

Bazaar (`bzr`)

> https://bazaar.canonical.com/

Codeville (`cdv`)

> http://freecode.com/projects/codeville/

Concurrent Versioning System (`cvs`)
>   https://www.nongnu.org/cvs/

Darcs (`darcs`)
>   http://darcs.net/

Fossil (`fossil`)
>   https://fossil-scm.org/

Git (`git`) https://git-scm.com/

GNU arch (`tla`)
>   https://www.gnu.org/software/gnu-arch/

Mercurial (`hg`)
>   https://www.mercurial-scm.org/

Monotone (`mtn`)
>   https://monotone.ca/

Perforce (`p4`)
>   https://www.perforce.com/

Subversion (`svn`)
>   https://subversion.apache.org/

SVK (`svk`)
>   https://svk.bestpractical.com/

There is also support for the patch management system `quilt` (`https://savannah.nongnu.org/projects/qui`
See Section 26.5.4 [vcs_info Quilt Support], page 444, below for details.

To load `vcs_info`:

```
autoload -Uz vcs_info
```

It can be used in any existing prompt, because it does not require any specific `$psvar`
entries to be available.

26.5.1 Quickstart

To get this feature working quickly (including colors), you can do the following (assuming,
you loaded `vcs_info` properly - see above):

```
zstyle ':vcs_info:*' actionformats \
    '%F{5}(%f%s%F{5})%F{3}-%F{5}[%F{2}%b%F{3}|%F{1}%a%F{5}]%f '
zstyle ':vcs_info:*' formats        \
    '%F{5}(%f%s%F{5})%F{3}-%F{5}[%F{2}%b%F{5}]%f '
zstyle ':vcs_info:(sv[nk]|bzr):*' branchformat '%b%F{1}:%F{3}%r'
precmd () { vcs_info }
PS1='%F{5}[%F{2}%n%F{5}] %F{3}%3~ ${vcs_info_msg_0_}%f%# '
```

Obviously, the last two lines are there for demonstration. You need to call `vcs_info` from
your `precmd` function. Once that is done you need a *single quoted* `'${vcs_info_msg_0_}'`
in your prompt.

To be able to use `'${vcs_info_msg_0_}'` directly in your prompt like this, you will need
to have the `PROMPT_SUBST` option enabled.

Now call the `vcs_info_printsys` utility from the command line:

```
% vcs_info_printsys
## list of supported version control backends:
## disabled systems are prefixed by a hash sign (#)
bzr
cdv
cvs
darcs
fossil
git
hg
mtn
p4
svk
svn
tla
## flavours (cannot be used in the enable or disable styles; they
## are enabled and disabled with their master [git-svn -> git])
## they *can* be used in contexts: ':vcs_info:git-svn:*'.
git-p4
git-svn
hg-git
hg-hgsubversion
hg-hgsvn
```

You may not want all of these because there is no point in running the code to detect systems you do not use. So there is a way to disable some backends altogether:

```
zstyle ':vcs_info:*' disable bzr cdv darcs mtn svk tla
```

You may also pick a few from that list and enable only those:

```
zstyle ':vcs_info:*' enable git cvs svn
```

If you rerun `vcs_info_printsys` after one of these commands, you will see the backends listed in the **disable** style (or backends not in the **enable** style - if you used that) marked as disabled by a hash sign. That means the detection of these systems is skipped *completely*. No wasted time there.

26.5.2 Configuration

The `vcs_info` feature can be configured via `zstyle`.

First, the context in which we are working:

> `:vcs_info:`*vcs-string*`:`*user-context*`:`*repo-root-name*

vcs-string is one of: `git`, `git-svn`, `git-p4`, `hg`, `hg-git`, `hg-hgsubversion`, `hg-hgsvn`, `darcs`, `bzr`, `cdv`, `mtn`, `svn`, `cvs`, `svk`, `tla`, `p4` or `fossil`. This is followed by '`.quilt-`*quilt-mode*' in Quilt mode (see Section 26.5.4 [vcs_info Quilt Support], page 444, for details) and by '`+`*hook-name*' while hooks are active (see Section 26.5.7 [vcs_info Hooks], page 447, for details).

> Currently, hooks in quilt mode don't add the '`.quilt-`*quilt-mode*' information. This may change in the future.

user-context

is a freely configurable string, assignable by the user as the first argument to `vcs_info` (see its description below).

repo-root-name

is the name of a repository in which you want a style to match. So, if you want a setting specific to `/usr/src/zsh`, with that being a CVS checkout, you can set *repo-root-name* to `zsh` to make it so.

There are three special values for *vcs-string*: The first is named `-init-`, that is in effect as long as there was no decision what VCS backend to use. The second is `-preinit-`; it is used *before* `vcs_info` is run, when initializing the data exporting variables. The third special value is `formats` and is used by the `vcs_info_lastmsg` for looking up its styles.

The initial value of *repo-root-name* is `-all-` and it is replaced with the actual name, as soon as it is known. Only use this part of the context for defining the `formats`, `actionformats` or `branchformat` styles, as it is guaranteed that *repo-root-name* is set up correctly for these only. For all other styles, just use '`*`' instead.

There are two pre-defined values for *user-context*:

`default` the one used if none is specified

`command` used by vcs_info_lastmsg to lookup its styles

You can of course use '`:vcs_info:*`' to match all VCSs in all user-contexts at once.

This is a description of all styles that are looked up.

`formats` A list of formats, used when actionformats is not used (which is most of the time).

`actionformats`

A list of formats, used if there is a special action going on in your current repository; like an interactive rebase or a merge conflict.

`branchformat`

Some backends replace `%b` in the formats and actionformats styles above, not only by a branch name but also by a revision number. This style lets you modify how that string should look.

`nvcsformats`

These "formats" are set when we didn't detect a version control system for the current directory or `vcs_info` was disabled. This is useful if you want `vcs_info` to completely take over the generation of your prompt. You would do something like `PS1='${vcs_info_msg_0_}'` to accomplish that.

`hgrevformat`

`hg` uses both a hash and a revision number to reference a specific change-set in a repository. With this style you can format the revision string (see `branchformat`) to include either or both. It's only useful when `get-revision` is true. Note, the full 40-character revision id is not available (except when using the `use-simple` option) because executing hg more than once per prompt is too slow; you may customize this behavior using hooks.

max-exports

> Defines the maximum number of `vcs_info_msg_*_` variables `vcs_info` will set.

enable A list of backends you want to use. Checked in the `-init-` context. If this list contains an item called `NONE` no backend is used at all and `vcs_info` will do nothing. If this list contains `ALL`, `vcs_info` will use all known backends. Only with `ALL` in `enable` will the `disable` style have any effect. `ALL` and `NONE` are case insensitive.

disable A list of VCSs you don't want `vcs_info` to test for repositories (checked in the `-init-` context, too). Only used if `enable` contains `ALL`.

disable-patterns

> A list of patterns that are checked against `$PWD`. If a pattern matches, `vcs_info` will be disabled. This style is checked in the `:vcs_info:-init-:*:-all-` context.

> Say, `~/.zsh` is a directory under version control, in which you do not want `vcs_info` to be active, do:

> ```
> zstyle ':vcs_info:*' disable-patterns "${(b)HOME}/.zsh(|/*)"
> ```

use-quilt

> If enabled, the `quilt` support code is active in 'addon' mode. See Section 26.5.4 [vcs_info Quilt Support], page 444, for details.

quilt-standalone

> If enabled, 'standalone' mode detection is attempted if no VCS is active in a given directory. See Section 26.5.4 [vcs_info Quilt Support], page 444, for details.

quilt-patch-dir

> Overwrite the value of the `$QUILT_PATCHES` environment variable. See Section 26.5.4 [vcs_info Quilt Support], page 444, for details.

quiltcommand

> When `quilt` itself is called in quilt support, the value of this style is used as the command name.

check-for-changes

> If enabled, this style causes the `%c` and `%u` format escapes to show when the working directory has uncommitted changes. The strings displayed by these escapes can be controlled via the `stagedstr` and `unstagedstr` styles. The only backends that currently support this option are `git`, `hg`, and `bzr` (the latter two only support unstaged).

> For this style to be evaluated with the `hg` backend, the `get-revision` style needs to be set and the `use-simple` style needs to be unset. The latter is the default; the former is not.

> With the `bzr` backend, *lightweight checkouts* only honor this style if the `use-server` style is set.

> Note, the actions taken if this style is enabled are potentially expensive (read: they may be slow, depending on how big the current repository is). Therefore, it is disabled by default.

check-for-staged-changes

> This style is like check-for-changes, but it never checks the worktree files, only the metadata in the .${vcs} dir. Therefore, this style initializes only the %c escape (with stagedstr) but not the %u escape. This style is faster than check-for-changes.
>
> In the git backend, this style checks for changes in the index. Other backends do not currently implement this style.
>
> This style is disabled by default.

stagedstr

> This string will be used in the %c escape if there are staged changes in the repository.

unstagedstr

> This string will be used in the %u escape if there are unstaged changes in the repository.

command

> This style causes vcs_info to use the supplied string as the command to use as the VCS's binary. Note, that setting this in ':vcs_info:*' is not a good idea.
>
> If the value of this style is empty (which is the default), the used binary name is the name of the backend in use (e.g. svn is used in an svn repository).
>
> The repo-root-name part in the context is always the default -all- when this style is looked up.
>
> For example, this style can be used to use binaries from non-default installation directories. Assume, git is installed in /usr/bin but your sysadmin installed a newer version in /usr/local/bin. Instead of changing the order of your $PATH parameter, you can do this:
>
> ```
> zstyle ':vcs_info:git:*:-all-' command /usr/local/bin/git
> ```

use-server

> This is used by the Perforce backend (p4) to decide if it should contact the Perforce server to find out if a directory is managed by Perforce. This is the only reliable way of doing this, but runs the risk of a delay if the server name cannot be found. If the server (more specifically, the host:port pair describing the server) cannot be contacted, its name is put into the associative array vcs_info_p4_dead_servers and is not contacted again during the session until it is removed by hand. If you do not set this style, the p4 backend is only usable if you have set the environment variable P4CONFIG to a file name and have corresponding files in the root directories of each Perforce client. See comments in the function VCS_INFO_detect_p4 for more detail.
>
> The Bazaar backend (bzr) uses this to permit contacting the server about lightweight checkouts, see the check-for-changes style.

use-simple

> If there are two different ways of gathering information, you can select the simpler one by setting this style to true; the default is to use the not-that-simple code, which is potentially a lot slower but might be more accurate in all possible cases. This style is used by the bzr and hg backends. In the case of hg

it will invoke the external hexdump program to parse the binary dirstate cache file; this method will not return the local revision number.

get-revision

> If set to true, vcs_info goes the extra mile to figure out the revision of a repository's work tree (currently for the `git` and `hg` backends, where this kind of information is not always vital). For `git`, the hash value of the currently checked out commit is available via the `%i` expansion. With `hg`, the local revision number and the corresponding global hash are available via `%i`.

get-mq   If set to true, the `hg` backend will look for a Mercurial Queue (`mq`) patch directory. Information will be available via the '`%m`' replacement.

get-bookmarks

> If set to true, the `hg` backend will try to get a list of current bookmarks. They will be available via the '`%m`' replacement.

> The default is to generate a comma-separated list of all bookmark names that refer to the currently checked out revision. If a bookmark is active, its name is suffixed an asterisk and placed first in the list.

use-prompt-escapes

> Determines if we assume that the assembled string from `vcs_info` includes prompt escapes. (Used by `vcs_info_lastmsg`.)

debug   Enable debugging output to track possible problems. Currently this style is only used by `vcs_info`'s hooks system.

hooks   A list style that defines hook-function names. See Section 26.5.7 [vcs_info Hooks], page 447, below for details.

patch-format
nopatch-format

> This pair of styles format the patch information used by the `%m` expando in formats and actionformats for the `git` and `hg` backends. The value is subject to certain %-expansions described below. The expanded value is made available in the global `backend_misc` array as `${backend_misc[patches]}` (also if a `set-patch-format` hook is used).

get-unapplied

> This boolean style controls whether a backend should attempt to gather a list of unapplied patches (for example with Mercurial Queue patches).

> Used by the `quilt` and `hg` backends.

The default values for these styles in all contexts are:

formats   " (%s)-[%b]%u%c-"

actionformats
> " (%s)-[%b|%a]%u%c-"

branchformat
> "%b:%r" (for bzr, svn, svk and hg)

```
nvcsformats
          ""

hgrevformat
          "%r:%h"

max-exports
          2

enable    ALL

disable   (empty list)

disable-patterns
          (empty list)

check-for-changes
          false

check-for-staged-changes
          false

stagedstr
          (string: "S")

unstagedstr
          (string: "U")

command   (empty string)

use-server
          false

use-simple
          false

get-revision
          false

get-mq    true

get-bookmarks
          false

use-prompt-escapes
          true

debug     false

hooks     (empty list)

use-quilt
          false

quilt-standalone
          false

quilt-patch-dir
          empty - use $QUILT_PATCHES
```

`quiltcommand`
> quilt

`patch-format`
> *backend dependent*

`nopatch-format`
> *backend dependent*

`get-unapplied`
> false

In normal `formats` and `actionformats` the following replacements are done:

`%s`   The VCS in use (git, hg, svn, etc.).

`%b`   Information about the current branch.

`%a`   An identifier that describes the action. Only makes sense in `actionformats`.

`%i`   The current revision number or identifier. For `hg` the `hgrevformat` style may be used to customize the output.

`%c`   The string from the `stagedstr` style if there are staged changes in the repository.

`%u`   The string from the `unstagedstr` style if there are unstaged changes in the repository.

`%R`   The base directory of the repository.

`%r`   The repository name. If `%R` is `/foo/bar/repoXY`, `%r` is `repoXY`.

`%S`   A subdirectory within a repository. If `$PWD` is `/foo/bar/repoXY/beer/tasty`, `%S` is `beer/tasty`.

`%m`   A "misc" replacement. It is at the discretion of the backend to decide what this replacement expands to.

> The `hg` and `git` backends use this expando to display patch information. `hg` sources patch information from the `mq` extensions; `git` from in-progress `rebase` and `cherry-pick` operations and from the `stgit` extension. The `patch-format` and `nopatch-format` styles control the generated string. The former is used when at least one patch from the patch queue has been applied, and the latter otherwise.

> The `hg` backend displays bookmark information in this expando (in addition to `mq` information). See the `get-mq` and `get-bookmarks` styles. Both of these styles may be enabled at the same time. If both are enabled, both resulting strings will be shown separated by a semicolon (that cannot currently be customized).

> The `quilt` 'standalone' backend sets this expando to the same value as the `%Q` expando.

`%Q`   Quilt series information. When quilt is used (either in 'addon' mode or as a 'standalone' backend), this expando is set to quilt series' `patch-format` string. The `set-patch-format` hook and `nopatch-format` style are honoured.

> See Section 26.5.4 [vcs_info Quilt Support], page 444, below for details.

In `branchformat` these replacements are done:

%b   The branch name.

%r   The current revision number or the `hgrevformat` style for `hg`.

In `hgrevformat` these replacements are done:

%r   The current local revision number.

%h   The current global revision identifier.

In `patch-format` and `nopatch-format` these replacements are done:

%p   The name of the top-most applied patch (`applied-string`).

%u   The number of unapplied patches (`unapplied-string`).

%n   The number of applied patches.

%c   The number of unapplied patches.

%a   The number of all patches.

%g   The names of active `mq` guards (`hg` backend).

%G   The number of active `mq` guards (`hg` backend).

Not all VCS backends have to support all replacements. For `nvcsformats` no replacements are performed at all, it is just a string.

26.5.3 Oddities

If you want to use the %b (bold off) prompt expansion in `formats`, which expands %b itself, use %%b. That will cause the `vcs_info` expansion to replace %%b with %b, so that zsh's prompt expansion mechanism can handle it. Similarly, to hand down %b from `branchformat`, use %%%%b. Sorry for this inconvenience, but it cannot be easily avoided. Luckily we do not clash with a lot of prompt expansions and this only needs to be done for those.

When one of the `gen-applied-string`, `gen-unapplied-string`, and `set-patch-format` hooks is defined, applying %-escaping ('foo=${foo//'%'/%%}') to the interpolated values for use in the prompt is the responsibility of those hooks (jointly); when neither of those hooks is defined, `vcs_info` handles escaping by itself. We regret this coupling, but it was required for backwards compatibility.

26.5.4 Quilt Support

Quilt is not a version control system, therefore this is not implemented as a backend. It can help keeping track of a series of patches. People use it to keep a set of changes they want to use on top of software packages (which is tightly integrated into the package build process - the Debian project does this for a large number of packages). Quilt can also help individual developers keep track of their own patches on top of real version control systems.

The `vcs_info` integration tries to support both ways of using quilt by having two slightly different modes of operation: 'addon' mode and 'standalone' mode).

Quilt integration is off by default; to enable it, set the **use-quilt** style, and add %Q to your **formats** or **actionformats** style:

```
zstyle ':vcs_info:*' use-quilt true
```

Styles looked up from the Quilt support code include '.quilt-*quilt-mode*' in the *vcs-string* part of the context, where *quilt-mode* is either **addon** or **standalone**. Example: :vcs_info:git.quilt-addon:default:*repo-root-name*.

For 'addon' mode to become active **vcs_info** must have already detected a real version control system controlling the directory. If that is the case, a directory that holds quilt's patches needs to be found. That directory is configurable via the 'QUILT_PATCHES' environment variable. If that variable exists its value is used, otherwise the value 'patches' is assumed. The value from $QUILT_PATCHES can be overwritten using the 'quilt-patches' style. (Note: you can use **vcs_info** to keep the value of $QUILT_PATCHES correct all the time via the **post-quilt** hook).

When the directory in question is found, quilt is assumed to be active. To gather more information, **vcs_info** looks for a directory called '.pc'; Quilt uses that directory to track its current state. If this directory does not exist we know that quilt has not done anything to the working directory (read: no patches have been applied yet).

If patches are applied, **vcs_info** will try to find out which. If you want to know which patches of a series are not yet applied, you need to activate the **get-unapplied** style in the appropriate context.

vcs_info allows for very detailed control over how the gathered information is presented (see Section 26.5.2 [vcs_info Configuration], page 437, and Section 26.5.7 [vcs_info Hooks], page 447), all of which are documented below. Note there are a number of other patch tracking systems that work on top of a certain version control system (like **stgit** for *git*, or **mq** for *hg*); the configuration for systems like that are generally configured the same way as the *quilt* support.

If the *quilt* support is working in 'addon' mode, the produced string is available as a simple format replacement (%Q to be precise), which can be used in **formats** and **actionformats**; see below for details).

If, on the other hand, the support code is working in 'standalone' mode, **vcs_info** will pretend as if **quilt** were an actual version control system. That means that the version control system identifier (which otherwise would be something like 'svn' or 'cvs') will be set to '-**quilt**-'. This has implications on the used style context where this identifier is the second element. **vcs_info** will have filled in a proper value for the "repository's" root directory and the string containing the information about quilt's state will be available as the 'misc' replacement (and %Q for compatibility with 'addon' mode).

What is left to discuss is how 'standalone' mode is detected. The detection itself is a series of searches for directories. You can have this detection enabled all the time in every directory that is not otherwise under version control. If you know there is only a limited set of trees where you would like **vcs_info** to try and look for Quilt in 'standalone' mode to minimise the amount of searching on every call to **vcs_info**, there are a number of ways to do that:

Essentially, 'standalone' mode detection is controlled by a style called '**quilt-standalone**'. It is a string style and its value can have different effects. The simplest values are: '**always**' to run detection every time **vcs_info** is run, and '**never**' to turn the detection off entirely.

If the value of `quilt-standalone` is something else, it is interpreted differently. If the value is the name of a scalar variable the value of that variable is checked and that value is used in the same 'always'/'never' way as described above.

If the value of `quilt-standalone` is an array, the elements of that array are used as directory names under which you want the detection to be active.

If `quilt-standalone` is an associative array, the keys are taken as directory names under which you want the detection to be active, but only if the corresponding value is the string 'true'.

Last, but not least, if the value of `quilt-standalone` is the name of a function, the function is called without arguments and the return value decides whether detection should be active. A '0' return value is true; a non-zero return value is interpreted as false.

Note, if there is both a function and a variable by the name of `quilt-standalone`, the function will take precedence.

26.5.5 Function Descriptions (Public API)

`vcs_info` [*user-context*]

> The main function, that runs all backends and assembles all data into `${vcs_info_msg_*_}`. This is the function you want to call from `precmd` if you want to include up-to-date information in your prompt (see Section 26.5.6 [vcs_info Variables], page 447, below). If an argument is given, that string will be used instead of `default` in the *user-context* field of the style context.

`vcs_info_hookadd`

> Statically registers a number of functions to a given hook. The hook needs to be given as the first argument; what follows is a list of hook-function names to register to the hook. The '`+vi-`' prefix needs to be left out here. See Section 26.5.7 [vcs_info Hooks], page 447, below for details.

`vcs_info_hookdel`

> Remove hook-functions from a given hook. The hook needs to be given as the first non-option argument; what follows is a list of hook-function names to unregister from the hook. If '`-a`' is used as the first argument, `all` occurrences of the functions are unregistered. Otherwise only the last occurrence is removed (if a function was registered to a hook more than once). The '`+vi-`' prefix needs to be left out here. See Section 26.5.7 [vcs_info Hooks], page 447, below for details.

`vcs_info_lastmsg`

> Outputs the last `${vcs_info_msg_*_}` value. Takes into account the value of the `use-prompt-escapes` style in '`:vcs_info:formats:command:-all-`'. It also only prints `max-exports` values.

`vcs_info_printsys` [*user-context*]

> Prints a list of all supported version control systems. Useful to find out possible contexts (and which of them are enabled) or values for the `disable` style.

`vcs_info_setsys`

> Initializes `vcs_info`'s internal list of available backends. With this function, you can add support for new VCSs without restarting the shell.

All functions named `VCS_INFO_*` are for internal use only.

26.5.6 Variable Description

`${vcs_info_msg_N_}` (Note the trailing underscore)

>   Where N is an integer, e.g., `vcs_info_msg_0_`. These variables are the storage for the informational message the last `vcs_info` call has assembled. These are strongly connected to the **formats**, **actionformats** and **nvcsformats** styles described above. Those styles are lists. The first member of that list gets expanded into `${vcs_info_msg_0_}`, the second into `${vcs_info_msg_1_}` and the Nth into `${vcs_info_msg_N-1_}`. (See the **max-exports** style above.)

All variables named `VCS_INFO_*` are for internal use only.

26.5.7 Hooks in vcs_info

Hooks are places in `vcs_info` where you can run your own code. That code can communicate with the code that called it and through that, change the system's behaviour.

For configuration, hooks change the style context:

>   `:vcs_info:vcs-string+hook-name:user-context:repo-root-name`

To register functions to a hook, you need to list them in the **hooks** style in the appropriate context.

Example:

>   `zstyle ':vcs_info:*+foo:*' hooks bar baz`

This registers functions to the hook 'foo' for all backends. In order to avoid namespace problems, all registered function names are prepended by a '+vi-', so the actual functions called for the 'foo' hook are '+vi-bar' and '+vi-baz'.

If you would like to register a function to a hook regardless of the current context, you may use the `vcs_info_hookadd` function. To remove a function that was added like that, the `vcs_info_hookdel` function can be used.

If something seems weird, you can enable the 'debug' boolean style in the proper context and the hook-calling code will print what it tried to execute and whether the function in question existed.

When you register more than one function to a hook, all functions are executed one after another until one function returns non-zero or until all functions have been called. Context-sensitive hook functions are executed **before** statically registered ones (the ones added by `vcs_info_hookadd`).

You may pass data between functions via an associative array, **user_data**. For example:

```
+vi-git-myfirsthook(){
    user_data[myval]=$myval
}
+vi-git-mysecondhook(){
    # do something with ${user_data[myval]}
}
```

There are a number of variables that are special in hook contexts:

ret   The return value that the hooks system will return to the caller. The default is an integer 'zero'. If and how a changed **ret** value changes the execution of the caller depends on the specific hook. See the hook documentation below for details.

hook_com   An associated array which is used for bidirectional communication from the caller to hook functions. The used keys depend on the specific hook.

context   The active context of the hook. Functions that wish to change this variable should make it local scope first.

vcs   The current VCS after it was detected. The same values as in the enable/disable style are used. Available in all hooks except **start-up**.

Finally, the full list of currently available hooks:

start-up   Called after starting **vcs_info** but before the VCS in this directory is determined. It can be used to deactivate **vcs_info** temporarily if necessary. When **ret** is set to 1, **vcs_info** aborts and does nothing; when set to 2, **vcs_info** sets up everything as if no version control were active and exits.

pre-get-data
        Same as **start-up** but after the VCS was detected.

gen-hg-bookmark-string
        Called in the Mercurial backend when a bookmark string is generated; the **get-revision** and **get-bookmarks** styles must be true.

        This hook gets the names of the Mercurial bookmarks that **vcs_info** collected from 'hg'.

        If a bookmark is active, the key `${hook_com[hg-active-bookmark]}` is set to its name. The key is otherwise unset.

        When setting **ret** to non-zero, the string in `${hook_com[hg-bookmark-string]}` will be used in the `%m` escape in **formats** and **actionformats** and will be available in the global **backend_misc** array as `${backend_misc[bookmarks]}`.

gen-applied-string
        Called in the **git** (with **stgit** or during rebase or merge), and **hg** (with **mq**) backends and in **quilt** support when the **applied-string** is generated; the **use-quilt** zstyle must be true for **quilt** (the **mq** and **stgit** backends are active by default).

        This hook gets the names of all applied patches which **vcs_info** collected so far in the opposite order, which means that the first argument is the top-most patch and so forth.

        When setting **ret** to non-zero, the string in `${hook_com[applied-string]}` will be available as `%p` in the **patch-format** and **nopatch-format** styles. This hook is, in concert with **set-patch-format**, responsible for %-escaping that value for use in the prompt. (See Section 26.5.3 [vcs_info Oddities], page 444.)

gen-unapplied-string

Called in the **git** (with **stgit** or during rebase), and **hg** (with **mq**) backend and in **quilt** support when the **unapplied-string** is generated; the **get-unapplied** style must be true.

This hook gets the names of all unapplied patches which **vcs_info** collected so far in order, which means that the first argument is the patch next-in-line to be applied and so forth.

When setting **ret** to non-zero, the string in **${hook_com[unapplied-string]}** will be available as **%u** in the **patch-format** and **nopatch-format** styles. This hook is, in concert with **set-patch-format**, responsible for %-escaping that value for use in the prompt. (See Section 26.5.3 [vcs_info Oddities], page 444.)

gen-mqguards-string

Called in the **hg** backend when **guards-string** is generated; the **get-mq** style must be true (default).

This hook gets the names of any active **mq** guards.

When setting **ret** to non-zero, the string in **${hook_com[guards-string]}** will be used in the **%g** escape in the **patch-format** and **nopatch-format** styles.

no-vcs   This hooks is called when no version control system was detected.

The 'hook_com' parameter is not used.

post-backend

Called as soon as the backend has finished collecting information.

The 'hook_com' keys available are as for the **set-message** hook.

post-quilt

Called after the **quilt** support is done. The following information is passed as arguments to the hook: 1. the quilt-support mode ('addon' or 'standalone'); 2. the directory that contains the patch series; 3. the directory that holds quilt's status information (the '.pc' directory) or the string **"-nopc-"** if that directory wasn't found.

The 'hook_com' parameter is not used.

set-branch-format

Called before 'branchformat' is set. The only argument to the hook is the format that is configured at this point.

The 'hook_com' keys considered are 'branch' and 'revision'. They are set to the values figured out so far by **vcs_info** and any change will be used directly when the actual replacement is done.

If **ret** is set to non-zero, the string in **${hook_com[branch-replace]}** will be used unchanged as the '%b' replacement in the variables set by **vcs_info**.

set-hgrev-format

Called before a 'hgrevformat' is set. The only argument to the hook is the format that is configured at this point.

The 'hook_com' keys considered are 'hash' and 'localrev'. They are set to the values figured out so far by **vcs_info** and any change will be used directly when the actual replacement is done.

If `ret` is set to non-zero, the string in `${hook_com[rev-replace]}` will be used unchanged as the '`%i`' replacement in the variables set by `vcs_info`.

pre-addon-quilt

This hook is used when `vcs_info`'s quilt functionality is active in "addon" mode (quilt used on top of a real version control system). It is activated right before any quilt specific action is taken.

Setting the '`ret`' variable in this hook to a non-zero value avoids any quilt specific actions from being run at all.

set-patch-format

This hook is used to control some of the possible expansions in `patch-format` and `nopatch-format` styles with patch queue systems such as quilt, mqueue and the like.

This hook is used in the `git`, `hg` and `quilt` backends.

The hook allows the control of the `%p` (`${hook_com[applied]}`) and `%u` (`${hook_com[unapplied]}`) expansion in all backends that use the hook. With the mercurial backend, the `%g` (`${hook_com[guards]}`) expansion is controllable in addition to that.

If `ret` is set to non-zero, the string in `${hook_com[patch-replace]}` will be used unchanged instead of an expanded format from `patch-format` or `nopatch-format`.

This hook is, in concert with the `gen-applied-string` or `gen-unapplied-string` hooks if they are defined, responsible for %-escaping the final `patch-format` value for use in the prompt. (See Section 26.5.3 [vcs_info Oddities], page 444.)

set-message

Called each time before a '`vcs_info_msg_N_`' message is set. It takes two arguments; the first being the 'N' in the message variable name, the second is the currently configured `formats` or `actionformats`.

There are a number of '`hook_com`' keys, that are used here: '`action`', '`branch`', '`base`', '`base-name`', '`subdir`', '`staged`', '`unstaged`', '`revision`', '`misc`', '`vcs`' and one '`miscN`' entry for each backend-specific data field (N starting at zero). They are set to the values figured out so far by `vcs_info` and any change will be used directly when the actual replacement is done.

Since this hook is triggered multiple times (once for each configured `formats` or `actionformats`), each of the '`hook_com`' keys mentioned above (except for the `miscN` entries) has an '`_orig`' counterpart, so even if you changed a value to your liking you can still get the original value in the next run. Changing the '`_orig`' values is probably not a good idea.

If `ret` is set to non-zero, the string in `${hook_com[message]}` will be used unchanged as the message by `vcs_info`.

If all of this sounds rather confusing, take a look at Section 26.5.8 [vcs_info Examples], page 451, and also in the `Misc/vcs_info-examples` file in the Zsh source. They contain some explanatory code.

26.5.8 Examples

Don't use `vcs_info` at all (even though it's in your prompt):

```
zstyle ':vcs_info:*' enable NONE
```

Disable the backends for `bzr` and `svk`:

```
zstyle ':vcs_info:*' disable bzr svk
```

Disable everything *but* `bzr` and `svk`:

```
zstyle ':vcs_info:*' enable bzr svk
```

Provide a special formats for `git`:

```
zstyle ':vcs_info:git:*' formats       ' GIT, BABY! [%b]'
zstyle ':vcs_info:git:*' actionformats ' GIT ACTION! [%b|%a]'
```

All `%x` expansion in all sorts of formats (`formats`, `actionformats`, `branchformat`, you name it) are done using the 'zformat' builtin from the 'zsh/zutil' module. That means you can do everything with these `%x` items what zformat supports. In particular, if you want something that is really long to have a fixed width, like a hash in a mercurial branchformat, you can do this: `%12.12i`. That'll shrink the 40 character hash to its 12 leading characters. The form is actually '%*min.maxx*'. More is possible. See Section 22.37 [The zsh/zutil Module], page 382, for details.

Use the quicker `bzr` backend

```
zstyle ':vcs_info:bzr:*' use-simple true
```

If you do use **use-simple**, please report if it does 'the-right-thing[tm]'.

Display the revision number in yellow for `bzr` and `svn`:

```
zstyle ':vcs_info:(svn|bzr):*' \
       branchformat '%b%{'${fg[yellow]}'%}:%r'
```

If you want colors, make sure you enclose the color codes in `%{...%}` if you want to use the string provided by `vcs_info` in prompts.

Here is how to print the VCS information as a command (not in a prompt):

```
alias vcsi='vcs_info command; vcs_info_lastmsg'
```

This way, you can even define different formats for output via `vcs_info_lastmsg` in the ':vcs_info:*:command:*' namespace.

Now as promised, some code that uses hooks: say, you'd like to replace the string 'svn' by 'subversion' in `vcs_info`'s `%s formats` replacement.

First, we will tell `vcs_info` to call a function when populating the message variables with the gathered information:

```
zstyle ':vcs_info:*+set-message:*' hooks svn2subversion
```

Nothing happens. Which is reasonable, since we didn't define the actual function yet. To see what the hooks subsystem is trying to do, enable the 'debug' style:

```
zstyle ':vcs_info:*+*:*' debug true
```

That should give you an idea what is going on. Specifically, the function that we are looking for is '+vi-svn2subversion'. Note, the '+vi-' prefix. So, everything is in order, just as documented. When you are done checking out the debugging output, disable it again:

```
zstyle ':vcs_info:*+*:*' debug false
```

Now, let's define the function:

```
function +vi-svn2subversion() {
    [[ ${hook_com[vcs_orig]} == svn ]] && hook_com[vcs]=subversion
}
```

Simple enough. And it could have even been simpler, if only we had registered our function in a less generic context. If we do it only in the 'svn' backend's context, we don't need to test which the active backend is:

```
zstyle ':vcs_info:svn+set-message:*' hooks svn2subversion
```

```
function +vi-svn2subversion() {
    hook_com[vcs]=subversion
}
```

And finally a little more elaborate example, that uses a hook to create a customised bookmark string for the **hg** backend.

Again, we start off by registering a function:

```
zstyle ':vcs_info:hg+gen-hg-bookmark-string:*' hooks hgbookmarks
```

And then we define the '+vi-hgbookmarks' function:

```
function +vi-hgbookmarks() {
    # The default is to connect all bookmark names by
    # commas. This mixes things up a little.
    # Imagine, there's one type of bookmarks that is
    # special to you. Say, because it's *your* work.
    # Those bookmarks look always like this: "sh/*"
    # (because your initials are sh, for example).
    # This makes the bookmarks string use only those
    # bookmarks. If there's more than one, it
    # concatenates them using commas.
    # The bookmarks returned by 'hg' are available in
    # the function's positional parameters.
    local s="${(Mj:,:)@:#sh/*}"
    # Now, the communication with the code that calls
    # the hook functions is done via the hook_com[]
    # hash. The key at which the 'gen-hg-bookmark-string'
    # hook looks is 'hg-bookmark-string'. So:
    hook_com[hg-bookmark-string]=$s
    # And to signal that we want to use the string we
    # just generated, set the special variable 'ret' to
    # something other than the default zero:
    ret=1
    return 0
}
```

Some longer examples and code snippets which might be useful are available in the examples file located at Misc/vcs_info-examples in the Zsh source directory.

This concludes our guided tour through zsh's `vcs_info`.

26.6 Prompt Themes

26.6.1 Installation

You should make sure all the functions from the `Functions/Prompts` directory of the source distribution are available; they all begin with the string 'prompt_' except for the special function 'promptinit'. You also need the 'colors' and 'add-zsh-hook' functions from `Functions/Misc`. All these functions may already be installed on your system; if not, you will need to find them and copy them. The directory should appear as one of the elements of the `fpath` array (this should already be the case if they were installed), and at least the function `promptinit` should be autoloaded; it will autoload the rest. Finally, to initialize the use of the system you need to call the `promptinit` function. The following code in your `.zshrc` will arrange for this; assume the functions are stored in the directory `~/myfns`:

```
fpath=(~/myfns $fpath)
autoload -U promptinit
promptinit
```

26.6.2 Theme Selection

Use the `prompt` command to select your preferred theme. This command may be added to your `.zshrc` following the call to `promptinit` in order to start zsh with a theme already selected.

`prompt [ -c | -l ]`
`prompt [ -p | -h ] [ theme ... ]`
`prompt [ -s ] theme [ arg ... ]`

> Set or examine the prompt theme. With no options and a *theme* argument, the theme with that name is set as the current theme. The available themes are determined at run time; use the `-l` option to see a list. The special *theme* 'random' selects at random one of the available themes and sets your prompt to that.
>
> In some cases the *theme* may be modified by one or more arguments, which should be given after the theme name. See the help for each theme for descriptions of these arguments.
>
> Options are:
>
> `-c`   Show the currently selected theme and its parameters, if any.
>
> `-l`   List all available prompt themes.
>
> `-p`   Preview the theme named by *theme*, or all themes if no *theme* is given.
>
> `-h`   Show help for the theme named by *theme*, or for the `prompt` function if no *theme* is given.
>
> `-s`   Set *theme* as the current theme and save state.

prompt_*theme*_setup

> Each available *theme* has a setup function which is called by the **prompt** function to install that theme. This function may define other functions as necessary to maintain the prompt, including functions used to preview the prompt or provide help for its use. You should not normally call a theme's setup function directly.

26.6.3 Utility Themes

prompt off

> The theme 'off' sets all the prompt variables to minimal values with no special effects.

prompt default

> The theme 'default' sets all prompt variables to the same state as if an interactive zsh was started with no initialization files.

prompt restore

> The special theme 'restore' erases all theme settings and sets prompt variables to their state before the first time the 'prompt' function was run, provided each theme has properly defined its cleanup (see below).

> Note that you can undo 'prompt off' and 'prompt default' with 'prompt restore', but a second restore does not undo the first.

26.6.4 Writing Themes

The first step for adding your own theme is to choose a name for it, and create a file 'prompt_*name*_setup' in a directory in your **fpath**, such as ~/myfns in the example above. The file should at minimum contain assignments for the prompt variables that your theme wishes to modify. By convention, themes use PS1, PS2, RPS1, etc., rather than the longer PROMPT and RPROMPT.

The file is autoloaded as a function in the current shell context, so it may contain any necessary commands to customize your theme, including defining additional functions. To make some complex tasks easier, your setup function may also do any of the following:

Assign **prompt_opts**

> The array **prompt_opts** may be assigned any of "bang", "cr", "percent", "sp", and/or "subst" as values. The corresponding setopts (**promptbang**, etc.) are turned on, all other prompt-related options are turned off. The **prompt_opts** array preserves setopts even beyond the scope of **localoptions**, should your function need that.

Modify precmd and preexec

> Use of **add-zsh-hook** is recommended. The **precmd** and **preexec** hooks are automatically adjusted if the prompt theme changes or is disabled.

Declare cleanup

> If your function makes any other changes that should be undone when the theme is disabled, your setup function may call

> > prompt_cleanup *command*

where *command* should be suitably quoted. If your theme is ever disabled or replaced by another, *command* is executed with `eval`. You may declare more than one such cleanup hook.

Define preview

Define or autoload a function `prompt_name_preview` to display a simulated version of your prompt. A simple default previewer is defined by `promptinit` for themes that do not define their own. This preview function is called by '`prompt -p`'.

Provide help

Define or autoload a function `prompt_name_help` to display documentation or help text for your theme. This help function is called by '`prompt -h`'.

26.7 ZLE Functions

26.7.1 Widgets

These functions all implement user-defined ZLE widgets (see Chapter 18 [Zsh Line Editor], page 183) which can be bound to keystrokes in interactive shells. To use them, your `.zshrc` should contain lines of the form

```
autoload function
zle -N function
```

followed by an appropriate `bindkey` command to associate the function with a key sequence. Suggested bindings are described below.

bash-style word functions

If you are looking for functions to implement moving over and editing words in the manner of bash, where only alphanumeric characters are considered word characters, you can use the functions described in the next section. The following is sufficient:

```
autoload -U select-word-style
select-word-style bash
```

`forward-word-match, backward-word-match`
`kill-word-match, backward-kill-word-match`
`transpose-words-match, capitalize-word-match`
`up-case-word-match, down-case-word-match`
`delete-whole-word-match, select-word-match`
`select-word-style, match-word-context, match-words-by-style`

The first eight '`-match`' functions are drop-in replacements for the builtin widgets without the suffix. By default they behave in a similar way. However, by the use of styles and the function **select-word-style**, the way words are matched can be altered. **select-word-match** is intended to be used as a text object in vi mode but with custom word styles. For comparison, the widgets described in Section 18.6.7 [Text Objects], page 221, use fixed definitions of words, compatible with the **vim** editor.

The simplest way of configuring the functions is to use **select-word-style**, which can either be called as a normal function with the appropriate argument, or invoked as a user-defined widget that will prompt for the first character of the word style to be used. The first time it is invoked, the first eight -match functions will automatically replace the builtin versions, so they do not need to be loaded explicitly.

The word styles available are as follows. Only the first character is examined.

bash   Word characters are alphanumeric characters only.

normal   As in normal shell operation: word characters are alphanumeric characters plus any characters present in the string given by the parameter $WORDCHARS.

shell   Words are complete shell command arguments, possibly including complete quoted strings, or any tokens special to the shell.

whitespace
          Words are any set of characters delimited by whitespace.

default   Restore the default settings; this is usually the same as 'normal'.

All but 'default' can be input as an upper case character, which has the same effect but with subword matching turned on. In this case, words with upper case characters are treated specially: each separate run of upper case characters, or an upper case character followed by any number of other characters, is considered a word. The style subword-range can supply an alternative character range to the default '[:upper:]'; the value of the style is treated as the contents of a '[...]' pattern (note that the outer brackets should not be supplied, only those surrounding named ranges).

More control can be obtained using the zstyle command, as described in Section 22.37 [The zsh/zutil Module], page 382. Each style is looked up in the context :zle:*widget* where *widget* is the name of the user-defined widget, not the name of the function implementing it, so in the case of the definitions supplied by select-word-style the appropriate contexts are :zle:forward-word, and so on. The function select-word-style itself always defines styles for the context ':zle:*' which can be overridden by more specific (longer) patterns as well as explicit contexts.

The style word-style specifies the rules to use. This may have the following values.

normal   Use the standard shell rules, i.e. alphanumerics and $WORDCHARS, unless overridden by the styles word-chars or word-class.

specified
          Similar to normal, but *only* the specified characters, and not also alphanumerics, are considered word characters.

unspecified
          The negation of specified. The given characters are those which will *not* be considered part of a word.

shell   Words are obtained by using the syntactic rules for generating shell command arguments. In addition, special tokens which are never command arguments such as '()' are also treated as words.

whitespace
> Words are whitespace-delimited strings of characters.

The first three of those rules usually use $WORDCHARS, but the value in the parameter can be overridden by the style **word-chars**, which works in exactly the same way as $WORDCHARS. In addition, the style **word-class** uses character class syntax to group characters and takes precedence over **word-chars** if both are set. The **word-class** style does not include the surrounding brackets of the character class; for example, '-:[:alnum:]' is a valid **word-class** to include all alphanumerics plus the characters '-' and ':'. Be careful including ']', '^' and '-' as these are special inside character classes.

word-style may also have '-subword' appended to its value to turn on subword matching, as described above.

The style **skip-chars** is mostly useful for **transpose-words** and similar functions. If set, it gives a count of characters starting at the cursor position which will not be considered part of the word and are treated as space, regardless of what they actually are. For example, if

```
zstyle ':zle:transpose-words' skip-chars 1
```

has been set, and **transpose-words-match** is called with the cursor on the X of foo$X$bar, where X can be any character, then the resulting expression is bar$X$foo.

Finer grained control can be obtained by setting the style **word-context** to an array of pairs of entries. Each pair of entries consists of a *pattern* and a *subcontext*. The shell argument the cursor is on is matched against each *pattern* in turn until one matches; if it does, the context is extended by a colon and the corresponding *subcontext*. Note that the test is made against the original word on the line, with no stripping of quotes. Special handling is done between words: the current context is examined and if it contains the string **between** the word is set to a single space; else if it is contains the string **back**, the word before the cursor is considered, else the word after cursor is considered. Some examples are given below.

The style **skip-whitespace-first** is only used with the **forward-word** widget. If it is set to true, then **forward-word** skips any non-word-characters, followed by any non-word-characters: this is similar to the behaviour of other word-orientated widgets, and also that used by other editors, however it differs from the standard zsh behaviour. When using **select-word-style** the widget is set in the context :zle:* to **true** if the word style is **bash** and **false** otherwise. It may be overridden by setting it in the more specific context :zle:forward-word*.

Here are some examples of use of the styles, actually taken from the simplified interface in **select-word-style**:

```
zstyle ':zle:*' word-style standard
zstyle ':zle:*' word-chars ''
```

Implements bash-style word handling for all widgets, i.e. only alphanumerics are word characters; equivalent to setting the parameter WORDCHARS empty for the given context.

```
style ':zle:*kill*' word-style space
```

Uses space-delimited words for widgets with the word 'kill' in the name. Neither of the styles word-chars nor word-class is used in this case.

Here are some examples of use of the word-context style to extend the context.

```
zstyle ':zle:*' word-context \
        "*/*" filename "[[:space:]]" whitespace
zstyle ':zle:transpose-words:whitespace' word-style shell
zstyle ':zle:transpose-words:filename' word-style normal
zstyle ':zle:transpose-words:filename' word-chars ''
```

This provides two different ways of using transpose-words depending on whether the cursor is on whitespace between words or on a filename, here any word containing a /. On whitespace, complete arguments as defined by standard shell rules will be transposed. In a filename, only alphanumerics will be transposed. Elsewhere, words will be transposed using the default style for :zle:transpose-words.

The word matching and all the handling of zstyle settings is actually implemented by the function match-words-by-style. This can be used to create new user-defined widgets. The calling function should set the local parameter curcontext to :zle:*widget*, create the local parameter matched_words and call match-words-by-style with no arguments. On return, matched_words will be set to an array with the elements: (1) the start of the line (2) the word before the cursor (3) any non-word characters between that word and the cursor (4) any non-word character at the cursor position plus any remaining non-word characters before the next word, including all characters specified by the skip-chars style, (5) the word at or following the cursor (6) any non-word characters following that word (7) the remainder of the line. Any of the elements may be an empty string; the calling function should test for this to decide whether it can perform its function.

If the variable matched_words is defined by the caller to match-words-by-style as an associative array (local -A matched_words), then the seven values given above should be retrieved from it as elements named start, word-before-cursor, ws-before-cursor, ws-after-cursor, word-after-cursor, ws-after-word, and end. In addition the element is-word-start is 1 if the cursor is on the start of a word or subword, or on white space before it (the cases can be distinguished by testing the ws-after-cursor element) and 0 otherwise. This form is recommended for future compatibility.

It is possible to pass options with arguments to match-words-by-style to override the use of styles. The options are:

-w	*word-style*
-s	*skip-chars*
-c	*word-class*
-C	*word-chars*
-r	*subword-range*

For example, `match-words-by-style -w shell -c 0` may be used to extract the command argument around the cursor.

The `word-context` style is implemented by the function `match-word-context`. This should not usually need to be called directly.

bracketed-paste-magic

The `bracketed-paste` widget (see Section 18.6.6 [Miscellaneous], page 215, in Section 18.4 [Zle Widgets], page 195) inserts pasted text literally into the editor buffer rather than interpret it as keystrokes. This disables some common usages where the self-insert widget is replaced in order to accomplish some extra processing. An example is the contributed `url-quote-magic` widget described below.

The `bracketed-paste-magic` widget is meant to replace `bracketed-paste` with a wrapper that re-enables these self-insert actions, and other actions as selected by zstyles. Therefore this widget is installed with

```
autoload -Uz bracketed-paste-magic
zle -N bracketed-paste bracketed-paste-magic
```

Other than enabling some widget processing, `bracketed-paste-magic` attempts to replicate `bracketed-paste` as faithfully as possible.

The following zstyles may be set to control processing of pasted text. All are looked up in the context ':bracketed-paste-magic'.

active-widgets

A list of patterns matching widget names that should be activated during the paste. All other key sequences are processed as self-insert-unmeta. The default is 'self-*' so any user-defined widgets named with that prefix are active along with the builtin self-insert.

If this style is not set (explicitly deleted) or set to an empty value, no widgets are active and the pasted text is inserted literally. If the value includes 'undefined-key', any unknown sequences are discarded from the pasted text.

inactive-keys

The inverse of `active-widgets`, a list of key sequences that always use `self-insert-unmeta` even when bound to an active widget. Note that this is a list of literal key sequences, not patterns.

paste-init

A list of function names, called in widget context (but not as widgets). The functions are called in order until one of them returns a non-zero status. The parameter 'PASTED' contains the initial state of the pasted text. All other ZLE parameters such as 'BUFFER' have their normal values and side-effects, and full history is available, so for example `paste-init` functions may move words from BUFFER into PASTED to make those words visible to the `active-widgets`.

A non-zero return from a `paste-init` function does *not* prevent the paste itself from proceeding.

Loading `bracketed-paste-magic` defines `backward-extend-paste`, a helper function for use in `paste-init`.

```
zstyle :bracketed-paste-magic paste-init \
       backward-extend-paste
```

When a paste would insert into the middle of a word or append text to a word already on the line, `backward-extend-paste` moves the prefix from `LBUFFER` into `PASTED` so that the `active-widgets` see the full word so far. This may be useful with `url-quote-magic`.

`paste-finish`

Another list of function names called in order until one returns non-zero. These functions are called *after* the pasted text has been processed by the `active-widgets`, but *before* it is inserted into 'BUFFER'. ZLE parameters have their normal values and side-effects.

A non-zero return from a `paste-finish` function does *not* prevent the paste itself from proceeding.

Loading `bracketed-paste-magic` also defines `quote-paste`, a helper function for use in `paste-finish`.

```
zstyle :bracketed-paste-magic paste-finish \
       quote-paste
zstyle :bracketed-paste-magic:finish quote-style \
       qqq
```

When the pasted text is inserted into `BUFFER`, it is quoted per the `quote-style` value. To forcibly turn off the built-in numeric prefix quoting of `bracketed-paste`, use:

```
zstyle :bracketed-paste-magic:finish quote-style \
       none
```

Important: During `active-widgets` processing of the paste (after `paste-init` and before `paste-finish`), BUFFER starts empty and history is restricted, so cursor motions, etc., may not pass outside of the pasted content. Text assigned to BUFFER by the active widgets is copied back into PASTED before `paste-finish`.

`copy-earlier-word`

This widget works like a combination of `insert-last-word` and `copy-prev-shell-word`. Repeated invocations of the widget retrieve earlier words on the relevant history line. With a numeric argument N, insert the Nth word from the history line; N may be negative to count from the end of the line.

If `insert-last-word` has been used to retrieve the last word on a previous history line, repeated invocations will replace that word with earlier words from the same line.

Otherwise, the widget applies to words on the line currently being edited. The `widget` style can be set to the name of another widget that should be called to retrieve words. This widget must accept the same three arguments as `insert-last-word`.

cycle-completion-positions

> After inserting an unambiguous string into the command line, the new function based completion system may know about multiple places in this string where characters are missing or differ from at least one of the possible matches. It will then place the cursor on the position it considers to be the most interesting one, i.e. the one where one can disambiguate between as many matches as possible with as little typing as possible.
>
> This widget allows the cursor to be easily moved to the other interesting spots. It can be invoked repeatedly to cycle between all positions reported by the completion system.

delete-whole-word-match

> This is another function which works like the `-match` functions described immediately above, i.e. using styles to decide the word boundaries. However, it is not a replacement for any existing function.
>
> The basic behaviour is to delete the word around the cursor. There is no numeric argument handling; only the single word around the cursor is considered. If the widget contains the string `kill`, the removed text will be placed in the cutbuffer for future yanking. This can be obtained by defining `kill-whole-word-match` as follows:
>
> ```
> zle -N kill-whole-word-match delete-whole-word-match
> ```
>
> and then binding the widget `kill-whole-word-match`.

up-line-or-beginning-search, down-line-or-beginning-search

> These widgets are similar to the builtin functions `up-line-or-search` and `down-line-or-search`: if in a multiline buffer they move up or down within the buffer, otherwise they search for a history line matching the start of the current line. In this case, however, they search for a line which matches the current line up to the current cursor position, in the manner of `history-beginning-search-backward` and `-forward`, rather than the first word on the line.

edit-command-line

> Edit the command line using your visual editor, as in `ksh`.
>
> ```
> bindkey -M vicmd v edit-command-line
> ```

expand-absolute-path

> Expand the file name under the cursor to an absolute path, resolving symbolic links. Where possible, the initial path segment is turned into a named directory or reference to a user's home directory.

history-search-end

> This function implements the widgets `history-beginning-search-backward-end` and `history-beginning-search-forward-end`. These commands work by first calling the corresponding builtin widget (see Section 18.6.2 [History Control], page 204) and then moving the cursor to the end of the line. The original cursor position is remembered and restored before calling the builtin widget a second time, so that the same search is repeated to look farther through the history.

Although you `autoload` only one function, the commands to use it are slightly different because it implements two widgets.

```
zle -N history-beginning-search-backward-end \
        history-search-end
zle -N history-beginning-search-forward-end \
        history-search-end
bindkey '\e^P' history-beginning-search-backward-end
bindkey '\e^N' history-beginning-search-forward-end
```

history-beginning-search-menu

This function implements yet another form of history searching. The text before the cursor is used to select lines from the history, as for `history-beginning-search-backward` except that all matches are shown in a numbered menu. Typing the appropriate digits inserts the full history line. Note that leading zeroes must be typed (they are only shown when necessary for removing ambiguity). The entire history is searched; there is no distinction between forwards and backwards.

With a numeric argument, the search is not anchored to the start of the line; the string typed by the use may appear anywhere in the line in the history.

If the widget name contains '`-end`' the cursor is moved to the end of the line inserted. If the widget name contains '`-space`' any space in the text typed is treated as a wildcard and can match anything (hence a leading space is equivalent to giving a numeric argument). Both forms can be combined, for example:

```
zle -N history-beginning-search-menu-space-end \
        history-beginning-search-menu
```

history-pattern-search

The function `history-pattern-search` implements widgets which prompt for a pattern with which to search the history backwards or forwards. The pattern is in the usual zsh format, however the first character may be ^ to anchor the search to the start of the line, and the last character may be $ to anchor the search to the end of the line. If the search was not anchored to the end of the line the cursor is positioned just after the pattern found.

The commands to create bindable widgets are similar to those in the example immediately above:

```
autoload -U history-pattern-search
zle -N history-pattern-search-backward history-pattern-search
zle -N history-pattern-search-forward history-pattern-search
```

incarg   Typing the keystrokes for this widget with the cursor placed on or to the left of an integer causes that integer to be incremented by one. With a numeric argument, the number is incremented by the amount of the argument (decremented if the numeric argument is negative). The shell parameter `incarg` may be set to change the default increment to something other than one.

```
bindkey '^X+' incarg
```

`incremental-complete-word`

>This allows incremental completion of a word. After starting this command, a list of completion choices can be shown after every character you type, which you can delete with `^H` or `DEL`. Pressing return accepts the completion so far and returns you to normal editing (that is, the command line is *not* immediately executed). You can hit `TAB` to do normal completion, `^G` to abort back to the state when you started, and `^D` to list the matches.

>This works only with the new function based completion system.

>```
>bindkey '^Xi' incremental-complete-word
>```

`insert-composed-char`

>This function allows you to compose characters that don't appear on the keyboard to be inserted into the command line. The command is followed by two keys corresponding to ASCII characters (there is no prompt). For accented characters, the two keys are a base character followed by a code for the accent, while for other special characters the two characters together form a mnemonic for the character to be inserted. The two-character codes are a subset of those given by RFC 1345 (see for example `http://www.faqs.org/rfcs/rfc1345.html`).

>The function may optionally be followed by up to two characters which replace one or both of the characters read from the keyboard; if both characters are supplied, no input is read. For example, `insert-composed-char a:` can be used within a widget to insert an a with umlaut into the command line. This has the advantages over use of a literal character that it is more portable.

>For best results zsh should have been built with support for multibyte characters (configured with `--enable-multibyte`); however, the function works for the limited range of characters available in single-byte character sets such as ISO-8859-1.

>The character is converted into the local representation and inserted into the command line at the cursor position. (The conversion is done within the shell, using whatever facilities the C library provides.) With a numeric argument, the character and its code are previewed in the status line

>The function may be run outside zle in which case it prints the character (together with a newline) to standard output. Input is still read from keystrokes.

>See `insert-unicode-char` for an alternative way of inserting Unicode characters using their hexadecimal character number.

>The set of accented characters is reasonably complete up to Unicode character U+0180, the set of special characters less so. However, it is very sporadic from that point. Adding new characters is easy, however; see the function `define-composed-chars`. Please send any additions to `zsh-workers@zsh.org`.

>The codes for the second character when used to accent the first are as follows. Note that not every character can take every accent.

>! Grave.

>' Acute.

>	Circumflex.
?	Tilde. (This is not ~ as RFC 1345 does not assume that character is present on the keyboard.)
–	Macron. (A horizontal bar over the base character.)
(	Breve. (A shallow dish shape over the base character.)
.	Dot above the base character, or in the case of i no dot, or in the case of L and l a centered dot.
:	Diaeresis (Umlaut).
c	Cedilla.
_	Underline, however there are currently no underlined characters.
/	Stroke through the base character.
"	Double acute (only supported on a few letters).
;	Ogonek. (A little forward facing hook at the bottom right of the character.)
<	Caron. (A little v over the letter.)
0	Circle over the base character.
2	Hook over the base character.
9	Horn over the base character.

The most common characters from the Arabic, Cyrillic, Greek and Hebrew alphabets are available; consult RFC 1345 for the appropriate sequences. In addition, a set of two letter codes not in RFC 1345 are available for the double-width characters corresponding to ASCII characters from ! to ~ (0x21 to 0x7e) by preceding the character with ^, for example ^A for a double-width A.

The following other two-character sequences are understood.

ASCII characters

These are already present on most keyboards:

<(	Left square bracket
//	Backslash (solidus)
)>	Right square bracket
(!	Left brace (curly bracket)
!!	Vertical bar (pipe symbol)
!)	Right brace (curly bracket)
'?	Tilde

Special letters

Characters found in various variants of the Latin alphabet:

ss	Eszett (scharfes S)

D-, d-	Eth
TH, th	Thorn
kk	Kra
'n	'n
NG, ng	Ng
OI, oi	Oi
yr	yr
ED	ezh

Currency symbols

Ct	Cent
Pd	Pound sterling (also lira and others)
Cu	Currency
Ye	Yen
Eu	Euro (N.B. not in RFC 1345)

Punctuation characters

References to "right" quotes indicate the shape (like a 9 rather than 6) rather than their grammatical use. (For example, a "right" low double quote is used to open quotations in German.)

!I	Inverted exclamation mark
BB	Broken vertical bar
SE	Section
Co	Copyright
-a	Spanish feminine ordinal indicator
<<	Left guillemet
--	Soft hyphen
Rg	Registered trade mark
PI	Pilcrow (paragraph)
-o	Spanish masculine ordinal indicator
>>	Right guillemet
?I	Inverted question mark
-1	Hyphen
-N	En dash
-M	Em dash
-3	Horizontal bar

:3	Vertical ellipsis
.3	Horizontal midline ellipsis
!2	Double vertical line
=2	Double low line
'6	Left single quote
'9	Right single quote
.9	"Right" low quote
9'	Reversed "right" quote
"6	Left double quote
"9	Right double quote
:9	"Right" low double quote
9"	Reversed "right" double quote
/-	Dagger
/=	Double dagger

Mathematical symbols

DG	Degree
-2, +-, -+	- sign, +/- sign, -/+ sign
2S	Superscript 2
3S	Superscript 3
1S	Superscript 1
My	Micro
.M	Middle dot
14	Quarter
12	Half
34	Three quarters
*X	Multiplication
-:	Division
%0	Per mille
FA, TE, /0	For all, there exists, empty set
dP, DE, NB	Partial derivative, delta (increment), del (nabla)
(-, -)	Element of, contains
*P, +Z	Product, sum
*-, Ob, Sb	Asterisk, ring, bullet

RT, O(, OO   Root sign, proportional to, infinity

Other symbols

cS, cH, cD, cC

Card suits: spades, hearts, diamonds, clubs

Md, M8, M2, Mb, Mx, MX

Musical notation: crotchet (quarter note), quaver (eighth note), semiquavers (sixteenth notes), flag sign, natural sign, sharp sign

Fm, Ml   Female, male

Accents on their own

'>   Circumflex (same as caret, ^)

'!   Grave (same as backtick, ')

',   Cedilla

':   Diaeresis (Umlaut)

'm   Macron

''   Acute

insert-files

This function allows you type a file pattern, and see the results of the expansion at each step. When you hit return, all expansions are inserted into the command line.

```
bindkey '^Xf' insert-files
```

insert-unicode-char

When first executed, the user inputs a set of hexadecimal digits. This is terminated with another call to **insert-unicode-char**. The digits are then turned into the corresponding Unicode character. For example, if the widget is bound to ^XU, the character sequence '^XU 4 c ^XU' inserts L (Unicode U+004c).

See **insert-composed-char** for a way of inserting characters using a two-character mnemonic.

narrow-to-region [-p *pre*] [-P *post*]
          [-S *statepm* | -R *statepm* | [-l *lbufvar*] [-r *rbufvar*]]
          [-n] [*start end*]

narrow-to-region-invisible

Narrow the editable portion of the buffer to the region between the cursor and the mark, which may be in either order. The region may not be empty.

narrow-to-region may be used as a widget or called as a function from a user-defined widget; by default, the text outside the editable area remains visible. A **recursive-edit** is performed and the original widening status is then restored. Various options and arguments are available when it is called as a function.

The options -p *pretext* and -P *posttext* may be used to replace the text before and after the display for the duration of the function; either or both may be an empty string.

If the option -n is also given, *pretext* or *posttext* will only be inserted if there is text before or after the region respectively which will be made invisible.

Two numeric arguments may be given which will be used instead of the cursor and mark positions.

The option -S *statepm* is used to narrow according to the other options while saving the original state in the parameter with name *statepm*, while the option -R *statepm* is used to restore the state from the parameter; note in both cases the *name* of the parameter is required. In the second case, other options and arguments are irrelevant. When this method is used, no recursive-edit is performed; the calling widget should call this function with the option -S, perform its own editing on the command line or pass control to the user via 'zle recursive-edit', then call this function with the option -R. The argument *statepm* must be a suitable name for an ordinary parameter, except that parameters beginning with the prefix _ntr_ are reserved for use within narrow-to-region. Typically the parameter will be local to the calling function.

The options -l *lbufvar* and -r *rbufvar* may be used to specify parameters where the widget will store the resulting text from the operation. The parameter *lbufvar* will contain LBUFFER and *rbufvar* will contain RBUFFER. Neither of these two options may be used with -S or -R.

narrow-to-region-invisible is a simple widget which calls narrow-to-region with arguments which replace any text outside the region with '...'. It does not take any arguments.

The display is restored (and the widget returns) upon any zle command which would usually cause the line to be accepted or aborted. Hence an additional such command is required to accept or abort the current line.

The return status of both widgets is zero if the line was accepted, else non-zero.

Here is a trivial example of a widget using this feature.

```
local state
narrow-to-region -p $'Editing restricted region\n' \
  -P '' -S state
zle recursive-edit
narrow-to-region -R state
```

predict-on

This set of functions implements predictive typing using history search. After predict-on, typing characters causes the editor to look backward in the history for the first line beginning with what you have typed so far. After predict-off, editing returns to normal for the line found. In fact, you often don't even need to use predict-off, because if the line doesn't match something in the history, adding a key performs standard completion, and then inserts itself if no completions were found. However, editing in the middle of a line is liable to confuse prediction; see the toggle style below.

With the function based completion system (which is needed for this), you should be able to type TAB at almost any point to advance the cursor to the next "interesting" character position (usually the end of the current word, but sometimes somewhere in the middle of the word). And of course as soon as the entire line is what you want, you can accept with return, without needing to move the cursor to the end first.

The first time `predict-on` is used, it creates several additional widget functions:

`delete-backward-and-predict`
> Replaces the `backward-delete-char` widget. You do not need to bind this yourself.

`insert-and-predict`
> Implements predictive typing by replacing the `self-insert` widget. You do not need to bind this yourself.

`predict-off`
> Turns off predictive typing.

Although you `autoload` only the `predict-on` function, it is necessary to create a keybinding for `predict-off` as well.

```
zle -N predict-on
zle -N predict-off
bindkey '^X^Z' predict-on
bindkey '^Z' predict-off
```

`read-from-minibuffer`
> This is most useful when called as a function from inside a widget, but will work correctly as a widget in its own right. It prompts for a value below the current command line; a value may be input using all of the standard zle operations (and not merely the restricted set available when executing, for example, `execute-named-cmd`). The value is then returned to the calling function in the parameter `$REPLY` and the editing buffer restored to its previous state. If the read was aborted by a keyboard break (typically `^G`), the function returns status 1 and `$REPLY` is not set.
>
> If one argument is supplied to the function it is taken as a prompt, otherwise '? ' is used. If two arguments are supplied, they are the prompt and the initial value of `$LBUFFER`, and if a third argument is given it is the initial value of `$RBUFFER`. This provides a default value and starting cursor placement. Upon return the entire buffer is the value of `$REPLY`.
>
> One option is available: '-k *num*' specifies that *num* characters are to be read instead of a whole line. The line editor is not invoked recursively in this case, so depending on the terminal settings the input may not be visible, and only the input keys are placed in `$REPLY`, not the entire buffer. Note that unlike the `read` builtin *num* must be given; there is no default.
>
> The name is a slight misnomer, as in fact the shell's own minibuffer is not used. Hence it is still possible to call `executed-named-cmd` and similar functions while reading a value.

`replace-argument`, `replace-argument-edit`
> The function `replace-argument` can be used to replace a command line argument in the current command line or, if the current command line is empty, in the last command line executed (the new command line is not executed). Arguments are as delimited by standard shell syntax,

If a numeric argument is given, that specifies the argument to be replaced. 0 means the command name, as in history expansion. A negative numeric argument counts backward from the last word.

If no numeric argument is given, the current argument is replaced; this is the last argument if the previous history line is being used.

The function prompts for a replacement argument.

If the widget contains the string **edit**, for example is defined as

```
zle -N replace-argument-edit replace-argument
```

then the function presents the current value of the argument for editing, otherwise the editing buffer for the replacement is initially empty.

replace-string, replace-pattern
replace-string-again, replace-pattern-again

The function **replace-string** implements three widgets. If defined under the same name as the function, it prompts for two strings; the first (source) string will be replaced by the second everywhere it occurs in the line editing buffer.

If the widget name contains the word 'pattern', for example by defining the widget using the command 'zle -N replace-pattern replace-string', then the matching is performed using zsh patterns. All zsh extended globbing patterns can be used in the source string; note that unlike filename generation the pattern does not need to match an entire word, nor do glob qualifiers have any effect. In addition, the replacement string can contain parameter or command substitutions. Furthermore, a '&' in the replacement string will be replaced with the matched source string, and a backquoted digit '\N' will be replaced by the Nth parenthesised expression matched. The form '\{N}' may be used to protect the digit from following digits.

If the widget instead contains the word 'regex' (or 'regexp'), then the matching is performed using regular expressions, respecting the setting of the option **RE_MATCH_PCRE** (see the description of the function **regexp-replace** below). The special replacement facilities described above for pattern matching are available.

By default the previous source or replacement string will not be offered for editing. However, this feature can be activated by setting the style **edit-previous** in the context :zle:*widget* (for example, :zle:replace-string) to **true**. In addition, a positive numeric argument forces the previous values to be offered, a negative or zero argument forces them not to be.

The function **replace-string-again** can be used to repeat the previous replacement; no prompting is done. As with **replace-string**, if the name of the widget contains the word 'pattern' or 'regex', pattern or regular expression matching is performed, else a literal string replacement. Note that the previous source and replacement text are the same whether pattern, regular expression or string matching is used.

In addition, **replace-string** shows the previous replacement above the prompt, so long as there was one during the current session; if the source string is empty, that replacement will be repeated without the widget prompting for a replacement string.

For example, starting from the line:

```
print This line contains fan and fond
```

and invoking `replace-pattern` with the source string 'f(?)n' and the replacement string 'c\1r' produces the not very useful line:

```
print This line contains car and cord
```

The range of the replacement string can be limited by using the `narrow-to-region-invisible` widget. One limitation of the current version is that `undo` will cycle through changes to the replacement and source strings before undoing the replacement itself.

send-invisible

This is similar to read-from-minibuffer in that it may be called as a function from a widget or as a widget of its own, and interactively reads input from the keyboard. However, the input being typed is concealed and a string of asterisks ('*') is shown instead. The value is saved in the parameter `$INVISIBLE` to which a reference is inserted into the editing buffer at the restored cursor position. If the read was aborted by a keyboard break (typically ^G) or another escape from editing such as `push-line`, `$INVISIBLE` is set to empty and the original buffer is restored unchanged.

If one argument is supplied to the function it is taken as a prompt, otherwise 'Non-echoed text: ' is used (as in emacs). If a second and third argument are supplied they are used to begin and end the reference to `$INVISIBLE` that is inserted into the buffer. The default is to open with `${`, then `INVISIBLE`, and close with `}`, but many other effects are possible.

smart-insert-last-word

This function may replace the `insert-last-word` widget, like so:

```
zle -N insert-last-word smart-insert-last-word
```

With a numeric argument, or when passed command line arguments in a call from another widget, it behaves like `insert-last-word`, except that words in comments are ignored when `INTERACTIVE_COMMENTS` is set.

Otherwise, the rightmost "interesting" word from the previous command is found and inserted. The default definition of "interesting" is that the word contains at least one alphabetic character, slash, or backslash. This definition may be overridden by use of the `match` style. The context used to look up the style is the widget name, so usually the context is `:insert-last-word`. However, you can bind this function to different widgets to use different patterns:

```
zle -N insert-last-assignment smart-insert-last-word
zstyle :insert-last-assignment match '[[:alpha:]][] [[:alnum:]]#=*'
bindkey '\e=' insert-last-assignment
```

If no interesting word is found and the `auto-previous` style is set to a true value, the search continues upward through the history. When `auto-previous` is unset or false (the default), the widget must be invoked repeatedly in order to search earlier history lines.

transpose-lines

Only useful with a multi-line editing buffer; the lines here are lines within the current on-screen buffer, not history lines. The effect is similar to the function of the same name in Emacs.

Transpose the current line with the previous line and move the cursor to the start of the next line. Repeating this (which can be done by providing a positive numeric argument) has the effect of moving the line above the cursor down by a number of lines.

With a negative numeric argument, requires two lines above the cursor. These two lines are transposed and the cursor moved to the start of the previous line. Using a numeric argument less than -1 has the effect of moving the line above the cursor up by minus that number of lines.

url-quote-magic

This widget replaces the built-in **self-insert** to make it easier to type URLs as command line arguments. As you type, the input character is analyzed and, if it may need quoting, the current word is checked for a URI scheme. If one is found and the current word is not already in quotes, a backslash is inserted before the input character.

Styles to control quoting behavior:

url-metas

This style is looked up in the context ':**url-quote-magic:***scheme*' (where *scheme* is that of the current URL, e.g. **"ftp"**). The value is a string listing the characters to be treated as globbing metacharacters when appearing in a URL using that scheme. The default is to quote all zsh extended globbing characters, excluding '<' and '>' but including braces (as in brace expansion). See also **url-seps**.

url-seps Like **url-metas**, but lists characters that should be considered command separators, redirections, history references, etc. The default is to quote the standard set of shell separators, excluding those that overlap with the extended globbing characters, but including '<' and '>' and the first character of **$histchars**.

url-globbers

This style is looked up in the context ':**url-quote-magic**'. The values form a list of command names that are expected to do their own globbing on the URL string. This implies that they are aliased to use the '**noglob**' modifier. When the first word on the line matches one of the values *and* the URL refers to a local file (see **url-local-schema**), only the **url-seps** characters are quoted; the **url-metas** are left alone, allowing them to affect command-line parsing, completion, etc. The default values are a literal '**noglob**' plus (when the **zsh/parameter** module is available) any commands aliased to the helper function '**urlglobber**' or its alias '**globurl**'.

url-local-schema

This style is always looked up in the context ':**urlglobber**', even though it is used by both url-quote-magic and urlglobber. The values form a list of URI schema that should be treated as referring to local files by their real local path names, as opposed to files which are specified relative to a web-server-defined document root. The defaults are `"ftp"` and `"file"`.

url-other-schema

Like `url-local-schema`, but lists all other URI schema upon which `urlglobber` and `url-quote-magic` should act. If the URI on the command line does not have a scheme appearing either in this list or in `url-local-schema`, it is not magically quoted. The default values are `"http"`, `"https"`, and `"ftp"`. When a scheme appears both here and in `url-local-schema`, it is quoted differently depending on whether the command name appears in `url-globbers`.

Loading `url-quote-magic` also defines a helper function 'urlglobber' and aliases 'globurl' to 'noglob urlglobber'. This function takes a local URL apart, attempts to pattern-match the local file portion of the URL path, and then puts the results back into URL format again.

vi-pipe

This function reads a movement command from the keyboard and then prompts for an external command. The part of the buffer covered by the movement is piped to the external command and then replaced by the command's output. If the movement command is bound to vi-pipe, the current line is used.

The function serves as an example for reading a vi movement command from within a user-defined widget.

which-command

This function is a drop-in replacement for the builtin widget `which-command`. It has enhanced behaviour, in that it correctly detects whether or not the command word needs to be expanded as an alias; if so, it continues tracing the command word from the expanded alias until it reaches the command that will be executed.

The style `whence` is available in the context `:zle:$WIDGET`; this may be set to an array to give the command and options that will be used to investigate the command word found. The default is `whence -c`.

zcalc-auto-insert

This function is useful together with the `zcalc` function described in Section 26.10 [Mathematical Functions], page 485. It should be bound to a key representing a binary operator such as '+', '-', '*' or '/'. When running in zcalc, if the key occurs at the start of the line or immediately following an open parenthesis, the text `"ans "` is inserted before the representation of the key itself. This allows easy use of the answer from the previous calculation in the current line. The text to be inserted before the symbol typed can be modified by setting the variable `ZCALC_AUTO_INSERT_PREFIX`.

Hence, for example, typing '+12' followed by return adds 12 to the previous result.

If zcalc is in RPN mode (`-r` option) the effect of this binding is automatically suppressed as operators alone on a line are meaningful.

When not in zcalc, the key simply inserts the symbol itself.

26.7.2 Utility Functions

These functions are useful in constructing widgets. They should be loaded with 'autoload
-U *function*' and called as indicated from user-defined widgets.

`split-shell-arguments`

This function splits the line currently being edited into shell arguments and
whitespace. The result is stored in the array `reply`. The array contains all
the parts of the line in order, starting with any whitespace before the first
argument, and finishing with any whitespace after the last argument. Hence
(so long as the option `KSH_ARRAYS` is not set) whitespace is given by odd indices
in the array and arguments by even indices. Note that no stripping of quotes
is done; joining together all the elements of `reply` in order is guaranteed to
produce the original line.

The parameter `REPLY` is set to the index of the word in `reply` which contains the
character after the cursor, where the first element has index 1. The parameter
`REPLY2` is set to the index of the character under the cursor in that word, where
the first character has index 1.

Hence `reply`, `REPLY` and `REPLY2` should all be made local to the enclosing
function.

See the function `modify-current-argument`, described below, for an example
of how to call this function.

`modify-current-argument` [*expr-using-*$ARG | *func*]

This function provides a simple method of allowing user-defined widgets to
modify the command line argument under the cursor (or immediately to the
left of the cursor if the cursor is between arguments).

The argument can be an expression which when evaluated operates on the
shell parameter `ARG`, which will have been set to the command line argument
under the cursor. The expression should be suitably quoted to prevent it being
evaluated too early.

Alternatively, if the argument does not contain the string `ARG`, it is assumed
to be a shell function, to which the current command line argument is passed
as the only argument. The function should set the variable `REPLY` to the new
value for the command line argument. If the function returns non-zero status,
so does the calling function.

For example, a user-defined widget containing the following code converts the
characters in the argument under the cursor into all upper case:

```
modify-current-argument '${(U)ARG}'
```

The following strips any quoting from the current word (whether backslashes
or one of the styles of quotes), and replaces it with single quoting throughout:

```
modify-current-argument '${(qq)${(Q)ARG}}'
```

The following performs directory expansion on the command line argument and
replaces it by the absolute path:

```
expand-dir() {
  REPLY=${~1}
  REPLY=${REPLY:a}
}
modify-current-argument expand-dir
```

In practice the function `expand-dir` would probably not be defined within the widget where `modify-current-argument` is called.

26.7.3 Styles

The behavior of several of the above widgets can be controlled by the use of the `zstyle` mechanism. In particular, widgets that interact with the completion system pass along their context to any completions that they invoke.

break-keys

> This style is used by the `incremental-complete-word` widget. Its value should be a pattern, and all keys matching this pattern will cause the widget to stop incremental completion without the key having any further effect. Like all styles used directly by `incremental-complete-word`, this style is looked up using the context ':incremental'.

completer

> The `incremental-complete-word` and `insert-and-predict` widgets set up their top-level context name before calling completion. This allows one to define different sets of completer functions for normal completion and for these widgets. For example, to use completion, approximation and correction for normal completion, completion and correction for incremental completion and only completion for prediction one could use:
>
> ```
> zstyle ':completion:*' completer \
>         _complete _correct _approximate
> zstyle ':completion:incremental:*' completer \
>         _complete _correct
> zstyle ':completion:predict:*' completer \
>         _complete
> ```
>
> It is a good idea to restrict the completers used in prediction, because they may be automatically invoked as you type. The `_list` and `_menu` completers should never be used with prediction. The `_approximate`, `_correct`, `_expand`, and `_match` completers may be used, but be aware that they may change characters anywhere in the word behind the cursor, so you need to watch carefully that the result is what you intended.

cursor
> The `insert-and-predict` widget uses this style, in the context ':predict', to decide where to place the cursor after completion has been tried. Values are:
>
> **complete** The cursor is left where it was when completion finished, but only if it is after a character equal to the one just inserted by the user. If it is after another character, this value is the same as 'key'.
>
> **key** The cursor is left after the nth occurrence of the character just inserted, where n is the number of times that character appeared

in the word before completion was attempted. In short, this has the effect of leaving the cursor after the character just typed even if the completion code found out that no other characters need to be inserted at that position.

Any other value for this style unconditionally leaves the cursor at the position where the completion code left it.

list When using the `incremental-complete-word` widget, this style says if the matches should be listed on every key press (if they fit on the screen). Use the context prefix ':completion:incremental'.

The `insert-and-predict` widget uses this style to decide if the completion should be shown even if there is only one possible completion. This is done if the value of this style is the string **always**. In this case the context is ':predict' (*not* ':completion:predict').

match This style is used by `smart-insert-last-word` to provide a pattern (using full **EXTENDED_GLOB** syntax) that matches an interesting word. The context is the name of the widget to which `smart-insert-last-word` is bound (see above). The default behavior of `smart-insert-last-word` is equivalent to:

```
zstyle :insert-last-word match '*[[:alpha:]/\\]*'
```

However, you might want to include words that contain spaces:

```
zstyle :insert-last-word match '*[[:alpha:][:space:]/\\]*'
```

Or include numbers as long as the word is at least two characters long:

```
zstyle :insert-last-word match '*([[:digit:]]?|[[:alpha:]/\\])*'
```

The above example causes redirections like "2>" to be included.

prompt The `incremental-complete-word` widget shows the value of this style in the status line during incremental completion. The string value may contain any of the following substrings in the manner of the **PS1** and other prompt parameters:

%c   Replaced by the name of the completer function that generated the matches (without the leading underscore).

%l   When the **list** style is set, replaced by '...' if the list of matches is too long to fit on the screen and with an empty string otherwise. If the **list** style is 'false' or not set, '%l' is always removed.

%n   Replaced by the number of matches generated.

%s   Replaced by '-no match-', '-no prefix-', or an empty string if there is no completion matching the word on the line, if the matches have no common prefix different from the word on the line, or if there is such a common prefix, respectively.

%u   Replaced by the unambiguous part of all matches, if there is any, and if it is different from the word on the line.

Like '**break-keys**', this uses the ':incremental' context.

stop-keys

> This style is used by the `incremental-complete-word` widget. Its value is treated similarly to the one for the `break-keys` style (and uses the same context: ':incremental'). However, in this case all keys matching the pattern given as its value will stop incremental completion and will then execute their usual function.

toggle

> This boolean style is used by `predict-on` and its related widgets in the context ':predict'. If set to one of the standard 'true' values, predictive typing is automatically toggled off in situations where it is unlikely to be useful, such as when editing a multi-line buffer or after moving into the middle of a line and then deleting a character. The default is to leave prediction turned on until an explicit call to `predict-off`.

verbose

> This boolean style is used by `predict-on` and its related widgets in the context ':predict'. If set to one of the standard 'true' values, these widgets display a message below the prompt when the predictive state is toggled. This is most useful in combination with the `toggle` style. The default does not display these messages.

widget

> This style is similar to the `command` style: For widget functions that use `zle` to call other widgets, this style can sometimes be used to override the widget which is called. The context for this style is the name of the calling widget (*not* the name of the calling function, because one function may be bound to multiple widget names).
>
> ```
> zstyle :copy-earlier-word widget smart-insert-last-word
> ```
>
> Check the documentation for the calling widget or function to determine whether the `widget` style is used.

26.8 Exception Handling

Two functions are provided to enable zsh to provide exception handling in a form that should be familiar from other languages.

throw *exception*

> The function `throw` throws the named *exception*. The name is an arbitrary string and is only used by the `throw` and `catch` functions. An exception is for the most part treated the same as a shell error, i.e. an unhandled exception will cause the shell to abort all processing in a function or script and to return to the top level in an interactive shell.

catch *exception-pattern*

> The function `catch` returns status zero if an exception was thrown and the pattern *exception-pattern* matches its name. Otherwise it returns status 1. *exception-pattern* is a standard shell pattern, respecting the current setting of the `EXTENDED_GLOB` option. An alias `catch` is also defined to prevent the argument to the function from matching filenames, so patterns may be used unquoted. Note that as exceptions are not fundamentally different from other shell errors it is possible to catch shell errors by using an empty string as the

exception name. The shell variable `CAUGHT` is set by `catch` to the name of the exception caught. It is possible to rethrow an exception by calling the `throw` function again once an exception has been caught.

The functions are designed to be used together with the **always** construct described in Section 6.3 [Complex Commands], page 11. This is important as only this construct provides the required support for exceptions. A typical example is as follows.

```
{
  # "try" block
  # ... nested code here calls "throw MyExcept"
} always {
  # "always" block
  if catch MyExcept; then
    print "Caught exception MyExcept"
  elif catch ''; then
    print "Caught a shell error.  Propagating..."
    throw ''
  fi
  # Other exceptions are not handled but may be caught further
  # up the call stack.
}
```

If all exceptions should be caught, the following idiom might be preferable.

```
{
  # ... nested code here throws an exception
} always {
  if catch *; then
    case $CAUGHT in
      (MyExcept)
      print "Caught my own exception"
      ;;
      (*)
      print "Caught some other exception"
      ;;
    esac
  fi
}
```

In common with exception handling in other languages, the exception may be thrown by code deeply nested inside the 'try' block. However, note that it must be thrown inside the current shell, not in a subshell forked for a pipeline, parenthesised current-shell construct, or some form of command or process substitution.

The system internally uses the shell variable `EXCEPTION` to record the name of the exception between throwing and catching. One drawback of this scheme is that if the exception is not handled the variable `EXCEPTION` remains set and may be incorrectly recognised as the name of an exception if a shell error subsequently occurs. Adding **unset** `EXCEPTION` at the start of the outermost layer of any code that uses exception handling will eliminate this problem.

26.9 MIME Functions

Three functions are available to provide handling of files recognised by extension, for example to dispatch a file `text.ps` when executed as a command to an appropriate viewer.

zsh-mime-setup [-fv] [-l [*suffix* ...]]
zsh-mime-handler [-l] *command argument* ...

These two functions use the files `~/.mime.types` and `/etc/mime.types`, which associate types and extensions, as well as `~/.mailcap` and `/etc/mailcap` files, which associate types and the programs that handle them. These are provided on many systems with the Multimedia Internet Mail Extensions.

To enable the system, the function `zsh-mime-setup` should be autoloaded and run. This allows files with extensions to be treated as executable; such files be completed by the function completion system. The function `zsh-mime-handler` should not need to be called by the user.

The system works by setting up suffix aliases with 'alias -s'. Suffix aliases already installed by the user will not be overwritten.

For suffixes defined in lower case, upper case variants will also automatically be handled (e.g. `PDF` is automatically handled if handling for the suffix `pdf` is defined), but not vice versa.

Repeated calls to `zsh-mime-setup` do not override the existing mapping between suffixes and executable files unless the option `-f` is given. Note, however, that this does not override existing suffix aliases assigned to handlers other than `zsh-mime-handler`.

Calling `zsh-mime-setup` with the option `-l` lists the existing mappings without altering them. Suffixes to list (which may contain pattern characters that should be quoted from immediate interpretation on the command line) may be given as additional arguments, otherwise all suffixes are listed.

Calling `zsh-mime-setup` with the option `-v` causes verbose output to be shown during the setup operation.

The system respects the `mailcap` flags `needsterminal` and `copiousoutput`, see man page mailcap(4).

The functions use the following styles, which are defined with the `zstyle` builtin command (Section 22.37 [The zsh/zutil Module], page 382). They should be defined before `zsh-mime-setup` is run. The contexts used all start with `:mime:`, with additional components in some cases. It is recommended that a trailing `*` (suitably quoted) be appended to style patterns in case the system is extended in future. Some examples are given below.

For files that have multiple suffixes, e.g. `.pdf.gz`, where the context includes the suffix it will be looked up starting with the longest possible suffix until a match for the style is found. For example, if `.pdf.gz` produces a match for the handler, that will be used; otherwise the handler for `.gz` will be used. Note that, owing to the way suffix aliases work, it is always required that there be a handler for the shortest possible suffix, so in this example `.pdf.gz` can only be handled if `.gz` is also handled (though not necessarily in the same way).

Alternatively, if no handling for `.gz` on its own is needed, simply adding the command

```
alias -s gz=zsh-mime-handler
```

to the initialisation code is sufficient; `.gz` will not be handled on its own, but may be in combination with other suffixes.

`current-shell`

> If this boolean style is true, the mailcap handler for the context in question is run using the `eval` builtin instead of by starting a new `sh` process. This is more efficient, but may not work in the occasional cases where the mailcap handler uses strict POSIX syntax.

`disown`   If this boolean style is true, mailcap handlers started in the background will be disowned, i.e. not subject to job control within the parent shell. Such handlers nearly always produce their own windows, so the only likely harmful side effect of setting the style is that it becomes harder to kill jobs from within the shell.

`execute-as-is`

> This style gives a list of patterns to be matched against files passed for execution with a handler program. If the file matches the pattern, the entire command line is executed in its current form, with no handler. This is useful for files which might have suffixes but nonetheless be executable in their own right. If the style is not set, the pattern `*(*) *(/)` is used; hence executable files are executed directly and not passed to a handler, and the option `AUTO_CD` may be used to change to directories that happen to have MIME suffixes.

`execute-never`

> This style is useful in combination with `execute-as-is`. It is set to an array of patterns corresponding to full paths to files that should never be treated as executable, even if the file passed to the MIME handler matches `execute-as-is`. This is useful for file systems that don't handle execute permission or that contain executables from another operating system. For example, if `/mnt/windows` is a Windows mount, then
>
> ```
> zstyle ':mime:*' execute-never '/mnt/windows/*'
> ```
>
> will ensure that any files found in that area will be executed as MIME types even if they are executable. As this example shows, the complete file name is matched against the pattern, regardless of how the file was passed to the handler. The file is resolved to a full path using the `:P` modifier described in Section 14.1.4 [Modifiers], page 47; this means that symbolic links are resolved where possible, so that links into other file systems behave in the correct fashion.

`file-path`

> Used if the style `find-file-in-path` is true for the same context. Set to an array of directories that are used for searching for the file

to be handled; the default is the command path given by the special parameter **path**. The shell option **PATH_DIRS** is respected; if that is set, the appropriate path will be searched even if the name of the file to be handled as it appears on the command line contains a '/'. The full context is :**mime**:.*suffix*:, as described for the style **handler**.

find-file-in-path

If set, allows files whose names do not contain absolute paths to be searched for in the command path or the path specified by the **file-path** style. If the file is not found in the path, it is looked for locally (whether or not the current directory is in the path); if it is not found locally, the handler will abort unless the **handle-nonexistent** style is set. Files found in the path are tested as described for the style **execute-as-is**. The full context is :**mime**:.*suffix*:, as described for the style **handler**.

flags   Defines flags to go with a handler; the context is as for the **handler** style, and the format is as for the flags in **mailcap**.

handle-nonexistent

By default, arguments that don't correspond to files are not passed to the MIME handler in order to prevent it from intercepting commands found in the path that happen to have suffixes. This style may be set to an array of extended glob patterns for arguments that will be passed to the handler even if they don't exist. If it is not explicitly set it defaults to **[[:alpha:]]#:/*** which allows URLs to be passed to the MIME handler even though they don't exist in that format in the file system. The full context is :**mime**:.*suffix*:, as described for the style **handler**.

handler   Specifies a handler for a suffix; the suffix is given by the context as :**mime**:.*suffix*:, and the format of the handler is exactly that in **mailcap**. Note in particular the '.' and trailing colon to distinguish this use of the context. This overrides any handler specified by the **mailcap** files. If the handler requires a terminal, the **flags** style should be set to include the word **needsterminal**, or if the output is to be displayed through a pager (but not if the handler is itself a pager), it should include **copiousoutput**.

mailcap   A list of files in the format of ~/.**mailcap** and /etc/**mailcap** to be read during setup, replacing the default list which consists of those two files. The context is :**mime**:. A + in the list will be replaced by the default files.

mailcap-priorities

This style is used to resolve multiple mailcap entries for the same MIME type. It consists of an array of the following elements, in descending order of priority; later entries will be used if earlier entries are unable to resolve the entries being compared. If none of the tests resolve the entries, the first entry encountered is retained.

files   The order of files (entries in the `mailcap` style) read.
Earlier files are preferred. (Note this does not resolve
entries in the same file.)

priority   The priority flag from the mailcap entry. The priority
is an integer from 0 to 9 with the default value being
5.

flags   The test given by the `mailcap-prio-flags` option is
used to resolve entries.

place   Later entries are preferred; as the entries are strictly
ordered, this test always succeeds.

Note that as this style is handled during initialisation, the context
is always `:mime:`, with no discrimination by suffix.

mailcap-prio-flags

This style is used when the keyword **flags** is encountered in the
list of tests specified by the `mailcap-priorities` style. It should
be set to a list of patterns, each of which is tested against the
flags specified in the mailcap entry (in other words, the sets of
assignments found with some entries in the mailcap file). Earlier
patterns in the list are preferred to later ones, and matched patterns
are preferred to unmatched ones.

mime-types

A list of files in the format of `~/.mime.types` and
`/etc/mime.types` to be read during setup, replacing the default
list which consists of those two files. The context is `:mime:`. A +
in the list will be replaced by the default files.

never-background

If this boolean style is set, the handler for the given context is
always run in the foreground, even if the flags provided in the mailcap entry suggest it need not be (for example, it doesn't require a
terminal).

pager   If set, will be used instead of `$PAGER` or `more` to handle suffixes
where the `copiousoutput` flag is set. The context is as for `handler`,
i.e. `:mime:.`*suffix*`:` for handling a file with the given *suffix*.

Examples:

```
zstyle ':mime:*' mailcap ~/.mailcap /usr/local/etc/mailcap
zstyle ':mime:.txt:' handler less %s
zstyle ':mime:.txt:' flags needsterminal
```

When `zsh-mime-setup` is subsequently run, it will look for `mailcap` entries
in the two files given. Files of suffix `.txt` will be handled by running 'less
file.txt'. The flag **needsterminal** is set to show that this program must run
attached to a terminal.

As there are several steps to dispatching a command, the following should be checked if attempting to execute a file by extension *.ext* does not have the expected effect.

The command 'alias -s *ext*' should show 'ps=zsh-mime-handler'. If it shows something else, another suffix alias was already installed and was not overwritten. If it shows nothing, no handler was installed: this is most likely because no handler was found in the .mime.types and mailcap combination for .ext files. In that case, appropriate handling should be added to ~/.mime.types and mailcap.

If the extension is handled by zsh-mime-handler but the file is not opened correctly, either the handler defined for the type is incorrect, or the flags associated with it are in appropriate. Running zsh-mime-setup -l will show the handler and, if there are any, the flags. A %s in the handler is replaced by the file (suitably quoted if necessary). Check that the handler program listed lists and can be run in the way shown. Also check that the flags needsterminal or copiousoutput are set if the handler needs to be run under a terminal; the second flag is used if the output should be sent to a pager. An example of a suitable mailcap entry for such a program is:

```
text/html; /usr/bin/lynx '%s'; needsterminal
```

Running 'zsh-mime-handler -l *command line*' prints the command line that would be executed, simplified to remove the effect of any flags, and quoted so that the output can be run as a complete zsh command line. This is used by the completion system to decide how to complete after a file handled by zsh-mime-setup.

pick-web-browser

> This function is separate from the two MIME functions described above and can be assigned directly to a suffix:
>
> ```
> autoload -U pick-web-browser
> alias -s html=pick-web-browser
> ```
>
> It is provided as an intelligent front end to dispatch a web browser. It may be run as either a function or a shell script. The status 255 is returned if no browser could be started.
>
> Various styles are available to customize the choice of browsers:
>
> browser-style
>
>> The value of the style is an array giving preferences in decreasing order for the type of browser to use. The values of elements may be
>>
>> running   Use a GUI browser that is already running when an X Window display is available. The browsers listed in the x-browsers style are tried in order until one is found; if it is, the file will be displayed in that browser, so the user may need to check whether it has appeared. If no running browser is found, one is not started. Browsers other than Firefox, Opera and Konqueror are assumed

to understand the Mozilla syntax for opening a URL remotely.

x
Start a new GUI browser when an X Window display is available. Search for the availability of one of the browsers listed in the **x-browsers** style and start the first one that is found. No check is made for an already running browser.

tty
Start a terminal-based browser. Search for the availability of one of the browsers listed in the **tty-browsers** style and start the first one that is found.

If the style is not set the default **running x tty** is used.

x-browsers

An array in decreasing order of preference of browsers to use when running under the X Window System. The array consists of the command name under which to start the browser. They are looked up in the context :mime: (which may be extended in future, so appending '*' is recommended). For example,

> zstyle ':mime:*' x-browsers opera konqueror firefox

specifies that **pick-web-browser** should first look for a running instance of Opera, Konqueror or Firefox, in that order, and if it fails to find any should attempt to start Opera. The default is **firefox mozilla netscape opera konqueror**.

tty-browsers

An array similar to **x-browsers**, except that it gives browsers to use when no X Window display is available. The default is **elinks links lynx**.

command
If it is set this style is used to pick the command used to open a page for a browser. The context is :mime:browser:new:$browser: to start a new browser or :mime:browser:running:$browser: to open a URL in a browser already running on the current X display, where $browser is the value matched in the **x-browsers** or **tty-browsers** style. The escape sequence %b in the style's value will be replaced by the browser, while %u will be replaced by the URL. If the style is not set, the default for all new instances is equivalent to %b %u and the defaults for using running browsers are equivalent to the values **kfmclient openURL %u** for Konqueror, **firefox -new-tab %u** for Firefox, **opera -newpage %u** for Opera, and **%b -remote "openUrl(%u)"** for all others.

26.10 Mathematical Functions

zcalc [-erf] [*expression* ...]

A reasonably powerful calculator based on zsh's arithmetic evaluation facility. The syntax is similar to that of formulae in most programming languages; see Chapter 11 [Arithmetic Evaluation], page 31, for details.

Non-programmers should note that, as in many other programming languages, expressions involving only integers (whether constants without a '.', variables containing such constants as strings, or variables declared to be integers) are by default evaluated using integer arithmetic, which is not how an ordinary desk calculator operates. To force floating point operation, pass the option -f; see further notes below.

If the file ~/.zcalcrc exists it will be sourced inside the function once it is set up and about to process the command line. This can be used, for example, to set shell options; emulate -L zsh and setopt extendedglob are in effect at this point. Any failure to source the file if it exists is treated as fatal. As with other initialisation files, the directory $ZDOTDIR is used instead of $HOME if it is set.

The mathematical library zsh/mathfunc will be loaded if it is available; see Section 22.17 [The zsh/mathfunc Module], page 351. The mathematical functions correspond to the raw system libraries, so trigonometric functions are evaluated using radians, and so on.

Each line typed is evaluated as an expression. The prompt shows a number, which corresponds to a positional parameter where the result of that calculation is stored. For example, the result of the calculation on the line preceded by '4>' is available as $4. The last value calculated is available as ans. Full command line editing, including the history of previous calculations, is available; the history is saved in the file ~/.zcalc_history. To exit, enter a blank line or type ':q' on its own ('q' is allowed for historical compatibility).

A line ending with a single backslash is treated in the same fashion as it is in command line editing: the backslash is removed, the function prompts for more input (the prompt is preceded by '...' to indicate this), and the lines are combined into one to get the final result. In addition, if the input so far contains more open than close parentheses zcalc will prompt for more input.

If arguments are given to zcalc on start up, they are used to prime the first few positional parameters. A visual indication of this is given when the calculator starts.

The constants PI (3.14159...) and E (2.71828...) are provided. Parameter assignment is possible, but note that all parameters will be put into the global namespace unless the :local special command is used. The function creates local variables whose names start with _, so users should avoid doing so. The variables ans (the last answer) and stack (the stack in RPN mode) may be referred to directly; stack is an array but elements of it are numeric. Various other special variables are used locally with their standard meaning, for example compcontext, match, mbegin, mend, psvar.

The output base can be initialised by passing the option '-#*base*', for example 'zcalc -#16' (the '#' may have to be quoted, depending on the globbing options set).

If the option '-e' is set, the function runs non-interactively: the arguments are treated as expressions to be evaluated as if entered interactively line by line.

If the option '-f' is set, all numbers are treated as floating point, hence for example the expression '3/4' evaluates to 0.75 rather than 0. Options must appear in separate words.

If the option '-r' is set, RPN (Reverse Polish Notation) mode is entered. This has various additional properties:

Stack
: Evaluated values are maintained in a stack; this is contained in an array named stack with the most recent value in ${stack[1]}.

Operators and functions
: If the line entered matches an operator (+, -, *, /, **, ^, | or &) or a function supplied by the zsh/mathfunc library, the bottom element or elements of the stack are popped to use as the argument or arguments. The higher elements of stack (least recent) are used as earlier arguments. The result is then pushed into ${stack[1]}.

Expressions
: Other expressions are evaluated normally, printed, and added to the stack as numeric values. The syntax within expressions on a single line is normal shell arithmetic (not RPN).

Stack listing
: If an integer follows the option -r with no space, then on every evaluation that many elements of the stack, where available, are printed instead of just the most recent result. Hence, for example, zcalc -r4 shows $stack[4] to $stack[1] each time results are printed.

Duplication: =
: The pseudo-operator = causes the most recent element of the stack to be duplicated onto the stack.

pop
: The pseudo-function pop causes the most recent element of the stack to be popped. A '>' on its own has the same effect.

>*ident*
: The expression > followed (with no space) by a shell identifier causes the most recent element of the stack to be popped and assigned to the variable with that name. The variable is local to the zcalc function.

<*ident*
: The expression < followed (with no space) by a shell identifier causes the value of the variable with that name to be pushed onto the stack. *ident* may be an integer, in which case the previous result with that number (as shown before the > in the standard zcalc prompt) is put on the stack.

Exchange: `xy`

> The pseudo-function `xy` causes the most recent two elements of the stack to be exchanged. '`<>`' has the same effect.

The prompt is configurable via the parameter `ZCALCPROMPT`, which undergoes standard prompt expansion. The index of the current entry is stored locally in the first element of the array `psvar`, which can be referred to in `ZCALCPROMPT` as '`%1v`'. The default prompt is '`%1v> `'.

The variable `ZCALC_ACTIVE` is set within the function and can be tested by nested functions; it has the value `rpn` if RPN mode is active, else 1.

A few special commands are available; these are introduced by a colon. For backward compatibility, the colon may be omitted for certain commands. Completion is available if `compinit` has been run.

The output precision may be specified within zcalc by special commands familiar from many calculators.

`:norm`   The default output format. It corresponds to the printf `%g` specification. Typically this shows six decimal digits.

`:sci` *digits*

> Scientific notation, corresponding to the printf `%g` output format with the precision given by *digits*. This produces either fixed point or exponential notation depending on the value output.

`:fix` *digits*

> Fixed point notation, corresponding to the printf `%f` output format with the precision given by *digits*.

`:eng` *digits*

> Exponential notation, corresponding to the printf `%E` output format with the precision given by *digits*.

`:raw`   Raw output: this is the default form of the output from a math evaluation. This may show more precision than the number actually possesses.

Other special commands:

`:!`*line...*   Execute *line...* as a normal shell command line. Note that it is executed in the context of the function, i.e. with local variables. Space is optional after `:!`.

`:local` *arg* ...

> Declare variables local to the function. Other variables may be used, too, but they will be taken from or put into the global scope.

`:function` *name* [*body*]

> Define a mathematical function or (with no *body*) delete it. `:function` may be abbreviated to `:func` or simply `:f`. The *name* may contain the same characters as a shell function name. The function is defined using `zmathfuncdef`, see below.
>
> Note that `zcalc` takes care of all quoting. Hence for example:

```
:f cube $1 * $1 * $1
```

defines a function to cube the sole argument. Functions so defined, or indeed any functions defined directly or indirectly using **functions -M**, are available to execute by typing only the name on the line in RPN mode; this pops the appropriate number of arguments off the stack to pass to the function, i.e. 1 in the case of the example **cube** function. If there are optional arguments only the mandatory arguments are supplied by this means.

[#*base*]   This is not a special command, rather part of normal arithmetic syntax; however, when this form appears on a line by itself the default output radix is set to *base*. Use, for example, '[#16]' to display hexadecimal output preceded by an indication of the base, or '[##16]' just to display the raw number in the given base. Bases themselves are always specified in decimal. '[#]' restores the normal output format. Note that setting an output base suppresses floating point output; use '[#]' to return to normal operation.

$*var*   Print out the value of var literally; does not affect the calculation. To use the value of var, omit the leading '$'.

See the comments in the function for a few extra tips.

min(*arg*, ...)
max(*arg*, ...)
sum(*arg*, ...)
zmathfunc

The function **zmathfunc** defines the three mathematical functions **min**, **max**, and **sum**. The functions **min** and **max** take one or more arguments. The function **sum** takes zero or more arguments. Arguments can be of different types (ints and floats).

Not to be confused with the **zsh/mathfunc** module, described in Section 22.17 [The zsh/mathfunc Module], page 351.

zmathfuncdef [*mathfunc* [*body*]]
A convenient front end to **functions -M**.

With two arguments, define a mathematical function named *mathfunc* which can be used in any form of arithmetic evaluation. *body* is a mathematical expression to implement the function. It may contain references to position parameters $1, $2, ... to refer to mandatory parameters and ${1:-*defvalue*} ... to refer to optional parameters. Note that the forms must be strictly adhered to for the function to calculate the correct number of arguments. The implementation is held in a shell function named **zsh_math_func_***mathfunc*; usually the user will not need to refer to the shell function directly. Any existing function of the same name is silently replaced.

With one argument, remove the mathematical function *mathfunc* as well as the shell function implementation.

With no arguments, list all *mathfunc* functions in a form suitable for restoring the definition. The functions have not necessarily been defined by `zmathfuncdef`.

26.11 User Configuration Functions

The `zsh/newuser` module comes with a function to aid in configuring shell options for new users. If the module is installed, this function can also be run by hand. It is available even if the module's default behaviour, namely running the function for a new user logging in without startup files, is inhibited.

`zsh-newuser-install` [`-f`]

> The function presents the user with various options for customizing their initialization scripts. Currently only `~/.zshrc` is handled. `$ZDOTDIR/.zshrc` is used instead if the parameter `ZDOTDIR` is set; this provides a way for the user to configure a file without altering an existing `.zshrc`.

> By default the function exits immediately if it finds any of the files `.zshenv`, `.zprofile`, `.zshrc`, or `.zlogin` in the appropriate directory. The option `-f` is required in order to force the function to continue. Note this may happen even if `.zshrc` itself does not exist.

> As currently configured, the function will exit immediately if the user has root privileges; this behaviour cannot be overridden.

> Once activated, the function's behaviour is supposed to be self-explanatory. Menus are present allowing the user to alter the value of options and parameters. Suggestions for improvements are always welcome.

> When the script exits, the user is given the opportunity to save the new file or not; changes are not irreversible until this point. However, the script is careful to restrict changes to the file only to a group marked by the lines '`# Lines configured by zsh-newuser-install`' and '`# End of lines configured by zsh-newuser-install`'. In addition, the old version of `.zshrc` is saved to a file with the suffix `.zni` appended.

> If the function edits an existing `.zshrc`, it is up to the user to ensure that the changes made will take effect. For example, if control usually returns early from the existing `.zshrc` the lines will not be executed; or a later initialization file may override options or parameters, and so on. The function itself does not attempt to detect any such conflicts.

26.12 Other Functions

There are a large number of helpful functions in the `Functions/Misc` directory of the zsh distribution. Most are very simple and do not require documentation here, but a few are worthy of special mention.

26.12.1 Descriptions

`colors`   This function initializes several associative arrays to map color names to (and from) the ANSI standard eight-color terminal codes. These are used by the prompt theme system (Section 26.6 [Prompt Themes], page 453). You seldom should need to run `colors` more than once.

The eight base colors are: `black`, `red`, `green`, `yellow`, `blue`, `magenta`, `cyan`, and `white`. Each of these has codes for foreground and background. In addition there are seven intensity attributes: `bold`, `faint`, `standout`, `underline`, `blink`, `reverse`, and `conceal`. Finally, there are seven codes used to negate attributes: `none` (reset all attributes to the defaults), `normal` (neither bold nor faint), `no-standout`, `no-underline`, `no-blink`, `no-reverse`, and `no-conceal`.

Some terminals do not support all combinations of colors and intensities.

The associative arrays are:

`color`
`colour`   Map all the color names to their integer codes, and integer codes to the color names. The eight base names map to the foreground color codes, as do names prefixed with 'fg-', such as 'fg-red'. Names prefixed with 'bg-', such as 'bg-blue', refer to the background codes. The reverse mapping from code to color yields base name for foreground codes and the `bg-` form for backgrounds.

   Although it is a misnomer to call them 'colors', these arrays also map the other fourteen attributes from names to codes and codes to names.

`fg`
`fg_bold`
`fg_no_bold`
             Map the eight basic color names to ANSI terminal escape sequences that set the corresponding foreground text properties. The `fg` sequences change the color without changing the eight intensity attributes.

`bg`
`bg_bold`
`bg_no_bold`
             Map the eight basic color names to ANSI terminal escape sequences that set the corresponding background properties. The `bg` sequences change the color without changing the eight intensity attributes.

In addition, the scalar parameters `reset_color` and `bold_color` are set to the ANSI terminal escapes that turn off all attributes and turn on bold intensity, respectively.

`fned` [`-x` *num*] *name*
             Same as `zed -f`. This function does not appear in the zsh distribution, but can be created by linking `zed` to the name `fned` in some directory in your `fpath`.

`is-at-least` *needed* [*present*]
             Perform a greater-than-or-equal-to comparison of two strings having the format of a zsh version number; that is, a string of numbers and text with segments

separated by dots or dashes. If the *present* string is not provided, `$ZSH_VERSION` is used. Segments are paired left-to-right in the two strings with leading non-number parts ignored. If one string has fewer segments than the other, the missing segments are considered zero.

This is useful in startup files to set options and other state that are not available in all versions of zsh.

```
is-at-least 3.1.6-15 && setopt NO_GLOBAL_RCS
is-at-least 3.1.0 && setopt HIST_REDUCE_BLANKS
is-at-least 2.6-17 || print "You can't use is-at-least here."
```

nslookup [*arg* ...]

This wrapper function for the **nslookup** command requires the **zsh/zpty** module (see Section 22.35 [The zsh/zpty Module], page 379). It behaves exactly like the standard **nslookup** except that it provides customizable prompts (including a right-side prompt) and completion of nslookup commands, host names, etc. (if you use the function-based completion system). Completion styles may be set with the context prefix ':completion:nslookup'.

See also the **pager**, **prompt** and **rprompt** styles below.

regexp-replace *var regexp replace*

Use regular expressions to perform a global search and replace operation on a variable. If the option `RE_MATCH_PCRE` is not set, POSIX extended regular expressions are used, else Perl-compatible regular expressions (this requires the shell to be linked against the **pcre** library).

var is the name of the variable containing the string to be matched. The variable will be modified directly by the function. The variables `MATCH`, `MBEGIN`, `MEND`, `match`, `mbegin`, `mend` should be avoided as these are used by the regular expression code.

regexp is the regular expression to match against the string.

replace is the replacement text. This can contain parameter, command and arithmetic expressions which will be replaced: in particular, a reference to `$MATCH` will be replaced by the text matched by the pattern.

The return status is 0 if at least one match was performed, else 1.

run-help *cmd*

This function is designed to be invoked by the **run-help** ZLE widget, in place of the default alias. See 'Accessing On-Line Help' (Section 26.2 [Utilities], page 423) for setup instructions.

In the discussion which follows, if *cmd* is a file system path, it is first reduced to its rightmost component (the file name).

Help is first sought by looking for a file named *cmd* in the directory named by the `HELPDIR` parameter. If no file is found, an assistant function, alias, or command named **run-help-***cmd* is sought. If found, the assistant is executed with the rest of the current command line (everything after the command name *cmd*) as its arguments. When neither file nor assistant is found, the external command 'man *cmd*' is run.

An example assistant for the "ssh" command:

```
run-help-ssh() {
    emulate -LR zsh
    local -a args
    # Delete the "-l username" option
    zparseopts -D -E -a args l:
    # Delete other options, leaving: host command
    args=(${@:#-*})
    if [[ ${#args} -lt 2 ]]; then
        man ssh
    else
        run-help $args[2]
    fi
}
```

Several of these assistants are provided in the **Functions/Misc** directory. These must be autoloaded, or placed as executable scripts in your search path, in order to be found and used by **run-help**.

run-help-git
run-help-ip
run-help-openssl
run-help-p4
run-help-sudo
run-help-svk
run-help-svn

> Assistant functions for the **git**, **ip**, **openssl**, **p4**, **sudo**, **svk**, and **svn**, commands.

tetris   Zsh was once accused of not being as complete as Emacs, because it lacked a Tetris game. This function was written to refute this vicious slander.

This function must be used as a ZLE widget:

```
autoload -U tetris
zle -N tetris
bindkey keys tetris
```

To start a game, execute the widget by typing the *keys*. Whatever command line you were editing disappears temporarily, and your keymap is also temporarily replaced by the Tetris control keys. The previous editor state is restored when you quit the game (by pressing 'q') or when you lose.

If you quit in the middle of a game, the next invocation of the **tetris** widget will continue where you left off. If you lost, it will start a new game.

tetriscurses

> This is a port of the above to zcurses. The input handling is improved a bit so that moving a block sideways doesn't automatically advance a timestep, and the graphics use unicode block graphics.
>
> This version does not save the game state between invocations, and is not invoked as a widget, but rather as:
>
> ```
> autoload -U tetriscurses
> ```

tetriscurses

zargs [*option* ... **--**] [*input* ...] [**--** *command* [*arg* ...]]

This function has a similar purpose to GNU xargs. Instead of reading lines of arguments from the standard input, it takes them from the command line. This is useful because zsh, especially with recursive glob operators, often can construct a command line for a shell function that is longer than can be accepted by an external command.

The *option* list represents options of the **zargs** command itself, which are the same as those of **xargs**. The *input* list is the collection of strings (often file names) that become the arguments of the **command**, analogous to the standard input of **xargs**. Finally, the *arg* list consists of those arguments (usually options) that are passed to the *command* each time it runs. The *arg* list precedes the elements from the **input** list in each run. If no *command* is provided, then no *arg* list may be provided, and in that event the default command is 'print' with arguments '**-r --**'.

For example, to get a long **ls** listing of all plain files in the current directory or its subdirectories:

```
autoload -U zargs
zargs -- **/*(.) -- ls -l
```

Note that '**--**' is used both to mark the end of the *option* list and to mark the end of the *input* list, so it must appear twice whenever the *input* list may be empty. If there is guaranteed to be at least one *input* and the first *input* does not begin with a '**-**', then the first '**--**' may be omitted.

In the event that the string '**--**' is or may be an *input*, the **-e** option may be used to change the end-of-inputs marker. Note that this does *not* change the end-of-options marker. For example, to use '**..**' as the marker:

```
zargs -e.. -- **/*(.) .. ls -l
```

This is a good choice in that example because no plain file can be named '**..**', but the best end-marker depends on the circumstances.

The options **-i**, **-I**, **-l**, **-L**, and **-n** differ slightly from their usage in **xargs**. There are no input lines for **zargs** to count, so **-l** and **-L** count through the *input* list, and **-n** counts the number of arguments passed to each execution of *command*, *including* any *arg* list. Also, any time **-i** or **-I** is used, each *input* is processed separately as if by '**-L 1**'.

For details of the other **zargs** options, see man page xargs(1) (but note the difference in function between **zargs** and **xargs**) or run **zargs** with the **--help** option.

zed [**-f** [**-x** *num*]] *name*
zed -b   This function uses the ZLE editor to edit a file or function.

Only one *name* argument is allowed. If the **-f** option is given, the name is taken to be that of a function; if the function is marked for autoloading, **zed** searches for it in the **fpath** and loads it. Note that functions edited this way are installed into the current shell, but *not* written back to the autoload file. In this case the **-x** option specifies that leading tabs indenting the function according to syntax should be converted into the given number of spaces; '-x 2' is consistent with the layout of functions distributed with the shell.

Without -f, *name* is the path name of the file to edit, which need not exist; it is created on write, if necessary.

While editing, the function sets the main keymap to zed and the vi command keymap to zed-vicmd. These will be copied from the existing main and vicmd keymaps if they do not exist the first time zed is run. They can be used to provide special key bindings used only in zed.

If it creates the keymap, zed rebinds the return key to insert a line break and '^X^W' to accept the edit in the zed keymap, and binds 'ZZ' to accept the edit in the zed-vicmd keymap.

The bindings alone can be installed by running 'zed -b'. This is suitable for putting into a startup file. Note that, if rerun, this will overwrite the existing zed and zed-vicmd keymaps.

Completion is available, and styles may be set with the context prefix ':completion:zed'.

A zle widget zed-set-file-name is available. This can be called by name from within zed using '\ex zed-set-file-name' (note, however, that because of zed's rebindings you will have to type ^j at the end instead of the return key), or can be bound to a key in either of the zed or zed-vicmd keymaps after 'zed -b' has been run. When the widget is called, it prompts for a new name for the file being edited. When zed exits the file will be written under that name and the original file will be left alone. The widget has no effect with 'zed -f'.

While zed-set-file-name is running, zed uses the keymap zed-normal-keymap, which is linked from the main keymap in effect at the time zed initialised its bindings. (This is to make the return key operate normally.) The result is that if the main keymap has been changed, the widget won't notice. This is not a concern for most users.

zcp [-finqQvwW] *srcpat dest*
zln [-finqQsvwW] *srcpat dest*

Same as zmv -C and zmv -L, respectively. These functions do not appear in the zsh distribution, but can be created by linking zmv to the names zcp and zln in some directory in your fpath.

zkbd   See 'Keyboard Definition' (Section 26.2 [Utilities], page 423).

zmv [-finqQsvwW] [-C | -L | -M | -{p|P} *program*] [-o *optstring*]
  srcpat dest

Move (usually, rename) files matching the pattern *srcpat* to corresponding files having names of the form given by *dest*, where *srcpat* contains parentheses surrounding patterns which will be replaced in turn by $1, $2, ... in *dest*. For example,

        zmv '(*).lis' '$1.txt'

renames 'foo.lis' to 'foo.txt', 'my.old.stuff.lis' to 'my.old.stuff.txt', and so on.

The pattern is always treated as an EXTENDED_GLOB pattern. Any file whose name is not changed by the substitution is simply ignored. Any error (a substitution resulted in an empty string, two substitutions gave the same result, the destination was an existing regular file and -f was not given) causes the entire function to abort without doing anything.

In addition to pattern replacement, the variable $f can be referrred to in the second (replacement) argument. This makes it possible to use variable substitution to alter the argument; see examples below.

Options:

-f
    Force overwriting of destination files. Not currently passed down to the mv/cp/ln command due to vagaries of implementations (but you can use -o-f to do that).

-i
    Interactive: show each line to be executed and ask the user whether to execute it. 'Y' or 'y' will execute it, anything else will skip it. Note that you just need to type one character.

-n
    No execution: print what would happen, but don't do it.

-q
    Turn bare glob qualifiers off: now assumed by default, so this has no effect.

-Q
    Force bare glob qualifiers on. Don't turn this on unless you are actually using glob qualifiers in a pattern.

-s
    Symbolic, passed down to ln; only works with -L.

-v
    Verbose: print each command as it's being executed.

-w
    Pick out wildcard parts of the pattern, as described above, and implicitly add parentheses for referring to them.

-W
    Just like -w, with the addition of turning wildcards in the replacement pattern into sequential ${1} .. ${N} references.

-C
-L
-M
    Force cp, ln or mv, respectively, regardless of the name of the function.

-p *program*

    Call *program* instead of cp, ln or mv. Whatever it does, it should at least understand the form

        program -- oldname newname

    where *oldname* and *newname* are filenames generated by zmv. *program* will be split into words, so might be e.g. the name of an archive tool plus a copy or rename subcommand.

-P *program*

    As -p *program*, except that *program* does not accept a following -- to indicate the end of options. In this case filenames must already be in a sane form for the program in question.

-o *optstring*

> The *optstring* is split into words and passed down verbatim to the `cp`, `ln` or `mv` command called to perform the work. It should probably begin with a '-'.

Further examples:

```
zmv -v '(* *)' '${1// /_}'
```

For any file in the current directory with at least one space in the name, replace every space by an underscore and display the commands executed.

```
zmv -v '* *' '${f// /_}'
```

This does exactly the same by referring to the file name stored in `$f`.

For more complete examples and other implementation details, see the `zmv` source file, usually located in one of the directories named in your `fpath`, or in `Functions/Misc/zmv` in the zsh distribution.

`zrecompile`

> See 'Recompiling Functions' (Section 26.2 [Utilities], page 423).

`zstyle+` *context style value* [+ *subcontext style value* ...]

> This makes defining styles a bit simpler by using a single '+' as a special token that allows you to append a context name to the previously used context name. Like this:

```
zstyle+ ':foo:bar'  style1 value1 \
      +':baz'       style2 value2 \
      +':frob'      style3 value3
```

> This defines *style1* with *value1* for the context `:foo:bar` as usual, but it also defines *style2* with *value2* for the context `:foo:bar:baz` and *style3* with *value3* for `:foo:bar:frob`. Any *subcontext* may be the empty string to re-use the first context unchanged.

26.12.2 Styles

`insert-tab`

> The `zed` function *sets* this style in context ':`completion:zed:*`' to turn off completion when `TAB` is typed at the beginning of a line. You may override this by setting your own value for this context and style.

`pager`   The `nslookup` function looks up this style in the context ':`nslookup`' to determine the program used to display output that does not fit on a single screen.

`prompt`
`rprompt`   The `nslookup` function looks up this style in the context ':`nslookup`' to set the prompt and the right-side prompt, respectively. The usual expansions for the `PS1` and `RPS1` parameters may be used (see Chapter 13 [Prompt Expansion], page 39).

Concept Index

D

E

M

N

O

P

Q

R

S

T

Variables Index

505

Options Index

Functions Index

Editor Functions Index

Style and Tag Index

U

V

W

Z

www.ingramcontent.com/pod-product-compliance
Lightning Source LLC
Chambersburg PA
CBHW081452050326
40690CB00015B/2766